ALSO BY MARGOT PETERS

Charlotte Brontë: Style in the Novel
Unquiet Soul: A Biography of Charlotte Brontë
Bernard Shaw and the Actresses
Mrs. Pat: The Life of Mrs. Patrick Campbell

THE HOUSE OF
BARRYMORE

MARGOT PETERS

A TOUCHSTONE BOOK
Published by Simon & Schuster
New York London Toronto Sydney Tokyo Singapore

TOUCHSTONE
Simon & Schuster Building
Rockefeller Center
1230 Avenue of the Americas
New York, New York, 10020

Copyright © 1990 by Margot Peters

Library of Congress Cataloging in Publication Data
Peters, Margot.
The house of Barrymore / Margot Peters.—1st Touchstone ed.
p. cm.
Includes bibliographical references and index.
1. Barrymore family.   2. Motion picture actors and actresses—
United States—Biography.   I. Title.
PN2285.P48   1991
791.43'028'092273—dc20
[B]   91-16251
                                                       CIP

ISBN: 0-671-74799-1

FOR

Spencer Berger

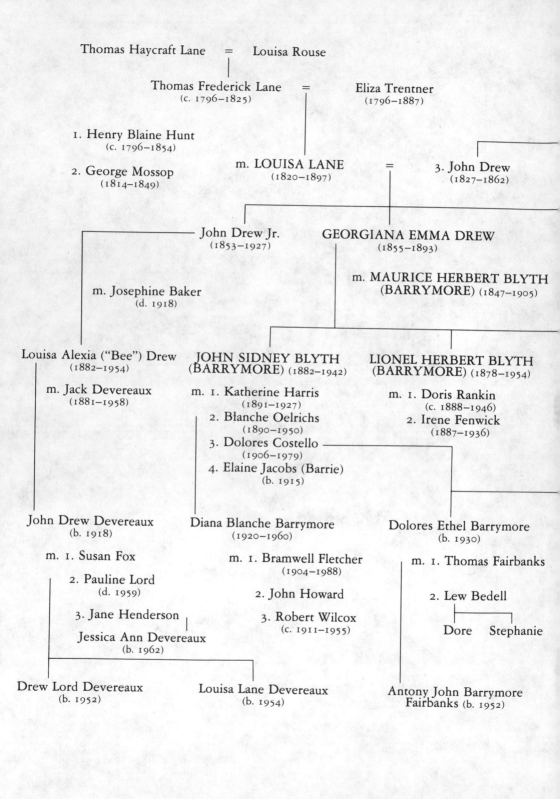

Thomas Haycraft Lane = Louisa Rouse

Thomas Frederick Lane = Eliza Trentner
(c. 1796–1825)   (1796–1887)

1. Henry Blaine Hunt
(c. 1796–1854)

2. George Mossop
(1814–1849)

m. LOUISA LANE = 3. John Drew
(1820–1897)   (1827–1862)

John Drew Jr.   GEORGIANA EMMA DREW
(1853–1927)   (1855–1893)

m. Josephine Baker   m. MAURICE HERBERT BLYTH
(d. 1918)   (BARRYMORE) (1847–1905)

Louisa Alexia ("Bee") Drew   JOHN SIDNEY BLYTH   LIONEL HERBERT BLYTH
(1882–1954)   (BARRYMORE) (1882–1942)   (BARRYMORE) (1878–1954)

m. Jack Devereaux   m. 1. Katherine Harris   m. 1. Doris Rankin
(1881–1958)   (1891–1927)   (c. 1888–1946)
                                   2. Blanche Oelrichs   2. Irene Fenwick
                                      (1890–1950)   (1887–1936)
                                   3. Dolores Costello
                                      (1906–1979)
                                   4. Elaine Jacobs (Barrie)
                                      (b. 1915)

John Drew Devereaux   Diana Blanche Barrymore   Dolores Ethel Barrymore
(b. 1918)   (1920–1960)   (b. 1930)

m. 1. Susan Fox   m. 1. Bramwell Fletcher   m. 1. Thomas Fairbanks
                                         (1904–1988)
2. Pauline Lord   2. John Howard   2. Lew Bedell
(d. 1959)

3. Jane Henderson   3. Robert Wilcox   Dore   Stephanie
Jessica Ann Devereaux   (c. 1911–1955)
(b. 1962)

Drew Lord Devereaux   Louisa Lane Devereaux   Antony John Barrymore
(b. 1952)   (b. 1954)   Fairbanks (b. 1952)

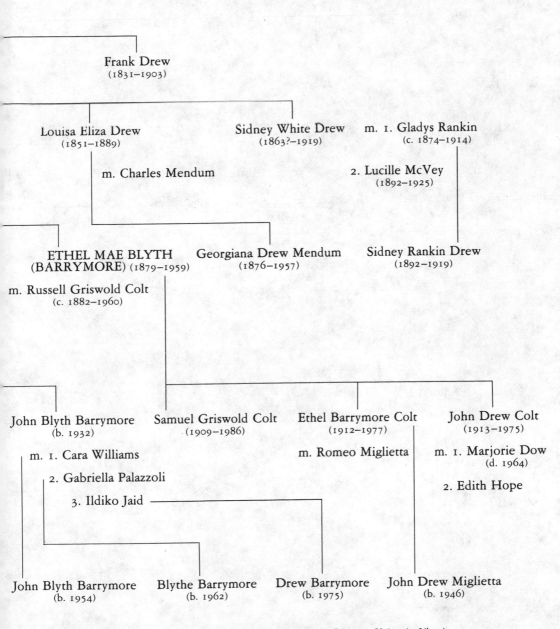

Frank Drew
(1831–1903)

Louisa Eliza Drew
(1851–1889)

Sidney White Drew
(1863?–1919)

m. 1. Gladys Rankin
(c. 1874–1914)

m. Charles Mendum

2. Lucille McVey
(1892–1925)

ETHEL MAE BLYTH
(BARRYMORE) (1879–1959)

Georgiana Drew Mendum
(1876–1957)

Sidney Rankin Drew
(1892–1919)

m. Russell Griswold Colt
(c. 1882–1960)

John Blyth Barrymore
(b. 1932)

Samuel Griswold Colt
(1909–1986)

Ethel Barrymore Colt
(1912–1977)

John Drew Colt
(1913–1975)

m. 1. Cara Williams

m. Romeo Miglietta

m. 1. Marjorie Dow
(d. 1964)

2. Gabriella Palazzoli

2. Edith Hope

3. Ildiko Jaid

John Blyth Barrymore
(b. 1954)

Blythe Barrymore
(b. 1962)

Drew Barrymore
(b. 1975)

John Drew Miglietta
(b. 1946)

Courtesy Mary Ann Jensen, Curator, Seymour Theatre Collection, Princeton University Libraries

CONTENTS

Illustrations follow pages 50, 210, and 370.

ACKNOWLEDGMENTS

I would like to acknowledge the assistance and encouragement I have received in my work from both individuals and institutions. Both the research for this biography and its writing were helped immeasurably by three grants: a Rockefeller Resident Fellowship at the Wisconsin Center for Film and Theatre Research, a Wisconsin Institute for Research in the Humanities Fellowship, and a Guggenheim Fellowship. I am deeply grateful to those colleagues who supported my applications for these fellowships. My thanks also to the University of Wisconsin–Whitewater for granting me released time for research and writing, and to Professor Ruth Schauer, chair of the Department of English, who has supported this and other writing projects over the years.

My thanks to the staffs of the following libraries and collections: the Billy Rose Theatre Collection at the Performing Arts Research Center, Lincoln Center; the Theatre Collection of the Museum of the City of New York; the Shubert Archives; the Hampden-Booth Theatre Library; the Manuscript Division of the Library of Congress; the Beinecke Rare Book and Manuscript Library, Yale University Library; Special Collections, Houghton Library, Harvard University; the Harvard Theatre Collection; the Seymour Theatre Collection, Princeton University Library; the Department of Rare Books, Cornell University Library; the Theatre Collection of the Free Library of Philadelphia; the Wisconsin Center for Film and Theatre Research, Madison; the Gene Fowler Collection, Special Collections, University of Colorado at Boulder Libraries; the Department of Manuscripts, the Henry E. Huntington Library; the Academy of Motion Picture Arts and Sciences; the University of Southern California Cinema-Television Library and Archives of Performing Arts; the Department of Special Collections, Library of the University of California, Los Angeles; the Turner Entertainment Company; and the Raymond Mander and Joe Mitchenson Theatre Collection, Beckenham, Kent. Special thanks to Mary Ann Jensen (Seymour Theatre Collection, Princeton University), Jeanne T. Newlin (Harvard Theatre Collection), Louis A. Rachow (Hampden-Booth Theatre Library), Mary C. Henderson (Theatre Collection, Museum of the City of New York), Geraldine Duclow (Theatre Collection, the Free Library of Philadelphia), Marianne Chach (the Shubert Archives), Nora J. Quinlan (Rare Books Room, University of Colorado at Boulder Library), Maxine Fleckner Ducey (Wisconsin Center for Film and Theatre Research), Audrey E. Kupferberg (Yale Film Study Center), Jan-Christopher Horak (George Eastman House), Howard B. Gotlieb (Special Collections, Mugar Memorial Library, Boston University), Edward S. Comstock (Archives of Performing Arts, University of Southern California), and Jilian Edwardes-Jones and Kenneth Carpenter (Raymond Mander and Joe Mitchenson Theatre Collection, Beckenham, Kent).

I am grateful to the following for permission to quote unpublished material: James D. Akins (Zoë Akins), Gwenn Thomas Avillez and Viviane Thomas Trimble (Michael Strange and Diana Barrymore), Eleanore Phillips Colt (Ethel Barrymore), Valerie Delacort (Gabriel Pascal), Antony Barrymore Fairbanks (John and Lionel Barrymore), Will Fowler (Gene Fowler), Peg Kocher (Theresa Helburn), Sesaly Gould Krafft (Charles B. Gould), John Miglietta (Louisa Lane Drew, John Drew, and Louisa Drew Devereaux), Princeton University Libraries (William Bartlett Reynolds), Lucilla Potter (Henry C. Potter), Shubert Archives (Lee Shubert), Screen Actors Guild (the Estate of William Hopper), George Towers (the Estate of George Cukor), and the Turner Entertainment Company (MGM files).

To the many people who talked or wrote to me about the Barrymores or otherwise offered assistance, my sincere thanks: Linda Aaron, Stella Adler, Eloise Arman, Lauren Bacall, Paul M. Bailey, Frank J. Baldassarre, David Beasley, Francesca Beaufort, Pandro S. Berman, Dr. J. Evan Blanchard, Professor David Bordwell, George D. Brightbill, Diana R. Brown, Kimberly Carson, Professor James Coakley, Eleanore Phillips Colt, Whitfield Connor, Enid Coors, Nena Couch, Professor Donald Crafton, Babette Craven, Allan Davis, Barbara Robins Davis, the Reverend John B. DeMayo, Oliver Dernberger, Armand Deutsch, Philip and Amanda Dunne, William D. Eppes, A. J. Feifarek, Father William Noe Field, Will Fowler, Bernard Geis, Nicholas Gordon, Charles B. Gould, Gene Graves, Susan Harley, Katharine Hepburn, Anne Higgins, Jeri Hill, Sara S. Hodson, Kim Hunter, James H. Hurson, Sonia L. Jacobs, Sol Jacobson, Eliot and Elizabeth Janeway, C. Lee Jenner, Mark H. Jones, Steven C. Jones, Nancy Prichett Jordan, the Reverend Monsignor Michael E. Kelly, John

Kobler, Dr. Richard Larson, Dan H. Laurence, Phillip Le Strange, Bertram Lippincott III, Toby Little, Betty Lord, Frank McGlinn, Dorothy McGuire, Gene Mailes, Linda Harris Mehr, Robert A. Mendelsohn, John Miglietta, Wallace Munro, Mildred Natwick, Herbert S. Nusbaum, Professor Robert J. O'Brien, Lisa Onofri, Evelyn Payson, Professor Edward Pfau, Phyllis Powell, George C. Pratt, Jeffrey Rankin, Michael Redmon, Philip Rhodes, Wallace Rooney, Donald R. Seawell, John D. Seymour, Alissa Simon, Robin Strausberg, Dorothy L. Swerdlove, Herbert Swope Jr., Elin Vanderlip, Richard Waring, and Georgianna Ziegler. Special thanks to James Kotsilibas-Davis.

My research in England was assisted by Sir John Gielgud, Emlyn Williams, Diana Forbes-Robertson Sheean, Laurence Irving, Rhiannon Bell, Kay Hutchings, Colin Mabberley, Susan Shaw, Allan Davis, Peter Graves, and Alfred Shaughnessy. My thanks to them and to Professor Gabriel Merle in Paris for his efforts to solve the mystery of Lionel Barrymore's daughter Mary.

I am very much indebted to Spencer Berger, Ray Ruehl, and Peter Ridgway Jordan, my husband, for their careful reading of the manuscript. Thanks too to Donna Lewis and her staff for hours of photocopying.

Peter Jordan lent his critical and research skills to this biography from its conception: my best thanks.

My gratitude to Robert Gottlieb, my editor, for his enthusiasm for this project; to my new editor, Victoria Wilson, for her encouragement; and to her assistant, Antoinette White.

With a generosity unparalleled in my experience as a biographer, Spencer Berger has given me unlimited access to his collection of Barrymore films, books, records, tapes, photographs, letters, articles, clippings, and notes. This largesse he has supplemented over the past years with informative letters, phone calls, taped interviews, introductions to people who knew the Barrymores, and personal visits. Though as a long-time friend and chronicler of the Barrymores he has decisive opinions about both their public and private lives, he has—with a tact that is as rare as his generosity—never sought to impose his viewpoint. Thanks are inadequate to express my enormous debt to this Barrymore colleague and friend.

THE HOUSE OF
BARRYMORE

PRELUDE

I N THE SUMMER of 1890 Ethel Barrymore made an important decision. Her father, Maurice Barrymore, was touring after his Broadway hit *A Man of the World*. Georgie Drew Barrymore, her mother, had captivated New York in *The Senator* that year and was also touring, though not with Maurice. Uncle Sidney and Aunt Gladys, herself a Rankin of the famous acting Rankins, had recently emerged as the comedy team Mr. and Mrs. Sidney Drew. Uncle John Drew had just closed another brilliant season at Daly's. The Drew family for as long as anyone could remember had been actors: the names Drew and, more recently, Barrymore *meant* acting to American audiences. "And here I am," said Ethel, eleven next month, "getting older every day and I haven't *done* anything!"

But mainly it was Mummum. Mummum (stress on the second syllable) was Mrs. John Drew, her grandmother. Mummum had made her debut at twelve months as a "crying baby." At seven little Louisa Lane was murdered in the tower in Junius Brutus Booth's *Richard III* and had an apple shot off her head by Edwin Forrest in *William Tell*. At eight Louisa made her New York debut; then, bored with merely starring, appeared just before her ninth birthday at the Chestnut Street Theatre in Philadelphia playing five parts in one play called *Twelve, Precisely*.

She had kept this pace all her seventy years, going through three husbands, all Irish comedians, and bearing three children in four years (or was it four in five?). In 1861 she assumed management of the important Arch Street Theatre in Philadelphia, a coup for a woman. To this theatre she not only lured the greatest actors of the day but headed the bill in a stock company that she trained and directed. At the same time she managed to convince Philadelphia that she was a pillar of Episcopalian respectability (another coup) and provide a home and support for her

3

own children, several dubiously connected offspring, and her daughter Georgie's three children, Lionel, Ethel, and John. This formidable woman was under five feet tall with plain features and large, popping blue eyes. She was called "the Duchess." The great Edwin Booth was said to be afraid of her.

With Mummum a star at eight, Ethel knew it was past time for her own debut. She chose *The Lady of the Camellias* because every great actress played it and because she'd seen Modjeska as Marguerite Gautier and simply *dissolved*. She persuaded an older boy also holidaying on Staten Island that summer to write a script and, though he'd forgotten most of the play, he obligingly produced three penciled scrawls. Ethel took them to her brothers, Lionel and Jack. Why not give a show, she told them, on the Fourth of July in the barn in back of Madame Bourquin's boardinghouse. They would charge admission. "It's about time we were doing something in the theatre," said Ethel seriously.

Lionel, twelve, and Jack, eight, groaned. True that after seeing *Les Chouans* they had dueled furiously up and down Mummum's stairs with fly swatters in imitation of their father's swashbuckling, but they were more interested this summer in sneaking cigarettes behind the barn or slipping off to play with the thirty-five huskies Maurice kept on the Island at a tumbledown farm. Lionel had not a shred of acting ambition and particularly loathed the idea of playing the lover; if anything he wanted to be the villainous Count de Varville. But Ethel wanted Lionel for Armand because he was tall, and got her way. She began to practice Marguerite's cough.

Since it was to be her pièce de résistance, the cough had to be rehearsed secretly, difficult in Madame Bourquin's crowded boardinghouse. Ethel chose the only bathroom; it was not soundproof. "Something must be done about that child," said Mummum in alarm. "She's started to bark like a dog!" Behind the door Ethel went on experimenting. On Saturday night the line of angry boarders clutching towels and soap grew longer as Ethel coughed on. At last Mrs. Drew swept among them. "My God, she's got a bone in her throat!" she cried, hammering at the door. In a few moments it opened and Ethel, very red, emerged.

Ethel's cough became famous among the summer people, and on the evening of the Fourth, thirty-seven paid a penny each for "orchestra seats" in the barn to see *The Three Barrymores in Camille*. The performance went over very well except with Mummum, who told them they had charged entirely too much. As manager, director, and star, Ethel paid herself seventeen cents and gave Lionel and Jack each a dime. They resented this but didn't complain because they got to stay up late and there was ice cream. Ethel produced more plays that summer; and Lionel and Jack went along, for the ice cream.

IT'S A CHARMING STORY that should be true because it captures the picture of the three, or at least the picture the Barrymores allowed to be painted. All three denied they wanted to act. Ethel dreamed of being a concert pianist. Lionel and John both wanted to be artists. Acting was only the family business that put food on the table. Yet Ethel had a precocious sense of duty. If the stage was her destiny (and she soon discovered it was), then she would give the stage her all. As in the story, Ethel's determination paved the way for her brothers' careers in the theatre. As in the story, Ethel would always star, Lionel always hate romantic roles, and John always prefer playing the rogue. (If Jack's Count de Varville showed flashes of genius, that too would have been right, as would Lionel's and Jack's immediately spending their take and borrowing Ethel's.) Certainly the story catches the relationship of the three: Ethel serious and morally superior, Lionel and Jack resentful but too intimidated to complain. "My sister Ethel always has awed me more and I have dreaded her criticisms more than that of any other person," Jack said a few years before his death. Perhaps that is why when the Barrymores met later in life the occasions tended to be formal. "My God!" said an observer of one of these reunions. "Don't you *know* each other?"

A charming story indeed; but is it true? Jack first told it to a reporter from the New York *Sun* in 1917. In 1933 it appeared, embellished, in a "truth about the Barrymores" serial in *American Magazine*, reportedly by John Barrymore himself, actually written by his friend Jerome Beatty. Significantly the episode was titled "Blame It on the Queen": Jack's not entirely playful way of accusing Ethel of roping him into an acting career. By the time he got around to telling the *Camille* story to his first biographer, Alma Power-Waters, in 1940, he had turned the tables on Ethel and Lionel who, he now claimed, divided the profits and paid him a pittance. Indignantly he had stormed in to his grandmother. "Ethel and Lionel are trying to cheat me! Since you are manager of the Arch Street Theatre, you can surely manage ours." Why, demanded Mummum, had he not had a proper understanding with them before he started? Jack grinned. As a matter of fact he had made friends with the box-office manager who had promised him a percentage without telling Ethel and Lionel.

Finally Jack has the story the way he wants it. Ethel had railroaded him into acting, but not only had he got the part in *Camille* he wanted, he had made three times what his siblings made and not given them a cent. Once again, however, Jack revived the *Camille* story in 1941 for a special radio broadcast honoring Ethel's forty years in the theatre as a star. This time he tells us that as the Count de Varville he wore long corn-silk mustaches dyed black and actually introduces a new character— Arthur Byron (later a popular Broadway and film actor). It is Byron who has the choice line when, with a wicked flourish, he tells Ethel, "Come, entice me further, pretty one, over a libation in the conservatory."

The story had become part of Jack's repertoire: like all actors he relished a good yarn, and this one could actually be told in public. If true, the *Camille* debut mattered little to Lionel or Ethel, however. Lionel himself never mentioned the agony of playing Armand one Staten Island summer and, more important, Ethel—the star of the tale—says nothing about this supposedly momentous occasion in her life.

But the innocent little *Camille* story only hints at the problem of writing about the Barrymores. Barrymore history is tangled, distorted, falsified, and just plain missing. Dates are wrong, records nonexistent, entries in the Family Bible contradictory, and newspaper accounts inflated. Frustratingly enough, the Barrymores themselves were supremely unconcerned with setting the record straight. Ethel kept few records, described a 1940 scrawl to the critic Alexander Woollcott as "almost the second letter I've ever written," said grandly that if anyone wanted to know about her they could check the index of the *New York Times*. Lionel was less forthcoming than Ethel. Though John told his friend James Montgomery Flagg, "You know what an onion I am as a scribe," he wrote ardently to the women he courted; letters to Michael Strange, Dolores Costello, and Elaine Barrymore, however, are still in private hands. John's friend, literary executor, and biographer Gene Fowler at least saw that many of the actor's papers were preserved; personal effects of Lionel and Ethel seem virtually nonexistent.

Does it matter if the *Camille* story is true? Probably only to the biographer struggling to separate fact from myth, knowing while she does that both stars like the Barrymores and the public prefer the myths.

PART ONE

IN THE WINGS

1878–1901

ONE

1878–1882

AND BEFORE

T HEY WERE BORN to Maurice and Georgie Drew Barrymore on
April 28, 1878, August 15, 1879, and February 14, 1882—or were
they. Lionel says his birthday was April 12. Ethel does not say, reference
books say August 15, her birth certificate says the sixteenth. The Family
Bible says John was born February 15, reference books say the fifteenth,
his birth certificate says February 14. Lionel's and Ethel's surname on
their birth certificates is Barrymore, John's is Blythe. In the Family Bible
Maurice Barrymore's real name is given as Herbert Blyth, no *e*; the
confusion between Blyth and Blythe remains to this day. Neither has
anyone explained why John was the only child given his father's actual
name. After this confusion it seems a minor matter that Ethel swears that
Dr. Mitchell delivered all three of them, whereas their birth certificates
show that Lionel and Ethel were delivered by "J. Bivens."

But they were born and in Philadelphia in houses leased by their
grandmother: Lionel and Ethel at 119 North Ninth Street, John (Jack or
Jake to the family) at 2008 Columbia Avenue. The only house they
remembered, however, was 140 North Twelfth Street, a dark-brick row
house between Cherry and Quarry streets with three prominent second-
story windows overlooking white marble steps and the narrow tree-lined
street. Georgie had nicknamed 140 the "Tomb of the Capulets" for the
prominent display across the street of a tombstone carver's urns and
angels; and it often seemed like a tomb to her children. To Ethel the
house was cavernous, filled with "the most alarming echoes." During
the day Lionel and Jack played pirates in the big drafty attic known as
the "Annex" or got their ears pulled by Mary Aggie, the cook. At night,
however, the Tomb of the Capulets could be sinister. Once, as punishment, a very small Jack was made to go up the long flight of stairs alone
to ponder his crimes in the Annex. "You can't hurt me," Ethel heard him
say as he disappeared into the darkness. "I have a wonderful power!"

The 140 North Twelfth Street menage was decidedly Gothic. The first-floor kitchen with its huge fireplace and chimney was ruled by a succession of Irish cooks and maids all called, after an early servant, "Mary Aggie." Forbidden the kitchen, the children hung over the stairs listening to the soft secret Irish laughter. Flitting through the cold halls was Mummum's dresser, Lily Garrett, called, mysteriously, "the pearl-handled knife," and her mother, Mrs. Garrett, who came to collect and deliver the washing. There was also Mrs. Garrett's daughter-in-law Kitty, the children's long-suffering nursemaid.

Dominating the second floor was a big front bedroom that Ethel dreaded to pass. It contained an old woman wrapped in the silences and smells of ninety years. Eliza Lane Kinlock (misspelled by Ethel as Kinloch because Mummum's *k*'s in the Family Bible look like *h*'s) had come with her child Louisa from England in 1827 to pursue a stage career in America. Though successful as "a sweet singer of ballads," Eliza's chief contribution to the theatre had been her daughter, Louisa Lane Drew. Now Eliza lay in bed surrounded by the faded souvenirs of her past and shook her bell whenever she wanted tea or a chamber pot. The bell rang often and was promptly answered. Mummum inspired Ethel's unreasonable terror of this relic: if the Duchess obeyed Grandmother Kinlock, the old lady must be awful indeed.

Just the opposite was "Aunt Tibby," a sweet, fragile creature whose eagerness to serve the family seemed a perpetual apology for her presence. Adine Kinlock Stephens Drew was the daughter of Mummum's younger half sister Georgiana Kinlock. Her father *may* have been Robert Stephens, an actor Georgiana met and perhaps married while touring Australia. In February 1862 Georgiana had returned from abroad without a husband but with a baby girl born in Melbourne. Perhaps Louisa Drew offered to take the child then and there, since the child's grandmother was already under her roof and since Georgiana was both poor and in poor health. Or perhaps Adine only came under Louisa's protection after Georgiana's death at thirty-five in 1864.

Ethel, however, had a different story from an ancient family retainer: that Mummum's husband, John Drew, had been in love with Georgiana until the forceful Louisa, seven years his senior, said "Nonsense!" and married him herself. That after the birth of her third child, Louisa had allowed John to undertake a long tour abroad with his former love Georgiana as his leading lady—the implication being that Louisa was tired of bedroom duties and willing to risk old embers bursting into flame. That they had burst indeed, and that a forgiving Louisa adopted Adine because the child was John Drew's.

It hardly mattered to the girl, for she never knew Stephens or John Drew. A few months after his return Drew complained of illness for several days before Tuesday, May 21, 1862, when, with Adine in his arms, he fell insensible to the floor and died hours later of congestion of the brain.

Then there was Uncle Googan, who occupied the other third-floor attic when he ran out of money. Uncle Googan was Sidney White Drew, and Adine's pedigree is a clear page compared to the mystery surrounding this Drew's origins. Some say that when John Drew returned from that long tour Louisa surprised him tit-for-tat with an "adopted" infant named Sidney White. This story fails to provide a father for Sidney, however, and to explain how Louisa could possibly have borne a child during the slightly more than three years her husband was gone, given that:

In 1859 she joined the Arch Street Theatre company, becoming such a reliable favorite during the 1859–1860 season that the board of directors decided to offer her the management. In the last months of 1860 she accepted the position and at once threw herself into redecorating the theatre, paying off debts, and assembling a company. Inaugurating "Mrs. John Drew's Arch Street Theatre" on August 31, 1861, she also played an incredible forty-two roles during that season. Now while a woman might possibly adopt a child during these years of furious public activity, it is almost inconceivable that she could carry and bear one, even given the concealing nature of women's dress in those days.

In the Drew Family Bible one may read in Eliza Kinlock's elegant hand, "N.Y. Aug. 28, 1863. Sidney, only son of Sidney & Maria White, son by adoption of Louisa Drew." That settles the matter—or does it. The adoption is still not explained and, while the birth date may be right, Eliza could have invented "Sidney and Maria White" to save her daughter's reputation.

Buried even deeper archivally is an entry in the *Catalogue of Matriculates of the College, University of Pennsylvania, 1748–1893:* "Sidney Drew White. b. at sea, September 28, 1863. s. John White and Maria Drew. Entered in 1879, and left during the Fresh. year [1883]. m. Gladys, dau. McKee Rankin." Despite discrepancies from the Drew Bible, this is incontrovertibly *the* Sidney, and at last Louisa has a motive for adopting him. Maria Drew is related to John Drew. Given Louisa's monumental sense of responsibility, nothing more natural than she should adopt a little nephew or cousin.

And so the truth is stumbled upon at last—or is it. Both Lionel and Ethel declared that Uncle Googan was Mummum's illegitimate son. "I am proud to claim kin to him," said Lionel, "although in her autobiography

. . . Louisa Lane Drew states that she had adopted Sidney. Mrs. Drew, of course, may say what she wishes in the matter, but Uncle Googan certainly *looked* like her." Ethel was firmer: "[My grandmother] proceeded to have four children: my Aunt Louisa, my Uncle John, my mother, and Sidney. Uncle Sidney may not have been the son of John Drew, but he was indubitably the son of Mrs. John Drew."

Whatever his parentage, young Uncle Googan was a favorite of his nephews, an easygoing sort who thought that the colony of white mice Lionel had established in his bedroom during his absence kept Philadelphia from being dull. Also making Philadelphia lively was the local pool hall. "Would you like to see Uncle Googan hit the pretty balls?" Sidney would ask; and uncle and nephews would make a stealthy exit for the poolroom. With Lionel and Jack standing by as mascots, Sidney would flourish his cue and invite customers unfamiliar with his skill to a match. Recouped, he would then vanish from Philadelphia and Lionel's white mice reclaim their territory.

But from Grandmother Kinlock in the best bedroom to the Mary Aggies in the kitchen, 140 North Twelfth was a matriarchy ruled by Mummum. The women in the family could be physically frail, but the men tended to lack both the physical and moral strength that radiated from Louisa Drew. Her father, Thomas Frederick Lane, died before she was five; her stepfather, John Kinlock, when she was eleven. Henry Blaine Hunt, an actor Louisa married when she was sixteen, lasted eleven years before she divorced him in 1847. Her second husband, George Mossop, drank himself to death a year after their marriage in 1848. John Drew, her third, died at thirty-five, leaving her after twelve years of marriage a widow of forty-one.

These elusive men were gregarious, feckless, and engaging. George Mossop was a popular Irish singing comedian. John Drew had talent, charm, and flashing black eyes, but the eyes roved and neither was Louisa happy with his relaxed approach to his profession. "Too early success was his ruin; it left him with nothing to do," she complained, but John Drew was quite satisfied entertaining audiences as a romantic Irish comedian.

Their son John inherited his father's charm and disinclination for struggle. He played his first role at the Arch at nineteen so coolly that his mother burst out in the middle of a scene, "What a dreadful young man! I wonder what he will be like when he grows up!" At her instruction, Lionel, Ethel, and Jack came nightly to Grandmother Kinlock's room to kneel and pray, "God bless Mother and Papa and Mummum and Grandmother and Uncle Googan; and please, God, make Uncle Jack a good actor." Uncle Jack became a good actor—*the* leading man of his day. Yet he was too content to play all his life the perfect gentleman onstage and off, a role that fit him like his expensive pigskin gloves. Only those who appreciated his magnificent Petruchio knew what the stage had missed because John Drew refused to grow into larger acting clothes.

John was a heavyweight, however, compared to Sidney, who played in popular stage and film "marriage comedies." Irrepressible Sidney preferred chorus girls to the Philadelphia young ladies Louisa chose for him and took his pool cue more seriously than his stage cues, inspiring his mother to remark acidly when he once announced he had turned dramatist, "Does someone in your play get killed with a billiard ball?" Not that Sidney didn't succeed. They all did, even the tippling George Mossop. But they didn't succeed Louisa Drew's way: the disciplined, serious way. In her uncompromising eye, none of them quite measured up.

Georgie Drew inherited her mother's taste in men. Maurice Barrymore, whom Georgie and her brother John brought to Philadelphia in 1875, fit the pattern. The current Mary Aggie turned scarlet in his virile presence, the cook stuck her head up the kitchen stairs to catch glimpses of him, ancient Eliza Kinlock threw him kittenish winks. He had an athlete's grace, a divine wit, startling physical beauty. He had a pedigree: he was actually Herbert Blyth, born in India of British parents with good connections. He had an Oxford education. He affected monocles and top hats. He was eccentric, mercurial, charming.

He also had the English gentleman's fatal propensity to take nothing seriously. Georgie didn't know this, Louisa suspected. Somber and straight of back, "Mother sat at the other end of the drawing room *snowing* on us," said Georgie. But even a Queen Victoria might be charmed by a Regency buck. When Maurice further assured her that Augustin Daly had just offered him a three-year contract, Louisa was forced to give in. They were such a striking, spirited couple. She wanted Georgie to be happy. On December 31, 1876, the Reverend Dr. William Rudder of St. Stephen's Episcopal Church came to North Twelfth Street to unite Georgiana Emma Drew and Maurice Barrymore in marriage.

Yet in years to come Louisa Drew often spoke slightingly of Maurice Barrymore, both as an actor and a family man. His children caught the tone of their grandmother's disapproval, contrasting sharply with her strong though undemonstrative affection for their mother Georgie. Lionel became precociously solemn, as though compensating somehow for his father's devil-may-care. Ethel never did believe in her father. Little John was very like his father temperamentally, yet deeply attached to his grandmother—fertile soil for conflict to thrive.

TWO

1882–1886

TO THEIR CHILDREN Maurice and Georgie seemed infinitely glamorous. Whenever they descended upon Philadelphia the tempo quickened. Blond, blue-eyed Georgie was like an older sister who rustled and smelled sweet, didn't scold, and could even make Mummum laugh. Maurice was earthier, though no less impressive. If he happened to be acting at the Arch, he might appear suddenly late at night in the Annex in flagrant violation of Mummum's bedtime rules. Begged for a story, he would launch into blood-and-thunder tales of the Indian Mutiny. His tour de force was the siege of Fort Agra with one lone British battalion holding out heroically against swarms of storming sepoys. Of course Lionel and Jack couldn't help bursting into cheers and bouncing up and down as Maurice impersonated the whole battalion slashing back the foe. A bed slat clattered to the floor. Mummum threw open the door, terrible in nightgown and cap.

"Well, *you*," she said witheringly (Maurice was always *you*), "is four o'clock in the morning the best time to scare the children!"

"I was only giving them a touch of India, Ma'am," said Maurice, who always addressed her as though she were Queen Victoria. "A soothing battle scene."

We were not amused. "I'd like to give *you* a touch of something," said Mummum. "A touch of intelligence, perhaps."

Every now and then their parents took them along. In 1882, for example, the great Polish actress Helena Modjeska had engaged Maurice as her leading man for an extensive American tour, agreeing that Georgie and the children be included. Mummum was against it, especially for infant Jack, already her favorite because (she said) he looked like the sweet little "Greengoose" of the fairy tale. But Georgie was still nursing and besides had hired an impeccably qualified nanny.

The militantly taciturn Lionel swears he doesn't remember this tour, but he and Ethel were not too young to feel its tensions. Their father, bad at memorizing, now had to cope with four Shakespearean roles as well as the male leads of *Adrienne Lecouvreur, The Lady of the Camellias,* and *Frou Frou.* They probably didn't see the last rehearsal of *Adrienne* when Maurice and Modjeska fell weeping into each other's arms, but they may have heard Georgie cue their father again and again for lines that maddeningly eluded him. They could hardly have avoided the electricity generated by the conjunction of their parents, Modjeska, and her husband, Count Bozenta Chlapowski. Maurice had met Modjeska the previous year in London; the attraction was immediate and, given the free-wheeling nature of each, immediately transferred to the bedroom. Back home Georgie read between the lines. Count Bozenta liked the Maurice business as little as he had liked Modjeska's flaming affair with the Nobel laureate Henryk Sienkiewicz. Georgie and Modjeska met head-on when Modjeska announced that her leading man would sleep in her private palace car while Georgie and the children could make shift with the supporting cast and the baggage. Georgie had her own priorities: Maurice was her husband and husbands slept with their wives. Modjeska gave in, and a strange attraction sprang up between the two women. Not that Modjeska gave up trying to get Barrymore into her bed.

Of the children who toured this season and again in 1883–1884, Ethel would be the most affected. Having lost her only daughter in childhood, Modjeska was drawn to the shy, eager child with enormous eyes that changed from blue to gray to black with her moods. Modjeska may have had mixed motives when she persuaded Georgie, ready to send the children back to Mummum, to let them stay (after all, they kept Georgie busy), yet she appeared genuinely fond of them and again, when the nanny got fed up with "theatre folk" and quit, she offered her own maids. As a result, a second powerful woman came into Ethel's life. The children were allowed behind the scenes at matinees, and Modjeska often felt Ethel's eager eyes following every move of a love scene with Orlando or her death scene as Marguerite.

But Modjeska's influence went further. Without Modjeska, Ethel would have become an actress, but she would not have become a Catholic.

Mummum was strict Episcopalian, paying Philadelphia social dues for those husbands and a stage career with her own pew in St. Stephen's and a silver offering dish engraved "L. Drew." But though she taught Sunday school, Georgie was apparently unmoved by the Episcopalian creed. Attracted now to Modjeska, she began to feel the appeal of Modjeska's religion. Since Georgie's voice is silent so is the real reason for her conversion. A declaration of independence from Mummum, perhaps.

Perhaps a bond that she hoped the predatory Modjeska might honor. Or perhaps just a need for a simpler faith. Given Maurice's casual approach to marriage, she would need all the miracles she could get.

Modjeska remembered the precociously adult Lionel on this tour lying for hours on his stomach in the aisle of the railway car drawing ships and trains or, in a restaurant where she took them for tea and cream cakes, sitting quietly while Ethel chattered on her lap. But for Lionel, Modjeska was not the star of this tour, an honor reserved for Billy Muldoon, a wrestler friend whom Maurice imported to play Charles the Wrestler in *As You Like It* when the original Charles deserted.

Nobody but an old friend would have dared to start tickling "Handsome Billy Muldoon" onstage during the bout when Orlando has Charles pinned to the ground. Muldoon writhed, swore, and was only saved from hysterics when Maurice released him to get on with the scene. Lionel knew nothing about Muldoon's vow of vengeance. Standing in the wings watching the next performance, he only knew that in the center of the ring where Orlando was supposed to be trouncing Charles, Maurice was suddenly seized by Muldoon, thrown over his knee, and walloped, while the Cleveland audience roared with laughter. Lionel paled. If Muldoon could punish his amateur middleweight champion father, what might he not do to a child.

Typically, Lionel confided his dread to no one. He managed to keep out of Muldoon's sight until St. Louis, where he was unexpectedly allowed to substitute in *As You Like It* as the "Second Banished Page." The pages were warbling their "hey noninos" when Lionel chanced to glance into the wings. There stood the terrible Muldoon. Lionel had no intention of being spanked in front of an audience or anywhere else. With a yell he bolted, leaving the First Page to finish the duet solo.

Back in New York in April before beginning the western lap of the tour, Georgie made her official conversion to Catholicism and arranged for the baptisms of her three children. Before the fatal day, however, Mummum paid a visit to the Judsons' boardinghouse in Gramercy Park where Drews and Barrymores often stayed. Georgie and the children were out, but a young Judson entertained Mrs. Drew while she waited with the news that there would soon be a christening.

"How nice," said Mrs. Drew conversationally. "And who is the lucky child? One of your little cousins?"

"Oh, no, Mrs. Drew," said the child, "it's your grandchildren. We've never been inside a *Catholic* church before!"

Catholic! Mrs. Drew rose and the child fled. *Her* grandchildren—Papists! This must be her degenerate son-in-law's doing. But when the family returned, she discovered to her utter chagrin that the renegade was her own daughter. Suddenly Maurice's Anglican pedigree made him an ally, and for a brief moment (as Ethel said later) Louisa was under the impression that she and Maurice had something in common—"one of her incredibly few errors." For as it turned out, Maurice reacted to his family's conversion as he did to most things, with infinite amusement.

According to legend, Mummum was not yet defeated. Since Lionel and Ethel were already baptized Protestants, the Catholic baptism, she argued, wouldn't "take." Little unbaptized Greengoose had no such protection. That night after Georgie and Maurice left for the theatre, she fled with Jack into the (surely dark and windy) night back to Philadelphia. The next morning at seven o'clock her coachman roused Dr. William Rudder and an hour later, with Uncle Googan and Aunt Tibby as godparents, little Jack was safely out of the clutches of the pope. Meanwhile that same day in New York Georgie rushed Lionel and Ethel to the nearest Catholic church. With Modjeska and the Count standing godparents for Lionel, and a woman who ran a theatrical boardinghouse and an "Italian" tenor for Ethel, Georgie defied her mother for the second important time in her life.

Another good story. If only records survived to prove it. If lack of evidence is no proof that John was *not* baptized, at least Dr. Rudder could not have performed the ceremony: his death in 1880 would have proved a decisive obstacle.

Having won over the wife, Modjeska tried again for the husband on a second tour. At her encouragement Maurice had written a play; performed in Baltimore and New York in February 1884, *Nadjezda* was well received and Barrymore hailed as a promising playwright. If Modjeska thought her patronage would bring Barrymore back into her arms, however, she was mistaken. In revenge she began to play cat and mouse with him: playing *Nadjezda* on the poorest drawing days of the week, encouraging her husband's jealousy of his rival, snubbing Georgie.

Suddenly Georgie's love affair with Modjeska was decidedly over even though she herself was now acting in Modjeska's company. In Boston she managed to subtly sabotage a Modjeska triumph in *The Lady of the Camellias*. Modjeska was furious. The next afternoon Modjeska had her revenge by deliberately dying too near the footlights so that when the curtain fell she and Maurice were stranded in front of it. As Maurice desperately maneuvered to get them behind, the curtain shot up then dropped again, leaving them still in full view of the now laughing audience. This time Maurice was furious.

Watching her idol from the wings, Ethel had no idea that Modjeska and her father had quarreled. When the stage was empty, she stole out and picked up the wreath of calla lillies from a fan that Maurice had so inexplicably flung away. She tapped at Modjeska's door and held out the wreath worshipfully. To her horror, Modjeska seized the flowers, hurled them to the floor, and stormed from the room. Ethel wept, not knowing that the superstitious actress loathed white lilies as a bad omen and thought that Maurice had sent Ethel deliberately to taunt her.

Ethel survived. "I was only four years old," she said much later, "but I remember Madame as Rosalind and Marguerite Gautier more vividly than any memory of Duse, Bernhardt, Réjane, or Ellen Terry. I don't remember Papa or Mamma in the plays at all. But Madame Modjeska was stamped on my mind and heart indelibly for my life. . . ."

As exciting as the Modjeska tours was the trip to London that followed. Retiring after twenty years as London's foremost actor-managers, Squire and Marie Wilton Bancroft invited Maurice to join them in a farewell season of their biggest successes. Of course Maurice was flattered, Georgie eager to see her husband's country, and the children not to be left behind. On July 5, 1884, Mummum came to New York to say good-bye to her family: John Jr. and his wife Josephine traveling with Augustin Daly's company; Adine, off on one of the few adventures of her quiet life; Georgie and Maurice with Lionel, Ethel, and two-year-old Jack.

Georgie hired a French governess to dress the children and generally keep them from harassing passengers and tumbling overboard while she and Maurice sparkled in the main salon. The governess did not keep them from pestering the captain with constant "When shall we get to Liverpool"s. "Captain Roberts is gracious to us," Lionel the solemn reported to his parents, "but keeps his own counsel and we can only hope soon to see land once more." When they finally docked they could see nothing but fog and flapping gulls, but everything about England was an adventure.

Maurice's London solicitors had found them a house with a walled garden in fashionably bohemian St. John's Wood Road. Maurice's engagement with the Bancrofts did not begin till fall so everyone was on holiday in London town, where Henry Irving and Ellen Terry reigned at the Lyceum Theatre, Burne-Jones and Browning presided over arts and letters, and cocky young men like Whistler, Wilde, and Shaw were challenging the establishment on all fronts. Temperamentally, Maurice was a carryover of the Regency rake: Byronic in his taste for pugilism, lowlife, bawdiness, eccentricity—for everything not middle-class. He indulged his Byronism now by installing exotic monkeys and birds in cages in the garden and, flush with $12,500 from a recent sale of English family property, splurged on servants, wine, and entertainment for the artistic people to whom the Barrymores' youth, promise, and glamour gave them instant introductions.

The children needed a nanny, and Polly came, more beautiful with her "crinkly red hair" (said Maurice) than the beautiful red-haired actress Mary Anderson. Georgie was more concerned with Polly's good judgment, suggesting, after a visit to Madame Tussaud's that kept Ethel screaming for weeks with nightmares, that future excursions be confined to parks and the British Museum.

Relatives had to be faced. Henry Wace, whose brother had married Maurice's sister Evelin, was the Principal of King's College, Cambridge, and Honorary Chaplain to Queen Victoria. The Barrymores, the children combed and curried, went to tea in Portland Place with misgivings: though actors were beginning to be taken up by society, Henry Irving's knighthood was eleven years away and the stage not yet a gentleman's profession. Henry and Elizabeth Wace dealt with Maurice's unfortunate career by ignoring its existence. The children had been instructed to behave, and conversation was proceeding neutrally until Lionel took his first sip of tea. "Ma'am," he announced in his best grown-up style, "this tea is damn hot!" There was a terrible silence. "Maurice," said Georgie with a straight face, "haven't I *warned* you not to let the children stray into the coachman's quarters, where they hear such language?" The Barrymores and Waces concluded family obligations with relief.

Far more successful were Georgie's "at-homes" in the St. John's Wood house, which quickly won a reputation as a "social, literary, and artistic centre." Georgie was a witty, lively hostess, and Maurice, though he hated society people who slummed with show people for thrills, was bonhomie itself. The children became used to brilliant and amusing gatherings that might include Ellen Terry, the prize fighter Ned Donnelly, George Grossmith (the inimitable performer of Gilbert and Sullivan patter songs), or Oscar Wilde.

The Barrymores had already met Wilde in New York, where Georgie had actually got the better of him. "America," Wilde had announced to an admiring crowd, "is a most uninteresting place. No antiquities, don't you know; no curiosities." "My dear Mr. Wilde, we shall have the antiquities in time," said Georgie, scanning his flowing locks, green velvet coat, enormous scarab ring, and patent pumps—"and we are already importing the curiosities!"

Despite a certain oiliness and a black front tooth that shocked when he laughed, the brilliant Oscar had become a fixture in London drawing rooms and was invited to the Barrymores'. At the Sunday at-homes, Ethel was invariably made to pass sandwiches and cake, which she did so shyly, her enormous eyes fixed on the carpet, that Georgie often teased her with a line from *The Lady of Lyons*, "Look up, Pauline!" One Sunday Ethel extended the cake plate toward a pair of patent pumps. "Look up, Pauline!" called Georgie from across the room. Ethel looked up into the decadent-Roman-emperor face of Oscar Wilde, shrieked, dropped the plate, and fled. Mamma and Papa might laugh over Lionel's performance at the Waces who, after all, were only relatives, but Oscar was a friend in their home. "My parents nearly killed me," said Ethel. "I don't remember ever being so severely punished for anything."

Critics praised Maurice's first appearance with the Bancrofts that November as Count Orloff in *Diplomacy*. Soon afterward, he began work with a friend on a second play, *Waldemar: or the Robber of the Rhine*; for convenience and research he took a flat in Store Street near the British Museum. Lionel was attending the Gilmore School in Warrington Crescent, Ethel and John amusing themselves with Polly, Aunt Tibby, the monkeys, birds, and dogs—but Georgie was hurt by her husband's defection. Yet it was not another woman she had to fear as much as Maurice's eternal willingness to go along with the crowd. "There was much—too much—good fellowship," said Maurice's journalist friend Harry St. Maur. "Barry had the kind of geniality that catches its glow from surroundings; he had to do what was being done to avoid what would have seemed to him unkindness."

Some Saturday evenings after the theatre, however, Maurice would take Georgie back to Store Street, and from time to time he would turn up in St. John's Wood, spar with his sons, cuddle Ethel, take them to the pantomime at Drury Lane or the zoo in Hyde Park, let them stay up till all hours ("owlingales," a friend called the children), slip them sovereigns—playing the good father as enthusiastically as he played the bon vivant. "While he was with you he was indivisibly yours," said one of Maurice's pals, ". . . but when the rest of the world captured him in its turn you became a negligible quantity. His engagements were recorded in air . . . he abandoned himself to any society that interested him." When his children ceased to interest him, Maurice would vanish as suddenly as he had come. While he was with them he was delightful, but he was not often with them.

The Prince of Wales himself chose the evening of July 20, 1885, for the beloved Bancrofts' final appearance on the London stage. For the great occasion Maurice brought Mummum and Sidney to London, Louisa

Drew's first return to the country she had left fifty-eight years before. Mummum's reaction to Maurice's Ernest Vane in *Masks and Faces* is unrecorded (Maurice would have been lucky to get a smile and a nod), but that evening, which capped his acclaimed appearance at the Haymarket, was the high point of Maurice's London career. The family took a cottage for the summer on the Thames at Weybridge; Maurice and Georgie talked of making England their permanent home. But this dream was permanently shattered on the evening of January 2, 1886, when the curtain fell on his unlucky *Nadjezda* to jeers and hisses. "He couldn't care much ever," said Harry St. Maur, "and after that—he cared not at all."

And so in June 1886 the Barrymores with the indispensable Polly and the dogs and birds and monkeys came back to New York to find Mummum waiting at the wharf to welcome them. London was finally too small for them: for Georgie, whose spirited performance in *Nadjezda* had been branded shockingly suggestive; for the bohemian Maurice who really preferred Broadway to the West End. Had their parents stayed in England, the theatrical careers of the three Barrymores—embedded in classical tradition—would have been very different. As it was, all three were life-long Anglophiles, and two of them would feel the challenge of conquering the London stage.

And finally there were summer days on Staten Island or at Pleasure Bay or Point Pleasant on the Jersey shore. Point Pleasant in those days was little more than half a dozen farms stretching from the Manasquan River through dense pine groves, green pastures, salty marshes, and white sand dunes to the broad blue sea. Mummum and the children would take the train, then a three-hour drive in a rickety stagecoach through hot, sweet pine woods to one of the rambling houses let to summer folk, and sometimes Maurice in white flannels or Georgie in fluttering summer skirts would come and play. The Davis family also summered in Point Pleasant, and young Charles and Richard Harding Davis had huge crushes on Georgie, who was so "wonderfully handsome" with a "marvellously cheery manner." The Davis boys remembered Ethel, "a sweet, long-legged child in a scarlet bathing suit running toward the breakers and then dashing madly back to her mother's open arms." Tattooed with mosquito bites, the children lived outdoors all day—swimming, sailing, fishing; climbing, falling. Ethel was called "the water rat" because she would dare anything in the water, but Lionel and Jack were equally skilled swimmers who calmly struck out for shore when the catamaran they'd built sank under them one summer at Pleasure Bay. At Point Pleasant they'd usually be on the beach all morning until Georgie would come racing out of the waves and up the beach calling "Come along, kids—lunch!" "It was lovely," said Ethel, "to hear her say 'kids.'"

Yet the Barrymore children never really knew Maurice and Georgie. Lionel was "interested" in his parents "what little time I saw them." Jack said flatly that he never knew his mother. Ethel said that both her father and mother were strangers. Georgie's "kids" was lovely because it was longed for, and rare.

THREE

1886–1892

IT WAS MUMMUM who seemed to anchor their young lives with a routine as invariable as her integrity. Weekdays she was driven in her black brougham to the Arch Street Theatre, where she arrived at ten to go over her books and oversee all arrangements for that evening's production. Typically, she insisted that her theatre be immaculately clean, that every scene-shifter, carpenter, and property man wear suits of white canvas, and that every foot be shod in felt while the play was in performance. A sign of her displeasure was a certain red paisley shawl; if she flung it about her shoulders every last employee knew he had better be on his best behavior. At two she emerged from the theatre to be driven home again. Promptly at three dinner was served by the current Mary Aggie. After dinner she retired to her room to read or rest. She took a cup of tea before leaving again for the theatre where the doors opened at quarter-past seven sharp and the performance began at quarter of eight precisely. Returning, she had a light supper of cheese and crackers or a cup of soup in her room, chased with a dram of rye whiskey before retiring.

Every Sunday she regally entered her pew off the center aisle on the gospel side as though it were *not* in the rear under the balcony, and sat upright through the longest sermons. On Sunday afternoons she entertained theatre folk and less snobbish Philadelphians in her drawing room where her grandchildren might appear silently in their Sunday best, for in Mummum's house children in the presence of grownups were not allowed "to utter." However chaotic their parents' lives, the children could predict Mummum's to the minute.

One forty North Twelfth seemed as uncompromisingly changeless as its chatelaine. The ornate silver tea service embossed with grapes and vines. The Victorian landscapes on the walls. The illustrated volumes of *The Ancient Mariner* and *Picturesque America*, so immense that the children

23

could scarcely hold them on their laps. The music box that chimed "Carnival of Venice." The white marble front steps up and down which they played for countless hours. One forty seemed as respectable as Philadelphia itself, whose satisfied residents considered anyplace else—especially New York—"out of town."

In her theatre, said the young actress Clara Morris, Mrs. John Drew ruled with "a certain chill austerity of manner, her weapons a sharp sarcasm, while her strength lay in her self-control, her self-respect." In her house too Mummum's word was final, her displeasure to be feared. "Whenever any member of the family appears upon the stage you are *never* to applaud!" commanded Mummum; the children never did. Lionel might complain that Mary Aggie pulled his ears. "*She pulls them with reason*," said Mummum. Jack might rush in late for dinner. "Oh, Mummum," he said in one desperate attempt at diversion, "have you ever seen a house *all painted black?*" "No," said his grandmother decisively, "nor have you. Sit down!" Sometimes the children's were not the worst crimes. Kitty came to complain that "Mr. Lionel was very naughty, Mrs. Drew. He kicked me, Mrs. Drew, he kicked me in the shins." "Shins, woman!" cried the Duchess. "What are *shins?* Leave the room!"

But Louisa Drew's real genius lay in creating the impression of stability, for in reality her professional life was as unstable as the acting trade itself. She had begun at the Arch as manager of a well-trained group of actors skilled in playing varieties of roles: this was theatre as she knew it. Gradually, however, her company was undermined by touring companies from New York that used local actors merely to support them. Louisa Drew heartily disliked being reduced to a booking agent, but Philadelphians now demanded more than resident actors. She held out stubbornly until 1876, watching the theatre she loved die on her hands, then tried a "combination house" of alternating stock and touring productions. Eventually even that compromise failed. In 1880, after thirty years at the Arch, she was forced to tour. A bitter blow: her ancestors had been strolling players, vagabonding about England; in managing her own theatre she had achieved a status far above the Kinlocks and the Lanes. However, the tour was not exactly punishment (though her son-in-law *was* in the cast). Joseph Jefferson's company was famous for *The Rivals*, Louisa's superb Mrs. Malaprop now gained wide recognition, her salary was enough to keep the Arch open, she did return. But the days she loved were dead.

These theatrical adjustments created violent fluctuations in her domestic economy. Sometimes there were new velveteen coats for her grandchildren, and concerts at the Academy of Music and treats of Dexter's White Mountain Cake. At other times toes were pinched in outgrown shoes and Jack, playing "Bean-porridge hot, bean-porridge cold" with Ethel, craved any porridge, even nine days old. Georgie's acting engagements were sporadic, it was "find your own dresses" at the theatre, and Georgie's personal wardrobe was lavish. She did little more to save money than Maurice, whose excesses, however, made her cry: good money squandered on a bear cub bought on impulse in Kansas City or spent at Georgiana Hastings's brothel in the notorious Tenderloin district at Sixth Avenue and Broadway.

And, despite her renowned self-control, Mummum's temper could be as unpredictable as her bank balance. Writing her memoirs in 1953, Ethel found herself struggling with the ambivalent feelings Mummum had aroused. Although she admired Mummum's "force without effort," she also felt the impact of her strong, dark, frequent moods as well as the oppression of "an exceptionally rigid and appallingly respectable household"—strong words from Ethel Barrymore, who seldom took the public into her confidence. Some things Ethel could not bring herself to say. Writing of Louisa Drew's "command tempered by sense and a quiet unspoken love," for example, she crossed out *love* and substituted *feeling*. Mummum was partial to Jack, but all three children felt the darker side of their grandmother's nature which denied them warmth, approval, and love.

Besides, Louisa Drew's own career often meant that they "had to be set aside." Thus it was Mrs. Griffiths when Mummum went on tour, or Kitty or Aunt Tibby or Polly who ran after the children and tried to make them behave. Out of Mummum's sight they were always falling into or out of something: Jack from a tree cutting open his head on a flowerpot, from which accident he carried a little triangular scar over his eyebrow that burned white when he was angry; Ethel, "fishing" over the third-floor banister, leaning over to untangle her line from Lionel's and plummeting two flights to land in the entrance hall unhurt.

Occasionally they were good. Near Mummum's theatre at 819 Arch Street William Clark had a shop where they spent hours sitting on his knee watching him cut patterns for ladies' dresses or drawing themselves on pattern wrappings—Lionel crayoning sailboats and trains puffing lots of steam, Ethel carefully printing the alphabet until, bored at *J*, she wrote the rest upside down and backward. Mrs. Clark often saw them in the neighborhood: "beautiful children," she thought them, "always accompanied by a nurse, not mingling much with other youngsters." She evidently did not see Kitty dragging Lionel and Ethel home in disgrace, their best clothes dyed indigo from their dip in Mrs. Garrett's big wooden blueing tub.

Or witness their inevitable internecine quarrels. Ethel was fiercely protective of Jack but ready to do battle with Lionel, a rivalry that often ended with the tall and strong Ethel delivering as good as she got. Since she was a girl, Lionel was usually blamed for the conflict; perhaps this is why Ethel always considered Lionel "unlucky." They both competed at being good: according to Jack Lionel was "a steady citizen" and Ethel, apart from spirited struggles with her older brother, "behaved herself perfectly." As they grew older, however, Ethel and her brothers grew apart. She found herself excluded from slingshot competitions and ghost-hunts, from stalking Iroquois in the shrubbery of the nearby Academy of Fine Arts and, of course, from pool-hall expeditions with Uncle Goo-gan. Lionel and Jack had boys' freedom, and Jack in particular was dangerously precocious.

There was the time, for instance, after a large dinner party that Mummum found him unconscious on the dining-room floor. The doctor came, noted the drained wine glasses. "The boy's drunk, ma'am," he said bluntly, to her shock and relief. There was the time Mummum missed a quantity of good stage jewelry. As she accompanied the detectives about the house her eye fell upon little Jack idling with elaborate nonchalance. The detectives were dismissed and Mummum went for the Green Slipper, an old Russian-leather castoff the children had learned to dread. But Jack freely admitted he was "a little more fruitful in untruth than his contemporaries." He often pilfered money from the residents of 140, so little at a time that it wasn't missed, stashing the loot in a secret hiding place in the Annex. And there was the time that Jack, newly enrolled at Seton Hall, was invited by Father Marshall to try out the gymnasium's parallel bars. Jack promptly swung himself into a handstand while out of his pockets tumbled, before the cleric's fascinated gaze, a pack of cigarettes, brass knuckles, and a half-pint of rotgut whiskey (Lionel's inventory), or a pack of cards, a razor, a loaded pistol, and a pair of dice (Gene Fowler's)—or perhaps all of the above.

And so it was rather perverse that Louisa Drew preferred bad little Jack among her grandchildren, just as (according to Jack) she favored the "very naughty" Sidney over her impeccably correct son John. Eventually the preference drove a wedge between the brothers. In the summer of 1892, Louisa had very little money; Maurice was touring, his children out of sight and therefore out of mind; and somehow Lionel and Jack were allowed to spend their vacation at Maurice's derelict farm on Staten Island in the care of Edward Briggs, an ancient Negro nicknamed, for his great dignity, "the Black Prince." It was paradise: no beds to make, teeth to brush, dishes to wash—until Mummum announced a visit.

"We worked for days cleaning up the place," said Jack, "scrubbing floors, clearing rubbish out of the yard. We even made our beds and tied up some of the dogs. On the appointed day the Black Prince donned his yellow and white striped shirt that he wore on quite important occasions. Lionel and I bathed and put on our best clothes."

But the day wore on and Mummum did not appear. Next morning, they received a telegram: Why had Lionel and Jack not come to Long Branch as invited? They reread her letter, discovered their mistake. Jack answered that they would be glad to come but they had no money. A few days later money arrived—for Jack.

A cruel, if unintentional, slight. Although he returned to Staten Island a few days later, "it was a long time before I got back to Lionel," said Jack. "My grandmother's favoritism had built a wall between us. It was years before he forgot." Unlucky Lionel.

While Louisa Drew was a rock to which her grandchildren could cling, Louisa Drew was also a stone that could bruise. Her chief legacy to her grandchildren, however, would be "the powerful and lingering influence that taught that one never disclosed one's deepest feelings." This reticence affected them to the degree she herself practiced it. Lionel and Ethel became deeply reserved. Because she loved Jack best he was the most spontaneous and at the same time the most uncertain of where his real allegiances lay.

IT WAS MUMMUM, without a day of formal schooling herself, who insisted the children not be "dragged about like urchins" when they returned from London. Georgie agreed—they would go to Catholic schools. At this Mummum "gave tongue": Who was paying and who was responsible for them in Philadelphia? Mother and daughter finally compromised. Lionel would board at the Episcopal Academy in town; Ethel would carry on the Modjeska-Georgie line at the Convent of Notre Dame. Jack, only four, would stay for the time being with Mummum.

At eight Lionel began his erratic progress through a series of classrooms he consistently failed to illuminate. Mummum was so unimpressed with his performance at the Academy that when an acquaintance boasted one day that Race Public School had made a man of him, she enrolled Lionel at Race. The boy was made a man of speedily. "Hello, Mary Aggie, you old sonofabitch!" he greeted the maid, who promptly ran to Mrs. Drew with Mr. Lionel's latest infamy. Lionel was hastily snatched from Race and Philadelphia, and Georgie had her way.

He was sent first, in 1887, to St. Aloysius Academy in Yonkers, where he learned little and was taunted as "Lord Cornwallis" for the English accent he'd still not shed. One February evening in 1888 in New York, Maurice opened his door at the Sturdevant House to a shivering and sooty truant. The nine-year-old had run away, walking through the dark, train-infested railroad tunnel that led into old Grand Central Terminal, then down to his parents' hotel at 1586 Broadway, thirteen long cold miles. Amused, Maurice took Lionel in, only remarking when a frantic wire from St. Aloysius announced Lionel's disappearance, "I hope they find him." Eventually Lionel was sent back, ran away again, and was transferred to Mount Saint Vincent, a foundation of the Sisters of Charity at Fonthill on the Hudson, where he lasted a semester.

Lionel says he attended Seton Hall in South Orange, New Jersey, from the age of ten to fifteen, where he continued to establish "an all-time record for resistance to knowledge." School records show him entering in 1889, boy number 1,366 to pass through the Catholic prep school doors since its opening in 1856. From first to last Lionel sat with the small boys in arithmetic class, the multiplication tables a mystery he had no intention of solving. He did better in English (until he chose to read aloud a passage from De Quincey about the prostitute Ann) and in Latin, to which he was drawn by something more powerful than intellectual curiosity. He had got hold of a book containing explanations of matters that "seemed to shine with glittering interest"; however, just when the mysteries of sex were about to be revealed before his popping eyes, the author would lapse infuriatingly into Latin. Lionel applied himself to Latin.

Little Jack stayed a year with Mummum before she gave up her favorite to the Catholics. Unlikely that Louisa Drew had mellowed. Perhaps, inspecting Ethel on weekends, she found no signs of popish degeneracy; perhaps at sixty-seven she was too concerned with dwindling theatre receipts to protest. So Jack went as a day scholar to the small boys' school attached to Ethel's convent, was made much of by apple-cheeked Sister Vincent, then went home to Mummum afternoons.

In Mummum's house the children had been fascinated with a big illustrated book showing avenging angels hurling the souls of the damned into a fiery pit. At the convent school a more impressively illustrated book came into Jack's hands, assigned by Sister Vincent as penance for hitting another boy in the ear with a hard-boiled egg. It was Dante's *Inferno*, illustrated with the tormented drawings of Gustave Doré. Instead of terrifying, Doré's drawings fascinated Jack; he egged the boy again to get another look. Soon Sister Vincent had to tell his parents that little Jack spent entirely too much time scrawling pictures in his books and even on the walls—lurid pictures of monsters and the Devil that frightened the other children.

"Why *do* you draw pictures of the Bad Man and monsters?"

"Because I see them in my sleep," said Jack.

An older John liked to blame Doré's infernal drawings for much that was macabre in his character. But that is cart before horse. Doré spellbound him because even then he thought of himself as "bad." Two kinds of stories emerge from Jack's thinly documented childhood: his "second-story capers" and his love of his supremely virtuous grandmother. Admiring goodness and believing oneself bad is an explosive combination that accounts for much of the self-hatred that afflicted John Barrymore.

In the fall of 1891 after a season of low receipts at the Arch, Mummum was again forced to tour with her friend Joseph Jefferson in *The Rivals*. With Mummum gone Jack was sent to join Lionel at Seton Hall. He seemed to be settling in until one day Mummum received a hair-raising scrawl from South Orange. "I was attacked by this huge fellow and without cause," wrote Jack in one version of the famous letter. "And, as the great brute advanced toward my desk, I tried to placate him; but he struck me a blow which felled me to the ground."

This at least was something her feckless son-in-law could handle. "My father's on his way to beat seven kinds of hell out of the entire faculty!" boasted Jack. "Blood will flow from here to Newark!" Suddenly he was the big man on campus. On the promised day, Jack and the boys watched from the shrubbery as the former middleweight champ clattered up in a hack, jumped out, and disappeared into the building housing the headmaster's study.

Inside, Maurice shook hands with Father William Marshall, a sophisticated and personable priest. The "great brute" turned out to be a junior instructor who had discovered Jack reading *Buffalo Bill's Adventures* inside the covers of a schoolbook and laid a reprimanding hand on his head. Enchanted with Jack's creativity, Maurice dismissed the incident and plunged into a lively debate with Father Marshall over the outcome of a recent murder case while in the shrubbery poor Jack tried to account to increasingly skeptical mates for the singular lack of fireworks in the administrative chambers. Eventually two figures emerged arm in arm from the hall, chatting cozily. "Tell the boy to look out and behave himself," Jack heard his father say as he jumped into the hack and was gone without a backward glance.

Not that Maurice did not contribute to his sons' educations. What they learned from him during sporadic visits to New York was, in fact, the real curriculum.

Maurice was an Oxford man; they learned to respect education while resisting it. Maurice was a great reader; they learned to respect words and books. (When Jack was twelve he discovered Victor Hugo and ran to Lionel with the great news. "Ethel and I read them all," said Lionel scornfully, "*years* ago.") Maurice had a rapier wit; they learned humor. Maurice knew everyone; they found that successful people taught life's real lessons. Maurice had no snobbery and little vanity. He was generous, spontaneous, and the most amusing company in the world. In all this he set his sons an example.

But Maurice was also irresponsible, thriftless, and lazy. The difference between what he could do professionally and what he did do was a source of despair to those who cared about the theatre. "There is no man on the American stage today who can play the melodramatic hero better than he if he wants to," wrote one frustrated critic; "none his superior in refined comedy would he only give his mind to it. When one knows what a really brilliant man Maurice Barrymore is, how far ahead he is in talent of most of the successful actors on our boards, one feels inclined to kick him as he shambles through his part."

He was intemperate, the victim of a culture that said that "real men" drank, smoked, swore, gambled, and preferred the company of other "real men." "Staggering is a sign of strength," Maurice would say; "weak men are carried home." It was no accident that Maurice Barrymore was the favorite leading man of male theatregoers. Fidelity to a woman was also a weakness. Women were a necessary evil. They didn't understand a man, and a man was a fool to trust them. Through Maurice, Lionel and Jack were exposed to every vice in the world.

Already older and in some ways more responsible than his father, Lionel admired him "inordinately" while escaping serious infection. Jack, however, was not only highly impressionable but fatally like his father. "He did not resemble Maurice Barrymore," said Lionel of Jack the man. "He resembled his mother more in looks. He did not . . . affect any mannerisms or techniques of Maurice Barrymore's on the stage. This would have been impossible, Jack being too young to observe these things (and not caring anyway) before his father died. But Jack was like Maurice. They seem[ed] to have . . . precisely the same talent, the same imbalance, the same oddly slanted curiosity, the same ennui with achievement once achieved, the same integrity—and the same capacity for hurting themselves. On stage they were brilliant and poised. Off stage, they invariably stumbled and barked their shins."

Augustus ("Gus") Thomas, the playwright and Maurice's closest associate, analyzed Maurice's legacy to his sons differently. Maurice himself was a contradiction: he combined the sturdiness of a Greek gladiator with the grace of a man who could sip a cup of tea in a drawing room. Maurice had bequeathed his gladiator quality to Lionel, thought Thomas, his teacup quality to Jack, whose features, so extraordinarily like his father's in the modeling, were poetic rather than manly.

Ethel did not share her brothers' admiration of their father. She hated the name he had given her after Thackeray's heroine in *The Newcomes*. ("Eethyl," Jack teased her.) She burst into tears when he pushed back her bangs and said she should wear her hair like "Alice's" with a round comb. His eccentricity embarrassed the child Mummum had taught never to display emotion in public. Once after the Giants lost a baseball game and Maurice was striding up and down the train platform "throwing his arms to heaven" and shouting "God! how could you do this to me?" she ran away from him and ended in a police station. And he broke promises. She never forgave him for telling her that she must go to Vienna and study piano with Theodor Leschetizky, then never mentioning it again. But of course she never knew the excitement of being partners in crime with her father: was never checked into the Lambs Club cloakroom and forgotten, like Jack, or introduced in a bar by Maurice to Mark Twain, like Lionel. To Ethel, Maurice was not admirable.

In the convent the blond, blue-eyed girl had promptly been dubbed "Little Ethel" and made a pet of by the sisters and the older girls. In unCatholic Philadelphia, the Convent of the Sisters of Notre Dame de Namur on the South Nineteenth Street side of Rittenhouse Square was considered fashionable, and many Protestant families sent their daughters there, though they preferred to call it "the Academy."

The sisters were gentlewomen: serious, high-minded, romantic, ever alert to save the souls of their charges from sin. Over the boarders presided Sister Julie de Saint Esprit, surveillance her creed, x-ray vision her genius. Not a scribbled note, an exploring hand, a cache of sweets, a secret crush, an undarned black stocking, or an unsaid prayer escaped her. Girls took baths in their shifts, rose at chilly dawn to hurry into dark serge uniforms decorated only by pink or blue good-conduct ribbons, walked out in twos under the eagle eye of a chaperone, were handed their letters with all improper sentiments blacked out by the convent censor. Among pupils and sisters went Sister Superior Agnes Mary, frowning sweetly, grasping the reins in a strong, gentle hand.

Ethel loved it, she said. Catholic mysticism may not have moved her, but Catholic discipline reassured her. She bloomed for the almost impossible to please music teacher, even though Sister Aloysius saw to it that Ethel's rendition of Beethoven's Thirteenth Sonata took second place in the contest to May Heizmann's "Nearer My God to Thee with Variations." She claims she dreaded Recitation Days, waiting with cold hands while other girls rattled off Shakespeare with the confidence of amateurs. Her classmate Mary Hagerty said, however, that Ethel "could memorize to beat the band. Boy, could she reel off Longfellow!" She had "butter hair," said Mary, and "her uniform never slipped off her shoulders like the other girls'." During recess she played tag and guessing games with the rest of the girls in the walled garden, but was a bit of a show-off, thought Mary—promising to wear her Grandmother Drew's jewels to school the following Monday.

On weekends she went home to 140. Saturday afternoons, off and on, she attended Professor Asher's dancing class in an old hall on South Broad Street, her long curls bobbing as she skipped over the floor. Most of the time she spent in her room with her nose in romantic novels like *Robert Elsmere* and *David Greve* unless she was sitting in Mummum's box at the Arch, lost in the passions of the Saturday melodrama. She was dreamy, serious, and reserved, with a winning personality and a lovely smile. She was very, very good and conscious of it.

So they grew, their childhoods both privileged and poor. Their name—Barrymore—wasn't even real but something their father had taken off a theatre poster. They were brought up like gentry, yet thoroughly steeped in the stage. Every family saying was a quotation from some play or another: if Maurice wasn't reciting the bawdiest passages of Shakespeare or Georgie calling to Ethel, "Look up, Pauline!" then they were being sent to bed with "Stand not upon the order of your going, but go at once!" or admonished at the table "to eat wisely and slow." They were drilled in family protocol, yet as a family were seldom together. When they were with their parents there were mysterious quarrels and Maurice's vanishings. The power of one woman created their only security. There was always 140 North Twelfth Street in Philadelphia. There was always Mummum when their parents failed.

But in 1892 Mummum began to fail them.

FOUR

1 8 9 2 – 1 8 9 7

IN 1 8 9 2 Louisa Drew looked at the red ink in her ledger and knew her days at the Arch Street Theatre were over.

There had been other losses. Eliza Kinlock had died in 1887 at ninety-two; Ethel didn't dread passing the big bedroom anymore. In cold January 1888 Adine died of lung congestion after twenty-eight uncomplaining years. ("I cried a lot over Aunt Tibby," said Ethel.) More tragically for Mummum, her older daughter Louisa was only thirty-seven when she died in Boston in 1889.

But with the Arch, where in her first three seasons alone she had acted ninety-two roles, Louisa Drew was losing her spiritual home. "This is much worse for me than it is for you," she told the audience who had applauded *The Widow Green* without suspecting it was Mrs. John Drew's last performance. "It is a wrench for me, I confess it. . . ." Her voice broke as she fought back tears. "This week has been a very happy one for me. The only drawback was, it was the last. To hear these walls resound with applause for simply acting and nothing more, the acting of an old comedy, merely acting, is something to make an actor's heart almost burst with joy. I thank you sincerely. . . ." Outside, the sign MRS. JOHN DREW, SOLE LESSEE came down. Thirty-one years as a theatre manager "better than any man in the country" were over.

With no Arch and no savings (she'd plowed back most of her earnings into her theatre) she also had to give up 140 North Twelfth Street— home for only eleven years but the only home Lionel, Ethel, and Jack knew. Maurice and Georgie had an apartment in New York on Fifty-ninth Street; after nearly forty years of housekeeping in Philadelphia, Louisa retreated there. Her gray-streaked brown hair had thinned, but her figure was still neat and her will indomitable. At seventy-two she began "to look about for something to do."

Paradoxically, the change in theatrical taste which had forced Louisa

Drew from the Arch was making stars of her children John and Georgie. Audiences had always cherished the Keans, Macreadys, Irvings, Terrys, Cushmans, McCulloughs, Booths, and Bernhardts, but equally they had cherished their Hamlets and Macbeths, Cleopatras and Ophelias. Now the public craved "personalities": actors who won audiences by being themselves in realistic dramas that eschewed ranting and melodrama. Louisa Drew disliked the new style—"a lazy stroll-about school of so-called repression," she called it, "empty and wearisome."

There were many reasons for this change, but none so important as the new respectability of the theatre. Plays now tended to mirror upper-class manners and mores. Larger audiences, ignorant of the classics, came to the theatre to learn to light a cigarette with elegance or accept a husband's infidelity like a lady. Actors who most convincingly aped on-stage the ideal patterns were taken up by society as a reward for good behavior. They helped maintain the illusion in the face of such realities as the recent influx of "undesirable" immigrants from Eastern European countries that the world was still comfortably Anglo-Saxon. At the same time the new mass-circulation tabloids, hungry for gossip and sensation, magnified the importance of this new generation of stage stars, making their every move offstage as important as their acting on. The result was enormous popularity, publicity, and salaries undreamed of by an older generation of actors.

No one was more aware of this changing taste in the theatre than Charles Frohman, the son of a German-Jewish peddler and himself one of a new breed of theatrical entrepreneurs. Actors like Irving, the Jeffersons, the Booths, and Mrs. Drew had managed themselves. As the theatre increasingly became big business, the entrepreneur stepped in to lift sordid financial details out of the new gentleman actor's hands. Powerful syndicates and trusts gained control of theatres nationwide until virtually no actor could appear without contracting himself to one of the monopolies. Frohman's ruthlessness was masked by a civilized manner, his shrewd eye for big money tempered by respect for big talent. Big talent meant Drew and Barrymore.

For years John Drew had been the biggest of Augustin Daly's "Big Four," collaborating with Ada Rehan, Mrs. G. H. Gilbert, and James Lewis in highly polished ensemble performances. Frohman guessed that John Drew's already considerable drawing power could be immense. He dined him on terrapin, let him win largely at poker, and finally offered him more money than Daly offered any actor in his palmiest days. "Frohman," Drew was told, "is the coming man."

On October 3, 1892, John Drew appeared as "The Big One" under

Frohman's management in *The Masked Ball* with a new leading lady named Maude Adams. Mummum, Georgie, and John's wife Josephine watched his triumph. Afterward the new star appeared before the curtain to gracefully thank his "friend and preceptor" Augustin Daly who, across the street in his darkened theatre, moaned "My boy, my boy!" like a parent robbed of a favorite child. Critics went wild over the Frohman-Drew combination, praising "every point of Mr. Drew's personality" with more notices in a week than many actors achieve in a lifetime. Frohman had created his first big star.

After a career interrupted by marriage and childbearing, Georgie had emerged in 1890 in *The Senator* as a sparkling comedian. In the summer of 1891 she accepted the lead in Frohman's production of William Gillette's *Mr. Wilkinson's Widows*. The first night launched her as "Georgie Drew Barrymore," a personality whose signatures were a tall graceful figure, an odd voice with a delightful break and quaver, and high spirits laced with witty repartee. After the performance Louisa Drew went backstage. She kissed Georgie's cheek and squeezed her hand, leaving Georgie to interpret these gestures as approval, for Louisa Drew did not expand.

For Lionel, Ethel, and John the center of family life was now an apartment in New York, where Georgie usually wasn't, Mummum sometimes was, and Maurice might arrive as dawn was breaking over the East River, or might not since he kept three other establishments for his convenience. Still, someone usually managed to be there when the children came on holiday, and whether the family was broke or flush, a holiday mood prevailed. Lionel and Jack stared at their father and the actor Richard Mansfield—both got up in circus tights, sashes, and astrakhan hats—peddling tandem down Fifth Avenue on that new craze, the bicycle. While Lionel solemnly spooned a huge ice-cream confection, Ethel watched Georgie and Maurice waltz to Maurice's own song "Hast Thou Forgot" under lantern-lit trees at an open-air restaurant on the Hudson— tears in her eyes because they were so handsome, so admired, so gay.

And then that autumn of 1892 Georgie was off touring as the star of a company called Frohman's Comedians. It seemed long ago that she had wrecked the apartment of a female rival for Maurice's affections and left her calling card among the shambles, or that early one morning on those marble steps she'd met her husband returning from a brothel and had answered his "Where are you going?" with "I'm going to church and you can go to hell!" She had always been a match for Maurice in talent and energy, but her career had suffered with her marriage. Now she was in demand, well paid, applauded and, according to Otis Skinner, the most delicious comedienne on any stage.

But in San Francisco where her spirited comedy brought down the curtain in bursts of applause, Georgie began to cough. She'd had bronchitis before, but not this sudden loss of breath that left her gasping. She refused to rest even when Maurice, alerted by Frohman, wired money for a sea voyage, but finally it was too much for her. She sailed for New York via Panama in January 1893, arriving tanned and rested and insisting she would open with Frohman's Comedians in February. She did, brilliantly, but in March an understudy took her place. Six weeks in Bermuda only postponed the inevitable. When the coughing began again she had to face the seriousness of her condition. For the first time in her life she became depressed and silent; for perhaps the first in his, Maurice realized how much he depended on her courageous gaiety. Like the exotic animals he collected, Maurice had never been successfully domesticated. Now, however, he gave up his bachelor evenings to be with her; he became afraid.

And so two weeks before summer vacation was to begin, Ethel was told to take her mother to Santa Barbara. She was tall and responsible for her age, but she was only thirteen and kept praying she would "be all right and not too shy and scared" of the mother she worshipped but hardly dared speak to. To Lionel and Jack the whole thing seemed like a holiday, with Mummum and Uncle Googan and Aunt Gladys at the North River pier, and Augustus Thomas, who admired Georgie, arriving with a beribboned china teapot stuffed with chocolate creams. Did Georgie share those chocolate creams with Lionel and Jack (as one story goes) or (as another) forget to offer them. The latter seems right here: Georgie clutching the teapot and begging Maurice not to forget her, the boys wondering why Mamma was hoarding such delicious-looking creams, Ethel dimly aware that she was witnessing tragedy.

What Georgie felt and thought these last weeks of her life is unrecorded; there are only Ethel's fragmentary yet vivid impressions. Georgie, as young as her daughter, chatty and gay during long sunny days on the boat. Georgie in the lower berth of their small cabin sobbing, "What's going to happen to my poor kids?" (it wasn't lovely to hear her say "kids" now) and smothering her cough so she wouldn't wake her daughter who, terrified, could never let her mother know she'd heard because in this family "one's deepest feelings were never disclosed." Then in Santa Barbara not the "lovely little house covered with roses" of Ethel's memory, but apartments at Bath and Arrellaga streets, and "a great and wonderful gentleman" who was their Chinese cook and retainer. Dr. Otto, who listened to Georgie's chest and was very grave when he heard she had only her daughter to care for her. Unpacking brocaded evening gowns and brocaded slippers: her mother must have brought everything she owned. Warm sun, bright flowers, red tile roofs, blue sea, soft Pacific air. Georgie out of doors, feeling so much better that she accepted an engagement for the next season. The news that Maurice was coming west on tour and bringing Lionel and Jack. Everyone in Santa Barbara so very kind. . . .

On Sunday, July 2, when they had been there three weeks, Ethel carried up her mother's breakfast tray. Georgie was cheerful and said that Ethel must run off to mass because *she* was feeling very well and was going for a carriage drive with the mayor Edward Gaty and his wife. She put on one of the lovely dresses, carefully rouged her cheeks which the sun had failed to color, took up her blue parasol, and waited for the Gatys' arrival at eleven.

Ethel was walking home slowly in the sunshine from eleven o'clock mass, kicking stones and every now and then doing a little dance in the middle of the road, when she looked up to see a girl running toward her.

"Oh, Ethel," called Mabel Gaty, "hurry home! Your mother has had a hemorrhage."

Dr. Otto had come. Georgie was just alive, the lovely dress ruined, and did not know her daughter before she died. The Chinese houseman quickly did things to the room to make it look "as if no terrible thing had happened." Very calm, Ethel set about doing what had to be done. She telegraphed Maurice and Uncle Sidney. She accepted the condolences which began pouring in. The next day she ordered black mourning. A telegram came from Mummum: Georgie must be brought home to Philadelphia; Ethel must travel with the coffin overland by train. Ethel made arrangements with the undertaker and the Southern Pacific railroad. Then she went upstairs to pack, and there, at the sight of all the lovely dresses and lovely shoes that Georgie would never wear again, she broke down at last.

In New York Gus Thomas had intercepted Ethel's wire at the Lambs Club and took it to Palmer's Theatre where Maurice was rehearsing. Maurice read the message, stared at Gus in bewilderment and, muttering something about the ferry, stumbled out of the theatre. Gus caught up with Maurice, persuaded him to wait at the Lambs Club while he made arrangements, bought a ticket, and wired Ethel that her father would meet her in Chicago. Then he collected Maurice, took him to the station, and sat with him for two hours during which Maurice did not say a single word.

Many kind people were at the station in Santa Barbara when the coffin was loaded into the baggage car for the eight-day journey. Ethel was determined to be brave and was, comforting Madame Modjeska, who met the train in Los Angeles and could not stop crying. "I did not cry," said Ethel. "I knew that the strangers on the car knew and cared nothing about my trouble. I read four or five books a day, turning over the leaves but not knowing what I read." There was no dining car on the train and Ethel was afraid to get off at the periodic restaurant stops. After twenty-four hours someone noticed her plight and brought her sandwiches and an apple.

In Chicago Maurice met a tall serious young woman in a black cloak. The day after Georgie's death Ethel had pinned up her ash-blond hair in a symbolic coming-of-age gesture; womanlike, she now comforted Maurice. She made arrangements for the final lap of the journey, walked with her weeping father behind the coffin as it was transferred to another train, held Maurice's hand as the train rumbled toward Philadelphia, though she herself would never cry in public. Finally she stepped off the train at the Broad Street Station into Mummum's arms.

Louisa Drew called her daughter Georgie's death "the keenest sorrow of my life." She refused to honor her Catholic conversion, arranging for the funeral to be held at Saint Stephen's. On July 12 the church was crowded with friends and kin. Ethel and Maurice, in a frock coat he had worn in *Frou Frou*, followed the blue-velvet-draped coffin crowned with Maurice's wreath of laurel and blue immortelles. Mummum followed, very straight and holding tight to Sidney, then Lionel and Aunt Gladys. Lionel rode in the carriage to Glenwood Cemetery with Maurice and his actor friend Eben Plympton. Still dazed, Maurice tugged incessantly at his high stiff collar until Plympton took out a cigarette, put it between Maurice's lips, and lit it. "It's not true," Maurice kept saying, "it's not true." Lionel saw the cigarette go out.

Jack said that Mummum sent for him and told him of his mother's death: "She wanted to be alone with me then." Much later he realized how frustratingly little was known about Georgie Drew Barrymore. "Much has been written by actors and playwrights and literary people of Maurice Barrymore, my father—he was a great wit and his conversation kept people up willingly all night—but little has been said about my mother. . . . The people who knew both my mother and my father remember my mother best. Clever as my father was, he never pulled one of his famous lines upon her. He simply could not get away with it."

Georgie is supposed to have called her children "my little shooting stars." Georgie is supposed to have said, "All my children have Drew eyes and Drew hair . . . and Drew courage." Once when he was fishing in Nassau, Jack met a lady who said she'd been living in the same house in Santa Barbara when Georgie died and that his mother's last words had been, "Oh, my poor kids, whatever will become of them?" Not a hint of what happened to all the lovely shoes and dresses.

ETHEL'S INITIATION into adulthood was rapidly followed by Lionel's. He and Jack had been safely stowed away at Seton Hall that fall when a telegram summoned Maurice to South Orange. "Even if he dies," said Lionel fiercely as his parent entered Father Marshall's study, "he should not have said my mother was disgusting!"

Lionel and Jack (it emerged) had joined the baseball team for a smoke in the locker room, where the shortstop had produced a fresh box of Sweet Caporals. Besides the forbidden cigarettes, each box contained a souvenir picture card of some famous athlete or actor—in this case the photo of a handsome blond woman in plumed hat, long gloves, and stylish gown.

"It's Mamma!" said Jack. "Look, everybody!"

Lionel grabbed the card. "It's Mamma all right. What an honor! Look, isn't she wonderful? She's my mother!"

Almost everyone was impressed. "*I* think," said one righteous teammate, "it's disgusting."

Lionel's fist connected with the jaw of the offender who fell, striking his head on the edge of a locker. The boy finally recovered, but Father Marshall, though sympathetic, was firm. Lionel left Seton Hall to join Maurice in New York, where he was spending most of his time at the Patten mansion on West Eighteenth Street.

After Georgie's death, Maurice had given up the flat on Fifty-ninth and taken a room at the Lambs. One of the many people who tried to cajole him back into society was Ernestine Patten, the widow of one of Maurice's oldest theatrical friends and now married to the banker Thomas G. Patten. Ernestine had a daughter named Mamie. She was blond and lovely and inexplicably unmarried at twenty-eight, for surely her teenage crush on Maurice Barrymore hadn't kept her single. Now she threw herself at Maurice headlong. Maurice was at first indifferent; then flattered, aroused, and conquered.

Unaware that his mother's "honor" was again threatened, Lionel spent days roaming about the large house, copying the fake Corots that hung on the walls and learning simple passages of Bach fugues by placing his fingers on the Pattens' player piano and going along with the mechanism. He might have lingered there indefinitely if Mummum had not descended upon New York and handed him his fate "like juice before breakfast." He would be an actor.

Chiefly to give Mummum work, Uncle Googan had put together a tour of *The Rivals* and *The Road to Ruin*. Lionel joined the tour, far more interested in the locomotives and lunchboxes than in launching his stage career. When Mummum announced that in Kansas City he would play the part of Thomas in *The Rivals*, he was horrified. He was more horrified when he discovered that no one was going to tell him how to play it.

Somehow Lionel's inadequacy went unnoticed in rehearsal. He himself was all too aware of it, however, and in Kansas City on the Saturday afternoon of October 28 crept wretchedly onto the stage of The Auditorium. His livery was too loose, his boots too small, his gray wig unconvincing. Worse, his voice was changing and he sounded like nothing so much as an automaton in need of an oil can. That evening he was obliged to repeat the agony; anticipating failure, he was worse. In the wings he stumbled past Mummum, scrubbed off his make-up in the little hole that passed for his dressing room, and went out to forget the debacle in the streets of Kansas City. He had not succeeded by the time he returned to the boardinghouse. Propped on the bureau was a letter in familiar purple ink.

> My Dear Lionel [he read]: You must forgive your Uncle Sidney and me for not realizing that when Sheridan wrote the part of Thomas he had a much older actor in mind. We feel that we were very remiss in not taking cognizance of this—although we are both happy that you are not at the advanced age you would have to be in order to be good in this part.
>
> We think, therefore, that the play as a whole would be bettered by the elimination of the front scene and have decided to do without it after this evening's performance. Sincerely and with deep affection, your Grandmother,
>
> Mrs. Drew.

Lionel flew to say his customary good night to his grandmother, who was sitting in front of her fire with crackers, cheese, and the tumbler of whiskey and water. At the sight of her grandson her eyes filled with tears; she held out her arms. Then she saw his face.

"This is odd, sir. I find the occasion rather distressing, but here you arrive garlanded in smiles. Speak frankly, my boy. What portion of my letter exalted you?"

Nothing would give him greater satisfaction, Lionel explained, than the elimination of the front scene.

"So. Well, dear boy, what would you like to do then?"

"Perhaps I could paint scenery. Or would you rather send me home?"

There wasn't any home. "We'll keep you around," said Mummum. "Perhaps something will come of this after all. I am forced to remember that your father was not so distinguished an actor either when he first started."

With a deep aversion to acting—his acting, *all* acting—Lionel stayed with the tour as odd-jobber and martini mixer to Uncle Googan, pretending that the stage was a pregnant girlfriend he didn't have to marry. But in New York he was informed that he would make his Broadway debut on Christmas Day at the Fourteenth Street Theatre as a lowly footman in *The Road to Ruin*. No lines, which gave him enough confidence to invite his old terror, Billy Muldoon, to witness his performance. Muldoon sat through the whole play and didn't see Lionel. "You must have blinked just as I made my entrance," mused the boy. And so Lionel continued to tag along with Mummum and Uncle Googan, hoping that something would save him.

THAT SEPTEMBER Ethel exchanged her black dress for the convent uniform. She continued to dream of becoming a concert pianist: surely Maurice would pay for lessons, or prosperous Uncle Jack. But the last thing Maurice was thinking of was piano lessons, and debonair Uncle Jack's interests did not include his niece's musical career.

Sometime this year Ethel discovered that Jack had not been baptized a Catholic—perhaps from Jack himself, perhaps from Mummum, stopping to deliver Christmas gifts at the convent where Jack was spending the holiday with Ethel because he had nowhere else to go. Strange that Georgie herself hadn't seen to Jack's baptism, but so it was, and Ethel decided to take the matter into her own hands. She hunted down a boy named Sam McGargle, a pupil of Sister Vincent's who looked old for his twelve years, and pressured him until he consented to be Jack's godfather. Feeling like Saint John the Baptist, Ethel dragged Jack and Sam to Saint Patrick's near the convent. No record of this ceremony exists, but a lay person can baptize. One can imagine Ethel and Sam mumbling their best guess at the formula, dashing holy water at Jack, and making a speedy exit.

In February Superior Sister Agnes Mary sent for Ethel and handed her a clipping announcing that Maurice Barrymore and Mamie Floyd had been married secretly two months before. The report was false; the marriage would not take place until July. But whether Maurice secretly married Mamie six months or a year after Georgie's death, Ethel was profoundly hurt and contemptuous. "It was years, really years" before she could "take it in stride."

This convent year was the last in which Ethel was not forced to make a living. In June Mummum sent for her to join the *Rivals* tour in Montreal. Ethel, just fourteen, was bitter, but she had no choice: there was no money, no home—and as for the piano, "No one talked about it, no one talked about it at all, ever." No one told her how to act Julia Melville either, or how to make up. Ethel experimented lavishly with both.

"What have you got on your face?"

"Make-up."

"Go wash it all off."

Aunt Gladys was playing Lydia Languish. Ethel managed an entrance and took her place on the sofa rigid with terror. One look at the glazed, idiotic expression on Aunt Gladys's face, however, told her that she was not the one in trouble and suddenly she found herself asking questions and answering them in her best grammar school manner—getting through. In the wings she saw Mummum fold her fan and give a little nod as if to say, "That's all right." Unlike Lionel's Thomas, Ethel's Julia stayed in the production. She was launched.

She quickly learned the uncertainties of the actor's trade when Mummum left the company to fulfill another engagement and Mrs. McKee Rankin, Gladys's mother, took her place. This meant new plays, and Ethel was demoted to playing the piano in the orchestra pit between acts. Unfortunately, Mrs. Rankin didn't draw, and in St. John, New Brunswick, Ethel agonizingly had to leave the trunk containing all her worldly possessions at the hotel as the company slipped out of town on the midnight train, Aunt Gladys very fat because she was wearing five dresses. In Halifax, Nova Scotia, a scene in *Oliver Twist* so terrified her that she forgot her lines. In Bar Harbor, Maine, she had mixed emotions when girls she'd known in Philadelphia came to the orchestra pit to talk to her: *they* didn't have to work, but were they having such adventures!

She did what she was told and got no salary, and when the tour ended she was moved like a pawn to New York to join Mummum, who was living with Uncle Jack and Aunt Dodo (as everyone called Josephine) at the Sherman Square Hotel at Broadway and Seventy-first Street. Everything seemed to have collapsed. Mummum had no more engagements and sat in her room, enormously dignified and silent, gazing out over "the sinister rooftops," not admitting that being out of work was living hell. Although her father and uncle might have opened doors, Ethel was told to look for work at the theatrical agencies and did, wishing that someone would explain the sudden collapse of a world that for so long had pivoted around her grandmother. From September 1894 into the next year she pounded pavements or took the five-cent horsecar around Manhattan. She waited hours and hours in outer offices, but no one gave Ethel Barrymore work or seemed to care that generations of acting blood flowed in her veins.

JACK DURING THESE YEARS is difficult to trace. He may have lived with Maurice and Mamie at 161 West Ninety-seventh Street and gone to public schools or perhaps stayed with Uncle Jack at his hotel. In his thirteenth year, however, someone decided that he needed a restraining hand, and on October 16, 1895, he was delivered to the Jesuits at George-town Preparatory School in Rockville, Maryland.

"Slim and pale as a church candle," looking like "a Siamese office boy" under black bangs, Jack was a volatile combination of dreaminess and profanity, sensitivity and waywardness. He was a voracious reader, president of the junior tennis team, assistant editor of the school maga-zine. He managed to score 94.5 out of 95 points on an exam in "the English branches." He delivered an exceptionally well done recitation of "Orpheus and Eurydice." *The Academy* published a short story and two poems rife with "dells and dingles," "murmuring rills," "snowy mantles," and "wingèd steeds"—but very clever for his age. He continued to draw: spidery monsters; mordant, sexless young women; the Bad Man who began to look more and more like Jack Barrymore.

At fifteen Jack combed back and parted his hair in the middle, giving his pale face the look of a perverse saint. Licking his chops, an elderly actor friend of Maurice half jokingly offered to adopt him. ("Do you wish to adopt my son, sir, or *adapt* him?") But Jack was also tempting to women. On a holiday visit to Maurice, Jack was lured into his stepmother's bed-room and seduced. It was not a sentimental seduction, but an abrupt initiation by the hungry and versatile Mamie into varieties of sexual in-tercourse not commonly experienced by boys of fifteen.

Dr. Samuel Hirschfeld, who later treated John and knew his early history, diagnosed him as "more or less a chronic drunkard since the age of fourteen." If the seduction story is true, perhaps fifteen was the age he took seriously to alcohol. Of course Mamie is the villain: the pretty slut who lured Maurice from the memory of the incomparable Georgie and then, not satisfied with that victory, corrupted her husband's son. But Jack shared in the cuckolding of his father, and what better solvent for the conscience than alcohol?

Jack understandably blamed Mamie for what happened—and by extension all attractive women. Yet there were also madonnas whom one loved romantically. Back in Philadelphia little Jack had spent his stolen money to buy a rosary for "a symmetrical lady" many years his senior with whom he'd fallen in love. On Long Island one summer he'd kissed the hand of a red-haired enchantress named Henrietta and got kneed in the stomach for his chivalry. At sixteen he would fall solemnly in love with a policeman's daughter. Yet he remembered the advice of Maurice, who had witnessed Henrietta's blow: "My boy, that kick was symbolic of what happens whenever men like ourselves fall in love. Remember from now on to keep your eye on 'em, before, during, and after you kiss."

Jack experienced another cataclysm that fifteenth year. With everyone else in the family acting that summer of 1897, Louisa Drew had gone on June 1 to a boardinghouse in Larchmont, New York, on Long Island Sound. She was seventy-seven and, though she regarded illness as the kind of faux pas no well-bred Drew would commit, seriously ill. Since there was no one else, Jack went to Larchmont to be with his grandmother, or perhaps she summoned him.

Attending a sick old woman is no adolescent's idea of summer fun, but Jack—to his eternal credit—looked after his grandmother tenderly. After breakfast he helped her slowly negotiate two flights of stairs down to the large front porch, where he installed her in a rocking chair and handed her one of the innumerable paperbacks that she held in her hands without reading. Instead she gazed out over the Sound, half dozing, half dreaming of old days and old faces. Jack was often beside her, sketching, and sometimes her thoughts would sound out loud.

"The greatest sorrow of all," she said on one of these occasions, "is for a mother to outlive her children." "Waves and actors," she mused another time, "are much alike. They come for a little time, rise to separate heights, and travel with varying speed and force—then are gone, unremembered. Our good friend Joseph Jefferson has correctly observed, 'Nothing is as dead as a dead actor.' "

Lionel came to consult the grandmother who had sacked him about his career, but found her in such pain, "though she gallantly and lightly denied it," that he talked instead of Ethel's recent and great successes in London, where she had gone with William Gillette's company. Though her doctor told Lionel she hadn't long to live, Mummum was contemptuous. "There is nothing the matter with me at all. I am merely resting between plays. And I must be up soon for a new rehearsal." So Lionel left her with Jack, realizing again that he was not the favorite.

Every night Jack bathed his grandmother's swollen legs and feet as she sat in a chair in her third-rate hotel room. Then he helped her into bed and sat with her, while through the window came the laughter of girls and music from the carousel and beer tent. He did not leave until his grandmother dropped off to sleep, and he returned early, though he "desperately wanted to go about nights and stay out until any hour." He was living up to his grandmother's code.

On the last day of August Jack bathed Mummum's feet as usual, helped her into bed, and sat down to wait. By then Louisa Drew must have known there would be no new season for, in an unusually expansive gesture, she reached out and patted Jack's arm. She died at three o'clock that morning in a convulsion, of heart and Bright's disease.

She was brought back to Philadelphia to be buried on September 5 at Glenwood Cemetery beside her husband John, her half-sister Georgiana, Adine, and her beloved Georgie. John Drew, rushing in from Salt Lake City, contributed a wreath of white roses and wild flowers. From London Sidney wired a pillow of roses and asters with the words "Mother, from Sidney" in blue immortelles. Joseph Jefferson, the last of the generation that had called her "Louisa," sent a huge heart of autumn leaves. A great throng traveled to the cemetery in trolley cars and stood outside the family enclosure while John Drew and a few close friends bowed their heads as the small coffin was lowered into the ground. Some reports say that the grandson standing next to John Drew was Lionel, others say Jack.

The previous December, 1896, Maurice Barrymore had celebrated twenty years on the American stage with an emotional after-curtain speech in Boston. On March 29, 1897, Maurice created quite a different sensation when he became the first legitimate actor to appear in that entertainment of the masses, vaudeville. ("Well, *you!*" one hears an outraged Mummum saying.) It shocked many of the acting world who were slow to realize how much tradition had already been buried in Philadelphia with Mrs. John Drew.

FIVE

1895–1901

ETHEL'S SUCCESS had not come overnight. Through Frohman, Uncle Jack had finally got her "a little tray-carrying" at the Empire. Ethel gritted her teeth. She knew she knew nothing but acting, and little of that. She wanted to eat.

She was understudying Elsie de Wolfe's Kate Fennel in *The Bauble Shop* when one day de Wolfe could not go on. Hearing that John Drew's sixteen-year-old niece was going to step into Elsie's fabulous Paquin gowns as a sophisticated woman of thirty-five, the cast shuddered. They had brought the popular play to a pitch of ensemble perfection. Ethel was not only green but sizes smaller than de Wolfe. Nerves were not calmed when Frohman himself was reported in the audience.

They needn't have worried. "The girl came from Miss de Wolfe's dressing room laughing as if school had just been let out," remembered one of the cast. "She crossed to the entrance where we were all gathered, turned with a laugh to [Arthur] Byron, and then walked on the scene with as much composure as if she were about to recite her geography lesson." Of course Ethel was terrified but so impressed Frohman that he gave her the part of Kate Fennel in the touring production. In Chicago they called her "an opalescent dream."

The next season she had a small part in a bad play, toured as an understudy with her uncle and Maude Adams, played Zoe in *The Squire of Dames*. In her third season at the Empire, however, she sailed onto the stage in a short skirt, low bodice, and starched cap as the maid Priscilla in *Rosemary*. Her entrance was applauded. In one scene she had to make love to a ponderously polysyllabic gentleman. She widened her enormous eyes. "Your words r-oll and r-oll and r-oll," she drawled in a voice that was "something between a cello and a delicious caramel sauce." Her exit was applauded. It was the first real sign that the Drew-Barrymore magic might be surfacing in the younger generation.

When *Rosemary* went on tour, Ethel discovered another kind of success. Wherever she went she was immediately taken up by the best society. It didn't matter that she stayed in cheap boardinghouses and owned only one thin blue serge cape and two convent uniforms that she elaborated with a handmade blue velvet collar. Society loved her. She was escorted to the Baltimore Hunt Ball, to Harvard Class Day, and to Boston Symphony Orchestra concerts. In Boston she knew Jack and Sally Fairchild and the Sears and the Thayers. In Chicago she hobnobbed with Marshall Field, Delia Caton, and Medill McCormick. In Washington she knew John Hay, future ambassador to the Court of St. James's, and his popular daughters, Helen and Alice. Wherever she went there were luncheons and teas, balls and cotillions, carriage drives and picnics—and people fought to invite and escort her.

She was equally popular with the artistic set, particularly writers: Dick (Richard Harding) Davis, who remembered the scarlet bathing suit from Point Pleasant summers; Finley Peter Dunne, and George Ade. Sara Teasdale and a young man on the fringe of the St. Louis group named T. S. Eliot. And in San Francisco she talked books with Frank Norris, Ambrose Bierce, and Jack London.

"Often and often I have been asked how, when I was a young, shy girl staying in cities I had never seen before, I came to know so many people," said Ethel. And she had to admit she hadn't the faintest idea: "All of a sudden I just knew people and they were my friends."

There were explanations. One was that she was a Barrymore touring with the enormously popular John Drew. Although shy, she was also spontaneous and unaffected with a frank way of talking that refreshed without shocking. She was passionately interested in everything: music, books, painting, politics, baseball, boxing, and above all people. She was a working girl, interesting in itself. And she had the lovely, unexpected beauty of a startled fawn.

Then one night in St. Louis, Uncle Jack handed her a telegram from Frohman: WOULD ETHEL LIKE TO GO TO LONDON WITH GILLETTE IN SECRET SERVICE? Ethel was ecstatic. She'd been longing to get back to London; she had a raging crush on the lean-jawed William Gillette, whom she'd worshipped through countless Thursday matinees.

"Do you really want to go?" said Uncle Jack, astonished.

"More than anything in the world."

"Death!" said Uncle Jack, relenting. "What nonsense!"

Back in New York she packed everything she owned in a small bag and was given a steamship ticket. Maurice had promised to see her off at the boat; she hadn't seen him since his marriage to Mamie. He didn't come, as she'd told herself he wouldn't, but she forgot him when she saw coming toward her across the deck the tall, austere hero of her dreams. For all her poise, there could hardly have been anyone more sexually naïve than Ethel Barrymore at seventeen: convent-raised, steeped in Sir Walter Scott, Frances Hodgson Burnett, and matinees. A young actor in the company performed introductions, Gillette bowed low over her hand. And with that gesture smash went her dreams. She hadn't wanted artificial, automatic flattery. Oh, he was common after all! And Gillette, a bachelor not known for his enthusiasm for women, lost his most ardent fan.

But nothing could spoil London. When she got off the train at Waterloo and smelled the wooden platforms wet with rain she felt as though she'd come home. She took cheap lodgings in Chapel Street; they might have been a palace. She had letters of introduction from Sally Fairchild to the formidable Sidney and Beatrice Webb and to Bernard Shaw, but she was far too timid to use them or to announce that Maurice Barrymore's daughter and John Drew's niece was in town.

She didn't need letters. Overnight Ethel Barrymore was a greater success in London than at home. It was as though she'd run up to society's great front door, knocked lightly and, without realizing she needed an invitation, skipped blithely in. Her two good dresses, a black and a white, carried her triumphantly through introductions to the Duke of York, a waltz with Lord Kitchener, and the Queen's Diamond Jubilee garden party where she was the sole actress invited. At dinner she might be seated next to Alfred Rothschild, Whistler, Henry James, Alfred Lyttelton, or Anthony Hope. The theatre welcomed her: Ellen Terry, Ben Webster, who became "Uncle Ben," and his wife, May Whitty, who quickly became her confidante.

In the melodrama *Secret Service*, which opened in May at the Adelphi, she had the small part of a Civil War nurse. One day, however, Odette Tyler, the female comedy lead, fainted in the wings and Ethel, still in her nurse's uniform, was told to go on. Knowing the play by heart, she "went straight at the difficult fence and cleared it beautifully." And then, just when she thought the part was hers, she'd walked back into the theatre the following afternoon to find a new girl rehearsing the part and herself again in nurse's uniform. She was hardly comforted when the Duke of York told her he liked her much better than the new girl in the part.

When *Secret Service* closed in August she found herself still deep in the social whirl but out of work. Actor-managers who had seen her at the Adelphi all said, "Oh, you must stay in London," only none of them offered her a job. Her money was almost gone: when she wasn't invited out to dinner she existed chiefly on handfuls of dates. Finally (though it was not the months and months it seemed in retrospect), she swallowed her pride and went to Uncle Jack, who was in London and about to sail for America. "Of course, of course," said Uncle Jack; she could play the French maid at the Empire that fall. And so Ethel went sadly back to Chapel Street and began to pack.

Of all the versions of what happened next, the most dramatic is this: she was struggling to keep her tears from falling on the beautiful dresses she was packing for Uncle Jack's new leading lady when a hansom clattered up to the door and a note was handed up to her. "Dear Little Bullfinch [it read]. I hear you're going back to America. Come down to the theatre tonight to say goodbye to Sir Henry and me."

The royal command came from Ellen Terry, leading lady of the Lyceum where Irving reigned as the chief actor-manager of the day. So Ethel quickly bathed her eyes and took a hansom to the Lyceum where Ellen, past fifty but as young in heart as Ethel, told her to go in and see The Chief.

"So you want to go back to America?" said the great actor.

"No, Sir Henry, but I can't find anything to do."

And the great man said, "How would you like to stay here and be our little leading lady?"

Ethel floated down the stairs to Mr. Loveday's office where a contract was waiting, then floated along to the Savoy where a farewell dinner was in progress for Uncle Jack. She said nothing; and everyone, knowing how heartbroken she was about leaving London, was very kind until the dark and beautiful Mrs. Patrick Campbell called down the table insincerely, "We are so sorry that you are sailing tomorrow." Mrs. Pat was the vogue, competitive, and very nervous about playing Ophelia to Johnston Forbes-Robertson's Hamlet that fall.

Ethel waited for the sympathetic murmurs to subside. "Oh, but I'm not," she said brightly. "I have a very pleasant engagement. I have just signed a contract with Sir Henry Irving and Miss Terry. I am going to be their leading lady."

Consternation.

Ethel's coup, however, was less the reward of talent than of the fact that Sir Henry's younger son Laurence was madly in love with her and that Ellen Terry was an enthusiastic matchmaker. And although Ethel attacked the role of Annette in *The Bells* with her usual energy, the engagement wasn't quite as transporting as she'd imagined. On the first day of rehearsal word had come of Mummum's death, and then the Lyceum company resented the intruders. Besides Ethel, Irving had hired two other American actors, one "a red-haired jade" named Suzanne Sheldon. The British actors didn't stop to consider that Irving's American tours kept the huge Lyceum operation solvent; they just knew they could play any role better than Ethel Barrymore, Robert Taber, and Suzanne Sheldon. Worse still, Irving was horribly grim with everyone that fall except little Bullfinch, who could always make him smile; and then Laurence not only insisted on endless rehearsals of his *Peter the Great* but also decreed that the juicy part of Euphrosine, the Tsarevich's mistress, go to Ethel. Ethel and Suzanne were left severely alone on that tour and became great friends, though much of Ethel's time was taken by Laurence Irving.

He was an intense, untidy young man of twenty-six, an ardent disciple of Tolstoy and all that was gloomy in the Russian temperament. He had studied in St. Petersburg for the Foreign Service, changed his mind, and come home to act, then—infuriated that he was not welcomed at the Lyceum—shot himself Slavically in the chest while on tour in Belfast. Britishly surviving, he turned to writing grim plays in the Russian manner. Ethel was at the Websters one night when Laurence came to read his *Godefroi and Yolande.* He called for silence, cleared his throat. "The play begins with a chorus of lepers," he announced somberly. The silence gave way "to dreadful laughter." Laurence had stormed out in a fury; but somehow he had forgiven her, and now they walked the suicidally bleak streets of Hull and Sheffield, Ethel feeling with every step more and more Russian until eventually they were both paddling cozily side by side in the black waters of nihilism. She read Nietzsche and Voltaire late at night in bed and was profoundly impressed with the anguish of existence.

Back in London in December, Ethel and Suzanne took a flat at 21 Bedford Street over the publishing offices of William Heinemann, right across the street from the Websters and within five minutes of any stage door in the West End. As occupants of Bedford Street's "Left Bank," they became the nucleus of "the Gang" that congregated at the Websters after the theatre for little suppers of kidneys and toast, hot ham, and corn fritters. Ethel and Suzanne introduced a whole contingent of Americans, who quickly got in the habit of cabling ARRIVE SATURDAY HAVE PARTY.

One of these was Dick Davis, a correspondent who collected wars and was of course in love with Ethel. They had wonderful adventures like the time their cab got lost in thick yellow fog on Christmas Eve on the way to Ellen Terry's in Barkston Gardens. Horse and cab went round in circles, slipping on the asphalt, Ethel biting her lip in terror until it bled, until finally the cab jammed itself against an area railing and the horse fell, at which Ethel and Dick left the hansom and groped their way to the nearest door for help. Dick was wearing war decorations and a

Louisa (Mrs. John) Drew, one of the great comediennes of her day (she was best known for her role as Mrs. Malaprop in *The Rivals*), also managed the Arch Street Theatre in Philadelphia.

John Drew Sr. (Louisa's third husband) was successful as a romantic Irish comedic actor. Louisa and John Drew were the grandparents of Ethel, John, and Lionel.

Their sons. John Drew Jr. (LEFT) made his acting debut in 1872 at his mother's Arch Theatre, and Sidney (with his wife, Gladys Rankin Drew) appeared in many popular stage and film "marriage comedies."

LEFT: Maurice Barrymore in the role of Captain Swift, 1888. The photograph is signed "To Ethel from her affectionate father."
ABOVE: Georgie Drew Barrymore.
BELOW: Left to right, John, Ethel, and Lionel Barrymore in late 1882

Georgie Drew Barrymore with her childen Ethel, Lionel, and John, 1890

ABOVE: Lionel and Julie Herne in *Sag Harbor*, 1900. RIGHT: Ethel as Euphrosine in the 1898 London production of *Peter the Great*. BELOW: John with Emily Dale on the beach near Greenwich, Connecticut, August 1907

Ethel in 1901 in her breakthrough role as Madame Trentoni in *Captain Jinks of the Horse Marines*, and (INSET) in her dressing room at the Savoy Theatre during the 1902 run of *Carrots*

John, Ethel, and Lionel, 1904

Bruce McRae, John, and Ethel in *Alice-Sit-by-the-Fire*, 1905

ABOVE: Constance Collier and John in *Peter Ibbetson*, 1917. BELOW: Evelyn Nesbit

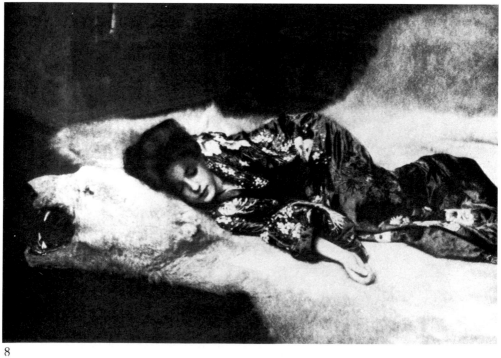

Lionel as Milt Shanks in *The Copperhead*, 1918

TOP: John with his wife Katherine Harris Barrymore in Central Park, circa 1915. LEFT: Ethel on vaudeville tour. ABOVE: Russell Colt, 1909

Ethel with her children Sammy (age five) and Jackie (one year old), 1914

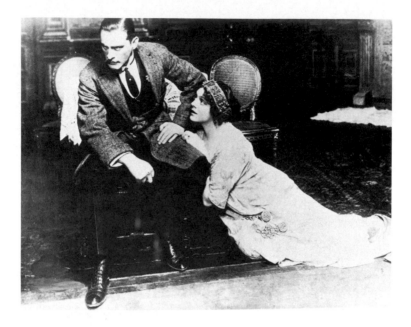

ABOVE: John and Ethel as Mr. and Mrs. Hyphen-Brown in *A Slice of Life*, 1912. BELOW: Doris Rankin Barrymore and Lionel filming *The Copperhead*, 1920

ABOVE: Ethel in the film *The Final Judgment*, 1915. BELOW: Lionel (left) and John in *The Jest*, 1919

John (LEFT) as Richard the
Third in the 1920 Arthur
Hopkins production, and
(BELOW) in *Dr. Jekyll and
Mr. Hyde*, 1920

LEFT: Lionel as Macbeth in
the ill-fated production, 1921.
BELOW: Ethel and Vernon
Steele in the popular
Déclassée, 1919

John as Hamlet in the epoch-making 1922 Arthur Hopkins production

luxurious fur coat, and for some reason he said out of the blue, "We must get back to the Duchess's for the night." "Yes, Duke," Ethel answered calmly. Suddenly the householder and servants were all agog and "Your Gracing" and "Your Ladyshipping" them until they thought they would burst laughing and had to stumble out into the fog again. At last, guided by a man with a bicycle lamp and a linkboy, they found their way back to the Justin McCarthys', from where they'd started, and Ethel was given whisky and quinine to stop her teeth from chattering and sent to bed.

On the Left Bank glorious poverty reigned. Ethel and Suzanne owned a single evening gown between them which, with added lace and undersleeves, could double for afternoons. Ethel complained bitterly that Suzanne lingered too long at tea parties for her to wear the dress to dinner. Suzanne accused Ethel of monopolizing the one pair of long kid gloves. But they were cheerful, except for days when Laurence came for tea. After one of these lugubrious sessions Ethel might wake in the middle of the night, fling her arms to heaven, and moan, "God! How bored I am!" though Suzanne noted she fell instantly back to sleep. Gloom was also thick at the Lyceum, where even Ellen Terry was "nigh dead from anxiety" over Laurence's *Peter the Great* and unhappy with the "new actors."

And in fact *Peter* was heavy cake for the public, though after the first performance a bald, beetle-browed man Ethel didn't know (it was the dramatist Arthur Wing Pinero) came up and said, "My dear, you're the most natural thing I've ever seen on the stage." The rejection of his play drove Laurence, and with him Ethel, to new depths of intimate depression. As a result, after a particularly dismal performance, Ethel decided they might as well marry and be delightfully miserable together.

"What! gobbled up by Barrymore?" Bernard Shaw replied to Ellen's announcement that Laurence had finally engaged himself to Euphrosine "after having been refused by Her Highness about half a dozen times." Ellen decided she'd like "to bang them both," but Maurice, when Ethel cabled him hoping he might care, replied affably, CONGRATULATIONS LOVE FATHER.

And then something awful happened. Overnight Laurence grew cheerful. After a few deplorable days of this new happiness, Ethel was forced to conclude that Laurence's philosophical pessimism was a sham: he'd only been unhappy because she'd refused to marry him. Suddenly he was a totally different person and, unfortunately, no longer a man she could admire. At least that is Ethel's charming story. To it may be added her real aversion at eighteen to the idea of marrying anyone.

It required a great deal of courage to break the engagement when she was still acting in Laurence's play and when her decision was likely to mean throwing away the unlimited advantage of Irving's and Terry's patronage. She continued as Euphrosine with the company treating her like one of Laurence's lepers, then played Annette again in *The Bells*. She thought herself bad in both roles but was slightly comforted by Maurice's reply to her cable that she was not marrying Laurence after all: CON-GRATULATIONS LOVE FATHER.

Suddenly realizing that it might have a field day with the fickle young beauty, the American press began to see how often it could engage Ethel Barrymore. Any man she smiled at was fair game: Dick Davis or his brother Charles; the novelist Anthony Hope; the young Duke of Man-chester and the handsome Earl of Ava; Herbert Stone, the publisher; C. D. Wetmore, a popular clubman from an old Rhode Island family; Arthur Byron, acting in Uncle Jack's company; Prince Kumar Shri Ran-jitsinhji. And then Americans following their princess's triumphs read in the *Telegraph* of June 28 that she was engaged to Gerald du Maurier, and this happened to be true.

That summer tiaras were in fashion. Ethel did not have one, so she made a wreath of oak leaves to crown her ash-blond hair. Soon everyone was calling her "Daphne" after the nymph who was changed into a tree, and it was this tall, lovely, laureled Daphne who stunned young du Mau-rier. Like Laurence, Gerald had a famous father (Sir George, author of *Trilby* and *Peter Ibbetson*) and was full of promise, though as an actor he had hardly progressed beyond lighting cigarettes gracefully. Unlike Lau-rence he was debonair and witty. He swept Ethel off her feet and she thought, "*This is it!*"

That summer, too, another American actress became an intimate of the Left Bank: Gertrude Elliott, whose flamboyantly beautiful sister Max-ine with her husband, Nat Goodwin, had come to England to conquer society at Jackwood, their estate near Shooters Hill. Ethel had spent long nights at Jackwood debating whether she should marry Laurence; now she discussed Gerald's virtues endlessly with Gertrude and Suzanne. Like the Barrymores, the trio had favorite catch lines from plays that would double them up with laughter. Their favorite was "Do nothing til you hear from me," but they didn't say it about darling Gerald, who was so right for Ethel in every way. And again Maurice approved, this time in person.

Maurice, Mamie, and Jack had all arrived in London, Maurice to play *The Heart of Maryland* at the Adelphi, Jack to further his education. It had ended abruptly at Georgetown Prep when, caught at a local house where he was "merely chatting with a nice lady in the parlor," he refused to rat on his otherwise occupied companions. He was promptly expelled and sent to his father.

"But Father, I just went along. I didn't . . . you know."

"Well, for God's sake," said Maurice, popping his eyes, "why not?"

Jack was enrolled at King's College at Wimbledon Common, where his relative Henry Wace was headmaster. He quickly excelled at running, jumping, and sparring, and displayed talent for freehand and mechanical drawing. But suburbia was not Jack's style. He became an expert at "bunburying": inventing urgent business in London where, with or without Maurice, every temptation lay open to the sixteen-year-old boy.

He moved in with Ethel for the summer "hols," a disconcerting mixture of sophistication and shyness. The Websters took him under their wing, but "found it hard to understand what further education was supposed to be acquired by a youth whose extensive knowledge of life left them gasping." And yet when Ethel gave a big tea party for the American cast of *The Belle of New York,* Jack broke into such a cold sweat at the thought of coming in to mingle that Ethel gave up coaxing him. He was happier playing Red Indian games on Hampstead Heath summer afternoons with Ethel and Gerald. Yet Ethel herself on these romps was having doubts.

Mrs. du Maurier and Gerald's sisters had doubted too that Daphne could make their beloved Gerald happy. Of course she was very "pretty, and undeniably charming, and of course one knew who were her people, and she seemed very talented and all that"—but she was also very young, very spoiled, and very self-willed. But when Gerald was so very happy they had relented; Daphne might be teachable. Mrs. du Maurier had thus initiated long instructional conversations with Daphne about what she must provide for Gerald's supper and what warm clothes she must make him wear in winter. Daphne listened, and suddenly all she could think of was getting home to the four walls of a dressing room. She fled to May Whitty. She could not marry Gerald and May must tell him so. Accordingly, May spent several hours closeted with Gerald while the rejected suitor strode about the room "beating his forehead and calling upon God." He was so distraught that May suggested Ethel accompany him and two friends to Ireland on a fishing trip and there decide once and for all.

They stayed at the Bay View Hotel in Waterville, and Ethel, looking fourteen and adorable with her hair in a pigtail and a crimson tam-o'-shanter, was temperamental because her light-hearted swain had been replaced by a tedious martyr who, at Kerry Beach, waded into the surf up to his neck and stood waiting with folded arms for the rising tide to end his misery. Of course Ethel sobbed, "Gerald, Gerald, come back!" wetting her toes, and of course he eventually waded, grim and chilled, to shore. She asked if they couldn't be brother and sister, but Gerald did not feel fraternal, so she returned to London, left money with the Websters to be prudently doled out to Jack at Wimbledon Common, and bought a cheap ticket back to the States with her last pounds.

"Gerald saw me off at the train. I felt heartbroken. I was crying, tears pouring down my cheeks. Gerald was running along the platform. I almost jumped off the train. I was still in love with Gerald, but I knew I couldn't go through with the marriage."

As Ethel later dramatized it, she arrived at Grand Central Terminal with one quarter in her purse and no idea what would become of her, dazedly told a cabby (for no earthly reason) to take her to the luxurious Waldorf-Astoria, and then booked a room and languidly asked a clerk, "Will you pay my cab, please?" In fact Uncle Jack was staying at the Waldorf and the papers had already announced her engagement with Frohman that fall. Ethel also said she had no idea why the Waldorf staff greeted her with such deference, but it was impossible for her not to know that her London success had made her a celebrity.

She said further that when the door of her room closed behind her she realized for the first time that America was where she really belonged. But the realization had come earlier. After her engagement at the Lyceum ended she had had no offers. She had seen for herself that most London leading ladies were halves of couples: Kembles, Kendals, Bancrofts, Irving and Terry, Charles Wyndham and Mary Moore, William Terriss and Jessie Millward, Johnston Forbes-Robertson and Mrs. Patrick Campbell—and that those stage knots had been tied by Cupid. Moreover, no American actress had ever permanently conquered the London stage. Ethel had left London because she wanted to conquer. America was her battlefield.

Stardom did not happen overnight. That October she appeared in *Catherine* at the Garrick. Not only was Madeline a minor part, but two beautiful dresses cost her $100 of her $35 weekly salary. And yet so well had the press done its job that she was greeted on opening night with a tremendous ovation, embarrassing since the play offered her no way of earning it. Inevitably some critics found her disappointing: perhaps they'd expected her to get engaged onstage. Yet she was also called "that glamour girl," and though she protested she hadn't a clue what that meant, the public's enthusiasm must have given her a hint of her power.

She had moved back to Mrs. Wilson's boardinghouse on Thirty-sixth Street, where Georgie Drew Mendum, the cousin from Boston, had also come to live. Eyeing Georgie as a puny infant, Mummum had said, "Humph, that crow will never live!" and certainly, compared to Ethel, Georgie was short and plain. But she was also witty, clever, and ready for any adventure, and she and Ethel were deep conspirators. Mrs. Wilson's was chiefly famous, however, as the residence of Maude Adams, one of the most interesting phenomena of the American stage and a lesson to Ethel, had she realized it.

After Maude Adams's success with John Drew in *Rosemary*, Frohman had looked for a starring vehicle for her and found it in James Barrie's *The Little Minister*. With Barrie's approval, Frohman shifted the interest from the minister to Lady Babbie, surrounded Maude with an excellent cast, and opened her at the prestigious Empire Theatre in 1897. *The Little Minister* ran 300 nights, most of them to standing room only, and Maude Adams became America's favorite star.

But there was a catch to fame. Frohman not only made stars but, if they were women, managed their lives. He was married to the theatre; he expected his actresses to take the same vow.

Ethel had got to know Maude on tour; they'd shared crackers and cheese and secrets in cheap lodgings in Buffalo and Detroit. Looking at Ethel, Maude was always reminded of George Meredith's line, "Beautiful she looks, like a tall garden lily"; Maude was also impressed with Ethel's "delightful young seriousness about her work." As for Maude, she'd been gay and friendly, just the girl who had grinned spontaneously in her first publicity photographs.

Frohman changed all that. He decided that Maude's trademark would be mystery. She would seldom appear in public, not talk when she did, and reduce her smiles to a wistful gaze. She would not marry, not even be seen with a man. Maude's mother moved into Mrs. Wilson's to chaperone her daughter. Now when Ethel came home after the theatre and up the stairs lit by a shaded gas lamp held by a Nubian slave, she found Maude's door firmly shut. The press nicknamed the boardinghouse "Maude Adams' Adamless Eden"; Maude had become the original "I want to be alone" girl. To Ethel it was all very puzzling and rather sad.

On tour with *Catherine* during the winter of 1898–1899, Ethel had ecstatic reunions with friends across the country, as well as being the only bridesmaid at Dick Davis's wedding and receiving a handsome diamond brooch in memory of the scarlet bathing suit and the London fog. And then with enough money finally saved she cabled the Websters ARRIVE SATURDAY HAVE PARTY and sailed back to the scene of her splendid social triumphs the year before.

Jack had borrowed two pounds from the Websters so he could meet her boat at Southampton, but no Jack appeared. Two days later he turned up at her lodgings at 18-A Clifford Street, disheveled and dirty and explaining that he had got as far as the dock when some sailors had proposed a game of billiards. Sighing, Ethel realized again that her beloved brother had much in common with his father.

The Gang always vacationed on the Thames between Maidenhead and Henley. This summer it was Cookham, where E. H. Sothern's brother Sam rented a picture-postcard cottage. Jack had become a member of the Gang because he had to report to the Websters for pocket money. He had become so addicted to May's comfortable society that though he was always rising and saying, "I e'en must fly," he was always sitting down again to talk for another hour. Somehow Jack was fitted into the bursting Cookham cottage and Ethel would come down on the train after a party, still in one of the beautiful *Catherine* dresses, sit up most the night talking and smoking, and wake ready to go punting on the river.

Most of them were beginners, overbalancing on the pole and taking headers as the punt shot out from underneath them. Seeing Mrs. Sam capsize in this undignified way, Jack dropped his pole and dove manfully to the rescue into three feet of water while Mrs. Sam simply gathered up her skirts and waded heartlessly to shore. Sam rewarded Jack by the loan of some smart summer clothes, but correct dress quickly eluded him. He stripped one day in a willow-hemmed backwater, leaving all his clothes in the boat where Sam was fishing. Sam eventually drifted down-river, forgetting Jack, and Cookham village was treated to the sight of the young Adonis strolling down the main street back to the cottage, stark naked. Or so legend has it.

For the most part, however, brother and sister inhabited different worlds. Ethel knew nothing of Jack's escapades with a fast older crowd headed by the jockey Tod Sloan, and hated Sloan when Jack had him to tea. She was happier with the handsome Earl of Ava, who nicknamed her "Cinderella" and introduced her to his brothers Terence and Basil Blackwood, to whom she was soon sending little notes like

> Oh, most foolish BTB
> Come and take a walk with me
> In the park this afternoon
> Not too late and not too soon
> As I must hie to many teas . . .

Then she was scooped up by the beautiful and brilliant hostess Millie, Duchess of Sutherland, was often at Stafford House and in August at

Dunrobin, the Earl's fairy-tale castle at the top of Scotland, perched high above a seaweed-strewn shore.

Of course she already knew the Asquiths, and on her way Londonward stopped at the decidedly lesser castle they'd rented near Aberdeen. There'd been just family at Dunrobin, but at the Asquiths' she sat down to dinner with Chesterton, Balfour, and Lord Rosebery. It was said that Henry Asquith didn't care what damned duchess he had on his right as long as he had Ethel on his left. Ethel knew you had to be intellectually on your toes to dine out in England, and yet once Asquith had leaned over and asked with apparent sincerity, "Tell me, Ethel, have you ever heard of an American named Alexander Hamilton?"

And then on to Alfred and Edith Lyttelton's little summer place in Scotland where she was forced to make a fourth at bridge with their only other guest, Balfour again; then to Herbert and Dolly Gladstone's and then . . . summer was over and her money gone and no matter how much they all loved her, there really was nothing to stay on for. Few of them, anyway, realized that she had to work for a living: she was just that charming American Daphne who miraculously appeared to decorate house parties in need of youth, beauty, and high spirits.

Summer was over for Jack too, who was transferring from Wimbledon to London University to take art or perhaps literature courses, whichever met later in the day. Ethel had had a hundred summer flirtations, but Jack (legend says) had gone to bed with a duchess and with an actress whose husband had not sued for divorce only because of the humiliation of naming a seventeen-year-old corespondent. Ethel still believed in love's young dream. Jack, more pursued than pursuing, was coming to believe that you had only to scratch a lady to find a whore.

Back in New York Ethel guiltily pawned Dick Davis's diamond brooch at Simpson's around the corner from her boardinghouse, its first of many visits to that shop. Then she went to see Frohman in his third-floor office at the Empire. She'd loved Irene Vanbrugh in London in *His Excellency, the Governor*. Clasping her hands tightly to keep them from trembling, she said, "I hear you are going to do *His Excellency, the Governor* this autumn. I want to play Stella de Gex."

"Do you, indeed?" said Frohman, shifting his inevitable cigar. "So does Ellen Terry."

To humor her he gave her a script and promised vaguely to hear her someday. Ethel went home, learned the part, returned. Startled but obliging, C.F. waddled downstairs to the darkened theatre and watched as Ethel, dimly lit by a single spot, gave her impersonation of a sparkling, high-comedy adventuress. Sheer agony, but afterward C.F. said kindly: "You're amazingly like your mother, Ethel. You're all right."

She could not have asked for higher praise; she idolized her mother. But that fall she also discovered that her father could be a superb actor. She was in the audience September 12 for the opening of Mrs. Fiske's *Becky Sharp* at the Fifth Avenue Theatre. Even the New York *Tribune*'s frosty William Winter admitted that Maurice's Rawdon Crawley was "a signal triumph." Ethel could not remember Maurice's acting when she was a child; now she hurried backstage to congratulate him and the two ended celebrating his triumph quietly together at Delmonico's. Maurice's marriage to Mamie was virtually dead, so it was pleasant to be with his daughter, so much like Georgie, with nothing this time to apologize for.

Frohman was impressed enough with Ethel's reading to send her on tour as Stella de Gex. Reclaiming the diamond brooch with an advance on her eighty-dollar weekly salary, Ethel set out in February 1900 with *His Excellency, the Governor*. "Beautiful Ethel Barrymore won a distinct success," said the Boston *Herald*. ". . . Her performance last night furnished convincing proof that she has developed more rapidly in the past two years than any other actress on the American stage. In fascination of manner and charm of personality she greatly resembles her brilliant mother, and has the added advantage of being a singularly beautiful girl."

Interviewed, Ethel allowed that, yes, she wanted to be a star, but only after five or even ten years' hard work. Yet she had already discovered for herself one of Georgie's most effective techniques: throwing away a comic point rather than underlining it. She had also absorbed much of John Drew's utterly natural behavior onstage. The secret of good acting, she believed, lay in disguising the workings of one's technique. At twenty Ethel Barrymore had found her style.

THE SAME COULD NOT be said for Lionel at twenty-one, Lionel who had been utterly excluded from Ethel's and Jack's adventures in England. He had matured into a tall (five-feet-eleven) young man with straight-combed light brown hair and Drew blue eyes. He was handsome, even very handsome; yet he stubbornly hid his sex appeal behind careless clothes and a truculent manner. Compared with Jack's already notorious sex life, Lionel's was a deep secret. But 25,000 prostitutes hustled Broadway between Madison and Herald squares. No passing male could avoid "Only costs a dollar and I got the room," and Lionel passed that way often. On the surface he seemed thoroughly Maurice's boy: he saw lots of bars, booze, and brawls. Yet fundamentally he was a serious person, serious about wanting to paint, about knowing good music—about everything except his destined career.

Like Ethel he had to eat. McKee Rankin, currently producing Sidney Drew because Sidney had married Rankin's daughter Gladys, decided to capitalize on that need. Lionel acted any part not nailed down in light comedies like *The Bachelor's Baby*. Then rather mysteriously he turned up in Miss Georgia Cayvan's company during 1896–1897, Cayvan's first tour as a star. Just nineteen, Lionel was given the impossible part of the old roué Lord Silversnake in *Squire Kate*. When Miss Cayvan first laid eyes on Lionel's personally hand-crafted eyebrows, she fell to the floor and beat the boards with her hands. "Oh, you're a fright!" she howled. "Can't you do *anything* right?" But *Squire Kate* got excellent reviews when it played at Palmer's in New York, and in Chicago critics found Lionel "a manly young chap and a good match for his sister Miss Ethel."

Next he dropped thirty years as Adolphus Drayton Lennox, a cadet in the romantic drama *Cumberland '61,* then was picked up again by Rankin, who had teamed with Nance O'Neil for summer repertory in Minneapolis. There, like Ethel in *The Rivals*, he found he was born to act. Rankin was more occupied with Nance O'Neil than casting, with the result that in *Oliver Twist* Lionel found himself already onstage as Toby Crackit and supposed to enter as Joey. "There was a window, left center," said Lionel. "In my extremity, I used that window. I walked over to it and addressed Joey through it. Joey answered me—in another voice." Lionel not only fooled the audience but so charmed Rankin that he kept the scene, Lionel's ventriloquism saving him the price of another actor.

Lionel's roommate and boozing companion during that Minneapolis stand was Frank Butler, a former newspaperman turned actor, whose breath was enough to wilt the flowered bonnets in the first three rows. Rankin had to fire him, but Butler, deftly nabbing a vacationing Minneapolis journalist's place, got his revenge. "Last night's performance provided as wretched an evening as these old eyes have witnessed since being compelled to see twelve men hanged in a row by a bungling sheriff," he wrote gleefully under his own by-line. Yet, incredibly, one performance had stood out more hideously than the rest. "A deplorable young actor whose name I am able conveniently to forget, although it smacks of Barrymore, appeared only once in a figment of a role but enacted it so balefully that the audience was terrified all evening lest he come back on stage." After his friend's review, Lionel had little to fear from an enemy's.

From a compulsive sense of privacy as well, perhaps, as from a sense of unworth—Ethel and Jack had always been the favored ones—Lionel hated playing himself onstage. He would do anything to disguise his virile good looks with gray wigs, a bent back, and a shuffle. It was as though he had been born old. Character parts were also, however, an escape from a trade he claimed he hated. When the public loved you as "John Drew" or "Maude Adams" there was no escape. But as long as it was some crusty colonel or peg-legged sailor behind the footlights, Lionel Barrymore could disappear and forget the whole damned business. He was unhappy, therefore, as Lieutenant Young in a touring production of Augustus Thomas's hit *Arizona* that season of 1899–1900. Eleanor Robson was in the cast and sat up nights on the jolting train listening to Lionel read Kipling's *Jungle Book*, forgetting the endless miles in the adventures of Kaa and Rikki-Tikki-Tavi just as Lionel was trying to forget his romantic duties as Young. He was pleased in April during the company's long return Chicago run to be promoted to playing the heavy, Captain Hodgman, acting so well that James A. Herne came backstage to offer him the young male lead in a New York production of his own play *Sag Harbor*.

"I *hate* romantic leads," said Lionel.

"I'll give you more money," said Herne.

AMERICA FOR A CAREER, but England for real society! Ethel sailed again that summer of 1900, eager for reunions and new conquests. One thing was clear: Frohman's actress could no longer bat about London in hansom cabs and walk-up lodgings; she must take a room at the Savoy, where he was staying. The Duchess of Sutherland, however, declared the Savoy no place for a young lady. Ethel shifted her suitcase to Stafford House, following a servant up the great branching gold and white staircase rising in a spectacular hall that soared the full height of the mansion. ("I have come from my house to your palace," Queen Victoria had once told then Duchess Harriet.) But Stafford House was just home to the all-conquering Ethel Barrymore.

She did not forget less exalted friends. Dissatisfied at the Lyceum, Suzanne Sheldon had gone to Australia, but Gertrude Elliott was now Johnston Forbes-Robertson's leading lady, another theatrical knot tied by Cupid. One day Ethel and Gertrude decided to wire a joke cable to Suzanne, abbreviating their old "Do nothing til you hear from me" to DO NOTHING. Suzanne meanwhile had engaged herself to a sheep rancher and written Gertrude the news. Wires crossed; the cable appeared to be a dire warning. To her fiancé's utter bewilderment, Suzanne icily broke the engagement and started packing for London. Old Left Bank ties were still strong.

Jack had more than survived his year in London, some of it spent at the Slade School of Art, still more in pubs, gaming houses, music halls, and ladies' bedrooms. Ethel discovered, however, that his delightful charm and wit had won him an entrée to society at many levels. Some of his friends she liked: Max Beerbohm, for example, or the artist Will Rothenstein—*not* the professional debauchee George Moore, "like something under a stone." To rescue him from such companions she spirited him away to Dunrobin overlooking the North Sea, where the air, food, and company were more wholesome. It was a relief to her too to escape London, for though Mafeking had been relieved at last and Pretoria had fallen, the bloody Boer War cast a pall over the city. The handsome Earl of Ava had been shot dead early that year in the siege of Wagon Hill. He had called himself Prince to her Cinderella; she had been rather chagrined to find half the ladies of her acquaintance in black mourning.

Since Maurice was more impressed with Jack's expenses than his progress, Jack sailed to New York with Ethel at summer's end. Jack's return coincided with the breakup of Maurice's marriage to Mamie; he had moved to a rambling farmhouse at Coytsville, New Jersey. Jack spent a lot of time at the farmhouse, where theatre people flocked on weekends, shocking the locals with drinking and horseplay. The place was overrun with animals, hangers-on, and Maurice's women. Jack felt right at home.

Maurice and Jack were together on September 26, 1900, for Lionel's third assault on Broadway in Herne's *Sag Harbor*, a realistic drama about a small Long Island fishing village. Carpenters were pounding the last nails in Oscar Hammerstein's new Republic Theatre as Lionel unhappily made up as Frank Turner, the younger of two brothers in love with Martha, played by Herne's lovely daughter Julie. He need hardly have bothered. In that season of Maude Adams's *L'Aiglon*, William Gillette's *Sherlock Holmes*, Mrs. Leslie Carter's *Zaza*, John Drew's *Richard Carvel*, E. H. Sothern's *Hamlet*, and the *Florodora* Sextette, critics gave Herne's quiet play a cool reception. And although Maurice and his sons toasted Lionel's first night at the Lambs, critics damned Lionel next day for playing the young sailor in "too saturnine and brutal a way," thus winning not a bit of sympathy.

Lionel was so bad, in fact, that Herne had to fire him. Herne blamed himself for a casting mistake, though Lionel also suspected he was concerned about Lionel's interest in Julie and her pretty sister Chrystal. But Lionel left the company with Herne's daughters undeflowered and a warm feeling for the great actor-manager-playwright: not even Mummum had dismissed him more kindly.

Sag Harbor was not a total loss, however. Lionel had wrenched from the unfriendly *Times* the admission that there was promise in his acting. He'd also had another warning that he had better avoid parts with romantic clinches and lines like, "Will you kiss me for auld lang syne?"

Jack meanwhile had made an acting debut of sorts with Maurice in a benefit performance of *A Man of the World* for the Coytsville Hose Company No. 1. Casual as always, Maurice gave Jack no hint how to make up for the small role of a young seducer. Jack therefore simply took his cue from Maurice's mustache and lavishly applied black hair until he was satisfied that his reflection in the mirror looked "terribly dangerous." Maurice stared in amazement at the entrance of his top-heavy son while the Coytsvillians hooted. Lionel would have suffered agonies, but Jack, who didn't care, coolly burlesqued his role and later told Maurice that having a go at the lead would be a cinch. Impressed by Jack's aplomb (or suddenly in need of an actor), Maurice summoned him that October to Cincinnati where his *Man of the World* headed the vaudeville bill. Jack had made his debut.

Having no intention of taking up the family profession, however, Jack persuaded Maurice that fall to finance lessons at the Art Students League. Informed eventually that Jack had attended exactly one session, Maurice was philosophical, only wondering what had inspired him to turn up once. Jack continued to drift aimlessly, sometimes sleeping at the Coytsville farm, sometimes hanging out with Lionel. But it was Ethel as usual who rescued him, insisting he move into Mrs. Wilson's with her so she could keep an eye on him. Ethel who, unsuspected by all but Frohman, was about to burst upon the public as a star.

She'd returned from London broke as usual and gone straight to Frohman. C.F. did not fail her. "Ethel, I have a nice part for you at last," he said, handing her a copy of Clyde Fitch's new play *Captain Jinks of the Horse Marines*.

Fitch was currently the hottest playwright on Broadway, a consummate craftsman who so subtly denigrated the vapors and vanities of his heroines that actresses fought for the parts. In *Jinks* Madame Trentoni sports false "waterfall" curls, cries buckets, cannot travel without forty-eight pieces of luggage, and is ready to throw away a brilliant career for love. But she also has an enchanting sense of humor and "is quite the most lovely creature that ever came, like Venus Aphrodite, from the sea." The right actress could make a sensation in the bravura role. Frohman shrewdly decided to gamble on Ethel.

Fitch wanted an established actress. Tugging luxuriant dark mustaches and puffing gold-tipped cigarettes, the perfectionist playwright was everywhere at rehearsals, fussing over the lighting, sets, and the stunning 1870s costumes that were half the show. He fussed at Ethel too, until he discovered she was a quick study and a hardworking pro. More enthusiastic, he began to write her personality into the part: Madame Trentoni's wildly enthusiastic reception at the boat dock, for example, parodied Ethel's own enormous transatlantic popularity. And when Ethel finally appeared in her third-act costume of white tarletan showered with rosebuds over a billowy skirt and frothy train, a wreath of pink roses in her hair, Fitch capitulated completely.

Jinks was to open in Philadelphia. Frohman may have thought he was doing Ethel a favor, but Ethel would have far preferred to fail—she was sure she would fail—before an audience less conscious of her theatrical lineage. In a paroxysm of first-night nerves, she begged that the curtain be held a moment until she talked to the manager. "I haven't any money," she pleaded. "Do you think you could let me have five dollars until salary day?" If *Jinks* sank she would at least have train fare back to Mrs. Wilson's.

Despite a heavy snowstorm that night of January 7, 1901, the old Walnut Street Theatre was packed from pit to gallery. Her appearance at the top of the gangplank with a small dog in her arms was greeted with a burst of applause. She was supposed to run gaily down and cry, "Hip! hip! hurrah! Here we are at last on American soil—planks—never mind, *soil—E Pluribus Unum!*" It was not the easiest entrance in the world and in her nervousness she didn't get the lines across.

"Speak up, Ethel," called a solicitous voice from the gallery. "You Drews is all good actors!"

"We loved your grandmother, Ethel," called another voice, "and we love you too!"

Nine curtain calls seemed to prove it. Afterward, friends assured her that everything had gone splendidly, and she admitted she felt so too. The next morning she eagerly scanned the theatrical columns. "If the young lady who plays Madame Trentoni had possessed beauty, charm, or talent," she read, "this play might have been a success . . ."

Other critics did not like Fitch's play but praised Ethel Barrymore. It didn't matter: the bad review wiped out all the rest. All through the Philadelphia run and the two weeks of one-night stands that followed she was miserable, praying that *Jinks* would close, begging Frohman not to bring it into New York. But Clyde Fitch's vanity prevailed. With three plays running on Broadway, he wanted to go for a record fourth.

Much as she'd suffered, it was only on opening night at the Garrick that she experienced "genuine 18-karat stage fright," a "little dying," an "agony of terror" that made her vomit uncontrollably and turned her hands to ice. Because this wasn't Recitation Day at the convent or a small part or even the kind of ensemble playing Uncle Jack had done at Daly's. *Captain Jinks* was Ethel Barrymore pure and simple. If she failed the play failed. "Why am I doing this?" she moaned as the clock ticked inexorably toward eight-thirty. "Why didn't I try to do something else?" On her dressing table sat a big shiny red apple, a talisman from Uncle Jack, who was acting that night and couldn't be there. "Speak your piece well and you'll get a big red apple"—she'd heard it dozens of times as a child. Oh God, couldn't there be an earthquake or a tidal wave—anything to stop that curtain from going up and her going on!

The house was crowded not only with first-nighters but with Ethel's friends and with people who had known the Drews and Barrymores for years on both sides of the curtain. Jack, pale and nervous, shared a box with Aunt Dodo. Maurice and Gus Thomas, however, had only standing-room tickets. Maurice's last tour had been a disaster, not only because *The Battle of the Strong* had bad lines but because Maurice couldn't remember them. His behavior had grown increasingly bizarre. All he'd brought back from the tour was a suitcase bulging with twenty-two fourteen-dollar suits of the identical cut, fabric, and color; yet along Broadway he sported fantastic getups of dirty trousers, carpet slippers, and top hat. His once brilliant conversation had degenerated into incoherent diatribes against enemies, fate, God, and the United Booking Office. Afraid of how his friend might react on this emotional occasion, Gus Thomas had suggested that they watch Ethel's New York debut from the back of the house.

Fitch had calculated every moment of the opening scene to build suspense for the entrance of Madame Trentoni. At last Ethel did appear at the top of the gangplank, tall and ravishing in a whipped-cream hat, ermine tippet, and full flounced skirt. There was a hush, then a burst of spontaneous applause as she ran down the plank. She stood waiting with a smile as the applause swelled. In the back of the theatre Maurice's eyes stung with tears. "Oh, God," he whispered to Gus Thomas, "isn't she sweet!"

But Fitch also knew Ethel had not yet convinced New York that she could act. He had therefore provided her with a line calculated to disarm critics. In one scene Madame Trentoni is brought face to face with the mother of the man who has won her hand. "But," the old gentlewoman protests, "you are an actress?" "There seems to be some question about that," replies Madame Trentoni with adorable modesty. The line was greeted with a roar of laughter; hearts not already won melted.

When the curtain finally fell on the flower-strewn stage, Jack could hardly fight his way backstage through the throngs pressing to congratulate her. "Where's Father?" said Ethel. "He promised he'd be here." After all her admirers had finally laid their bouquets at her feet, Maurice appeared. "It was wonderful, darling," he said, kissing her; then he was gone.

Ethel walked back to Mrs. Wilson's just around the corner from the Garrick and sat up all night waiting for the reviews. She knew that the welcoming applause had been for "the much-engaged Miss Ethel Barrymore," a fabulous press-created monster having little resemblance to herself; she knew the audience had been heavily laced with friends. What she wanted to know was whether her hard work had paid off: had she made a critical success?

If the sheer space devoted to her in the morning papers was any indication, she had. But there were demurs. Curmudgeonly William Winter found her "a juvenile performer, still in the experimental stage." The *Times* only admitted she would bear a good deal of watching. But there was much to make her happy, particularly the *Sun*'s judgment that in effortless, debonair comedy she was "the full equal of Georgie Drew Barrymore." To Ethel then and long afterward, that morning in her dark little hall bedroom was the happiest of her life.

With her salary improved to $125 a week, Ethel moved to the large second-floor front bedroom, which had a kind of "friar's cell" where Jack could sleep if so disposed. *Captain Jinks* packed the Garrick, the curtain continued to fall on ecstatic applause. Young Wallace Stevens's reaction to Ethel's magic was typical. Seeing the play the first time, he went home enraptured and immediately began writing for her a romantic comedy called *Olivia*. Raving about her the next day to his host, he was told "that Ethel Barrymore actually took grapes—I mean luncheon—in this house one day last summer. Oh Heavens!" He went to see her again: "Beautiful angel!" Back again six nights later "to see his ardor through," he found her "charming in the last act in that white and green dress with the roses." All New York seemed to share that ardor. The Garrick's box office was the busiest on Broadway.

Yet Ethel still did not expect what happened one night three weeks into the run. As she and her maid rounded the corner of Thirty-fifth Street, something about the Garrick marquee struck her as different, though she couldn't say what. Suddenly she stopped short. What was different was the name ETHEL BARRYMORE blazing in big lights above the title of Fitch's play.

The next day she hurried to Frohman's office. "It was a wonderful thing for you to do!"

Frohman shrugged, led her to the window. "They did it," he said, jerking his thumb at the crowds below in the street.

They had, and would. Ethel Barrymore had come, been seen, and conquered.

PART TWO

CENTER STAGE

1901–1925

SIX

1901–1902

THE BROADWAY that Ethel conquered that year of 1901 was flashy and sybaritic. Carriages deposited ostrich-plumed women and top-hatted men at Delmonico's and Sherry's for roast beef dinners before the theatre. At the theatre, "What a magnificent sight it was from the stage in those days!" said one actress, remembering the men's dazzling white shirt fronts and the waves of perfume pulsing across the footlights. The rich, the powerful, and the beautiful were regular first-nighters: Diamond Jim Brady with a statuesque blonde, Mrs. Stuyvesant Fish, Tammany chief Richard "Boss" Croker, Charles Dana Gibson, Stanford White, William Randolph Hearst with a woman on each arm. After the theatre crowds poured into the Café Metropole, Bustanoby's, Churchill's, and the Astor for midnight suppers of oysters, lobster, steak, and champagne. And there was Rector's, where an ambitous actress might hook a diamond bracelet or—if she were a *Florodora* girl—a twenty-carat engagement ring. With forty-one theatres, New York boasted more marquees than any other city in the world. Theatre was *the* entertainment, a hot time in the old town at night. Diamond Jim Brady had christened Broadway "the Street of the Midnight Sun." It was also the street of midnight sin: of extravagance, venery, and hangovers.

Miss Ethel Barrymore with her aura of "rare, radiant girlhood" seemed a contradiction. True, she could be seen smoking cigarettes at Sherry's or lunching at her regular table in the Palm Room of the Waldorf-Astoria. But her tastes were simple, her ideals high. She still wore black for the street and white for balls, sewing many of her dresses herself with mea-sured, convent-learned stitches. She still "ate" books: Henry James, Pope, Kipling, "Mr. Dooley," Jack London, Conrad, and even George Eliot for, though she preferred male writers, Mary Ann Evans was "more like a man than a woman." She was passionate about ideas and fond of saying "Bully!" Her companion at Sherry's or the Waldorf might be Uncle Jack, and when she relaxed after the theatre by going for a drive in a hansom, her cousin Georgie or another girl chum shared the cab. As for the diamonds that *Florodora* girls found buried in their bouquets, "I shall have to send it back," said Miss Ethel, surveying with distaste a magnificent solitaire.

"Why not accept it as a tribute to your art? I hear that's being done in London."

"But this is *not* a tribute to my art."

In fact, Ethel embodied the new young woman who had emerged with the suffragist movement in the nineties. This girl was taller, stronger, and far more active than her Victorian sister. She was a decidedly Anglo-Saxon beauty, her blond hair, blue eyes, and red-rose complexion coinciding with the ideal of an America recoiling from waves of "undesirable" Eastern European immigrants. She exuded high spirits. She had a brain and was not ashamed to use it. Her free and frank manners paradoxically proclaimed her innocence: only virtue could be so unselfconscious. Adults loved her like a daughter. Young men found her "the best fellow in the world." But she was also a woman's woman, the kind of girl who had as many idolizers at Smith and Vassar as at Princeton and Yale. This was Ethel Barrymore: "our Ethel," the epitome of the American girl, a national treasure.

Newspapers bombarded their readers with her. Young women everywhere tried to copy her upswept hairdo, her throaty drawl, the way she leaned forward earnestly as she talked and clasped her hands. Whatever she did was received with breathless interest. When a yacht she was aboard sailed past a floundering passenger liner in New York Harbor, the event was reported MISS BARRYMORE SEES VESSEL SINK. Gentlemen were instructed that suitable topics for the debutante sitting next to them at dinner might be platonic love, the relative merits of Harvard and Yale, and Ethel Barrymore.

She adored hansom cabs, her fans were told. Her first remembered fight with her brother Lionel had ended in a draw. She swam, golfed, and drove a mean tennis ball. She was terribly happy that her hips were flat. She had literary ambitions and wrote plays and short stories. Her favorite composers? Beethoven, of course, but she also loved playing Schumann, Sibelius, Rachmaninoff, and Liszt. Queried about the invention of the phonograph she declared rather obscurely that it was "delightful to see mechanism performing the duties of genius."

About two things she was perfectly clear. First, remembering Mummum, she never revealed anything private to the press. Second, she dismissed all nonsense about her position in high society conflicting with her art. If she had "views" of the actress in society, said Ethel, it was that "the more she knows of life the better is her art, and that she can learn life more agreeably and with less damage to her skirts in society than in the slums."

Ethel thus installed herself in the camp of actors like Uncle Jack, Maxine Elliott, and Mrs. Patrick Campbell for whom society was as much a profession as the stage. Ethel often felt compelled to defend her position. "Yes, I have a good many friends in society," she would say, "but that doesn't matter. I like them just as well." At the same time she was incorruptible and militantly loyal to her profession. Perhaps this was why Charles Frohman accepted Ethel's frenetic socializing with good grace. Besides, society's darling Ethel offered a dramatic and profitable contrast to his other star, Maude Adams.

JACK, REGULARLY REPORTING to the worried Ethel, had been trying his best to keep track of their increasingly erratic father. On March 28, with *Captain Jinks* into its eighth triumphant week, he followed Maurice to Harlem, where he was appearing at the Lion Palace Vaudeville Hall. The moment Maurice came onstage Jack knew from his distraught manner there would be trouble, and there was. Instead of reciting poetry, Maurice launched into a wild attack on the monopolizing Theatrical Trust, Jews, and the human race in general. "Down with the Trust! Death to the Syndicate! Charles Frohman is doomed!" he shouted, striding up and down the stage waving his arms. The stunned audience began to laugh as the stage manager frantically tried to wave him off. Ranting, tears streaming down his cheeks, Maurice was oblivious. Finally the curtain was rung down.

When Maurice burst from the theatre, Jack pursued him twenty blocks to the Fort Lee ferry dock at West 130th Street where he found his father harassing the waiting passengers, so outraging one couple that the man went for a policeman. Blows were exchanged, but Jack helped pull Maurice off, rashly promising to take charge of his father, and the officer did not make an arrest, for after all this was Maurice Barrymore, or what was left of him. Meanwhile Maurice was entertaining the crowd with boasts and obscenities. "I am Maurice Barrymore, the greatest actor this country ever saw. . . . Why, I'm greater than Lincoln. Mankind will forget Lincoln, Webster, Booth, and Barrett, but they'll remember me!"

Jack could not let his father make the crossing to New Jersey alone. Scared and sick, he waited for the ferry with Maurice. But as he trailed him up the gangplank, Maurice suddenly spun round and shoved. Jack staggered and landed on the dock on his back. As debarking passengers rushed to help him, the gangplank lifted and the ferry pulled away.

After the evening performance Ethel went straight to Mrs. Wilson's to wait for Jack and his news. It was after two before he came in with Gus Thomas; he sobbed as he described Maurice's tirade at the Lion Palace and his crazed behavior at the ferry landing. When the three separated hours later they still had not decided what to do about their father and friend.

At ten that morning Ethel was still sitting in a chair staring out the window when she heard raised voices in the hall. Seconds later Maurice burst through her door. "Death to the Syndicate," he cried. "Charles Frohman is dead! The White Rats have killed him! And I am the greatest theatrical manager in the world."

Ethel was on her feet. Her father's hatred of her benefactor chilled her. "That's true, Father," she said quietly, and smiled. He seized her by the throat; she kept very still, smiling into his eyes. Momentarily subdued, Maurice dropped his hands.

Mrs. Wilson had sent for Jack. He followed his father when he rushed from Ethel's room and across Thirty-sixth Street to the Lambs, raving again. A hastily gathered council of Lambs friends convened in Ethel's rooms. Fortunately she had an attorney, William Redding, who recommended a medical examination.

When the doctor arrived at the Lambs, he found Maurice pathetically exhausted. There was only one course: Ethel and Jack must commit their father to temporary restraint pending a thorough examination at the Pavilion for the Insane at Bellevue. The thought appalled them, but there was nothing else to do. The problem of luring Maurice into the waiting cab was solved by his friend Digby Bell's urging him to go downtown to file a formal complaint against the policeman who had attacked him the day before. Maurice leapt at the idea but once in the cab sank back against the cushion and seemed to forget his mission.

In the admitting room at Bellevue Jack tried to answer routine questions about his father, but again broke down and wept. At this Maurice took the stage. "My son has an exaggerated idea of my condition," he said and proceeded to swagger his replies as though giving a command performance. He finally asked for paper, scrawled two pages, folded them, and handed them to Jack, who watched him disappear flanked by two attendants. Outside, still crying, Jack opened the letter. It was almost indecipherable. "I have traversed the whole country . . . big audiences . . . Applause . . . Think that I should come to this: to be barred. . . ."

Finally it was Jack Barrymore, "art student, nineteen years old, resident at No. 61 West Thirty-sixth Street," who testified that Maurice Barrymore was dangerous to himself and his family. Meanwhile Ethel had gone to the theatre, where, besides the familiar bouquet of gardenias from "L'inconnu," she found her dressing room heaped with consolatory cards, telegrams, and flowers. Word of Maurice Barrymore's breakdown had spread like wildfire; the theatre was packed with people who wanted to see how his daughter was "taking it." She thought she would break down but did not, though afterward she would see no one but Gus Thomas and Frohman. Frohman was leaving for England, but told her that he had instructed his office to advance her whatever money she might need for whatever cause.

The next morning the papers had a field day, sweeping aside Ethel's explanation that her father had never recovered from an attack of the grippe the year before: MAURICE BARRYMORE IS A RAVING MANIAC IN BELLEVUE. HIS DAUGHTER IS ON THE VERGE OF NERVOUS PROSTRATION. IT IS FEARED THAT BARRYMORE WILL NOT RECOVER. Ethel was not on the verge of nervous prostration: night after night she survived the bravura Madame Trentoni role. But she began to faint rather regularly during the performance, and her leading man, H. Reeves-Smith, grew used to catching her as she fell.

On April Fools' Day Ethel and Jack went to Bellevue to learn the results of their father's examination. They happened to arrive just as Mamie Floyd Barrymore was deposited at the entrance. The meeting was not warm—neither for Ethel, who had never gotten over her father's remarriage, nor for Jack, confronted with his seductress. The three waited for the doctor in silence.

One part of his report they had anticipated. Maurice Barrymore was incurably insane. The other part they had not. Maurice's insanity was due to syphilitic paresis of the brain.

> He's been treated in every known way,
> But his spirochetes grow day by day;
>   He's developed paresis,
>   Has long talks with Jesus,
> And thinks he's the Queen of the May.

Of course in 1901 the doctor would not have put it so callously, yet the three must have recoiled. It was Ethel who signed the commitment papers to the Long Island Home for the Insane at Amityville and Jack who escorted Maurice there. Maurice went quietly, convinced that he was on his way to fill an acting engagement in Philadelphia.

AGAIN LIONEL HAD NOT taken part or perhaps was excluded by a sister who preferred her brother Jack. Since being relieved of his duties in *Sag Harbor*, Lionel had been intermittently employed by managers needing someone for the week in Buffalo, Hartford, or Newark. In town he was sharing a drafty tenement on Thirtieth Street with two friends named Jack Gallatin and William Carpenter Camp. They called it "Running Water" because the bathtub dripped relentlessly. No plumber could ever get in to fix it because they slept all day.

Lionel was drinking a lot of beer, playing a lot of baseball, painting. Chancing to go to a concert, he heard Schubert's "Unfinished" Symphony, and suddenly he was mad about music—about playing music, about composing. He bought books but found that reading was no help. He began to haunt concert halls. Wagner became a god.

Occasionally he expressed a need for gainful employment; thus one day over a couple of beers he was advised to look up three newcomers from Syracuse who were going to put on a Broadway show. Acting on the suggestion, Lionel introduced himself to a small, harassed man named Sam Shubert and bravely told him he could act.

"What's your salary?" said Sam, getting to the point at once.

Thirty-five a week had always gotten Lionel, but what the hell. "Seventy-five."

Sam survived the news. Maybe he thought Lionel could get him Ethel. "This is a dressy part, you know."

Lionel and any kind of dress suit were strangers, but what the hell. He went into rehearsal immediately for a melodramatic British farce called *The Brixton Burglary* with a stage manager so tough that even seasoned actors dropped out. Since it was either insult or starvation, Lionel stuck. But this didn't necessarily mean that he buckled down. One afternoon he was awakened by thunderous pounding at the door. "What in the hell's the matter with you, Barrymore?" It was Sam, and the rehearsal had been important. "Get up! Get out of there! Come to work! How do you ever expect to amount to anything lying there stinking in bed?"

Camp loaned Lionel a dress suit and *The Brixton Burglary* had a decent success in New York, where it kept Lionel at the Herald Square Theatre for seven weeks. With the $525 he left Running Water for rooms near Carnegie Hall. He hired Henry Hadley, a composer-conductor and

Lambsian, to give him lessons in music theory and composition, he took piano lessons, and he persisted with his painting, unaware that William Gillette, Joseph Jefferson, Johnston Forbes-Robertson, and Richard Mansfield (to name a few) had all wanted to be painters and had all made their living on the stage.

Militantly modest, Lionel would always maintain for publication that he owed his Broadway career to Ethel: his engagement that fall of 1901 with John Drew at the Empire in *The Second in Command* as well as the successes that followed. That Ethel, dining that summer with Frohman in Paris, had primed the sugarholic with éclairs and marrons glacés, and then said firmly, *"Now what about Lionel?"* And undoubtedly Ethel with her strong sense of duty and even stronger sense of their Drew-Barrymore heritage did recommend Lionel to Frohman. But Frohman was a businessman, not a philanthropist. Not only was the very name Barrymore a draw, but critics had called Lionel "one of the best leading juveniles on the stage," who "gives every promise of being a far better actor than his father." Besides, Lionel's indifference to acting was largely a pose. During the run of *The Brixton Burglary* he had confided to Sam Shubert that his great desire was to accede to the high position in the theatre occupied by his father, Maurice Barrymore. Ethel did not get Lionel hired at the Empire; Lionel did.

THAT SUMMER Ethel had again returned to England where stories of new social triumphs immediately began to burn the wires. Given the nunlike regime decreed by Frohman, Ethel's chief rival, Maude Adams, had a harder time making headlines. That summer, however, she almost upstaged Ethel by entering a Catholic convent in Tours disguised as an American heiress in need of a rest cure. She was happy there canning cherries and making butter until one day she was moved to confess her profession. The nuns screamed in horror, but Maude had become such a great pet that they wiped their damp brows and unanimously voted she could stay. And then this adventure was capped by the news that Sarah Bernhardt wanted to play Romeo to Maude's Juliet.

Ethel retaliated with Winston Churchill. Winston was twenty-six, famous for his Boer War exploits, and already in the House of Commons. He was half an inch shorter than Ethel's five-foot-seven, with pale red hair and a slight lisp. Though he'd been in love before, he had not considered himself financially able to marry. Now, however, he had just earned 10,000 pounds from lecture tours and writing. Ethel was ravishing, with an American vitality like his mother's. She was witty, intelligent.

They moved in the same social circles. Ethel began to notice that wherever she went young Winston Churchill just happened to be a fellow house guest. She liked him, but Churchill himself fell deeply in love.

BESIDES CHAPERONING his father, Jack had been employed since November 1900 as a political cartoonist for the *Evening Journal*, making fifty dollars a week and surviving the fury of Ella Wheeler Wilcox, a writer of the saccharine kind of verse then popular. Jack had been assigned to illustrate her poems and had responded with his usual morbidities. Enraged, Ella telephoned the *Journal*'s editor, Arthur Brisbane: "Don't let that pessimistic old swine, Barrymore, illustrate anything more of mine!" Jack's charm had often prevented Brisbane's firing him on the spot; he sent Jack now to work it upon Mrs. Wilcox at the Hoffman House. Jack knocked diffidently at her door.

"I am Barrymore," said Jack to the woman in flowing blue velvet.

"Didn't your father," demanded Mrs. Wilcox, "have enough courage to come up here himself?"

Jack humbly confessed that he was the despised illustrator and that, besides being naturally morbid, he always had to draw his characters in long robes or tall grass because he hadn't yet had lessons in rendering feet. Ella was enchanted and immediately telephoned Brisbane to say she would have no other illustrator but Jack Barrymore.

Jack just might have missed the feet lesson. Carl Strunz, with whom he was currently studying, began his classes at 9:00 a.m. Jack would stroll in about eleven-thirty, pull out a sketching pad, and draw a few lines, upon which Strunz would bawl him out. After an hour or so Jack would leave, cutting afternoon class. When he stayed for the still-life class he ignored the subject to do macabre sketches of his own. He impressed the other students as conceited, spoiled, and rude. He wore "different" clothes and his hands were always dirty. He was sullen; had no apparent wit. He seemed to be floundering, trying to find himself, and unhappy much of the time.

He *was* making progress, though Ethel wasn't satisfied. At one of those Palm Garden luncheons she said to her dear friend the actress Cissie Loftus, "Isn't it a pity that Jack can't get recognition for his work?"

"*Work?*" said Cissie, never having associated the word with Jack.

Informed that Jack was an illustrator, Cissie persuaded Daniel Frohman to commission a poster from him advertising her appearance that fall with E. H. Sothern in *If I Were King*. But Ethel really wanted Jack with her in the theatre. She had returned to a triumphant New York reopening of *Jinks*, then set out on tour. In Philadelphia a young actor had to leave the cast temporarily and of course Ethel thought of Jack. He was to come immediately, memorizing his lines on the train.

Jack approached the task with his usual zeal, with the result that in a first-act exchange with Captain Jinks he stopped dead. "I've blown up," he announced affably to Jinks and audience. "Where do we go from here?" The rest was improvisation with the cast sweating bullets and Ethel so convulsed with laughter that the other actors had to say her lines. Jack then capped his performance by detaching himself after the huge round of applause for Ethel's second-act dance and taking a low bow solo. He then led the star forward for *her* bow. Frohman happened to be in the audience that night. "With a better memory," he told Jack, "you might make a comedian some day."

Back in New York, Jack submitted "The Hangman" to the Press Artists League show, a Munch-like drawing of an executioner trudging down a road, his shadow thrown behind him like a gallows and the bloated faces of his victims leering above. Dropping by the gallery one day Jack was astounded to find a SOLD sign, more astounded to find that the purchaser was Andrew Carnegie. He split the ten dollars with the League, which was impressed enough to award him a scholarship for 1902 to study with the reputable artist George Bridgeman.

Then in January 1902 *Cosmopolitan* published four of his drawings—"Despair," "Unrest," "Fear," and "Jealousy"—accompanied by a critique that credited him with not only anatomical correctness but "strength of the kind that arrests and holds the eye"—though, the reviewer concluded, Barrymore would only achieve greatness when he flung away his vision of man defeated to show man triumphant. That Jack was not about to do. (Uncle Jack was always fond of a particularly bizarre drawing called "The Web of Life" accompanied by an editorial note that began, "This is not an unpleasant picture when looked at properly.") Jack's pictures were meant to be unpleasant—weird mixtures of Blake, Fuseli, Daumier, and Doré in the tradition of gothic romanticism that produced *Frankenstein, Dracula*, and *Dr. Jekyll and Mr. Hyde*. Were they good drawings? Well, if Jack had not been a Barrymore his work probably would not have received such attention. On the other hand, far inferior work was published every day.

But Jack spent most of his time simply being a young bohemian in New York. He had a "studio"—a third-floor hall room in an old brownstone on Fourteenth Street, subsidized of course by Ethel. It had a north window, a gas plate, and a sink, and was furnished with burst cartons of Maurice's books. Jack didn't mind because he wasn't there most of the time. Sometimes he would bunk at Minnie Hay's boardinghouse on

Thirty-fourth Street, a hangout for the newspaper crowd whom Jack had gotten to know through Lionel's old pal Frank Butler, now a writer for the *Herald*. The boys at Minnie Hay's were a tough bunch, as raw and uncouth as the tabloids that thrived on scoops and scandal. Jack was sensitive, imaginative—still "silk," as gangsters say of a recruit. He was ashamed of being silk and did everything he could to coarsen the fabric of his mind and body.

And he could always grab a few winks (like Maurice he didn't seem to need sleep) at the old Aulic Hotel on Thirty-fifth where the artist Rip Anthony managed to pay rent by whipping out drawings for newspapers with incredible speed. In return for a night on his floor Jack would pose, sometimes as Custer, sometimes as a mourning Roman matron at the tomb of her son.

Jack, Rip, and Butler—the Three Musketeers—were such entertaining company that cronies would stand them booze or supper just to hear them talk. When that didn't work, Rip had a different scam. He and Jack would enter a restaurant but defer ordering because they were "waiting for someone." A waiter would bring rolls and butter which Rip would pocket along with the pepper and salt. After a decent interval he would summon the waiter. "When Mr. Vanderbilt asks for us, tell him we couldn't wait any longer and have gone on to Sherry's. He will understand." Indulgent waiters did understand, allowing Rip and Jack to work the trick up and down Broadway. Next morning, the Aulic maid would come up with hot shaving water. Rip would salt and pepper it, lay out stale rolls and butter. "Get up, Jack. We have bouillon this morning—bouillon, my boy!"

Butler could be equally inventive, especially when his big gold front tooth was missing, a sure sign of poverty. One night when he and Jack had a dime between them, strategy was required. Butler walked into Thorpe's all-night restaurant around the corner from the *Herald* building and ordered large, filling butter cakes (three for five cents) and a cup of coffee. When he had consumed half the meal, Jack burst in and whispered in his ear. Butler leapt to his feet. "My God, isn't that terrible!" he cried, grabbing his hat and racing for the door, obviously on his way to the *Herald* where a big story had broken. Jack moved in, rapidly devoured the remaining butter cakes and coffee and joined Butler around the corner.

Jack had promised to lodge Butler for the feed. But when they finally climbed the long flight to Jack's studio Butler knew he'd been taken. He could have slept on any number of floors without sharing his butter cakes. The outraged victim had to make the best of it and burrowed under heaps of Maurice's books "as though they were snow." Eventually his "A Night with Great Authors" piece earned him fifteen dollars. Relenting, he gave five to his host.

If Jack's earnings were sketchy, he was also perennially broke because he spent every cent he made. One expensive item was women. There'd been any number of girls but none—he thought now, staring across architect Stanford White's opulent Tower Room at the small, perfectly turned figure of a girl with coppery curls and pouting mouth—none so devastating as Evelyn Nesbit, an artist's model and the most sensational of the new *Florodora* Sextette.

Their first meeting (as Evelyn later told it) had been sensational. Stanford White had taken pity on Jack one day when he'd walked into the Knickerbocker Grille in rumpled evening clothes, sat down at an uncleared table, put his head in his arms, and gone to sleep. Recognizing a Barrymore, White ordered a stiff highball and shoved it under his nose. Revived, Jack told a pathetic tale of jumping a milk train back to New York from an out-of-town revel without a dime. He was killing time until he could get in touch with Ethel.

White had numerous apartments around Manhattan, including the notorious mirrored Tower Room atop his own creation, Madison Square Garden. He liked his mistress Evelyn Nesbit to be waiting in one or another; she was used to receiving his little notes explaining that he "needed impetus for his free artistic impulses." Discovering her wrapped in furs would provide this impetus, or sleeping between white silk sheets, or posed on the red velvet swing in the Tower Room wearing only black stockings and a red garter. That day he wanted to find her in the pink, white, and mauve apartment curled up like a sleeping nymph on the huge polar bear rug. Evelyn dutifully stripped, arranged herself nymphally on the rug, and closed her eyes. A key turned in the lock. When she opened her eyes she saw not White's hot heavy face but the startled face of a young god. White had given Jack the wrong key.

So Jack knew the score about Evelyn Nesbit, though he may have believed she was White's slave because the villain had given her too much champagne and raped her. He also knew he was here now in the Tower Room as White's guest. But Evelyn's demure sexiness drove everything else from his mind. He had grown a little eyelash of a mustache; he fingered it now as he telegraphed love across the room to Evelyn, who smiled shyly. When White briefly left the room Jack was at her side. "Quick! Your address and phone number!" He scribbled them on his cuff. That night at the Knickerbocker Theatre where she was dancing in *The Wild Rose*, Evelyn found a bunch of violets with a single American

Beauty rose buried in its center. Mixing floral metaphors wildly, Jack had written, "To a quivering pink poppy in a golden, windswept space."

Since the appeal of an attraction like Evelyn Nesbit was inaccessibility, her manager had made her sign a stiff contract: not to become engaged or contract a marriage; not to appear in restaurants or cafés within one mile of any theatre, be photographed or sit for paintings, ride in streetcars or omnibuses, issue autographs, carry or lead a dog in public, appear without face veiling, use stimulants, become facially tanned, accept presents, employ any dentist or doctor not approved by the management or wear any gowns, hats, gloves, and shoes ditto. None of the clauses prohibited her from being White's mistress.

But then Jack began to haunt the stage door. And when Stanford White incautiously left town on a fishing trip, Jack persuaded Evelyn to go to Rector's, for which she'd always had a weakness. Heads turned at the beautiful young couple; whispers ran around the tables that White's private pond was being poached. At supper, where Ethel's photograph was among the beauties gazing down at them from the walls, their laughter made the other diners envious. Evelyn ordered milk and Jack plucked a petal from a rose and set it delicately afloat in her glass. "That is your mouth," he said, and Evelyn thrilled to his Villonesque charm.

She did not always avoid stimulants. There was the night that she and Jack had far too much red wine at a little Italian restaurant and decided it was more prudent to retreat to Jack's studio than face Mrs. Nesbit in the suite White paid for in the Hotel Audubon. Jack tenderly wrapped the shivering Evelyn in Maurice's old Orlando cloak and, folding her in his arms, laid her down to sleep among the old books "the heavy dreamless sleep of youth." That was Evelyn's story at any rate, and perhaps true, for Jack was very capable of romantic gestures.

When Jack returned Evelyn to the Audubon late the next morning both White and Mrs. Nesbit dismissed the "dreamless sleep" story with contempt. "Your reputation is ruined!" cried Mrs. Nesbit, voicing society's view that a girl may sin with a rich man but not with a poor one. White, however, still owned Evelyn and proved it by ordering that doctor of millionaires Nathaniel Bowditch Potter to keep Evelyn under lock and key without food until she confessed to intercourse with Jack Barrymore. "Is it true?" Potter grilled her throughout the day. "Did Jack Barrymore seduce you?"

Evelyn did not break down. The next day White summoned the two criminals to the Tower. Browbeaten but unbowed, Jack stubbornly insisted that their relationship was strictly platonic. Then turning to Evelyn he said, "Will you marry me?"

White raged. Impossible! Evelyn was his; besides, what would they live on?

"Love," said Jack simply. "Don't move, Eve." Evelyn had placed herself under a lamp that sparked the copper in her hair. "You look beautiful there. Why not marry me, Eve?"

"I don't know," said Evelyn, knowing.

In the next days Mrs. Nesbit inveighed constantly against marrying "that penniless little pup." White played a stronger hand. "Barrymore is a little crazy," he told Evelyn. "His father is in an insane asylum. The whole family is queer."

Together they only inspired Evelyn to resist, though she knew marrying Jack was absurd. As a result, White shipped her off to the DeMille girls school at Pompton, New Jersey, for after all she was only sixteen. Jack came to Pompton often, and when he couldn't see her left passionate love notes tucked into the gates and shrubbery.

This turbulent sequence coincided roughly with Jack's being fired from the *Journal*. In May 1902 a sensational fraternal murder-suicide inspired Arthur Brisbane to plant a long moral diatribe on the editorial page where a large space was left for an illustration by Jack. Jack came in late with the deadline minutes away, dashed off a sketch of a hulking brute branded with the mark of Cain, and rushed it to the photoengraving department. There was no time for the department to do a decent job of reproduction. When Brisbane saw the blot that was to have pictorially enhanced his sermon, he sent for Jack. His family were actors, right?

"Yes, sir," said Jack, eyeing the domelike brow and thick-lensed glasses that gave Brisbane the goggly look of one of Jack's creatures.

All things considered, Jack should think seriously of pursuing the family trade.

"Yes, sir."

Over a bottle of red wine, Lionel was not consoling. There was no escape for a Barrymore. "We are in the cul-de-sac of tradition."

But neither tried seriously to escape. One of Lionel's and Jack's favorite myths was that they hated acting and fought strenuously to avoid it. Sheer rot. Had they really had such an intense aversion to the stage they could have driven a hansom cab or sold men's haberdashery.

Jack still pretended to pursue other work. He applied to the *Telegraph*, was given Gainsborough's portrait of the Duchess of Devonshire to copy in line. Twenty minutes later he turned in the unsigned drawing, it was passed up to the editor, and Jack was shown the door. A clothing firm sometimes paid him a dollar a drawing, and then there was that job of soliciting testimonials for an after-shave lotion called Schaeferine. He'd got it because Uncle Jack had agreed to endorse the product. Mr. Schaefer was delighted; now if he could get Ethel's name he would change the product from an after-shave to a general face lotion. Jack boldly promised his sister's endorsement, telegraphed her on tour, waited in suspense. Finally Ethel replied. "Dear Sirs: I have received your—I can't remember the damned thing's name—but I think it's the best table water I ever drank." Comedian Nat Goodwin, also plied by Jack for a testimonial, did in fact send one but wired Jack himself, "I have used your Schaeferine— my lawyer will see you in the morning." But Jack did not suffer the indignities of solicitation for long. Selling for thirty cents a bottle and costing fifty cents to make, Schaeferine folded with mathematical inevitability.

Ethel still tried to help, guilt-stricken that she the sister should have succeeded so brilliantly while her brothers languished in comparative obscurity. Her dear friend Finley Peter Dunne ("Mr. Dooley") had hinted that he might be able to do something for Jack. "If you are managing all these papers," Ethel wrote him, "do you think there is a chance for him to get steady work or something? I hear he's been sick & as I've not heard from him directly, feel rather worried. If you have time & could send for him to come in to see you & give him a good talk & say what you want is some one who will *work*, etc. perhaps some good may be done. I shall be eternally grateful dear Peter—& I know you will find him clever. Don't let him know I've written or suggested anything . . . I'd rather just now he didn't think I was doing anything for him." But nothing came of Ethel's efforts.

ETHEL'S INCREDIBLY SUCCESSFUL *Jinks* tour finally ended in June in Boston, where she outdrew the great Mrs. Patrick Campbell and Minnie Maddern Fiske. And now the big question was, "What next?"

With actors who first make their mark in a great role, the second role is crucial; in the case of "personality actors" the second outing simply has to allow that personality free play. Ethel was a personality actress. As one critic had remarked, Clyde Fitch had absolutely nothing to do with the success of *Captain Jinks*: Ethel Barrymore and her "kaleidoscopic voice" had done it all. Now Fitch was tailoring a new play to Ethel's measurements. She would inaugurate her 1902–1903 season with *The Flirt*.

Swishing new beaus behind her like her frothy *Jinks* train, Ethel again sailed for England. And again Winston Churchill turned up wherever she went, more in love than ever with the beautiful creature he called "my harp with the golden sling." The romance was not going as well as he could hope. Ethel was effervescent and heartbreakingly popular; he was

awkward, with no patience for romantic small talk. To test her potential
as a mate, he gave a small dinner in London for Neville Chamberlain,
Lloyd George, and Lord Rosebery. As usual Ethel shone in conversation
as though she hobnobbed with world leaders every day, but she did not
say what Winston wanted to hear: that being a politician's wife seemed
more desirable than being on the stage.

When Clyde Fitch fell ill and couldn't finish *The Flirt* for her opening
at the Savoy, Frohman decided on *Carrots*, a curtain raiser with Ethel as
a boy of fifteen, to be followed by the lightly satiric *The Country Mouse*,
in which Ethel could wear lots of lovely white clothes. Flush with the
success of his "star factory," Frohman was attempting his biggest season
yet with imported English stars including Irving and Terry, Charles Wyndham, George Alexander, and Mrs. Patrick Campbell. Frohman still doled
out Ethel's salary paternally: "No matter what you get, Ethel, it'll go."
Instead of regular raises he gave her a bonus at the end of each season.
This summer she refused the bonus. She had been neglecting Lionel of
late; her preference for Jack showed. Instead of the bonus she now asked
Frohman to give Lionel the part of the organ grinder in John Drew's
tenth season Empire opener *The Mummy and the Hummingbird*.

"But Giuseppe is already cast."

"Well, that's all I want and I really think Lionel should have it," said
Ethel, looking rather like Mrs. John Drew.

Lionel got it, and was on hand to greet Ethel when the *Philadelphia*
docked. In fact (as reporters gushed), Ethel's two "cavaliers" were always
the last to bid her goodbye and the first to welcome her home—quite
probably since they were always looking for handouts. But they were
beginning to be recognized as a trio: THE BARRYMORES, WINNING FAME
WHILE THEIR FATHER IS DYING. Ethel loved it when the press called
them "The Flying Barrymores," and now it was Lionel's turn.

Lionel's first thought was that Frohman had given him Giuseppe hop-
ing he would blow it sky high. His second was that despite the difficulties
Giuseppe was the part of a lifetime. He went to two Italian actors who
took him in hand "like a pair of rooster owners training a cock for battle."
They even rounded up a real Italian organ grinder. Every night for three
weeks over beer at the Casino Roof, Lionel, George Barnum, Ralph
Delmore, and the organ grinder thrashed out the creation of Giuseppe.
To their suggestions Lionel added the mannerisms of the Italian waiter
at Plavino's and every other Italian he'd ever run into. By the dress
rehearsal Lionel was so Sicilian that people swore they could smell the
garlic three blocks away. He could even grind an organ, rather a departure
from his musical ambitions, but what the hell.

To Lionel's amazement, Frohman accepted this incredible accomplishment as though Lionel had been playing Sicilian organ grinders from the cradle. And then the dress rehearsal did not go smoothly. At the culmination of his great emotional scene, Lionel had to snatch a knife from his belt, kiss it fiercely crying, "Vendetta! Vendetta!" then collapse sobbing into a chair as the curtain slowly descended. Lionel kissed the knife, burst into real tears, flung himself at the chair and—missed.

Serene as custard, Frohman raised a pudgy hand. "I'm glad you did that tonight, Barrymore. Because you will never do it again."

On September 4, Ethel joined the carriage trade for the Empire opening. But although the applause at John Drew's entrance lasted five minutes, the triumph that night was Lionel's. While Ethel watched with "flushed cheeks, humid eyes, parted lips, and heaving breast," Lionel swept the audience with his passion. When the curtain fell, Ethel turned to a Roman count in her party. "What do you think of the Italian?" she asked triumphantly. "He is *not* Italian," said the Count, "he is Sicilian!" Ethel laughed with delight.

"The one vital character in the play was the organ grinder of young Lionel Barrymore," said the *Daily Tribune* the next day. Other critics raved about "the hulking, handsome Barrymore" whose Giuseppe is "the genuinest thing ever put on the stage." Lionel had earned the big red apple Jack sent in what, compared to Ethel's Madame Trentoni, was a very small part. Whether he liked it or not, he was an actor.

John Drew was not used to being played off his own stage. A few nights after the opening a friend at the Players Club asked how he was holding up. Drew cocked an expressive eyebrow. "Well enough, thank you, considering that every night I have to play second fiddle to that preposterous nephew of mine!" In fact, he declared Lionel's Giuseppe "a revelation."

SEVEN

1902–1905

MORE THAN A YEAR after he was given six months to live, Maurice Barrymore was physically alive at Amityville. For twenty dollars a week Ethel had bought her father a large ground-floor room in a detached villa with views of woods and ground. Guilt as well as duty prompted her, for Maurice had been heard to rave, "Oh, Ethel, Ethel, don't look at your father like that!"—and her lifelong estrangement and even hostility to her father troubled her now, as did her own brilliant success coinciding with his fall.

At first he had seemed to improve until Ethel and Jack even talked about his coming back to Broadway and the Lambs. But periodic remission is characteristic of advanced paresis, and Maurice soon lapsed back into hallucination. His obsessions had narrowed to two. Charles Frohman had become the supreme villain in his universe, and Maurice spent hours plotting how he would escape and murder him. An interesting delusion since compared to the theatre monopolists Abe Erlanger and Marc Klaw, Frohman was a prince, and interpretable in part as jealous rage at Frohman's becoming the father-provider to Ethel that he had never been. Maurice's other obsession was his failed career. Sane, he would not have begrudged Ethel her success. Mad, his daughter's triumph seemed to goad him into a fury he directed at her mentor.

More important to Maurice than acting was authorship. After all, he was a sophisticated, widely read Oxford man whose wit outsped Oscar Wilde's more languid paradoxes. He could have been, like Wilde, a brilliant playwright had luck not somehow always been against him. Now he wrote feverishly, confident that he was finally creating the masterpiece that had eluded him. "I have a new play," he said to Gus Thomas, who visited him often. Maurice's voice was urgent. "Run your eyes over this." He had covered a hundred pages with the sentence "It was a lovely day in June."

85

Ethel and Jack came regularly, Lionel less often. At first Maurice welcomed his sons; then he became suspicious and hostile. He refused to believe that Jack sold drawings or that Lionel had acted at the Empire. When he confused Ethel with Georgie he lapsed into rambling, sentimental conversations about the old days. When Ethel was Ethel, he became contentious and cruel. Ethel left drained and depressed. To the public Maurice Barrymore was already dead. To his children he had become an unburied corpse.

That autumn Ethel moved out of Mrs. Wilson's into the first place she was able to call her own: an eight-room apartment on Central Park South, three doors from the Plaza. She unpacked boxes and boxes of books and music, bought a Sohmer piano and a statue of the Winged Victory. She hung copies of Flandrin's *The Pearl Diver* and some Whistlers on the white walls, laid oriental carpets. Her creation, she decided, had a distinctly Pre-Raphaelite air.

That October she opened at the Savoy in the twin bill *Carrots* and *The Country Mouse*, in which the attractive, reliable Bruce McRae made the first of seven appearances as her leading man. Whether she wore pants or crinolines, the public welcomed her ecstatically, but Ethel's favorite role that autumn and for years to come was Carrots, the suicidally unhappy red-haired boy who learns he must keep his heart open to love. Those who thought she could play only fluff like Madame Trentoni were amazed at the depth of tragic feeling with which she infused the misunderstood lad; critics talked of "a touch of genius." But Ethel had higher ambitions. She wanted to equal her mother, whom she thought the greatest American comedienne of all time; she wanted to surpass her even by playing Rosalind and Lady Teazle.

But she was reckoning without Frohman. Perhaps the shrewdest judge in the business of what would "go," Frohman generally avoided both classics and experimental drama in favor of popular plays and playwrights. Frohman was far less interested in Ethel's development as an actress than in finding showcases for her personality. Because he hid this motive behind generosity, soothing paternalism, sentimentality, and a genuine love of the theatre, Ethel did not feel the steel fist in the velvet glove. Critics were wiser, saying that the "sincere flirt" she played in *The Country Mouse* was nothing more than Ethel Barrymore being utterly and charmingly Ethel Barrymore. Ethel bitterly resented the judgment. Just because, like Uncle Jack, she made it look easy did not mean she wasn't acting.

Yet it was hard for Ethel to be more than Ethel Barrymore when she was so loved and successful, when she could hardly walk up Broadway for the numbers of people stopping to congratulate and admire her, when she was so much in demand by so many people that the papers dubbed her "The Girl Who Never Rests." Indeed there was something frantic in her violent socializing, in her restless search for love. Her cousin Georgie would set the clock ahead so that Ethel would get to bed before dawn; yet even after withdrawing into her bedroom she would keep up a running fire of repartee over the transom. As for love, Ethel herself admitted, "I was always trying to let myself get married." Perhaps it was the sheer strenuousness of being Ethel Barrymore which caused the sudden illness that closed the Savoy unexpectedly at the end of November. There were rumors of a nervous collapse, the press hinted darkly at "too many cig-arettes," and Ethel fled far from the madding crowd to Lakewood, New Jersey, forced to rest at last.

She recovered in time to appear with E. H. Sothern in January 1903 in a benefit for Georgia Cayvan—Georgia Cayvan, who had sat down and screamed at Lionel's eyebrows, now in a sanitarium, her career wrecked by a scandalous divorce, nearly blind and going mad. Then Ethel took her double bill on tour, delighting audiences from Philadelphia to Chicago and in Boston receiving the tribute of a letter from John Singer Sargent requesting a sitting. Ethel took the elevator to the top floor of the Mont-gomery Sears home, which Mrs. Sears had turned over to Sargent for a studio, and Sargent alternately played the piano for her entertainment and drew her.

"That's you, plus Sargent," observed a friend when Ethel displayed her portrait.

"Yes, and minus resemblance," said Ethel. Yet the portrait became one of her most treasured possessions.

In Washington she sat next to Theodore Roosevelt at lunch: she and Alice Roosevelt were bosom friends, even though the president objected to Alice's "selling herself" by pouring tea at five dollars a cup for charity as Ethel did. (Alice poured anyway.) Finding a husband for the spirited daughter of the president was becoming as much of a national pastime as engaging Ethel. "Alice Blue Gown," like Ethel, would become a media-created celebrity.

After the tour Ethel sailed for England on May 6, feeling as she stepped off the boat train that she hadn't been gone an hour. Laurence Irving had just married the actress Mabel Hackney, but she found Win-ston Churchill not too occupied as the new leader of the free trade movement to court her, though his absorption in his own career did nothing further to persuade her he would be the ideal husband for an equally self-absorbed actress.

To the smitten Winston, Ethel's popularity was tormenting. She was the darling of Stafford House, where she was again the guest of the Duchess of Sutherland. She was equally popular during a visit to Millie's sister Daisy at Warwick Castle. There were endless balls and yachting parties, and then she was given "the costliest dinner of the season" at the Carlton by E. Clarence Jones, a Wall Street broker vainly pursuing her. After Parliament adjourned in August, Winston could follow Ethel up to Scotland, but then Jack came over (on Ethel's money) and Ethel was painfully more affectionate with him than with Winston, who never seemed to be able to abandon himself to pure fun like sister and brother. So that when Ethel sailed back late in September nothing still was certain except that the enchanting young woman had again eluded him.

Frohman had a play waiting, but first she went to Uncle Jack's summer home on Long Island, the ivy-covered, many-verandahed Kyalami Cottage at Easthampton. Sporting impeccable riding and yachting clothes, John Drew had become "the Squire" of Easthampton. Forty carriages often lined the drive on weekends; on weekdays old-timers sunning themselves on the village green would nod with pride as Drew strolled by flourishing his walking stick. At Kyalami Ethel caught up with family news. That Georgie, "the Mutt of the Drews," had married the actor Alan Parsons. That Uncle Jack's daughter "Bee" (so Drewish-looking she was a caricature of the family) wanted, despite a fancy French education, to be an actress. That Lionel, visiting Kyalami with his pal Jack Gallatin, had almost drowned in the surging tide. So like the unlucky Lionel, mused Ethel, to be dragged to shore while Jack had actually saved the life of a young lady floundering in the Easthampton surf.

That fall they all returned to Broadway under Frohman's aegis: Uncle Jack in *Captain Dieppe*, based on the Anthony Hope story, Lionel as "a great, rough, sturdy, broad-shouldered Boer" in *The Best of Friends*, Ethel at the brand-new Hudson Theatre in *Cousin Kate*. Even Jack, not yet Broadway material, would make his legitimate debut in Chicago playing Max von Wendelowski in the McKee Rankin–Nance O'Neil production of *Magda*.

Rankin might have been a competent manager were he not always worrying about money and lusting after Nance O'Neil. He had absently put Lionel onstage as two characters at once; Jack had an equally traumatic experience as he was buttoned into a form-fitting German frock coat not made, however, for *his* form. Everything handy was grabbed and stuffed into the coat and Jack made his entrance with a magnificent barrel chest, which, gradually conforming to his natural slouch, shifted by the second act to a beer belly. After the performance Jack repaired to a warm saloon to wait his notices. There was only one. Maurice's great fan, the Chicago

Tribune critic Amy Leslie, was terse: "The part of Max was essayed by a young actor who calls himself Mr. John Barrymore. He walked about the stage as if he had been all dressed up and forgotten." The big red apple from his Broadway kin only underlined his failure.

Again the Drew-Barrymore name was more a curse than a blessing. Jack was simply tossed into the water and expected to swim through a role for a gifted actor. But nothing Jack did that autumn in Chicago was right. Invited to a luncheon by Ethel's friends and asked where he was staying, Jack casually mentioned the name of a notorious bed-and-sex hotel that had been recommended to him by an acquaintance. No amount of suddenly clashing silverware could disguise this terrible breach of decorum; after that Jack gave the Cleveland Theatre as his address. Ethel's friends recovered enough to threaten to come and see him act. Jack kept putting them off: "Just wait till next week when we do Elizabeth. I shall be good in that, for I'll have a real part." But the friends grew impatient and came instead to *Leah the Forsaken*. Spotting this terrible jury through the peephole, Jack dashed back to his dressing room to slap on a wig and more greasepaint. Ethel's friends were baffled by the creature in the shingled blond wig until he had to utter his one line, "Throw her in the river." Then a howl went up from the front rows, and Jack knew he was through.

The Barrymore cry for aid had always been "Help Cassius, or I sink," but Jack had cried "Cassius" too often of late. Something stronger was needed: perhaps Ethel might be moved by "For Christ's sake send me fifty dollars." It was not profanity, Jack explained to the Western Union clerk: George W. Christ was the manager and the company would be stranded in Chicago if the message was not sent. Jack got his fifty dollars and caught the next train to New York, where Ethel as usual was packing them in.

Lionel's and Uncle Jack's unfortunate vehicles had closed, but Ethel was still enchanting audiences as Cousin Kate. Naïve and sentimental by today's standards, the story of an independent novelist of twenty-nine who frankly falls in love with a man at first sight and, after routine complications, triumphantly marries him was fresh air in 1903. Daniel Frohman thought the combination of Ethel and Bruce McRae equaled the felicity of John Drew and Ada Rehan; today we can only imagine how Ethel and the dark, energetic McRae must have scintillated.

While Ethel Kated through the season, Frohman had another role for Lionel: Kid Garvey, based on the real middleweight champion Kid McCoy, in a play written for him by Gus Thomas. Kid Garvey was a natural for Lionel, who had a middleweight boxing champion for a father and worshipped fighters like Billy Muldoon, John L. Sullivan, and "Gentleman" Jim Corbett. But Lionel took no chances, going to Kid McCoy's Broadway Café to study the boxer himself and working out with McCoy's brother at Wood's Gymnasium—impressing him as "a young man of boundless ambition to become a great actor." On opening night the audience gasped at his entrance. Lionel had disappeared into the Kid, right down to the checked short jacket and curly hair. But Lionel's Kid Garvey was no mere imitation, it was essence of boxing champ distilled from all his experience and observation of sporting men. With a talented cast including Drina and Elsie de Wolfe, *The Other Girl* kept audiences howling with laughter for 160 performances. Critics called Lionel's Kid "a more remarkable performance than his other triumphs" and "one of the successes of the season." On the third night Frohman put LIONEL BARRYMORE up in lights on the Criterion marquee. He was a star.

Yet he was terrified that Frohman wanted to turn him into that self-satisfied monster, the Great Actor; he had only scorn for the breed:

The Great Actor always must act. He must make a ceremony of waking up in the morning. He must sit in his room and act so that his whole body vibrates to the thrill of it. Forever he must be a poseur. Every last second of his life must be pose and posture. He must be such a poseur as to be blinded against all rational points of view. He must live in roles and love them. He must be another fellow. Ridicule must pass him by. If, by any chance it grazes him, the Great Actor must view it with pitying kindness. His last week's failure must be more than forgot—it never happened. Above all, the Great Actor must have no sense of humor. When he looks at himself in the mirror he must do so through a telescope. And everything admirable that he reads or sees or hears must be his. Let the most profound, the most classic line fall from his lips, he must be unconscious of the fact that he is not the author of it.

Unlike the Great Actor, Lionel found it hard to take himself seriously. And yet on first nights when the audience shuffled in and the orchestra scraped the overture—then any actor *had* to take himself seriously. First nights were nightmares. It took him two days to recover—if he ever did.

Jack too dreamed other dreams that year, pouring his rebellion into a painting of a hard-drinking actor friend that he titled "Corse Payton Defying the Drama." But "Corse" went unhung at the Academy and the drama undefied. Instead Frohman cast him as the press agent Corley in

Clyde Fitch's *Glad of It*. Not much of a play, but Jack made such a hit in the theatre skit that everyone wanted him back in the other acts. Frohman responded by shifting him to the larger role of Polk, stage manager of the Savoy, but *Glad of It* was simply not substantial enough to let Jack do more than tantalize.

In 1904 Jack as an actor was more like Ethel than Lionel. He too played more or less himself: in his case an insouciant, incorrigibly charming young man. He had Ethel's natural grace and comic timing. He had Ethel's magnetism, her glamour. But he had none of her commitment or ambition. He took the matter of his Broadway debut hands-in-pockets, though with Frohman he didn't dare stop the show again with, "I've blown up. Where do we go from here?" He was a poor study and didn't try to improve. His voice was flat and furry, and he didn't bother cleaning it up. While the perfectionist Lionel labored over his creations, Jack breezed through a role. Lionel suffered; Jack laughed.

Lionel would always feel that Jack's success came easily. "I suppose I have worked," he told the theatre critic Ashton Stevens. "I'm not as clever as my brother Jack, who can't help but get along. I remember one day my father asked, 'Who killed King Arthur?' and before I could get in with my strictly truthful answer, Jack was there with 'Henry Irving.' "

But it was a great event when Jack joined Ethel and Lionel on Broadway that season of 1903–1904. Acting families are not rare: at any given time there might have been three Kembles or Guitrys or Terrys or Davenports on the boards. The three Barrymores were special, however. There was their heritage: Mrs. John Drew, Georgie Drew Barrymore, Maurice Barrymore—not only actors but celebrities when that word described both personality *and* accomplishment. There was their youth: twenty-five, twenty-four, twenty-one. There was their good looks. There was "the Barrymore Curse," which considerably heightened their glamour. Every time Ethel coughed, Lionel got drunk, or Jack did something eccentric there were dark prognostications. And there was what acting families of the past did not have: Frohman's "star system" and the new mass-circulation dailies that constantly fed the doings of these stars into the public's gaping maw. And finally there was their undisputed talent. They were a phenomenon. Thus in 1904 they were the talk and the hope of the legitimate theatre. Great things lay before them.

Ethel at least felt their uniqueness. "The Flying Barrymores," she said proudly: "three—count 'em—three!" These three were not, had not been emotionally close, yet they seemed to embody in their natures the three stages of life. That is, Lionel was from the beginning old, Ethel even as a girl maternal with a middle-aged sense of responsibility, Jack irrepressibly young. And they would psychologically maintain these three stages of one life all their lives.

Now for the first time since Philadelphia or the brief summer holidays, Lionel, Ethel, and Jack were together in the same place at the same time. Not only on Broadway, but together on Wednesday and Saturday matinee days in Ethel's suite at the Algonquin, which Frohman had provided for its convenience to the Hudson Theatre. They were a happy trio. Much as Lionel and Jack still resisted acting, neither could completely resist the sudden celebrity, the lionizing, and the regular paychecks. Ethel had been right: there was something to this family trade after all. Exuberant, the three worked up a music hall routine with Ethel at the piano, Lionel and Jack soft-shoeing, and all three exiting with a shuffle-off-to-Buffalo. They went over so well at private parties that Ethel proposed the act to Frohman for the Actors Fund Benefit. *"No,"* said C.F.

But their trio was already threatened by Lionel's romantic involvement with a pretty dark-haired girl of sixteen. Doris Rankin was practically family: McKee Rankin's illegitimate daughter, the half sister of Gladys who had married Uncle Googan and Phyllis who had married Harry Davenport of the acting Davenports. To Lionel, Doris had always been just part of the scenery on tours and at the Davenports' farm near White Plains. But in the spring of 1903 Lionel had visited the farm—and suddenly little Doris Rankin had turned into the girl he'd been looking for. As Lionel said simply, "We fell in love." A year later, in April, they became engaged. Few people were in on the secret: Lionel was the most private of persons, but Ethel heartily approved this theatrical liaison.

With Lionel engaged, Ethel felt more than ever like letting herself get married. She preferred Englishmen and certainly there would be opportunity, for she was going to London again in May, this time with a play. Frohman's empire encompassed London (he had ten plays running there in 1904); he decided now that London was ready for Ethel. She had shone in *Cousin Kate*; Frohman would combine the playwright Hubert Henry Davies and the actress again in Davies's *Cynthia*. Ethel was terrified. She hadn't acted in London since her appearance with Sir Henry Irving six years before, and rather badly then. Although John Drew was always heartily welcome in London, she knew that English audiences were notoriously more critical than American. Then too, her English friends refused to take her career seriously, if they were aware of it at all; they would come to Wyndham's in the spirit of amateur night. One comfort was that darling Gerald du Maurier was to play her young husband. Gerald, now happily married but still sentimental enough to name his daughter Daphne after her.

Winston Churchill sent flowers on opening night. The audience was all she could desire: James Barrie, her old friend Anthony Hope, Arthur Wing Pinero, W. S. Gilbert, and her many, many other friends. And yet after the performance Winston hurried to her dressing room and threw his arms around her. "Oh, my poor darling!" he consoled her. Ethel herself pronounced *Cynthia* a failure, and the play's run—four weeks instead of the intended six—seems to indicate a general disappointment.

Max Beerbohm, the critic for the *Saturday Review*, called *Cynthia* "rather hard to analyse," but was intrigued with Ethel's androgynous charm. She was best summed up, he thought, as a Pierrot. "Pierrot was irresistible, and we mourn him. In Miss Barrymore, surely, he has come to life again." Other critics were more predictable. "An actress of greater skill and force than Miss Ethel Barrymore might have been less successful than she in being Cynthia—for she was Cynthia, and not merely a clever young actress playing the part, and this is the highest praise. We must wait for other work ere judging her as a player." And so the highest praise was again no praise: Ethel was only being herself.

As Ethel was closing shop at Wyndham's, Lionel and Doris decided to marry. On Saturday, June 18, Doris left the Davenport farm to be met in New York by McKee Rankin, who escorted her the next day to St. Francis Xavier's Church on Sixteenth Street where Lionel was waiting with the ring. Uncle Googan, Aunt Gladys, and Jack were the only guests at a wedding so secret that by the time word leaked out on June 22 Lionel and Doris had disappeared on an equally secret honeymoon. Of the wedding Lionel remembered only one thing clearly. While the priest was still intoning the ritual, it occurred to him bleakly that in taking him on "this nice girl, only sixteen, hadn't the slightest idea what she was getting into." She would soon learn.

Ethel did her best to follow Lionel's act. "There was a friend of many friends of mine named Harry Graham, a gay, brilliant creature of great charm and attraction who had written several books of verse. He liked me, too, and there I was again with a faint hope that this time was it." Harry Graham had good connections: The Duchess of Portsmouth was a cousin; he was private secretary to Lord Rosebery; his father, Sir Henry, whom Ethel saw for the first time hurrying through the Gothic arches of the House of Lords, his full-bottomed wig askew, was a K.C.B. Harry was a captain in the Coldstream Guards and wrote light verse under the name Col. D. Streamer. Ethel accepted gracefully the dedication that spring of Harry's latest slim (very slim) volume *Misrepresentative Men*. So much jollier than hearing how Winston had earned the reputation of a violent and reckless political adventurer that year by switching from the

Tory to the Liberal party. So much more appealing the good looks of the tall dashing captain than Winston's pink face and ginger hair.

Graham did not go with her to County Kerry on holiday with some of the old Bedford Street gang: Ben and May, the Harry Esmonds, Anthony Hope, Cissie Loftus, and Gerald. The eight took over the small inn—there was only the inn and a few mean huts and pigs and amazingly beautiful Irish girls with black eyelashes so long they "seemed to sweep the dust." All day long they swam and fished and bicycled along the coast road, and Muriel du Maurier did not have to worry about the evenings, for Ethel the all-American girl was virtuous. And then suddenly it was September and still another English summer was gone.

Ethel sailed home trusting that Frohman would have a good part for her. *Cynthia* had not been a happy experience; more than ever she wanted to show the public that she could be more than Miss Ethel Barrymore. Still, that role had its compensations. Playing in Boston, Ethel had hurried over to the Colonial Theatre to see Henry Irving die as Louis XI. It was the last American tour for the great actor whom both she and Jack worshipped. Because she was Miss Barrymore she was allowed to watch the death scene backstage and, looking into the wings, Sir Henry recognized "little Bullfinch."

"And so you're a great star now," he said when she came to sit beside him.

"Oh, no, Sir Henry. That's the system here."

"What's the matter. Aren't you happy?"

"No, not very."

"What do they say about you?"

"Oh, they say I look all right and I have this and that and the other, but that I am always Ethel Barrymore."

"See to it," said Irving, laying his long aristocratic hand over her capable square one, "that they never say anything else."

Theoretically she did have an un-Etheline character to play that November at the Hudson: an orphan raised in a mining camp, Miss Sunday of Silver Creek. Wearing red-checked gingham with her hair in double braids, she said "Damn!" and pronounced bureau "bew-rah"—and she had good reason, after inventing a Southwestern accent for herself, to be furious when William Winter said that the role suited her style of speech. But alas! *Sunday* again was judged a play that gave Ethel a part particularly suited to her "peculiar personality," and again her adoring public packed the Hudson to see her be irresistibly Ethel. Ethel was grim. "I'll make you cry yet," she vowed.

In the unpredictable way such things happen, *Sunday* gave Ethel the line that became her trademark. In the second act Sunday reads a letter from the miners but stops when she comes to a part she doesn't want her aunt to hear. "Go on, Sunday," says the aunt, but Sunday runs off the stage without a word. Ethel didn't like it.

"It seems so rude," she told Frohman. "I think I ought to say something to her."

"Well, well," said Frohman rather testily, "what do you want to say?"

"Oh, maybe something like 'That's all there is, there isn't any more.' "

Just a way to get her gracefully offstage, but the line had poetry and caught. After that, anyone doing an Ethel Barrymore imitation just had to drawl huskily, "That's all there is, there isn't any more" to get applause. Ethel herself scoffed at the deep significance people tried to attach to the line, yet she found it a useful way to get herself out of more curtain calls, welding it to herself absolutely.

If possible, the tempo of her life accelerated that late fall. There were letters from Winston Churchill and Harry Graham to ponder and answer. There were endless teas, benefits, receptions, dinners, balls, and luncheons. She was badgered by innumerable requests for interviews: the public seemed to have nothing else to read about—irritating to the young woman who "gladly would have paid *not* to have been written about." The few interviews she did grant were about serious subjects, chiefly the stage ("I have a tremendous respect for the stage; I think only amateurs have not") and literature. A *Daily Mail* reporter who cornered her in December went away with nothing juicier for his gossip-hungry readers than Ethel's current taste in plays. She had immersed herself in Ibsen, but found him too morbid. She deplored French plays because they were interminably about a wife, a husband, and a lover. As for Bernard Shaw, at last emerging as an important playwright, she found him trivial. "He has reverence for nothing, always the indication of a small intellect," said Miss Ethel. "He makes you laugh, of course, but you afterwards are disposed to reproach yourself for frivolity." After all her public avowals of high seriousness, it is disconcerting, then, to find her writing privately to Clyde Fitch, "Now, Clyde, I would give an awful lot if you would write me another wonderful part. There's no one like you—you know—& I know so well you'd do me another great turn. So please, as soon as you can, come & chat with me about it." And yet a Fitch play doubtless would have her playing Ethel Barrymore again.

She was never too busy to applaud Jack, who had opened in April at the Criterion in her friend Dick Davis's farce *The Dictator*. Charley Hyne, a tippling wireless operator, was a step up for Jack: a better part in a better play with William Collier, an enormously popular actor and a lesson in comic technique every time he stepped onstage. Though Jack was still an amateur by Ethel's definition because he did not take the stage seriously, his acting improved considerably. And as audiences took to Jack, Jack began to feel the power of The Audience, "the great hulking monster with four thousand eyes and forty thousand teeth . . . a wonderful monster with one great mind that makes or breaks men like me." The monster haunted his dreams. "I shouldn't be at all surprised," said Jack, "if some of those bug-house cartoons of mine were subtle impressions of an audience."

Lionel continued to agonize internally, though on tour with *The Other Girl* he delighted his public all the way. Boston audiences "fairly howled with glee" over a play that was one continuous laugh—and clean besides! "Lionel Barrymore is not a coming actor—he has arrived," declared the *Record*. Doris trooped along as she had since the cradle with the Rankins, but soon discovered that the young man whom she had married because he at last had a successful career now wanted to chuck it. Doris was very young and very much in love, and anything that big, handsome Lionel wanted she wanted too. If she had ambitions to act with Lionel she would squelch them. But so far he was only muttering. There was a western tour of *The Other Girl* scheduled for 1905 and an announcement that Lionel's next vehicle would be *Davy Crockett*. One didn't just wire Frohman I QUIT.

ON MARCH 25, 1905, at Amityville, Maurice Barrymore suddenly roused himself from semiconsciousness, looked at the nurse, and said clearly, "Our trade falls heavily upon these feeble folk." It was a line from the play whose failure he never forgot, his own *Nadjezda*. Five minutes later he died, only fifty-five but almost unrecognizable from the ravages of syphilis.

Lionel was in El Paso with *The Other Girl*, Jack in Buffalo with *The Dictator*, Ethel in Philadelphia with *Sunday*. Frohman's office wired the news of Maurice's death to Ethel's manager with instructions not to tell Ethel until after the Saturday matinee. Ethel had expected her father's death, perhaps even longed for it; still she fainted twice. Then she set about doing what had to be done, wiring Lionel and Jack and escaping through the quickly gathered crowd to the Broad Street Station, where she caught the train to New York, then to Amityville. Shocked at the appearance of the dead man, she decided that the funeral must be private. When she returned to her house at 94 Park Avenue (the restless young woman had moved again), Jack was waiting. The press had to be dealt with. Ethel ordered a pillow of orchids and gardenias for the coffin, wired

Uncle Jack for permission to bury Maurice next to Georgie in the family plot in Philadelphia. She and Jack attended the funeral on Wednesday. Temperamentally the outsider, Lionel was so now by chance: at Chicago he realized he could never make the funeral and turned back. DEAR OLD DAD, he wired Ethel, —BUT THANK GOD IT IS OVER. HE IS BETTER OFF.

The largest floral tribute at the funeral was from Maurice's imagined enemy Charles Frohman. He and many others viewed Maurice Barrymore's life as a tragic waste, and indeed Maurice had admitted as much in composing his own epitaph:

> He walked beneath the stars
> He slept beneath the sun;
> He lived a life of going-to-do
> And died with nothing done.

Going-to-do has its fascination. Maurice left his potential to the imagination. Perhaps his greatest charm was that he gave prodigally of his wit and talent, exacting little return. To those who are firmly their own best friends, there is something irresistible about a man who is his own worst enemy—and Maurice flung his talents away with a recklessness that could almost be called courage. As an actor he might have achieved anything, had he cared. "Your father was the best Captain Absolute I ever had," Joseph Jefferson told Lionel, ". . . and the worst." His most dangerous legacy to his sons was his indifference to what he did well and his longing to do what others did far better. This romantic dissatisfaction he passed on to Lionel and Jack. Ethel inherited the Drew realism.

As a result she, the trouper, acted at the Garrick the evening of her father's funeral, though it wasn't easy now to say, "That's all there is, there isn't any more." The audience had stood at her entrance in tribute to Maurice Barrymore; at the end they stood again, this time cheering his daughter. "Thus ended a chapter in my life," said Ethel, "that has always seemed tragically incomplete."

For Jack too a chapter had ended. After the funeral he had told the cab to take him to 140 North Twelfth Street, the magic house of childhood with its big rooms and secret stairways and the three white steps that he and Lionel and Ethel had jumped up and down in their countless comings and goings. A slatternly woman was washing those steps now, though they weren't getting any whiter in the process. He went inside and looked into the old rooms where he had played and went up the dark steps to the Annex and found the place where he'd hidden his pirate's loot. But though he could still feel the powerful presence of Mummum, all was cramped and dark and fusty. He rushed out of the house past the woman, for the first time glad he had the theatre to go back to where there was a future and room to breathe. The death of the parent means the death of the child one was; no wonder Jack had not been able to find him in the house on North Twelfth Street.

Maurice's death liberated Lionel too. Suddenly he could think of nothing but getting back to paintbrush and canvas. "I think I should quit the stage and go the Arts Students League again," he told Doris.

"Why go there?" said his adoring wife. "Go after the real thing. Go to Paris."

Lionel was persuaded.

What happened next can be roughly reconstructed. Not having saved a dime, Lionel wired Frohman's office from Colorado Springs on April 29 requesting an advance of $1,500, presumably for steamship tickets to France. Frohman refused. In Denver Lionel quit and headed east, according to press reports (1) suffering from the high altitude, (2) suffering nervous prostration, and (3) suffering a delayed reaction to the death of his father. The ever helpful Ethel arranged for him to stay in the quiet country house of a friend, perhaps at Richard Harding Davis's farm near Mount Kisco that he had bought with the proceeds of *The Dictator*. And of course Lionel was genuinely suffering—from wanting to do something besides what he was good at.

And Ethel too, now that she was no longer a daughter, tried to put away the girl she was. Lionel and Doris had read Ibsen's *A Doll's House*; Ethel *must* play Nora Helmer. Ethel reread the play, shelved her Ibsen prejudice, and wired Frohman, "I MUST DO THIS PART. MAY I?" "OF COURSE," replied Frohman gallantly.

In Chicago on April 27, acting as her own stage manager, Ethel presented a matinee of Ibsen's revolutionary exposure of marriage. Jack had agreed to share the experiment, playing Dr. Rank, a deep, serious, psychological character who, like his own father, is dying of syphilis. He had never acted a serious part before, and after a dramatic scene to which for the first time in his life he gave everything he had, he felt the theatre become deathly quiet. For the first time in his life he realized he had got hold of an audience, that some spiritual transference had taken place between them. When he left the stage the sensation left him, but he was weak and trembling and wet with sweat.

Ethel was standing in the wings. "You were very, very good, Gus," she said. When Ethel felt cheerful she called him Gus. "You are a serious actor, not a comedian." And for the first time, Jack felt he was.

Ethel was so encouraged by the critics' opinion that Nora Helmer had revealed her as "a thorough artist instead of the public's petted darling" that she persuaded Frohman to let her bring *A Doll's House* to the Lyceum in New York for a matinee in May. But New York was critical. Surely it was her claque of admirers who had caused the curtain to be raised six times after the first act and eight after the second? Surely she was often out of her depth and quite unsuccessful at portraying Nora's sense of revolution. Surely her eating of macaroons as though she'd had them before, liked them, and quite intended to have them again was shockingly soulless. At least the *Dramatic Mirror* congratulated her for "intelligent and spontaneous playing," conceding that if her Nora was not a complete victory neither was it a defeat. But Ethel felt it was.

A Doll's House was her first appearance in a major play since *The Rivals*, when she was fifteen. But the public didn't want her to be grown up and serious. Its opinion was expressed in an "Open Letter to Miss Ethel Barrymore": "Let those who are fond of issues, of discordant and nightmarish problem plays hack away at Ibsen's 'messages'—those awful questions of sex and madness and disquieting stage discussions. Be our Cousin Kate again, Miss Barrymore, and for the love of those who love you as a woman, and not as a streak of feminine perversion, leave Mr. Ibsen alone—completely, now and evermore."

Ethel never played Ibsen again. Ibsen didn't draw, and Frohman wasn't running theatres for charity. Yet the public's refusal to let the ideal American girl grow up was juvenile itself and would injure Ethel's career in the long run.

EIGHT

1905–1909

ETHEL'S 1905 SUMMER was distinguished by the rise of Harry Graham, the defeat of Winston Churchill, and the attention of James M. Barrie.

Barrie had no more dedicated admirer than Charles Frohman, but this year climaxed their collaboration, for Frohman had bought Barrie's *Peter Pan* for Maude Adams in America. For Frohman *Peter Pan* was not a play but a religion of which he was the prophet. Incredibly, Barrie himself had so little faith in *Peter Pan* that he gave Frohman another play as collateral against its failure. He had written *Alice-Sit-by-the-Fire* for Ellen Terry who, fifty-eight and no longer acting with Irving, was finding little to do in the theatre. Barrie considered *Alice* a sentimental little potboiler that wouldn't tax Terry's increasingly poor memory, but Ethel liked it when she saw it at the Duke of York's and was flattered that Frohman wanted it for her. She saw herself naturally as the daughter Amy rather than as the mother Alice, Terry's role. Barrie, however, insisted she play Ellen's part.

"But why?" asked Ethel.

"Because you have 'the mother thing,' " said Barrie.

With *Alice* at the Duke of York's was Barrie's *Pantaloon* with Gerald du Maurier as the sad old pantomime character tormented by Joey the Clown. Ethel cried so hard over *Pantaloon* that she immediately wanted the one-act for Lionel. Perhaps it would keep him on the stage where he belonged. Frohman agreed.

She saw Barrie often that summer and delighted the shy, moody Scot as she delighted everyone. Sometimes she came to Frohman's suite at the Savoy, where the two men often sat in silence, Barrie chewing his pipe, Frohman puffing cigars and dreaming of Peter Pan flying into the hearts of America.

"Wasn't he wonderful?" C.F. asked Ethel one day after Barrie had gone. "What do you suppose he was thinking about?"

"I don't suppose he was thinking about anything," said Ethel, stunning C.F. with her soullessness.

The last day of June she went to Barrie's Black Lake Cottage near Farnham in Surrey for a week of cricket. The cottage was surrounded by thick pine woods with not another house in sight. Gerald du Maurier's dark-haired sister Sylvia was there with her son Michael, one of the five Llewelyn Davies boys whose power over Barrie's emotions had inspired *Peter Pan*. The cottage was packed with cricket enthusiasts, the overflow housed at the local inn at Barrie's expense for this eighteenth competition between writers and artists: Barrie's Allahakbarries versus Edgar Horne and his Shackleford eleven. On this occasion there was a new team member, invited on Ethel's account.

She had been delighted to find Harry Graham still witty, charming, and very much in love. Together they strolled the lawns, explored the lake that inspired the lagoon in *Peter Pan*, vied in the croquet and badminton tournaments that Barrie organized. But the cricket match was the main agenda, and the women watched from under huge floppy hats as Barrie unflinchingly met the fastest balls, though his team lost two to the artists. But then the writers triumphed at last and there was a noisy return to the cottage, where a banquet was quickly spread. Photographs survive of that cricket week: the men in white flannels and straw boaters, Barrie clasping little Michael by the hand, Harry Graham tall and mustached and a little detached. Blurred in the distance in one photograph are the slender figures of two women walking together—Ethel and Sylvia?—as graceful in their long white skirts as the Edwardian days which, in retrospect, were so clearly numbered. Ethel would remember such grace, such friends as paradise lost forever.

That summer Harry Graham was a steel filing drawn by the magnetic Ethel from house party to house party and finally back to London, where at Ethel's flat in Berkeley Square he met Jack, in London with Willie Collier's *The Dictator* company. Jack quickly agreed that Graham was "the right sort—fine man." As a result of Jack's and her friends' approval and her own conviction that she really *should* marry, Ethel announced on July 13 in the *Morning Post* that she was officially engaged to Captain Harry Graham, D.S.O. The wedding would take place in New York the coming winter or spring with Lionel giving the bride away. She had no intention of giving up her profession.

Winston Churchill conceded defeat. "I was so in love with her! And she wouldn't pay any attention to me at all." More than two years later those close to him still sympathized. "You were in love really once," wrote his brother Jack, "—and you know what that meant. But you had other things to think of. Your career and your future filled more than half of your life. I love the same way you did—but I have no other thoughts." Winston recovered: in 1908 the twice-engaged and very popular Clementine Hozier agreed to marry him. Yet in one respect he remained faithful. People who knew both Ethel and Clemmie noted their remarkable physical resemblance.

That summer therefore, for the first time since cross-Atlantic rumors had begun to fly in 1898, Ethel's fans were rewarded. When the *Deutschland* docked at Hoboken, New Jersey, on August 17 and Ethel and Jack ran down the gangplank to meet Lionel, she could flash a pearl, ruby, and diamond engagement ring and tell reporters, "Yes, I am!

"And he's very nice and has heaps of brains and is reconciled to the fact that I am not going to leave the stage after our marriage."

"And she answers his letters," added Jack solemnly, "something without precedent in the history of our family."

Ethel's friends generally rejoiced. "I'm glad she isn't going to marry an actor," said one. "I hope the Englishman's able to take good care of her."

"Oh, that'll be all right," said Ethel's dear friend Peter Dunne. "Jack and Lionel will support them on what Ethel gives Lionel and Jack."

ETHEL HAD PERSUADED Frohman to add Jack to the cast of *Sunday* for the autumn tour. But if she expected a new seriousness in her brother after his Dr. Rank epiphany, she was disappointed. Jack missed rehearsals, showed up drunk, chased any good-looking actress in the cast, though he had still not got over Evelyn Nesbit, now the wife of the young millionaire Harry K. Thaw. Much as it distressed her, she had to keep telegraphing Frohman to telegraph Jack that he was fired. Upon receipt of one of these wires, Jack would appear waving the piece of paper. "Here's a telegram from Frohman. You've got to do something about it."

He would not have spoken to her in days. "Then you've got to pull yourself together," Ethel would say in Mummumish tones.

And now and then he did, and was "awfully good" when he wanted to be.

Meanwhile, like a nun preparing to take the veil, Maude Adams was preparing for *Peter Pan*. She had not very much liked Ethel getting *Alice-Sit-by-the-Fire*: Barrie was *her* playwright, but jealousy was now forgotten in her absorption in her role. She isolated herself in the Catskills, immersing herself in the play's creed of the sacredness of childhood and the imagination; she invented her costume of leaf-patterned tunic and feathered hat. Halfway through opening night at the Empire, the audience knew that Frohman, Barrie, and Adams had a stunning success. London had liked *Peter Pan*; New York, a young city, went wild. *Peter Pan* ran longer at the Empire than any other play before Adams set out to take the cause to the masses. Children and adults everywhere fell under the enchantment of nurseries, Saint Bernard dogs named Nana, pirates, red-skins, and lagoons; and when Maude came down to the footlights to plead, "Do *you* believe in fairies?" the thundering *"Yes!"* rocked theatres across the land.

Throughout her career Ethel Barrymore publicly had nothing but praise for her fellow actors. Now she said she was delighted that Maude Adams was doing *Peter Pan*. She would scarcely have been human, how-ever, had she not felt a twinge of jealousy. For comfort she could tell herself that all Maude Adams had was her art: no social life, no gifted brothers, no Captain Graham. Like "the boy who wouldn't grow up," Maude was arrested in her make-believe-land, the stage. Ethel would boast that she kept her professional and private lives strictly separate: once the curtain came down she put make-believe sternly aside. And what actress after all would want to play a boy? But she lied when she told the press Alice was her favorite role. She knew it was second-rate Barrie; she remembered how much she had loved playing Carrots, the unhappy boy.

On Christmas Day 1905 *Alice-Sit-by-the-Fire* and *Pantaloon* opened at the Criterion. It was the first time the Barrymores ("three, count 'em—three!") shared a theatre at the same time, though they still did not all appear together in one play. The night was "a triumph for the Barrymore family," though generally the verdict was "John Barry-much, Lionel Barry-more, and Ethel Barry-most." Jack seemed to universally please, however, playing the Clown with an exaggerated cockney accent and in *Alice* the young Stephen Rollo with (thought many) Maurice's looks and manner, and some thought Lionel's powerful mixture of comedy and pathos as Pantaloon the finest achievement of all. And Ethel was attacked. Though she had streaked her hair with white and worn long earrings, almost every critic seized on her youth, ignoring Barrie's point that Alice is younger than any of her children. What actually bothered the critics, however, was the fact that the ideal American girl had dared to put aside "her chiefest charm of rare, radiant girlhood" to play a sexually experienced woman with a husband and three children. New York critics weren't ready for that. But again Ethel made a distinction between critics, who didn't matter, and the public, who did, especially the female contingent.

The fact that she could sway an audience of women as Alice proved she was right for the part.

Asked at year's end to wish New York a happy new year, Ethel said, "The best greeting I could offer would be to wish everyone to be as happy as I am." She liked her play, her two brothers were with her, they had proved themselves fine actors. But it was Jack she adored, Jack she tried to draw close to. In January they sparkled in Dick Davis's little one-act *Miss Civilization* for the Actors Fund Benefit, where Ethel was cheered and called back so loudly and long that she finally told the stage manager to douse the lights to stop the demonstration. They then gave a joint interview to the *Dramatic Mirror*. Even though the young woman in plays always wins, "I love character parts," said Ethel. "I am quite willing to make myself unattractive on the stage if it serves the right purpose."

"Oh, *Ee*-thyl," snorted Jack. "Be honest!"

But Jack's irresponsibility continued to torment the utterly professional Ethel. One night as Stephen Rollo, for example, he did not appear on cue. Ethel tried to save the situation. "Here he comes," she ad-libbed. "He's walking up the path . . . He's ringing the bell." Meanwhile the stage manager, James Kearney, hurried to Jack's dressing room, where he found him sprawled dead drunk and naked on the sofa. There was nothing for Kearney to do but play Jack's role for the whole three acts.

Despite Ethel's strong will that had brought them all together in one theatre, their unity was mostly illusion. Why couldn't they, for example, have all appeared together in one play—either Lionel playing Ethel's husband in *Alice* or Ethel playing Columbine in *Pantaloon*? Incestuous, perhaps, but surely audiences would have granted them "that willing suspension of disbelief." More potent than the taboo against Lionel or Jack making love onstage to Ethel was the competition that had existed from childhood between Lionel and Ethel. Jack could act with them both, they could not act with each other; even in their childish "playing stage" games Lionel had been only "Pop" while Ethel had been "Madame." Although Ethel was militantly loyal to Lionel in print ("Someday I'll be known as Lionel's sister"), the praise seemed a substitute for the love she had never spontaneously felt. Add to this Lionel's resentment at having been lured back by Ethel to the theatre when he wanted only a paintbrush and canvas, and clearly the Barrymore idyll could not last.

There are two versions of what happened on the spring 1906 tour of *Alice* and *Pantaloon*, but they agree on one point: both Lionel and Ethel were reported "stricken with nervous prostration."

According to Ethel, "It was during this season that Lionel got a nervous terror of the theatre and became almost obsessed with the idea that he was going to forget his lines. He never did forget them, but the fear was so strong in him that he came to me one day and said he could not go on—that he must stop."

According to Lionel, he wanted Paris *now*. There was only one person in the world who would finance Paris. So one raw night in March in Chicago after the performance, he came to Ethel with a piteous tale of quaking stomach and fraying nerves. And of course he *was* suffering— from the thought he would have to act the rest of his life. He didn't dare say this to Ethel; on the contrary, he tried to persuade her that a break from the stage would bring him back a better actor. They sat up all night in Ethel's suite arguing, and finally toward dawn she weakened. All he was asking was to study at the Art Students League again.

"You went there," said Ethel reluctantly. "Why don't you do it right and go to Paris."

"I don't have enough money," said Lionel, and waited to catch the plums as they fell.

They fell. Ethel's financing Lionel was a way for her to assuage her guilt over her own great success (girls were not supposed to excel over boys), her guilt over their competition. Lionel caught the next train east and lay low at his Rocky Point, Long Island, home while the press reported him stricken with pneumonia. Eventually he and Doris sailed on a fifth-rate liner: no cheering relatives at the dock, no champagne. Lionel knew he was ruthlessly exploiting his sister, but then the artist is ruthless. As the Statue of Liberty receded in the distance, he felt intensely happy. He knew he had set foot on the stage for the last time.

ETHEL HAD NOT recovered from Lionel's defection when Jack told her he was leaving to join Willie Collier's *On the Quiet* company in New York for a tour that would take them to Australia. Again Ethel was reported prostrated. Finally she was genuinely ill: on April 4 she was rushed to the Bay State Hospital in Boston with an attack of acute appendicitis and operated on the next day.

During her weeks in the hospital Ethel had Harry Graham's letters to read and read again. He had no objection to her career, he repeated. It had become clear to him, however, that he could not leave his post as Lord Rosebery's secretary, his clubs, his friends. She must come to England to live.

And now Ethel understood at last why her engagements had never taken. They had all been to Englishmen and, much as she adored England, she was an American after all. America was where her work was: above all she needed her work. She wrote Harry that she could not make the sacrifice. She agonized: it was a fine and rare human being she was hurting. At the end of April she returned to New York and, as Graham arrived to discuss the matter, fled to a friend's cottage in New Hampshire, leaving behind the brief, harsh statement "All this stuff that has been printed about my marrying Captain Graham is a pack of lies." Whether she saw Graham or not is unknown, but her decision was plain: ETHEL BARRYMORE PREFERS U.S. TO HUSBAND. The public drew a collective sigh; Ethel's friends were amazed and disappointed. But then, as Ethel said firmly, "I really can not marry someone for my friends."

COLLIER HAD TAKEN Jack back in a spirit of masochism. He had almost fired him a dozen times from the *Dictator* company, would have had not Frohman pleaded, "Don't do it, Willie, it'll break Ethel's heart." "If I keep him, it will break mine," Collier had said; and here he was with the train about to pull out and all the rest of the company present and accounted for, but no Jack. Finally at the last "All aboard!" Jack sauntered onto the platform in evening clothes. "So nice of you to come," said Collier. If oversleeping was a problem why the hell hadn't he left a call at his hotel?

"I did," said Jack innocently, "but I couldn't tell where I would stop last night so I left calls at six or seven hotels. Only I didn't hit the right one."

Collier thought grimly of the months ahead.

They arrived in San Francisco where, in the small hours of April 17, Jack felt a shock rock the house of a friend where he was staying the night. Hurriedly he pulled back on his evening clothes and staggered into the tilting hall. His friend was a collector of Chinese glass. "Come and see what has happened to the Ming Dynasty!" Jack shouted. They found the valuable collection reduced to powder.

The streets were chaos. Everywhere whole sides of houses had sheared away, leaving their occupants wandering about in nightgowns in full view. In Union Square opposite the St. Francis Hotel where he'd been staying, Jack recognized a familiar figure in bedroom slippers and dressing gown. "Go west, young man," called Collier cheerfully, "and blow up with the country." Caruso, whom Jack had heard sing *Carmen* the night before, was supervising the loading of his trunks in a van. " 'Ell of a place!" he kept muttering. "I never come back here. 'Ell of a place!" In front of the Palace Hotel Jack met that inveterate New York first-nighter Diamond Jim Brady. Brady was highly amused to see Jack picking his way through the rubble in evening clothes: Jack's "dressing for an earthquake" became one of Diamond Jim's favorite stories.

Overcome with sleepiness, Jack finally went back to the St. Francis where the clerk assured him there wasn't the slightest chance of another tremor. The words were no sooner out of his mouth than a second quake rocked the hotel. The clerk dove over the counter out into Union Square, but Jack merely went upstairs and slept like a baby until late afternoon when excitement in the square and the smell of burning woke him.

Eventually he ended up with little more than the clothes on his back in suburban Burlingame where—as everywhere—he found friends to put him up. He was perfectly happy: the Collier company must have sailed by now and he'd never wanted to go on the damned tour anyway. After six days, however, he was reminded that he should probably let Frohman and his family know he was alive. So he borrowed a bicycle and a badge that looked official in case he was stopped, and started pedaling. All the familiar San Francisco landmarks were gone and the streets deserted except for some soldiers from the Presidio who, seeing his badge, did stop him and put him to work bossing a gang clearing debris.

Finally escaping, he discovered to his chagrin that he was just in time to sail with Collier from Vancouver. Since, however, he had only ten dollars and the clothes on his back, he decided to appeal to Ethel in terms strong enough to command a hundred dollars. In Boston Ethel read to Uncle Jack a letter painting horrifying scenes of death and destruction and Jack's own ordeal when an army sergeant put a shovel into his hand and made him dig rubble for twenty-four hours. John Drew was strangely unmoved.

"What's the matter, Uncle Jack," said Ethel. "Don't you believe it?"

"Every word," said John Drew. "It took a convulsion of Nature to get him out of bed and the United States Army to put him to work."

Whatever Jack had expected of Australia, he was not prepared for the tedium of rattling from outpost to outpost with a company who'd been together so long they'd milked all their good stories dry. Even Melbourne rolled up the sidewalks after the theatre, and the company had to retreat to a little room lent them over a delicatessen, where night after night they sat in boredom, having literally no place else to go. When Jack and Collier did venture out one night they were arrested for laughing in the streets after 9:00 p.m.

Two feminine interests relieved Jack's tedium. One was Grace Palotta, more beautiful than Evelyn Nesbit and like her a singer and dancer. Grace had played in the wildly popular American import *Florodora*, as had Evelyn; her manager was American: perhaps that is how she and Jack met. On the other hand, Jack—with his mobile eyebrows, deep-dimpled chin, and teeth "like deepwater gems"—didn't need formal introductions to beautiful women, and Grace Palotta, according to his sworn testimony, was one of the loveliest creatures on earth.

The other was news from America about Evelyn Nesbit herself. On the night of June 25 Evelyn and her husband Harry Thaw had been seated at a table on the roof of Madison Square Garden waiting for the performance of the musical *Mamzelle Champagne* to begin when Harry got up, walked over to the table where Stanford White was seated, pulled out a pistol, and pumped three shots into White's shirt front. "He ruined my wife," Thaw told the arresting policeman—rather a belated conclusion, but poor beautiful Eve seemed to do irrational things to men. Reading of the scandal, it did not occur to Jack that he, as one of her lovers, might be involved in the murder trial.

He returned with Collier from Australia in early September, toured the west into November, then gravitated back into Ethel's orbit to take up his role of Stephen Rollo in *Alice*. After the Harry Graham rupture, Ethel had avoided England that summer; that autumn had been the first in four years that Frohman hadn't had a new play waiting for her. But audiences didn't seem to mind what she acted just as long as they could watch her lovely comedy, listen to that "lost-in-the-dark" voice. She therefore revived *Captain Jinks* with Jack in the cast until, in the last week of January 1907, he was jolted by a summons from the Manhattan district attorney. Harry Thaw was pleading insanity: he had lost control after Evelyn had confessed how she had waked in White's bed to hear him saying, "Don't cry, kittens. It's all over. Now you belong to me." The prosecution, on the other hand, was trying to prove that there had been dozens of men before Evelyn married Thaw—including John Barrymore.

Jack obeyed the summons, found he was not yet needed as a witness, returned to *Jinks* in Boston. There, however, he began to realize his predicament. Not only were the coppery curls and pouting red mouth still vivid, but as a witness he could only damage Evelyn's reputation further. Lionel was already adept at taking ill in moments of crisis; Jack now followed his example, the press faithfully announcing him "Threatened with pneumonia and gone to a sanitarium." Maine in February suddenly seemed attractive. Jack arrived in Rockland on February 8, then headed for Poland Spring while national headlines trumpeted him as THE LATEST FIGURE IN THE THAW, WHITE, AND NESBIT CASE. In Poland Spring Jack secluded himself at the Mansion House, reportedly in "an angry and excited state." Meanwhile in a Manhattan courtroom Evelyn blanched as a Dr. Carlton Flint was called to the witness stand. No, swore Evelyn, she'd never seen the gentleman before.

"Did you never go to [this] gentleman for medical treatment in this city?"

"No, sir."

"Did you not go with Jack Barrymore to this Dr. Carlton Flint's office in his house in New York City?"

"No, sir."

Nobody believed her. In the face of a widely circulated rumor that Jack had taken Evelyn to Flint for an abortion, the testimony that followed revealed that Evelyn had had three operations: two in New York and one at the DeMille School where White had sent her after her affair with Jack. Curiously, all the operations had been "appendectomies."

"Was the operation performed on you at Pompton a criminal operation?"

But here Thaw's lawyer jumped up and said that Evelyn could hardly testify to that since she'd been under anesthesia. Nor was Flint allowed to violate personal confidence by testifying.

Jack never had to testify and escaped further involvement; fortunate, for had Harry Thaw known the man Evelyn really loved he would have murdered Jack Barrymore. Stanford White was only one victim in this crime that proved that women had no existence apart from their sexual relation to men. Jack had probably been the kindest of Evelyn's lovers. But now she was dead, socially and professionally. As she said, "Stanny White was killed, but my fate was worse—I lived." Clever Ethel: so defiantly *Miss* Ethel Barrymore, the chaste Diana of the American stage. *Her* appendectomy had been real.

BUT AT TWENTY-EIGHT, Miss Ethel Barrymore was decidedly unhappy with the progress of her career. "There's almost no kind of role I wouldn't like to attempt," she'd told a reporter two years before, "including Phèdre." Yet what had she been acting? A little whimsy by Barrie and a revival of *Jinks*. She would have made, with training and experience, a fine Portia, a Juliet, a Rosalind. But not only was Frohman anti-Shakespeare, his star system also precluded her having a leading man strong enough for serious plays. Frohman maintained it was a case of simple economics: what manager would hire two stars when one could fill the house? And a star like Ethel Barrymore could make the most vacuous play glitter in a market flooded with trash that made *Alice-Sit-by-the-Fire* look like a masterpiece.

Frohman brought *Captain Jinks* into New York in February 1907, Ethel's first time at his prestigious Empire Theatre as a star. And if possible, this Madame Trentoni was even more successful than her first. There were terrific demonstrations after the final curtain and cries of "Speech! Speech!" Ethel would say, "Oh, no" with a little smile and vanish. Oh, no: you're not getting me to thank you for loving me as Madame Trentoni when I'm longing to play Rosalind and Phèdre! Or Mrs. Jones in a play by John Galsworthy called *The Silver Box*, which she had read and loved.

"Can't we do it?" she asked Frohman.

"It is very tragic."

"I don't mind. I want to do it so much!"

To his eternal credit, Frohman let her play the downtrodden charwoman Mrs. Jones. To do so she had to drop the mannerisms that audiences loved but wiser critics deplored: the adorable giggles and tosses of the head, the widening in surprise of her enormous eyes, the throaty drawl. And she did, metamorphosing completely into Galsworthy's drab, broken-spirited little char. "Few actresses could have suggested better the hopeless pathos of the character," wrote the critic of the *Dramatic Mirror*. "Miss Barrymore's future lies in character parts, however much many of her young women admirers may revolt at the thought." And revolt they did, hating their heroine, as did most critics, in a vehicle that had "nothing for her charms." *The Silver Box* lasted only twenty performances before Frohman rushed on a revival of *His Excellency, the Governor* (with Jack playing Captain Carew "capitally") and *Cousin Kate*, then sent her touring with *Jinks* and *Carrots*. Ethel smoldered.

Impressing a reporter in Minneapolis with a handshake that might have been mistaken for Teddy Roosevelt's, Ethel wanted one thing made clear: "I do not like New York and I do not like to play there." Had her next vehicle been successful she might have relented, but Clyde Fitch's *Her Sister*, written especially for her, was called "spineless" even though the Toledo *Blade* said, "If Charles Frohman were to 'present' Ethel Barrymore in a dramatization of a dictionary she would pack the house." She brought *Her Sister* into New York to the Hudson Theatre that December. Little matter that some admired her skillful acting. "I hate New York critics and New York audiences," raged Ethel. "They go to carp, not to laugh or cry." What really outraged her, however, was the defection of her once most enthusiastic fans, the New York 400. "Society and I have nothing in common," declared this new Ethel. "I now and then am compelled to dine with men and women who have gained social distinction. And I am bored to death. I don't know what to talk about."

Her anger was interpreted as the "nobody loves me anymore" pout of a child or as female unpredictability: "Like most of her sex," the critic Burns Mantle pronounced, "she is a temperamental extremist." But Ethel didn't think she was being either childish or temperamental. Next year she would be thirty. She was tired of being "our Ethel, the American girl" for a public who wouldn't let her grow up. And yet the despised *Silver Box* had changed the course of her career.

THE COURSE OF JACK'S CAREER too was changing. Whether or not the Thaw trial had shocked him into a little sobriety, he now let go of Ethel's apron strings. With eleven plays under his belt, he found himself in four that would take him to the threshold of stardom. In Chicago the critic Amy Leslie at first greeted Jack's Tony Allen in *The Boys of Company B* coolly: "He has twenty faults which he can, but probably will not correct, because the Barrymores never correct anything or change the even tenor of their wilful ways." But Jack granted her an interview and, like Ella Wheeler Wilcox, she became an instant convert. Jack Barrymore, she raved, was "a lighted taper of inexhaustible humor," as "sweet, bubbling and irresponsible as the flight of a zephyr." He was well bred, courteous, kind, and could even act.

Jack admitted he was trying to settle down at last. "I'm so good these days my halo pinches."

"Your father never wanted you to be an actor?"

"Well, yes he did, after he saw what I did in art."

Audiences were delighted that Jack had abandoned art. "Everybody likes the Barrymores, they're so classy," sighed a matron in the sixth row. The first rows were jammed with young ladies going mad over Jack, clapping him back for curtain call after curtain call. By March 1908 *Vanity Fair* was calling him "an irresistibly fascinating matinee idol." Next he was irresistible as Lord Meadows in a Clyde Fitch concoction called *Toddles*, playing a gay blade who "doesn't want to get married, doesn't want to break the engagement, but chiefly doesn't want to get out of bed." TWO BARE BARRYMORE FEET ONLY SENSATION IN TODDLES, claimed one critic, but others noted happily that Mr. Barrymore's comedy shone as he scored "a pronounced personal success."

Still he hadn't a clue about managing money, wiring Ethel that he was determined to start saving, only the telegram cost a dollar, which he didn't have, so could she please stake him until he could begin? Naturally he spent the stake, so that when *Toddles* closed in Atlantic City he was broke. A set of prized lapis lazuli cuff buttons had already been pawned and Jack was dining alone on shrimp bisque and contemplating a hotel bill compounding every day he avoided paying it, when the theatrical manager Mort Singer paused at his table. He was putting on a new musical in Chicago. Would Jack like a part?

"Oh, I don't know," said Jack as casually as a man could who hadn't the price of his dinner. "I've got something in mind that I'm considering."

"How would a hundred and fifty a week do?"

Having never been paid more than fifty, Jack was struck mute.

"Well, then," said Singer, misinterpreting his silence, "make it a hundred and seventy-five. If you want some money now, here's a hundred dollars."

Jack found his voice and accepted.

A Stubborn Cinderella opened at the Princess Theatre in Chicago in June 1908 with Jack in a role that required him to sing, dance, clown, and wear a Charles I wig with long corkscrew curls. The audience seemed only mildly responsive the first night, so Jack, the author, and the stage manager huddled all night at the Bucket of Blood Café trying to decide how to save the play. They could as well have slept, for the early papers pronounced A Stubborn Cinderella the best show to hit Chicago in years. "The only, irresistible, brilliant, and idolized Barrymore!" sang Amy Leslie, and Chicago packed the Princess until the end of the year to watch Jack cavort with his charming leading lady, Sallie Fisher. Yet Jack was nonchalant about his talents.

"What do you consider the prime requisite for a musical comedian?" he was asked.

"A latent inadequacy," said Jack.

Ethel followed his successes hungrily. When Jack opened in The Boys of Company B, she'd run up an enormous phone bill in one day having his notices telegraphed to her hotel in Grand Rapids. For A Stubborn Cinderella she'd come to Chicago from Milwaukee to watch a rehearsal and declared herself downright envious of the lively, pretty Sallie Fisher: "Oh, what I wouldn't give to play those scenes once with Jack!" When A Stubborn Cinderella came to New York in 1908 at the Broadway, Ethel had Jack play the whole first act for her privately. She was indignant when New York didn't seem as ready to accept Jack as unconditionally as Chicago had. She found him delicious in April in The Candy Shop (which the critics labeled fluff), particularly when he broke into the song "Just We Two." She adored him possessively, willing him to succeed, jealously listening to her friends rave over his charm and beauty.

She was feeling more and more in the mood to marry if only she could find the Right One. Her dear friend Alice Roosevelt, the other girl the American public loved to engage, had married Nick Longworth, rounding herself appropriately into a wife. And a recent experience had particularly disconcerted her. Chloese Hatch, another friend, had asked her out to Tuxedo Park for lunch, so she'd rented a car since there was no other way to get there. Then Chloese rang back. Could she bring another guest whose car had broken down? Ethel picked him up and delivered them both to Chloese. And then after lunch he had wandered off into the woods with a very pretty girl and they'd come back engaged. Everybody had been delighted, but Ethel had to drive him back and deposit him at his door. She was not delighted. It was not her custom to chauffeur men around the countryside so they could get engaged. Besides the man was very rich. At least he could have paid for the car.

Her turn was at hand. One day as she was lunching at Sherry's with Uncle Jack, Aunt Dodo, and Bee, a young man strolled by the table and Uncle Jack said, "Hello, Hungry. Sit down." Russell Colt (nicknamed "Hungry" after a DeWolf ancestor) was a tallish young man of twenty-seven with dark brown eyes and already thinning hair. Jack knew him and Ethel had once asked him to introduce them, but nothing had happened. Ethel naturally knew something about the millionaire Colts.

Samuel Colt, the legendary inventor of the six-shooter, was Russell's great-uncle; his father, Colonel Samuel Pomeroy Colt, the president of the United States Rubber Company. In Bristol, Rhode Island, the Colts, Howes, and DeWolfs, all intermarried, were in and out of each other's houses continually. Colonel Colt or "Unkie"—the patron saint and sinner of Bristol—owned the magnificent Linden Place as well as the acreage of Poppasquash Farm. On his land was a big stone barn where he bred Jersey cattle he named "Nancy Dear" and "Darling Ruth" after various female conquests. Overlooking the western arm of the bay he had built a casino where he presided over reputed orgies; at least he did enjoy slapping the behinds of pretty guests as they ran down to swim in their "Annette Kellermans." Add to the splendor of his possessions Unkie's reputation as an exploiter of cheap immigrant labor in his factory and one had the archetypal ruthless millionaire whose motto was "If you don't love money, you won't get it."

Rather hard to say what his son Russell did for a living besides belong to some golf clubs; yet he was not a "society type" or "man about town." He had a fine speaking voice, low and strong, thought Ethel now, gazing at him with her huge eyes. They were all going down to Kyalami Cottage for the weekend, and since it turned out that Russell was going to East-hampton too, he took the same train. Once they got there, he drifted away and Ethel wondered whether she was imagining the wonderful thing that was happening, but then he came back to Kyalami after dinner—

"and after that, well, it just happened." And after all the agonizing and tears and consultations with friends and returned engagement rings, she was amazed how simple it was.

Her new maturity was echoed in her new play that fall: Somerset Maugham's *Lady Frederick*. Frohman had again permitted her an adult role. Ethel took it on a tour that was marked by another outburst in the press, a curious one, considering. Under the headline MILLIONAIRES' SONS BRAINLESS, RICH WOMEN PRIGGISH, Ethel was quoted in St. Louis as calling the elite "Useless, brainless and purposeless." "If a plague were to wipe out the entire society element of New York, the city would be none the worse for it. . . . Never, never, will I marry the son of a millionaire. The millionaire would be bad enough, but the son of one, no. Why the average son of a millionaire hasn't enough brains to interest a playful kitten."

Uproar. Ethel issued an immediate denial, then betrayed herself by claiming she had been in a train wreck in Springfield, Illinois, and in St. Louis hadn't known what she was saying. In fact, a young reporter had come to interview her in St. Louis. Ethel had liked her and invited her back the next day for a "woman to woman talk." The reporter had published Ethel's off-the-record confidences.

Interesting, this attack on millionaire's sons in light of Ethel's later claim that during the six months of her engagement to Russell Colt she never tried to escape and was never troubled by doubts. Apparently she was not only troubled but appalled at Russell's type, though much attracted to Russell himself. And perhaps a little appalled at herself, for though she prided herself militantly on not being a snob, she was rather overwhelmed by the Colt pedigree and the splendor of Linden Place. But it was time to marry. She'd been trying to let herself get married for at least a dozen years.

Russell took a seat at the Hudson for the entire ninety-six-night run of *Lady Frederick*. Not caring as much now that the critics found Lady Frederick middle-aged and unsuitable to the American girl, she played to Russell or his empty seat. Only close friends knew they were engaged: ironically this real engagement went unreported in the press. In the new year, 1909, she took *Lady Frederick* to the eastern cities, but came back to New York as often as she could by the late train to be with Russell. On March 2 the play moved to the Hollis Street Theatre in Boston and, tired of the love commuting, Ethel and Russell decided to marry. First they must break the news to Colonel Colt. Ethel was elected, and on March 7 came to New York and was shown into Colt's huge cold parlor at the Holland House.

"I can't understand why you want to marry my son," said Unkie in his gravelly voice. "I have no money." There had been a recent panic on Wall Street and the rich man was feeling poor.

"I don't want money," said Ethel.

"How are you going to live?"

"I make enough money, but I think it would be a good thing if Russell had some kind of job."

The engagement was formally announced three days later and greeted skeptically.

"Do you really think she will marry him?" wondered a friend in Chicago.

"It's possible, but it isn't customary."

In Boston Ethel went to Bishop O'Connell to arrange for a dispensation to marry a Protestant. After Russell signed the necessary papers in the bishop's office he said, "That's the most charming man I ever met. How do you get to be a Catholic?" Ethel was thrilled, but Russell never mentioned converting again. Finally she was granted four dispensations: for marrying a Protestant, for marrying on Sunday, for marrying in Lent, and for marrying in a rectory. Ethel usually got what she wanted.

Before the wedding day Ethel tore up the contents of two big red dispatch boxes of letters containing the passionate protestations of Laurence Irving, Gerald du Maurier, Winston Churchill, Harry Graham, and dozens of other smitten swains—showing a fine regard for Russell's feelings but no regard at all for history. After the Saturday performance they left the Hotel Bellevue where they'd both been staying, and drove eight miles to Dedham to the house of Ethel's dear friends Jack and Sally Fairchild. The next morning, March 14, they were married by the Reverend Father James Chittick in the rectory of the Church of the Most Sacred Blood in Hyde Park. Jack and Russell's brother Roswell were the only witnesses; the only guests afterward at the wedding breakfast were Ethel's stage manager James Kearney and his wife.

The public announcement was to be made at the Hollis Street Theatre on Tuesday by Kearney. Russell and the Fairchilds occupied a balcony box, Russell with a magnificent bouquet of violets ready to toss at his bride's feet. The announcement that Miss Ethel Barrymore was now Mrs. Russell Colt was greeted by surprised and enthusiastic applause. Her color coming and going rapidly, very self-conscious about the big new ring glittering on her finger, Ethel bent to retrieve the violets. For perhaps the first time Russell realized how much he would have to share Ethel with her public. As for the audience, it realized that "our Ethel" was no longer their darling American girl.

In his first interview as Ethel's husband, Russell sounded like Jack, which may explain a good deal of the attraction he had for Ethel. His father had got him a junior partnership with a Wall Street firm, but he wasn't ready to step into the job yet: "It'll be a funny honeymoon at first. Bride working, husband loafing."

When would Mrs. Colt get back from her West Coast tour?

"You mean *we* get back," corrected Russell. "Bless your heart, I'm going too. Don't for a minute think I'm going to be left behind."

Was his wife's career a problem then?

He denied it. "One of my pre-engagement promises—I might properly say *plea*-engagement promises—was that I would in no way interfere with her business and professional plans. What Miss Barrymore is going to do next season depends upon herself and Mr. Frohman."

At last, the real reason Ethel married Russell Colt. She could rule him, she thought. Without ambition or a profession himself, he could accommodate his life to hers. She was still intact, still "Miss Ethel Barrymore." For this reason she was willing to overlook his "lighthearted irresponsibility," which, after all, like Jack's, was part of his charm. In fact, the marriage would be a tragic mistake: the union of a strong, gifted woman to the very kind of millionaire's son she had deplored.

NINE

1909–1912

THREE MAJOR EVENTS occurred in the Barrymore world that fall of 1909. Lionel gave up his dream of being an artist, Jack became a star, and Ethel became a mother.

For Lionel, Paris was a mixed experience. On the one hand, the Barrymore name meant nothing there so that he was just one of many students who came to the Académie Julien, worked as long as he could pay his fees, and trembled as the master Jean Paul Laurens, his interpreter at his heels, approached to criticize his canvas. Ethel's checks came regularly, Doris did pleasant things with fish and sauces on a tiny burner, and they could bear the squalor of Latin Quarter walk-ups because they were young and in love. Lionel grew a shaggy beard and felt like an artist, though when the actress May Irwin visited them she didn't know whether to laugh or to cry.

On the other hand, they were pathetically isolated. True, Lionel made some friends among the students and even knew Gertrude Stein a little. But with successful artists he failed to make contact. He could watch Picasso drink absinthe at the Café de Dôme, but dared not approach him. He could sneer enviously at the work of a current favorite like Lucien Simon in the galleries, yet never cross his path. Even the classes at the Académie were impersonal. Like every new student Lionel stood drinks his first day. "You want to remember this, Barrymore," an old student told him, "because it will be the only day in your life here that you will be noticed." The fellow was right. If a kind word was ever said about his paintings, Lionel didn't hear it. He didn't even have a finished canvas to show: every Friday he wiped it down for a fresh start on Monday. And Ethel expected progress.

Still, had Ethel not married, Lionel and Doris might have lingered in Paris indefinitely. When the announcement came of her marriage it was clear that she was planning a family of her own, and Lionel knew that his days as "a remittance man" were over. That August 1909 he and Doris arrived in New York on the *Pennsylvania* after an absence of more than three years.

With them were their daughters Mary and Ethel—or were they. Of all the mysteries of Lionel's very private life, the fate of Mary is the deepest. There were two infant girls: Lionel has said so. Ethel saw her namesake when she visited Lionel and Doris in Paris shortly after the child's birth in August 1906. Mary was supposedly the elder, yet Ethel does not mention her. Doris Rankin is mute on the subject, as on all others. As an old man Lionel said that Mary died at two and Ethel in infancy. Mary may have died in Paris. She remains an unknown quantity.

Lionel planned on making a living as an artist in New York when he returned, he said. He said, however, that he found the Impressionism he'd studied in Paris knocked cold by the new Ash Can school of American artists who painted backyards, boxing rings, saloons, and slums with a fresh, tough realism. From the Continent, too, the Modernists had arrived and were on exhibition at Alfred Stieglitz's revolutionary photo succession gallery, 291. Before he had even started, Lionel knew he was passé. Finally, when he went to apply for illustrating work and found the magazines employing the very artists he couldn't hope to emulate, he gave up, he said. However, had Lionel studied *seriously* in Paris, one of the most sophisticated art centers of the world, surely he would not have been bowled over by Ash Canners or Modernists. Had he really felt himself a good artist or even been truly committed to being an artist, surely he would have persisted. The conclusion seems inescapable that Paris was a last desperate attempt to avoid doing the thing he was born to do.

He had not been a starving artist in Paris, and now checked in at Billy Muldoon's health farm near White Plains, New York, to try to shed his bulk before reporting to Frohman. When he'd left the stage he had been Barrymore number two, except to those few critics who had found his rich character acting superior to Ethel's poignant comedy. Since then not only had Ethel established her maturity with *The Silver Box* and *Lady Frederick*, but Jack had scored a triumph in *The Fortune Hunter*.

That summer of 1909 Jack had been tapped for Winchell Smith's comedy about a young man determined to marry an heiress. As these things go, he was not very good at rehearsals, and after the first night in New Haven the management hesitated to send him into New York. Fortunately for the play—and for Jack—someone had faith in the careless young actor.

On the night of September 4, Jack eyed the three red apples on his dressing table, applied the finishing touches to his make-up, puffed furiously at a cigarette in the wings, and sauntered onto the stage of the Gaiety to give a knockout performance as the engaging Nat Duncan. Though a few critics hedged ("John Barrymore Nearly Acts," said the *Telegraph*), everyone else knew that Jack had scored a huge success. Reviewers raved over his "lightness and ease," the "happiest sort of frank assurance" of his playing, his "firm touch in making points which creates the impression of spontaneity" as well as a new sort of "undercurrent of sympathy and feeling that gave tenderness to the laughter." His performance made one forgive *The Candy Shop* and (almost) *Toddles*: John Barrymore, it was devoutly to be hoped, was now lost to vapid musical comedy forever. What critics did not analyze was Jack's peculiar combination of tension, sensitivity, recklessness, and grace that electrified his audience that night. He generated excitement. Men envied him, women wanted to love and comfort him. (Many tried.) Interestingly enough, Jack, like his father Maurice, was not a Frohman creation. He had found his way to stardom himself.

On October 28 Jack threw a party at the Gaiety for about 1,500 fellow actors and friends. After a scintillating performance for an audience that included Uncle Jack, Aunt Dodo, Bee, Georgie Drew Mendum, and Johnston Forbes-Robertson, Jack appeared in front of the curtain to calls of "Speech!" Cocking an eyebrow just like John Drew, he threw a mischievous glance at his uncle's box. "Oh, Uncle John," he laughed, "isn't it nice to be on Broadway?"

Lionel watched the triumph from the back of the house, detached as usual. "I'm not as clever as my brother Jack," he'd always said, "who can't help but get along." Jack and Ethel both had it—that charisma, that fascination no matter what they did. And no matter how hard Lionel worked, he hadn't. And now he was certain that Broadway, "that long street with a short memory," had forgotten him altogether.

Ethel had just left Broadway to become a mother. She had been very eager to have children (she said) as a Catholic and a propagator of the Drew-Barrymore line. She had conceived immediately upon marrying— or was it just before. When she discovered she was pregnant she felt at last that her decision to marry Russell Colt had been right, yet she had no intention of letting children or husband interfere with her career. She had gone back to *Lady Frederick* the day after her wedding; touring that spring of 1909 she avoided doctors because she was afraid they might tell her to quit and go home. Indeed, her behavior during this first pregnancy seems like denial rather than acceptance of motherhood, unless one takes into account her passionate need to keep working.

The *Lady Frederick* tour had ended in California in July, and Ethel, four months pregnant and rather nervous, arranged to travel back to New York with Uncle Jack and Aunt Dodo because Aunt Dodo was the nearest thing to a mother she had and she wanted to talk about having a baby. Aunt Dodo only promised to get her a good nurse when the time came, so that holidaying in Connecticut that August where she and Russell were "the important people" at the fashionable Belle Haven resort, Ethel still hadn't seen a doctor. She was concerned enough to train into New York one day to try to find Mummum's old physician, but Dr. Bagg's boarded-up brownstone displayed the sign "Back in September." Rather desperate, she returned to Greenwich and, as luck would have it, after a dinner party that week two young women asked her about her doctor. She had to confess she didn't have one. Promptly the young women recommended a Dr. Danforth, also summering at Greenwich, and Ethel, five months pregnant, had medical advice at last.

That early autumn the Colts took the August Belmont house at 46 East Thirty-fourth Street, an appropriate setting for the birth of an heir. Mrs. Frings, sent by Aunt Dodo, came to take care of Ethel who, in September, "retired temporarily to assume the duties of motherhood." These duties began in earnest on November 28 when Dr. Danforth told the girl who never rests that she was *not* visiting the Peter Dunnes in Garden City that day but staying home and having a baby. Lionel and Jack were summoned to usher in the sixth generation. Heavily fortified with drink, they waited downstairs until a boy was born to Ethel at eleven that night.

"I'm trying to feel like an uncle," Jack told a waiting reporter.

"And how do you feel?"

"Like King Lear."

Ethel made a great deal of the child's being a premature baby of three and a half pounds, but was contradicted by the *Telegraph*'s report that "[It] is not generally known that Master Colt tipped the scales at eleven pounds at his debut." The only significance of a full-term baby is the chink it would betray in Miss Ethel Barrymore's virginal armor. One does not dislike her for the possibility.

Although she claimed she adored motherhood, her curiously detached account of a famous photograph taken soon after the baby's birth again suggests ambivalence. "It was [Mrs. Frings's] idea," said Ethel, "that a photograph should be taken of the baby and me immediately. . . . I was propped up in bed with pillows, a lace cap put on my head and, I suppose, [I] registered maternity under the stern orders of Mrs. Frings [as] the small son was placed in my arms." Then she had not yet chosen a name for the baby. Though Lionel and Jack called him Mike and her friends were sure she would name it Maurice, at Unkie's request, Ethel tardily named the baby Samuel after the inventor of the Colt revolver and Colonel Colt himself.

Jack seemed always to be the one on hand for solemn occasions like weddings and funerals; along with Peter Dunne he was present now as godfather at St. Patrick's Cathedral for the baptism of Ethel's child. Creedless himself (despite his baptism by Ethel), he enjoyed ritual, though he took it lightly enough. "I believe in God the Father Almighty," he began confidently, "Creator of Heaven and earth—" He stopped. "That lets me out!" he said cheerfully, leaving Peter Dunne, purple with laughter, to finish the formula and Ethel, as usual, both horrified and amused.

Ethel may have had other reasons for not asking Lionel to stand godfather, but in fact that January of 1910 they were quarreling. Afraid of Broadway, Lionel had opened in Chicago in December as Abdullah, a dragoman, in *The Fires of Fate*. Though Arthur Conan Doyle's play was dismissed as "melodrama, pure and simple," Lionel had lost none of his genius. Critics were surprised at the added flesh, but called his Abdullah "unusual acting . . . really wonderful." Everything was set for a Broadway opening when Lionel was "stricken" and hurried east at the end of December for an appendicitis operation. It is hard to believe in this operation from which he supposedly recovered at Ethel's house when appendicitis was a euphemism for everything from abortion to a nervous breakdown; it seems likely that Lionel had undergone another revulsion from the stage.

Ethel did not quarrel with this but with Lionel's decision to join Uncle Sidney and Aunt Gladys in vaudeville. Maurice had been the first legitimate American actor to defect to vaudeville, but then she'd been too young to be shocked. She was shocked now: Lionel the wonderful actor, Lionel the senior Barrymore. There was no excuse: vaudeville was treason. Ignoring her pleas and threats, Lionel made his debut at Hammerstein's on January 31, 1910. She was undoubtedly delighted that *The Jail Bird* flopped, Lionel being "lost in a hopeless morass of stagey talk and utterly false theatricals" in a sketch "not interesting for a minute."

She herself had broken records by returning to rehearsals three weeks after Sammy's birth.

"Ethel, I have a big play," Frohman had told her, "but it is dark and sad. I don't think you want to do it."

Ethel listened to him read Arthur Wing Pinero's *Mid-Channel*, then turned to him impulsively. "You are wrong. I want to play this part very much."

FROHMAN REGARDED ACTRESSES who married as traitors. Children were beyond the pale, but Ethel Barrymore was a law unto herself and C.F. had to make the best of it. Making the best of it meant capitalizing upon the new Ethel: no longer the ideal American girl but, by grace of losing her virginity at last, the ideal American woman. "There is to be no more light work for Ethel Barrymore," Frohman announced. "Miss Barrymore is a woman. . . . She is capable of strong emotion—strong dramatic work—and it is with that line she is to be identified hereafter."

But audiences not prepared for the physically new Ethel Barrymore gasped as she made her entrance at the Empire the night of January 31, 1910. The lithe Daphne, the startled fawn, was gone forever. Ethel had flouted Dion Boucicault's three commandments for an actress: (1) Keep your figure, (2) Keep your figure, (3) Keep your figure. This new Ethel Barrymore was "fair, fat, and forty." Some critics may have projected their dislike of Ethel's bulk onto Pinero's play when they claimed it had "not one redeeming feature in four acts." The discerning recognized that this new Ethel Barrymore was a revelation. "As Zoe Blundell she had a triumph," said Daniel Frohman, C.F.'s brother. "The sweetness and girlishness now stood aside in the presence of a somber and haunting tragedy that was real. Miss Barrymore literally made the critics sit up." Mrs. Jones, the charwoman of *The Silver Box*, had ushered in this new Ethel Barrymore; Zoe Blundell marked even more clearly the evolution of her career.

Perfectly aware that she had shocked a large portion of her following, Ethel remained calm. She had her own three rules for an actress: "the first is to think, the second is to think, and the third is to keep on thinking." "The most wonderful thing in life is to grow," she told her public, "to develop new capacities." She did not regret the lost girl. The womanhood that society decreed could only be won through marriage and motherhood was at last hers.

Her pregnancy had sparked debates in the press over Motherhood and Art. Were they incompatible? "Yes!" said Mary Garden, Julia Marlowe, Maxine Elliott, Mrs. Leslie Carter, and Maude Adams—all childless. "No!" said Gertrude Elliott, Réjane, and Bernhardt—actresses and mothers. Ethel herself was crisp. "Well, here *I* am," she said, "and there's my brother Jack and my Uncle John and my Cousin Louise and Uncle Sidney and my mother and father, and grandmother and grandfather, and we were all born—and yet there has been considerable acting in the family ever since." She went further, claiming that she had done her best work as an actress since her son's arrival.

In Chicago where *Mid-Channel* eventually arrived on tour, Barrymore admirer Ashton Stevens met Mrs. Russell Colt, wife and mother.

"Have you the remotest idea what we shall talk about?" said Ethel, leaning back and reaching for a cigarette with a resigned but hospitable smile.

"You might fetch Baby—eh?"

"Sam-u-el is where he belongs. At home."

Stevens found it good news.

"Shall you stick?"

She merely nodded that, yes, she would stick.

"Still stage-struck?"

"Yessss"—those inimitable sibilants—"still stage-stricken. I guess it's in the blood. We don't seem to be born for anything else."

Were the stage and marriage incompatible?

"Not in any way, my dear friend." She raised huge eyes as Russell wandered in looking for a nail file.

Stage and marriage, no; vacuity and marriage, yes.

DORIS BARRYMORE also had to consider the conflicting claims of stage and motherhood that season. In place of the disastrous *Jail Bird* Sidney Drew quickly substituted a new short play by Lionel with a part for Doris—their first appearance together. Though some considered the prostitution theme of *The White Slaver* unfortunate, more agreed that Lionel Barrymore scored heavily in a strong sketch. Quiet and controlled, Doris also emerged as an intelligent actress. Then in March, while they were still playing at Hammerstein's, any conflict Doris felt about motherhood and a career was tragically resolved.

On March 23 little Ethel became so seriously ill that Lionel and Doris rushed her from their home at 70 West Forty-seventh Street to Dr. Bull's sanitarium at 33 East Thirty-third. At 6:00 p.m. the following day the eighteen-month-old child died. Dr. Rudmann explained that a swelling of lymphoid tissues throughout the body particularly endangered the child by lowering her powers of resistance; sudden death was common. If Mary had already died, Lionel and Doris were now childless.

Ethel considered the death of her namesake another piece of Lionel's bad luck. Some people have said that Lionel subconsciously never forgave Doris for the loss of his daughters, irrationally believing that some congenital weakness in her had blasted his wish to be a father. Lionel and

Doris took the small casket to Philadelphia to be laid in Greenwood Cemetery beside her grandparents and great-grandparents, then set out to tour the vaudeville circuit across the country. It seemed particularly cruel that Lionel should have lost his second child just when Ethel's motherhood was splashed across all the newspapers. Though Doris was only twenty-one, there would be no more children.

ETHEL MEANWHILE was discovering that the man who hadn't bothered about converting to Catholicism was not going to be bothered doing much of anything. Colonel Colt had got Russell a position with the Wall Street firm H. L. Norton, but Russell took it lightly. "What train do you take to New York?" asked a friend. "Oh," said Russell, "I usually miss the ten thirty-seven." And though Russell had been reputed to be worth a million with the prospect of ten million more, Ethel found they were living chiefly on her salary, a circumstance that she, with no idea in the world about money except that it came regularly from Frohman, accepted far too meekly.

She had been prepared for Russell's lighthearted irresponsibility, but there was a darker side to his nature that he displayed publicly by smashing his fist into the jaw of a curb broker who approached him in the lobby of the Hotel Knickerbocker. Fortunately Jack got Russell by the coattails and pulled him off before the management ejected him. But Ethel had already felt Russell's fists herself, one night six months after their wedding when she asked him why he had come home so late. She hadn't suspected that he was a womanizer like his father or that he would use physical violence. Russell might have complained that marriage to the magnificent Ethel had proved overwhelming, a constant threat to his fragile ego. Yet a man who would beat a pregnant wife was, even in the euphemism of the day, a bully and a cad.

Searching for stability in a marriage that was already disintegrating without having really begun, Ethel decided that she must have the country. To her relief Unkie was no longer feeling poor, but then he also found her decidedly attractive. "You find a place and I'll give it to you," he said. She found it at last twenty-one miles from New York in Mamaroneck at the end of Taylor's Lane. "What a lovely hall for a little boy to throw his cap in!" she exclaimed, already seeing the big, rambling house on ten acres painted white and green and apple trees and roses in bloom. Russell didn't like the place at all and thought her crazy to want it, but Russell had lost his authority. So they had their country retreat: New York seemed a million miles away. She designed a new "Adamsy" fireplace for the library—she had to have fireplaces in every room—planted fruit trees, filled the game room with Maurice's collection of boxing and baseball photographs. Though her father-in-law had bought the place, she soon discovered that her income would pay for the English butler, the cook, the groundskeeper, the chauffeur, and the maids as well as for all upkeep and taxes. It didn't matter. She had found a home.

AT TWENTY-EIGHT Jack was thinking of marriage himself. Since Evelyn Nesbit there had been a parade of actresses and chorus girls in and out of various bedrooms: Irene Frizzelle, Hazel Allen, Lotta Faust, Bonnie Maginn, Vivian Blackburn. But Jack was also an idealist about women. It was typical, for example, that his chivalry had been roused at the rudeness and violence displayed toward women during the recent Hudson-Fulton Celebration. Men had elbowed them out of the way and refused them seats in streetcars. Jack promptly joined the "Seats for Women" movement, distributing "True Blue" buttons to Lambs and Players members. "I know the boys are going to kid me on this, but I am serious about it. Good manners are decaying so rapidly in New York that it is time that those who believe in courtesy as a fine art should do something about it." That the "New Woman" might have found such chivalry patronizing would have puzzled Jack.

The women in his life could not live up to the madonna he searched for. Irene ("Frizzy") Frizzelle, a pseudosweet ninety-pound blonde known as "the pocket Venus," was shopworn before she and Jack became lovers. He soon discovered that Hazel Allen was all too familiar to male patrons of the lobster palaces. Lotta Faust's white, firmly fleshed back was famous on both sides of the Atlantic, but though Jack admitted he liked "to grab a handful of back," the scandalous dancer fell short of his romantic standards. Curvacious Bonnie Maginn had too many sugar daddies waiting for her at the Weber and Fields Music Hall stage door. Vivian Blackburn was a professional fencer as well as a showgirl, but could Jack pledge true love to the queen of the cigarette-picture girls? Certainly not in that day of vicious sexual double standards.

The women's practicality also doomed these affairs. Jack was divinely handsome, amusing, and charming, but he could not afford the diamonds that were a girl's best friend. Evelyn Nesbit had married the millionaire Harry K. Thaw. Irene Frizzelle left Jack for the Wall Street investor Jay Ward, then left Ward for Felix Isman, a multimillionaire real estate investor. When they divorced—Isman charging adultery with, among others, John Barrymore—Irene consoled herself with another prosperous Wall

Street man, James F. O'Brien. Hazel Allen married Isman. Bonnie Maginn married a man handsomely equipped with a multimillionaire father. Jack just wasn't in their league.

As a matinee idol he could of course marry into society himself, as Ethel had done, though his reputation was *not* the ideal American boy's. So likely, in fact, was it that an infatuated society woman might snatch handsome Jack that his managers, George M. Cohan and Sam Harris, were inspired to take out a $50,000-a-year insurance policy on the star of their *Fortune Hunter*. Part publicity stunt, the insurance policy also confirmed that marriage could destroy a matinee idol's appeal as much as a chorus girl's. Thus on April 30, 1910, Jack signed the statement, "I am not now engaged to be married nor do I contemplate marriage."

And yet that season Jack fell in love. Exploring his pockets one rainy night after the theatre, he had found among his cigarettes an invitation to a debutante's ball. He hesitated, then told the cabby to drive him uptown. The debutante of the evening was Katherine Corri Harris, seventeen, honey-colored hair, blue blue eyes. Like Ethel at that age she was tall and lanky with wide shoulders; her voice had the slightest, most fascinating lisp. Jack had met Katherine before at Newport where she visited her aunt, Mrs. Herbert Harriman. He knew Katherine came from a well-connected family, that her mother, though divorced from Sidney Harris, a well-known lawyer, lived in style on alimony and an inheritance from her uncle of half a million. None of this, including Katherine, had penetrated before. But tonight, like Lionel's suddenly seeing Doris Rankin for the first time, Jack found himself bewitched by a madonna with both position and money.

Sidney Harris did not intend his daughter for an actor. When the romance became public, he immediately threatened to cut off alimony payments to her mother and ordered Katherine to a Paris convent. Cowed by the threat and the fact that Katherine was not yet of age, mother and daughter sailed in July, Harris following to make certain Katherine was out of harm's way. It was all very melodramatic and only made Katherine want Jack more.

But Jack, who had always appealed to older women too, found an unexpected champion in Katherine's grandmother, Mrs. Brady, who happened to see Jack for the first time walking down the street and hurried home to write her granddaughter:

Don't let your father keep you over there. Come back with your mother. You cannot be shut up. The more he is against Jack

Barrymore, the more you will like him. Do not be afraid of Mr. Harris. He helped to bring you into the world. That was all.

Aunt May and Uncle Herbert are bitterly against Jack, but don't you care. Come home to see him. A lady told me today that the Barrymores go everywhere in Philadelphia. Excellent family. Excellent position.

Jack looks as if he wants a woman's care. . . . He is so handsome. If I were a young woman I would be crazy about him myself.

On August 3 Katherine and her mother returned to New York. Headlines announced BARRYMORE IS TO WED, BUT NOT JUST YET. "There is little romance about the affair," Jack rather heartlessly told a reporter. "It is just a regular engagement coming after a long friendship." On August 11 he went with Katherine ("unchaperoned in a taxi"!) to take out a marriage license, squelching rumors that he might break the engagement. The next day Katherine left for Canada as her father's ship docked in New York. Informed that his daughter was indeed engaged to Jack Barrymore, Sidney Harris was outraged.

On September 1 Jack and Katherine were married at St. Francis Xavier's Church where Lionel and Doris had pledged their vows almost six years before. Gazing at the couple, Ethel thought "how beautifully radiant they both looked with the sun shining on them through a stained-glass window." After the ceremony Ethel took Katherine—of whom she approved in every way—back to Mamaroneck where the couple would live temporarily, while Jack reported to the Gaiety. Messrs. Cohan and Harris were not unduly upset, but Jack's marriage cost Lloyds of London $50,000.

Shortly afterward, *The Fortune Hunter* ended its supremely successful 345-performance run and Jack, with Katherine, went on tour. Katherine began the inevitable process of discovering that an actor is far more glamorous onstage than off. Privately Jack began to think of his marriage as a "bus accident."

BY NOVEMBER 1910 the disastrous Colt marriage erupted into headlines. On tour in New Orleans, Ethel became almost hysterical while denying rumors of an estrangement. At the same time Colt was seen about the city with his arm in a sling. He had "caught it in a taxicab door," yet one remembers that in fights with Lionel Ethel gave as good as she got. The next day Ethel denied absolutely all reports of marital discord.

Yet no press coverage for the next half year did not mean that the marriage was not in trouble.

In July 1911 in Los Angeles Ethel went with her cousin Bee to draw up papers against Russell, while friends testified to Ethel's complaints that "her young husband was not only of no assistance to her in her work, but that he annoyed her and made her labor doubly hard with his objections and opinions." But there was only one divorce charge that Ethel was making: Russell's adultery with more than one woman. This story had hardly hit the street when Ethel, surrounded by a phalanx of friends, relatives, and tour managers, again denied everything and refused all comment. In the East Russell professed surprise at the charges, Jack interest and concern, Aunt Dodo no surprise. "We knew it was coming before she left New York, and, of course, all our sympathies are with her." On July 12 Ethel filed for divorce amid speculation that Mrs. Frings, Ethel's blond, attractive nurse, was the other woman—a rumor that was scotched when little Sammy was reported staying in St. John, Canada, with Mrs. Frings and her husband Eugene.

Then Ethel traveled east incognito, and though everyone recognized her in a plain gingham dress and old hat, such was her power that no one dared approach her. Looking ill and worn and accompanied by Bee and Georgie Drew Mendum, she avoided Grand Central Terminal by slipping off the train at 125th Street. She was next spotted in Canada visiting her infant son. Then on August 5, stopped for reckless driving on Long Island, Russell tried bribery.

"I will buy a case of wine. At any rate, please don't detain me now. I must start for Canada tonight to keep an appointment with my wife. She is Ethel Barrymore. May I go?"

And because she was Ethel Barrymore, he could.

Eight days later the Mamaroneck house was ablaze with lights when a reporter knocked at the door. It was answered by a testy Mr. Colt.

"All that has been printed about us is lies," he snapped. "The stories of divorce are all lies. We are perfectly happy and always have been perfectly happy."

"Now, Russell," drawled a famous voice from the drawing room, "don't become so angry." The goddess herself appeared on the threshold. No, there was absolutely nothing to the divorce suit.

"But David Gerber, your attorney, admitted it," said the reporter.

Ethel smiled her crescent smile. Mr. Gerber could not have admitted anything since there was nothing to admit.

Shortly after the reconciliation Ethel found herself pregnant again. Touring that fall in *Witness for the Defense* before its Empire opening, she almost miscarried in South Bend, Indiana. The doctor was astonished that she wanted to keep the child: she was an actress, wasn't she? Ethel, a Catholic determined to have "the mother thing," felt like killing him.

At the same time, Ethel's favorite cousin Georgie was also having trouble with corespondents. Georgie had been tipped off that her husband, Alan Parsons, was living in Chicago with a woman who called herself his wife. Georgie had recently played a female detective onstage. Armed with her methods, she stormed the apartment house, winning the confidence of the maid to the bogus Mrs. Parsons as well as collecting evidence of Parsons's adultery from elevator operators, janitors, and butcher boys. Her clever but disillusioning work won her a quick divorce in October 1911.

A nearly blind actress had once whispered to a theatre companion, "That girl must be a Drew. There is something in her voice that reminds me of Mrs. John Drew." "They tell me I am more like Georgie Drew Barrymore than any of her children," said Georgie Drew Mendum—and there was a resemblance in the big light gray eyes, the break and quaver voice, the drollery and high spirits. But Georgie found her Drew inheritance crippling: "I'd rather be Susie Smith; people wouldn't expect so much of Susie Smith at first."

Yet Joseph Jefferson had told her, "You have the brightest jewel in an actor's crown, the spirit of comedy." No less a critic than Ashton Stevens thought her "a capital comic." Comparing cousins, one critic actually called her "the brightest grandchild of Mrs. John Drew," only lacking Ethel's fostering and polishing under Frohman. Some got impatient. "Can't someone make Georgie Drew Mendum stop wasting her energies and talents and realize her unquestioned gifts?" an admirer complained. "She has only to concentrate her forces, be less prodigal of her vitality, devote herself exclusively to the dramatic stage and refuse odds and ends from the dramatic scrap-heap. She has much more talent in comedy than Louise Drew and Ethel Barrymore."

But now Ethel held out her strong hands and drew Georgie back into her orbit. Georgie resented being offered the meager part of Jane the maid in the January 1912 revival of *Cousin Kate*—another odd bit from the scrap heap, yet it was flattering that Ethel wanted her, not only onstage but off as chief confidante. She should have fought Ethel tooth and nail, for whether Ethel intended it or not, Georgie could not be seen to advantage in her cousin's blaze.

IF ONLY ETHEL could find another great role like Zoe Blundell. She'd acted Rose Trelawny in Pinero's wonderful *Trelawny of the Wells*. But even Pinero, Ethel, and the British actress Constance Collier could not keep *Trelawny* at the Empire for more than six weeks, the fate also of *Witness for the Defense* which followed, though Ethel had a meaty part in Stella Ballantyne.

She'd had to go back to dear Barrie: a revival of *Alice-Sit-by-the-Fire* with Louisa Drew as her daughter Amy and no one complaining now that Ethel looked too girlish for the mother Alice. In fact, many thought *The Twelve Pound Look*, played as a curtain raiser, referred to Ethel's new bulk. And yet the role of Kate in Barrie's one-act drama of female emancipation became Ethel's signature role: Kate, the woman who earns twelve pounds to buy herself a typewriter and independence from her obtusely arrogant husband, Harry Sims. "How quickly you do it!" says the new Lady Sims, watching Kate's fingers flash at the keys. "It must be delightful to be able to do something, and to do it well." Not only delightful but essential to a woman's survival, Ethel knew. She undertook to bring Kate's message of economic independence to the women and men of America. She was rewarded by the opinion that in *Alice* and *The Twelve Pound Look* she had again carried off the acting honors of the year by being "so good, so perfect, that any mere words seem almost inadequate. Suffice to say that one is glad to be alive in the same generation which produced an actress such as Ethel Barrymore."

She also did a bit of Barrie fluff called *A Slice of Life*. Frohman had almost died laughing over it in London, and Ethel too thought it brilliant, but, more important, "Jack came back to me for this play," she said, betraying in eight words her adoration for her younger brother. While they were rehearsing that January 1912, Frohman was holed up in the Hotel Knickerbocker with rheumatism that made movement agony. When he could stand it no longer, he would send a message to the Empire: "Send Ethel over to rehearse, I want to forget my pain." And the suffering man would double up with laughter at the antics of Jack and Ethel as Mr. and Mrs. Hyphen-Brown, a couple who are at last forced to admit that neither has had the exotic sexual past they've pretended.

Audiences doubled up as well. After the January 19 opening, the usually telegraphic Frohman wrote effusively to Barrie:

> . . . I just want to tell you that there is absolutely no comparison, in performance, as the play is given here and the way it was given in London. . . . Ethel Barrymore never did better work. Her emotional breakdown, her tears, her humiliation—when she confesses to her husband that she had been a good woman even before she met him—all this is managed in a keener fashion, and with

even a finer display of stage pathos than she showed in her fine performance in *Mid-Channel*.

As for the husband, Jack Barrymore is every inch a John Drew. He feels, and makes the audience feel, the humiliation of his position. When he confesses, it is a terrible confession. . . . So these artists step out in the light—before a houseful of great laughter; one feels that they have struck the true note of what you meant your play should have.

At the end of March Ethel went to Mamaroneck to wait for her baby, giving birth on April 30 to a girl. Lionel and Jack were not on hand to usher in this baby, but reporters called and Dr. Danforth answered the telephone. When Ethel came out of the ether she found to her horror that he had told the press that the baby's name was Ethel. She claims it was too late to contradict him, but that is nonsense; she must have felt some pleasure in having a namesake. Still, she herself firmly substituted for her daughter the generic name "Sister."

AFTER *The Fortune Hunter* everyone had expected Jack Barrymore to expand his stardom in bigger and better plays. Instead he had gone right back to light comedies like *Uncle Sam*, "a real scream" to many but to the distinguished *New York Times* critic Alexander Woollcott "an obscenely witless opiate." Jack next sauntered charmingly through *Half a Husband*, then left with Katherine for Los Angeles for five weeks of summer stock in the equally light *On the Quiet, The Honor of the Family*, and *The Man from Home*. His enormous popularity continued. He had only to open his mouth and the audience gratified him by laughing. But he was only treading water, doing the debonair young blade in third-rate vehicles he could act without thinking. *The Affairs of Anatol* in New York in the autumn of 1912 was better: Arthur Schnitzler's sophisticated, picaresque tale of an Austrian bon vivant. Though Jack was thoroughly American, he brought to Schnitzler his deft timing, his grace, his insouciance. Many thought Jack's performance the most brilliant comedy they had seen in years.

During these years Jack had many imitators, of course, but one lookalike in particular amused himself by dawdling along Broadway twirling a cane and tugging his mustache, frequently fooling even Jack's acquaintances. Apparently it was easy to be Jack Barrymore—except for Jack. "What the hell has happened?" he'd asked Lionel after the smash success of *The Fortune Hunter*. *"Who am I?"*

Marriage had only intensified the confusion. He had his madonna and found she expected romantic passion. Contrary to rumor and appearance, Jack felt vastly insecure in the boudoir. One-night stands were not a problem: he had hit upon the trick of giving out a "banshee screech" at his moment of climax, so unnerving a strange partner that she forgot she'd not had her own. But sex as developing intimacy, trust, or love was beyond this insecure egotist.

To his horror he discovered that Katherine expected the kind of romantic treatment he gave his leading ladies, but Jack had no intention of fascinating his wife as he fascinated female audiences. Even the greatest thoroughbreds, he explained, don't gallop away from the racetrack. He found himself developing a passionate fondness for a pipe, slippers, and a good book; the more Katherine wanted a night on the town or a soiree with her society friends, the more he craved solitude. And then her profound vacuity! Had he ever thought her bright and amusing? He scornfully christened her "the Mental Giantess" and fled to his male turf of bars and clubs where a man could find real companionship.

Rather a normal marriage, perhaps. But Jack Barrymore was far from normal: he was impossible to live with because he could not live with himself. Many have tried to analyze the torment that drove this brilliant young man to self-hatred, suicidal drinking, and escape from the love he craved. The most percipient was Mercedes de Acosta, a friend who understood the devastating conflict in Jack between his "masculine" and "feminine" natures. Many geniuses are androgynous: Shakespeare, Shaw, Chaplin, Garbo. Jack's androgyny was the source both of his great gifts and his equally great destructiveness. One critic would even divide his face into masculine forehead and nose, feminine mouth and chin, but the division went far deeper in the sensitive boy raised in a "man's man" world that taught him to be ashamed of any hint of vulnerability. To mask his vulnerability, he adopted a supermasculine pose: hard-drinking, profane, whoring, cynical. He lived in terror of being unmasked. It could happen any time, for example, when he got into a fight with a barber over a haircut in Los Angeles and the papers with enormous sarcasm announced JACK BARRYMORE MANAGES TO LICK SOMEONE AT LAST. Or when the comedian Arnold Daly called his Anatol "intermediately sexed," then "sissed it" in a take-off of Jack at the Palace. Or when another critic called his profile "epicene." Or if his barber revealed that his stage mustache was false.

Because he despised what he considered this "feminine" weakness, he could not love himself and therefore was unable to believe that anyone could love him. This was the source of his mad jealousy over any woman close to him. His fear of "feminine" weakness also goes far toward explaining his antipathy to acting. As Sarah Bernhardt said, acting is essentially a feminine craft. That is, the art of making up, display, emoting and, especially, yielding oneself completely to the audience-other has traditionally been the role of women rather than men. Add to this the feminizing of the American theatre at the turn of the century—the dominance of the actress and of plays for and about women—and one understands why Jack thought all acting "sissing it" and despised his natural talent. Lionel shunned sissy hero roles for rough, masculine character parts, but Jack was the beautiful romantic hero par excellence.

Though her acting ambitions had been furthered by appearances with Jack in *Uncle Sam, Princess Zim-Zim*, and *On the Quiet*, the uncomplicated Katherine was bewildered by her husband. She did not understand why he preferred solitude or the company of other men to hers. She did not understand why, when they did go out with friends, he would drift away to the bar for the evening or simply fall asleep in his chair. She rarely saw him: most nights he came home late, read until dawn, woke late the next afternoon, left for the theatre. She didn't understand the violent shifts from tenderness and gaiety to fury and contempt. Like many women, she'd thought she could change him; she discovered she had no influence at all. The more she pleaded, fought, and wept, the more he drank.

LIONEL WAS STILL TOURING the vaudeville circuit with Sidney and Gladys, their son, Sidney Rankin Drew, and Doris. He was making $850 a week (peanuts, however, compared to the $3,000 pulled in by top-billed stars) but finding that vaudeville audiences were extremely difficult to please. *Bob Acres*, a sketch from *The Rivals* with Uncle Googan as Bob and Lionel as Sir Lucius O'Trigger, drew only a few laughs from audiences who wanted something "snappy," though in Chicago Ashton Stevens recognized that "Lionel Barrymore can do virtually everything he attempts to do in the theatre. . . . I do not remember a performance of Sir Lucius quite so round and pat to Sheridan as Mr. Barrymore's is." Lionel had avenged his disastrous Thomas in Kansas City eighteen years before.

Aunt Gladys rescued them by writing *Stalled*, a witty modern sketch of an auto's breaking down on a lonely road, and if *Stalled* lacked Sheridan's immortal lines, vaudeville audiences liked it that way. Gladys came up next with *The Still Voice*, another "easy hit" with Lionel, still refusing romantic roles, playing a doctor and cousin Sidney as the young man Doris loves. An extraordinary cast: five (count 'em, five) members of the "celebrated Barrymore and Drew family." But then, just when they seemed to have found the formula, Uncle Googan and Doris flopped dismally in *A Model Young Man*. "Even Sidney Drew is expecting too much in asking its acceptance," said *Variety* severely.

But a revolution was brewing that would lure Lionel from a career as one of America's greatest, if unhappiest, stage actors. As if anticipating the devastating political upheaval that would sweep away an elitist culture, a handful of men were working to develop a new entertainment for the masses called (variously) the vitascope, the Kinetoscope, the nickelodeon, and finally the motion picture show. By 1910 there were at least 10 million moviegoers across the country; by 1916, 25 million fans would spend $735 million a year at the motion pictures. The flickering fast-paced action on the screen matched the new speed of life outside the movie palaces as honking automobiles elbowed horse-drawn vehicles from the avenues and trendies like Jack Barrymore and Bee Drew bunny-hopped and fox-trotted wherever they could find a patch of dance floor.

Interestingly, the coming of motion pictures also coincided with a renaissance in the theatre. As though pawning off its bad habits on the new medium of film, the theatre began to replace stereotyped characters and melodramatic plots with realism. Much of the new drama came from England in the greatest flood of talent since the Renaissance: Shaw, Wilde, Pinero, Jones, Synge, Yeats, Barrie, Granville-Barker, Maugham, Galsworthy—drama that Ethel and Jack, with their naturalistic styles, were particularly suited to act. But American dramatists like Elmer Rice, Ned Sheldon, Augustus Thomas, and Steele MacKaye were also turning American drama toward naturalism with realistic plays about American subjects like slums, racism, and women's rights.

Ironically, this new vitality in the theatre came in part from its release from bondage to the masses. The vast American public now went to the picture show for its thrills and chills, allowing the legitimate theatre to grow up. At the same time, the theatre became an elitist form of entertainment, the fate of any amusement superseded by entertainment with a broader appeal. (Eventually television would eliticize the movies, promoting them from mass entertainment to an art form studied in universities.)

The theatre reacted to motion pictures in several predictable ways. Most legitimate actors dismissed the movies as a crude mechanical form of entertainment that had nothing to do with the art of acting which—after all—depended chiefly on the art of speech. Underlying the scorn was fear, fear that grew as theatre managers across the United States began realizing that projection booths were cheaper than green rooms. Some theatre people were stoutly optimistic, like Daniel Frohman, who declared that "as long as civilization endures, the stage will form one of its chief sources of amusement"—though for safety, Frohman became a partner in a movie company. And then there was Lionel's point of view.

Bob Acres was not going over well in vaudeville; Lionel was broke as usual and still afraid of Broadway: "Perhaps I might have caught on again on the Broadway stage, perhaps not. At any rate, nothing rewarding was offered me and I had heard at the bars and at The Players of a new thing, motion pictures, for which an actor could work anonymously at easy hours and low pay. . . . I went down to 11 East Fourteenth Street to call on D. W. Griffith, whom I had met at lunch, and offered myself as a motion picture actor. . . . He looked me up and down, peering over that fine, cantilevered nose of his, and he said:

" 'I am not employing stage stars.'

" 'I am not even remotely any such creature,' I said. 'I will do anything. I mean absolutely anything. Believe me, I'm hungry. I want a job.'

" 'All right,' said Griffith, 'we'll put you on. You be here tomorrow afternoon at two o'clock in a dress suit.' "

Lionel would be humble indeed to doubt his catching on again on Broadway. Not only had he been recognized as an extraordinarily gifted actor since his 1902 performance as Giuseppe in *The Mummy and the Hummingbird*, but the Barrymore name was a sure job ticket. The movies appealed, however, to an actor terrified of forgetting his lines (though he was a remarkably quick study), to an actor who took three nights to get over an opening, to an actor who said, "No one more intelligent than a calf expects anything from audiences." To an actor who hid behind elaborate disguises (Griffith's actors had no names). To an actor who claimed he was constitutionally lazy. And finally to a man who took satisfaction in being a loner. He knew most legitimate actors despised motion pictures. He'd show Ethel.

But where were Ethel's cries of outrage when she discovered that "the genius of the family" (she'd called him that in print) had disgraced the Barrymore name? Vaudeville had been bad enough; movies were lower than low. But there was reason for Ethel's silence now.

Ethel not only needed to make more money with two children, Mamaroneck, and Russell to support, she was restive under Frohman's management. Other actresses had captured the limelight: Laurette Taylor in 1912 with 607 performances of *Peg O' My Heart*. Maude Adams, this time in Frohman's spectacle *Chantecler*. Billie Burke and Marie Doro, who had both become full-fledged Frohman stars. "I didn't like any of the plays that Mr. Frohman gäve me to read that summer [of 1912]," said Ethel, "and at last I went to him and suggested that I play *The Twelve Pound Look* in vaudeville. He threw up his hands in horror.

"I said, 'Why not? Irene Vanbrugh, who originally played the part in London, is playing it in the halls there. Bernhardt has played in vaudeville. Why all this snobbishness, or whatever it is, about it?' "

She might well ask. In a breathtaking turnabout, La Barrymore herself joined Martin Beck's Orpheum circuit. Compared with motion pictures, vaudeville suddenly looked quite respectable. Besides, vaudeville would pay her $3,000 a week—far more than Frohman could offer. And as attractive as the money was the opportunity of spreading the feminist word of *The Twelve Pound Look* to wider audiences. Times were changing, so must she.

At the end of 1912, therefore, Mummum might well have despaired. Jack seemed supremely content sauntering through silly comedies. Ethel shared the bill with trained seals and acrobats. Lionel was grinding out one-reelers. The inheritors of the American stage had deserted their post.

TEN

1912–1916

"FIVE DOLLARS!" said little Lillian Gish after making her first movie. "For doing so little!" Mary Pickford also agreed that movies were great between stage jobs: "I'm earning more than I ever have before—much more!" "I saw you in the picture play," said Frohman to his star Marie Doro. "What a lot of money you make!" And there is no use pretending that movies meant much more than easy money to the actors who gravitated to the decaying brownstone where D. W. Griffith and his cameraman Billy Bitzer ground out the one-reelers that were making cinematographic history.

Some of the Broadway actors who condescended to a few days' work at the Biograph studio treated the whole business with contempt. "But from the moment he stalked through D.W.'s door," said Mary Pickford of Lionel, "we liked him!" His very presence at Biograph reassured Lillian and Dorothy Gish: movies couldn't be too sinister if a Barrymore was involved. Lionel made his first picture, *The Battle*, in 1911 with Blanche Sweet, then *Friends* with Pickford in 1912. Despite studio opposition, Griffith had Bitzer move his camera in to shoot Mary waist-up, eliminating stereotyped posing and gesture but outraging the men who owned Biograph and didn't care about art: they paid Mary $100 a week and they wanted every inch of what they paid for. Loathing them, Griffith went ahead, his way.

Mary discovered she would need a different kind of make-up for a closer camera; Lionel discovered something else. "Am I really that fat?" he asked, staring at the pitiless camera's revelation. "I want you to tell me the truth, little girl." Mary told him. During the unhappy years—the frustrated painting, his daughters' deaths—Lionel packed 260 pounds on his five-eleven frame. Now he began to cut down on the beer, frequent gymnasiums, and jog around the Central Park reservoir sweating under four layers of wool. Since he couldn't melt overnight, Griffith cast him literally as a heavy.

Griffith had a stable of performers chosen to portray the five standard ingredients of the one-reeler: Heart Interest, Drama, Danger, Comedy, Rescue. Blanche Sweet, Claire McDowell, Florence Lawrence, and Mae Marsh were Heart Interests, but Lillian Gish and Mary Pickford were more important because they photographed "young." Henry B. Walthall, Owen Moore, and Bobby Harron were Heroes to the Rescue. Lionel, Harry Carey, Donald Crisp, and James Kirkwood provided Drama, Danger, and Comedy—though Lionel, said Lillian Gish, could play any part.

Miming broadly before viewers spellbound in darkness, the actors in these early films remained anonymous until 1910 when "The Biograph Girl" won billing at a competitive studio as Florence Lawrence and became the first screen star. Griffith remained the star at Biograph. In a wide-brimmed desperado hat, with piercing blue eyes and a bony prow of a nose, he was everywhere—brainstorming a whole movie on the spot, driving his actors, constantly experimenting. A lifelong student and appreciator, Lionel recognized that Griffith was reaching for new forms for a new art that was evolving day by day. Many of the one-reelers Lionel made with Griffith were uninspired, Lionel fighting endlessly identical battles until, his number up, he bit the dust with appropriate agony. Of the twenty-one films he made in 1912, however, he recognized one as superior.

For twenty-five dollars Griffith bought the script of *The New York Hat* from a schoolgirl who signed herself A. Loos—Anita, who would write the classic *Gentlemen Prefer Blondes*. Cast as a New England minister, Lionel vindicates his reputation when he proves to his outraged congregation that he bought little Mary Pickford a fancy hat not to corrupt her but because her dead mother had left him money to buy her daughter "little bits of finery from time to time." Inspired by something fresh in the story, Griffith wanted the camera in closer than ever. When Bitzer was reluctant, Griffith sent out for beer: "Two bottles," said Bitzer, "brought the camera almost as close as he was trying to get it." Theatre audiences had to reach out with their senses across a fixed space toward life-sized actors. When Mary Pickford's tear-stained face suddenly filled the screen, the movies found their power. A machine could create life larger than life itself.

Griffith respected the legitimate stage and felt deeply the conflict between it and the motion picture, but he also recognized his calling. Overhearing an actress sneer at "flickers," he exploded. She wasn't working in some third-rate theatrical company now, he told her. "What we do here today will be seen tomorrow by people all over America—people all over the world! Just remember that the next time you go before the camera!" Lillian Gish was one of the performers Griffith could leave trembling; Lionel tried to comfort her. It wasn't so long ago, he explained, that Griffith himself had talked scathingly of "flickers" and "galloping tintypes." But now he was convinced that he was pioneering in a new art. That was why he drove his players—and himself—so hard.

CAST AS FATHER, son, uncle, nephew, minister, Union soldier, wagon driver, woodsman, cattle buyer, bartender, farmer, business backer, doctor, bandit, desk sergeant, policeman, ranchero, Japanese ambassador, counterfeiter, bum—even lover, Lionel acted in fifty-six Biograph films as well as directing five and writing three. In the 1913 *Just Gold* he is still overweight, mimes by rubbing his chin or running his hand vigorously over his hair. Compared to the exaggeration of much early film acting, however, Lionel's is usually restrained and believable. Griffith must have been satisfied, yet Lionel didn't stick with Griffith after the director broke with Biograph in 1914. Why didn't Lionel follow a pioneer whose vision he acknowledged?

The answer may be as simple as Lionel's not wanting to pull up stakes in the East: Griffith was moving to California. Money was also undoubtedly a factor. Griffith liked his actors anonymous, choosing not to rely on Broadway stars to draw audiences. Griffith knew that if actors had their names publicized they would demand more money, and Griffith worked a tight budget, paying even himself only a modest sum. After *The New York Hat* Mrs. Pickford had demanded $300 a week for Mary. Griffith wouldn't pay it; five years later Mary was commanding a weekly $10,000. In a good week when Griffith bought one of his scenarios like *The Burglar's Dilemma*, Lionel might hand in a voucher for $125—a pittance compared to what he made in vaudeville. He might make more at another studio. Finally, personalities inevitably came into play. Griffith was a molder, coaching every movement of actresses like Pickford and Gish. Lionel was a seasoned actor whom Griffith was forced to leave to his own devices, a Drew-Barrymore who'd had his name in lights on a Frohman marquee.

Then too Lionel was not passionately committed to motion pictures like Griffith and his followers, perhaps even rather ashamed of them. Though Mary Pickford spoke of Lionel stalking through the front door, Raoul Walsh, also acting at Biograph, remembered Lionel sneaking down the alley to the studio and coming in the back way because he didn't want anyone to see him. And there was a frustrating lack of power to movie acting compared to stage. Mrs. John Drew had had ultimate power as manager, director, and actress. Managed by Frohman, Ethel had less but still personally commanded her audiences. But between the movie actor and autonomy stood not only the studio but the director and the camera, moving him two squares further from control. So Lionel stuck with the movies for the extra money they put in his pocket and the relief they gave him from arduous stage appearances, drifting from Klaw-Erlanger to Vitagraph, Kinetophote, World Film, Life Photo, Pathé—while Griffith the visionary went on to make *The Birth of a Nation* and *Intolerance*.

LIKE MOST LEGITIMATE actors who "descended" to vaudeville, Ethel had nothing but praise for her fellow performers and audiences. Vaudeville sharpened the wits, she declared. You were only a turn between the slack-wire artists and the performing seals: if you didn't hit the wire or catch the ball on your nose, your act was dead. Vaudeville was also democratizing: everyone was a star and no one. (Yet La Barrymore would have been furious had she not headed the bill.) Vaudeville was also lucrative: it was exciting to open your envelope every Saturday and find $3,000, though it melted just as fast as $500. And it was wonderful to be reunited with Suzanne Sheldon in *The Twelve Pound Look*, Suzanne whom she'd rescued after the handsome British actor Henry Ainley had walked out on her the year before. If not for the fatal telegram, would Suzanne be happily married to the Australian sheep rancher? Ethel prayed not.

Most satisfying was spreading the word of *The Twelve Pound Look*. "Don't think me gushing or sentimentalizing," Ethel told an interviewer. "On the contrary, I'm the most practical of persons. But when I speak those lines of Barrie I feel as if I were preaching a sermon to every married man and woman in the world. I just have to get that message across." She did—rudely waking thousands of husbands from a deep sleep of complacency, galvanizing an equal number of weary wives. She woke critics and audiences as well to the new depth of her acting. "In 'The Twelve Pound Look,'" wrote Alan Dale, "all her latent emotionalism emerged. How many times I saw that admirable little sketch! Night after night I used to watch it, just as much for the sake of Ethel Barrymore as for its intrinsic value. No trace of the old ingenue now remained."

That spring of 1913 the papers were also full again of Ethel on motherhood: "Motherhood the Greatest Joy . . . Ethel Barrymore Wonders How People Can Get Along Without Children . . . Childless Homes a Tragedy," and so forth. This was important to assert not only because she was pregnant again but because she did much of her mothering "by wire"—a "very practical method," she insisted. She had rented a house on Sixty-first Street for the family when she was in New York, however, and had another wonderful nurse, a big, stolid Swede named Ida. Russell also cooperated, at least for the cameras, dandling Sister on his knee with Ethel saying in the caption, "You see, Russell is exceedingly domesticated." Of course motherhood was important. If it wasn't, then her marriage was a sham, a tragedy, a sick joke.

On September 6 Ethel was prominent in an orchestra chair at the Casino Theatre. On September 9 John Drew Colt (Jackie) was born. Like Mummum and Georgie, Ethel had now produced three heirs to the great tradition. She even had an Ethel and a Jack—Lionel left out in the cold again. And she herself did not let down the great tradition for a moment. Two hours after Jackie was born she was on the telephone.

"I will be ready for rehearsals very soon and I have an awfully nice little boy."

Strangling noises on the other end. "It is impossible for you to be talking!" cried Charles Frohman.

Ten days later she was on the stage of the Empire rehearsing *Tante.* Not only the great tradition but competition goaded her: Elsie Ferguson had emerged as an appealing new emotional actress, Billie Burke had had her greatest success with Pinero's *"Mind-the-Paint" Girl.* More important, despite the first-night agony of nerves, acting was her life—her escape: there was "a blessed sanctuary, every night, in those two and a half hours in the theatre." John Drew had the privilege of opening every Broadway season at the Empire; Ethel now followed him on October 28 as Madame Mercedes Okraska—"Tante."

As Tante, Ethel had to play the piano and she played it, said the young British actor James Dale in the audience, "like an angel or an expert." To him she was unforgettable: "her hands poised over the keyboard ready to pounce unerringly, melodiously, her neck arched like a swan, her scowl fixed upon the ivory keys." She intrigued him immensely. "I hoped that she was not suffering actually, though she seemed to be doing neck exercises: she would duck her chin, then all of a sudden stretch it so that it stared at the ceiling. The rusty vowels would crawl stiffly out of that so welcome voice, ignoring their attendant consonants. . . . I did not know what I was watching, but I was fascinated by it. It was so alone, so private, so exotic. She was a new experience entirely. She was being someone. But who? A highly complicated state of soul seemed to be seething behind the bridge of the Grecian nose which made, with the eyebrows, a letter 'T,' a capital 'T' of course."

She was suffering. That year [her 1921 deposition would say] Russell struck her several times in a New York hotel, as a result of which brutal treatment she suffered nervous shock and required medical treatment. In defiance she clung closer to the children, delighting to hug little Sammy when he asked, after listening to "Little Miss Muffet," "But where was her mother?" To comfort him after the children all flew away in *Peter Pan*, when he cried, "Where do that mother and father think those children *are?*" And the more she clung to the children the more resentful Russell became in the face of this overwhelmingly virtuous wife and mother. In a Kinemacolor film made that autumn of 1913 of "theatrical personalities as they appear in private," Ethel and Sammy are smiling, Russell is not. That was the year, said Ethel witheringly, that "Russell discovered bronchitis and decided it was necessary for him to spend the winters in Palm Beach."

Perhaps because her private life was in shambles, Ethel took the drastic step in January 1914 of signing a contract for a reputed $10,000 with All Star Feature Corporation to make a motion picture called *The Nightingale* written especially for her by Augustus Thomas. For this story of a young woman's rise from street singer to diva she had as a romantic lead Conway Tearle, a handsome actor who had toured with her in *Mid-Channel* in 1910, the year her marital difficulties first erupted into print.

Few actresses were better known or loved, but Ethel was not really a natural for motion pictures in 1914. She was going on thirty-five when the brutal camera of the day photographed so old that even the teenage Lillian and Dorothy Gish asked to be filmed at dawn or dusk when the lens was kinder. And Ethel was decidedly overweight: with each baby she'd put on pounds she hadn't bothered afterward to shed. "Just to satisfy the public," the *Dramatic Mirror* pleaded, "I wish she would train down a bit. Those comments, 'matronly,' 'heavier,' 'quite a big woman now,' 'stout,' are not pleasant. . . . Other actresses may acquire avoirdupois, and the addition may be accepted humorously. But in the case of Miss Barrymore it is really resented."

And the motion pictures in 1914 were not really satisfactory vehicles for Ethel Barrymore. Early silent film genres were predominantly masculine: melodramas, spectacles, shoot-'em-up westerns, slapstick comedies. It was impossible to transfer the kind of subtle verbal dramas that Ethel acted onstage to the silent screen. And yet such was her immense charm and magnetism that *The Nightingale* did not hurt her career, perhaps because the movies and the theatre were such different spheres. Yet there would be fierce competition: "Why pay a dollar to see Ethel Barrymore," a Boston movie house would advertise when Ethel was in town onstage, "when you can see her in pictures for a dime?"

As if in recoil she fled from All Star Feature to the past: the red velvet and gilt Empire, Uncle Jack, and an old carpenter-made play by the once popular Victorien Sardou. It was delightful to play with Uncle Jack again and not carry a tray; Uncle Jack who, with his thirty-two-inch waistline, *could* have been in movies but humorously declined to risk second billing to Flash the Wonder Dog. After Russell, Uncle Jack's old-fashioned courtesy was a healing: who else would have insisted she take his number one dressing room. Naturally she refused. When he was not playing, perhaps, but never when he was there—

"Nonsense," said Uncle Jack, "it's where you belong."

Belong she did, playing Suzanne de Ruseville with such deft comedy that retrieving *A Scrap of Paper* from the dramatic dustbin actually seemed worthwhile. Certainly it was worth a great deal to see the uncle's urbane, brittle comedy parried by the niece's ripe charm. Delicious as Ethel was, however, critics could not resist little jabs at her weight. The *Star*, for example, claimed, "Miss Barrymore, as Suzanne, is handsomer than ever—in fact, a little more so, because there is a little more of her."

Back to vaudeville in *Drifted Apart*, such "a weak, rickety vehicle" about a husband and wife still in love but growing inexorably apart that it was nothing short of a miracle the way she tore people's hearts. Then finally she could retreat to Mamaroneck and the children. This time, Ethel had heard the critics: she launched into a strict regime of riding, swimming, and dieting. When Russell joined her, his bronchitis temporarily cured, a slim and radiant Ethel could almost believe that her marriage might be saved.

Actually they had a strong bond in their love of society and sports: had they not been wife and husband they might have been good friends. Ethel was passionate about boxing, baseball, tennis, and polo. ("I might have liked football, but I always had Saturday matinees and couldn't get to games.") IN FOUR HOURS I SHALL BE IN THE DEGRADING ACT OF ENTRAINING FOR LINCOLN, NEBRASKA, she had telegraphed one midnight to Ashton Stevens at his newspaper office. MEANTIME WILL YOU PLEASE WIRE ME HOW MANY ROUNDS AND WHO WON TONIGHT'S FIGHTS? YOURS FOR THE HIGHER EDUCATION OF WOMEN, E.B. She knew the batting averages and pitching records of every player in the major leagues; during the World Series she hung over her radio. So rabid was her enthusiasm for these competitions—far more rabid than her brothers'—that they seemed outlets for an aggression she could not exercise in her own life. Though she drove a mean tennis ball and loved a game of poker.

That summer, she thought as she and Russell watched the graceful

Davis Cup players in white flannels move back and forth on velvet green courts under the bright blue sky, seemed more perfect and peaceful than any summer before. Or was it only so in retrospect? For most Americans the war did not begin until America entered three years later. For Ethel, whose English ties were strong, the war began that fourth of August when the country she loved declared war against the Central Powers and began to send a generation of its best young men to die.

Nearly all the young men Ethel had known went bravely to give their lives "by a chivalry for which the new world had no use." Some Americans also responded. Dick Davis, watching from a window of the U.S. embassy in Brussels, sent back his famous description of the gray German armies cutting Brussels in two "like a river of steel." Her dear friend the journalist Herbert Bayard Swope left for Berlin from where he sent back ominous reports of German U-boat sinkings. Her cousin Sidney Rankin Drew volunteered for the Lafayette Escadrille. And that autumn Russell left to drive an ambulance in France, where he could be someone besides Ethel Barrymore's husband. Clearly he was happier when they were apart.

She found it easy the following January 1915 to play Berthe Tregnier in *The Shadow*, the barren wife who discovers that her beloved husband and her best friend are lovers with a child. For the entire first act Berthe is a paralytic sitting motionless in a chair; that too was not hard. But the height of emotion comes with Berthe's lament that she has been denied the greatest joy in the world: the joy of having a child in the image of the one she loves, that she might crush it to her heart.

"What is Mama crying for?" asked six-year-old Sammy anxiously from the wings. In the house both star and audience were awash.

"Your mother is not really crying, Sammy," said Ethel's maid.

"She must be crying," said Sammy, "or else why are those tears on her face and dress?"

"They are not real tears, my dear," said the maid soothingly. "Now come with me and we'll play soldier."

"I don't *like* acting," said Sammy, led sobbing away.

Ethel herself never could utter Berthe's words about the child without crying; sometimes she could not stop for ten minutes afterward, try as she would. And yet, she told herself, she was not at all like Berthe Tregnier. She was furious when people said, "Poor Ethel Barrymore, she must have a miserable life at home or she couldn't be so sad on the stage." She kept—had always kept—her private and theatrical emotions strictly separate. And yet Berthe Tregnier so fit her mood that people were saying it was by far her best performance. She did not know that it was to be her last at Charles Frohman's Empire Theatre.

The Shadow fit Frohman's mood as well. In constant pain, walking only with a cane he called "my wife," he felt his own failing powers sapped by the terrible changes the war was making. The Jewish boy from Sandusky, Ohio, who had adopted the code of the British gentleman in his private and personal dealings now saw his world being swept away: a world of manners, taste, and ethics that for him—as for the Drews and Barrymores—had been personified by British culture. For Frohman the war became an obsession.

"You and I have seen our period out," he told his intimate, Paul Potter. "What comes next on the American stage? Cheap prices, I suppose. Best seats everywhere for a dollar, or even fifty cents, musical shows excepted. Authors' royalties cut to ribbons; actors' salaries pared to nothing. Popular drama—bloody, murdererous—ousting drawing-room comedy. Crook plays, shop-girl plays, slangy American farces, nude women . . ."

"And then?"

"Chaos. Fortunately you and I won't live to see it."

With this black mood upon him, yet outwardly stoical and even cheerful, Frohman chose to book passage on the *Lusitania*, scheduled to sail the first of May. He greeted all protests serenely. "As far as I am concerned," he told Sothern and Marlowe, "when you consider all the stars I have managed, mere submarines make me smile." He had been uncannily able to predict hits and stars; some premonition now touched his actions these last days. When Marie Doro came to say goodbye, Frohman was leafing through a little red pocket notebook. "Queer," he said, "but the little book is full. There's no room for anything else." Usually telegraphic, he wrote warm and unexpected notes to acquaintances, adding to a routine communication to John Drew, "Our last talk before you left for the West gave me much happiness." Ethel too had premonitions, feeling a sudden urge to see him before he sailed.

"What are you doing here, Ethel?" said C.F. when she appeared unexpectedly from Boston the morning of April 26. As usual he was indulging in a box of his favorite Smith's Delicious Cream Patties made in St. Paul.

"I thought I would come down to say good-by, Mr. Frohman." (She always called him "Mr. Frohman.")

"They don't want me to go on the boat," said C.F. There had been mysterious letters and phone calls; even Franz von Papen, the German military attaché in Washington, had warned him off the *Lusitania*. But Barrie had begged him to come over early to help save a failing play. He couldn't let Barrie down.

As Ethel lingered they talked of the old days and the stars he had made: Georgie Drew Barrymore, John Drew, Lionel, and of course his shining Ethel. When she said goodbye he kissed her cheek, something he had never done before, and she saw tears glistening in his eyes. That night in Boston just before she went on there was a telegram: NICE TALK, ETHEL. GOOD-BY. C.F. John Drew had sent his own message to Frohman, calculated to match his manager's nonchalance: IF YOU GET YOURSELF BLOWN UP BY A SUBMARINE I'LL NEVER FORGIVE YOU.

Directing his own last curtain, a showman to the end, Frohman refused a place in the lifeboats that May 7 when the *Lusitania* was struck broadside by a torpedo off the Head of Kinsale eight miles from the Irish coast. While others clutched at life belts, Frohman puffed a cigar. "Why fear death?" he told his companions. "Death will be an awfully big adventure." The words were scarcely said when the ship lurched and a huge cliff of water hurled him away to drown with 1,197 others.

The line was from *Peter Pan*. "All I would ask is this," Frohman had once said of his epitaph: " 'He gave *Peter Pan* to the world and *Chantecler* to America.' It is enough for any man." Both plays were Maude Adams's, the only Frohman actress who had dedicated herself to the theatre as wholly as he. After her mentor's death, Maude played *Peter Pan* and *The Little Minister* as he had arranged before he sailed, but though she lived until 1953, her fabled career essentially ended when Charles Frohman died.

Ethel was attending a luncheon for Elsie Ferguson in Chicago when she was called to the telephone. She returned to the table, stricken. For the rest of the afternoon she and Elsie just kept looking at each other and saying "Mr. Frohman . . . Mr. Frohman." God had died. "For many years he had been my very best friend," said Ethel. "He had taken the place of parents and I had gone to him with not only my theatre troubles, but all my troubles. . . . Nothing was ever quite the same after that for me."

Yet Frohman probably would not have survived a postwar theatre that rejected his Barries, Fitches, and Pineros as old hat. He had already been learning with much cost that the public wanted strong drama, intrigue, action, sex. He had been feeling out of touch with public taste for years. "I'm all in," he'd said to Paul Potter. "The luck is against me. The star system has killed my judgment. I no longer know a good play from a bad. The sooner they scrap me the better."

With his usual acumen but without his old energy, Frohman had sensed the shift on Broadway from personalities to plays. Certainly the theatre would still have stars: Laurette Taylor, Helen Hayes, Katharine

Cornell, the Lunts, and John Barrymore were in the wings. But the biggest stars would no longer be the creation of the theatrical manager but of a studio, a director, and a camera. Motion picture stars by virtue of their mass appeal and circulation would obscure theatrical stars.

That summer of 1915 Russell came back from France because he did not like being called an *embusqué* (danger-dodger) by men often facing less hazard than he. He left almost immediately for a month of military training while Ethel stayed with the children at Mamaroneck. She didn't much care: "It was at such periods that my children and I would have uninterrupted good times." That winter, she knew, he would go to Palm Beach for his "bronchitis." She tried not to care; and she had a new play that she liked.

After her tragic Berthe Tregnier, Frohman had shrewdly chosen *Our Mrs. McChesney* as a complete contrast—and his agenda would be carried out by his loyal lieutenant Alf Hayman as though he were still chewing his cigar in his office at the Empire. Edna Ferber's stories about a traveling petticoat saleswoman had been sensationally popular; Frohman himself had summoned Ferber from Chicago to turn the stories into a play. But Ferber, fashioning a play for the grand Ethel Barrymore and America's foremost management, wasn't happy.

She thought the play that she was writing in collaboration "clumsy, inept, and spiritless." She found the manners of the director Augustus Thomas, who insulted everyone but Ethel Barrymore, boorish. And she didn't think the part right for Ethel. "Emma McChesney was crisp, alert, businesslike, magnetic. Ethel Barrymore was glamorous, beautiful, the aristocrat, the star who was just right in English drawing-room plays." Disliking everything about the production, Ferber however succumbed to Ethel's spell.

"At rehearsals Ethel Barrymore behaved like an angel," said Ferber. "She was tireless, uncomplaining, never demanding. She never tried to steal a line or a scene. Everyone in the company adored her. I had heard stories of her brilliant wit, and they were true. She took direction gratefully." From Ethel, Ferber learned how a star might conduct herself in the theatre—might, because Ferber never again encountered anyone like her.

On the road tryout Ethel played Sibelius to the company on a smeary hotel piano with her blunt-fingered, almost masculine hands. She carried a large flat scarlet box of Pall Malls everywhere, chain smoking. Cigarettes did not seem to affect the wonderfully throbbing voice, the amazingly fine poreless skin. And they were absolutely essential for tryout night nerves in Atlantic City.

That day Ethel begged Ferber to come round to her apartment in the Shelburne Hotel because she couldn't bear to be alone. There were one or two others there and Ethel stuck her head out of the bathroom door to greet them. Her hair was all about her shoulders, she clutched a towel in her hand, and her face was dripping with water "like a morning glory with the dew on it." She insisted on going out. She couldn't digest anything and she couldn't sit still. They spent the afternoon going up and down the Boardwalk, and Ethel bought hat after hat—nothing she would ever wear. Between purchases she would excuse herself to go vomit. Naturally the tryout went beautifully, but that didn't help Ethel opening night, October 19, at the Lyceum in New York.

"She was terribly nauseated," said Ferber, with her in her dressing room before the curtain. "Between seizures she went on carefully making up. The call boy made his rounds. Half-hour, Miss Barrymore! . . . Mr. Frank, the house manager, came round to report on the Names in the house. . . . Fifteen minutes, Miss Barrymore! She looked like one waiting for the tumbrel to take her to the guillotine. . . . Overture, Miss Barrymore! . . . First-act curtain, Miss Barrymore!"

Ethel rose, searched her face one last time in the brilliantly lit mirror, made a last dab with her rabbit's foot, stood in the wings setting herself, threw over her shoulder a "gay desperate self-amused look," and walked on with a group of traveling men, her little suitcase in her hand.

At least one critic agreed with Edna Ferber that glamorous Miss Barrymore had little to do with snappy Mrs. McChesney. But the public as usual adored her, and Ethel herself was so elated at playing a business-woman that she began thinking of producing her own plays. *She* thought she was Emma McChesney to a T: "For the first time in my career I am almost acting myself."

As happy as she was with *McChesney*, however, Ethel went back to movies, hitting the screen as her tour ended in April 1916 in *The Kiss of Hate* accompanied by the announcement that she had signed a four-picture contract with Metro-Rolfe at $40,000 a film. Critics called *The Kiss of Hate* "a piece of melodramatic junk" that did more than $40,000 damage to her reputation; yet Ethel this year came out publicly on the side of the movies. From the office of Metro Film Corporation came the improbable news that Miss Ethel Barrymore had abandoned the stage. "She believes in pictures," swore the article, because "in them she believes she has a larger field for her art than the stage." Ethel did not counter the lie.

Perhaps one reason was that D. W. Griffith's first feature-length film, *The Birth of a Nation*, had had an enormous impact on both the public and the motion picture industry, proving that the business of movie-making could be an art. More important, Frohman was gone, and with him security. But Ethel still disliked movies. She signed with Metro-Rolfe for the money. If her marriage to Russell was indeed over, there was to be no question to whom the children belonged. This was the motive too behind the growing stream of assertions that career and motherhood were compatible, the increasing numbers of photographs of Mother Ethel flanked by her little brood. Filming in New York, moreover, allowed her to be conspicuously close to her children and home, as touring did not. Movies were useful.

NOT SURPRISINGLY, the Barrymore who had tagged along in the family profession chiefly for the "ice cream" had also discovered that motion pictures offered a double scoop. Jack made his film debut in 1914 in *An American Citizen*—or did he. A 1912 trade paper lists four Lubin Company films with "Jack Barrymore" in supporting roles. This itself seems dubious: why would John Barrymore, a star since *The Fortune Hunter*, settle for third billing with a third-rate company? On the other hand, how improbable the existence of two Jack Barrymores. Chances are that Jack did do a little moonlighting with the Lubin Company in Philadelphia, keeping—given the disreputability of the movies in 1912—his profile low. The puzzle is probably unsolvable: the films are missing, presumably destroyed when the Lubin vaults exploded and burned in 1914, and neither stills nor publicity releases have survived.

Jack made *An American Citizen* with Adolph Zukor's top-echelon Famous Players, formed in conjunction with Daniel Frohman to film "famous players in famous plays." Unlike Griffith at Biograph, Zukor recognized the drawing power of theatre stars; he also discovered, however, that favorites like James O'Neill, James K. Hackett, and Minnie Maddern Fiske lacked the appeal on screen that they had on the stage. Zukor thus had doubts about contracting John Barrymore until his director J. Searle Dawley told him, "Mr. Zukor, he's the best actor I've ever had the privilege to handle." Zukor signed Jack; Jack delighted movie audiences with an inimitable light touch that made a conventional romance "joyous." It was no coincidence that Ethel signed for her first film with All Star thirteen days later. Jack's success as a star, not Lionel's anonymous appearances with Biograph, persuaded her.

As Metro-Rolfe with Ethel, Zukor's office had Jack publicly declare motion pictures a superior art form to the theatre, more indicative of the infant industry's inferiority complex than of Jack's opinion. "The film determines an actor's ability, absolutely, conclusively," Jack was quoted.

"It is the surest test of an actor's qualities. Mental impressions can be conveyed by the screen more quickly than vocally. The moving picture is not a business. It is an art." Later Jack would say that making silent movies was like "making frantic and futile faces to try to express unexpressible ideas—like a man behind a closed window on a train that is moving out of a station, who is trying, in pantomime, to tell his wife, on the platform outside, that he forgot to pack his blue pajamas and that he wants her to send them to him in care of Detwiler, 1032 West 189th Street, New York City." But then the contradictions between what Jack said publicly and privately about the movies would span his career.

When Jack was on the set Zukor found him "all business." The problem was getting him there. Al Kaufman, Zukor's brother-in-law, was usually delegated to storm Jack's apartment in Gramercy Park and argue him out of bed or, if he was up, argue him into the mood for film making. Sometimes Al returned from Gramercy Park alone. After a few days Zukor would then send the studio propman to comb the waterfront bars, beginning with Jack's favorite saloon on Twelfth Avenue. Jack's indifference inspired a lot of good stories. At the same time, his drinking—it was always the drinking—played havoc with studio finances.

As the drinking did with his marriage. "Their voices could be heard all over the building," said a resident at number 36. "When the contretemps became too frequent, several of the tenants held a meeting to discuss what must be done. It was eventually decided to write a letter of complaint to the landlord . . ." But the next day Jack, sober, and Katherine would emerge into the square arm in arm, and the letter never got mailed.

Then Jack would drink again. One night he picked up a two-handed medieval sword and went for her. Katherine ran from the apartment in her nightgown and hid in the small park where she could hear Jack pounding door to door and bellowing, "I want my wife!" The policeman she appealed to for help made sexual advances. She managed to fight him off, get back into the building, and eventually make peace with Jack. The next day, however, she took the sword to James Montgomery Flagg's studio for safekeeping.

Flagg, the popular illustrator, had known the Barrymores for years. "There never were such people on sea or land," he said. "They are the most charming humans, the most talented, the wittiest, the most delightful people ever given the bum's rush out of Heaven; and at the same time probably the most self-centered, spoiled, irresponsible leprechauns ever to crawl out of a hollow tree. It was like this. Either you took them as they were—or else!"

Flagg had sailed home from England on the *Deutschland* the summer

Ethel had been engaged to Harry Graham and Jack had been dated up for necking in the shadow of the lifeboats with a different girl every night. The captain had given a dinner in honor of Ethel's twenty-sixth birthday and *she* had given everyone presents. Next to Jack, thought Flagg, "Big Ethel" was the best company in the world. And now there was Katherine, to whom Jack had said "I will" when (thought Flagg) he should have said, "The hell I will!" Katherine was a decided temptation, though Flagg preferred Jack—Jack who would come to his studio afternoons to look through his art books ("He couldn't draw for nuts!") and leave the taxi meter ticking for hours. "As many-faceted as a fly's eye," thought Flagg. Lovable. Mad.

The Barrymores and Flagg and his wife Nellie always had a table Sunday evenings at the Claridge. Jack spent the pre-dinner hour swallowing double Dubonnets at the bar. When he finally sat down he would look at his dinner with a pop-eyed grin and wave it away. If he was feeling possessive, he would whip out a pocket handkerchief, grab Katherine by the chin, and savagely wipe off her lipstick. His attitude toward his wife was proprietary, bored, jealous, or amused. "She walks exactly like a cinnamon bear!" he confided to the Flaggs.

Fond as he was of Jack, Flagg saw his opportunity with the quarreling couple. The lecherous artist offered Katherine a shoulder to cry on, and more. Katherine spent more and more time in Flagg's studio; Jack, whose jealousy could flare without reason, this time had one. He confronted Flagg: "You've been living with my wife!"

"No, John," said Flagg ruthlessly. "You've been living with her. I've been sleeping with her."

Drunks do not make good lovers.

He retreated more than ever to hard-drinking pals like fellow actors Corse Payton and Jack Prescott; sometimes he would be missing for days at a time. Yet one very different kind of friend had gained more influence over him in the past year than either his drinking cronies or his wife.

This was the playwright Edward Sheldon, a young man with clear brown eyes and cheeks polished so rosy he might just have come in from ice skating. Sheldon was disarmingly modest, despite the fact that when Jack met him in 1911 he was the talk of Broadway with three important plays behind him. Sheldon's real genius, however, was for people. Anyone who spent an hour with Ned came away feeling inches taller. He had an instinct for seizing upon the best in people and making them live up to it. How someone in his early twenties could have achieved such self-confidence and spiritual poise was a mystery. He seemed almost too good to be true.

Ostensibly the wealthy, moral, straight-A Harvard man had nothing in common with the hard-drinking, unstable Jack Barrymore. That was the attraction. Carefully brought up by protective parents, Sheldon was irresistibly drawn to the glamour of the theatre—and if any actor exemplified that glamour it was Jack Barrymore. Conversely, Jack, undeceived by the glitter, longed for Ned's self-assurance. Mary Strong Sheldon, the remarkable mother to whom Ned was deeply attached, didn't like Jack and could not understand why Ned did. "What do you see in him?" she complained. "I like to be with him," said Ned flatly.

Besides, there were similarities. Both were dynamically imaginative with a huge flow of conversation about the most improbable subjects. Both were romantics, searching for the unobtainable ideal. And, like Ned, Jack could go out to people; more than Ned, seem to blend himself in others, even disappear. In fact Jack's outstanding ability was "to make *anyone* to whom he spoke or *listened* feel that that person was the only one in his immediate confidence, the only one to be entrusted at the helm." A feminine trick, an actor's trick—but one that made Ned feel he was the most important influence in Jack's life. And then Jack *could* show his tender side with Ned and not be hurt. With Ned he could show he was "silk."

They had met during the trial run of Sheldon's *Princess Zim-Zim* in Albany; Ned would drop by Jack's dressing room or after the performance they would go out for beer and talk. When *Zim-Zim* folded out of town, the friendship was transferred to Gramercy Park where Ned also had an apartment (indeed, that may be why Jack moved there), and to the Players Club, a stone's throw from their front doors. Jack was happy in Ned's bachelor digs: thick black carpets, book-lined walls, old prints, and for a splash of color, brilliantly plumed macaws on perches. As their friendship deepened, Ned's sense of mission grew. Was Jack really satisfied wasting himself on trifles like *Believe Me, Xantippe* and *The Yellow Ticket* when great parts like Hamlet waited? He owed it to the American theatre to stop wasting his gifts. There was nothing, Sheldon told him, he could not achieve.

In the summer of 1914 the men had a further bond. Sheldon had broken his engagement to the actress Doris Keane, saying, "I would make a very poor sort of husband for you, Doris," and had gone to Europe. Bored himself with summers of tennis, teas, and fox trotting, Jack spent obligatory weeks with Katherine at various holiday resorts, then rushed to Europe to meet Ned in the playwright's favorite city, Venice.

Jack had long nursed a taste for the Gothic, a taste reflected in his Bosch-like drawings, his love of stained glass and gargoyles and old furniture which he antiquated further by boring wormholes with an ice pick. Now the two romanticists had a glorious escape, riding in gondolas, prowling the city by dark, by day soaking themselves in the Gothic splendors of Santa Maria Glorioso dei Frari and the Ca' d'Oro. Then they went to Rome. They walked the Appian Way, gazed at the frescoes of Michelangelo, found Keats's grave and the resting spot of Shelley's heart in the little English Cemetery. And in Rome a new spirit seized Jack, a broader more generous spirit than Gothicism, a spirit that whispered of the nobility of the human spirit and imagination in tones very like those of Ned Sheldon. Intoxicated, exploring and discussing endlessly, the two went from Rome to Florence—to the Uffizi, the Ponte Vecchio, the Bargello Palace, to the cafés and bistros where red wine flowed into morning. The last night in Florence they were both too excited to sleep; finally it was Jack who proposed getting up into the cupola on top of the roof of the hotel to see the sun rise. In pajamas they scrambled through a trap door and onto the tiles, and there in the dissolving gray Florence emerged, its domes and crosses and river glittering in the sunlight as church bells began to peal. "All this seems highly improbable," said Jack, gazing in awe. But the summer with Ned had wakened in him the possibility of the improbable.

The next day they said goodbye, Ned starting for London, Jack for Paris where he intended to buy fox furs for Katherine as a peace offering. More pacifying to Katherine was a 51 percent interest and a role in Jack's new play that autumn at the Longacre. *Kick In* was not exactly what Ned Sheldon had imagined for his friend—one of Frohman's despised crook plays; yet the saga of Chick Hewes, a converted convict, gave Jack more to get his teeth into than any previous role. "People thought [Al] Woods was crazy to trust me with the part," said Jack: why try to make a poor character actor out of a good comedian? But Al Woods, an astute producer, guessed that Jack had both character and comedy, and Jack scored an even greater personal success in *Kick In* than he had in *The Fortune Hunter*.

Ned Sheldon wasn't satisfied, however, and came backstage to tell Jack so. "If I were you I should play a part without a bit of comedy in it," he advised. "As long as you do both comedy and straight work in one play, they will always think you a comedian."

Jack fingered his beloved mustache, signature of the gay Broadway blade. "I suppose I might try it," he said. "I could paste down my mustache."

Kick In ran into 1915 with 188 performances, but Jack seemed no closer to sacrificing his John Drew adornment. In fact he deliberately seemed to turn his back on Sheldon, returning to Famous Players to kick up his heels in the farcical *Are You a Mason?*, *The Dictator*, and *The Incorrigible Dukane*. In *Dukane*, the only one of the films to survive, Jack plays a construction company boss's no-good son who is sent West and made a man of almost in spite of himself. In the opening scenes Jimmy Dukane emerges from bed late in the afternoon in his shoes, vest, and underwear. He is not attractive. He shampoos in the shower while chugging whisky. Dressed at last and sporting the inevitable straw hat and boutonnière, he still does not charm. His face is puffy, his shoulders round, he slouches. His movements are nervous, jerky. And he does not know what to do with his hands, those strangely large, thick hands that Jack, comparing them to the rest of his finely wrought anatomy, always feared were an eruption of his ugly, darker nature. He looks old. And are his pigeon-toed walk and the acrobatic mayhem as he is kicked, hurled, trampled, chased, attacked, dragged, beaten, blown up, and knocked flat twenty-two times really very funny? Jack does not look a happy actor in *The Incorrigible Dukane*. There is a kind of furtive uneasiness about his playing. And yet according to the reviews, the movie was superior to many that year of 1915 and Jack Barrymore a popular comedian.

Ned did not give up on Jack, though his own situation might have driven everything else from his mind: he was finding it increasingly difficult to move without stiffness and pain. Doctors talked of a progressive, crippling arthritis probably linked to a systemic infection. Ned was only twenty-seven. His life had been magically blessed with fame, wealth, friends. Surely the stiffness that made walking, bending, and reaching agony would disappear when the infection was conquered. He could imagine nothing less. He turned back to the play he had been reading, John Galsworthy's *Justice*.

This story of the grinding mechanical "justice" meted out to a check-forging junior clerk had stunned London in 1910. So dispassionate and real was Galsworthy's depiction of office, courtroom, and prison that audiences felt they were not observers but part of the drama unfolding onstage. *Justice* was so real that Galsworthy was accused of being "cinematographic," that is, of having no art; it was so real that it inspired new demands for prison reform. But what intrigued Sheldon was the character of the junior clerk, William Falder.

"A pale, good-looking young man, with quick, rather scared eyes," Falder is no hero but an ordinary, weak, rather uninteresting clerk tending toward hysterics, with no scruples about trying to fasten blame for the forgery upon an innocent colleague. He has no great speeches; much of the time he is mute. But the moment when he raises his fists and beats helplessly against the door of his solitary cell is a moment of horror, and his suicide a tragedy. Sheldon put down the play haunted by the fate of the weak, sensitive, doomed man. Falder was just the part for his friend Jack Barrymore. The vulnerability of the two was the same. Forget Jack's drinking, his laziness, the voice that was shallow and thin, the slovenly diction. All these could be conquered if Falder could conquer Jack as he had Sheldon.

Ned contacted his Harvard friend John D. Williams, a producer formerly associated with Frohman and a man of independent taste and judgment. Williams too was ready to gamble; together they proposed the role of Falder to Jack. The light comedian fingered his mustache and swallowed hard.

Sheldon and Williams needed all their faith. In February, March, and April 1916 three more Barrymore films hit the movie palaces. In *Nearly a King* Jack played a jobless actor and the Prince of Bulwana. In *The Lost Bridegroom* he was smashed on the head and induced to rob his fiancée's home, a film *Variety* dismissed as cheap, trivial, and inconsequential except for Barrymore in the stellar role. *Variety* fell upon Jack himself in *The Red Widow*: his obsolete mugging and slapstick methods "a three-day 'nut' comedian would hesitate to use" turned the film into a low-class nickelodeon stunt. Jack himself called *The Red Widow* the worst movie ever made.

Meanwhile *Justice* was in rehearsal.

ELEVEN

1916–1917

INSPIRED BY *Justice* Jack stopped drinking absolutely. For the first time in his life he threw himself completely into creating a role, thinking himself into the mind of the timid little clerk William Falder while at the same time re-creating himself physically for the part. He adopted a quite flawless cockney accent. He became thinner, paler, a little stooped. He had his hair clipped short, leaving a little pat to stand out from the crown of his head. This pat had to stand out just a little, yet droop; he saw Falder as that kind of man. The British actress Cathleen Nesbitt, playing Ruth Honeywill, the woman for whom Falder changes a check from nine to ninety pounds, marveled at the completeness with which Falder subdued Barrymore. And yet at the same time Jack stood outside his creation, watching himself critically. He would never be the Great Actor of Lionel's definition. He was too conscious, and he had a sense of humor. But he was no longer the man who scoffed, "Acting—all you have to do is paint your nose red and go on."

Justice tried out in New Haven in March while Jack's latest farces convulsed movie audiences, then moved to New York for a few rehearsals before the opening. Unlike Ethel, Jack did not vomit from dread; instead, discovering huge posters in the lobby of the Candler Theatre with BAR-RYMORE blazoned across the top, he furtively pasted strips of paper over his name. If he failed, he would fail less conspicuously.

He did not fail. The night of April 3, 1916, marked an epoch not only in the career of Jack, who overnight emerged as the distinguished actor John Barrymore, but in the American theatre. *Justice* was a real play at last, and the audience *rose* to it. *Justice* marked a coming of age for Broadway; a new hope for the American theatre flared into being. And a new hope in John Barrymore. Here was a new kind of tragedian whose sincere and sensitive performance excited audiences intellectually as well as emotionally.

For the young Brooks Atkinson, looking down from the second balcony at John Barrymore acting Falder was "a little like looking at a flame." The "lean, handsome, magnetic" actor gave such "a burning performance" that Atkinson could feel the heat of it at the top of the house. Barrymore, he thought, "cut through the darkness of the theatre like a sharp, glittering penknife."

For Cathleen Nesbitt the most affecting moment of Jack's performance was his reply to the prosecuting attorney: "I keep thinking over and over again how it was I came to do such a thing and if only I could have it all over again to do different." Jack said it very simply, but to her it conveyed all the anguish of Lear's "Never, never, never, never, never!" and every night she wept at Falder's despair.

For some the scene of solitary confinement was almost unendurable. Falder paces his cell in his stocking feet trying to catch some human sound, sinks back into inertia, picks up his convict's work of making buttonholes in a shirt, drops it, springs up again to listen at the door, returns, picks up and stares into the lid of a tin of food as though trying to find a friend in his own face, drops the lid. Silence. Then gradually a dull beating sound on thick metal becomes audible. Suddenly the cell is flooded with light. As the sound swells, Falder creeps toward the door, his hands beginning to move as though his spirit has already joined the drumming protest of his fellow convicts in solitary. The sound crescendos. Raising clenched fists, panting violently, Falder flings himself at the door, hammering and hammering as the curtain falls.

Ethel would have played such a role six hundred times and looked forward to the six hundred and first. "I have played Zoe Blundell for months," she said back in 1910 of *Mid-Channel*, "and I have never gone on for a performance without making the effort to improve my work in it, to make it more real, more finished, more effective, and now after having played it for nearly two seasons I still feel that I am just started on it, that I could go on for years more without ever growing tired of it or feeling that there was nothing more for me to learn from it."

Brilliant actor though he was, Jack had no patience for endless refinement. As Falder began to bore him he began to invent little amusements for himself onstage. He was not the first: Ellen Terry giggled and whispered, Mrs. Patrick Campbell stuck pins into her leading men, John Drew conscientiously tried to break up his fellow actors. Now Jack began to play with the final scene: Falder lying dead and Cokeson, the senior clerk, saying to Ruth Honeywill, "Don't cry, my pretty. No one will touch him now, never again. He's gone to Gentle Jesus." O. P. Heggie, from the original British cast, had to say this dangerous line without a trace of

self-consciousness—impossible to do when Jack was muttering obscenities, pretending to squash cockroaches, or faking the onset of a sneeze.
Florence Reed in *The Yellow Ticket* had rung the curtain down on Jack
for just such fooling. Heggie warned Jack, then the next night walked
out before his curtain call, leaving a note that demanded an apology and
a written oath that Jack would in future behave.

"Tell the old boy I'll be good next week," said Jack lightly, but next
week there was no Heggie. After three days a chastened Jack had his
lawyer draw up an agreement, and Heggie returned to a bottle of truce
champagne from Jack, who never fooled again—at least in Heggie's
scenes.

Jack's stunning success in *Justice*, coupled with his new faith and growing self-confidence, caused him to break away that spring from what he
had outgrown. Katherine, the pretty socialite, had been the choice of
Jack Barrymore, the debonair matinee idol. John Barrymore was ready
to move on. He left 36 Gramercy Park to move in with Ned Sheldon,
the friend whose vision had changed the course of his career. When
Katherine pleaded for reconciliation, he was adamant: their temperaments
were too different. (That he had not left her after discovering her infidelity
with Flagg is surprising, considering his intense jealousy.) Ned concurred
with his decision, supported him—Ned who had renounced Doris Keane
at the advent of Jack. In June (having insisted on a break from *Justice*
before the fall tour) Jack accompanied Ned to Santa Barbara, where
doctors hoped the mild climate might ease the increasing stiffness in his
joints. Katherine tagged along, an outsider. When Jack left to join the
Justice tour, she stayed behind to establish the year's residence needed
for a divorce. She would sue for desertion.

Justice on the road was not the sensation it had been in New York:
Buffalo and Toledo did not seem to realize that a great American actor
had been born. The play was too heavy for popular taste: Grand Rapids
suggested that Jack might whip up business by autographing play copies
in a department store window. Yet the play's message was not lost. Wherever they played, the company was invited to tour the local prison. In
Boston they were shown the facility by such a charming and articulate
young man that Jack invited him to the play and supper afterward.

"I'm afraid I have two more years to do before I can accept any
invitations," said the young man.

"*You're* doing time?" stammered Jack. "Whatever for?"

"Forgery."

Another, more decisive, confrontation took place during the *Justice*
tour. Seasoned actors in the cast like Whitford Kane and Bertha Mann

saw that John Barrymore was the one man on the American stage with enough charisma to revive interest in the classical theatre. On trains, in roadhouses after the performance, these actors prophesied to Barrymore his great future. *Justice* was only a prelude to Romeo, Iago, Hamlet: the whole classical repertoire was his to command. Sipping nonalcoholic Bevo, Jack was suspicious, then noncommittal. They persisted. How could he in all conscience evade his destiny? At last Jack admitted that if it was a question of Shakespeare he was more interested in Richard III than in Hamlet. They cheered. "I like to think that we in the *Justice* company had something to do in persuading Barrymore to take his theatre more seriously," said Whitford Kane. Yet they might have prophesied that John Barrymore would never make a trouper. By November the monotony of the towns and the nightly repetition were driving Jack wild. Abruptly he canceled the tour and returned to New York.

If Jack thought he could forget what he had wrought in *Justice* and slip back into film mugging and pratfalls, however, he was mistaken. If he would not take his destiny into his hands, others would. One day the British actress Constance Collier appeared at Ned Sheldon's door clutching a much-rejected playscript of George du Maurier's novel *Peter Ibbetson*. Staging *Peter Ibbetson* had become for Constance an obsession. British managers had refused it; in America the story was the same. No Broadway producer wanted anything to do with an old-fashioned, feverishly romantic play about two lovers who defy separation and death by "dreaming true." Besides, the script was weak and the action impossible: how could the hero appear onstage in triplicate—lying on a sofa dreaming that he saw himself as a young man talking to the boy he had been. The public wouldn't buy it even if he could.

So Constance did what everyone did: she went to Ned. A du Maurier addict like herself, Ned saw the weaknesses immediately but just as immediately knew the play must be done—with John Barrymore as Peter Ibbetson. Constance had always seen Jack in the role but couldn't believe such a popular actor would be interested in a purely artistic venture. She left the play with Ned, who cut and reworked John Raphael's script until he felt he had a stageworthy vehicle; then he approached Jack.

"But I thought I was going to do *The Lonely Heart*," said Jack who, however, loved du Maurier's novel, which had also been Maurice's favorite.

"My play is not unlike this one in certain respects," admitted Ned. "The yearning of the dead to return to the ones they loved on earth."

"Well, then, let's do your play."

"No," said Sheldon, "Peter Ibbetson will be a better part for you."

But who could play the thankless, utterly unsympathetic role of Colonel Ibbetson, the vicious guardian with the dyed mustaches whom Peter
murders? Ned invited Lionel to visit him.

Lionel listened, unmoved. "Yes, yes indeed. Pour me one." He did
not mind taking Jack's career seriously as long as he had no part in it.
He, Lionel, had steady work in pictures. He was composing and playing
the oboe. He was painting a few pictures. Why should he return to the
sweat, the nerves, the uncertainty of the stage? But since Ned was such
a hard person to refuse, Lionel made insincere agreeing noises over his
beer, certain that a production would never materialize.

Meanwhile Constance was at work. She talked some money out of
Lee Shubert, who thought she was crazy, and more out of friends like
the wealthy brewer Benjamin Guinness. But a manager still had to be
found. Finally she and Jack went to Al Woods, who'd had luck with Jack
in *Kick In*. Valiantly they tried to explain *Peter Ibbetson*'s "There is no
death" theme to the producer of bedroom farces and crook shows.

"I don't understand the play at all, sweetheart," said Woods. "There's
a boy in it. Then we see him grow up. Then he's dead, but comes back
all the same. It sounds nuts!"

"Well," said Jack, "there's one scene in it where Lionel calls me a
bastard and I hit him over the head with a club and knock him cold. It's
the end of the second act."

"You're on, sweetheart."

Lionel was informed that there would be a production and that he
had promised Ned to be in it. He squirmed and swore, but you had to
live up to promises made to Ned.

The *Peter Ibbetson* spell continued to work. More money was needed.
"If you only would let us have the $6,000 and then take no more notice
of us until the dress rehearsal," Constance Collier wrote Lee Shubert, "I
know how delighted you would be. The money is only sitting in the bank
doing nothing, with all your other money, and there must be so much
there, that this sum, one way or another, can make very little difference."
Shubert put up the $6,000. Florenz Ziegfeld lent them his lighting stands
to create the special dream-play effects. Maude Adams came forward to
volunteer her lighting expertise. Laura Hope Crews joined the cast. Al
Woods came to rehearsals and sobbed helplessly into his sleeve, though
he swore he hadn't the faintest idea what the play was about. But not all
problems were solved.

Lionel the perfectionist found he couldn't get a grip on Colonel Ibbetson. His circle of acquaintances just then did not include any villains

from whom he could extract a performance. Though he locked himself up for endless hours, he found he couldn't memorize his lines. An all too familiar panic seized him, undispelled by a conversation overheard between Constance and Jack.

"But Jack, the dress rehearsal is almost upon us and so far he has done absolutely nothing."

"Yes, yes, Constance, quite so. Well, perhaps that Personage you're always calling upon will be able to help us."

"Personage?"

"God."

That night Lionel reluctantly agreed to attend a performance of *The Newcomes* at the invitation of its star and Constance's former manager, Sir Herbert Beerbohm Tree. He took his script with him and was still studying it hopelessly when the curtain rose. And then suddenly his attention was riveted. There in Sir Herbert's Colonel Newcome was the Colonel Ibbetson he had been struggling to realize, from the balding head and tufted eyebrows to Tree's own idiosyncratic breathings and gurglings. He fastened upon Tree, memorizing him. The next day, to the utter amazement of Constance and Jack, Lionel gave an astounding performance of Colonel Ibbetson—subtle, cruel, gay, exuding a horrible charm as well as the scent of patchouli with which he had drenched himself for decadent effect. So powerfully did the patchouli come to convey the Colonel's evil, in fact, that Constance could never smell it in the wings without shuddering.

Sir Herbert himself attended the first dress rehearsal and confronted Lionel afterward. "Congratulations, Lionel. Very good. Very good indeed. By the way, old man, I seem to know that old fellow of yours. All through the performance I kept asking myself again and again: Tree, where have you seen this fellow before? I should say he must have been drawn from life?"

Jack had his own problems with characterization. He had played the hero who gets the girl many times, but now he had to act that very different thing, a lover. The essence of the male lover is his emotional identification with, even subordination to, the woman he loves—a role patently open to ridicule and disturbing to Jack, who was concerned with being a "real man." The beard, copied from du Maurier's illustrations of Peter, looked manly, but then Tree knocked that prop away when he said, "Makes you look like a dentist, old boy, like a dentist. If you don't shave instantly, the romance will fly out the window." Jack fretted about the loss of the beard and also about the pale reddish wig he had to wear. It made him look, he complained, just like a geranium. What Constance observed, apart from all his complaints, was Jack's intense competitiveness with Lionel.

On the night of April 18, 1917, the Republic Theatre was jammed. Jack had an enormous following, and people were eager to see Lionel again after his twelve-year furlough from Broadway. Many loved du Maurier's novel, and finally it was the fact that this *Peter Ibbetson* managed to capture du Maurier even more than the unusual acting that turned opening night into such a triumph. The beauty and nostalgia of the story gripped the audience from the beginning, a lucky thing since a catastrophe occurred that might have ruined the whole enterprise.

Heavy machinery and dreams were incompatible enough; the machinery *must* work. One scene change was particularly difficult: the scene in the forest which, in the lovers' dream, is supposed to fade into the opera house where Adelina Patti is singing. Jack and Constance were alone on the stage, walking in ecstasy up to the wide-open opera house doors when, to their horror, the scene slowly began to collapse. As they stood paralyzed, the entire opera house came down around their heads, exposing stagehands, guy ropes, and bare brick wall. Someone had the presence of mind to ring down the curtain on Constance wringing her hands and Jack swearing vilely as his mulatto valet Paul hurried to dust him off. There was nothing to do but try to rebuild the opera house and start the act all over again—if there was anyone left to act to.

Incredibly, the hypnotized audience remained quiet in their seats, so powerfully had the play moved them and so sympathetic were they to du Maurier's lovers. When the curtain rose again there was not even a titter. And even though the actors themselves were shaken out of their best performances, the audience roared its approval at the final curtain. Constance Collier had been right about *Peter Ibbetson*.

Critics applauded John Barrymore's "grave, beautiful, romantic, and lovelorn Peter" to whom he brought a quality of "starfire." Alexander Woollcott raved about the flawless characterization of Lionel's "artfully and richly played" Colonel: the prodigal had returned and "the greeting that awaited him must have warmed the cockles of his foolish heart." Heywood Broun thought that Lionel gave even a better performance than John. For some it was the two Barrymores together that gave the evening its magical quality. As for Constance Collier, *Peter Ibbetson* won her more friends in America than she had ever had before.

Although Jack said, "Railway accidents don't happen twice in the same place," incredibly the next night the opera scene collapsed again at exactly the same point and, incredibly, the spellbound audience again waited quietly while the scene was rebuilt. *Peter Ibbetson*, in fact, became a cult. Jack could not get over his astonishment that the audiences were made up so largely of people who had seen it before: one woman told him she had actually seen it forty-five times. To the amazement of Woods, Shubert, and everyone involved in the production, *Peter Ibbetson* turned out to be the biggest theatrical draw in town—even though less than two weeks before its opening America had grimly committed itself to the Great War. But then *Peter Ibbetson* offered an escape from the reality that newspapers blared daily, returning romance to a theatre which had lost it, dreams to those whose dreams were being shattered.

Of course not everyone was uncritical. Channing Pollock said that the best way to see the play was to stay home and read the book: du Maurier did not translate well. Some objected to the sentimentalizing of the original text. While the novel ended with Peter sternly dead in his coffin, for example, the play provided an afterworld in which Peter and the Duchess of Towers were reunited, needing (groaned Pollock again) "only mica to suggest a Christmas card, or a frame of painted clouds to recall Little Eva in Heaven." Actually the play skated on very thin ice. As Alec Woollcott said, if someone had laughed, John Barrymore's career might have ended there and then.

But no one laughed. Jack kept the play from the brink of absurdity by a quality of acting that critics struggled to define. "Clear and cool . . . fine edge of light . . . silver suggestiveness." What they seemed to be reacting to was a fine tension in his performance, a nervous sensibility generated by his own inner tensions: Jack the poetic, the vulnerable versus Jack the mocker, the dissolute. This tautness kept Peter Ibbetson and *Peter Ibbetson* from slackening into sentimentality. The ice was thin, but it did not crack.

Women were particularly receptive to this thoroughbred quality in John Barrymore. He was, thought Blanche Thomas, as she sat with a party of friends, "a poetry of head and throat," the lyrical epitome of romance. There was in his beauty "a fatal kind of fineness, an unearthliness, which you could not but see through tears, because it was not of life, but only as in our secret hearts we dream that life might be." Surely the audience that watched him with their hearts in their throats, thought Blanche, could now believe in a love that triumphed over the misfortunes of life and even over life's cessation.

Mrs. Leonard Thomas had been born Blanche Oelrichs into a family even more elite than Katherine Harris's, well entrenched in New York–Newport–Palm Beach circles. Yet Blanche could hardly have been more unlike Katherine. Endowed with anarchistic self-confidence, she had been a rebel from childhood. She could match school capers with Jack, having mined her teachers' chairs with explosive caps, tripped fire alarms, and laced her math teacher's soup with whiskey. Unlike Ethel, Blanche lasted only three months at her convent, expelled for eating foie gras sandwiches in bed after lights out. Marriage to a wealthy banker and two children had not tamed her. She was an ardent suffragette, smoked cigarettes, bobbed her hair, and sported George Sandian trousers. She wrote poetry, stories, and plays under the pseudonym Michael Strange. Unfortunately she was rich, which meant that she neither disciplined her work nor was taken seriously as an artist. *She* took herself very seriously indeed. She was slim, with black hair, eyebrows that she drew into wings, and smoldering dark eyes. The fashionable artist Paul Helleu had pronounced her "America's most beautiful woman," but she looked more like a healthy Arab boy.

She certainly had not thought Jack Barrymore America's most beautiful man when at fourteen she had seen him dining at the Hotel Knickerbocker with a heavily made-up older woman. The star of *The Fortune Hunter* had looked pasty-faced and heavy-jowled, with "a drooping mustache" and "dazed eyes." Then she met him again after the transforming miracle of Ned Sheldon, *Justice*, and Bevo to find him—well, fascinating.

Blanche says they met when the playwright Philip Moeller came up to her at a Theatre Guild party to ask if he might present Mr. Barrymore, who wished to meet her. "So he wishes to meet me?" she thought, remembering seeing him a few days before bending over a case at Cartier's and noting how well he contrived to look to one side of his beautiful profile without moving his head. She watched him now as he approached with Moeller, his "slanted, oblique walk" seeming to say that "his clothes irked his skin." Introduced, Jack bowed and smiled, and she studied him with more leisure. He looked "very slim and nervously poetic, with greyish greenish hazel eyes of immense fascination, because they seemed to mirror back oneself in flatteringly mischievous terms." He looked "elfin and forsaken" and "very highly strung." An amazing metamorphosis from the dazed creature at the Hotel Knickerbocker.

Cathleen Nesbitt says, however, that during the run of *Justice* she met Blanche Thomas who immediately invited her to lunch because (Cathleen discovered) she wanted Cathleen to bring Jack Barrymore with her.

"Good God, no!" said Jack, informed. "I never go to lunch parties given by society bitches." But Cathleen had promised Blanche she'd bring him, and Jack finally gave in.

When Cathleen and the reluctant Jack arrived, Leonard Thomas told them that Blanche was finishing some work in her studio. After suspenseful minutes, Blanche finally appeared, looking like a Gypsy in a burgundy velvet tea gown with close-fitting medieval sleeves, one of which, Cathleen noticed immediately, had a large ragged hole at the elbow. How too embarrassing: surely her maid ought to have fixed it, or was Blanche going to change for lunch? Blanche did not change. During lunch she completely ignored her other guests, totally engrossing Jack. After they left she took Jack upstairs to see her studio while Cathleen twiddled her thumbs below. That night Jack burst into Cathleen's dressing room.

"My God! that's a fascinating woman. Where did you meet her? What eyes, and did you notice that cute little hole with her elbow peeping through? I do like a woman who doesn't get herself all tarted up like everybody else!"

Jack began to appear at a few of the Thomas's parties, "a more or less silent, charming, and very decorative guest." Blanche noted the astute way he handled himself, at the same time concealing the astuteness so that he appeared vulnerable and shy. All the magnetism of success reinforced his natural charm—not the rakish, straw-hat kind of success that had won Katherine, but success born of discipline and purpose, refining his nature (she thought) as those in training for a high purpose are refined.

Jack in turn was fascinated by the beautiful, wealthy *enfant terrible*. She seemed daringly different, a woman with brains, sex appeal, and a masculine vigor and confidence. That she was a wife and a mother deepened her appeal. He read her poetry: "I am Unrest, / The furtive scratching / Of secret itch, / The galloping rear / Against mountains' feet / The brow-heaving sight / Over chasms at night." Why, he might have drawn the allegory himself.

He began to meet Blanche outside her home, to follow her on her social rounds, coming to Lakewood, New Jersey, for example, where she was weekending at a fashionable hotel. A friend of Blanche's watched them as they joined a group of young people playing poker—Blanche, poised, vivacious, Jack very handsome, dashing and graceful, yet very tense, his pupils strangely enlarged. "He seemed under great stress," said the friend; he was laboring (she guessed) under "a new and complex love." When Leonard Thomas left for the war as a commissioned first lieutenant, Blanche and Jack began to see each other openly.

As a child Blanche had seen Ethel "bewitchingly tilting herself forward in a hansom cab as she called out directions to the cabby through the trap." To Blanche, Ethel Barrymore had always seemed a brilliantly fortunate person; she marveled at the astonishing coincidence of beauty, charm, and talent so dazzlingly merged in one lovely, unspoiled being.

Now, however, as they sat around the small table, she felt herself more drawn to Lionel.

She observed him as he sat silently. He was quite thin now, his shoulders slightly hunched, his face lined. He seemed less of the theatre than Jack and Ethel, she thought. He didn't bother to *project* as they did; he was not "on." Instead he was receptive, self-effacing, and quite indifferent to the impression he was making.

Even more silent was his wife Doris, whom Ethel called "Da"—a striking-looking young woman with "huge gray eyes shot with glints of green" and a white, heart-shaped face. She seemed to deliberately affect old-fashioned clothes; she looked like an Emily Brontë or a Lorna Doone in a particularly somber mood. To what "extraordinarily rich form of self-effacement," wondered Blanche, had this woman been inured to appear so consciously patient, so alert yet withdrawn, so determined not to be anybody? Jack had told her that Lionel adored his wife; she believed it when they rose to go and she saw Lionel surreptitiously kiss Doris's cloak as he laid it across her shoulders.

IF ETHEL WAS less charming than Blanche expected, there were reasons. Ethel's sympathies were not with "Mrs. Thomas," as she scrupulously addressed her, but with Katherine Harris Barrymore, serving out her year's residence in Santa Barbara. Ethel had liked Katherine as a wife for Jack partly because she was no competition; she saw immediately, however, that Blanche Thomas had a will as powerful as her own. She saw her beloved Jack being taken over by this woman, her own influence undermined. If it came to marriage, Blanche would never honeymoon with Jack at Mamaroneck, for example, as Katherine had. Blanche even had the audacity to assume that she could help Jack with his career, assistance that had always been Ethel's prerogative. She was polite to Mrs. Thomas, just.

Besides, Ethel's own marriage had sunk to new depths of misery that spring. Russell had as usual spent the winter in Palm Beach, curing his "bronchitis" with any number of sympathetic women who understood how harrowing life with a famous actress must be. Ethel had gone to Jacksonville to film the last scenes of *The Call of Her People* for Metro-Rolfe, then to Palm Beach to join Russell. It was a mistake. Among the palms and the sun and the endless parties, she spent "two of the most miserable weeks" of her life. She finally came north when America declared war against Germany that April, while Russell got his commission at last and left for France.

Not everyone wanted America to go to war. People sang "I Didn't

Raise My Boy to Be a Soldier," "Don't Take My Darling Boy Away,"
and "We're With You, Mr. Wilson" while the president opposed America's entering the conflict. But war fever grew quickly, and for the first
time in history actors as a class were used politically to sell patriotism
and fill the war chests. Julia Marlowe recited "The Battle Hymn of the
Republic" and "In Flanders Fields." E. H. Sothern took *If I Were King*
across America, receipts to America's ally Great Britain. Nora Bayes sang
George M. Cohan's "Over There" at the Thirty-ninth Street Theatre:
after a few bars the audience leapt to its feet cheering. Elsie Ferguson
sold $85,000 worth of Liberty Bonds in less than half an hour on the
steps of the New York Public Library. Ten theatre stars, including Minnie
Maddern Fiske and James K. Hackett, went on tour for the Red Cross,
giving their talents free and paying their own expenses. Ethel, Lionel,
and Jack were filmed in a Red Cross Pageant—together for the first time
in a movie, though not acting together. Hollywood picture stars, however,
were the most successful moneymakers. In Chicago Mary Pickford raised
over a million dollars in subscriptions for the Loan Drive, auctioning off
her curls for $15,000 apiece, far surpassing the efforts of theatre stars
like Margaret Anglin and John Barrymore. Still, the theatre came through.
It was, said President Wilson, "one of the most potent contributing factors
to American victory in the World War."

"I was never able to do very much," said Ethel, "but I did all that I
could, as we all did." With Jane Cowl and Mrs. Patrick Campbell she
helped net $50,000 entertaining a posh audience at the Strand with fa-
mous scenes from their plays. She posed as "America" and "a widowed
European mother" for charity tableaux. At the Allies Ball at Madison
Square Garden she was "magnificent" as "Devastated Belgium" in nunlike
robes and veils of black chiffon. She was so nervous about reciting "The
Battle Hymn of the Republic" for a Red Cross benefit at the Metropolitan
Opera House that she asked Lionel to stand by in the prompter's box.
Sure enough, just before the last verse her mind went blank. In her terror
she heard muffled roars coming from the box, but they sounded only like
the strange cry of some jungle beast. And then just when she was ready
to faint or run, the words rushed back. To recite "Ode to the Allies" in
the stadium of New York University she firmly clutched a piece of parch-
ment and read the piece.

Needing money, she kept on making movies, only one of which she
thought any good: *The Awakening of Helena Ritchie*, a woman-with-a-past
drama that allowed her to act with depth and sympathy. She made it clear
that she thought motion pictures slumming: when she discovered a scene
was to be shot in front of a Park Avenue mansion which she frequented

socially, she insisted the cameras move elsewhere. In *The White Raven*, in which she played Nightingale Nan, a dance-hall singer, she barred even the director B. F. Rolfe from a scene which required her to wave her arms and wiggle in a scanty red dress. She managed her little shimmy sweetly and decorously, but obviously Ethel felt far happier in nunlike robes and veils of black chiffon. For *Life's Whirlpool* she was reunited with Lionel, who both wrote the script and directed. There was nothing original about Lionel's story: a tight-fisted husband and his carping sister, the unhappy wife, the other man. The best thing about the film was Ethel, whose profound understanding "of the realities of life," said *Variety*, "set her apart from other actresses." But Ethel hated making movies and never bothered to see hers. She didn't watch herself on stage, why should she watch herself in motion pictures?

She was looking for great parts, triumphs. With the arrival of John Barrymore as the theatre's most exciting talent, her own position had been challenged. Back in 1905 she had been "Ethel Barrymost"; now *Justice* and *Peter Ibbetson* had vaulted her little brother to the heights. She had always wanted to do large roles—Shakespeare, Sophocles, but her financial and emotional dependence on Charles Frohman had forced her to bow to his repertoire. "I think I've played every bad part ever written," she said rather ungraciously. "I'd play a Hottentot if only it were a good role." But now Alf Hayman, manager of Frohman's enterprises, promised her a repertory season. Of course she knew exactly what her first role would be.

She had met Ned Sheldon through Jack. But though Ned was the perfect confidant of "older women," soothing the damaged egos of Julia Marlowe, Minnie Maddern Fiske, Edith Wharton, and Mrs. Patrick Campbell, Ethel would never bare her soul like the others; she had learned Mummum's proud reticence too well. Still, she found Sheldon characteristically ready to help her. That autumn of 1917 he quickly revamped Dumas's creaking *La Dame aux Camélias*. Finally Ethel would play Marguerite Gautier as Réjane, Bernhardt, Nazimova, and her beloved Modjeska had before her.

Unfortunately, Sheldon was not the right dramatist for her purpose. What *The Lady of the Camellias* needed was a pruning hand to expose the core of tragedy in the story of a consumptive prostitute's futile effort to evade death in love. The weakness of all Sheldon's plays, including his version of *Peter Ibbetson*, was sentimentality. This combined unhappily with Ethel's prudery, for surely it was she who excised frankly sexual lines like Marguerite's "Let me tell you, my friend, that no young lover I ever had stayed with me longer than a month or so," or Armand's "I don't mean that you're pretty, that I want to live with you! Of course I do, but that's not everything." Was it Sheldon or Ethel who replaced the dramatic end of the first act—Marguerite, having fallen in love with Armand, tearing up a letter from her lover, the Prince d'Aurec, and tossing the pieces to her maid, saying, "Give him that!"—with, instead, the curtain slowly descending on Marguerite with outstretched arms crying, "I love you! I love you! I love you!" The changes in Ethel's script are in her hand.

Ethel also needed pruning again: at thirty-eight she was not quite the fragile consumptive of Dumas's story. She dieted severely and decided on a blond wig for Marguerite (Jack's lovely pinkish hair had gone over well in *Ibbetson*). Conway Tearle would be her Armand, a sensually handsome matinee idol who had acted with her in *Mid-Channel* and *The Nightingale* and was reputedly as amorous offstage with Ethel as on.

The public was primed: CAMILLE TO BE HER GREATEST EFFORT, headlines announced, establishing her once and for all as a great emotional actress. Ned Sheldon came East for the Christmas Eve opening at the Empire; the house was packed for the great event. And Ethel's loving public thought her ravishing in floating white skirts and blond curls. They wept copiously as Marguerite coughed her life away, they came back again and again. Two particular friends came to every matinee and cried so hard that they had to pin their large soaked handkerchiefs to the backs of the seats in front of them to dry. Sometimes on dates these same friends would suddenly be seized with an irresistible urge. "Oh, let's go and see her die!" they'd say, and drag their unwilling escorts over to the Empire in time to watch Ethel expire in Tearle's arms.

But Ethel wanted the kind of critical ecstasy that Jack had inspired in *Justice* and *Peter Ibbetson*, and she didn't get it. Difficult to decide whether the actress or the vehicle was wanting. One critic, commenting acidly on "Mr. Sheldon's inordinate affection for piccolos, fife and drum corps, love birds, harps, choirs, music boxes, military bands, street organs, and victrolas in the wings" observed that "music off" was to Sheldon what "clothes off" was to Ziegfeld. And Sheldon had added to three full acts a prologue and an epilogue in which the tragic story was revealed to be a dream. Yet Ethel might have overcome these drawbacks: after all *Peter Ibbetson* was a dream play, a period piece which had also endured Sheldon's sentimentalizing hand.

The truth was she did not rise to Marguerite's tragedy because she could not make Marguerite a prostitute. The bite of Dumas's story lies in the contrast between Marguerite's sexual promiscuity and her sense of honor. Her giving up Armand because she loves him means nothing if she has not previously been shown to be a sexually reckless and cynical woman. But Ethel made Marguerite a "good" woman through and through. As a result the kind critics praised her "exquisite grace and charm," her "youthful and joyous Camille." But the verdict that stuck was "an uninspired performance."

Ned Sheldon's physical condition had improved so markedly after Jack's triumphs in *Justice* and *Peter Ibbetson* that he had even tried to enlist in the army. The failure of *The Lady of the Camellias* set him back severely. He had hoped as much as Ethel that the play would establish her as an American Bernhardt. As for Ethel, she had dreamed of playing Camille ever since she, Jack, and Lionel had charged a penny for their performance that summer in the barn. Little comfort now to receive from the great Bernhardt her own copy of *La Dame aux Camélias* with the note "My Dear: I have heard such beautiful things of your Marguerite that I wish I could come to see it, but that is impossible. I think this book, which Dumas once sent to me, ought to be yours now." Ethel had challenged Jack and, tragically, she had failed.

AND THEN JACK came out with the best movie he had done so far, the only film he made in 1917, *Raffles*. From the first shot showing him standing slim and poised on the ship's deck smoking a cigarette, he is obviously a different actor from the uncouth comic of *The Incorrigible Dukane*. He is suave, fleet; his movements have poise and assurance. His face, slack-jawed in *Dukane*, is refined and taut, the left side particularly expressive: the nostril cut high, the crooked smile dimpling the cheek, the eyebrow arched high. His eyes dance; he scintillates. Gerald du Maurier had had a terrific success playing the "amateur cracksman" in the coolly impassive British manner. Jack's Raffles has the energy of mischievous amusement, of taut nerves under steely control. When the detective exclaims at Raffles' final getaway, "Well, I'm deucedly glad he's escaped. He's splendid!" movie audiences enthusiastically agreed. *Raffles*, as *Variety* said, was "a super show."

Obviously this was an extraordinarily versatile talent: at home in comedy, tragedy, romantic drama. An enormous talent, yet housed in a sadly unstable human being. Take the run followed by the tour of *Peter Ibbetson*, for example. Jack closed *Peter Ibbetson* in June in the teeth of sold-out houses because he didn't want to work any longer—an irresponsible act. He delayed the August opening because he was "rather ill." When Shubert and Woods scheduled the play for Chicago in October, Jack declined to go because "legal matters" made it imperative he remain in New York. As a result, Shubert and Woods plucked *Ibbetson* from the Republic and dropped it into the 48th Street Theatre, where business declined sharply. Jack was often late and took the matter lightly. "Aren't you sorry you haven't more Barrymores to wait for?" he would tell the fuming manager. The tour was launched in Philadelphia late in November of 1917; the following January Jack pleaded off a Monday matinee in Washington because he had to be in New York on Sunday. On February 18 he was again unable to play (for reasons to be explained), but real trouble didn't develop until March when Constance Collier wired Shubert that the company couldn't play Holy Week because both she and Jack had New York business. Shubert wired back tersely that they could not cancel Holy Week under any circumstances.

This backed Jack into a corner. ALL ARRANGEMENTS MADE, he telegraphed Shubert on March 16. MUST BE OPERATED ON HOLY WEEK WITH DOCTORS IN NEW YORK. DO NOT WISH ANYONE BUT YOURSELF TO KNOW BUT PARTICULARLY MY FAMILY AS IT WOULD WORRY THEM UNNECESSARILY. MUST BE IN HOSPITAL AT LEAST THREE DAYS.

Shubert was not deceived, again wiring crisply that it was impossible to cancel the Detroit Holy Week engagement. Desperate for any out from the (to him) grueling tour, Jack dug in his heels and complained about the Sunday night performances in Chicago. "I might as well come right out with it, Mr. Shubert, I'm sure I won't be able to manage them. It is just a question of physical endurance with me now, day in and day out." A doctor in Buffalo had told him he was "very nearly all in"; he had taken on a trained nurse for the rest of the tour. If he were a well man, he would, of course, etc. etc. Obviously Jack Barrymore was sick of *Peter Ibbetson*, which collapsed in Chicago in May as Constance wired Shubert that it "would be good to go on" but obviously hopeless. Despite efforts to engage substitutes for John Barrymore, there was no one to replace him. *Peter Ibbetson*, which Ethel would have played for years, was over.

To explain Jack's struggle against *Peter Ibbetson* on practical grounds won't do. Yes, he might have canceled the play in June to film *Raffles*, yet actors made movies while doing legitimate theatre. Jack's "legal business" in New York? A stagehand had sued him for $10,000 damages for punching him, but no one named John Barrymore would have had to remain in New York on that account. More seriously, Katherine's divorce was final on December 6, but that could not have been the legal business that detained him since by that date he'd already left for Philadelphia. The operation? No information survives about this operation that was obviously never performed. In Chicago Jack rolled up a trouser leg for Ashton Stevens to display the varicose veins that had kept him out of the army. His leg undoubtedly was troubling him. But there is little doubt that what was really troubling Jack was the tedium of transforming himself every night into the lover of Mary, Duchess of Towers, when the real woman he loved was back in New York.

The story is that from the time he committed himself to *Justice*, Jack kept off liquor for two years. Constance Collier, however, said that she was amazed how Jack could come drunk to the theatre, apply his make-up with a steady hand, and perform flawlessly onstage. The two years would have ended in about March 1918, exactly the time Jack started wiring Lee Shubert that he couldn't go on. The disciplined period, as far as alcohol went, was over.

Lionel himself had left the tour just after it began, not because he was tired of Colonel Ibbetson but because the producer, John D. Williams, wanted him to star in Augustus Thomas's drama of a Union spy, *The Copperhead*.

Lionel had been deeply moved at his reception in *Peter Ibbetson* which, said *Vanity Fair*, was "chiefly worth seeing for a wonderful performance by Lionel Barrymore, the man who came back." "I'm surprised that New York seems to remember me," the almost impossible to interview actor told a reporter. "Usually it forgets anyone who merely goes out for a drink." His enthusiasm for the theatre was rekindled; *Peter Ibbetson* had been like coming home.

"Salary apart," he was asked, "which would you prefer to act for, stage or movies?"

"Well, which *would* one prefer?" replied Lionel. "Singing before an audience in Carnegie Hall or into a phonograph?"

When his contract with Metro-Rolfe expired that year, Lionel did not renew it. Instead he began to worm his way into the heart of Milt Shanks, the Civil War "copperhead" who grows old despised by family and village because he cannot reveal his true allegiance to the North. If Ethel thought she had only Jack to compete with, 1918 would disabuse her. Lionel was going to knock Broadway (as he would say) for a row of Chinese pagodas.

TWELVE

1918–1919

NOTHING COULD EQUAL the enthusiasm of that young actor over a mere reading of the script," said Augustus Thomas, amazed to find at rehearsals that Lionel quickly knew more about the hostilities between the North-South border states during the Civil War than he did. He was both impressed and exasperated with Lionel's passion for detailed characterization, a passion which "quite exceeded" Thomas's own demands and "really taxed the patience of his associates." And again by opening night at the Shubert on February 18, Lionel Barrymore had disappeared completely. Only Milt Shanks, the Copperhead, remained.

Jack was supposed to play *Peter Ibbetson* that night in New Haven, but arranged with Lee Shubert to buy out the full house with his own money so that he could be in New York for his brother's opening. He and Ned Sheldon were conspicuous in the first row of the balcony, adding considerably to the excitement. "This seat cost me $3,000," said Jack to Ned. "If Lionel doesn't put on a good show I'll kill him!" Ethel, playing at the Empire in *The Off Chance*, had been ill with bronchitis the previous week and decided to extend that engagement through Lionel's opening night. Shortly before curtain time she was smuggled incognito into the gallery.

The tragedy of Milt Shanks is that both his wife and soldier son die believing him a traitor to the North. Shanks's vindication finally comes when, to save his granddaughter's happiness, he decides to reveal his true role in the Civil War. In front of his detractors, he brings out a box of letters. He takes down a plaster cast of Lincoln's head and sets it under a lamp. He brings out another cast of Lincoln's hand and holds his own next to it. "Bigger man'n me, every way," says Shanks. Finally he opens the box and takes out a yellowed letter. "Dear Milt," he reads, though he knows the words by heart, "Lee's surrender ends it all. I cannot think of you without a sense of guilt, but it had to be. I alone know what you did—and even more what you endured. . . ." Gradually Milt Shanks unfolds his story: the midnight meeting with Lincoln in the Executive Mansion . . . the clock ticking on the mantel . . . Lincoln pulling a small flag from his pocket, laying Shanks's hand on the stars and covering that hand with his own. "I need you, Milt," says the president, mustering Shanks into the nation's service. "Your country needs you." And as Lionel spoke and the light shone on Lincoln's head and hand, Lincoln himself materialized there on the stage of the Shubert just as though the audience were seeing him with their own eyes. Like hypnosis, like a visitation, Lionel Barrymore filled the Shubert with Lincoln's presence—real as life, larger than life.

In the final scene, his most bitter enemy helps Milt Shanks into the blue coat of a Grand Army colonel. "God!" says Shanks, drawing a deep breath. "It's wonderful—to hev friends again!" As the curtain falls Lionel stands alone on the stage, Lincoln's small flag in his hand, his face lit uncannily with joy.

Dead silence. Then suddenly the audience were on their feet as applause burst from orchestra, balcony, and gallery. Up and down the curtain went while the demonstration grew louder and Jack furiously tried to check his tears and failed. John Williams, the producer, pushed Gus Thomas onto the stage. He stood there, helpless, as the audience chanted, "Barrymore! Barrymore! Barrymore!" Finally they let him begin, but as soon as he spoke Lionel's name the demonstration began again: "Barrymore! Barrymore!" They cheered him on and on, longer than anyone remembered any actor's being cheered by a Broadway audience before. When after fifteen curtain calls they finally let him go, they poured out into the street, still seething with excitement. Lionel himself was awed at the tremendous ovation but typically laconic. "Gosh," he was heard muttering as he left the stage, "I hope this isn't a dream."

The next day Jack went to Lee Shubert's office to pay up.

"That's all right, Jack," said Lee.

"What do you mean?" said Jack. "You closed the theatre for one night and lost $3,000. I saw my brother on the biggest night of his life and I'm glad to pay for it."

Lee's brother Sam had been killed in a railroad collision not long before. "You don't owe me anything," said Lee now. "I'm glad to do it for you. You see, I liked my brother too."

As *The Copperhead* settled in as a solid hit, Ethel forgot that Lionel was the unlucky one and added her voice to the chorus. "He has such a sense of the theatre, such a brain and such humor! If he had to be a *dwarf*, he would make you think he was one." His genius had nothing to do with make-up but what he did with his face. His teeth, for example.

Lionel's were good, but as an old man he worked his mouth as though his teeth were "trick piano keys." And his legs, they were *old* legs; even the feet in the shoes seemed old. "And it's so wonderful because Lionel has none of those tricks of the theatre to indicate old age. He doesn't come on shaking a trembly stick. He doesn't do that terrible thing that some do, to be oh so sweet that you wish they were dead. And it is all because his acting comes out of his head." She considered Lionel not a character actor but an actor who could realize any character. "I can't imagine," said Ethel, "Lionel going wrong."

His triumph bemused some critics. "Lionel is the one that fascinates me the most," wrote P. G. Wodehouse, comparing Barrymores. "He is like the pea under the thimble. Now you see him, now you don't. He pops up and makes a sensational success, and then he thinks he's earned a vacation, so he knocks off for ten years or so; and then, just when you think you are never going to see him again, up he bobs once more and makes everyone else look like enthusiastic amateurs reciting pieces at church sociables."

The press descended upon Lionel, who greeted all reporters "with the air of an early Christian martyr." He was restless, puffing a black cigar, turning away questions about what part he would like to play next with, "Don't know. Any part that's good." He admitted a spiritual kinship with Joseph Jefferson who, as Rip Van Winkle, had also won fame by playing both a young and an old man in one play. He brusquely dismissed the eternal question of why he would not play the lover. It was a question of temperament: as he preferred the oboes and bassoons in a symphony so he preferred the more deeply shaded role in a play. He took his sensational success in *The Copperhead* quietly: "I'm glad everybody likes me in it, if they do."

Acting both Milt's bitter drudge of a wife and his granddaughter, Doris was even more reticent, though Heywood Broun, among others, had called her excellent. "My husband's part is truly wonderful," she told a reporter in a rare interview, "though of course we mustn't tell him so." She admitted that though she had acted as a child with Mrs. John Drew and McKee Rankin, when she married Lionel she had given up the legitimate stage until now. She had nothing to say about her own performance except, "I have always been cast to represent suffering womanhood." One wonders whether these, Doris's only surviving words about herself, might refer also to her offstage role.

The stirring patriotism of *The Copperhead* spoke strongly to a nation at war; houses continued packed. But as so frequently happens after the dazzle of a star's performance stops blinding the critical eye, the play and rest of the cast eventually came up for scrutiny. "Most of the actors were inarticulate," complained Arthur Hornblow. "One had to guess at half they said. When will correct diction be insisted upon as an important part of an actor's equipment?" Wodehouse was blunter: "I have never seen a play which died in its tracks so dismally as did *The Copperhead* in the intervals between the Barrymore scenes. The other players sat about and chatted in a dispirited sort of way until he came back." *The Copperhead* was Lionel Barrymore pure and simple.

ETHEL COULD NOT boast anything like Lionel's success that season. She had followed the disappointing *Lady of the Camellias* with the drawing-room comedy *The Off Chance*—unconvincing, thought many, when German troops were smashing the Allied lines and casualty lists mounting with horrifying speed. Not impressed with the play either, a young actress in the cast named Eva Le Gallienne was deeply impressed with Ethel's genius for making something out of nothing. Her second-act curtain line, for example, was totally banal. She was with two men, and they were all on their way to a poker game. They were hemming and hawing, and finally Miss Barrymore said, "Are we ready? Why don't we go?" Absolutely nothing—yet the way she said it, the line got a roar of applause.

She did A. A. Milne's *Belinda* next, a production, said one critic severely, "that was hopelessly beneath the standard that the Empire once prided itself on maintaining." Not the repertory season she had imagined; yet so tightly did she have the affections of her audiences wound around her charming finger and so clever was she at making something out of nothing, that she herself was never faulted. Moreover, she directed and produced herself, and if the plays were below standard the acting was not, critics conceding that with Cyril Keightley, E. Lyall Swete, and Le Gallienne she had "quite the best cast in town."

But she needed a good play. One night when she was having supper at the Algonquin with Uncle Jack and Aunt Dodo after the theatre, the actress Jobyna Howland came to their table to say hello. With her was a dark young woman whom Ethel didn't know but who said in an odd accent at parting, "I've written a play for you."

"Who was the Polish girl with Joby?" asked Ethel.

Uncle Jack said, "I think her name is Zoë Akins."

Shortly afterward Alf Hayman handed Ethel two acts of a play. She tucked the script under her arm and climbed into her De Dion-Bouton, and was already in New Rochelle when she rapped on the glass and told her faithful chauffeur Britt to drive straight back to the Empire. When she got there she seized Hayman. "Where is the third act? Get it as quickly as possible. I've got to do this play!"

But the third act was not ready and so she returned to Metro to film two of her stage successes, *Our Mrs. McChesney* and *Lady Frederick*, retitled *The Divorcee*. "Films of this kind are not seen often enough," said *Variety* of *Our Mrs. McChesney*, which many thought the best thing she'd appeared in to date. But neither praise nor money could reconcile Ethel to making movies. She waited impatiently for the last act of Zoë Akins's play.

JACK WAS HAPPIER making movies. Audiences adored him as Robert Ridgeway in the breezy farce *On the Quiet*. How, they marveled, had the camera managed to catch some of Jack's incredible stunts—jumping out a window, somersaulting in the air, and crashing through the hood of an automobile where a beautiful heiress is waiting to elope? Dashing Jack Barrymore had movie audiences in a continuous uproar of laughter, audiences who had never heard of *Peter Ibbetson* or would hardly have recognized him as the pale, furtive William Falder.

But he could be serious, so serious that when Katherine was announced to appear this year at the 48th Street Theatre as Katherine Harris-Barrymore, Jack (and Lionel and Ethel) were outraged at her use of the great Barrymore name. He had forgiven her the marriage and even her sleeping with James Montgomery Flagg. "You know, Monty, I can't really blame her," he'd said, speaking again to Flagg after a silence of several years. "I was drunk most of the time." But using his name professionally was another matter. In fact, Jack's elaborate indifference to the theatre and his acting heritage was pretty much a hoax, as much a hoax as the three Barrymores' elaborate pretenses that they were not all rivals. Katherine had gone too far.

Since his divorce Jack had left Ned's apartment for quarters on the top floor of an old four-story house off Washington Square. As he had once created a pirate's cave in the shadowy reaches of the Annex, he now undertook to create for himself a retreat that he named the "Alchemist's Corner." No women were allowed to climb the stairs to the top floor and few men, yet a great attraction of the place was his widowed landlady, Mrs. Juliette Nicholls.

Mrs. Nicholls had not wanted the notorious Barrymore as a tenant: only Jack's paying his rent far in advance and the agent's assurances that he would behave like a gentleman persuaded her. But when Jack began sending her charmingly boyish notes signed "Top Floor," she melted and they quickly became friends. Jack was capable of warm friendships with older women. They were a relief from the advances of female fans and society women for, like most Don Juans, in love Jack was more pursued than pursuing. He had drawn emotional comfort in his lonely childhood from Mummum; he now drew considerable comfort from his indulgent concierge.

She innocently agreed to let him fix up his eyrie at his own expense. Jack hired a decorator to do his bedroom and bath in *Peter Ibbetson* style. Pink striped wallpaper, black woodwork, a flowered burgundy carpet. Doors converted into mirrors framed in black. Bathroom and bathtub tiled in glittering glass squares. Bedroom windows draped in mauve taffeta fringed with white beads, curtains of piped glass backed with crystal drops, filets of crystal festooning the moldings. A French white marble fireplace. And facing the fireplace a hard, narrow bed: a single bed, said Jack, a celibate bed, for once.

Inspired by the transformation, Jack himself attacked the larger studio. He created a bay window, then fitted a flanking window with squares of Italian blue glass. He swathed a large skylight in saffron chiffon to create a mysterious glow. He did the walls in dull Chinese gold, then lit candles and smoked them until the gold was properly "aged." He smoked the furniture, further aging old carved chests and moldy pews. He added tapestries, a Chinese rug, and a prie-dieu with stools. He draped the baby grand he could not play in embroidered gold brocade and ensconced a bronze pheasant among its folds. Candles in tall standards flickered in Venetian mirrors. And scattered about the room was the riot of his imagination: old gilded leather books, a gold and red shrine, old green and amber bottles, canoe paddles, paints and brushes, old guns and maps, make-up boxes, rare chess sets, antique pipe racks and tobacco boxes, antique dolls and puppets—everything that a man searching for himself in the exoticism of the past could buy. A "tall, pallid and very beautiful Madonna" provided the only feminine presence that Jack would allow.

Mrs. Nicholls was out of town when Jack decided to expand his kingdom. "You have been so lenient in permitting me to exercise my fancy on the studio," he wrote her. "Would you mind very much if I did a few ornamental things to the roof, at my own expense, of course? I'd like to build a little stairway to it, and place a few plants there, with perhaps a small pavilion in which I could sit when the locust blossoms come to the courtyards of Greenwich Village. It would be like living in Paris in the twelfth century. Yours entreatingly, Top Floor."

A few ornamental things, indeed! Jack got an old carpenter to fashion a steep, crooked "medieval" staircase to the roof, the rope railing secured with rusty iron clamps to the side sinister. On top of the roof Jack instructed the old man to build a kind of ship's cabin, then promptly stole his rules, squares, and levels. "I want everything crooked or off-center," he explained, "like a Nuremberg poet's home." He then imported thirty-five tons of topsoil from Long Island that had to be hauled up from the street in burlap bags by block and tackle. While roof beams groaned below, Jack planted eight-foot cedars, wisteria, arborvitae, cherry trees, and grapevines. What was missing? A fountain. He had one installed and set it flowing. Beehives added a Yeatsian touch. Crooked walks of broken flagstone wound through the flora; sunlight flashed from shards of colored glass embedded in the fire walls. The fountain splashed. He surveyed his kingdom and found it good.

Mrs. Nicholls gasped, but did not complain. There was, after all, a weird beauty about Jack's production, and then he was so childishly pleased as he fed "his birds" and basked in his reflected sunlight. But Jack also spilled over into the lower floor where the hallway choked on potted plants and floral boxes and the table spilled perfumed notes. The potted plants reappeared on the roof, the flowers went to hospitals, and every Sunday the accumulated mail went unopened into the furnace, bills included.

"A lot of fool women," said Jack, dismissing the correspondence with a wave of his hand.

"Don't you even open telegrams? Might be something important."

"Opened one once. Nothing in it."

Jack permitted a cleaning woman to invade his sanctuary once a week, giving her strict instructions not to disturb the cobwebs or the rivers of candlewax that had overflowed their sconces. Ned could not manage stairs, so few people besides Lionel had access to the Alchemist's Corner where Jack, in a mood of dedication, was attempting to transmute baser metals into gold.

Others knew the value of John Barrymore. During the past few years a group had formed around the actor whose purpose was to save the self-destructive man both from himself and from those eager to prey upon his susceptibility. The president of this Barrymore Board of Regents was Ned Sheldon. Constance Collier was an enthusiastic member as was Alexander Woollcott, the brilliant, waspish, partisan theatre critic. John Williams, the producer of *Justice*, had tried to be another, but Jack had broken with Williams. As a result, a new and very important "regent" came into Jack's life: a quiet, round-faced, unassuming little man by the name of Arthur Hopkins, who happened to be the most progressive producer on Broadway. Jack, for a change, had actually come to Hopkins, hearing that he wanted to produce Tolstoy's powerful drama *The Living Corpse*. Hopkins had only been waiting for the right actor to play Fedya Vasilyevich Protosova. He had the Plymouth Theatre cheaply through a generous arrangement with the Shuberts. They would open, Hopkins told Jack, with the Tolstoy play, rechristened *Redemption*. Afterward Jack would stay at the Plymouth for three years building an outstanding repertory which he would then take on tour. Jack listened, thought the plan "rather overburdened with hope," but agreed.

Blanche Thomas was not a member of the Board, yet she exerted more sway now over Jack than anyone else. Ned had first wakened "The Sleeping Beauty" (as Woollcott called Jack); Blanche kept him wide awake. It was she who encouraged him to do *Redemption*, making an adaptation from a literal Russian translation herself. Despising actors as a class, she had the highest ambitions for the aristocratic John Barrymore who, single-handedly, would restore classical acting to the American stage. And she had the highest ambitions for herself, Michael Strange the poet. Together they would soar to undreamed-of heights.

Lazy Jack Barrymore seemed a thing of the past as Jack threw himself into the creation of Protosova. The role was congenial, a study of the degradation of a man who abandons his wife by faking his death, then, after her remarriage, becoming indeed a "living corpse." Fedya called for wild eyes, matted hair, and palsied limbs—all of which Jack was more than eager to provide. No detail was too small. In the first scene in the Gypsies' den, for example, Fedya's hands appear slowly above the back of a couch. Jack did not want those hands to be his own: those hands that to him seemed some monstrous excrescence, like Cain's brand or Byron's clubfoot. He painted his hands white, then outlined each finger in black. The result was the sinister, incredibly tapering white hands that Cornelia Otis Skinner would remember twenty-six years later. Jack also hired a Russian to coach him in accent and flavor, an effort that backfired when Hopkins pointed out that since none of the other actors had accents he sounded like a foreigner among his own people.

Hopkins was impressed with the dedication of the actor about whose instability he'd been warned. But just as Jack's real hands were there underneath the make-up, the profane Jack lurked beneath the earnest actor. Hopkins would be startled by sudden bursts of profanity or scatology. It was, he thought, as if John Barrymore was afraid of losing touch with Jack Barrymore and had to take his pulse from time to time to reassure himself that Jack was alive and well.

Because *Redemption* was a high experiment in every sense, Hopkins brought in Robert Edmond Jones to design the sets and lighting. Jones had been profoundly influenced by Gordon Craig's revolutionary theory that the simpler the set the more powerful its impact, as well as by Max Reinhardt's experimental staging on the Continent. Tolstoy's play itself was modern, proceeding naturalistically in a series of scenes alternating with tableaux, some of them only minutes long. For these Jones designed utterly simple flat backgrounds, achieving the Russian atmosphere by a play of light and shadow that made the groupings of actors look like paintings. With Hopkins's sensitive direction, a huge cast of talented actors, and John Barrymore's intense dedication to creating Fedya, it is probable that Broadway had never before staged a production of higher artistic merit than it did with *Redemption* at the Plymouth Theatre the night of October 3, 1918.

But artistic merit didn't sell tickets. "The play opened," said Hopkins, "receiving laudatory but forbidding reviews. They stressed the Russian melancholy. What had looked like certain success now had disturbing aspects of failure." No matter that John Barrymore had created a Fedya that could be ranked with the best acting of that generation. Business was bad; business continued bad; Russian melancholy plus a raging flu epidemic kept people away in droves. Hopkins and Jack huddled: perhaps they should close. And yet the enthusiasm of the small audiences goaded them to continue. They were right. Like a patient hovering between life and death, *Redemption* survived the crisis: the fever broke, the patient sat up, life surged back. Ignoring the critics, the public began flocking to see the remarkable thing going on at the Plymouth. Receipts climbed. The only dissenter seemed to be Tolstoy's solemn, bearded son, who sat unsmiling through a special performance as Jack acquitted himself magnificently. "But where is Fedya's beard?" he demanded of Hopkins afterward. And yet John Barrymore was supreme in *Redemption*.

Two people were disappointed that *Redemption* was a hit. John D. Williams had been trying to sign Lionel and John since the summer of 1918 to play the Mayo brothers in a new play, *Beyond the Horizon*, by an exciting new playwright named Eugene O'Neill. O'Neill had been dismayed when *Redemption* was announced with John Barrymore, but told himself that such an exotic play could not run long. Week by week he waited for it to fold, but he had underestimated both John Barrymore and the outstanding production.

Lionel visited the Plymouth, though not the way Jack had visited the Shubert for *The Copperhead*. One night Lionel persuaded an actor who had a small part as a Gypsy to let him go on in his place. He disguised himself in a big bushy beard and, armed with his lines written on a scrap of paper, walked onstage and seated himself, placing the scrap on the table in front of him. "So it's you," Jack greeted him on cue. "Yes," came a strangely familiar voice through the beard, "it is I." Jack's antenna quivered; he spotted the scrap of paper. "All right," he said, snatching it, "let's proceed." Since Lionel hadn't a word in his head, Jack adeptly turned the scene into a monologue. But then, thought Lionel sardonically, Jack had always been the clever one.

THAT NOVEMBER 11 bells rang out across the nation proclaiming the end of the Great War, the bloodiest war in history, the war to end all wars. New Yorkers danced in the streets in showers of tickertape; euphoria reigned as the doughboys came marching home.

Russell Colt returned from France to find Ethel touring as usual. Perhaps because the war was over at last, perhaps because the flu epidemic had subsided, or perhaps just because Ethel Barrymore was her usual irresistible self, audiences couldn't seem to get enough of the very *Off Chance* that critics had panned in New York. Russell seemed, as usual, extraneous. The children—now eight, six, and five—were boarding in exclusive private Catholic schools and didn't seem to need him either. There was nothing for him to do at Mamaroneck, so common sense advised him to go back to nursing his bronchitis in Palm Beach.

Leonard Thomas also came home. He found his wife Blanche in love with John Barrymore.

Many did not come home, among them Sidney Rankin Drew, shot down in flames behind the German lines. After his wife Gladys's death in 1914, Uncle Googan had met Lucille McVey on the Vitagraph lot where they were both making movies. Lucille was only twenty-four, less than half Sidney's age, pretty, clever, and fun. Losing no time, Sidney married her the same year Gladys died, then teamed with her in a series of movies scripted by Lucille that introduced a clean, more subtle kind of domestic comedy to the screen. For Sidney the fun ended with the death of his only child.

Uncle Googan had not intended his son for show business: the proudest moment of his life had been the time young Sidney, in his military academy uniform, had invited a bellboy who mistook him for a rival to step out of the hotel and knocked him cold. Yet Sidney could no more resist the family destiny than his cousins Lionel, Jack, and Ethel. Encouraged by Lionel, he had gotten into the movies and gone on to a promising career in film acting and directing as S. Rankin Drew. The war ended that when he was twenty-six. His father did not care to live much longer, taking ill on the road and dying in April 1919. Lionel missed him most: all those martinis he'd spirited to Uncle Googan between Buffalo and St. Louis. The death of Sidney Drew left the mystery of his birth as dark as ever.

AS ETHEL WAS entertaining audiences evidently eager to believe that the world was still a drawing room, Lionel was storming the same cities with *The Copperhead*. On December 2 a first-night Chicago audience "stamped, whistled, and yelled for ten minutes until the star, recalled from his dressing room, reappeared and made a speech." Critics next day out-hyperboled themselves over the sensational triumph at the Garrick. Lionel smiled grimly.

The old terror was gripping him: the horror of drying up onstage before thousands of eyes. He tried reasoning with himself: Lionel, you just want to get out of this damned business and go back to your painting and music. It didn't help. His nights were tortured, he woke in cold sweats, he thought of Maurice and knew he was going crazy. Desperate, he sought out an alienist, in those days the last step before the insane asylum. The psychiatrist probed, but no psychic snakes uncoiled: no suppressed desire for his mother or hatred of his father. He loved his wife; he didn't fool around.

"O.K.," said the analyst. "You have a phobia. Everybody has a little phobia of some sort. Keep it. Good thing. I wouldn't tell anyone about it if I were you, but you won't forget your lines."

Thus reassured, Lionel could again express enthusiasm for the stage. "The movies?" he said in Toledo. "Certainly they are all right, but personally I don't think they are any rival for the legitimate." Yet something was missing in Toledo, specifically the fine big theatre he'd played in last time. Told it was now a movie palace, Lionel was startled. Yet he couldn't believe that movies were threatening the legitimate as much as people believed. Granted, there were fewer and fewer touring companies, but that, he insisted, was the only difference. He was right about the touring companies. With 15,000 movie houses in the country, most of them converted theatres, the old road companies that used to play New York hits like *East Lynne* and *Uncle Tom's Cabin* from city to city were a vanishing breed.

Yet in a season in which (to quote Channing Pollock) there had been not half a dozen plays above the mental level of a ten-year-old, revolutionary breezes were sweeping Broadway. Not only *Redemption* but Arthur Hopkins's season of Ibsen plays with Alla Nazimova. In Barrie's *Dear Brutus* the durable William Gillette supported by a young and remarkably talented actress named Helen Hayes. The experimental Wash-

ington Square Players, that year becoming the nucleus of the Theatre
Guild. Out of town there was equal vitality. George Pierce Baker's 47
Workshop at Harvard continued to turn out promising playwrights. On
a fish wharf the Provincetown Players were giving exciting productions
of new talents like Eugene O'Neill. On the West Coast the Pasadena
Playhouse was setting new standards for good theatre. And Broadway
was about to be clobbered again by all three Barrymores.

Early in 1919 it became apparent that neither the torturous operation
Ned Sheldon had undergone in hopes he could walk again nor the more
torturous stretching treatment that followed had done the slightest good.
"If I only knew what I have ever done to bring all this upon me!" Ned
cried to his mother. That said, he deliberately turned back to the play he
was adapting for Jack from Sem Benelli's *La Cena delle Beffe*. Set in Florence in the days of the Medici, *The Jest* tells of the terrorizing of an effete
young painter, Gianetto Malespina, by the brutal Neri Chiaramantesi and
his brother—the timeless conflict of the weakling and the playground
bully. Gianetto had, in fact, been played by a woman onstage, giving point
to Neri's taunt, "Are you cock or hen?" Central to the quarrel is Ginevra,
Gianetto's betrothed, whom Neri also loves. In the end the persecuted
Gianetto manages to turn the tables on his tormentors, causing Neri to kill
his own brother and go mad. *The Jest* would reunite Jack and Lionel: the
lurid melodrama appealed immensely to both brothers. Rape, blood, lust,
and murder—*The Jest*, said Jack, was like a bullfight in a brothel.

Following his policy of doing two plays a season no matter what the
business, Hopkins called rehearsals in March 1919 for *The Jest* while
Redemption was still selling out the Plymouth. He was looking forward to
working with Lionel, whose performance in *The Mummy and the Hummingbird* had made a deep impression, but shocked to shake hands with
a bent, gray, shuffling old man. How could this ancient play the powerful,
ruthless, drunken Neri? What Hopkins didn't know was that Lionel
checked his own personality like an overcoat whenever he took on a part,
and he had been playing Milt Shanks for more than a year. In the next
days he transformed himself into a big rip-roaring brute who in a struggle
could carry six men on his back and more than thrash both Willard and
Dempsey. It was, thought Hopkins, uncanny.

Magnificently set and lit with fire and moonlight, *The Jest* opened cold
on April 9 and overnight was the sensation of the season, perhaps the
decade. "*The Jest* has fallen across the sky of the declining season like a
burst of sunset color," rhapsodized the *New York Times* as people
stampeded the Plymouth eager to be bathed in the lurid glow. Some were
stunned. "My God!" a dazed playgoer was overheard to exclaim at in-

termission. "I brought my *mother* and my *sister* to this?" Couples argued and friends fell out over the merits of the two performances. Was Lionel better as the bullish, sadistically humorous Neri, or John as the spiritual yet perverse Gianetto? Many ended by agreeing that the American stage had never witnessed finer acting.

Everyone felt the *physicality* of the brothers. Lionel's muscular legs were bare, his arms huge, his heavy sensual face half hidden by long matted hair; for the first time onstage he kissed a woman "long and lingeringly." Jack was aspen-slim but sizzling with sexuality. No woman had ever been costumed more provocatively than this Gianetto: with a crotch swollen by padding and green tights that left nothing to the imagination, Jack made sure Gianetto was a cock. Even more sensual was his portrayal of the artist's psyche: Gianetto is a coward who yet gets a voluptuous thrill out of being in personal danger, an effeminate youth who burns with sexuality. Watching him boil and froth in the presence of his stage lover Ginevra, Blanche suffered the jealousy of the woman who must share her lover with every man and woman in the audience. Jack himself, however, was characteristically flippant about his sex appeal, declaring that in the infamous green tights he resembled nothing more dangerous than "a decadent string bean."

The Barrymores were so spectacular that the other actors tended to be overlooked, but Blanche at least was intrigued with the way Maude Hanaford played Ginevra, the woman who has inflamed both Gianetto's and Neri's passions. Jack himself had insisted that Ginevra not be warm and sensual: harlots, he argued, were not passionate but cold. Maude agreed and made Ginevra remote, almost indifferent. "Sandwiched between the frenzies of Lionel and Jack," said Blanche, "Ginevra, the bone of contention . . . moved with a plastic caution, her hands usually crossed on a slightly protruding belly, her eyes downcast, mysteriously seeming to portray by her presence and in her detachment, a kind of stylization of contempt for the insane virility of these passions she had impishly aroused."

While some argued that Jones's sets and costumes made *The Jest* a sensation, others claimed it was all Barrymore. Woollcott, for example, thought the designer's contribution wildly overrated: without the Barrymores, *The Jest* would be "unthinkable"; with the Barrymores it could be played in a high school auditorium and no one would notice the difference. Dorothy Parker agreed. The Barrymores were, indubitably, "*quelque* family." She had only one piece of advice for those who still had not fallen under their spell: "park the children somewhere, catch the first city-bound train, and go to the Plymouth Theatre, if you have to trade in the baby's Thrift Stamps to buy the tickets. . . . You ought to be able to get nice comfortable standing-room any time after Labor Day."

One standee could have had Booth Tarkington's seat after the first act. "I could write a book about that play and about New York's spasms of ecstasy over it—the paeans from the critics," complained Tarkington to John Peter Toohey. "Penrod wrote plots like that—especially the tantin' of the scoundrel in a celar; and I haven't seen such acting since the old time elocution teacher left the Boys' Classical School in Indianapolis in 1884 to join Jas. C. Milne the preacher-actor. This is confidential, however: the Barrymore boys are friends of mine. They have got the innocentest nerve I ever saw and New York is—well, I can hardly bear it alone: you *bet* it's a Jest!"

In their more rational moments, some spectators came to agree with Tarkington, for Sheldon's script teetered on the ludicrous. Lionel complained that there never was a script at all, just jottings on scraps of letters, envelopes, napkins, and menus—and much of it invented on the spur of the moment at rehearsals. And what invention! For Neri's mad scene, Ned simply borrowed an advertisement for *The Book of Knowledge*: "Why do flies walk upside down? Where does the wind begin? Why do the stars come out?"—lines interpreted as deeply symbolic by the critics. The critics found oaths like "By the twenty-four thumbs of the Twelve Apostles" and "By the holy slipper of Saint Babingoose" profound as well, and were evidently delighted by the "Shakespearean" richness of epithets showered upon Ginevra: chuck, dove, turtle, little macaroon, quail, cheesecake, mustard-pot, trull, dumpling, bird of God, little bowl of lard—an extraordinarily indigestible muddle. But thanks to the Barrymore magic the public ate up *The Jest*.

John Barrymore's acting not only intrigued the general public, however. So persuasively did he play neurotic heroes torn by inner conflict that at least one doctor was inspired to analyze the plays which he made famous. As far back as *Peter Ibbetson*, for example, the noted brain and nerve specialist Dr. Smith Ely Jelliffe had begun a series of articles for medical journals analyzing Peter, Fedya, and now Gianetto as men whose inability to deal with reality leads them to escape in defensive dreaming (Peter), alcoholically induced fantasy (Fedya), and the submission of his essentially good nature to the lower impulses of hate and revenge (Gianetto). In this heyday of Freudianism, Jelliffe naturally attributed all three men's conflicts to the Oedipal complex. In each case the mother-lover figure has been corrupted (either in reality or in the hero's imagination) by a powerful male: Colonel Ibbetson, Victor, and Neri. As a result, Peter kills the Colonel, Fedya kills himself, and Gianetto causes

Neri to kill his own brother and go mad. Just how deeply Jack himself delved into the psychological impulses of his characters is uncertain. He apparently was a friend of Jelliffe, who also knew Hopkins, and Hopkins was profoundly influenced by Freudian theory. More likely, however, Jack's similar conflicts—he was himself a prime escapee from reality—permitted him to play Peter, Fedya, and Gianetto with such truth that plays which in themselves might not have attracted the attention of analysts appealed to some as virtual case histories.

The Jest roared on. In June it got the biggest gross in Times Square: $18,259—triple the take of most theatres and the only show not affected by a heat wave that left Jack and Lionel drenched after their strenuous performances. The Jest, in fact, made Broadway history by being the first play ever to draw more than a musical comedy. But Jack and Lionel didn't care. Again they'd had enough, and Hopkins closed the wildly successful play a week early at their request.

ETHEL TOO WOUND UP her extraordinarily successful Off Chance tour in the Midwest the summer that Prohibition became law. Announcements that she, Lionel, and Jack would make a movie version of Peter Ibbetson came to nothing because the three stars proved too costly for Famous Players–Lasky; as a result the public and posterity lost the chance of seeing John and Ethel make love to each other on film. Instead Russell joined her in Toledo for the Dempsey-Willard fight, putting a great deal of money on Willard while Ethel bet her shirt on Dempsey. With her winnings she went to White Sulphur Springs, West Virginia, in August for the baths and golf, which she played with authority. She celebrated her fortieth birthday there with, among other pleasures, the third act of Zoë Akins's wonderful play. She would begin rehearsing Déclassée as soon as she got back to New York.

But when she got there and was going to visit her cousin Georgie on Forty-fifth Street, she found the streets so crowded that Britt couldn't get the De Dion-Bouton through and she had to get out and walk to Georgie's apartment.

"What are all those people doing?"

"Don't you know? It's the actors' strike."

"Strike?" said Ethel, who hadn't been reading the papers. "What for?"

The pampered star might well ask. Charles Frohman and now Alf Hayman had always treated her well. But most actors were at the bottom of the ladder as far as pay, benefits, and rights went—even though they *were* the show. The Actors Equity Association had been founded in 1913; many actors, however, were anti-union. Incredibly, Minnie Maddern

Fiske, who with Maurice Barrymore and Sarah Bernhardt had battled the Syndicate at the turn of the century, hated the very word "union" because it implied that acting was not an art but a trade. William Collier also thought unions and strikes degrading: "I don't want stagehands calling me Willie," a sentiment shared by E. H. Sothern and George M. Cohan, who refused to join Actors Equity. Now, however, the majority of actors, led by Frank Bacon, who had toured for thirty years before reaching Broadway, were on strike. They were protesting not only low pay but such injustices as being left stranded when a tour suddenly folded and rehearsing ten weeks (eighteen for musicals) without pay. They wanted an end to slavery.

There in Georgie's apartment, Ethel suddenly knew whose side she was on. "I ought to belong to Equity," she said.

"You damn fool," said Georgie, staring, "you're a life member. [Ethel had the habit of signing things without reading the large print.] You should go and show yourself at headquarters and be there, as everyone else is."

"Oh, no," said Ethel, not believing that her presence would matter. But she finally agreed because Georgie was so passionate about it.

In the streets milling crowds surrounded them and swept them along with such force that Ethel, terrified, thought of tumbrels and guillotines. But by the time they reached Equity headquarters, something had happened. The crowds of extras and chorus girls had recognized her and suddenly a great shout of welcome rang out, a shout that seemed to come from the very souls of these people who were her people. It rocked her, left her trembling and exalted. Then she was half carried up the steps and into the brownstone and lifted onto a table. People were sobbing and grabbing her hands and kissing them and kissing the hem of her skirt. "It's all right," they were crying. "We've won! We've won!"

She was too shaken to give a speech. "I'm with you, whatever it is," she said tremulously. "Stick. You will win, for you are right." Suddenly, miraculously, she was their leader, a goddess descended among mortals. Yet those who had seen her as Barrie's Kate and Emma McChesney should not have been surprised.

She took hold as she always had. She promptly telephoned Uncle Jack in Easthampton, and though that well-heeled actor had no personal grievance against the managers, there was no question of his loyalty. Ethel wrote the statement he read the next day at an Equity meeting: "While my entire theatrical career has been associated with but one management from whom I have received only fairness and consideration, I feel that the traditions of my family and my personal predilections ally me, logically and irremediably, with the members of my profession in the Actors Equity Association." Drew then announced that both Lionel and John Barrymore had asked him to announce their allegiance with the strikers. The Drew-Barrymores had again closed ranks.

On August 24 Ethel issued a declaration of independence to the *New York Times*:

> People understand, I think, that all my experience under one management has been a happy one. Mr. Frohman never made a contract and always kept his word. . . . The change began with the great combinations of managers. From that time on, making more money, at any sacrifice of standards, has been their one end. . . . A good many managers appear to think they are simply merchants and the actors are their stock in trade. When they think more money can be made that way, they put on plays that the best of the profession are ashamed of. . . . Of all the childish things that have been said against us, the funniest is that the *actors* are forgetting the dignity of their art! . . . All we are working for is democracy in the theatre, justice, equality, truth. I have never thought of leaving the cause. I believe with my whole heart that it is right. But if I felt less conviction than I do, I would not leave. These are my people.

On August 26 Alf Hayman called a rehearsal of *Déclassée* for the next day. Ethel replied that she would not attend any rehearsal until the strike was settled. On August 28 at the Hotel Astor she and Uncle Jack led the Grand March at the Actors Equity ball, which raised $27,000 for the strike. The next day a furious Hayman told Ethel he could postpone rehearsals no longer and was cabling Mrs. Patrick Campbell to come over and play Lady Helen Haddon. "I'm sure she will be very good," said Ethel.

Because the actors were getting hungrier, Equity then organized three weeks of benefit performances at the Lexington Opera House. Everyone not a Fido (a member of the anti-union Actors Fidelity Association) pitched in. When the Shuberts issued an injunction against Ed Wynn's appearing on a stage, Wynn delivered his comic monologue from the house. Eddie Cantor and Eddie Foy also drew roars from the crowd, which was suddenly hushed, however, by the strains of "Plaisir d'Amour." Ethel's entrance as Marguerite Gautier for a scene with Conway Tearle and Lionel as Monsieur Duval was applauded for three minutes. ". . . Miss Barrymore's voice!" raved Woollcott. "But then how can a hum-drum day-by-day reviewer of dramatic entertainment hope to describe that enchantment. It would be like measuring the music of a purling brook and that calls for a poet." Lionel's Monsieur Duval was even better than Ethel's Marguerite, however: visually superb, remarkable in characterization. And then Lionel came back again and blew everyone away with the Lincoln scene from *The Copperhead*.

On September 6 the managers finally capitulated and called a meeting with Actors Equity. Ethel, Frank Gillmore, Francis Wilson, and Lillian Russell represented the actors; Al Woods, William Brady, Arthur Hopkins, and John Golden management. According to Golden, it was "more like a love feast than the settlement of a bitter strike." Management gave in on every point, in some cases actually offering more than the actors had demanded. The strike was over. The actors had won.

The following Monday at the Empire Ethel found a sullen Alf Hayman though no sign of Mrs. Patrick Campbell. In the next days Hayman made it very clear that he had not forgiven the renegade. *Déclassée* needed a classy setting, but Hayman provided nothing but repainted backdrops and old warehouse furniture. When Ethel pointed out that the first act required a large sofa, Hayman sulked and said he did not choose to buy one. Desperate, Ethel went out and bought a beautiful piece herself, expecting reimbursement. She never got it.

Lionel, Doris, and Jack attended Ethel's final dress rehearsal. "If I hadn't gone she would never have spoken to me again," Jack wrote Blanche, vacationing in Paris. "Doris said Lionel and I looked in the taxi cab like 'two heiffers [*sic*] led to the slaughter.' " By now Jack was head over heels in love with the woman he called "my weeny beloved my own darling fig." Blanche, however, was jealous of Katherine, whom Ethel had got a good part in *Déclassée*; well aware of Ethel's favoritism, Blanche feared Jack's ex-wife would try to worm her way back into his affections. Jack reassured her: "I saw Katherine. She came and sat with us during an act when she wasn't on the stage—and asked me about you and I said 'I am more fond of her than anything I've ever known and I hope you are glad and wish me well.' She was really terribly nice. . . ." About Ethel's performance he said nothing, but then he seemed to be there under protest in the first place.

Amid rancor and coldness backstage, *Déclassée* opened at the Empire on October 6. The failure of *The Lady of the Camellias* still rankled; Ethel needed a hit. And this first play by a young woman from Missouri would be one of Ethel Barrymore's greatest successes.

THIRTEEN

1919–1920

WITHOUT KNOWING Ethel Barrymore personally, Zoë Akins had distilled her essence in Lady Helen Haddon. Aristocratic, extravagant, self-admittedly a very ignorant woman, Lady Helen still knows something about everything in the world because she is eager and intelligent. Above all, there is a magnificence in her blood, a reckless urge to squander life and fortune precisely because life and fortune have been so lavishly kind. But then she is the last of the "mad Varricks" and doomed by blood. "The Curse of the Barrymores" echoes through *Déclassée* like the clank of chains.

Dramatically, too, Akins's play dealt Ethel the kind of hand she played best. English drawing rooms, hotel lounges, Park Avenue mansions. Entrances "curiously aflame" or "like a violent goddess walking on the wind." Waiters to summon, cigarettes to light, champagne to sip. Exits—Mozart playing in the background, friends hovering. "It's like the theatre—when they turn out the lights before the curtain rises—on the next act," murmurs Lady Helen before her head falls forward and "the last shudder tears her breath from her lips." Zoë Akins was a clever Barrymore tailor.

The first-night audience went insane, but Alf Hayman was still sulking. "Well, it may be all right," he told Ethel after the curtain came down positively for the last time, "—if that audience is on the level."

It was. Again the word swept New York: "Oh, let's go see her die!" Firemen were called in to handle the crowds in front of the theatre, and finally Alf Hayman himself could be seen in a second box office chewing on a cigar as he raked in ticket money. "A brilliant play!" fluted Woollcott. "Beg, borrow, or steal, but get to the Empire Theatre!" urged Heywood Broun. "If, during my theatre-going lifetime, there has been any other performance so perfect as the one [Ethel Barrymore] gives," said Dorothy Parker, ". . . I can only say that I had the hideous ill luck to miss it."

But then, said Ethel, those same raving critics mysteriously began taking back their wildly enthusiastic reviews. *Variety* was a case in point. "Miss Barrymore has done in this piece far and away the finest work of her artistic career. Nothing else approaches it. . . . It is indeed so fine that it is questionable if it will enjoy popular appeal—by which is meant that the play is probably over the head of the average playgoer." A month later *Variety* was cold as November. *Déclassée*, it said, was "interesting at least." What had inspired this incredible turnabout?

Certainly second thoughts on first nights could fault *Déclassée*. Lines like "My life is like water that has gone over the dam and turned no mill wheels" could be considered—well, corny. Drawing rooms, butlers, and a code of honor that makes a tragedy out of cheating at cards were all, moreover, distinctly passé. And Lady Helen's death. Wasn't it just another case of the "woman with a past" sentenced to die because she was normally sexed? A modernist like Bernard Shaw would have wed Lady Helen to the Jewish millionaire who loves her, uniting old blood with new money to the improvement of both. Akins's ending could be dismissed as reactionary.

And yet *Déclassée* was a parable for the times. Lady Helen's descent from her London drawing room to the millionaire's mansion where she finds *her* ancestral portraits gracing his walls symbolized the defeat of the aristocracy by the capitalist classes that had been completed by the Great War. Lady Helen dies after she is struck by a "noisy little taxi," that taxi a symbol of the new mobility of the middle classes in a competitive world in which Lady Helen cannot survive. And Akins has prepared for this death by emphasizing Lady Helen's love of the past, her obsolete code of chivalry. No: finally what was wrong with *Déclassée* was that people in 1919 were not supposed to sympathize any longer with aristocrats like Lady Helen Haddon—and Zoë Akins had.

According to Ethel, the critics' change of heart had nothing to do with the quality of *Déclassée* at all. It was jealousy pure and simple: the jealousy of the "Vicious Circle" at the Algonquin, where, said Ethel scornfully, "the wisecrack often passed for wit." She meant, of course, the Round Table, that group of ten or so regulars who met for lunch at Frank Case's "Algonk" on West Forty-fourth Street. Alexander Woollcott, Franklin Pierce Adams, Heywood Broun, Ruth Hale, John Peter Toohey, Robert Benchley, George and Beatrice Kaufman, Harold Ross, and Dorothy Parker formed its nucleus—the glitterati of their day. Zoë Akins was decidedly not a member.

Interestingly enough, the Round Table was born that winter of 1919–1920 when *Déclassée* looked as though it would run forever. None of the regulars could boast a smash hit on Broadway that season, reason enough to whet their malice. Perhaps if Zoë Akins had gone down on her knees like Edna Ferber, who pleaded, "Could I maybe lunch at the Round Table once?" the Vicious Circle might have relented. But Zoë refused to petition. Actually critical opinion proved to have no impact on *Déclassée*'s enormous popularity, something that two years later the Round Table had neither forgotten nor forgiven when they got up an evening of vaudeville skits called *No Siree!* The funniest skit, "Zowie, or the Curse of an Akins Heart," set in "Printemps 1922," poked delicious fun at society tragedies, with Ruth Gillmore as Zhoolie Venable giving a brilliant imitation of Ethel's Lady Helen. And perhaps the Round Table did indeed have the last laugh. No Pulitzer drama award was made in 1919, the year *Déclassée* was an obvious contender. Zoë Akins's Pulitzer Prize for *The Old Maid* in 1935 seemed an admission that she should have won in 1919 for *Déclassée*.

But quite apart from *Déclassée*, Ethel resented the Round Table wits. Long before Woollcott et al. discovered it, the Algonquin had been *her* hotel: hers and John Drew's and Jack's. Its theatre-loving owner, Frank Case, had previously managed the Lambs Club; when he took over the Algonquin he rolled out the red carpet for the Drews and Barrymores. It was understood that they occupied a certain table against the wall which commanded the entire room. When Jack was down and out, he had always been able to count on a free bed at the Algonquin and, if his own clothes were too disreputable (and they usually were), Frank Case's personal wardrobe. And it was at the Algonquin that Zoë Akins had told Ethel, "I've written a play for you."

Besides, Ethel was quite accustomed to wits. Maurice could have laid the Round Table flat. Georgie would have shone. Ethel herself could be just as malicious as Alec Woollcott, that modern Madame Defarge. Moreover, some of the members were friends: the brilliantly loquacious Herbert Bayard Swope, for example, who always called her "Ekett" because that's how her name looked in signature. As for the "little baby New Jersey Nero," whatever knives he may have thrown at table, Woollcott had salaamed to the Barrymores in print for years. To Ethel, therefore, the Barrymores were an institution at the Algonquin, the Round Tablers mere snipers. Not only were they undaunting, she found them pathetically childish.

She was daunting to a young actress dubbed "The Baby of the Round Table." Tallulah Bankhead's aunt had chosen the Algonquin as a residence for her beautiful, fey, stage-struck Alabaman niece who had come to conquer New York at the ripe age of sixteen. Tallulah had worshipped at Ethel's shrine ever since *Déclassée* had opened; she not only knew Lady

Helen's lines by heart but had perfected the most subtly amusing take-off of Ethel Barrymore in New York. Still, she was unprepared when she entered the Algonquin elevator one day to find herself face to face with her idol. "I had to lean against the wall of the car to keep from collapsing," said Tallulah, "so overpowered was I by her presence. Her imperious manner, the scorn in her voice, the contempt in her eyes, the great reputation in which she was cloaked, made a violent impact on me. When introduced to her by Estelle Winwood, I was struck dumb. In view of my vocal record, what higher proof can I offer of my awe, my devotion?"

Desperate for any kind of attention, as well as for food and a Broadway part, Tallulah often sang for her supper by giving clever imitations of Broadway stars. So when Frank Crowninshield, the editor of *Vanity Fair*, asked her to do Ethel Barrymore one evening, she was ready, ready until Crowninshield said, "Miss Barrymore is one of my guests. What's more, she has asked you to do it." Tallulah could not refuse. When she entered the room where the guests were gathered, Ethel was sitting immediately in front, imperial in blue-black silk and pearls. "Licked by the flames of hell," Tallulah launched into her very witty impersonation. When she finished to applause, she went to Ethel and said, "Miss Barrymore, please forgive my impertinence."

Ethel gave her a withering glance; Ethel had no superior as a witherer. "But my dear," she drawled, "you make me look so fat."

"But Miss Barrymore," said Tallulah, trembling but irrepressible, "I was imitating *you*."

At which, like a violent goddess walking on the wind, Ethel rose and slapped her.

Jack was hardly less overwhelming. One day as he was dining at the Algonquin with Ethel and Estelle Winwood, Tallulah felt his eyes follow her as she table-hopped across the room. She saw him lean to question Estelle, saw Estelle beckoning. Then she found herself seated next to not only the most exciting actor but the most Greek-godly handsome man in New York. She was shocked at his impact.

Jack began dropping into the Algonquin rather frequently—not, said her spy, to see Ethel. There were developments. "I hope you don't think me cheap," Tallulah told the actress Margalo Gillmore. "But I've allowed Jack Barrymore to kiss me." Finally there was a note bidding her to his dressing room at the Plymouth after a matinee of *The Jest*. Outwardly calm, she made her way backstage while less fortunate females in the audience went home to dream of John Barrymore into their pillows. Was he going to offer her a role in a play or a roll in the hay? Tallulah looked sophisticated, even a tart, but she was still "silk."

Jack's opening gambit staggered her. He was about to film *Dr. Jekyll and Mr. Hyde*. Would she, Tallulah, like to be his leading lady?

Offered what an actress might kill for, Tallulah heard herself declaring that she wasn't interested in movies, that she wanted to make her mark on the stage, that flattered though she was she must decline his offer.

Jack accepted her refusal gracefully, then attacked on a different front. Making little animal noises in his throat, he rose and began pulling her toward the casting couch. Offered what any woman would have killed for, Tallulah again declined. Jack pleaded. Tallulah fled and found herself on the cold pavement of West Forty-fifth Street.

Years later Tallulah would say that she never could make up her mind who she was more in love with, Jack or Ethel. Jack finally admitted defeat. "For the good part of a season I wore myself out trying to impress Tallulah," he said. "I felt like a bullfighter who makes his kill and is then publicly given the boot. . . . In all truth, I must report that our relationship was loathsomely platonic."

Tallulah became a friend of Ethel's. Ethel adored Jack, and Tallulah was much like him: gifted, wild, breathtakingly impractical—who else on an allowance of fifty dollars a week would spend twenty-five on a French maid? Like Jack too, Tallulah tried to solve her conflicts with drugs. She did not drink, but she used cocaine in these years when fashionable invitations read, "Will you come to my snowball?" and guests received hypodermic needles in ultrachic vanity cases. Cocaine didn't solve her problems any more than alcohol solved Jack's; it made her "dirty and rude" to people, and whenever Estelle could find her friend's stash she flushed it down the toilet. With Ethel, however, Tallulah was always on her best behavior. She copied her idol's tastes in people and politics; she became just as much of a baseball fanatic. She was adoring and loyal and had class; and Ethel invited her to court.

At the same time he was pursuing the silky-haired ingenue from Alabama, Jack was pledging deathless love to Blanche, currently in Paris setting the wheels of her divorce in motion.

> My darling my own tiny fig—my baby [wrote Jack]. . . . I'm sure you meant that the deceit of other people regarding us—to *each other*—would roll off our love like frogs off a crystal mountain— and leave us shining and smiling with our tiny hands grown together like a lovely tree and the brown earth. . . . I *know* I can *never* be happy til my tiny soul is sitting on the pinnacle—the *utter* top—with *nothing* above it but the sky! and no initials carved on trees by people who have been there before—I want to sit beside

you in a place where no foot has ever been and the wind that fans our faces is virginal as off a hitherto unseen and undiscovered snow—Oh my own *darling* beloved I love you so terrifically like a spark from Vulcan's forge purified by centuries of unsatisfied desire—There is more quivering strength in one slender attenuated line of my love for you than in the bulk and surge of all the lovers that have ever lived my darling—It is like Astarte and the horn of Isis wrapped in the light of some white-flaming cross—or a saint's heart with a burning snake in it—or the pallid breathless soul of moonlight dipped in blood! My beloved I am going to lie down now and close my eyes and think of resting my passionate head in the Lethe of your body—and forgetting everything but its fragrance and the soul-rest of your lovely skin—Good by my darling I love you—tiny one.

Though the insecure man did not stop pursuing other women, Jack had soared to new heights in his love for Blanche. He loved her "incomparably more wonderfully" than he ever had thought it possible for him to love. And yet these new heights were dizzying and dangerous. He sensed that Blanche had an ego as rapacious and a will stronger than his own. The tender words he showered upon her—tiny fig, my baby, tiny one, little Genius Fish, little wife—spoke of his yearning for true intimacy but also his need to defuse her power, to reduce her to something tiny, safe, sweet, manageable. Blanche was none of these.

She had great power over him because she had not yet decided to marry him. Her parents were horrified at her divorcing Leonard for a man like Jack Barrymore. He had not reformed: despite promises to stop drinking, he was seen staggering in the street. She must think of her two sons. Blanche did think—of her sons, her social position, Jack's instability. Her cables and letters stopped.

OH MY BABY WHAT IN THE NAME OF GOD COULD MAKE YOU SO COLD TO ME [Jack wired her frantically] I HAVE BEEN SO WRETCHED I HAVE WRITTEN YOU LETTERS THAT WERE LIKE THE LAST WAIL OF THE DAMNED IN THE VALLEY OF THE DEAD AND TORN THEM UP OH MY BELOVED MY DEAREST BELOVED I HAVE WAITED AND LONGED AND PRAYED AND CURSED FOR YOU ALL MY LIFE LIKE A MAROONED SOUL ON A DESERTED COAST PLEASE FOR THE LOVE OF HEAVEN BELIEVE THAT YOUR FUTURE IS STREWN WITH LITTLE PIECES OF MY HEART FOR YOUR FEET TO

WALK ON SO THEY NEED NOT TOUCH THE EARTH I LOVE YOU
I LOVE YOU I LOVE YOU

And then Blanche wrote again and Jack shot up to the heavens—until he began to agonize about the men she must be sleeping with in Paris. And then he would prowl the purlieus of the Algonquin or any other hunting ground. Filming *The Test of Honor* in New York that season with Jack, Constance Binney found herself literally being chased around the room by the handsome actor. "You remind me of a beautiful white dove on a black velvet cushion," panted Jack. "But Mr. Barrymore," protested Constance, "that's what you told my sister last week!"

BREAKING ALL BOX-OFFICE records, *The Jest* could have run indefinitely. It had shot Arthur Hopkins to the front rank of American theatrical producers and Lionel and John to the top of their profession. Still, it was clear who was the star. When Lionel left the production at the end of 1919, business did not fall off seriously, everyone agreeing that Alphonz Ethier also made an excellent Neri. But when a severe case of the grippe forced Jack to quit, receipts plummeted. Gilda Varesi took his place, but though Gianetto had been acted by a woman in Europe, people complained that Varesi could not possibly counterfeit the sexuality vital to the part. Jack returned in February and business boomed again, but no matter how popular, *The Jest* was in its last days. Hopkins was not interested in producing hits but in building a repertory for America's most exciting actor. Next, Shakespeare.

Some years before, Jack and Ned had been strolling through the Bronx Zoo when Jack's eye had been caught by a particularly evil-looking red tarantula, its back rubbed bald from struggling to squeeze out of its cage.

"He looks just like Richard the Third," said Jack, staring fascinated.

"Why don't you play him?" said Ned.

Always intrigued by the sinister and the deformed, Jack had debated playing Richard from that day. Now the time had come. *Richard the Third*, designed by Robert Edmond Jones, would open on the first of March.

None of the acting versions Hopkins studied had satisfied him. Shakespeare was not dated; Kean, Booth, Forrest, McCullough, and Barrett were. Hopkins went back to the text itself, treating it like any other new play, though in the event he did not despise Richard Mansfield's acting version which, combining scenes from *Henry the Sixth*, showed Richard as a boy poised at the crossroads of good and evil. He deliberately recruited a cast with no Shakespearean experience and no accents, British or regional. He discarded traditional stage business, handing the actors their lines typed without any directions; he forbade old-fashioned declamation and rhetorical gesture. He urged the cast not to treat Shakespeare with reverence: reverence could turn a rousing melodrama into a funeral. He asked them to immerse themselves spontaneously in "the rich flow of the play."

Yet sheer spontaneity would not do for the star. Jack had no Shakespearean training, nor had he sat at the knees of classical actors like E. H. Sothern and Walter Hampden. Richard Mansfield had been a great Richard III, but Maurice had not taken his son to see the American actor. Although Jack had worked with a speech coach for *The Jest*, he could still lapse into an ugly slovenliness, sounding, complained his Uncle Jack, "like a ruffian from Avenue A." Nor did his voice have the range and timbre for Shakespearean iambics. Certainly he lacked the physical robustness of the tragedians who had stormed through *Richard the Third* in the past.

The solution turned out to be the actor Walter Huston's sister Margaret Carrington. Margaret, an imposing Wagnerian-soprano kind of woman, was a gifted singer and teacher of speech whose unusual methods could turn crows into nightingales. A wealthy woman, she would accept no money, only working with pupils who intrigued her. With John Barrymore she had never been so intrigued. Five hours a day they worked on his diction, voice control, and rhythm. Quickly the comb-and-paper voice took on sonority, elasticity, precision. Consonants rapped, vowels sang, periods rang with force and authority. The change was phenomenal. Jack called Margaret Carrington a white witch.

Inspired, Jack threw himself into creating Richard. He sketched two suits of armor and a two-handed sword, then ferreted out an old German metalworker in Newark who could produce them. To achieve Richard's "swift limp" he hit upon the technique of pointing his right foot inward toward his left instep, then forgetting about it. "I did not try to walk badly," said Jack, "I walked as *well* as I could." As for Richard's mentality, Jack imagined him imbued with all the Machiavellian subtlety of the Italian Renaissance. His Richard would be an intellectual with a mordant sense of humor, beautiful in deformity like a *fleur du mal*. As Gianetto in *The Jest* had created a protective armor of mockery to shield his weakness, this Richard would shield his physical deformity with total ruthlessness. Subtle, cruel, vain, this was not an inhuman but a superhuman Richard, as titanic as Lucifer surveying his kingdom of Hell.

Above all, this Richard would be magnificent. Jones's dark, nakedly somber sets were designed to throw the brilliantly colored king into strong relief. Richard in a glowing orange doublet on a glossy black horse. Richard wrapped in a scarlet cloak astride a white steed, inviting the little princes into the cold gray Tower. Richard at Bosworth Field, flashing in coppery armor. The white horse, incidentally, drove the usually calm Hopkins to despair by constantly rattling its bit and pawing the floor. Rehearsals ground to a stop until Jack said mildly from the saddle, "But Hoppy, isn't that exactly what a horse *would do?*"

Finally the eagerly awaited premiere had to be pushed forward to March 6: Jack needed more time. Indeed, he was near exhaustion. In the last four years he had risen to the top of his profession with *Justice, Redemption, Peter Ibbetson,* and *The Jest,* at the same time continuing to make movies. While he was plumbing the depths of Russian despair nightly as Fedya, for example, he had been shooting a pull-out-all-stops farce called *Here Comes the Bride* during the day. And then in November 1919 he had begun filming *Dr. Jekyll and Mr. Hyde.* The movie was a revelation. Many stage stars tried film acting; many failed. In *Jekyll and Hyde* John Barrymore proved that a great stage actor could transfer that talent to the screen *and* be appreciated by a public who had never entered a theatre in its life.

Of course the dual role of a good doctor transformed by an evil potion into a monster was intensely sympathetic to Jack, who was himself possessed by "dark urges" and whom alcohol could literally transform from a courteous, charming fellow into a foul-mouthed beast. In Robert Louis Stevenson's novel, Mr. Hyde is an ordinary little man whose evil is betrayed only in his sickly smile. Richard Mansfield had played the transformation with no make-up, just a change of lights and expression. Jack used first facial distortion then make-up to create an obscene monster with lank locks falling from a head peaked as though corruption had erupted through the skull. Jack's portrayal of Hyde's degeneration from lust to murder was also masterful. Its culmination—Hyde raising his head from his victim's neck, his face lit with obscene joy as he tastes human blood for the first time—remains one of the most horrific moments on film. Underlining the horror of Hyde is the astonishing beauty of Dr. Jekyll: the contrast shocks, like a maggot at the heart of a rose. And yet there is a flaw in that beauty: Jack's own ugly, blunt hands that he so loathed. Surely it was his idea to ride Jekyll's sleeves well above the wrists as he lifts the potion to his lips, displaying the hands as a symbol of the good doctor's potential for harm.

Despite his enthusiasm for the movie, Jack claimed disappointment at the result. "We had a good scenario," he said, "and yet when I saw the picture, as released, just one incident was right, and that the one in which

Dr. Jekyll tells his valet that a man described as Hyde is to run his house." No one agreed. Though the film was "decidedly not for women or children," *Dr. Jekyll and Mr. Hyde* broke all house records at the Rivoli in New York and drew a chorus of praise. "Unlike many players with stage reputation," said the *Times*, "[John Barrymore] has come to the screen with an understanding of the requisites for acting before the camera and the ability to suit his acting to the understanding. No actor needs fewer subtitles, or leaders, to make him intelligible. He belongs conspicuously in the relatively small class of actors in motion pictures who are really motion picture actors."

But now New York awaited *Richard the Third*. On the gusty night of March 6, a limousine pulled up to the striped awning in front of the Plymouth Theatre and a dark woman wrapped in sables emerged. Followed by a woman friend, she handed the doorman her ticket which, he saw with surprise, was not for the coveted first ten rows but for the balcony. Blanche Thomas was intentionally early for the premiere of *Richard the Third*; she wanted to savor every moment. Because this Richard, she told herself, was as much hers as Jack's. It was she who, on her return from Paris, introduced him to Margaret Carrington. She herself had lived the part with him, going over every line, watching rehearsals from the dark front of the house. After a scene he often left the stage to confer with her rather than with Hopkins. Yet although she was deeply involved with the production, she did not want to be conspicuous. Her affair with John Barrymore had made her notorious. Tonight she would be hidden from the curious, hovering like a good angel among the gallery gods.

One person with an equally big stake in tonight's performance would not be there. Ned Sheldon could no longer leave his bed, paralyzed by an arthritis whose severity baffled his doctors. Jack had played his Richard for Ned in private, but that was far from seeing the Shakespearean debut of the friend whose rise he had spurred.

By curtain time, the theatre was as charged with electricity as a summer thunderstorm. The combination of John Barrymore, Arthur Hopkins, and Robert Edmond Jones promised the kind of excellence that had been missing from the American theatre since Richard Mansfield and Augustin Daly had left the scene. And the audience was not disappointed. This sinister Richard, his face "like a dagger—now glittering, now dull," was a gorgeous creation, as was the voice that delivered Shakespeare's lines. No one would have recognized in this strong, sonorous instrument the slouching diction into which the old John Barrymore could fall.

The applause was tumultuous. Called before the curtain after the second interval, John made a neat little speech begging tolerance for his "audacious plunge." He was cheered. The delight of the audience boiled over again when, their own plays over, John Drew, Lionel, and Ethel entered a box to a burst of applause. The Royal Family of actors had gathered. They were, thought many, the closest thing America had to royalty with their artistic lineage, their class, their charm. Ethel could have withered Queen Mary; George V looked common next to John Drew. And, unlike most royal families, the Drew-Barrymores were entertaining.

Richard ran so long that first night that one wit was overheard thanking his hostess for the lovely *weekend*, yet John held the audience riveted until nearly one in the morning, an extraordinary feat. When the last curtain fell, the audience rose to cheer. John appeared, clad in the coppery armor, pale, exhausted, triumphant. The curtain rose and fell, rose and fell as Blanche leaned forward in her seat, smiling down on a triumph she felt was half her own. When it was over at last the audience knew that America had the great Shakespearean actor of its generation.

The morning papers brought criticism, of course. The tent scene in which Richard is visited by the ghosts of his victims was tepid. The battle of Bosworth Field lacked fireworks, partly because Barrymore's heavy armor prevented lightning action. And Hopkins's Shakespearean inno-cents had decidedly backfired. Alec Woollcott called half the players "intolerable" and the other half, "—well, tolerable," while other critics accused Jack of demanding a mediocre company so he would shine, a groundless charge.

But acclaim burst like a fanfare. John Barrymore had turned from a spoiled theatrical Prince Hal into a superb actor. "His voice is now beau-tifully placed, deep and sonorous and free," said the critic of *The New Republic*. "And his body, once a rather shiftless tenement, is now a man-sion, or rather a house in which there are many mansions." Arthur Horn-blow called his Richard "wonderfully brilliant, daringly bold and insistently fascinating." Woollcott found it richly satisfying, "like a sudden dish of rare and enrapturing meat served to one who had been dieting overmuch on hearts of lettuce and very thin sandwiches." Heywood Broun declared Jack's Richard "the most inspiring performance which this generation has seen." Kenneth Macgowan proclaimed it "the finest moment in American theatre." All marveled at "that rapid, unexpected ascent which began four years ago with the production of *Justice*, and which has been unparalleled in the theatre of our time."

No one was more proud of Jack than Arthur Hopkins, who thought his Richard "unforgettable": dazzlingly compounded of "fire, beauty, humor, cajolery, chilling cruelty." Hopkins's pride was reflected in the audience's. America had long nursed an inferiority complex about its Shakespeare. Now it had an actor whose name could be pronounced with the names Kean, Macready, Irving, and Forbes-Robertson. John Barrymore must play Romeo, Malvolio, Hamlet, Lear. And—the thought was irresistible—what an Iago he would make to Lionel's Othello!

Richard the Third became a hit, ash-barrel posters proclaiming SEATS EIGHT WEEKS IN ADVANCE as it easily led the town for a nonmusical. And second and third? Ethel Barrymore in *Déclassée* and at the Criterion Lionel Barrymore in *The Letter of the Law*. It was this season of 1919–1920 that the term "Broadway's Royal Family of Actors" was coined as the name BARRYMORE blazed from three separate playhouses. It was this year that would go down in theatrical history as the great Barrymore year.

For all his modesty, Lionel was not averse to seeing his name alone illuminating a marquee; he had left *The Jest* because John D. Williams had offered him a starring role. And yet though he was again turning in a performance of consummate skill, he was still running third. His acting was as good as Ethel's and John's (some thought it better), but he lacked their allure and excitement. Another problem was the play. Slow-moving and heavily burdened with the technicalities of the French legal system, *The Letter of the Law* only came alive when Lionel as Mouzon, the brutal prosecutor, held the stage. Acting again with her husband, Doris did onstage for Lionel what she did off, serving as "an excellent foil for the star, feeding him just the stuff he [is] so well adapted to turn to full theatrical advantage." Indeed, Lionel's heartless, ambitious French attorney was another brilliant creation, as different from Milt Shanks as Milt Shanks was from Neri. As *Variety* recognized, "There is this about Lionel Barrymore: he never seems the same. His brother has something he hasn't got but John Barrymore is always John Barrymore. He does not submerge himself as this man does and has without any tricks of make-up in this carefully staged and presented play by Brieux."

And yet Lionel could never catch up with Jack. He too had a film released this year, but *The Copperhead* only proved that some plays do not translate into movies. The play had only reached greatness during Lionel's long tour de force evocation of Abraham Lincoln. Little of this could be conveyed by pantomime. Attempting to compensate, the film introduced an actual Lincoln, not only robbing the story of its only great scene but adding nothing since Lincoln was played by a totally inadequate actor. Misdirected by Charles Maigne, *The Copperhead*, unlike *Dr. Jekyll and Mr. Hyde*, did nothing to convince movie audiences that this Barrymore too was a great actor.

THANKS TO IRONIES like "I enjoyed the first five hours of *Richard*," the curtain at the Plymouth Theatre now came down at eleven-thirty. Still, it was a strenuous three hours for the star. His armor was so heavy that Richard's backward falls in battle shocked Jack's skull and bruised his spine and so hot from spot and footlights that the armor had to be hosed with cold water before Jack's valet Paul could extract him. On matinee days Harry Davenport and his wife Phyllis Rankin sent Jack his supper because he was too tired to go out and get it, but after three weeks Jack insisted on cutting Thursday matinees because of the intense physical strain. His temper snapped one night when his "A horse, a horse! My Kingdom for a horse!" was greeted with a guffaw. "Hold, make haste to saddle yon braying ass!" cried Jack without missing a beat. He brought down the house, but this did not improve his disposition.

Then too, a few critical arrows had finally pierced that heavy armor. Admitting that John Barrymore "allures and dazzles," Ludwig Lewisohn objected both to the histrionics that canceled "the note of ultimate sincerity" and to the actor's self-consciousness: "We watch John Barrymore doing marvelous things, and he watches himself with an eager appreciation and applause." And as enthusiastic as Woollcott was about this Richard, the critic said frankly that the actor must take two final steps to reach the heights. First, he must learn to respect his audiences as he had learned at last to respect the theatre and himself: if he did not act the good host he would never "set a winning and ennobling character upon the Plymouth stage." Second, if John Barrymore was really to take the place of great actors of the past, he must tour. He could not hope to be to America what Booth and Mansfield were if he played only to select audiences in New York.

But the greatest pressure came not from the critics nor the physical ordeal onstage but from Blanche. Because this was no romance with a society girl of seventeen like Katherine, but a *grande passion* that demanded the utmost physical and emotional commitment. "O comrade, in that strange illicit dialogue of our perfectly matched fancy," Blanche apostrophized Jack in a poem:

Then my thoughts of you pressing upon your mouth—
Your evasive—flippant—tragic mouth
A kiss—sharp—evanescent

And drawing you for ever after its insinuation
That you should know yourself further—
Upon tasting it again . . .

O the cool fragrant breathing of this night
Savouring my breast—
And becoming the caress of my bridegroom's
Ivory and scented fingers . . .

Leave your mouth well over into the moonlight
So that I may kiss it full, O chance—
Press me into your pungent arms. . . .

Rather heavy going, but Blanche was incapable of striking less than twelve. She had a huge ego, supreme self-confidence, an iron will. When she confided her intention of marrying Jack to her friend Mercedes de Acosta, Mercedes was dubious.

"When you do, I wonder who'll kill the other first."

"What do you mean by that?"

"You are both such egomaniacs that you will some day start a fight to the finish, and one of you will do the other in. I'm not sure which one."

Blanche laughed. "I can tell you that right now. It will *not* be me."

During the run of *Richard*, she took rooms in Atlantic City to be alone to work on a play, a fantastic verse drama with a remarkable part for Jack. She had every right to seclusion, yet nothing could have been harder on her lover. Nightly after being extricated from the copper armor, he taxied to Penn Station and caught the train for Atlantic City. Undoubtedly Blanche expected a night of passion but, as Sir Laurence Olivier has observed, an actor "can't be more than one kind of athlete at a time" and Jack's onstage athletics were formidable. Little wonder that he would oversleep the next day, then rise foggily, tear himself from his beloved, train back, and dash to the theatre to start making up for the evening performance. To make things worse, Blanche's Paris divorce was dragging on and on, slow as the legal machinery in *The Letter of the Law*. If only they were married he might have some peace; but they could not marry.

Blanche herself was suffering. She continued to be under great pressure not to marry Jack, from family, friends, her lawyer, and even her druggist who, one night after she made a late call, flung up a window as she was starting her car and called, "Now don't you go and marry John Barrymore!" She herself had doubts about marrying an actor; actors' wives, she thought, were martyrs to their husbands' cause. Doris Rankin, for example. She had seen Doris standing in the wings while Lionel was rehearsing *The Jest*, "laden with everything he might need from a pencil to a sandwich," waiting for his notice or approval. And wives had constantly to fight off female fans. There was one so enamored of Jack that she ordered duplicate costumes of whatever role he was playing, then threw herself at him as he entered the Algonquin lobby, inviting him to take her on the spot. "My dear," the promiscuous Beerbohm Tree's daughter Iris had told her, "in the end actors always give in. I know!" All these terrors Blanche of course confided to Jack, whose nervous system reacted accordingly. Ecstasy, turmoil, raging quarrels: their love had everything but security.

On the last day of March, a shocked audience noticed that John Barrymore was fumbling his lines and seemed exhausted and confused. Several times he all but collapsed and only finished the performance with the greatest difficulty. The next night patrons were turned away with a refund at curtain time. Next day ticket sales were halted; then came the announcement from Arthur Hopkins that his star had suffered a nervous breakdown. According to Blanche, Jack had indeed "indulged" in a nervous breakdown—after "a brilliantly inquisitorial display" as he was simultaneously applying his make-up and hurling at her head a volley of unsavory "facts" he had unearthed about her conduct. Jack himself denied a nervous breakdown: "Certainly not. That's all rot." But the cause hardly mattered. After all the work and hope lavished on the production, the beautiful, searing, wildly acclaimed *Richard the Third* was forced to close after three weeks and four days.

On the advice of Ethel's Dr. Danforth, who declared the actor suffering from intense fatigue, Jack retreated to Billy Muldoon's health farm. The press was solicitous for the fallen star, but unwilling to swallow whole the story of overwork. *Variety* zeroed in on the disturbing Blanche. John Barrymore, it reported, had held curtains waiting messages from her, had ended the successful run of *The Jest* to take a trip with her, and had finally brought down the curtain on *Richard* after quarreling bitterly with her. Certainly Blanche seemed to be at the heart of the storm. But, as she had promised Mercedes, she would not be the one done in.

ETHEL AND RUSSELL had rented a house at 130 East Sixty-fifth Street for the season. She was in her bedroom one night after a performance when Russell came upstairs. Coldly, contemptuously, she charged him with adultery with a certain woman. Enraged, Russell struck her in the face with something he held in his hand, a cigarette case, perhaps; she only felt it. He hit her again and again. He beat her terribly, then left the room. When her maid, Anne Patterson, came in to turn down the bed, she found Ethel in shock, bleeding about the face, both eyes swelling purple. Anne called Dr. Danforth, who ordered Ethel to bed. She did not leave her room for five days, *Déclassée* closing due to the star's "laryngitis."

It was the end. After eleven years of pretending she had a marriage, she went to Cardinal Hayes and told him she was divorcing Russell.

"Oh, no. You can't do that," said the cardinal.

Eloquently and at length Ethel explained that she could.

"All right," said the cardinal at last, "but you mustn't marry again."

She had not the least intention of marrying again. Marriage had been a ghastly mistake. She had been right about Laurence Irving, Gerald du Maurier, Winston Churchill, and all the others, right to feel she should not give her heart away. Except to Jack and the children, "those three separate and adorable justifications for my existence," her children who sometimes seemed the only excuse for her life.

"RUSSELL COLT," said Ethel's friend the actress Barbara Robins Davis, "so *small*, so *insignificant!* How could he be Ethel Barrymore's husband?"

There was a second view. "Oh, I don't know," said another friend. "Think of the guts it took to lay a hand on Ethel Barrymore."

FOURTEEN

1920–1921

A T MULDOON'S SANITARIUM in the Westchester Hills Jack was taken in hand. Up at dawn (his usual bedtime), cold shower, workout in the gym, breakfast, two-hour rest. Five-mile trot, Muldoon riding rifle to make sure he didn't break pace. No cigarettes, no liquor. Jack had any number of friends ready to smuggle him Prohibition booze, but the experienced Muldoon foiled all attempts and eventually put the telephone off limits. Brooding over his breakdown and his tormenting duality, Jack continued his lifelong occupation of drawing himself: half hero, half monster whose spidery tentacles menace the dreamy idealist. On April 13 he displayed his charming side in a letter to the essayist John Jay Chapman:

> I know you must think me most damnably gauche—not to have answered your delightful letter sooner than this—but I have been in such a maelstrom of labor garnitured by exhaustion that I have put off everything—like some swimmer in the Atlantic Ocean might say, I'll put off telephoning till I land! I have landed at last more or less on my back—as playing that dynamically ruthless old buck eight times a week for all one is worth—after being pretty much "all in anyway"—was like trying to break 10 seconds flat in the hundred yard dash after walking up a long long hill!
>
> I loved every word of your letter and what is more it helped me like the devil as I believe firmly everything you said. Richard is a melodrama and all melodrama especially of the pageant-quality-background ought to gallop along like a mad stallion. I was *new* at the Shakespeare game and was watching *myself* instead of the *sweep* of the thing. I wish you could have been on the sidelines before—to yell at them "You're all dieing on your feet!!" I'll do it again sometime. He is *enormous* fun as he is so utterly

207

unequivocal or sentimental or good-to-his-mother or noble or
sweet or sincere or *romantic* or any of the God-awful things actors
have to be as a rule. I suppose that is the reason they are all
potential murderers off the stage!

Bless you for taking so much trouble to write me that letter
that I shall always keep. It is so *sane* and illuminating and kindly
and enthusiastic and *alive*. . . . I hope I may have the good fortune
to see you soon again.

Then finally the news that he had been waiting for: Blanche's divorce
was final. Suddenly he found himself quite recovered and on May 14
returned to New York, yet with no plans for stage or camera until fall.
Hopkins, who had hoped he would revive *Richard*, was bitterly disappointed, less because the production's curtailing had left him in debt than
because he loved Jack's performance. And now it was over, for who knew
what the unpredictable actor would do in the fall. Instead he was sucked
back into Blanche Thomas's exhausting vortex. Rumors continued to fly:
were they married, would they be? "They are both temperamental," said
one columnist flatly, "and should marry and be done with it."

Would they have married had Blanche not confirmed in early August
that she was pregnant? Probably. Jack had a fatalistic attitude toward
these "bus accidents" as well as a chivalrous belief that one owed a lady
marriage. On August 5 they surprised everyone by quietly taking vows
before a flower-decked cross in a friend's sitting room at the Ritz-Carlton.
Present were Blanche's mother Tibi, her brother and his wife, and Ethel,
Lionel, and Doris. Blanche's father, Charles Oelrichs, remained entrenched in his library at Newport, fortified with stiff drink. Blanche's
two children—Leonard, nine, and Robin, five—were not invited. Immediately after the "I do's" Tibi pulled Lionel aside. "But has he married
the Baby at all?" she asked, tear-stained and nervous. "I heard no mention
of the name Barrymore." Lionel explained that Barrymore was a stage
name borrowed by Maurice to spare his family's feelings, and that John
had been christened Blyth. "Oh," said Tibi, turning to the couple in a
fresh burst of sobs, "you both look like children, and have no business
to get married!"

Liking the White Plains area, Jack had bought a white farmhouse as
a wedding gift to Blanche, "a mound of mischievous plaster set in a gnarl
of / Still strange green," wrote Blanche, always adept at obfuscation. He
decided to sublet the Alchemist's Corner to which he was still tied, writing
Mrs. Nicholls, "I can see you tearing your hair and saying, 'My word,
neither marriage, plague, nor earthquake can evict him! He is lashed to

the house forever, unless death or fire intervene!' " Nevertheless he hugely enjoyed turning the farmhouse into a combination Catholic church and medieval castle. A kind of "crazed spirituality" had early permeated his and Blanche's relationship; it found expression now in icons, stained glass, fireplace andirons shaped like Holy Grails and, above the fireplace, to seal the visitor's bewilderment, the carved legend "Behold I send my angel before thy face."

Jack never did go back to 132 West Fourth Street. Meanwhile the sublessee of the Alchemist's Corner woke one morning to find rain pouring onto the bed through buckling ceiling beams. Mrs. Nicholls finally realized what Jack had wrought when hauling away the Long Island topsoil and reinforcing the beams with steel girders cost her $1,500. She never sent a bill. "I think," said Mrs. Nicholls kindly, "he was a confused child."

THE WONDERFUL CHILDREN . . .

In her hotel suite Ethel seizes a letter from the afternoon mail and tears it open. Her face glows as she reads.

"Ah, Ethel, they still write," says Ashton Stevens, who no longer interviews her but drops round to smoke a cigarette and chat.

"It's the first I've had from *him*. Listen." She reads it through. "And please send me $3. . . . Yours very truly, Sam." And she passes the precious paper to Stevens.

And yet she had to admit they were certainly not Drews or Barrymores, though Sammy's requests for money had a familiar ring. At eleven he was a tall, fair, stoutish child, spoiled into perfect manners in public and rule breaking behind his mother's back. He had charm, sensitivity, but no fire; and he hated the theatre, she thought with a sigh, remembering how she had adored Modjeska from the wings. More understandable was little Ethel's terror at Uncle Jack in *Dr. Jekyll and Mr. Hyde*—even though she had pushed the children's heads down during the scary parts; yet Sister was *not* going to be a beauty like her mother. Sammy and Sister were Colts through and through, but Jackie was a changeling, neither Colt nor Barrymore: a little dark horse who was growing up with the conviction that he had not been wanted. And Sammy hated his father. That was all right, mused Ethel, as long as they adored her. And they did, with mingled terror and worship.

If they were not Drews and Barrymores it was her own fault. Mummum and Georgie had married actors; the family profession was clear. But Ethel had married into society, brought up her children in society. They had nursemaids, ponies, the best private schools, country-club swimming pools, Unkie's lavish presents as well as the run of Linden Place.

Moreover, their father was ambiguous. What exactly did he do besides shuttle between Newport, Palm Beach, and New York? And Mama herself they saw less as an actress than as a social favorite who provided them with passports to a life of moneyed leisure they quickly took for granted. Fiercely proud of her profession, Ethel preferred to shield her children from its hardships. They lapped cream, unaware of the labor that produced it.

As long as they adored her. . . . Was anyone more adored than Ethel Barrymore as *Déclassée* closed that May to paeans like "God knows when we have seen such good acting!" Borne into the Equity Ball in a sedan chair, dazzling in red velvet and spun-sugar curls, with Jack as her page and Lionel, Bruce McRae, and Conway Tearle among her twenty courtiers. The belle of the ball given by the Motion Pictures Directors Association at the Biltmore. Playing Portia at an Equity benefit. Donating $30,000 of her own money in her and her brothers' names to endow a room for actors at the Fifth Avenue Hospital. Voted Actors Equity vice president 2,922 votes to her opponent's 833. And forever having men fall in love with her at first sight. Introduced to Ethel by Zoë Akins, the Irish playwright St. John Ervine was *startled* by the beauty of her hair—"thick and wavy and very fair . . . sunburnt, as if sunlight, mellowed by moonshine, had suffused it!"—and by her even more beautiful eyes, eyes that had "the grave beauty of an antelope's," haunted eyes "full of nervous disdain and elusive trouble." He pledged his heart to her on the spot.

And yet after the applause, after the little suppers at the Algonquin with friends or Uncle Jack, Ethel returned to the empty house on East Sixty-fifth Street. Her maid, Anne Patterson, eased her passage to bed. There, propped against pillows, she read biographies or detective stories until blank daylight threatened her windows. No Sister Julie de Saint Esprit patrolled the halls, but in some respects she might have been back at the convent in Rittenhouse Square.

MEANWHILE LIONEL AND DORIS were forging ahead just as though fate in the guise of Shakespeare and a certain blond actress weren't waiting in the wings. This year, 1920, Lionel left Metro for the prospering First National, which had also lured Chaplin and Mary Pickford with million-dollar contracts. Lionel's was a fraction of that amount, yet an improvement over Metro and a chance to work with the producer Whitman Bennett on four pictures designed to enhance Lionel's reputation as a serious actor with the kind of solid, dramatic parts at which he excelled. In *The Master Mind*, an avenging brother ultimately finds "the fruit of revenge like ashes in his mouth." In *The Devil's Garden*, an ambitious

RIGHT: Lionel in the early 1920s.
BELOW: John in *Sherlock Holmes*,
1922

RIGHT: Lionel and Irene sail for Rome, where they would be married, 1923. BELOW LEFT: John (center) with Jack and Harry Warner in Hollywood, 1925. BELOW RIGHT: John with his wife Blanche, circa 1920

ABOVE: Ethel on an MGM set with Elinor Glyn. BELOW:
Gloria Swanson and Lionel in *Sadie Thompson*, 1928

John with Clementine on his shoulder in *The Sea Beast*, 1926

ABOVE LEFT: John and Dolores Costello on their wedding day, November 24, 1928. ABOVE RIGHT: John and Dolores on the set of *When a Man Loves*, 1927. BELOW: Lionel directing Catherine Dale Owen in *His Glorious Night*, 1929

ABOVE: John and Mary Astor in *Don Juan*, 1926. BELOW: Lionel and John at the premiere

ABOVE: John and Dolores in *When a Man Loves*, 1927. BELOW:
Dolores and John christening the *Infanta*, 1931

RIGHT: Ethel at Tower Road
in the late twenties. BELOW:
Lionel, as director, with
Lawrence Tibbett on the set
of *The Rogue Song*, 1930

ABOVE: Dolores, John, and
Baby Dolores (Dede), 1931.
RIGHT: John, Dolores, and
their children, John Jr. and
Dede, leaving for a cruise,
1933

LEFT: John and Marian Marsh in *Svengali*, 1931. BELOW: John, in costume as the clubfooted "Mad Genius," with fellow Warner star George Arliss on the Burbank lot, 1931

ABOVE: Lionel and Norma Shearer in *A Free Soul*, 1931. Lionel received an Oscar for Best Actor. BELOW: Garbo and Lionel in *Mata Hari*, 1931

ABOVE: Lionel and Marie Dressler accept their Academy Awards
for, respectively, *A Free Soul* and *Min and Bill*, 1931. BELOW:
Lionel and John in their first film together, *Arsène Lupin*, 1932

Ethel brings her children Jackie, Sammy, and Ethel to Hollywood during the filming of *Rasputin and the Empress*, 1932

ABOVE: Lionel, Joan Crawford, and John in *Grand Hotel*, 1932. BELOW: John and Lionel with Lewis Stone near the set

ABOVE: Lionel (Rasputin), Ethel (Empress Alexandra), and John (Prince Chegodieff) in *Rasputin and the Empress*, 1932. BELOW LEFT: In a lighter moment between takes, John, Diana Wynyard, and Ethel. BELOW RIGHT: Lionel as Rasputin—an etching he made of his reflection in a mirror

Family reunion in Hollywood, 1932. Seated, left to right: Irene and Lionel with John Jr.; Ethel; Dolores and Ethel Colt with Dede. Standing: Jackie Colt, John, and Sammy Colt

servant kills the master who has seduced the woman he loves. In *The Great Adventure*, an artist sees his chance to escape fame by posing as his dead butler. In *Jim the Penman*, a man innocently forges a girl's name on his dance program and falls into a life of fraud.

Doris played opposite Lionel in the last three, emerging as a competent actress. Her dark hair is demurely coiffed, her face oval, her chin dimpled, and a bow-shaped mouth exposes pretty teeth. Everything she does is quiet, sincere. As on the stage, Lionel is different in each film, but good, strong, and handsome in a manly way. He wears his straight hair long; his faunlike ears are tight to his head. He talks around a cigarette dangling loosely in his mouth. When an evil thought crosses his mind, he looks very much like John—the same diabolical smile, narrowed eyes, lowering brows. He also kisses his hand with irony like John, or vice versa. Yet despite the demands of silent films, he seldom overemotes, a notable exception occurring when he fiendishly padlocks the yacht's cabin in the last scenes of *Jim the Penman*. There is too in Lionel a kind of chained sexuality. He and Doris never catch fire in their scenes together. He pecks her cheek, pats her shoulder. The sexuality is there, yet Lionel or the director refuses it. And except for *The Great Adventure*, he ends alone, baffled in his quest for human contact.

All four films won him the highest critical praise as well as congratulations on having a wife as talented as he, a verdict more chivalrous than accurate. Yet fine as these films were, they could not match in popularity Douglas Fairbanks's *The Mark of Zorro*, Pickford's *Pollyanna*, or Chaplin's Little Tramp. The chief reason is that Lionel had not developed a screen persona like Fairbanks's swashbuckler or Pickford's all-American sweetheart. His appearance and character changed with each role: he was an *actor*. Another reason is that his innate reticence controls his performance: he seldom plays to the camera and hence to audiences. Though his acting had force and authority, there is something irascible, introverted, and remote about his screen presence—not the prescription for box-office triumphs. *Motion Picture Classic* could even call all four films "an awful celluloid flop."

Perhaps it was sour grapes that inspired his diatribe against movies even while making them. "The art of movies? Pah!" His opinion of the movies was "fifty degrees below zero." He denied that the public wanted good stuff. "This is the age of insincerity. The movies had the misfortune to come along in the twentieth century, and because they appeal to the masses there can be no sincerity in them. Hollywood is tied hand and foot to the demands for artificiality of the masses all over the world." But Hollywood itself was guilty. Not only were its citizens "intellectually nothing to write and tell mother about," but fundamentally they cared about nothing but the size of the weekly paycheck. And frankly, that's why he was in the damned business himself. Lionel, the unashamed mercenary.

That late summer in a tangle of rumor and counterrumor, plans for John and Lionel doing *Othello* in repertory with *Redemption, The Jest*, and *Richard the Third* again surfaced. This time John Williams was named as their likely manager, a challenge to Hopkins, who had long dreamed of repertory with all three Barrymores and who had not only lost John in *Richard* but had been sued by Williams because he had lost Lionel to *The Jest*. In the end the whole repertory scheme blew up in both their faces when, in November, Jack finally announced that, on the advice of his doctor, he would not act again until the fall of 1921. In actuality, marriage to Blanche was completely absorbing him.

But that fall of 1920 Lionel was free for another Hopkins dream, *Macbeth*. No ordinary *Macbeth*, but the radium of Shakespeare released from the vessel of tradition through totally abstract sets and a heavily Freudian interpretation. Macbeth's bloody deeds would spring not from ambition but from irresistible and unconscious forces set in motion by a childless Lady Macbeth who projects her maternal ambitions onto her husband-son. Robert Edmond Jones's vast, actor-dominating sets reinforced this power of the unconscious: the stage, said Hopkins, became "an expanse of ominous, witch-infested space. Figures came out of the dark into the light and were enveloped by the dark again. There was the quality of an evil dream in which visible objects had a nightmarish distortion. There was no sense of reality. The whole was pervaded by the poisonous brew of the witch's cauldron." Jones also robed the characters in symbolic colors: red for evil, blue for good, white for repentance. Thus although Lady Macbeth would appear in lurid red, her scarf of blue symbolized that she was good in intent though evil in unconscious impulse. Arthur Hopkins's *Macbeth* was going to be a *Macbeth* no one had ever seen before. Well in advance the production was touted as revolutionary.

As the February opening approached, Doris lost Lionel completely. Hypnotized by the bloody Thane of Cawdor, he walked like a somnambulist, his mind somewhere in a Freudian Scotland. His eyes were a stricken madman's, his voice a writhe of pain. He produced an effect of almost unbearable horror. There was no snapping him out of it after a rehearsal; another spirit possessed Lionel Barrymore's body. Hopkins could only watch and wonder.

But one of the trio who had contributed vitally to Jack's success in

Richard the Third was missing: Margaret Carrington, who had turned John Barrymore into a Shakespearean actor. Why did she not undertake Lionel, the only one of the three Barrymores whose voice was distinctly "American"?

Lionel says that Hopkins considered his voice "all right"; on the other hand, he had been accused in *The Letter of the Law* of slovenly diction, a red alert for any actor attempting Shakespeare. Perhaps Hopkins thought training no use. Lionel could not detach himself from a creation as Jack could: what he did had little to do with acting, according to Hopkins, but "lay in another dimension of which we know little." Or perhaps Hopkins thought this *Macbeth* so untraditional that mastery of Shakespearean blank verse was irrelevant—or perhaps that what Lionel was doing with his Macbeth was right. Lionel himself agreed with Joseph Jefferson that a fine voice ruined more actors than whiskey. Perhaps he was determined not to be "trained."

The audience at the Apollo the night of February 17 vibrated at the highest pitch of expectation. Jack was on hand; Ethel was cheered as she entered her box, radiantly beautiful and on leave from Flower Hospital where she was being treated for such excruciating rheumatism that she had been forced to cancel her smash-hit tour of *Déclassée*. It was perhaps not coincidental that she was stricken just as formal divorce proceedings against Russell got underway. Yet in public, as usual, she was graciousness itself, though no less tense than the audience as it waited for the curtain to rise on Lionel Barrymore's *Macbeth*.

When it did, the house gasped. A bare stage hung with heavy curtains before which stood immobile three figures draped in lurid red staring through sexless silver masks. Light thrown upon them from the empty sockets of three huge identical masks suspended in velvet darkness above—these impassive visors symbolizing the forces that would spawn the tragedy: Macbeth's conflict between civilized and primitive urges, Lady Macbeth's twisted maternity, and the barrier to their ambitions presented by the living king. But the audience did not grasp this symbolism, nor did it want to. It wanted Shakespeare's "blasted heath," three crones, and a lot of cackling.

Jones's sets went from bold to worse. No castle or banquet room, only silver pointed arches that were moved about the stage seemingly at will. Jones meant these distorted Gothic arches to represent subconscious settings, echoed as they were in Macbeth's conical helmet, shield, and spear as a motif of soaring ambition thwarted. All the audience knew was that one moment Macbeth and his consort seemed to be inside an arch and the next outside without rhyme or reason. When the banquet room proved to be merely a series of madly soaring cubes, they gave up all hope of comprehending this *Macbeth*, which seemed to sacrifice the actors on an altar of baffling futurism.

Kelcey Allen, the influential critic of *Women's Wear*, was sitting next to the ticket broker William McBride. Halfway through the production McBride wondered aloud to Allen whether he should buy up a lot of seats for this *Macbeth*. At that moment onstage, Lionel flourished his sword and cried, "Lay on, Macduff!"

"Lay off, McBride!" whispered Allen. It proved sound advice.

Macbeth had the distinction of being that season's—that decade's—most spectacular failure. Good old Lionel had done it again. Not that Jones was spared. In this production, said Heywood Broun, Shakespeare was merely a collaborator in the *Macbeth* of Robert Edmond Jones. The audience that dispersed a little before midnight, agreed Woollcott, was suffering chiefly from shock: shock "that Mr. Jones, for all the three or four high moments of great beauty that he achieves, should have indulged in such impish antics of decoration as to become the star of 'Macbeth,' a 'Macbeth' that will be talked of till the cows come home—as an oddity." Jack would vow in years to come that Lionel was crucified by a bad production, and even Jones would admit his *Macbeth* was "a stunt."

That was only half the story. "The acting," said one critic, "proved to be hopelessly inadequate. Mr. Barrymore's Macbeth was just a gloomy, uninteresting oaf. There was no splendor, no vision of fatality, no tragic austerity to this rough, sordid and commonplace barbarian. . . . Mr. Barrymore made him a lout with a terrific grouch." Barrymore partisan Woollcott could hardly add a kinder word: Lionel Barrymore was "often good and occasionally very good," but never once "brushed greatness in all the length and breadth of the play." The *Forum*'s critic was bemused: ". . . Mr. Barrymore must have some particular reason for shouting at you as he waves his arms wildly about. Surely he has studied this play and found something that most of us have missed." Nothing could explain Lionel's spitting words and tossing arms, concluded the *Forum*, except that Mr. Barrymore not only believed Macbeth as Shakespeare conceived him insane, but Shakespeare and the audience insane as well. Speeding back to Flower Hospital, Ethel reminded herself that Lionel had always been the unlucky one.

Thus far Jones zero, Lionel zero. But finally the majority concurred with Kenneth Macgowan. Blaming Hopkins for too static a directorial pace, Macgowan nevertheless laid the blame squarely on Lionel's shoulders. "If he possessed the spiritual fire and strength that the part demands, the slow pace might not be evident. Certainly, if he did not give so absolutely tedious and unimaginative a performance, few would find the background anything but an exciting and immensely stimulating part of the drama enacted. As it is, Barrymore plods heavily through the play, dwelling endlessly on every vowel, never for a moment simulating any natural emotion appropriate to Macbeth. . . . Audiences that came looking for a Macbeth or a Barrymore were cheated of their satisfaction and fell back on cursing the settings. Never had a production called so for acting or been so ready to support it and raise it aloft; but without such acting, never was a production so vulnerable to popular prejudice."

Variety's critic had evidently seen a different play. "This brilliant, audacious pioneer [Hopkins] of the new stage art has transferred to the theatre a minute psychoanalysis of the tragedy in terms of the newest thought and in the light of the most recent research of psychotherapy, and the result is absolutely breathtaking. It can scarcely be a popular success, but it shatters all the stage traditions of Shakespeare piled up in the last 400 years." As for Lionel, "His performance marked a high peak in a notable career. His command of the classic role was apparent from the beginning, and he never lost his command of his character or the audience."

Publicly, Arthur Hopkins never went back on his assertion that Lionel created a great Macbeth. The trouble was his unconventionality. "Its effect was a puzzled and displeased audience, an audience which suffered new and forbidden emotions not to be classified with past theatre experience. The easiest escape from this discomfort was quick rejection, and in many cases angry rejection, yet there were a hardy few not easily confused by new and strange experience who knew that not only were they looking into the deep and infested well of Macbeth's soul, but were seeing a supreme portrayal that was far outside the realm of acting. This was the achievement that many of Lionel's admirers had been looking for, but when it came they were unequal to it. He had flown too far."

Ultimately, theatre depends on its audience, and Lionel's told him he had failed. Later in life, Lionel tried to rationalize the disaster: (1) Whitman Bennett at First National had not picked up his option after the four films and Lionel had agreed to do *Macbeth* in a fit of pique, (2) he did *Macbeth* only because he had to: grocers were yelping for cash (and Lionel was yelping over $10,000 of bootleg liquor stolen from his Hempstead, Long Island, basement), (3) unlike Jack, he had not prepared adequately, (4) Hopkins's complex Freudian interpretation of Macbeth's motivations confused him, (5) he had known in his heart he was not a Shakespearean actor.

Unsaid, but implied, was the conviction that Hopkins should have known better than to tempt him into deep water. "Probably it seemed like a fair enough wager that if one Barrymore could do Shakespeare so could the other, but they had the wrong Barrymore," said Lionel.

"They should have tried Ethel."

Macbeth closed ignominiously on March 12, having run less than a month. Lionel's pain went deep. The announcement on March 18 that he would create the movie character of the Chicago gunman Boomerang Bill was like a nasty laugh. No good telling himself that *Macbeth* was an unlucky play or that he could redeem himself in *Othello*, which Hopkins almost certainly could have been induced to stage with Jack as Iago. Like Byron, who boasted he only struck once like the tiger, Lionel retreated snarling to his lair. Just when he had almost reconciled himself to the theatre it had betrayed him. He had been right: acting was "a miserable and obscene way to make a living."

The wound would never heal. The contrast between Jack's triumph and his own catastrophe haunted and embittered him. Indeed, who could forget Kenneth Macgowan's devastating conclusion:

> Had John Barrymore played Macbeth, had Ben-Ami acted the part, if in fact any actor of first-rate ability had appeared against Jones's backgrounds, I am certain that the evening of February 17th would have been evident to everyone as an occasion of the very highest significance in the calendar of the American theatre.

Lionel never forgave the theatre and never forgave himself for having momentarily trusted it. He would soon leave it forever.

ON MARCH 3 a daughter had been born to Blanche and Jack. Blanche decided to name her Joan Strange Blyth: Joan for her heroine Joan of Arc, Strange for her pen name, Blyth for Jack. They were on their way to the christening at St. Ignatius where Lionel and Doris were to meet them, when Blanche suddenly changed her mind.

"I'm not naming her Joan. It sounds too much like John. This child must be an individual, not an echo of her father."

Jack bridled. "It may sound like John in that bastard British accent they use in Newport. But it doesn't sound like John to me. What name *are* you giving her?"

Blanche hesitated; then, "We shall call her Diana," she said.

"Very well, Fig," said Jack, yielding to the inevitable. "But to me she will be—Treepeewee."

They had left the White Plains farmhouse for a large brownstone on East Ninety-seventh Street. Blanche's children Leonard and Robin moved in with their governess, Miss Jones; the baby was installed in the nursery. Jack paid late-night visits to his daughter, contemplating the bundle from a distance. When Diana's nurse suggested he pick her up and hold her, Jack recoiled.

"Oh, no! She's too fragile! I'd break her!"

Once when Blanche rang imperatively, Nurse Dempsey transferred the baby to Jack's arms. When she returned he was standing rigid in the same spot holding the baby as though it were about to explode.

"Good God, never do that again!" he said, white-faced. "I might have dropped her."

Diana would grow up without stroking. Jack had already voluntarily waived paternal rights of guardianship so that Blanche had sole control until Diana reached twenty-one. Perhaps he felt he was protecting rather than rejecting her. Yet he remained aloof while Lionel, on the other hand, came often to the nursery to pick up Diana and nuzzle her.

MICHAEL STRANGE'S *Clair de Lune* was now finished. She had married Jack sure that he would release her genius. Jack did more, undertaking to produce her play on Broadway. He would play Gwymplane, the disfigured mountebank, and try to persuade Ethel to play the Queen.

"If I don't die," said Ethel when Jack came to Flower Hospital, her part in hand, "I'll play it."

The doctors had decided that the arthritis that shot in bolts of pain from her back to knee to hand was caused by a deadly streptococcus viridans infection lodged in her tonsils. As the operation was postponed again and again until she regained her strength, the news "Ethel Barrymore Leaves Husband" finally broke. She was clearly the moral victor: she would have sole custody, control, and education of the children, whom Russell would be allowed to visit at her convenience. While the columnist Dolly Madison wondered whether a certain young, much-photographed Long Island matron would be named corespondent, others noted that the announcement coincided with a marked improvement in Miss Barrymore's condition. But that was to ignore the effects of the finally performed tonsillectomy. Doctors also operated on her crippled hand. Before she went under the ether Ethel asked whether she would ever be able to play the piano again. Impossible, she was told.

Hopkins flatly refused to associate himself with *Clair de Lune*, but nothing could stem Jack's enthusiasm. He came again to the hospital to show Ethel his own scenic and costume designs. Though she was not enamored of Blanche, Ethel was touched: she had never seen Jack so excited about anything theatrical before. She was playing the Queen for Jack because the part was short, and because she wasn't ready to return to *Déclassée*.

Alf Hayman had finally been persuaded that anything with two Barrymores and a Strange couldn't lose; he was right. On the night of April 18 society clogged the doors of the Empire, causing the old doorman to grumble that it was "nothing short of a circus." Tickets sold at a record $25 and up, with some front seats going for an unheard-of $250 a pair, while 300 standees jammed the back of the house. Although Astors and Vanderbilts snubbed the opening, the place seethed with Drexels, Biddles, Dukes, Goulds, Condé Nasts, and Hearsts. Lionel, his "gentle face" begging people not to mention *Macbeth*, escorted Blanche, so nervous that she had put on a new dress backward. John Drew, his waist still thirty-two, escorted his thirty-nine-year-old daughter Bee. Just before the curtain Jack and Blanche held a last-minute counsel. "Now you'll show those sons of bitches, those society friends of yours, what you're made of!" said Jack. "This is your justification! Now they will have to accept you for what you are."

Society (or anyone else for that matter) had never seen the likes of Michael Strange's *Clair de Lune* on Broadway. Though based on Victor Hugo's *L'Homme Qui Rit*, the characters were pure Barrymore. A scornful queen: Ethel. A blueblood duchess perversely eager for a mountebank actor to seduce her: Blanche. The actor Gwymplane, sensitive and noble by birth but hideously marred by torture: Jack.

But it was what the characters said that confounded the audience. Everyone down to the last palace courtier was hopelessly entangled in festoons of verbiage:

Second Courtier: She is illusive. She is like a succession of masks, seen at dawn. In her there always appears a terrible wanness, right about the heels of a wonderful freshness.

If a minor character can talk like this, what wonder the contortions of a duchess?

The touch of your lips chills, burns me with forgetfulness. The touch of your lips is like a tide hushing, sucking my wakefulness down into depths of terrible oblivion.

Not only had Jack to listen to this rodomontade but to utter it:

I think you are something I have stolen out of a temple—a wonderful wingèd crownèd figure that I have stolen and profaned. I
feel as if we were in a black barge upon a scarlet sea, as if in a
moment it would dip over the horizon line and we should be lost
forever together. O, I feel as if all the light in the world were
flowing from behind the chalice of your pale face. I love you, I
love you.

As one critic said succinctly, John Barrymore could only have tolerated this "For love of Mike."

There were a few memorable moments. The house gasped as Ethel
swept on as the Queen, blindingly beautiful in white hoop skirts, powdered hair, and huge picture hat. She also clarified this un-*Clair de Lune*,
Robert Benchley observing that "under the warmth of Miss Barrymore's
voice, the lines assigned to her blossom into an unwonted state of lucidity
which at times gives the play the appearance of being very clever indeed.
And then she leaves the stage; the sun goes behind a cloud of murky
pathological poetry; the flood rises and you find yourself obliged to tread
water to keep your head up." In the audience Blanche complained to
Lionel that Ethel didn't know her lines, yet Ethel's ignorance imparted
to the evening its few moments of sense.

For his entrance in the last scene somersaulting followed by a pas de
seul, Jack had studied with a ballet master. In the climactic scene, torn
between the pure, blind woman he loves and the slut who tempts him,
he seizes a knife and cuts out his heart. As the slut tries to snatch the
dripping organ, Gwymplane thrusts it into the hands of the blind girl,
who presses it against her heart. Gwymplane expires while the slut falls
at his feet and "licks the blood from the heart of her dancer off the floor."
The gaping audience, swollen since eleven by Broadway actors so eager
to see the play that they hadn't wiped off their make-up, applauded
dazedly. Blanche appeared between Jack and Ethel for the curtain, not
quite as beautiful as before the airing of her play. The exit of the audience
was complicated by ushers shouting that only those with private cars could
leave by the front doors. After that no one would be caught dead leaving
by the sides.

Flinging down the reviews the next morning, Jack frothed and raved.
Woollcott in the *Times* and Heywood Broun in the *Tribune* had been
particularly venomous, Woollcott bemoaning that such a rich setting had
been wasted on a paste jewel. That night Jack stormed into Ethel's dressing
room: he was going to tell the audience what he thought of the filthy
swine who had trampled Blanche's play. Ethel was horrified. Jack must

remember who he was. She and Uncle Jack never paid attention to critics; Jack must not lower himself. When Jack refused to listen to reason, Ethel reached for her dressing room telephone and rang Lionel on Long Island. While the curtain was held, Jack fumed into the phone: "I'm going to talk about that pair of vultures in such clear and vigorous language that the story will make the front page of every paper in the country!"

"You are mistaken," said Lionel firmly. "The item on the front page will read 'Lionel Barrymore strangles brother Jack in dressing room before performance.' "

Jack desisted but sent copies of his speech to the *Times* and *Tribune*, neither of which printed his protest against "acidulated whirlwinds of lame invective" from critics who obviously never managed the feat of thinking and writing at the same time. Finally *Clair de Lune* had but one champion in Ludwig Lewisohn, who praised the play for its charm, Jack's costumes and scenic designs for their artistry, and Jack's Gwymplane for its fascinating display of "his personal genius, poetry, and pain."

Eventually Jack himself took the blame for the failure of *Clair de Lune*: "I know of nothing more that could have been done to distract attention from this charming play, except to have called upon Lionel to play a part in it. As it was, it seemed entirely filled with dwarfs and Barrymores. And Clair [de] Lune should never have had all these trappings or have been made a vehicle for stars or box-office reputations." Finally, however, *Clair de Lune* did manage to entertain: Nora Bayes took off on Ethel in *Clara de Loon*, a skit that was pronounced "far more amusing, logical, and convincing than the play it burlesques."

That same year Knopf published *Resurrecting Life* by Michael Strange, proving not so much that a distinguished publisher could be fooled by turgid prose labeled verse but that Blanche's notoriety was good business. As with *Clair de Lune*, pretension swells every line. One can imagine Michael in her velvet gown with the ragged sleeve flinging grand emotions onto the page. A sense of proportion which tells a writer that she is not the first to have loved, laughed, and suffered is completely missing: Michael Strange's poetry took itself more seriously than anything in the world.

Jack and Blanche still took their great romance seriously too; but professionally Jack was drifting. Plays starring John Barrymore were announced, retracted. "Nothing in the theatre, it seems," said the *Times* dryly, "is quite so ephemeral as the plans of the Brothers Barrymore." When he and Blanche fled from *Clair de Lune* in July 1921 to France, he had been on the stage only eleven weeks and four days in the *last sixteen months*. No wonder he and Alf Hayman (who had died during the run) had demanded an unprecedented five dollars per ticket for the eight-week run of Blanche's play. Yet it was not enough to keep him and Blanche in style, though she had her own money. Consequently, on his return from abroad he signed with First National to film *The Lotus Eater* under the direction of his old pal, the talented, hard-drinking Irishman Marshall Neilan.

Since Jack would not leave Blanche to go to California, shooting for the island scenes had to be done off Miami, where cast and crew went by boat. Colleen Moore, Jack's love interest, had heard about his drinking and womanizing and was scared to death to meet him. But Jack behaved charmingly, giving her acting tips and sometimes gently turning her so the camera would catch her best angle. He was also without a doubt the handsomest man she had ever seen. When he climbed the tallest mast of the boat every evening after work and plummeted seaward, his bronzed body silhouetted against the sun, she would catch her breath at the sheer beauty of him.

It *was* breath-catching how little Jack's drinking had yet affected his looks. He was still "silk." It was as though somewhere his portrait, like Dorian Gray's, must be corrupting while he remained untouched—now through prodigious drinking bouts with Neilan. When the company returned to New York to shoot interiors, Jack would excuse himself from the set for an hour "to go see Treepee." After two days Neilan would go in search; both would return days later suffering from the obvious effects of a gigantic souse. Yet in Grecian tunic, gold-laced boots, and long curling hair, Jack looked like a young god in *The Lotus Eater*. Luck and an incredibly tough constitution were still with him.

AFTER HER ILLNESS and *Clair de Lune*, Ethel too needed money badly, so she fell back on *The Twelve Pound Look* in vaudeville at the Palace. Again she filled houses, though there were plain hints that she should look for another vehicle: "Only a Barrymore could immortalize a sketch in which she is off at the curtain, in which she hasn't a ringing line, and in which she wears a go-to-work suit." But then Ethel never listened to critics.

In August Colonel Colt—Unkie—died at his beautiful Linden Place. And it had been Unkie and Linden Place which had really impressed Ethel when Russell was courting her. Unkie had been as successful in his field as she in hers; he admired her, courted her. Taking her place with his mistress Minnie Perry, she had often acted as his hostess: the Barrymore glamour had veiled the Colt reputation for ruthlessness. And he had been generous with her—Mamaroneck, the De Dion-Bouton, the fabulous $3,500 canopied bed in which she and Russell were supposed to have been happy, the jewelry (though the jewelry, along with two of Georgie's rings, her only keepsakes, had all been stolen from a hotel room).

Now he left her $25,000 and the Mamaroneck property, $50,000 each to her children. The rest of his estate, apart from bequests and a trust fund for the surviving grandchild, went equally to his brother, Senator Lebaron Colt, and his sons, Russell and Roswell. They promptly challenged the will, charging that the multimillionaire had been of unsound mind and unduly influenced. Approached in Boston where she was now appearing in *Déclassée*, Ethel refused comment. Though Russell was said to have a personal fortune of one million dollars, she had supported the household throughout their marriage. Of what concern were Russell's millions now?

ARTHUR HOPKINS had taken the *Macbeth* failure almost as hard as Lionel, but Lionel was the vulnerable one. Hopkins knew that Lionel's great—though denied—enthusiasm for the theatre had suffered a terrific blow. He also knew that Lionel had "no appraisal of his own gifts"; he was far too easily convinced of their frailty. Hopkins therefore had quickly followed *Macbeth* with a play tailor-made for his disgraced star, Henri Bernstein's *The Claw*.

The Claw tells the sordid tragedy of Achille Cortelon, a Socialist newspaper publisher who at forty-five marries a sexually experienced, ambitious woman of twenty-one. Sixteen years of adoration on his part and infidelity on hers reduce him to a senile, babbling fool, and the play ends with Cortelon awaiting imprisonment for bribery while a jeering mob stones his windows. Hopkins gave Doris the ungrateful part of the daughter who resents her father marrying a woman her own age. For Antoinette, the wife-adventuress, Hopkins engaged Jack's old flame Irene ("Frizzy" Frizzelle) Fenwick.

Charles Frohman had spotted the chorus girl in 1910 and decided to turn her into a legitimate actress under a more genteel name pronounced British-style, "Fennick." She had scored a success in Ned Sheldon's pseudoscandalous *Song of Songs* and gone on to play the bad woman so often that she felt obliged to protest, "I like clean plays and clean things. . . . [But] women like to see wicked women on the stage, and women rule the theatre." She divided critics on her acting, though Alan Dale was probably right when he said, "Miss Fenwick is not inordinately talented. She is competent, pretty, wistful, and earnest. The actors of a previous generation would laugh at the idea of her stellar qualities and well they might." She divided critics too on her appearance. Amy Leslie spoke of her "faintly exotic beauty, her die-away delicacy . . . her little wan, transparent face." Irene's face was indeed wan, almost skeletal, as were her sticks of arms: clearly she had an eating disorder; she looked anorexic. Though she claimed thirty-one, she was thirty-four, a year younger than Doris. She must have possessed a brittle, worldly charm.

Lionel fell deeply, passionately in love.

FIFTEEN

1921–1923

LIONEL HAD FALLEN solidly in love, but Jack and Blanche's marriage veered insanely between torment and ecstasy. Jack could not respect a woman he could dominate and could not live with one he could not. And Blanche was accustomed to getting her way in everything. On her part, Blanche discovered that she had married an alcoholic. When Jack downed the terrible potion, charm, humor, balance fled. She tried to stop his drinking, hiding bottles, smashing cases of champagne. Jack retaliated by drinking the alcohol out of her curling iron and gargling her perfume. Their battles were violent, theatrical, dangerous—tennis games in hell, Iris Tree described them, where nobody misses a ball.

Blanche's friend Mercedes de Acosta also witnessed the Barrymore battles. After one violent row during which Jack had slammed out of the house on his way (thought Blanche) to "his nanny—Ned Sheldon," Blanche telephoned Mercedes to come stay the night. After dinner Blanche was reading Mercedes her adaptation of *L'Aiglon* in front of the fire when they heard a noise in the cellar. Armed with pokers and kitchen knives, they went to investigate and discovered Jack lying stoned among a wreck of gin bottles. They managed to get him upstairs to bed, where the next morning he explained he had only pretended to leave. When Mercedes left, Jack and Blanche were twined about each other as though nothing had happened.

But it had, and did—again and again. One night Martha, the cook, woke to the sound of fury. Opening her window, she saw Blanche in a thin nightgown running toward Madison Avenue shouting, "I'll throw myself under the first streetcar!" She did not, but after another all-night row the maid found Jack's pajamas shredded to ribbons, and one night when Blanche came into the nursery to kiss Diana good night, her eye was black and her arm in a sling. "I stumbled over a case of champagne in the dark," said Blanche, fooling no one though the two rooms between

224

the bedroom and the nursery were stacked shoulder-high with cases of bootleg bubbly.

They could be twin spirits. They dressed alike. Jack had his black velvet trousers pleated like Michael's black velvet skirts. They wore the same soft shirts with loose pointed collars designed by Jack and known as "the Barrymore collar," set off by identical flowing black ties. They both wore broad-brimmed black hats cocked at the same angle. John let his hair grow as long as Michael's short bob, and Michael looked delicately masculine and Jack virilely feminine. And they had uncannily similar feelings about many things: Christ and war, poetry and critics. "To have been comrades walking off together a little unsteadily from our wine," wrote Michael Strange, saluting this intense union of souls—

To have returned entered in lain down among dazed surges of
    loving—
To have felt sleep at length aplay from your eyelids onto mine—
And our handclasp's gradual relaxing—

Whatever life can get it will have of you of me perhaps—
Yet I doubt if life can produce more than once for you or for me
    a comrade—
I doubt if life ever gives twice to whatsoever persons such love—
The love of brothers young children mates.

And then one would strike a raw vein of ego in the other, with violent repercussions. Two tender spots were their careers and sex.

"You go on acting, as the whole world wants you to," Michael would charge, "and although I can't say I know who wants me to write poetry, and my books don't sell, still I feel I must, and it's difficult to, in the sort of life we have!" His work was important, hers was not; *she* had to sacrifice.

Sex was a more inflammable subject. Because of his own insecure promiscuity, Jack's distrust of women was profound.

"I suppose you want to have people in to tea again."

"Why not?"

"Is tea any other thing than a sex projection?"

"Sex projection? Oh, my God! and I suppose there was no sex projection in 'The Jest' now, was there!"

Mayhem.

Jack was violently homophobic, refusing, for example, to do *The Portrait of Dorian Gray* because he loathed Oscar Wilde. They had both admired Walt Whitman until the subject of his homosexuality arose.

"So, you do not care that a poet whom you admire above all others—am I to understand above all others—"

"You are!"

"—is rumored to have had homosexual relationships?"

"Why not?"

"Why not! Is there nothing ridiculous to you in the idea of a venerable poet with a long white beard—and a bus-boy?"

"What have his pleasures to do with his greatness? What concern are they of mine? I'm not the bus-boy! I'm his reader!"

"You are a poet, and no doubt you feel that a poet should follow his emotions wherever they might lead him."

"Of course!"

Jack leaps up and sweeps the glasses off the table with a crash. "Then in God's name, what security is there in life with such a person?"

The quarrel was not really about Whitman, of course, but about Blanche, her lesbian friend Mercedes de Acosta, and finally about Jack himself.

Suicide was their favorite threat. Paris. Jack bursts from their apartment in the Impasse de Conti shouting that *this time he is going to do it.* "Go ahead!" screams Blanche, banging the door behind him. Moments later, remorse. "Jack!" she cries, tearing out of the apartment, running for the Seine, careening off bookstall browsers, calling, weeping. A glimpse of a man poised at river's edge on the cobbled road under the Quai. "Jack!" A scramble down to the water. A fisherman baiting his hook as he contemplates the Seine. Hours of wild searching, giving up, limping back to the Impasse de Conti framing the story she will give to the police. Looking poetically innocent, Jack asleep in their bed.

Her "suicide attempts" are equally flamboyant. Wild announcements from behind various locked bathroom doors that she has swallowed iodine. When in the mood, Jack shouts that unless she opens up he will brain himself against the door. A horrific crash, then silence. She flings open the door, crouches by his side, frantically searches for signs of life. Practiced at holding his breath at slow curtains, Jack enjoys her agony until at last, morosely, he is forced to sit up and breathe.

And insofar as their marriage was a drama, Jack was Blanche's superior in experience and talent. Yet she was exhausting the energies he should have been giving to the theatre. And the less they both worked the more they quarreled.

Finally Jack deigned to go to London to make a movie that excited him. He had studied Conan Doyle's Sherlock Holmes for months, poring over the drawings of Doyle's definitive illustrator, Frederic Dorr Steele. He had persuaded an old German actor named Gustav von Seyffertitz to play Moriarty. He had sketched the set for the great detective's famous sitting room complete with Persian slipper, cigars in the coal scuttle, and V.R. spelled above the mantel in bullet holes. Yet when Albert Parker, the director, arrived in London he couldn't find his star anywhere. Days later he tracked him down in a little attic room at the Ritz. Jack was sitting up in bed, blind drunk. The room was chaos; there were even gin bottles in his shoes.

Once coaxed to the studio, he could be charming to his fellow actors or beastly. He immediately liked Roland Young, a youthful, self-effacing actor playing his Watson, and gave him tips on business so that in the completed film he, John Barrymore, would not obliterate the novice. He was affable with a bit player named Hedda Hopper, who had not only gone on the stage after falling in love with Ethel in *Jinks* but had seen *The Jest* six times. Yet he took an intense dislike to the actress playing the love interest the film felt obliged to provide for Holmes in place of cocaine. With only one take remaining, Jack suddenly said, "I'm not going to do another shot with that woman!" and walked off the set. Parker had to use Carol Dempster's maid as a stand-in, and Jack played the final scene to her shadow, indistinguishable from Dempster's.

"I was fond of him," said Albert Parker, "and I think he was fond of me. But he was absolutely crazy, mad as a hatter, not good for himself at any time, but lovable." *Sherlock Holmes* proved not good to Doyle or to Jack's vision of Doyle on film. Lacking Holmes's and Watson's vivid verbal exchanges, the film also lacked action, a crucial flaw. Jack contributed a few moments of nervous intensity and a great deal of profile: he *looked* a marvelous Holmes. But acting honors (if any) were carried off by von Seyffertitz, the young William Powell in a minor role and, according to Jack, Roland Young: "The quiet, agreeable bastard had stolen not one, but every damned scene!"

AFTER THE DEBACLE of *Macbeth*, Lionel roared back with *The Claw*. There was only one excuse for exhuming Bernstein's drama, critics decided, but it was an excellent one: "Mr. Barrymore did the finest, most moving acting of his career." His Achille Cortelon was a tour de force, "a Barrymore holiday." "He wasn't acting at all, in the usual way," Spencer Tracy, a young college student with acting ambitions, remembered. "Everything he did, his little movements and gestures, was so basic and natural that people didn't notice them. He coughed right in the middle of a speech, and it was part of the characterization. He was . . . just being."

Ludwig Lewisohn seized upon Lionel's gift for turning himself into utterly different characters as an opportunity to compare him with John:

> The ambition of the average American actor is not to interpret drama or create character, but to be John Barrymore. In regard to Mr. Barrymore's artistic intelligence and fascinating gifts there can be no question. But as Fedya in *Redemption*, as Gianino [*sic*] in *The Jest*, and as Richard III he played but variations upon the theme of himself. There was the same *morbidezza*, the same sense of inferiority becoming fierceness or malign splendor, the same white profile, the same stricken grace. In each piece one became primarily aware not of a creature of a given world and kind, but of John Barrymore's somewhat hectic idealization of himself. It was not, first of all, acting, but superb day-dreaming upon the stage.
>
> Mr. Lionel Barrymore, devoid of his brother's poignant charm, is a far more scrupulous practitioner of his art. His Neri in *The Jest* was shaggy, boisterous, full of excess and gorgeous wildness; his Mouzon in *La Robe Rouge* [*The Letter of the Law*] was polished, quietly cynical, hard, and graceless in an inimitably truthful modern way. The two creations had nothing in common but his intelligence, his powers of observation, his ability to project what he had grasped and seen. The contrast illustrates this brief argument and sums it up. To emulate John Barrymore is both foolish and impossible; to imitate his brother is to have a just and fruitful notion of the actor's art.

In Chicago on tour that March 1922, Lionel had enough restored faith in the theatre to telegraph Theodore Dreiser, WOULD YOU CONSIDER MAKING PLAY OF SISTER CARRIE AM ENORMOUSLY INTERESTED IN POSSIBILITY OF PLAYING HEIRSTWEND [*sic*] IT WOULD MAKE A GREAT PLAY. Had Dreiser converted his novel, Doris would not have played Carrie. She had come along on the tour, trying to ignore evidence of her husband's infatuation with Irene Fenwick, hoping to save their marriage. But when she awoke in their Pullman sleeping compartment night after night to find Lionel's bunk empty, she finally left the tour in despair and humiliation.

Irene was thoroughly "the other woman." She had been divorced by one millionaire for adultery; her current husband, the broker James F. O'Brien, could make the same charge. Her method was direct. When an admirer once told her at a party that he had seen *The Song of Songs* ten times and still dreamed of her, Irene said promptly, "Then why don't we go upstairs?" This kind of frank sexuality thrilled the shy Lionel. Doris was good, undemanding, self-effacing. Irene was bold and sophisticated and made an old married man of forty-four feel dangerous again.

The family rallied round Doris. When she wasn't calling Irene "the Skeleton," Ethel called her "that bitch." She promptly offered Doris a part in a forthcoming play and summoned Lionel to Philadelphia where she tried, but failed, to knock sense into him. Back in the States, Jack too tried to discourage his brother. "Don't do it," he urged. "I've fucked her. She's nothing but a whore." This was too much even for a man used to coming in second. Furious, Lionel cut communications with Jack. Arthur Hopkins's hopes of a repertory season with both Barrymores died on the spot.

On June 28 Blanche and Doris sailed together on the *Mauretania* for Europe—Blanche because she and Jack had decided to test each other apart, Doris because she was suffering and hoped her absence might bring Lionel to his senses. Lionel and Jack were both at the dock to bid their wives goodbye, but only Jack gave the steward six exquisite bouquets to be delivered to Blanche each day of the voyage.

Shaken by her departure, Jack asked Ethel for shelter at Mamaroneck; of course she gave it. He was very unhappy and at loose ends. There are many versions of what happened next, but Ethel said that she took Jack off to the health spa of French Lick, Indiana, where he was even more restless until she produced a little red Temple edition of *Hamlet* and told him to learn one of the soliloquies. Though neither was satisfied with his rendition, Ethel at least "knew the spark was there." Jack says that he went alone with the Temple edition to White Sulphur Springs where he repaired to the woods and recited to the trees. He was amazed at how simple *Hamlet* seemed to be and bewildered that something of such lucid beauty should have inspired centuries of comment. For him Goethe had summed it all: "Shakespeare sought to depict a great deed laid upon a soul unequal to the performance of it. . . . Here is an oak tree planted in a costly vase, which should have received into its bosom only lovely flowers; the roots spread out, the vase is shivered to pieces."

Ethel said that when they came back to Mamaroneck, Britt drove them both to lunch with Margaret Carrington at her Greenwich, Connecticut, estate; that a few days later Jack asked for Britt and the car; that Britt came back, but that Ethel didn't see Jack again until November.

Blanche heard from him before that. She and Doris had progressed to a friend's chateau in the mountains above Grasse, and there, despite primitive communication facilities, a telegram from Jack found its way up the mountainside. In allowing her to go on this jaunt, he cabled, he had "forced himself to go desperately against his grain." Apparently he could not give her what she wanted. It would be better if they never met again.

Blanche understood. She went into Doris's room where doves were cooing under the eaves, and handed her the cable; she began to cry hard, as though she were seasick. "I never thought Jack would do such a cruel thing," Doris said over and over. "He will pay for it."

"WHAT A HAPPY SUMMER that was," said Margaret Carrington; "we worked six, eight hours a day—sometimes into the night. In the garden— and the woods. The day [Jack] arrived, he was carrying an armful of books. The *Hamlet* variorum, histories of the play as interpreted by actors of the past. I suggested that we put the books away and find out for ourselves what the play was about. We . . . studied the play as we would a modern script that had never been performed."

The idea of approaching Shakespeare as a new playwright had been Hopkins's in *Richard the Third*. Yet in one sense, this Hopkins-Barrymore *Hamlet* would not be modern at all. It had been the practice of nineteenth-century actors like Irving, Mansfield, and Tree to disembowel Shakespeare at will, slashing other parts to pad their own. At the end of the century a genuinely modern movement had begun in England to play Shakespeare without cuts and with the minimal scenery of the Elizabethan stage. But John Barrymore was a star; the play was not the thing. By the time Hopkins, Jack, and Carrington came up with their version of *Hamlet*, they had cut more than 1,250 lines. The modernity of this *Hamlet*, therefore, lay not in presenting Shakespeare *virgo intacta*, but in Jack's Freudian interpretation. His Hamlet would be a tragic hero who lacked the courage not of his convictions but of his complexes.

Though Jack is said to have consulted with psychiatrists during his shaping of Hamlet, there is more evidence that he spontaneously felt this the right interpretation: that Hamlet's feeling for his father is not so much reverence as fear and jealousy, that he has an ill-suppressed passion for his mother, that his hatred of Claudius stems chiefly from Claudius's having usurped his, young Hamlet's, place in his mother's bed. Jack's close friend Gene Fowler once asked him what had gone through his mind while playing the role. Jack answered with a burst of violent obscenity: "That dirty, red-whiskered son-of-a-bitch! That bastard puts his prick in my mother's cunt every night!" Finally, it was the forbidden sexual conflict raging in Hamlet that charged Jack's performance.

Jack would always place his Hamlet second to his Richard because he felt that with Richard he entered more deeply into the character's subconscious. Onstage he thought and felt like Richard; offstage he carried the king's psyche with him, even dreaming Richard's, not Jack Barrymore's, bloodily ambitious dreams. Since Hamlet possessed him less, he thought it the inferior creation. But the spontaneous affinity Jack felt for Hamlet did not mean a lesser but a freer, more natural performance precisely because Hamlet came to him more easily. Certainly this Hamlet would have Jack's masculinity complex: Jack was determined to avoid all traces of the romantic Peter Ibbetson or the effeminate Gianetto. "I want him to be so male," he told Hopkins, "that when I come out on the stage they can hear my balls clank." But this clank had little to do with sex appeal: to Jack the play was about a man, for men. "Seriously, I have often wondered why women go to see *Hamlet* in the theatre. Perhaps it is because they bear male children. I don't know."

The first week in October Jack announced that he was ready, and Hopkins set the opening for November 16. For Ophelia he hired a young English ballad singer named Rosalinde Fuller. Blanche Yurka (Gertrude) had classical experience, however, and Tyrone Power II (Claudius) had been pronounced the one American actor of this generation really equipped to play Shakespeare. Other actors Hopkins recruited from the recently disbanded Sothern and Marlowe Shakespeare company.

Long before the cast assembled, an air of mystery had gathered about this *Hamlet* at the Sam H. Harris Theatre. At the first rehearsal the actors exchanged greetings, then stood about the bare stage waiting expectantly. Finally Arthur Hopkins appeared, short, rotund, looking rather like a small boy caught stealing apples. He greeted the cast shyly and took a seat near the footlights to wait like the rest. At last John Barrymore strolled onto the stage, cigarette in hand. He conferred briefly with Hopkins in low tones, then greeted various members of the cast. Hopkins asked the actors to draw their chairs in a semicircle; they would read through the play making cuts as they went. The actors discovered that Hopkins had kept all the lines traditionally cut and eliminated those usually spoken so that Laertes, Horatio, and Polonius had virtually new parts. Though Jack read sotto voce, he was word-perfect. Both he and Hopkins insisted again and again that this production was not going to be Shakespearean in any traditional sense.

The creative ecstasy was again upon Jack. "Of all the actors I have known," said Hopkins, "he was the most conscientious and untiring in preparation. Nothing was too much trouble. He would go to the costumer, the bootmaker, the wig maker, the armor maker, twenty times each, forty if necessary to get everything right. He was the first to know his part. He would rehearse each time as though it were a performance. He was never late, never made excuses. He would rehearse scenes with other actors as long as they wanted. He never grew tired. To him perfection was the aim, and its attainment could not be too much trouble."

Acting the First Player, John Lark Taylor agreed. He'd heard that Barrymore was a perfect fiend—impossible to rehearse with, to act with hell. Instead Taylor found him the soul of kindness and courtesy. "He rarely directed any one; occasionally he would make a suggestion, and always a good one. His efforts, always, so far as I could see, were to get the best effect for the whole thing, and he seemed to want each individual actor in the cast to get the most he could out of his part." Yes, as long as that part did not interfere with his own. Blanche Yurka quickly discovered that Jack had planned his performance down to the last gesture, and that the other actors better be found in places where his movements required them to be. There was no question of John Barrymore's being "only an instrument in an orchestra": he was solar, pivotal, the star.

Many of the costumes for this *Hamlet* came from the ill-starred *Macbeth*, though not, of course, John Barrymore's. After a great deal of trouble, Jack finally hit upon a simple tunic of black silk duvetyn, the sleeves especially designed to end in long, hand-disguising points. He made up the way he did in movies, very pale, his eyes ringed with kohl. To give fullness to his head he wore a piece of false hair in back secured by a thin rubber band completely concealed by his own brushed-back hair. But where, wondered Taylor, were the beautifully turned, symmetrical legs of Gianetto in *The Jest*? Even with padded calves, Jack's legs in tights were thin, ungraceful. Taylor worried even more about the beautiful voice. Jack's progress about the stage was marked by cigarette butts; inevitably a cigarette burned between his fingers.

Whitford Kane, who had toured with Jack in *Justice*, came into rehearsals during the third week for the gravedigging scene. The British actor had heard many lurid rumors about the new *Hamlet*; the air of mystery shrouding rehearsals was irritating to a trouper who had seen forty *Hamlet*s in his time. If he simply asked whether he was standing in the right place for the grave trap, three or four assistant managers would come running and intimate slyly that indeed he was. Obviously, thought Kane, there was a big surprise coming from somewhere. He knew what it was when he laid eyes for the first time on Robert Edmond Jones's set.

Undaunted by accusations that his *Macbeth* set had extinguished the actors, Jones had designed for *Hamlet* a stage-filling flight of steps culminating in a huge arch. The action would take place up and down these steps, longer scenes on platforms at different levels. Side and overhead spots created the feeling of vast darkness pierced by shafts of light. Feeling very old and mid-Victorian, Kane found himself thinking that Jones's usurping staircase looked depressingly like a tomb. Jack nicknamed it "Penn Station."

There were other shocks for traditionalists. Ophelia was not the sweet maid of yore: the fragile, waiflike Rosalinde Fuller imbued her madness with a lewd sexuality that appalled some of the company, though Hopkins and Jack enthusiastically approved. More unsettling still, the ghost of Hamlet's dead father turned out to be nothing more than a spotlight hovering somewhere up in interstellar space. Awesome perhaps to some, but Kane found it silly and regrettable that this splendid-looking Hamlet had been sired by an electric light.

For Jack was undeniably beautiful: extraordinarily young, all fire and ice and princely grace. Chagrined that, though seven years younger, she was playing mother to this stripling, Blanche Yurka made herself as youthful as possible. The result—the slender, black-clad Hamlet wooing a lovely Gertrude whose fair hair cascaded over her scarlet dress—was breathtaking and uncannily real. For the first time Kane felt he was seeing not two actors but Gertrude, Queen of Denmark, and her son. "I was," said the veteran, "excited." He was not alone. Jack had been underplaying, but one day let himself go in one of the soliloquies. Afterward Tyrone Power seized John Lark Taylor. "By God! He's going to be great," said Power. "He's going to make the hit of his life in this part!" In fact, the whole company had jumped at Jack's performance, as though a bolt of lightning had shot through them.

MEANWHILE BLANCHE AND DORIS had returned. Informed by reporters that her husband was going to do *Hamlet*, Blanche granted he should be wonderful: "It will not be so trying as *Richard the Third* where he had to wear that heavy armor." Doris did not find Lionel waiting for her and Blanche discovered that the Barrymore Board of Regents had closed protectively around their genius. First she'd been cast off by Jack for "moral turpitude"; now his friends were trying to eliminate her from his life.

Difficult, since Jack constantly wavered. Firmly convinced she was an adulteress, Jack was suddenly told by a mutual friend that Blanche was merely "a lost and bewildered child." That threw him into confusion. Blanche had no right to be lost and bewildered: that was *his* forte; still, perhaps informants had exaggerated her insidiousness. He stormed the house on Ninety-seventh Street; for hours they hurled bitter truths at each other, the little triangular scar above Jack's left eyebrow burning white. Having exhausted vituperation, they gradually felt the rosy warmth of reconciliation steal over them. Soon Jack was on the telephone brutally denouncing the false friends who had turned him against his own tiny Fig. But with this manic couple no truce could last. Blanche sailed for Paris again, taking the children with her. The tug of egos recommenced across the Atlantic as Blanche cabled him daily to join her. Fortunately for the American theatre, Jack resisted. Yet this *Hamlet* was John Barrymore's first season in three years.

ONE DAY just before opening, Ethel came to a rehearsal. It was the company's first uninterrupted run-through, and Jack was excited about that and about his sister's presence. Though the cast wore street clothes and the stage was bare, everyone that afternoon was inspired. "I suppose it was the greatest experience I ever had in a theatre," said Ethel, moved to tears. "He was superb, magnificent, unforgettable, and had in some mysterious way acquired that magical ease, as if he really were Hamlet. It was for me the fulfillment of all I had ever hoped for him and more." Looking back, Hopkins thought Jack's performance that day—a gift to the maternal sister who loved him—his best.

For the opening-night audience at the Harris Theatre, John Barrymore's debut as Hamlet was an adventure, a triumph unequaled in the American theatre of his generation, perhaps of the twentieth century. "For me, Barrymore simply *was* the Prince of Denmark," said Helen Hayes, speaking for the majority. John Barrymore, the critics said, "seemed to gather together in himself all the Hamlets of his generation"; he was "an understandable, coherent Hamlet, Shakespeare's own Hamlet"; he was "the most interesting, intelligent, and exciting Hamlet of our generation"; he was "truly magnificent . . . unique in this generation" in "the finest production *Hamlet* had ever had in America."

Yet comparisons were inevitable, and in the following weeks the game began: who really was the greatest Hamlet in living memory? It was a riddle without an answer because each spectator brought to a performance his or her subjectivity. To those who remembered the dark force of Edwin Booth, Barrymore semed lacking in "tragic power" and "the inspiring spirit." To those who had witnessed Henry Irving's impersonation of a mind wavering on the brink of madness, Barrymore seemed implacably sane. To those who admired Walter Hampden's oratory, Barrymore seemed to lack eloquence. To those who thrilled to Johnston Forbes-Robertson's poetry, Barrymore seemed often to lapse into prose. Those who came fresh to John Barrymore's Hamlet, however, were completely conquered. This subversive Hamlet's clarity and lack of pretension, his bitter humor warring with a fundamental sweetness, his tense grace were qualities that spoke to a postwar generation no longer able to take seriously heroics or "the inspiring spirit."

Only one criticism moved Jack to respond: the accusation that this *Hamlet* was all John Barrymore. He posted his answer on the call board: "I cannot tell you how *utterly* the idea is repudiated by everyone I have talked to since last night, and how entirely and absolutely foreign this is to the manner in which the entire performance was genuinely received. The thing that makes this play go over the way it does is the extraordinary teamwork. . . . Everyone is speaking of it. . . ." John Lark Taylor was so touched by Jack's gesture that he wrote the star thanking him for his graceful generosity. For several days Jack gave no sign of having received Taylor's letter; then one night in the wings Taylor saw the glow of Jack's cigarette. "I sent your note to my wife," whispered Jack shyly. "She'll be tickled to death with it."

Embarrassed, Taylor said, "I envy her the pleasure she will have seeing your Hamlet."

Jack was silent, then he said huskily, "I don't know when she'll see it. She's in Paris, you know, and it's hard to make the trip with the children." His cue came and, after a few quick drags, he ground out his cigarette and walked onstage.

Jack did not respond to a more devastating criticism, the *Times*'s accusation that Hopkins and Jones had extinguished Shakespeare. The guilty party was "the new art of stage decoration, which Mr. Jones professes and Mr. Hopkins still patronizes, in spite of the mischief it has done him." In theory this new art was plausible enough: scenery should embody the theme of the play. But in this case Jones's symbolic stairs had "usurped the rightful domain of the players, the area needful to the creation of any genuine dramatic effect. One cannot play Shakespeare up and down the stairs." The chief limitation of John Barrymore's Hamlet was thus imposed by Hopkins and by Jones: "It must be kept in mind always when appraising the value of that spiritually elevated, intelligent and impassioned performance."

The question of whether there could exist two stars on the stage at the same time—Hamlet and Jones's set—was valid. But the actors and most of the audience had no trouble believing that the nunnery and the Queen's closet scene could be played on the same platform, for example, or that the foot of the stairs stood for both a castle interior and the graveyard. And though many considered Jones's *Hamlet* set "one of the glories of our theatre," John Barrymore's Hamlet won far more attention and praise.

Not a single critic, Jack complained, noticed his unique interpretation of the closet scene with the Queen. Very tender with his mother, Jack didn't like Hamlet's making rank accusations of adultery to her face. Beginning with the "Nay, but to live / In the rank sweat of an enseamed bed," therefore, he played as though the spirit of his dead father had gripped him and was speaking through him. A light struck him: he became rigid, his eyes staring, his voice hoarse and measured like the Ghost's; the light disappearing, he fell to his knees shrieking, "Save me, and hover o'er me with your wings, you heavenly guards!" as though suddenly released from the grip of his father's spirit. "Doing it that way makes Hamlet so much more decent," he told Taylor, then burst out, "God! How I would love to talk with Shakespeare about this play!"

As *Hamlet* played to capacity crowds that winter, one thing became clear: moody John Barrymore's impersonation of the moody Dane was never the same two nights in a row or even consistent during one performance. Blanche Yurka noted that he hardly ever sustained the entire performance at his top form, as though having to conserve limited energy; sometimes she wondered whether he would get through. Taylor thought he got slower every performance, playing between the lines and out-pausing Macready, famous for his long pauses. He would look at Taylor for a long time, raise his hand, open his mouth, look at Taylor again until the actor began to panic, then finally say, "Can. . . . . . you . . . play . . . . the murder. . . . . . . of . . . . Gonzago?" Eventually he added thirty minutes to a performance already long because the players had to run up and down Jones's interminable stairs. Certainly Jack was in constant trouble with his voice because he smoked so heavily, pausing every time he went onstage to fill his lungs even though he delayed the performance. Paul, his valet of nine years, constantly worked him over with ice bags and throat remedies, and Margaret Carrington often spent Sundays at his suite in the Ambassador tuning his voice for Monday. "My pipes are on the bum," Jack would explain cheerfully.

Hopkins thought that his performance grew more and more to resemble his Richard III, so that he lost some of the simplicity and sweetness of his original conception. Whitford Kane thought that Richard had been there all along, especially in Hamlet's "O villain, villain, smiling, damnèd villain" speech. Jack gave those lines "the sharpness of a knife thrust and the impersonality of an acid eating into metal. The man that could read the line like that would have killed the King in less than half an hour."

The critic George Jean Nathan also felt the ruthlessness: Barrymore's Hamlet was "like a diamond . . . glittering, vari-colored, brilliant—but cold, intensely cold." And sometimes, said Hopkins, Jack could be embarrassingly bombastic.

This happened when he most wanted to impress. One night he was told that the Shakespearean actors E. H. Sothern and Julia Marlowe were in the audience. "Ask them to come back and see me," he told the stage manager; then called after him, "No, no! Don't ask." He tried to outdo himself that night, and gave perhaps the worst performance of his life. Marlowe and Sothern left after the graveyard scene, an open snub. They said nothing to Jack, but Marlowe told the stage manager, "I have never seen a company so completely submerged."

He did it again one afternoon when the Moscow Art Theatre players, the renowned exponents of ensemble acting, came en masse to a matinee. Ethel was with them. She and Hopkins watched in horror as Jack played with a hysteria that exhausted even the spectators. After the first scene Hopkins hurried backstage and "begged him to alight," but "the stampede was on, and he never got back into the corral all afternoon."

Afterward Jack tried to hide behind the rest of the cast, but before he could disappear Ethel came bounding in calling loudly, "Jake! Jake! Oh, Jake! Here's Madame Chekova!"—sounding, to that perennial observer John Lark Taylor, like a raucous peacock. A large woman chattering Russian bore down. Jack took one look and dove into his dressing room, crying, "Ethel, I'm afraid!" Eventually there were lots of smacking kisses and hugs, but clearly the Moscow Art Theatre players were dazed. "Do you really do this eight times a week?" asked Madame Chekova incredulously. And yet in London Jack had passed Constantin Stanislavsky's test for actors with flying colors. They were dining when Stanislavsky ordered him into the next room, saying, "I will hide the pin. You come and find it." Jack reentered, lifted plates and glasses, ran his hand under the tablecloth and produced the pin. "You are engaged," said the co-founder of the Moscow Art Theatre. "I can tell a real actor by the way he looks for a pin. If he prances around the room, striking attitudes, pretending to think hard, looking in ridiculous places—in other words, exaggerating—then he is no good." That afternoon Jack had done a lot of prancing.

But no matter how packed the houses and enthusiastic the audiences, Jack quickly became bored with repeating *Hamlet* eight times a week. Indeed, no actor should have to endure that labor, yet Jack admitted that his enthusiasm lasted little more than a week. Bored, he would start to improvise, and when John Barrymore improvised, said Hopkins, it was time to run for the lifeboats. One night after the First Gravedigger had sung his quatrain, Jack whispered from the wings, "Sing it again, Whitford, you ought to be in opera." Kane was obliged to sing it three times before Jack made his entrance, leaving the senior actor a nervous wreck. As the weeks went on Jack cared less and less if he ruined a scene. One night one of the men bearing off the dead Hamlet almost dropped him and lunging, grabbed a ticklish spot. *"Ch-rrrist!"* the corpse yelped with a spasmodic jerk. The audience howled; the tragedy ended as comedy. "Why don't you keep on your job?" Jack told the bearer furiously. "Do you want to get a poke in the eye?" On the other hand, he could be charming, sending one actor a little note of apology: "I'm damned sorry I forgot my bally lines last night and amputeed two of your best lines. I must have been in *Patterson* instead of Denmark."

He was lonely, spending Christmas at the zoo; wild to see Blanche, torn with suspicion and jealousy. Rumors began to flit backstage that the play was closing, dismaying the cast who knew it was playing to $17,000 to $21,000 weekly houses. Finally on January 20 it was official: BARRY-MORE TO BREAK BOOTH "HAMLET" RECORD AND CLOSE. Indeed the challenge of breaking Edwin Booth's record 100 performances with 101 was all that kept Jack in New York, something he achieved as swiftly as possible by adding Tuesday matinees.

He was apologetic about deserting such a success. "God, I'm nearly crazy, I'm so worried about my kids," he would tell the cast. John Lark Taylor knew it was not the kids but Blanche. For the past two weeks Jack had fired off daily cables to Paris, "veritable books that must have cost a small fortune." Taylor wondered at the selfishness of the wife who not only refused to come and see her husband's great achievement but constantly urged him to join her. Clearly Jack was torn. "To sail or not to sail," as one wit parodied it.

The cast forgave him, he was so vulnerable, so distraught. Taylor tried to cheer him by relaying the comment of a psychic friend. "All through the performance," the psychic had said, "I sensed the great mental turmoil of the man, worried, nervous, irritable, but back of that something fine, a great sweetness and beauty. I got a strong impression that something wonderful, the thing he most desires, is coming to him."

Jack was superstitious, susceptible to any kind of suggestion. "Gee!" he said eagerly. "I hope so. Thanks for telling me, old man. I hope to God it's true."

The final house on February 9 had been sold out weeks in advance, but the announcement that standing room would be sold at seven-thirty created a line that stretched from the box office along Forty-fifth Street to Seventh Avenue. Finally 1,000 people were turned away. After the second act, Jack was compelled to make a little speech of thanks. About eleven, actors from the other theatres began to arrive to witness this historic one hundred and first *Hamlet*. The curtain did not fall to cheers and prolonged applause until twelve. Looking haggard, Jack exchanged goodbyes with the cast, then hurried from the theatre to board the *Majestic* which would sail the next morning.

But "something wonderful" was not coming to Jack, at least not in Paris. Something wonderful had already happened, but his triumphant Hamlet he perversely whistled to the wind.

SIXTEEN

1922–1925

No matter how brilliant Jack's Hamlet, Arthur Hopkins still was haunted by the aborted *Richard the Third*. He had dreamed of presenting America's greatest actor in repertory; Jack's unreliability had disillusioned him. Now he turned to the supremely reliable Ethel. Even at the height of their success, he felt, her brothers "never seemed to grow up to her." She had "an unfailing theater sense which they recognized and trusted." And to him, quite simply, she was the most fascinating, the most glamorous actress of her day.

Since Alf Hayman's death had severed her last ties to the Frohman organization, Ethel was free and eager to try repertory. In the summer of 1922, therefore, Hopkins announced Ethel Barrymore for two seasons at the Longacre in Shakespeare, Ibsen, Hauptmann, and America's most exciting young playwright, Eugene O'Neill.

Their first collaboration was Gerhart Hauptmann's *Rose Bernd* in which Ethel, though forty-three, played a tortured peasant girl who strangles her bastard infant. Hopkins thought her magnificent. Though disturbed by the "alien tragedy," Woollcott agreed in superlatives:

> Ethel Barrymore gave the finest performance she has ever given, a performance that at times reached a beauty that we, in our time, have never seen surpassed in the theatre. We have felt for some years that she was heir apparent in this generation to the magnificence that was Nell Gwyn's, Peg Woffington's, and Ada Rehan's. We have never felt surer of it than last night. . . . We suspect that many of Miss Barrymore's devoted admirers will be bored to rigidity and even torpor by *Rose Bernd*, but the lover of the theatre who lets such a warning frighten him away from the Longacre Theatre will miss a performance such as glorifies our stage only once in a long, long while.

Surely Arthur Hornblow had watched a different actress? "Miss Barrymore stumbles heavily through all the three long acts; she fidgets so nervously as to make Rose seem not just dull but lunatic; she groans her lines in a manner which suggests, more than anything, the roaring of her own brother as Neri; she stares madly. . . . Physically she is utterly unsuited to the role." Who is one to believe? Given the starkness of Rose Bernd's tragedy, this is probably another case of those who loved Ethel the Elegant loathing her as anything else. Ludwig Lewisohn, Hauptmann's translator, singled out two culprits for the failure: ignorant audiences who rejected "the greatest living dramatist," and Arthur Hopkins who manhandled Hauptmann's superb play. Little matter: for Ethel, *Rose Bernd* was another *Doll's House* or *Silver Box*. Audiences didn't want her to get serious.

The next play was to have been *As You Like It*, should have been *As You Like It*. With Jack's immense success as Hamlet, however, Hopkins decided it was more important for Ethel to play the comparably important Juliet. Ethel did not want to: she had learned Rosalind and, more important, Jane Cowl was going to play Juliet that season. She protested, but Jones had already designed the sets and—as usual—the sets prevailed. That, at least, is Ethel's story.

Of all Shakespeare's plays, *Romeo and Juliet* is the most passionate, heedless, fiery, ardent, sexual, and *young*. But Hopkins's goal, as with *Hamlet*, was a modern *Romeo and Juliet*. A muted, intellectual, naturalistic, sophisticated, staccato *Romeo and Juliet*. A *Romeo and Juliet* that would not assault the ear of a disillusioned "lost generation" with flights of embarrassingly overwrought eloquence. Ethel was to play Juliet like (in Bernard Shaw's words) "the decayed gentlewoman who has to cry laces in the street for a living but hopes no one will hear her." She must avoid offending both Romeo and the audience with her passion. And Ethel, to whom repression of feeling was only too natural, did not protest this sacrilege.

Inevitably plays are reinterpreted in the light of current taste and custom. But Hopkins and Jones this time had miscalculated. Critics were indeed offended—not by passion but by its total lack. This *Romeo and Juliet* was "a muffled dirge, with the most burning love speeches ever written trying vainly to burst forth from the blanket of repression." Ethel didn't have a chance.

"The public didn't like the scenery—they didn't like the company," said Ethel, "—and they didn't like me." Jack tried to comfort her: "It really, *really* is great. It is *truly* magnificent. The finest thing you've ever done."

Dear Jack. The critics disagreed. They fell upon her mercilessly, no matter that she had been a star for twenty-one years. She was a matronly Juliet, a dowdy Juliet. She spoke and moved in the balcony scene as if in a trance. In the potion and tomb scenes she had all the passion of a somnambulist. She was a dignified Juliet, a ladylike Juliet, a Juliet "bent upon no adventure," a Juliet who was almost—polite. And the company *took its pace from her*; Hopkins scot-free again. She was also blamed for the last-minute switch from Rosalind to Juliet, "one of those unfortunate quick decisions," critics said direly, "that frequently affects the whole course of a player's career." Little matter among the volleys of abuse that someone said her Juliet was often beautifully and sympathetically read. She was not sixteen, she hadn't acted sixteen. She had failed.

Hopkins gallantly defended her, at the same time covering himself: "Owing to my own failure to see that she was not well and was too exhausted to play and rehearse at the same time, she did not do herself justice as Juliet, although, as in anything she did, she had moments of unequaled beauty." Ethel was not consoled: "It was sheer misery for me all the time we were doing it, and when it was over, I felt as if a great burden had been lifted from me." To ease that burden during the play's four-week run, Ethel had begun to drink. Not like Jack, but not just Mummum's nightly tot of rye in water either.

To dramatize her failure, the Klauber-Selwyn production of *Romeo and Juliet* with the beautiful, youthful-looking Jane Cowl opened at the Henry Miller Theatre on January 24, 1923, just as Ethel's production ignominiously folded. If Ethel could have borne to read the reviews, she would have learned that "everything that was heavy and slow-paced about the ill-fated Barrymore production was here spirited and youthful. . . . Miss Cowl is easily the most beautiful and most gifted Juliet of our day. . . . With Juliet as the cornerstone of the classical repertoire she now plans to build up (she will add Shakespeare's Cleopatra and Viola next season), there is every reason to expect this actress will, within the next decade, take position as the first actress of the native theatre." The triumphant 160 performances of the Cowl Juliet contrasted with Ethel's failure was the hottest theatrical topic of the day.

A lesser actress, a lesser person than Ethel Barrymore might have thrown herself into the East River. Instead she roared back on February 12 in Alfred Sutro's *The Laughing Lady*, playing a woman so fascinating that in the course of a dinner party she makes the lawyer who had ripped her to shreds in court that very afternoon fall madly in love with her. Audiences fell in love right along with her victim, and Ethel "was immediately reestablished in the hearts of her adoring public." Ethel was not vindictive, yet she could not have been utterly displeased when Jane Cowl a year later played Cleopatra like a flapper, never once achieving tragic heights. Cowl never did play Viola; she did not become "the first actress of the native theatre." The public since 1901 had known who that actress was, despite her limitations. Their Ethel.

And then came a labor of pure love. Ellen Terry had immediately recognized that Ethel should play Lady Teazle. Her season at the Longacre over, Ethel went into a stunning Players Club production of *The School for Scandal* with Walter Hampden, McKay Morris, and Robert Mantell, William Seymour directing from Sheridan's original text and stage business. Ethel found the few performances with Uncle Jack as Sir Peter Teazle sheer joy.

Always discreet and formal, John Drew never publicly revealed his feelings for his niece. Bee, his tangoing, bunny-hopping daughter, had left the theatre to marry the film actor John Devereaux in 1917; the birth of John Drew Devereaux the next year had made the dapper Drew a grandfather. Bee might have become a good actress had she worked at it; she preferred café society. But Ethel was a trouper like her Uncle Jack. For years they had led the theatrical world, the undisputed royals of the stage. On March 23, 1923, Ethel presented a gold plaque to her uncle on the occasion of the fiftieth anniversary of his first stage appearance at his mother's Arch Street Theatre. No other actress could have lent to the tribute the same meaning. Had it been the old days, they might have trouped *The School for Scandal* across the country as Mummum trouped *The Rivals*. But it was not the old days.

After her emotionally exhausting season with Hopkins, "Our Lady of Vaudeville," as she had been dubbed, hurried back to Keith's to make money. In April papers had been served on Russell at a cigar stand in a hotel in Providence charging cruelty, assault, neglect, and failure to provide. The charge of adultery was conspicuous by its absence. That June reporters in Philadelphia tried to interview Ethel about the divorce, but "It's no use," the manager told them. "She won't see anybody, and if I ask again she'll walk out of the theatre, perhaps never to return." In the Providence Supreme Court John Drew testified to his niece's devoted care of both the children and Mamaroneck. Russell did not contest the divorce, which was finally granted July 6, 1923, the judge sealing all papers in the case.

Ethel had enrolled Sister at her old Convent of the Sisters of Notre Dame de Namur in Rittenhouse Square, where she now came to visit her. She was delighted to find it little changed. Many of the sisters were still there (Sister: was this the source of her daughter's name?). The same gong rang each hour, the same organ hummed in the little choir, every chair still seemed in place. Sister adored the convent, was very popular, and got such good grades that Ethel wondered. "My dear," said the Sister Superior, "we have to give them what they make." Almost as gratifying as being called "little Ethel" again by the dear, good ladies, as though she were still young and innocent once more.

DORIS RANKIN BARRYMORE'S divorce from Lionel for adultery had become final in March 1923. Lionel refused all comment; Doris is perennially mute. The only riveting piece of news in the affair was the announcement in at least two papers that *Doris was granted custody of their only child*. And yet Mary Barrymore, according to her father, died when she was two.

Eventually, Lionel tried to explain why the marriage had failed. ". . . I suppose that my frustrations as a painter, my preoccupation with music, and my obsession with the idea that I wanted to escape from the theater, contributed towards making me a difficult person to live with. These and all the other weaknesses and instabilities . . . made me abrupt, made me thankless, made me thoughtless, made me sour. I suppose that if Doris and I had had a small independent income and the leisure which goes with it, and could have pursued and patronized the many things we actually had in common, I suppose then that our marriage would have had a better chance. As it was, in part because I was a triptych personality, emotionally involved but unsatisfied in three arts, I made our marriage impossible and allowed it to dissolve. Doris was to blame in no respect. The only fault that can be laid to her is that in comparison with anybody else she always came off the better."

If the success of marriage depended on an independent income and leisure, most would fail. More relevant are "all the other weaknesses and instabilities." Drink was one: Lionel drank steadily, though he could control his drinking better than Jack. Irene was another. "When I saw him look at her," Doris said, "I knew. If he had only ever looked at me once that way in the sixteen years we were married." Irene divorced James O'Brien in April, shortly before announcing her engagement to Lionel. The look Doris longed for is evident in a photograph of Lionel and Irene taken on the liner *Paris* as they sailed for Italy where Lionel was to film *The Eternal City*. They were married on June 14 in Rome. One thing was certain: Irene would never wait in the wings with sandwiches. Instead, the Lionel who had been abrupt, thankless, thoughtless, and sour with Doris was already Irene's bond slave. By serving the new wife he might atone for exploiting the old.

In the fall of 1922 Lionel had been widely announced as the star of Eugene O'Neill's newest play, *The Fountain*, another exciting proposition which came to nothing. Instead he and Irene returned from Rome to something distinctly old-fashioned: David Belasco's production of *Laugh, Clown, Laugh!*, which offered Lionel the dual roles of Tito Beppi and Flik in a Pagliaccian drama of passion and revenge. Lionel never could decide whether *Laugh, Clown, Laugh!* was high tragedy or kitsch. The third act certainly qualified as the latter: Lionel going mad in a mirror-distorted room to the crashing accompaniment of thunder, lightning, and rain. Many thought Lionel's work in the second act, however, the best thing on Broadway that season—reason enough why *Laugh, Clown, Laugh!* carried Lionel and Irene through 1924 while Lionel kept searching for something sympathetic, moving, and above all, true. He thought he finally found it in *The Piker*, a tale of a broken-down bank manager who commits petty theft and comes to grief. Lionel went to Al Woods and told him he *had* to play Bernie Kaplan. Money was no object: *The Piker* was a masterpiece. "If you say so, sweetheart," said Woods and opened Lionel with Irene in the cast at the Eltinge on January 19, 1925.

Scanning the reviews, Lionel was angry enough to burst into print, which meant he had been dealt a knockout blow. He thought he had at last found a contemporary, truthful play; critics, however, obviously cared only for phony dramas about phony people. "Nothing profound or moving or tragic or terrible or pathetic or grotesque can happen to a citizen of New York," he complained. Bernie Kaplan's story was "the spirit and substance of great tragedy"—and critics had called him a moron! Well, the greatest story in the world had been written by Cervantes about a moron and a madman. Later he was terse: "This was a bleak role and I could do very little with it."

All the confidence Lionel had regained with *The Claw, The Letter of the Law*, and *Laugh, Clown, Laugh!* crumbled; he was plunged again into the blackest depression about his future on the stage. He stumbled from forty-four performances of *The Piker* into a revival of *Taps* which, said the critics without enthusiasm, "added another portrait to his gallery of stage art." Desperate, Lionel fled to Jerome K. Jerome's *Man or Devil* twelve days later. Most of these plays the infatuated man accepted because they had good parts for Irene; now, however, she collapsed shortly after the opening and entered Harbor Hospital to rest. A Barrymore might rehearse and perform three plays in five months, but Irene was no Barrymore.

Man or Devil was a twenty-performance disaster. Woollcott deplored it as "an elaborate and deeply unimportant fable," another rotten branch grasped by Lionel in his "tireless and groping search for a play of his own calibre." The critic's warning was dire. "Such stature as he has enjoyed in the American theatre cannot long stand the whittling process of such a season as he has just passed through."

Woollcott did not realize he was writing Lionel Barrymore's last Broadway review.

Ethel may have dismissed it as just Lionel's usual bad luck, but there must have been cogent reasons why this great artist could not find something worthwhile to do in the theatre. One problem was his own bad judgment. Others could choose roles for him: Ethel insisted on Giuseppe and Pantaloon, Gus Thomas tailored Kid McCoy and Milt Shanks to his measure, Sheldon commandeered him for Colonel Ibbetson and Neri. Left to his own devices, Lionel fumbled. Eugene O'Neill, for example, had wanted him for *The Fountain, Anna Christie*, and *Beyond the Horizon*, but Lionel had been "otherwise engaged." Another factor was sheer Barrymore arrogance, which afflicted even the most modest of the trio. No Barrymore would condescend to "off-Broadway"—even though some of the most interesting theatre was currently being staged by experimental groups like the Theatre Guild. Bernard Shaw had told Guild director Lawrence Langner that there were three actors who should play Dick Dudgeon, Minister Anderson, and Judith in his rousing *Devil's Disciple*: John Barrymore, Lionel Barrymore, and Ethel Barrymore. Shaw's casting was dead on the mark, the chance of three Barrymores playing for the Theatre Guild nil. Or of the three Barrymores playing together at all. Even humble Lionel dropped out of *Peter Ibbetson* and *The Jest* to star in other plays. Their taste in plays being very different, Ethel avoided her elder brother professionally (a benefit for Actors Equity was the exception). Jack and Lionel could work together as long as Jack's name came first. And then, Lionel tended to be old-fashioned, preferring highly colored dramas to the new realism—though his Mouzon and Bernie Kaplan were thoroughly modern portraits. As a result of these multiple handicaps, the only thing Lionel could think to do was tour *The Copperhead* again, a pathetic compromise when New York theatre was alive with opportunity.

On his way to the United Booking Office, his eyes on the pavement to avoid the huge Wrigley Chewing Gum sign at Broadway and Forty-fifth because both he and Jack believed looking at it was bad luck, Lionel collided with a small man and sent him staggering. He was indeed Small—Maury, Lionel's agent. Lionel confided his plan for a *Copperhead* tour.

"Don't do it," said Small. ". . . I think I can do better for you." (And for him.)

"How?"

"Movies."

Lionel had made eleven movies since the Whitman Bennett quartet, but though *America* had been directed by D. W. Griffith, none had made film history.

"Sounds prosperous. You have a carefully nurtured sucker on hand?"

"No sucker at all. B. P. Schulberg. . . . Here's my office, let's call him up."

To his horror, Lionel heard Small tell Schulberg he could get Lionel Barrymore for a mere ten thousand dollars.

"Five thousand," whispered Lionel, aghast. "Four thousand."

"Ten thousand isn't much," said Small, ". . . but he'd like a trip to California."

"For God's sake, don't kid around!" Lionel wheezed. "Take three thousand!"

Small hung up; the deal went through.

Had Lionel run into Small during *The Jest* or *The Claw*, had *Sister Carrie* or *The Fountain* materialized, had Arthur Hopkins offered another production, Lionel would have brushed Small aside. But as Hopkins said, his reception in *Macbeth* as well as the disastrous season he had just gone through made him easy prey for Hollywood: "It was not money that attracted Lionel. He cared nothing about it. He had lived happily for years without it. He was given to no extravagances, always lived a quiet and retired life, never knew what the glitter of Broadway meant. We never had a contract, and he never asked what he was to receive. After the successful opening of *The Claw* in Boston I told him what his share was to be. He objected because he thought it was too much. No, it was not money that drew him to Hollywood and certainly not love of the work. He wanted to get away from the theater, and Hollywood was the simplest escape."

Lionel did not care for money, true, but Irene Fenwick had been married to two millionaires and cared about it a great deal. Lionel could make a lot more money in Hollywood. Moreover, if she planned to retire from a stage career that had depended largely on youthful charm, her husband's income must take up the slack. She had recently been hospitalized; her health was not good after years of extreme dieting. Irene probably voted for Hollywood.

And perhaps, though he did not care about money, Lionel needed it.

Gene Fowler claimed that in 1925 Lionel became addicted to morphine, which he took to ease arthritic pain aggravated by a venereal disease that "responded to treatment." (Venereal disease . . . Irene, the "Pocket Venus," whom he married in 1923 . . .) Fowler was a responsible reporter, not given to scandal-mongering. If he is right—and Lionel had the addictive Barrymore constitution—Lionel then needed money to support a morphine habit which, according to some sources, Irene shared. So he turned his back on the theatre and went to Hollywood to make a mediocrity called *The Girl Who Wouldn't Work*. He was forty-six and had been on the stage twenty-eight years.

Lionel had impressed Arthur Hopkins as the most cultured and gifted man he had ever known, as the older brother to whom Jack "looked up in adoration to heights he could not attain." Hopkins was also among the many who thought Lionel the most gifted character actor of his day—"character" meaning an actor who does not play himself. "He more completely lost all personal identity in his portrayal than any other artist, man or woman, that it has been my privilege to observe. . . . Other great artists with whom I worked were not so successful in leaving themselves wholly off stage when the characters took the stage. This, of course, is the ultimate magic of acting, the complete legerdemain. No one knows how it is accomplished. It is a gift that cannot be transmitted to another. For me, at least, the miracle disappeared when Lionel left the stage only to be seen again in the too seldom flights of Laurette Taylor. We had experienced it earlier with Duse . . ."

Lionel would claim all the rest of his life that he never regretted leaving the stage. He lied.

AFTER THE CLOSING of *Hamlet*, Jack had hurried to Blanche in Paris. The ecstasy was brief. He didn't like Elsie de Wolfe's house that Blanche had rented for the winter, particularly Blanche's seductive bedroom. "Who is he?" Jack shouted, flinging a hand at the white satin walls. "Who is your lover? You might as well tell me!"

He didn't like Blanche's friends. During their separation she had fallen in with an ultrachic British set that included Oswald and Cynthia Mosley, Bridget Guinness, Lady Colefax, Duff and Diana Cooper. But no matter what friends she chose, Jack would not have liked them. He hated society: like many alcoholics he was comfortable only alone or with other heavy drinkers. He was also insanely jealous of any man Blanche glanced at. Now their few parties in Paris inevitably ended with Jack's fingering some anonymous man. "That's him, isn't it!" he would hiss in Blanche's ear. Quickly it became simpler not to go out or to eat somewhere outside

Paris. When they did choose some quiet place, however, Jack, who claimed he hated notoriety, would gaze with contempt at diners oblivious of the presence of John Barrymore.

His relations with the children were no better; the Catkins, Blanche called them: Leonard-Cat, Robin-Cat, and Diana-Cat. The trouble had begun early: Leonard had understood the servants' gossip when his father was in the army and "Mrs. Thomas was fooling around with that actor-chap." Jack gave Leonard soldiers, Leonard threw them in the garbage can. Jack baited his fishhook, Leonard pulled off the worm. Repulsing Jack's attentions, Leonard then felt distinctly aggrieved when he was not missed after an escape from his room via knotted sheets during one of Jack and Blanche's violent quarrels. The quarreling, the instability, Blanche's ambivalence, and their jealousy of Jack turned them away. Besides, a child himself, Jack was too insecure and egocentric to sustain close relations with children who, in any case, were constantly shunted off to nurses, nannies, tutors, and boarding schools. Diana remembered her mother's invariable, "Did you have a nice time, Catkin?" Seldom with her, Blanche had to ask.

Despite passionate reconciliations, therefore, the blissful reunion was anything but, and when Jack returned to the States in the summer of 1923 to make a film, Blanche stayed behind in Paris.

Jack had been making movies in New York and environs for eleven years. Now Hollywood wanted him—not one of the large, well-heeled studios but Warner Brothers, whose major star was Rin-Tin-Tin. The ambitious Jack Warner had come east to sign him, promising royal treatment and billing as "the world's greatest actor."

The resulting film was *Beau Brummel*, adapted from a Clyde Fitch play that Richard Mansfield had made memorable. Like *Sherlock Holmes* the film introduced a love interest into the life of a man who, in Brummel's case, cared only for clothes, faintly echoing *Peter Ibbetson*'s theme of love denied on earth consummated in death. It gave Jack a wonderful opportunity to show off his face and figure, and provided that favorite Barrymore stunt, a transformation—this time from handsome youth to mad old age.

There was some question whether Mary Astor, a beautiful girl with long rich auburn hair and huge dark eyes, would do for Lady Margaret, Brummel's love—until Jack laid eyes on her. "You are so goddamned beautiful you make me feel faint!" he breathed in her ear during a test take. Mary herself felt tongue-tied in the presence of the great actor until Jack put her at ease by talking and laughing about everything but the picture. She finally confessed she was just seventeen.

"It seems so long ago that I was seventeen—I'm forty now," said Jack, modestly dropping a year.

"*That's* not so old," said Mary, gazing at him with her big dark eyes. She claimed that then and there they fell in love.

An obstacle was her ambitiously protective parents, Otto and Helen Langhanke. They hovered over the child who was going to make their fortune like hawks over a fledgling. Now they were torn. Here was the world's greatest actor taking an interest in their little Mary. But what kind of an interest?

Jack was an old hand at disarming parents. Invited to the Langhankes' Hollywood apartment, he lavished praise on Helen's cooking and talked politics with Otto. Under Mrs. Langhanke's watchful eye he taught Mary how to read Shakespeare until "the tawdry little living room vibrated with magnificence." "He used all his charm on them," said Mary, "and he had more of it than any other man I have ever known."

But when the Langhankes did not let down their guard, Jack became impatient. He told them he must work with their daughter alone. "I feel she's too self-conscious. She's too afraid of what *you* are thinking, instead of listening to me." When they hesitated, Jack laughed the words right out of their mouths: "Don't be ridiculous! This is a *kid!*" Doubtfully, they began to allow Mary more freedom. Jack would send his car for Mary and her mother, and all afternoon Helen would sit on the verandah of Jack's Ambassador Hotel bungalow sewing and wondering what was going on inside. Mary herself did not fight Jack. She was eager for love and didn't give a dime for her father's prohibitions.

To be fair, Jack did mean to help her. Mary felt stimulated simply by his own respect for the theatre and the acting profession. He dismissed pictures scornfully as "the moo-vies" and turned any occasion into an acting lesson, even passing the butter at lunch.

"Before *any* scene go over how long you've known him or her," lectured Jack. "You even say 'Pass the butter' differently according to how you feel . . . There's always something *under* what you're saying— caused by a million things. Suppose, for instance, the guy says—maybe he's your husband—'I've quit my job' and your line is, 'Pass the butter, please.' O.K., now don't giggle like an ass. Listen, there'd be a world of difference if you think, 'Well, screw him, I'll get somebody else to buy me a sable coat.' Or if you feel happy that the guy's finally got nerve to do something that was your idea all along. Now let's try it. Let's improvise. I'll go out and come in and tell you I've quit my job. I'm, ah—let's see— a shoe salesman and I'll tell you I've quit my job and you invent something and let me *see* you thinking!"

She learned something about deportment just watching him on the set. Though his JOHN BARRYMORE star's chair was set apart and no underling dared approach it, Jack was without affectation, calling all the workmen by their first names and falling into long technical talks with them. On the other hand, they could get too close. "Hey, Jack!" a cameraman once yelled. Jack whirled, withered him with the Barrymore stare. "Why so formal? Call me kid." Yet he taught Astor a lesson she never forgot. Social conduct, he told her, was not a matter of impressing people but of acknowledging their existence, about which everyone needed reassurance. What he gave her most was beauty. His rooms were always filled with flowers. He would pick up one of the rare books he collected and flex the covers to display the fore-edge painting. He gave her books of philosophy, art, drama, and poetry. "He stretched my mind," said Mary, "in all directions."

As for *Beau Brummel* itself, the completed film was indeed interesting, though not an unqualified success. In powdered wig, swallowtail coat, white breeches, and buckled shoes, Jack displayed his beauty as never before—his beauty, in fact, became the purpose of the film. And yet unlike the stage on which he could create an extraordinarily youthful Hamlet, the camera is ruthless. Is that a dewlap marring that sweep of jaw, a tummy bulging those breeches? And his make-up is crude: dead-white face, lipsticked cupid's bow mouth, dead-black eyebrows. The real Beau Brummel, who affected an elegant simplicity in his dress and person, would not have recognized himself. Then too, the movie is static, with little action between endless dinners and parties. And Barrymore overdoes the mad Brummel with gaping mouth and glaring eyes that would have thrilled a theatre audience but are too exaggerated for the screen. An alert director might have tamed the madness, but John Barrymore was in Hollywood because he was the world's greatest actor. What director would have dared?

Yet John Barrymore's Beau Brummel is memorable. The disdainfully flared nostrils as though he's smelled something five days old. The self-mockery as he examines his figure in the glass. The fastidiousness with which he dislodges an innkeeper's hand from his shoulder. Mocking London society by exaggerating its vanities in his own dress and demeanor, Barrymore creates the quintessential dandy.

The film completed, Jack boarded the eastbound Super Chief, rehearsing *Hamlet* for the November 26 reopening with two porters standing in as the First Gravedigger and Polonius. He turned up the Saturday before the Monday performance at the Manhattan Opera House but took little part in rehearsals. Though the excellent Tyrone Power had left, the cast was predominantly the same, and Hopkins had yielded on one important point: the ghost was no longer a bit of blue ectoplasm floating above Elsinore's ramparts but the incarnate Reginald Pole who at the Sam Harris Theatre had been only a voice.

Again this revolutionary *Hamlet* played to enthusiastic, capacity crowds, but Jack's mind was on other things. Mary Astor arrived in New York to make a movie shortly after the play reopened. Waiting to be called to the studio, she spent the afternoons in Jack's suite at the Ambassador, where she donned burgundy satin lounging pajamas that Jack had specially tailored for her with the initials "M.A.B." on the pocket—charming, as long as she could forget there was a B.O.B. still married to Jack in London. The Langhankes swallowed Mary's need to "study Ophelia" with Jack every afternoon so thoroughly that Otto drove his daughter to the Ambassador and called for her at six. Or perhaps they only prayed she was working.

Jack believed her parents knew the score. "They are damn foxy, you know? They are shutting their eyes to what is really between us—it's their way of letting you out on a rope but keeping you feeling guilty, so they've got you."

"I just don't believe that. They're very straight-laced, truly."

"My ass!"

Jack was probably right. Mary's father had told her that in Europe men took their sons to older women for their sexual education. Evidently the Langhankes were chauffeuring Mary to Jack for hers.

Too soon, *Hamlet* left New York for a tour that began in New Haven. Since Jack dashed back to New York after every performance to see Mary, it was now, "CanyouplaythemurderofGonzago?" and the performance dropped an hour, to its improvement.

Jack took the tour far less seriously than he had the New York production: he had not yet learned to respect his audiences, particularly those in the provinces. He disconcerted the other actors with his fooling. John Lark Taylor, for example, lived in terror of blowing a line, knowing that Jack would worry it for the rest of the performance. One night instead of "Thoughts black, hands apt" Taylor came out with "Thoughts apt, hands black." For the rest of the evening Jack pretended to wash his hands, trying to break him up. Another time he wished Taylor a Merry Christmas that could be heard to the tenth row. He also began to indulge in little curtain speeches after the second act, improvising witty remarks about what his valet Paul thought of his Hamlet. Blanche Yurka thought them delightful since when the curtain rose again he was completely

Hamlet. Audiences also approved. In Boston *Hamlet* broke all Shakespearean records for both evening performances and matinees.

In Boston Jack was also invited to pose for John Singer Sargent as Ethel had many years before. The full-face crayon portrait was hardly flattering: Jack looks blank, puffy. Yet Jack was immensely proud of it and immediately had copies made for friends. He signed Blanche Yurka's "From your wildly incestuous son."

Charming, yet on New Year's Day 1924 the cast learns that the tour will close in Cleveland on January 27. They are dismayed: the play has been virtually sold out five weeks beyond that date. Rumors have been flying that the star has booked passage for England on the first of February, but the cast has discounted them. Now it appears they are true.

Philadelphia. Jack acts like a spoiled child, pretending to forget his lines, making silly speeches, referring to Philadelphia as "his dear old hometown." (Philadelphia loves it.) Washington. Margaret Carrington comes to try to persuade Jack not to abort the tour. She fails. Jack plays splendidly except on opening night when his bad mood ruins his performance for President and Mrs. Calvin Coolidge. Jack and Hopkins visit the White House the next day at noon, Jack making the supreme sacrifice of rising at eleven.

"Have you see many Hamlets, Mr. President?" asks Jack.

"Two. You and E. H. Sothern."

"And which performance did you like better?"

"Well, Mr. Sothern's clothes were prettier than yours."

Cleveland. Raging blizzard and subzero temperatures. Jack gives a stunning opening-night performance. "I'm glad to be in Arthur Hopkins' hometown," he tells the delirious audience. "Like the banker who seduced the lady, he made me what I am today." Yells and applause. "I'm always closing up on Arthur," he concludes, "like an oyster on a hungry man." More cheers and applause for a statement sadly true.

He is drinking heavily, in his hotel and in his dressing room. He plays sublimely, he plays the fool. Having thrown dice the night before with the cast, the next night he goes through all the motions of a crap game onstage, much to the audience's bemusement. That same performance he interrupts a dialogue to invite Taylor audibly to a party he is throwing the next night. The Gravediggers also receive the invitation as they are burying Ophelia, as do, eventually, most of the cast. The uninvited audience is privy to each summons.

The party takes place in the big ballroom of the Hollenden Hotel with the stars and chorus girls of the touring *Helen of Troy* company also invited. Despite Prohibition, bootlegged champagne, burgundy, and whiskey flow to the rhythms of a jazz band and everybody dances and drinks too much. In décolleté black velvet Jenny the wardrobe woman is the belle of the ball and Jack dances with her again and again, though Rosalinde Fuller is his partner when he stumbles and falls through the big bass drum, pulling her down on top of him. When they all finally sit down to supper, the women in the company find a hundred-dollar bill under their plates with a note of apology for closing so suddenly. The men get a handshake.

But Jack is full of plans for playing *Hamlet* in London. "For god's sake," he tells Taylor, gripping his hand hard, "fix it up with Arthur so you can go to London with me in April. Don't take anything you can't get out of."

A courageous move that Edwin Booth had tried in 1861 and 1880. In fact, Arthur Hopkins has been told, "If Barrymore has the audacity to come to London in *Hamlet*, they'll assassinate him."

SEVENTEEN

1924–1925

A RTHUR HOPKINS refused to produce *Hamlet* in London, though he promised Jack the costumes, Jones's set, and the electrician with the original switchboard. When Jack arrived in London to set up a production, however, he found no West End theatre manager willing to chance (1) Shakespeare, currently box-office poison, and (2) John Barrymore, an American actor.

Blanche had settled in London where she had become a member of a smart international set. Jack did not appreciate them, they did not appreciate the antics of Jack and Blanche, who became such a distressing spectacle that they had, said Blanche, the world pretty much to themselves. And wherever they fled that lovely spring—Normandy, St. Michael's Mount, Tintagel—they dragged their jealous quarrels with them like chains. Each seemed determined to destroy the other.

Baffled professionally and personally, Jack sailed home and went to Ned. Though he had greeted London skepticism thumb to nose, he had enough respect for four hundred years of British theatrical tradition to have qualms about challenging it. Ned would calm them.

Ned now lay rigid on his bed in his room in the apartment on Eighty-fourth Street which he would not leave again. And still he did not give in. His face was bronzed by daily sunbaths. He dressed impeccably in white turtleneck sweaters, shirts, ties, dinner jackets, and boutonnière. His voice was strong, his face cheerful. He looked, said one friend, "like a young man just lying down for a moment."

His case baffled doctors. One specialist in psychosomatic medicine believed the rheumatoid arthritis had an emotional source since Ned improved slightly when happy, deteriorated when moody or upset. Ned's regular physician tended to agree that his illness had its roots in "if not a subconscious retreat from life, at least a sort of self-immolation, of not moving forward into life." Ned's friend Mercedes de Acosta did not

255

speculate: "Jack was the love of his life and the suffering and emotional frustration he went through on account of it caused his illness." Straight-A, all-American Ned Sheldon was the type to be profoundly guilt-ridden by unorthodox feelings, and guilt can do strange things to mind and body. Worse still, he could never have admitted his passion to the homophobic Jack, who in turn may have sublimated the depth of his feelings for Ned. Ironically, Ned's illness prevented him from witnessing the very triumphs he had inspired, though this did not prevent him from offering constant encouragement. Now he assured Jack that the ghosts of British Hamlets past need not haunt him. He would get his West End theatre. His Hamlet could stand with the best of them.

Jack sailed again for England on November 5, 1924. He and Blanche took James McNeill Whistler's old house at No. 2 Cheyne Walk with a view of the Thames. Little Diana was installed in the nursery, Leonard and Robin in English schools. In December, while flares were lit against dense fog, Jack finally negotiated for the Theatre Royal, Haymarket, putting down $25,000 of his own money. He was delighted to have the Haymarket, not only because it was the classiest theatre in London but because Maurice had acted there. Although he had brought his American equipment, he would not, finally, trust an American cast. Instead he engaged his old friend Constance Collier for Gertrude, Fay Compton as Ophelia, and Herbert Waring for Polonius.

Margaret Webster, the daughter of Ben and May who were the nexus of Ethel's old Bedford Street gang, had heard of the coming of America's greatest actor and was dying to offer herself as a Court Lady but did not want to presume on the family friendship. Then one day Jack telephoned: he longed to set eyes on the old flat again; might he come to dinner? He came, greeted Ben and May with charming affection, then "strode into the drawing room and swept its contents with an eagle eye." He greeted the piano, books and pictures, fireplace fender, and sofa where he used to sleep when playing hooky from Wimbledon as old friends. The curtains and mirror above the fireplace, which hadn't been there in his day, he annihilated with a glance. Then he whirled on Margaret. "Constance talked to me about you. She tells me you have a good voice and can act. I guess it must be true because Constance knows all about acting. Would you like to be a Court Lady in *Hamlet*?" Later, over the fish course, he flashed her a dazzling smile. "There are some lines too."

Rehearsals began in January, a month of smothering fogs in which omnibuses overturned, autos collided, and pedestrians groped their way along area railings. Jack was in his element: back in the London he loved, his own director and producer, completely in tune with an intelligent and eager cast who pitched in from the first day, sensing that this was going to be exciting Shakespeare. Of course, there were patches of whitewater.

Fay Compton inconveniently insisted on being surrounded by flats while rehearsing so that the cast could not spy on her. And the Court. They were to be grouped on the upper steps as the curtain rose, Hamlet seated moodily below, chin on hand, gazing out into the audience. Jack wanted a rising frenzy of whispering as the lights dimmed and the curtain rose, to be cut off abruptly by the King's, "Though yet of Hamlet our dear brother's death." The Court whispered its damnedest, but suddenly Jack leapt from his chair with a piercing yell. "It won't do at all—not at all!" The paralyzed supers stared. Jack raked his hair. They had whispered, all right. "But it was the wrong *kind* of whispering. You've got to make the audience understand right away that this is a *very lecherous* Court!" Lechery was finally achieved, but afterward one of the Court Ladies appealed to the stage manager. "I would like to be assured that we were not picked for this scene as types. I could not continue with the production unless I am to be considered a character actress." But admonishing the women who carried Ophelia in the burial scene that they should remember they were virgins, Jack was confronted by a particularly seasoned veteran. "My dear Mr. Barrymore," she protested, "we are not character actresses, we are extra ladies."

The theatre cat watched the proceedings with detached calm, frequently sauntering across the stage just as Jack was delivering a soliloquy, as though to say, "I've seen them all; what are *you* doing here?" At the last dress rehearsal Jack formally thanked all the principals—Fay Compton for being the most enchanting Ophelia since Ellen Terry, Constance for investing the Queen with full-blown provocativeness, Waring for his happy combination of senility and sententiousness patinated by a kindly wisdom. Just then the cat strolled out to inspect the ranks. Jack scooped it up, caressed the blunt head. "As for you, my dear fellow," he added, "you are going to make a hell of a hit in one of my soliloquies."

London was "properly agog" at the prospect of this audacious *Hamlet*. Stalls had sold out early; in the small hours of February 19 a chilled line waited for first chance at pit and galleries. That evening as the brilliant first-night audience made their way to their boxes, the front house man bounced in and out of Jack's dressing room with the roster: Lord Dunsany, the Earl of Oxford and Asquith, Sir Squire Bancroft, Gerald du Maurier, Lady Diana Manners, Arnold Bennett, Dame Madge Kendal, Somerset Maugham, John Masefield. Jack lit a hundredth cigarette and contemplated a laurel wreath from Dame Nellie Melba with the detachment of a man going to the gallows. "Of course you know," said the front house man eagerly, "Mr. Shaw is in the house. . . ."

Asked by an influential friend if there was someone she would especially like to meet in London, Blanche had said, "Of course! Bernard Shaw." The great playwright had actually invited her to lunch. Though sixty-eight, Shaw had a lifelong avocation of flirting with young women, and was particularly vulnerable to "dark ladies." Blanche interested Shaw, who invited her to Adelphi Terrace again. At the door he asked inconsequently, "Why on earth did you marry an actor?"

Shaw liked actors when they acknowledged him as god. An actor who tampered with plays or subjugated an author's creation to his own personality, however, he deplored. He had spent five years as a critic attacking Sir Henry Irving for manhandling Shakespeare. Irving was Jack's idol. And Jack was taking liberties with Shakespeare.

All this would not have mattered had Shaw not escorted Blanche to Jack's opening night on a personal invitation she had wangled from her husband. Blanche had deliberately avoided Jack's New York *Hamlet* by sailing to Europe: after the debacle of her *Clair de Lune* the narcissistic woman could not have borne his triumph. Now she was conspicuously present with the foremost theatre figure of the day, one who was *bound* to dislike what John Barrymore did with Shakespeare.

One could argue that it didn't matter.

"I'm leaving you, Jack," Blanche had told him. "I can't take the fighting and the drinking and your genius for tormenting us both. You're destroying me as a person and an artist."

"Fig, if you leave me," Blanche says Jack said, "I'll quit the stage for good."

"I don't give a goddam what you do."

Jack had moved out of the Cheyne Walk house into the Ritz. Still it was cruel of Blanche to finally come to Jack's Hamlet with Bernard Shaw—a cruelty repaid by Jack in full with his triumph at the Haymarket that evening.

It is amazing to find today that there is still doubt that John Barrymore's Hamlet succeeded in London. It succeeded in the teeth of critics determined to look down their British noses at an American product. They did criticize aspects of the performance; they are paid to. Chiefly Jack was faulted for not giving the lines their full poetic value, critics remembering the sublimely poetic Hamlet of Sir Johnston Forbes-Robertson. Yet these same critics admitted that the Barrymore Hamlet gained clarity as a result, while some even praised Jack's "charming music."

A *Times* critic also decided that Jack appealed more to the judgment than the nerves ("I could only suppose the critic had none," said Margaret Webster). But when the dean of London critics, James Agate, concluded that John Barrymore's Hamlet "is nearer to Shakespeare's whole creation than any other I have seen. In fact, this *is* Hamlet"—why then Jack's success was beyond question. And this production was not just the star's *Hamlet*. Agate found the cast "brilliant almost throughout" and Jones's set "the most beautiful thing" he had ever seen on any stage. The critic of the *Daily News* concurred: "Barrymore may rest assured he not only made a personal triumph as Hamlet, but has given London one of the best performances of Shakespeare's play."

On the second night Jack thanked the "adorable audience"; adorable audiences continued to pack the house, extending the six-week run to nine. "It's terrible to have seen the play for the last time," Lady Diana Manners wrote Jack from France. "I'd sooner be in Denmark than here." More important was Jack's impact on three young actors. Margaret Webster called his Hamlet "a great performance in the truest sense of that much-abused adjective"; she went on herself to devote an acting life to Shakespeare. John Gielgud, not yet twenty-one, jotted his reactions on his theatre program:

> The "peasant slave" soliloquy excellent, and his opening scene fine. The nunnery scene was played as a love scene, tout simplement—effective but not right, I think. Setting very good. Real Gordon Craig precepts—and very suitable. Too many cuts, and rather too slow delivery. Barbarous to omit recorder scene—and "how all occasions."
>
> An enthralling and in some ways an ideal production although the last two acts are considerably less perfect than the first. . . . Barrymore is romantic in appearance and naturally gifted with grace, looks, and a capacity to wear period clothes, which makes his brilliantly intellectual performance classical without being unduly severe, and he has tenderness, remoteness, and neurosis all placed with great delicacy and used with immense effectiveness and most admirable judgment. Best in the Ghost scene and closet scene. Failed in climax in the play and graveyard scene.

Lecturing in 1986 at the National Film Theatre, Sir John Gielgud at eighty-two acknowledged that John Barrymore's "wonderful performance" had single-handedly revived enthusiasm for Shakespeare in London, no mean tribute from a Hamlet many thought the finest of his generation.

Seventeen-year-old Laurence Olivier was even more enthusiastic about Barrymore's Hamlet, however. ". . . I thought that it was burningly real," he said. "I believed that he was Hamlet, and I believed in the situations through which he was going. . . . He was stunning, so exciting, his voice, his high jumps." When Olivier eventually came to play his own Hamlet he tried to imitate John's virtuoso athleticism: "I must have been the most gymnastic Hamlet anyone has seen—not more than Barrymore, I suppose. I emulated him."

For many who would see both the Barrymore and Olivier Hamlets, however, Olivier was not in the same league. "Olivier was sleek," said the critic Herman Weinberg, "his voice was like music, his anger a true *actor's*. It was a performance, in short, 'of burnished gold.' " Barrymore, however, was "a suffering man, the well-springs of his voice glinted the words he spoke, making of them drops of sorrow." Every look, every gesture spoke of suffering, but above all "the hurt in his eyes that was reflected in his voice." No one who saw and heard him onstage could forget the moment when he interrupted himself—"Ay, there's the rub." "No one could forget the bitter smile and high inflection of voice with which he intoned that 'Ay.' All the contrariness of life [was] imbued there. . . ." In short, one could argue that Olivier *acted* Hamlet, Barrymore *was* Hamlet.

NO ONE CAN TOUCH the British for ceremony, and Jack was eminently fetable: the London theatre world turned out en masse to celebrate their American cousin's success. The Veuve Clicquot flowed at the Savage Club dinner, the Garrick Club dinner, the Old Players dinner, the Gallery First Nighters dinner. The English-Speaking Union gave Jack a luncheon, the Lyceum Club gave him a luncheon. At the latter Dame Madge Kendal sat next to Jack. She said charming things about his Hamlet but was chiefly interested in him because he was the son of Georgie Drew Barrymore, "one of the most brilliant women I have ever known," said Dame Madge. "Your mother made a perfect havoc of Maurice's witticisms— and he was supposed to have been much wittier." In the chair at the English-Speaking Union luncheon, the playwright Henry Arthur Jones first paid tribute to Hamlet's uncle, John Drew, then turned to Jack. "I have seen all the leading Hamlets of the English theatre since Fechter in 1869. Above them all was Henry Irving's. Irving's Hamlet at its best— sometimes it was very bad and incoherent—but at its best Henry Irving's Hamlet lifted itself out of all comparison with all other Hamlets of all ages. With that exception, John Barrymore takes his place in the front rank of great English and American Hamlets of the last two generations. It has fire and intensity, much tenderness, unity and consistency of conception, freedom from affectation and solemn pretentiousness, straightforwardness of simple elocution. . . . One word about John Barrymore the man. He is free from the vanities, affectations, and selfishness that are occasionally to be detected in leading actors. He delights to give every member of his company full scope to score to the utmost. I am very proud to claim him as my friend. . . ."

Jack was pleased, but much preferred off-duty drinking with Ethel's old suitors Gerald du Maurier and Winston Churchill, with the Prince of Wales, and with Feodor Chaliapin, singing his magnificent Boris Godunov at Covent Garden. The Prince of Wales was enthusiastic about Jack's Hamlet but wondered how he could sustain such an exhausting performance eight times a week. "Fervor and champagne," said Jack, who had a dresser waiting in the wings to hand him a glass every time he exited. It got him through one performance graced by Ellen Terry, the most memorable Ophelia of her day to Irving's Hamlet. Ellen was seventy-eight, deaf and befuddled, yet not befuddled about *Hamlet*, the words of which she recited loudly, keeping ten lines ahead of the actors throughout the entire play. Jack always tended to be dangerous during the duel with Laertes, but that night the cast ducked as rapiers whizzed about the stage like comets. By the last curtain call, Jack had calmed down, but when he sent for the great actress backstage he was informed that, deeply moved, she had hurried away in tears.

Into the midst of this celebration exploded Bernard Shaw's torpedo. The master of argumentative prose favored Jack with his reaction:

22 February 1925

My dear Mr. Barrymore

I have to thank you for inviting me—and in such kind terms too—to your first performance of Hamlet in London; and I am glad you had no reason to complain of your reception, or, on the whole, of your press. Everyone felt that the occasion was one of extraordinary interest; and as far as your personality was concerned they were not disappointed.

I doubt, however, whether you have been able to follow the course of Shakespearean production in England during the last fifteen years or so enough to realize the audacity of your handling of the play. When I last saw it performed at Stratford-on-Avon, practically the entire play was given in three hours and three quarters, with one interval of ten minutes; and it made the time pass without the least tedium though the cast was not in any way remarkable. On Thursday last you played five minutes longer with the play cut to ribbons, even to the breath-bereaving extremity of cutting out the recorders, which is rather like playing King John without little Arthur.

You saved, say, an hour and a half on Shakespear by the cutting, and filled it up with an interpolated drama of your own in dumb show. This was a pretty daring thing to do. In modern shop plays, without characters or anything but the commonest dialogue, the actor has to supply everything but the mere story, getting in the psychology between the lines, and presenting in his own person the fascinating hero whom the author has been unable to create. He is not substituting something of his own for something of the author's: he is filling up a void and doing the author's work for him. And the author ought to be extremely obliged to him.

But to try this method on Shakespear is to take on an appalling responsibility and put up a staggering pretension. Shakespear, with all his shortcomings, was a very great playwright; and the actor who undertakes to improve his plays undertakes thereby to excel to an extraordinary degree in two professions in both of which the highest success is extremely rare. Shakespear himself, though by no means a modest man, did not pretend to be able to play Hamlet as well as write it; he was content to do a recitation in the dark as the ghost. But you have ventured not only to act Hamlet, but to discard about a third of Shakespear's script and substitute stuff of your own, and that, too, without the help of dialogue. Instead of giving what is called a reading of Hamlet, you say, in effect, "I am not going to read Hamlet at all: I am going to leave it out. But see what I give you in exchange!"

Such an enterprise must justify itself by its effect on the public. You discard the recorders as hackneyed back chat, and the scene with the king after the death of Polonius, with such speeches as "How all occasions do inform against me!" as obsolete junk, and offer instead a demonstration of that very modern discovery called the Oedipus complex, thereby adding a really incestuous motive on Hamlet's part to the merely conventional incest of a marriage (now legal in England) with a deceased husband's brother. As producer, you allow Laertes and Ophelia to hug each other as lovers instead of lecturing and squabbling like hectoring big brother and little sister: another complex!

Now your success in this must depend on whether the play invented by Barrymore on the Shakespear foundation is as gripping as the Shakespear play, and whether your dumb show can hold an audience as a straightforward reading of Shakespear's rhetoric can. I await the decision with interest.

My own opinion is, of course, that of an author. I write plays that play for three hours and a half even with instantaneous changes and only one short interval. There is no time for silences or pauses: the actor must play on the line and not between the lines, and must do nine tenths of his acting with his voice. Hamlet—Shakespear's Hamlet—can be done from end to end in four hours in that way; and it never flags nor bores. Done in any other way Shakespear is the worst of bores, because he has to be chopped into a mere cold stew. I prefer my way. I wish you would try it, and concentrate on acting rather than on authorship, at which, believe me, Shakespear can write your head off. But that may be vicarious professional jealousy on my part.

I did not dare to say all this to Mrs Barrymore on the night. It was chilly enough for her without a coat in the stalls without any cold water from

yours perhaps too candidly
G. Bernard Shaw

One of Jack's most endearing traits was his habit of writing warm, appreciative notes to colleagues. Shaw's treatise hit him like the weight of the judicial system falling upon the unfortunate Falder. Shaw may have been technically right that Shakespeare should be played on, not between, the lines, yet Irving had created a great Hamlet playing between them. But Shaw's contention that Jack had made Hamlet the worst of bores was appallingly untrue. In fact, the letter was gratuitously cruel, a good example of why Henry Irving had announced himself ready to pay Shaw's funeral expenses at any time.

What made the letter even less excusable was the fact that Shaw was at the same time encouraging Blanche as an actress. She had, he told her, the right voice for his Saint Joan, adding, "If your husband lets you have the Haymarket I will rehearse you in some matinees of 'Candida.'" As a result, though she was estranged from Jack, though she knew his frail ego could not support such a personal challenge, and though Shaw had wounded her husband, Blanche asked Jack to give her the Haymarket afternoons for a *Candida* personally rehearsed by Bernard Shaw.

According to her, Jack looked blank, then sullenly incredulous, "like a small boy who suddenly finds himself pelted with his own marbles." He refused, but in the small hours of the morning she was wakened by the patter of gravel on the library window. Jack was standing under the TO LET sign nailed to the bare tree, overcoat collar turned up, hat pulled over his eyes.

"You can have the Haymarket."

"Hell!" said Blanche graciously. "I wouldn't take it for a million dollars."

That month the most discussed page in *Vanity Fair* was a portrait of Michael Strange by Ignacio Zuloaga painted in Paris a few months before. Clad in black doublet and hose, hands fondling a dagger at her belt, Blanche stands before Elsinore Castle dressed as Hamlet. Zuloaga's portrait is superlatively unpleasant: Blanche's face is smug, predatory, her hands claws, her neck vulturine. The portrait was accompanied by the rumor that Jack and Blanche were going to alternate Hamlets on the same stage. Certainly Blanche's ego was not frail.

On April 7 Jack cabled Mary Astor in Hollywood that he would be back in May. On April 18 he played his last Hamlet, a night he would look back upon as his most euphoric in the theatre. The whole cast was fired throughout the performance which ended to wild applause and cries of "Come back! Come back!" Afterward Jack triumphantly threw a party onstage for everyone, including the carpenters and chars, then staggered to the Ritz to fall into bed. He was done in. "What with labour, exhaustion, fatuous public utterances, the Flu, and eight or possibly nine times a week of this snappy Scandinavian farce," he wrote his English friend, Golding Bright, "whenever I had a moment to myself I occupied it by sitting down on the nearest thing at hand, however hard, and wonder[ing] vaguely through the accruing coma why I had taken up the theatre as a profession. There are so many other forms of endeavor equally lucrative and dishonest. . . .

"I shall be back in a few months. . . ."

But Jack never went back—to London or, with the exception of one late, unhappy venture, to the stage. He arrived in New York announcing that he would go almost immediately to Hollywood. Impressed by the box-office success of *Beau Brummel*, the increasingly affluent Warner Brothers had offered him a three-picture contract at princely terms: $76,250 a picture, $7,625 a week should shooting exceed three weeks, script and cast approval, a suite at the Ambassador, free lunch not to mention breakfast and dinner, and a chauffeured limousine. Warner Brothers was determined to bring a touch of class to its studio; no one had more than John Barrymore.

He negotiated another contract that spring, a separation agreement requiring him to pay Blanche $18,000 a year for her and Diana's support. Recognizing that neither had been a model spouse, they inserted a clause to prevent a divorce on the grounds of adultery, which would exact a stiff financial penalty from the guilty party. After less than five years, Jack's second marriage was over in all but name.

Blanche had coincided with the great years of John Barrymore's stage career: *Justice, Redemption, The Jest, Richard the Third*, and *Hamlet*. She had contributed to them, stimulating Jack with her vitality, ambition, and intelligence. He had accepted her challenge and reached high. And yet Blanche had also thwarted. In the nearly five years since their marriage in August 1920, Jack had worked a mere *thirty-eight weeks* in the theatre. Without discounting the alcoholism that was his chief enemy, marriage to Blanche had hurled him into a conflict of egos that exhausted him and sapped his creative energy. Blanche always claimed that Jack was the master at the sadistic games they played, yet the woman who could enjoy watching from a hidden doorway while her tardy husband paced back and forth in front of a restaurant until he gave up and left had her own flair. Blanche perhaps characterized them best when she called herself and Jack "two superlatively immature people."

"YOU CAN DO ANYTHING you want in any way," Robert Edmond Jones had written Jack after *Hamlet*. "There is nobody else in that position in the theatre today. There is Arthur, and Margaret, and me, and all the big roles that have ever been written. It is a great happiness to have something like this to look forward to."

Hopkins, Carrington, and Jones—and the American theatre—were robbed of their expectation. Some accused John Barrymore of greed. Some decided that a fatal laziness ran in the male Barrymores. Lionel thought that the letter from Shaw was a factor. Alexander Woollcott believed that "a real shyness, a certain pessimism, a crippling sense of humor, a horror at even seeming to take himself seriously"—that all these made it torture for Jack to display himself as "America's greatest actor." Though he believed Jack would return, Woollcott mourned even his temporary loss. There were, tragically, five Juliets these days for every Romeo; there simply were no "fit, articulate, romantic" male actors, a situation aggravated by the difficulty of getting the brothers Barrymore to act anything at all. Jack's "Aren't you sorry you don't have more Barrymores to wait for?" summed up for Woollcott the poverty of the American theatre in a nutshell. Lionel, thought Woollcott, was the better trouper, but had scuttled his own ship by insisting that Irene Fenwick always act with him. *That* was why he hadn't played O'Neill or Somerset Maugham's *Rain* or a dozen other dramas: sheer infatuation and wrong-headedness. Woollcott looked at the male contingent left in the American theatre and found the situation bleak.

Blanche, it should be noted, took the entire credit for Jack's abandoning the stage:

"Fig, if you leave me I'll quit the stage for good."

"I don't give a damn what you do."

Hopkins was more analytical. "He loved to create, but once that had been accomplished, he was like an artist who could not bear to look again upon a finished painting, or a writer who was nauseated by a glimpse of some past creation. . . . It is something akin to those forms in the animal world who must be restrained from devouring their young. That he would have had an unparalleled career there was no doubt, and he knew it. He did not forsake undreamed-of realms. His renunciation was with full knowledge of what he was leaving. He did not want the slavery that continuous service in the theater demands. . . . He was in no sense what the theater knows as a trouper, what his forebears had been, what his uncle John and sister Ethel were. The creative part of the theater he loved. Its repetition was unbearable. . . . His theater flights were like the nuptial flight of the bee—a glorious ascent into high, rarefied air, momentary exaltation and then quick death."

In other words, Jack was a romantic to whom desire is all, conquest boredom. "If you accept me," he had told a woman in *Beau Brummel*, "I shall hate you like the devil." The public and critics had accepted him with wild enthusiasm, wanted him to settle down in a long marriage with art. But John Barrymore was a philanderer.

Movies offered less work and far more money. They also offered wider recognition to a man who could be disgusted when restaurant patrons did not recognize him. Once in New York he had fought through crowds to the Lyric Theatre to see Douglas Fairbanks in *Robin Hood*. Though he was America's greatest actor and no stranger to films, he found himself disconcertingly just one of the crowd. In front of the theatre he watched the limousines draw up: Valentino, Richard Barthelmess, and Lillian Gish had arrived. The crowd rushed toward them. "Sure, that's him!" a female screamed in his ear. Had he been recognized at last? No, she was jabbing her finger at the handsome Barthelmess. Hollywood would cure the recognition factor.

At bottom, however, was the fact that Jack had not been able to take that final leap Woollcott had warned him he must take: he had never learned respect for his audiences, a respect which embodies responsibility to the public, loyalty to one's profession, and respect for oneself. Finally his failure to remain in the theatre was the failure he had seen so clearly in Hamlet: "Shakespeare sought to depict a great deed laid upon a soul unequal to the performance of it. . . . Here is an oak tree planted in a costly vase, which should receive into its bosom only lovely flowers; the roots spread out, the vase is shivered to pieces." The theatre was that oak, Jack the precious but fragile vessel.

"Most critics compare me to Irving," Jack said lightly to the reporters crowding the train platform on May 28; "they all agree he was better." On June 1 he arrived on the Santa Fe in Los Angeles to be greeted by a cigar-chomping Jack Warner. Lionel followed a month later. Their defection impressed Broadway as a Roman extravaganza at which gold plates are tossed into the river, doubly extravagant because both John and Lionel were at the river's edge. Difficult to say which was the more wasteful of his gold.

Ethel was devastated—and angry. No one had been prouder of the flying Barrymores—"three, count 'em, three!"—than Ethel during the many years their names had blazed on Broadway. Arthur Hopkins was sure that Jack's defection was the disappointment of her life. Now she was truly alone.

PART THREE

STUDIO AND STAGE

1925–1939

EIGHTEEN

1925–1927

ΙT IS DIVINE I AM CRAZY ABOUT IT, Ethel wired Zoë Akins about
her new play. But *A Royal Fandango* was a royal flop, again proving that
not even chefs Hopkins, Jones, and Barrymore could necessarily please
public taste. So Ethel simply did what she had done before: came right
back and knocked 'em into the aisles with *The Second Mrs. Tanqueray* in
which, as Paula, her "changing moods, bright wit, keen jealousy, dull
despair, and rebellious penitence" all evidenced "her supreme art." Yet
it was a step back rather than forward: Pinero's "woman with a past"
drama had made a star of Mrs. Patrick Campbell in 1893; this was 1925
and a different world. Playing a "highly satisfactory" Aubrey Tanqueray
was the English actor Henry Daniell. Daniell had acted in *Clair de Lune*
and had toured with Ethel in *Déclassée* and *The Laughing Lady*. He was
tall, dark, suave—good-looking in a sinister way.

And now it is time to talk about Ethel Barrymore's love affairs with
Conway Tearle and Henry Daniell, except that there is almost nothing
to say. Tearle and Ethel were decidedly together both onstage and off
during those years when her marriage to Russell was degenerating into
recrimination—together at parties, restaurants and, on tour, at hotels.
When Ethel played Los Angeles in 1924, it was Tearle who threw a party
in her honor; in a photograph they sit next to each other on the floor,
Ethel looking demure, Tearle either unhappy or supremely bored. People
understood that "they were together," but no gossip made the papers,
which always had been very tactful with Ethel Barrymore.

As for Daniell, "musty gossip" says that Ethel fell passionately in love
with her leading man during the run of *The Second Mrs. Tanqueray* but
that Daniell did not return her passion. Certainly both Tearle and Daniell
were the kind of men Ethel could have loved: British backgrounds, def-
erential, courtly, sophisticated, handsome, and in Daniell's case, "a gentle-

man who probably would've been happier in the 19th rather than the 20th Century." Worthy foils for the star.

It is pleasant to think of Ethel Barrymore passionately in love, yet there are those who believe she was not physically passionate. Her daughter called her "Victorian" and "nunlike," Eliot Janeway, a friend of the family, "a secular nun." "Her energies went elsewhere," said Barbara Robins Davis. And indeed there was something virginal about Miss Ethel Barrymore, as associates invariably called her: something fierce and Amazonian that made mere mortal men fear her, evoking in turn this goddess's quick scorn.

Ethel's friend Ruth (Mrs. Jacques) Gordon, however, believed there were affairs, but that given both Ethel's exacting standards and violent possessiveness, they could not last. "Ethel in her relationships with men," said Ruth Gordon, "was ready to give herself for twenty-four hours a day, seven days out of each week, and there wasn't a man alive who could take it. For this reason, her relationships with the men she cared about— and they were really very few—caused her great unhappiness. Somehow a change would come over her, and a possessiveness in her personality would emerge, and with it an unusual sort of touchiness." That Ethel could be possessive is believable; that "the girl who never rests" who had to will herself to marry and put her career above everything "was ready to give herself twenty-four hours a day" seems incredible. How much more likely that Ethel wanted to be loved singly and devotedly by a man who would understand that he came second to her career.

At any rate, at the end of the 1925 season, during which she had again been stricken with arthritis, she was suffering from fatigue, nerves, neuritis, and perhaps unrequited love. She had gained weight, she had not had a proper vacation for sixteen years. She decided that England would cure her.

And yet everything about beloved London seemed changed. Although the Webster-Whitty menage in Bedford Street was much the same, her closest Left Bank chum, Suzanne Sheldon, had died of pneumonia in a London nursing home the year before and the rest of the Gang had scattered. The theatre had changed, its gilt and red velvet faded, the great actor-managers—Irving, Tree, Alexander, Benson, Wyndham, Cyril Maude—all gone, only Arthur Bourchier and Gerald du Maurier still with theatres of their own. And she too had changed, they must have thought: no longer the slender Daphne who had captured all hearts. But where were they all? "Few people," said one columnist, "seem to be aware that Miss Barrymore is in London at the present time." Just six months ago Jack had been the toast of London; for Ethel, London evoked nostalgia.

Faithful Winston sent her a ticket for the Ladies Gallery in the House of Commons, where she listened to Lloyd George and afterward had tea with Winston in his rooms. He was now Chancellor of the Exchequer. Though she had not wanted to marry a politician, Ethel loved politics and political gossip, campaigning for Calvin Coolidge and visiting the White House when she played Washington. Still captivated, Winston invited her down to his country house, Chartwell, in Kent. They walked the grounds, Winston waving a pudgy hand. "All this," he said, "from my pen." It could have been hers, but at too great a sacrifice.

All the women had their hair bobbed, so she too took the plunge. She refused cocktails and high teas. When the *Olympia* docked in New York on August 22, her children gasped at their trim, shorn mother who radiated health. The effort had been made primarily for art: she was to team with Walter Hampden in *Hamlet* that autumn and was determined that her Ophelia, unlike her Juliet, would not be fat and forty.

Ophelia had been Ellen Terry's favorite Shakespearean role; Ethel herself had long wanted to play her—though the right time would have been twenty years earlier or at least before Jack's *Hamlet*. She tried not to believe her forty-six years a drawback: Ophelia was too often played by "little flibbertigibbets chosen apparently for both their youth and imbecility, so that when Ophelia does go mad, the shock which Shakespeare meant the audience to feel is no shock at all. I think she is really a very subtle, tragic and beautifully poetic character."

On opening night at Hampden's Theatre Blanche was conspicuous in a proscenium box brooding over the proceedings. But this *Hamlet* was no challenge to John Barrymore's; Hampden had played Hamlet before and was out to break no records. As Ophelia, Ethel succeeded as she had not as Juliet: if she could not act passion she could act virginal desire thwarted into madness. Woollcott yielded to the "shy, shimmering loveliness of this fair, this inexpressibly fair Ophelia," whose voice seemed to have been tuned all along for the "eerie cadences" of the mad scene. Still the production itself did not really excite fans of Hampden and Barrymore.

She went on to Portia, again with Hampden, in *The Merchant of Venice*. She found her first scene as difficult "as algebra or a complicated fugue," with the result that, on opening night, December 26, though she always suffered agonies, she was gripped in a vise of panic from which she felt she never would be sprung. Eventually she mastered her terror, as she always did, and her Portia began to move through the courts of Venice with authority. She had determined not to make the "quality of mercy" speech a showpiece. Thus when Portia says, "Then must the Jew be merciful" and Shylock replies, "On what compulsion must I? tell me that," Ethel said very simply, "The quality of mercy is not strain'd," then went on quietly to develop Portia's argument that mercy must temper justice. The audience reacted as she hoped: dead silence and then a gasp as they realized *Why that was the speech!* She took positive pleasure that winter thwarting the matinee schoolchildren who always whispered, "The quality of mercy is not strained" along with Portia, though Portia could do it very well herself.

James Dale, who had acted Gratiano with a white-haired Ellen Terry, thought Ethel's Portia a lady of "unimpeachable distinction. . . . Portia, choosing, depreciating and dismissing the various suitors, seemed to come so naturally from the lady with the faintly bored expression and sore drawl." And she looked so rich! "All the others, even Ellen Terry, seemed dowdy by comparison. This Portia manifestly believed in the clothes making the woman. She was obviously at home in the homes of the Estes and Borgias and Medicis. . . . She knew her place, and everybody else's into the bargain." No wonder, thought Dale, she made such an impression at court!

As an actress, however, Ethel continued to puzzle him. "What was she trying to get over? Her features would contract in a frown at the bridge of her straight nose as if she had encountered an unpleasant smell. This look of pain would appear before she took up a cue, and there would be a pause, as if of suffering, before the answer would scrape out in a drawl which was the most fascinating I can remember. There was no actress on the American stage who could rival her at this. But I got the impression that there was something there which was having difficulty in making itself clear. The whole performance appeared to be suffering. I felt sorry that she was having such trouble to say and do what was in her mind to say and do."

Contrast this impression with that of the great French actor Edouard Bourdet, who told Ethel she must bring Paula Tanqueray to Paris in English because a French audience "will understand every word you say." Ethel herself would have been outraged at Dale's judgment because simplicity was always her ideal. "For always, I have tried to leave my authors alone," she said. "You don't have to be bewildered by Shakespeare. There he is. Leave him alone. Say what he said and thank your God that he has given you a trumpet through which you may blow so sweetly. You don't have to be bewildered by Ibsen. There he is. Leave him alone. He will tell a woman's life in three hours, and there before you, like a golden gift, are those three hours. Thank your God for them, because if you are true to yourself, the very saying of them will make you an artist. That at least is what I feel about my own work. I say my lesson and have done. I want no mystery, no green lights, no Czecko-Slovakian [*sic*] producers or early Metro-Goldwyn wind machines. I want to speak and feel what I am speaking. And that is all I know."

Had Ethel considered Portia great drama rather than a lesson, perhaps *The Merchant* might have run longer than fifty-four nights. After it closed in February, she thought again of *As You Like It*. Zoë Akins told James Dale to try for the part of Orlando, and he went, quaking, to meet Ethel at Zoë's flat. He rang at length before the door was opened four inches and a pair of very black eyes pierced him to the quick. Brows drew together in a frown of annoyance. It was not Zoë.

What fine bone structure, he said to himself, and explained his mission. The scowl deepened. He ventured his name.

"Ye-e-e-ssss?" drawled the apparition, scraping the bottom of the sea.

Zoë had told him to come about *As You Like It*.

Abjectly he followed Portia into Zoë's parlor, suddenly sure that she had seen him as Joseph Surface and had disapproved. (He was right.) The great actress marched to the mantelpiece, scowled at the carpet in profile with beautifully arched neck, then bent her brows once more upon the supplicant. John Drew had asked the newcomer to the Players Club to "take wine." Not Ethel.

"I am a great admirer of your brother, Miss Barrymore," he ventured.

"Which one?"

"Well, Jack."

"That bastard!" Ethel swept to the window, flung aside the curtain to scowl down into the street.

He must say something. He began to praise her Portia extravagantly. "Yes, it was the only time I have seen *The Merchant of Venice* and been more interested in Portia than Shylock."

With a "rather jolly smile" she finally asked him to sit down.

"Yes, and I have never heard the Quality of Mercy better spoken. It was as if it had never occurred to you before, and line by line it was coming to you for the first time."

"O-o-oh?" drawled Ethel, seating herself rather near.

"Yes, and your Paula Tanqueray! I cannot imagine it better done by anyone."

"You liked i-it?"

Liked it! It was brilliant, original, unique. "And the best thing about it," he went on recklessly, "was that you contrived to suggest, here and there, that Paula was not *quite* out of the top drawer, so to speak."

Ethel rose, sailed like a thundercloud to the door and flung it open.

"You must have been thinking of Gladys Cooper!" she hissed as he fled.

Later Zoë called wanting to know what he had done to poor Ethel, who had asked if he was drunk. "*Were* you?"

"No," said Dale. "And *she* ought to know."

Dale's retort indicated not only that Ethel was drinking again but that she had become known as a drinker. She did no plays the rest of that season, was hospitalized in July for two weeks ("adhesion"), hurried back to vaudeville and *The Twelve Pound Look*. And then came a smash hit.

Somerset Maugham himself came over from England for rehearsals of *The Constant Wife*, a modern satire of marriage with Ethel as Constance and C. Aubrey Smith as John Middleton. Maugham fell madly in love with Ethel, as Englishmen tended to do, yet he was furious at the Cleveland opening in October when Ethel blew lines, introduced dialogue from other plays, and said in Act Three what she should have said in Act One. Even with the director George Cukor prompting her from the fireplace Ethel could not get a grip on herself. Somehow the curtain finally came down.

Maugham stormed her dressing room. "Oh, darling," cried Ethel, "I've ruined your beautiful play, but it'll run two years."

"She had," said Maugham, "and it did."

"She was *so* excellent in *The Constant Wife*," said the actress Barbara Robins Davis. "She had a beautiful, impeccable sense of comedy—easy, light, subtle. The audience understood everything that was going on. Her movements were magical, rather slow. Sometimes she would make a gesture, hold it until she had every eye in the audience locked, then speak. And those tears. She would be sitting on a sofa looking out over the audience, her face immobile. Suddenly huge, luminous drops would glisten in her eyes and roll down her cheeks. The effect was terrific: those huge globes springing from those huge eyes, larger than life like everything else about her. Yet you couldn't use her as a model for acting. Audiences loved whatever she did onstage because she was Ethel Barrymore."

But oh those critics. "The classical Mr. Heywood Broun," raged Ethel, who in the teeth of her success in *The Second Mrs. Tanqueray* had dared to say that in the play's most poignant moment she had impressed him as "a barge woman"! Or "the recondite Mr. Percy Hammond," who would never understand her art. In the last act of *The Constant Wife*, for example, she wept briefly before recapturing the spirit of sophisticated satire with which the plays ends. When she told the great Max Reinhardt that she could indeed weep every night, spontaneously, at just that moment, he paid the highest tribute to her art. Hammond, however, said Ethel bitterly, phrased it far more exquisitely than poor, ignorant Max Reinhardt: "Miss Barrymore indulged in a few vaudeville tricks in the last act."

And yet she knew her power. "But, Miss Barrymore," a young actor once objected when she directed him where to stand, "I'll be upstage of you then."

"Oh, my dear," said Ethel with her slow smile, "don't worry about me. Wherever I am is center stage."

The Constant Wife kept Ethel in money for three years, Somerset Maugham much longer: he often told visitors that Ethel Barrymore built his house at Cap Ferrat. He also declared that her Constance was the single most satisfactory performance he had ever witnessed in the theatre, and the play gave Ethel too more than money. Its felicitous comedy insulated her from a world she found increasingly ugly: ugly fashions, ugly politics, ugly scandals, ugly manners, ugly dances like the Charleston. Ugliest of all were the young "intellectuals" of the lost generation, as they took satisfaction in calling themselves: the Hemingways and Fitzgeralds who smeared their disaffection across the face of society. Jack, of course, could have taught the lost generation a few tricks, yet he had none of the self-pity that Ethel found their ugliest trait. Ethel, high priestess of gay gallantries in drawing rooms, was feeling the generation gap.

MANY THOUGHT HOLLYWOOD the ugliest phenomenon, spiritually and artistically, of all. "The most beautiful slave quarters in the world," said Moss Hart. "Siberia with palms," said Sir Cedric Hardwicke. Ben Hecht scorned film stars who got "tremendous sums of money for work that required no more effort than a game of pinochle." Hardwicke saw Hollywood as a sellout: "God felt sorry for actors, so he gave them a place in the sun and a swimming pool. The price they had to pay was to surrender their talent." Scott Fitzgerald called Hollywood "a mining camp in Lotus Land." Many agreed that Hollywood's mission seemed to be to seek and then misuse great talent.

Arthur Hopkins took the bleakest view of all. "The greatest slaves to the opinion of others that I have encountered are the people of Hollywood. There the servitude is so complete that it amounts to horror. The fear of failure is the specter that haunts their extravagant homes, rises before them out of their swimming pools, rides with them in their limousines, haunts their parties, hovers over their pillows at night and sits with them at breakfast in the morning. They even believe failure infectious. They shrink from talking to anyone who is regarded as a failure.

Not all the gold in the hills of Hollywood nor electric signs from Venus to Mars can compensate for such self-abasement."

Trailing interviews claiming that the art of the movies equaled the art of the stage, which he had *not* deserted for "the fleshpots of Hollywood and the swimming pools of Beverly Hills," America's Greatest Actor attempted the transformation to Movie Star. Jack was not really convincing in the role, nor at home in La La Land. Though protesting that he adored movies, he reeked of the stage. With his classical profile and voice, his picturesquely disheveled clothes, his new British valet Blaney, and Clementine, a pet monkey he had acquired, perched on his shoulder, he cut a foreign figure in the all-American world of Jackie Coogan, William S. Hart, Mary Pickford, and Lillian Gish. Compared with most movie stars he was erudite, intellectual, a connoisseur, a brilliant conversationalist. Sober, he had an old-world courtesy and respect for tradition that clashed with Hollywood's born-yesterday mentality.

He knew he was a misfit and displayed his scorn for the film colony by deliberately wearing clothes until they were ripe, spewing four-letter words, and "deeply and leisurely picking his classical nose." Ned Sheldon sensed his isolation. "I wish you were busy with a lovely wife who cared for you," he wrote by night letter, "and maybe a workshop behind the house where you made boats and practised Shylock, and one or two little Jacks that you would take fishing if they'd be very quiet. [Instead you keep] knocking yourself against the walls trying to find the little green door and desperately to get in. At least you have Clementine."

Jack's drinking also isolated him. Few actors, conscious that they must face the camera early the next morning, dared spend the night boozing with John Barrymore.

"That's a great makeup job," said Jack Warner as Jack emerged one morning from the bedroom of his bungalow suite at the Ambassador. The star's bloodshot eyes were saddled with pouches, his chin stubbled. "You'll make a tough-looking Captain Ahab."

"That's not makeup," said Millard Webb, the director of *Moby Dick*. "It's a hangover." Investigating, they discovered Jack's bathtub filled with champagne bottles, the hall closet bursting with Prohibition gin.

Jack's first film for Warners under his new contract was to have been *Don Juan*, but in deference to his loathing for "sweet-scented jackass" lovers they had agreed to let him do Herman Melville's saga of the white whale. Jack was fatalistically certain, however, that *Moby Dick* would not emerge from top Hollywood scenarist Bess Meredyth's typewriter as Melville had written it. "What we are going to do for a love interest I don't know. [Ahab] might fall in love with the whale. I am sure, however, Hollywood will find a way."

Hollywood did. In the completed script an invented New Bedford beauty replaced the great white whale as Ahab's passion, so that Ahab returns to sea not to pursue the white whale but to try to forget that Esther loves another. This other is an equally invented evil brother, whom Ahab eventually dispatches. In Melville's novel Ahab dies lashed to the white whale, a powerful metaphor. In the film Ahab returns to Esther's arms, a sop for the masses. At least Warner Brothers retitled the film *The Sea Beast*.

In the event, Jack had reason not to regret the emasculation of one of his favorite novels. Priscilla Bonner had been cast for Esther because Jack's choice, Mary Astor, was under contract to First National. One day, however, standing on the balcony of the Warner administration building, Jack looked down to see a trio of women who had stopped to give a begging war veteran money. One of them, a blond madonna who struck him as "the most preposterously lovely creature in the world," was fumbling for change in her purse but looked up under his intense gaze. Their eyes met for a moment before she hurried away. Then that evening he happened to be in the projection room on other business when suddenly her face flashed on the screen: limpid eyes, wistful mouth, a halo of fair hair. She was Dolores Costello, he was told, a bit player for Warners. "Get her here tomorrow morning," said Jack. The next morning Jack was waiting impatiently in Warner's office when Dolores was shown in. "Will she do?" asked Warner. She would. Priscilla Bonner was yanked from the cast.

The two women with Dolores turned out to be her lovely sister Helene and her formidable mother Mae. Like Evelyn's mother (indeed like the mothers of Katherine, Blanche, and Mary Astor), Mae Costello at first objected to Jack. As Wagnerian as Margaret Carrington, Mae dragonized her daughters and her husband Maurice, a stage actor for twenty years before becoming Vitagraph's first matinee idol. Maurice Costello had gone from romantic to character roles which became fewer the more he drank, until his wife and daughters lost all faith in him. So it was the Irish-Catholic mother who chaperoned her daughters on the lot, screened their escorts, waited up until they came home. Jack's all-out campaign to conquer her baby raised her hackles. After all, he was two years older than Mae and his reputation notorious.

Jack was undeterred. Dolores had little acting experience, but Jack was expert at putting leading ladies at ease. "No doubt you will be bewildered stepping into this thing with no preparation," he soothed her, "but whenever you feel uncertain tell me and we'll stop." Privately, he arranged to have the big love scene shot first: young Ahab bidding Esther goodbye in a moonlit garden beneath a tree showering blossoms. Ahab clasps Esther to his panting breast, sears her lips with a burning kiss. Millard Webb liked it and called "Cut!" Jack kissed on. "*Cut!*" Jack was deaf. "*CUT!*" Legend has it that when he finally released Dolores she was in a dead faint. Unslaked, Jack demanded the scene be shot four times more.

To pacify Mae he tried to curb his drinking and turned on his powerful charm. Actually he was very much drawn to her; like Mummum she made him want to behave. And Mae could not resist Jack's boyish enthusiasm. She began to welcome him to the house; they became so thick that some nights they would send "Winkie" to bed and gab the night away about old times in the theatre. "Are you sure it's *I* you want to marry and not my mother?" Dolores asked Jack. She found it hard to reconcile the cynical rake with the shy man whose idea of a good time was playing gin rummy with her mother.

Finally Maurice Costello exploded. "John Barrymore is no man for Dolores! In the first place, he's old enough to be her father. Why, he's *my* generation. In the second place, he's a married man. In the third place, I am something like Barrymore myself and that's the reason I don't want him for the husband of my baby."

"It is ridiculous to be prejudiced against a man because he is married," said Jack, informed of Costello's objections; "the divorce courts are made to take care of trivialities like that. As for the difference in our ages, an actor is no older than he admits." The Costello women themselves ignored Maurice until the day he called Jack a blackguard and ordered him out of the house. Then Mae slapped her husband's face and Dolores and Helene wept. Costello slammed the door. He was the plaintiff in the divorce suit that followed. He had tried to protect his daughter, he complained, but his family gave him to understand that he counted for nothing. He won his suit.

Maurice Costello was not the only Hollywoodite who objected to Jack, who had become "the most cussed and discussed" celebrity in Tinsel Town. He was accused of being high-hat, vain, selfish, insulting, cruel, and supremely egotistical. There was no crime he was believed incapable of committing.

Douglas Fairbanks Jr., a close friend of Jack's, tried to put the record straight:

. . . He has no conceit but rather a feeling of gross inferiority.
. . . His manner gives one the impression of a soul that has turned
bitter. This is not entirely the case. He is a dreamer whose dreams
became too true to be good. To protect himself he has erected a
wall of disdain and conceit and a wall of boredom. . . . There are
few men about whom there has been more vicious gossip. He is
reputed to have witnessed and indulged in every known vice. . . .
He is said to be the most conceited man ever to appear before
the public eye. . . . But his mind is thoroughly alert to all things
and his heart is gay with the joy of living. He makes himself
disliked for the purpose of keeping people away from him. . . .
Oftentimes when he is bored he will feign inebriation to rid himself
of the offending party. . . . He is cordial only to intimate friends
and to those who work with him; to strangers he is, at times,
inexcusably rude. . . .

He is a chap whom most men like and most women hate.
When he wants to be, he is as gentle and tender as a woman. . . .
He can be a grumbling scoundrel or a charming gentleman. He
can look like a tramp, or like a fashion plate, or like a king. He
is a Magnifico of the Middle Ages, transposed by a supreme and
happy gesture to the screen of today.

Released on January 15, 1926, *The Sea Beast* was a resounding success.
John Drew and Bee Devereaux were among the celebrities at the New
York premiere; in the following days five hundred to a thousand people
were turned away daily as people crowded to see "The World's Greatest
Actor" as a Hollywood star.

The opening closeup of Jack's leg and tapping foot is meant to emphasize Ahab's later loss of limb, but it is also a bit of cheesecake as the
camera draws back to reveal a manly chest and shoulders (Clementine
perched on one) and the beautiful left profile as Jack gazes from the
crow's nest over the sea. The pose deliberately announces that John
Barrymore is an object to be gazed upon like a woman, just as his lofty
perch clearly announces his eminence as an actor. And act John does with
a capital A, rejecting Melville's naturalism for a flamboyantly theatrical
romanticism. Ahab rages and snarls, bares his teeth as he obliterates with
a red-hot iron the tattooed "Esther" on his arm, stamps the deck on a
wooden leg. He is either convulsively in motion or arrested in a classical
pose designed to etch his image on the public brain. The Barrymore
gestures work overtime: hand flinging back poetic lock of hair, much

rubbing of chin and flexing of brows, head thrown back in a burst of derisive laughter. There is also the by now expected transformation, this time from handsome young whaling captain to wild-eyed madman. "I wanted to do some character with intestines," said Jack, and despite the interpolated love story, Jack does give Ahab grit, though the deliberate posing weakens his impact.

Jack's love scenes with Dolores thrilled audiences and catapulted her to stardom. Webb had strung all five of the takes together so that Ahab and Esther seemed to kiss forever. "That's not acting," mused Blanche when she saw the film in New York. "He's in love with the girl."

Filming in New York, Mary Astor could not take Dolores with such calm. Since the burgundy satin pajama days she had scarcely seen the man she still loved. Because she hid the love affair from her parents and friends, and since Jack too kept it quiet, she could almost believe it did not exist.

"I hear Miss Costello is really lovely," she said to Jack unhappily over the phone.

"She is. She's divine," Jack agreed, then evaded. "Don't worry, Goopher, she's just a chicken."

Jack was no longer in love with Mary, if indeed he ever had been. He had chosen her for his next film, *Don Juan*, but now tried to replace her with Dolores. With Priscilla Bonner suing the studio over her expulsion from *The Sea Beast*, Warners refused, but getting the part of Lady Adriana della Varnese was no victory for Mary. On the *Don Juan* set she would find Jack and Dolores huddled side by side in camp chairs laughing and whispering, just as she and Jack used to do when filming *Beau Brummel*. Jack himself was cold. Furious that he had to make love to a poor substitute for Dolores, he alternately ignored Mary between takes and taunted her by making passes at other actresses when Dolores wasn't around.

One of these was a beautiful tilt-eyed starlet named Myrna Loy, who received attention off the set as well as on. Her phone would ring in the middle of the night: "This is the Ham what am. Where are you?" She shied away from this Jekyll and Hyde star who at one moment cursed her and stuck pins into her and the next was all apologetic charm. "God knows," said Loy, "he was attractive, but he was really a rascal and I knew it. Actually, there was more to it than that. I sensed something going wrong in him, and it frightened me."

Prostituting himself for money was one of the things going wrong with Jack. He loathed "pansy parts" like Don Juan and tried to escape his usual way, appalling a reporter who cornered him at eight in the morning for an interview before he went on the set: "God, his breath! And those *red* eyes." Every day Jack submitted himself for hours to the make-up and costume departments, for this forty-three-year-old Don Juan was going to be more beautiful than the beauties he loves. The make-up man glued invisibly fine French muslin behind his ears with spirit gum and attached the muslin strings to a heavy rubber band around his head. Presto, a clean chin line. The same French muslin was glued to his sideburns, then pulled up and back and secured with another rubber band. Since his sideburns had disappeared, false hair was glued on to create a "natural" hairline. Jack's own gray-streaked hair was dyed blondish, then combed back to conceal the rubber bands and a fake piece added (as in *Hamlet*) to give the head fullness and disguise Jack's "juvenile bump." Because he was only five-feet-eight he wore lifts, even with the tights in which he was constantly condemned to display his legs. For $76,250 a picture you gave the public what it wanted.

Warner Brothers hyped *Don Juan* to the skies: heavily researched, a record four months in production, dangerous stunts that included John Barrymore's delivering and receiving 191 kisses in twelve reels. New Yorkers were treated to a huge animated sign above the Warners' Theatre at Broadway and Fifty-second Street that showed Barrymore and Astor gazing-kissing, gazing-kissing, gazing-kissing: JOHN BARRYMORE AS DON JUAN—INSPIRED BY THE LEGEND OF THE GREATEST LOVER OF ALL AGES. Poor Jack. "I made love all over the lot and on most of the locations in Southern California to girls, to old women, to trees, to flowers, to horses and buggies, to the moon, the sun, and most of the stars," he said. "In every scene I heaved like a fire horse. . . . I was the king sap of the universe." To the columnist Adela Rogers St. Johns he confided that on screen he looked like nothing so much as a male impersonator of Lilyan Tashman.

Don Juan was, however, a technical landmark, boasting a synchronized "Vitaphone" symphonic sound accompaniment on disc that included occasional sound effects: audiences gasped as they heard a mailed fist pound a door, the clash of metal during a duel, and a door slam for the first time in cinema history. Accompanying Vitaphone short subjects featuring songs and instrumental numbers almost eclipsed the main feature in New York: the ukulele playing of Roy Smeck enthralled audiences as much as Barrymore's leaps and lusts. Movie house pianists, organists, and orchestras may not have known it, but their days were numbered.

Don Juan made another kind of history as well, being more joyfully panned by New York critics than any movie in recent memory. Even Robert Sherwood, who liked it, admitted that "the backgrounds were awful, the costumes grotesque in their inaccuracy, the story dragged out and frequently confused, and Mr. Barrymore almost as bad, at times, as he was in *The Sea Beast*." And how Jack does ham! Evil sneers, diabolical leers, fierce grins. And he still does not know what to do with those orphan hands which he tries to keep busy with a lot of odd patting motions and finger shakings when he isn't holding one of them, limp-wristed, in his shirt front. As for his prowess as a lover, Mozart's Don Giovanni conveys more lust in one aria than Jack does "running broad osculation over the twelve-reel route."

He is superb, however, at the beginning of the film as Don Juan's father, Don José. The beard and aging make-up lend a convincing sensuality to Barrymore that he lacks as the young Don; the ruthlessness with which he orders his wife's lover bricked into an alcove in her bedroom to suffocate conveys the male libido more powerfully than any love scene. Don José is obviously a role he wanted to play. And Jack also demonstrates an athletic skill that challenges the swashbuckling Douglas Fairbanks: the superbly executed leaping duel with Montagu Love that the audience greeted with a burst of applause only climaxes twelve reels of vigorous acrobatics. Yet even these Jack satirizes with exaggerations, in keeping with his antipathy for the film.

Finally after a local preview, Warners could not even let the original ending stand but changed it to an impossibly speeded-up finale in which Jack, wreaking havoc on hordes of pursuers, snatches Mary Astor into his saddle as he whirls off into the sunset.

"I thought you made Don Juan for satire," said a reporter.

"I made it for money," said Jack.

Mary Astor had made it for love, or wanted to, but the evidence of Jack's infatuation for Dolores Costello was overwhelming. "Dear Goopher," said Jack rather sadly when she demanded a straight answer, "I'm just a son of a bitch." Mary blamed the drinking, her parents for not allowing her freedom, and finally Jack himself: "I decided he was—what he said he was." Much later she blamed herself. After the London *Hamlet*, Jack had talked of returning to England with *Richard the Third* and Mary as Lady Anne. Otto had instantly vetoed the idea: Mary was making the kind of money in films she could never command on the stage. Jack waited for Mary to tell Otto to go to hell, but Mary had been silent.

Fifteen years later Jack reminded her of her good luck. "It's a good thing I wasn't free to marry. And it's a good thing I couldn't get you away from your family. I would have married you, and you would have had a miserable life." Mary had rather a miserable life anyway: too much alcohol, too many men. "Can *I* help it," she said, "that I have this god-damned angel face?"

Now it was all Dolores. Jack had chartered an eighty-foot cabin cruiser after finishing *Don Juan* so that he could forget Hollywood on the blue seas. He wanted Dolores to come with him, but Mae would not allow her daughter to set foot on plank let alone make the voyage to Baja. Instead Jack kept a daily log for Winkie. " 'Winkie' saw him off," he wrote as Clementine capered on the deck of the *Gypsy*. "Only she is the very dearest smallest cat, and he is crazy about her, and hopes and truly believes they will be the very happiest things, if they have *any* sense at all! Wrote that small thing the longest letter, and went to bed after looking at its own curled up picture, and after praying that they both may be happy together for always."

This "voyage of yearning" was one of Jack's happy times: the dream was new, the beautiful woman unknown, the drinking more or less under control, the stage and movie set far away, the little green door almost within reach. "This West of hicks and sunsets, if properly used," he wrote hopefully, "may be a spiritual bath that will mean never living against one's own center again!"

He lay on deck smoking his pipe, gazing at Venus bright in the west. "Every evening," he wrote again, "I look at the fat, lovely, healthy, ever-young, ever-bright, ever-poised beacon of a star that is the symbol of 'Winkie's' and my life together, and, like the Angelus, say a gay, lifting, happy, husky, tiny spout of a prayer to it. It is as if the bottom of my soul, that has had so damned much happen above it, were stirring awake and saying, 'Hello,' like a child at something. . . ."

NINETEEN

1926–1928

C OMPARED WITH JACK'S touted Hollywood arrival, Lionel
sneaked in the back door. On the strength of his single film contract,
he and Irene had put up at the exclusive Town House on Wilshire Boulevard. The actress who had once insisted, "I like clean plays and clean
things," now tried to explain why Lionel had left the stage: "We love the
theater, but I can't see how anyone can blame actors and actresses who
stick to the films when the stage demands that they lower themselves and
do and say such coarse and common things. There is nothing like that in
motion pictures."

So her husband was rescued from the coarse and common stage. Lionel
himself thought motion pictures clean—too clean. Movies, he told an
interviewer, had to please the masses and therefore could be neither
experimental nor daring. Movies reflected a dream world: while in real
life success could be achieved by less than perfect people, in the movies
the race was won by the most flawless face or the best pair of legs. And
since the world worshipped make-believe, movies found vast audiences
to accept this pallid distortion of life.

The legs were clearly Jack's; Lionel could scarcely help compare his
younger brother's glittering career with his own. Jack the hero, Lionel
the heavy. And yet their acting reflected their personalities. The truculent
Lionel was all *down*, saturnine, earthbound, while Jack was all up, light,
mercurial. Jack's style was the more appealing, the more saleable.

Another reason why Lionel did not burst upon Hollywood like a
revelation, however, was that he was already an old-timer from the early
D. W. Griffith days at Biograph—ancient history now, though every director in Hollywood owed a debt to Griffith. Jack had been in films
thirteen years himself, but as the rakish Jack Barrymore, not John Barrymore, the great actor. The Lionel who arrived in Hollywood was essentially the same Lionel of *The New York Hat, Jim the Penman* and dozens

of other films in which he had proved his solid versatility. Good acting did not necessarily mean stardom, the dream of all Hollywood dreamers. Lionel found himself in the humiliating position of possessing the greatest American name in acting without being a star.

He hoped for extracurricular compensation. Since most movies took only two or three weeks to shoot, Lionel anticipated long days painting and listening to music. He had reckoned without Irene's taste for luxury, his own delight in indulging her, their drug addiction, and the Barrymore inability to save a dime. As a result, he bounced from studio to studio during the next years, at first for $10,000 a picture, eventually hiring himself out for $1,000 a week. In one or two of these films he got the girl: Marguerite De La Motte in *The Girl Who Wouldn't Work* and Pauline Starke in *Women Love Diamonds*. More often he lost her: Anna Q. Nilsson in *The Splendid Road*, Greta Nissen in *The Lucky Lady*, Renée Adorée in *The Show*, Greta Garbo in *The Temptress*. He was a father in *Children of the Whirlwind, The Barrier, Brooding Eyes, The Bells*, and everybody's father as Balzac's Père Goriot in *Paris at Midnight*. He was good, bad, vengeful, lustful, and suicidal. He was everything but box-office magic.

Perhaps he did his best acting in Henry Irving's old tour de force, *The Bells*, as Mathias, the Alsatian innkeeper whose vaulting ambition causes him to murder a rich Polish Jew stopping the night at his inn. In the play Irving had shivered spines in the scene where Mathias imagines the jingling of the murdered Jew's sleighbells coming nearer and nearer. Hollywood, however, superimposed images of the dead man and the ringing bells above Mathias's head, a clever camera device that, however, robbed Lionel of his best acting opportunity, a scene he would have done superbly. Jack complained that films lacked imagination. When they did so it was because they couldn't bring themselves to trust imagination.

In his first important role, Boris Karloff played a sinister mesmerist who intuitively discovers Mathias's guilt. Lionel intuitively recognized Karloff's talent, creating a special make-up to emphasize the British actor's cadaverous face; in his black cloak and top hat Karloff looked like nothing so much as William Butler Yeats. Karloff reciprocated the veteran actor's admiration. "Lionel was a stimulating man," he said, "a marvellous, a great man."

Grinding out one film after another, Lionel was able to buy a house at 802 North Roxbury Drive in Beverly Hills, a very good though not spectacular address. *He* would have preferred living in the suburbs, as he and Doris had on Long Island, but Irene wanted to be in the thick of things. They furnished 802 handsomely: Lionel at least had an artist's eye for interior decoration. He had little inclination for society, hated all card and parlor games and fancy luncheons, but he indulged Irene. She sent gold-engraved invitations to her luncheons for important people like Jeanne Eagels and Norma Talmadge; her tables gleamed with damask and crystal. She became aggressive: if someone she particularly wanted was already engaged, she invited that party to her party. Lionel chain-smoked, drank too much, grumbled a little, endured.

Because he had already blown the money from *The Bells*, he accepted $15,000 from Hal Roach to make a series of two-reel farces. All *Wife Tamers* proved was that Lionel had no gift for slapstick. He is not funny as he tries to light a match instead of a cigarette, gets hit over the head with a hose, staggers about with a drunken woman in his arms until they both fall forward into a pool. In New York Lionel's agent, Maury Small, certainly did not laugh; he took the next train to Hollywood.

"Are you crazy?" he demanded. "Are you mad? Don't you know what Roach is doing? He is hiring all the old-time stars like Theda Bara and Priscilla Dean and putting them into these comedies for people to laugh at. This will kill you in pictures. Even a Barrymore can't survive this."

"You don't know Barrymores," said Lionel. "We survive anything that pays."

Lionel made no more Roach comedies, yet his career slumped as he began to be cast second or third to film personalities who, in many cases, were poor actors. The crowning insult came when MGM decided to film *Laugh, Clown, Laugh!*—Lionel's stage triumph—and offered him a minor role supporting Lon Chaney. Lionel's "*No!*" reverberated through the studio.

JACK RETURNED FROM the *Gypsy* cruise more in love with his madonna than ever, a passion Dolores whetted by being slow to respond. Her languid beauty matched a languid temperament; she was the total opposite of Blanche. Besides, she'd grown up the daughter of an alcoholic actor and, though she wanted to trust Jack, had reservations about marrying one. Mae's constant vigilance also stimulated Jack's desire, as did Warners' insistence that their new star's image not be sullied by connection with the notorious rogue male—though he had made Dolores a star.

Jack was largely generous with women he loved and now insisted that his third Warner picture be a vehicle for Dolores, though she would still be paid only seventy-five dollars a week. In *When a Man Loves* Manon Lescaut, a beauty at the court of Louis XV, is banished to the New World with her lover, the Chevalier des Grieux. Jack deliberately gave Dolores every opportunity to display her beauty and talent, infuriating Ethel when she saw the rough cut: falling in love was one thing, but throwing your scenes unworthy of a Barrymore. Jack had another lover's role, but was happier playing the Chevalier than Don Juan: his love for Dolores springs from the screen in his ardent glances and spontaneous lovemaking. Again there is too much left profile; again there is acting in the high romantic style: John panting with love, wild with weeping, frozen in disbelief, exultant in triumph. It is a performance that has nothing at all to do with film acting in 1926; instead John Barrymore fuses the heroics of Kemble, Kean, Booth, Barrett, McCullough, and Irving in a performance that is pure theatre.

Critics either did not understand this grand romanticism, or disliked it. Even more they disliked the persistent left profile. Heywood Broun complained that "once John Barrymore walked the boards and used his entire head and not merely the lovely profile which he now edges into pictures like a beautiful paper knife." Even *Photoplay* disliked the way "John Barrymore goes into his scenes as one who says: 'Now watch what a fine actor I am! Please note my chiseled profile!' " "Inevitably predominating," said another, "is that left profile, hardening into a mask, rigid, chalky, disturbing. It is so perfect as to be uncanny. Exaggerated and obtruded, it becomes a visual irritant. This is not merely the fate of an actor who, having reduced himself to a profile, becomes automatically two-dimensional. It is, I think, the rather sad story of one who has played the Ladies' Delight too long and has been found out by the camera."

Sadly enough, Jack as a heroic lover *had* to look young and beautiful, and with the comparatively primitive lenses then used, full face shots were less flattering. But it was also the type of movies Jack was making that alienated many, particularly those who had loved John Barrymore on the stage. Stark Young was one of these; now he turned on him:

Of these moving pictures, people, looking at them and wondering afterward, can only observe that they are rotten, vulgar, empty, in bad taste, dishonest, noisome with a silly and unwholesome exhibitionism, and odious with a kind of stale and degenerate studio adolescence. Their appeal is cheap, cynical and specious. The only possible virtue in Mr. Barrymore's progress is a certain advance in athletics; he is more agile, he leaps, rides and hops to a better showing, promoted by the fine air of California and the exercise imminent to such a clime. Artistically, the only thing we could say about Mr. Barrymore's performances is that he brings to them remnants of his tricks and mannerisms that stiffen them slightly and perhaps convey the sense of acting to a public that has seen but little of it.

Percy Hammond had called John's Hamlet "so beautiful a picture, so clear an analysis, so untheatrical an impersonation, and so musical a rendering of Shakespeare's song." John's Broadway exodus turned Hammond sour. "The cinema has proved to Mr. Barrymore that Silence is Golden, and that in Hollywood's hushed shadows more money can be made and more happiness disseminated than in any other of the areas of make-believe. . . . Other hearts may be broken by that embezzlement of his art but this one remains intact."

Though he complained himself about his "asinine heroic activity," Jack could not admit that his films were bad, for that would indeed open an abyss under his feet. He did not act only for money, much as he often tried to give that impression. Dissatisfied with what Warners had offered him, he now accepted Joseph Schenck's offer to join the prestigious United Artists group founded by Pickford, Fairbanks, Chaplin, and Griffith: $100,000 per picture and a tempting 25 percent of the net. Believing Dolores's career his creation as well as jealously not wanting her out of his sight, Jack informed Schenck that Dolores would come with him. Warner Brothers did not agree. They slapped his wrist with a reprimand from Hollywood's moral watchdog, the Hays Office, but did not forget his arrogance.

Meanwhile he tried to escape again, this time on his own yacht, the *Mariner*, a ninety-three-foot gaff-rigged racing schooner that cost him, with the addition of three staterooms and conversion to a cruising yacht, $110,000. Jack was strictly a gentleman sailor, but he loved refurbishing the vessel as he had his Alchemist's Corner—designing silverware, selecting furniture, installing bookcases and exotic light fixtures. This time he succeeded in luring Dolores aboard, though she was accompanied by Mae; three days later the *Mariner* had to return to port, Mae violently seasick, Dolores's virtue intact. "My God!" said Jack. "I shall never again celebrate Mother's Day." Though the *Mariner* held the Southern California–Honolulu racing record, Jack had no better luck attempting that trophy, arriving in Honolulu conspicuously last after losing the wind en route. There the elusive star was met by the director Alan Crosland and the writer Paul Bern, both trying to pin down a script for Jack's first United Artists venture, a film about the poet-adventurer François Villon. Jack had long wanted to play Villon and took advantage of this studio's promise of greater creative freedom by collaborating with Bern on the script as they sailed back to Los Angeles, though he did not improve it by inserting a role for a friend's duck.

Jack had actually appeared in print this year, though his *Confessions of an Actor* was actually written by his hard-drinking friend Karl Schmidt.

Confessions was anything but: "You mustn't take it too seriously," warned one reviewer. "He obviously didn't. It is amusing, bright, witty." Jack devoted most space to his early years, the carefree times on Broadway with Frank Butler and Rip Anthony. He was generous with friends and so charmingly modest about himself that he left out almost everything of importance. He said little about his great years on the stage, devoting instead a whole chapter to the London *Hamlet* which, however, he capped with Shaw's letter, creating the *impression* at least that the playwright's severity had more than a little to do with his quitting the stage. He insisted again that he had been Mummum's favorite, ignored his first wife Katherine as well as Ethel, spoke of Blanche, briefly, as his wife. As she still was. And was in fact involving herself in Jack's Villon film by—characteristically—submitting her own treatment of the poet's life.

Jack let her down gently: now that they had stopped tormenting each other they could be chummy again. He wanted, he had told her, to do something different with his Villon—to burlesque the whole idea of romantic movie heroics. He intended that Villon "by his amazing dexterity and imagination" should maintain "a certain whimsical integrity, and prevent himself from looking like an ass, the audience being the only person he takes into his confidence. I think the picture of Villon skipping, bounding, and crawling on his stomach through a Gothic dimension of a dying chivalry and a brutal and slightly sacerdotal materialism," he concluded, ". . . is something that I can have genuine fun with and accomplish something real in the movies whose possibilities interest me exceedingly."

Whatever Jack intended, *The Beloved Rogue* did not successfully burlesque romantic heroics. He did not succeed in taking the audience into his confidence; as a result his Villon, "skipping, bounding, and crawling on his stomach through a Gothic dimension," often looks ridiculously theatrical. This is certainly Jack's most athletic performance: he shoots down banisters, scales towers, leaps from windows and rooftops. But what was the make-up department thinking of? With straggly shoulder-length hair, a pencil mustache, and wispy beard he looked in his feathered cap like an aged Peter Pan. And of course that left profile is stamped on the screen like the face on a coin.

Yet *The Beloved Rogue* is memorable. The Brueghelesque Paris designed by William Cameron Menzies with snow falling on towers and roofs is magical. Villon's antics with his mother are more appealing than the love scenes: he kisses her mouth and nose, gives her friendly raps on the shoulder—another wildly incestuous son. The beautiful Barrymore, too, finally emerges in the torture scene as he stands naked except for a loincloth, body glistening with sweat, muscles rippling. In total contrast is the scene in which, having been crowned the King of Fools in clown-face, Villon hears that he has been banished from his beloved Paris. Only the pain flickering across his mask betrays his anguish; then, kneeling, he slowly begins to wash off his make-up in the snow. But again, Hollywood betrays Barrymore's great acting. Instead of a convincingly medieval clown he is made up like a P. T. Barnum super: big red nose, garish lipstick, bald head, ragmop fringe—a travesty.

Jack had high hopes for his Villon movie until the night he slipped into an early public screening. Halfway through the film a derisive shout from the balcony startled the audience: "Call yourself an actor? My God, what a ham!" Many agreed; there was, indeed, a growing hostility to what John Barrymore was doing on film.

> It is getting so that the films of Mr. John Barrymore are be-coming more numerous than those of Rin-Tin-Tin [wrote one disaffected critic]. Recently three of his pictures were running simultaneously on Broadway, and that probably sets a record for man or beast. . . . The weakling was "The Beloved Rogue," the last to enter the lists and the first to go. Even the most devoted Barrymore enthusiasts can, I imagine, understand its lack of staying power. . . . It is almost as difficult to find a plot that will prevent him from running amuck as it is to contrive something that will prevent him from wearing tights, and that, as everyone knows, borders on the impossible.

Jack himself was baffled by the yawning gap between his intentions and the results. "In the theatre it is almost impossible for an actor who is sincere, and who knows something of his job, not to impress and excite an audience," he said. This was not true of movies; in fact if Garrick, Booth, Duse, and Bernhardt had had to submit to the camera "the result might be zero when the cutting room got through with it." In one of his scenes with Conrad Veidt, for example, the two actors had let themselves go for over two hundred feet of film; when the cameraman had to stop to reload there was a gigantic burst of applause from electricians, set hands, court ladies, and spectators. Jack anticipated a stunning scene, but when he saw it on the screen much of the effectiveness had been lost.

More of a problem was his hypertheatricality. In his first screen test he looked as though he had St. Vitus' dance. Even in long shots he came across like "an earthquake." And this was the actor who had played a clean, natural Hamlet onstage. Obviously in the movies less was more, but he was damned if he could make himself do less, like that master of the medium Buster Keaton, who had acquired "the facial impassivity of a blackboard in a grammar school, on which he slenderly traces patterns that photograph like Meryon's etchings." Because Lionel could be more reticent on the screen, as he was in life, he could be argued to be the better film actor.

After finishing *The Beloved Rogue*, Jack fled again on the *Mariner* for southern waters on December 20, accompanied by Clementine, his captain Doc Wilson and crew, and his "secretary" Karl Schmidt. The best place to spend Christmas, said the man who had always been "subconsciously embarrassed by the 'function' of Christmas and New Year's," was at sea, unless one could frolic with grandchildren under a tree—only there *were* no grandchildren in Hollywood. "I'll probably drink a lot on this voyage," said Jack. "I'm tired of the waiting, the silly mix-up of it all. Drink has been one of my two great weaknesses. I have tried, since meeting Dolores, to overcome the booze. Really I have. I do not want to hurt the one person I love more than I have ever loved anyone else, for she seems to adore me so trustingly."

The solution to "the silly mix-up" was in his hands, yet before sailing he denied publicly that Blanche was planning to divorce him. They'd been exchanging reams of Fig telegrams ever since he'd come to Hollywood, but there was no confusing which Fig was which because Blanche-Fig was always demanding money and Jack-Fig was always sending it. This Christmas they exchanged messages: DEAR FIG MERRY CHRISTMAS AND THE BEST ALWAYS FIG, and THANKS FOR YOUR WIRE SAME TO YOU BABY DELIGHTED WITH PRESENTS FIG. No wonder that rumors were only now surfacing in the press that the Barrymores weren't happy. Indeed, Jack vacillated about a third marriage and did not mention divorce to Blanche until Mae Costello furiously confronted him with a Hollywood column exposing his "secret romance" with Dolores. The time had come to make her an honest woman. Jack began to think of buying a home. He was drinking heavily.

THOUGH SUFFERING severe arthritic pain, John Drew still managed to make his acting look as effortless as ever and was the only member of the touring *Trelawny of the Wells* company never heard to complain. Even when his condition worsened, he kept on acting so that the rest of the cast would not be stranded on the road. Finally, however, he was rushed from Portland, Oregon, to a San Francisco hospital. His wife Josephine had died in 1918; now his daughter Bee and her husband hurried to his bedside. From the Hotel Mark Hopkins Bee wrote her cousin Georgie Drew Mendum on June 27:

Georgie darling—Both your wires came and I was so glad to hear from you. We are home for a moment as Papa seemed in no immediate danger. By that I mean, there was no sign of *immediate* collapse. He had a very bad collapse yesterday but he cannot keep up much longer. The doctors didn't expect to see him this morning. His vitality is too amazing. But what I'm really trying to say is this—when I bring his ashes back, I want you and Ethel, you two *only*, to meet me in Philadelphia to put them in Mama's grave. It's not to be prayed for that he should pull thro' this, as he'd be a hopeless invalid. If you could see him now, you would admire him more than ever, he is so wonderful. Tell Ethel, I don't write her as I'm afraid she might get it just before the performance. Jack Barrymore is coming up from Los Angeles tonight. Thank God my Jack is here or I should be a raving maniac.

Both Lionel and Jack came to San Francisco. Lionel had forgiven Jack for calling Irene a whore when Jack brought Dolores to meet him. "What I envy in Lionel is not his mind but his ability to believe," Jack had once told Arthur Hopkins. "If he never found love he would still believe that there was such a thing." Now Lionel was delighted with Jack's beautiful beloved: "Why, I bounced her on my knee when I came home drunk with her father," he said, remembering old Vitagraph days. The brothers were further united by grief for "The First Gentleman of the Stage," their uncle, who had always treated them as men of the world as well as loaned Jack his impeccable wardrobe. How long ago they had knelt in Grandmother Kinlock's bedroom to pray, "And please, God, make Uncle Jack a good actor." John Drew had become a good actor, so thoroughly of the theatre that the most appropriate gift Lionel, Ethel, and Jack could think of for his seventy-first birthday had been a leatherbound 1905 *Thespian Dictionary*. Privately he must have deplored his nephews' leaving the theatre, though Lionel could tell him proudly that his recent eight-week performance of *The Copperhead* at the Playhouse in Los Angeles had inspired cheers, rave reviews, and seventeen curtain calls.

Lionel had to return to filming; Jack, who still signed telegrams to his uncle "Greengoose," had no pressing commitment so he stayed by his bedside. John Drew lingered, increasingly weakened by rheumatic fever and septic poisoning. His last words to Jack on July 9 were characteristically gallant: "Stake," he whispered, "the nurses." On the fourteenth Ethel canceled her performance of *The Constant Wife* and met Bee in Philadelphia to bury John Drew's ashes in Greenwood Cemetery next to seven other Drews and Barrymores. Ethel had always despised people who called John Drew's acting superficial just because it looked natural, yet it was true that he had been "caught early by Augustin Daly and pressed and creased into formal lines like a pair of his best trousers." Still, his gala opening nights at Frohman's Empire Theatre were always the highlight of the New York season, while for more than fifty years audiences across the nation had looked forward to his yearly appearances as one looks forward to the visit of a witty, urbane, and entertaining friend. If he ever gave less than a deftly polished performance it is unrecorded. Few actors could boast the same.

THAT NOVEMBER Jack bought the director King Vidor's house on three acres at the very top of steeply winding Tower Road above Beverly Canyon, commanding a view like Ahab's from the crosstrees. Jack could not live on a mere street like Lionel: 6 Tower Road symbolized his eminence, at the same time serving as a fortress for his protection. "I may have to paint my face for a living," he would say, "but isn't it wonderful I can look down on the place where I have to do it." Immediately he began transforming the Spanish-Mexican structure. What he had done to Mrs. Nicholls's top floor he now did to 6 Tower Road on movie-star scale.

He bought four more acres. He had an enormous master bath built over the tennis courts. He turned the drawing room into a baronial hall with vaulted ceilings, archways, mahogany paneled walls, wrought-iron chandelier, and fireplace. He filled the whole house with badly bargained antiques from a Pasadena dealer he nicknamed "the Fairy Robber Baron." A pink Meissen chandelier cost him $8,500. Eventually he added to the main house a rathskeller with a mahogany bar from the Klondike and a cuspidor from Virginia City.

Massive wooden doors with old iron latches opened into a walled garden. He added two guest houses connected to the main building by arched colonnades. He installed a huge kidney-shaped pool with a stone cabana; in the middle he planted a massive antique sundial presented to him by McGill University on the occasion of a performance of *Peter Ibbetson*. He hired a Japanese gardener named Mark Nishimura to create wonders with Palestinian olive trees, Japanese dwarf shrubs, Italian cypresses, and the more exotic native blooms. He needed a bowling green, skeet-shooting range, new tennis courts, and a trout pond. And this was just the beginning.

As Tower Road was in process, Jack found himself a defendant in a lawsuit brought by Robert Gordon Anderson charging that Joe Schenck, United Artists, and John Barrymore had stolen his Villon book, *For Love of a Sinner*, for their film *The Beloved Rogue*. Jack was amazed to be included in the suit, but that was his reward for United Artists having given him nominal "creative freedom." The Anderson suit was eventually dropped, but the fracas was typical of the kinds of legal and financial difficulties in which Jack—a wealthy star without a clue about managing his affairs— continually found himself. But now he had Henry and Helios Hotchener.

The Hotcheners had sold Mary Astor one of their Moorish-style houses on Temple Hill Drive in the Hollywood Hills; Jack had met them there. The Hotcheners were Theosophists: Helios, considerably older than her husband, had studied with Madame Blavatsky and rubbed elbows with Annie Besant. Jack was intrigued with any form of the occult; besides, the Hotcheners had lived much in India, which interested Jack because Maurice had been born there. Helios was the kind of cheery, warm older woman with whom Jack felt at ease, Henry an income tax lawyer who took an immediate interest in Jack's affairs. He found them in chaos. Jack did not know the name of the manager of the New York bank which received his huge checks; he had not the least notion of how much money he had in the bank; he never kept receipts, statements, or business correspondence. When Henry finally untangled Jack's New York account he found that more than $100,000 was not earning a penny of interest. All this he explained to the careless actor. When Jack found himself deep in income tax trouble the following March, he thought of the kind, ever-smiling, soft-voiced Hotcheners and how much they had already done for him.

"Hank, for the love of God," pleaded Jack, "take over! Manage me."

The Hotcheners were delighted to do so, and Helios immediately drew up astrological charts to guide his business ventures and filming schedules. Jack acquired two parasites.

His next film, *Tempest*, was as tempestuous to film as its subject, the Russian Revolution. Because Hollywood was full of Russian émigrés who hated the Bolsheviks, the truth about 1917 could not be told, yet the film had to be larded with foreign names to give it "authenticity." The gifted Erich von Stroheim crafted an original screenplay especially for Jack and also wanted to direct but, for reasons of its own, von Stroheim's studio would allow him neither to direct nor receive credit for the script, which finally was put together by half a dozen scenarists. Three directors came and went, one of them the "too arty" White Russian Vyatcheslav Tourjansky, before Schenck decided that directorial credit would go to Sam Taylor.

Jack wanted Dolores for Tamara, the aristocratic Russian general's daughter; Warners would not release her. Greta Nissen, Carole Lombard,

Vera Voronina, and Dorothy Sebastian signed and withdrew. Finally Schenck imported a blond German actress who promptly became his mistress. Camilla Horn spoke no English, Jack no German. They managed.

"Sometimes he was drunk," said Camilla. "And when we were dancing together in one scene—a beautiful ballroom scene . . . he fell down with me on the floor because he was so drunk." The solution was a carousel. Jack and Camilla sat on opposite sides with their arms around each other, gazing into each other's eyes as the carousel whirled them round as though they were lost in each other's arms on the dance floor. Jack did not try to duplicate the position off camera; Camilla was intensely grateful that he made no passes.

By now a transformation scene was *de rigueur* in a John Barrymore film, this time Jack as an imprisoned soldier going mad. The scene was finely photographed by Charles Rosher using his own Kino-Portrait soft focus lens. Thanks to Rosher Jack could at last be shot full face without destroying his classical image; he emerges from *Tempest* a three-dimensional, less posed actor. Indeed *Tempest* might have been a very good film had not Hollywood studio politics plus the Hays Office reduced it to propaganda. The revolutionaries are one and all uncouth slobs who in reality could not take over the local tavern let alone Czarist Russia. The distortion hampers Jack's own interesting performance; once again the Hollywood mentality had betrayed him. As did United Artists. Jack had not insisted on a time clause in his contract: *Tempest* was the only film he made in 1928.

Trouble with *Tempest* reflected private upheavals. Jack now asked Dolores to marry him, but she agonized over his drinking. Mae was blunter: "Sober up, you son of a bitch, or leave my poor angel be." Jack could not. In March 1928 Mae took Dolores and Helene to Havana on a vacation that was really a separation from Jack. Dolores was wearing an engagement ring; she would marry him if he stopped drinking for six months. Jack did not, making news when he had his eye blackened by Myron Selznick, brother of David O., and was arrested for driving thirty-seven miles per hour on the wrong side of Wilshire Boulevard.

Something else was agitating him besides Dolores, something big: *Hamlet* in the Hollywood Bowl. His films had been largely unsatisfying; he needed to reestablish his claim as America's greatest actor; he longed for the kind of ovations that had greeted Lionel's Los Angeles *Copperhead* performances. He felt no triumph in film acting, no catharsis. He sat around idly between takes, barely aware of what the other actors were doing, making last scenes first or first scenes last, depending on how the cost-conscious producer or director grouped them. The applause after his *Beloved Rogue* scene with Veidt had brought back the thrill of a live audience, something he had not experienced the previous April when he made history by broadcasting readings from Shakespeare to the New York American Shakespeare Foundation banquet. At the same time he was terribly afraid.

In April Jack went to New York to secure Arthur Hopkins's electrician for *Hamlet* in the Bowl. Interviewed in his Ambassador suite, he was nervous and flippant, pulling constantly on a cigarette as he prowled the room. In another year or so, if plans worked out, he would take his yacht and person from the West Coast and return to New York and the stage. He liked "the climate" of the movies better than that of the stage, but that was the only comparison he chose to make. Meanwhile he was excited about Shakespeare in Hollywood. The Bowl was "such a tremendous place, set on the hills under the moon and stars," that he would be "the smallest Hamlet since General Tom Thumb."

As a pledge of his Shakespearean enthusiasm he recorded during his visit Hamlet's "Now I am alone" and Gloucester's "Ay, Edward will use women honourably" soliloquies for Victor Records. Widely sold and in the Victor catalogue for many years, these recordings were the closest listeners could come to the great *Hamlet* and *Richard the Third* stage performances of the early twenties.

The magnitude of the *Hamlet* plan next took him to Ned. Separated by 3,000 miles, they were still close. Jack constantly asked Ned's advice about stories for filming even though Ned himself would never see a movie: his sight was beginning to contract as well. But Ned was unfailingly cheerful, concerned, interested in everything from Tower Road to Clementine, who expressed thanks for her present in Jack's best style: "I wish to again tender to you, dear Uncle Ned, my great obligation for your kindness in the matter of the grapes."

Jack himself poured out his feeling for Ned on the train back:

> It is too fantastic to think that after we had talked—occasionally about myself if I remember—that we had been separated for more than a week—we felt just the same—like a divine room in the top of the house where the sun always comes in and where one went to play as a little boy when one wanted to be alone.
>
> You have no idea how much good it did talking to you. The burrs fell out of my whiskers in clusters and must be all over the floor. If the nurse steps on them ask her to throw them into the fire. I never want to see them again. . . .

Some burrs stuck. Returning from Havana, Dolores had run into Mary Astor on the boat, honeymooning with her new husband Kenneth Hawks, brother of the promising young director Howard. According to Dolores, Mary pounced on the ring, was not deceived when Dolores said she had bought it for herself. Still smarting, Mary took the trouble to air the lurid details of her affair with Jack. "It made me sick to hear of it," said Dolores. "I couldn't imagine why Mary found it necessary to tell me all those things." When she asked Jack about Mary he said flatly that Mary was making it all up.

IN JUNE 1928 the triumphant progress of *The Constant Wife* swept Ethel cross-continent to Los Angeles. After the many times she had housed him, Jack was now able to offer her superb accommodation, and there was the bonus, said Ethel, that he was a bachelor at the moment— "thank God!" Jack went to Ethel's first night at the Biltmore Theatre. Driving her back up the canyon road, he was curiously silent. Ethel always wanted strong black coffee after a performance, and finally when Jack had got the percolator going, he blurted, "Why don't they cough?" He had never reconciled himself to those "god-damned barking seals" who competed with the star.

"Oh, you mustn't let them cough."

"What the hell do you mean? They coughed in *Hamlet*."

Ethel was touched. As though Shakespeare were cough-proof.

"You mustn't *let* them cough."

"What do you mean? You can't stop them from coughing."

"Yes, you can. . . . I don't think the voice has anything to do with it, but maybe it has. You don't look at the cougher. You just know that they must not cough. That's all."

Which was why, she reflected, she was always so very tired after a performance. Onstage she could not forget the audience for a moment; uncannily she could *see* every face in the dark auditorium. She conquered them by sheer will. Was it worth it, she wondered, when for a fraction of the effort she might have a Tower Road of her own.

Lionel returned from filming in time for the reunion. As usual when they were all together they tried to outdo each other in a competition that dated from childhood. Lionel was mordant and crotchety and capable of mercilessly wicked jabs. He also was a rambler, cackling and growling through long, salty stories. Jack's humor mixed elaborate verbal embellishment with a Rabelaisian profanity lit by irrepressible mockery. Ethel, the most formidable, was perhaps the funniest because the contrast between her hauteur and her wickedness was so devastating. Irene was an outsider. Assessing Irene and her friends who jockeyed for social position in the film colony according to their husbands' incomes, Ethel dismissed them as "married whores."

She still could not dismiss another outrage: George Kaufman and Edna Ferber's *The Royal Family*, which had opened the previous December in New York. The play satirized a glamorous family of actors with a great theatrical heritage: Fanny Cavendish, the formidable matriarch; her glamorous daughter Julie; Tony Cavendish, a matinee idol who has recently deserted the stage for Hollywood; Julie's daughter Gwen, trying to decide whether to become an actress; and a suave theatrical impresario. Anyone familiar with the theatre could have recognized Mrs. John Drew, Ethel, John, young Ethel Colt, and the clan's favorite manager, Charles Frohman.

Kaufman and Ferber stoutly denied that their royal family was *the* Royal Family—except for Tony Cavendish, who was John Barrymore, or bits of him: "He was, of course," said Ferber, "too improbable to copy from life." At the same time they tipped their hand by actually hoping that Ethel, John, and young Ethel would play their parts. They sent Ethel the first two acts, meanwhile reading the play to the actress and Round Tabler Ruth Gordon, a fact that reached Ethel's ears. She never had liked the Round Table. She telephoned Ruth.

"Has George read you his new play?"

"Yes," said Ruth Gordon. "It's great."

"Is it about the Barrymores?"

"Yes. You'll love it."

Ethel slammed down the phone and engaged the prominent lawyer Max Steuer to sue Kaufman and Ferber. (The Marx Brothers, who did a famous Barrymore imitation, immediately announced that if the Barrymores sued so would they.) But Jack, whose support Ethel counted on, refused to talk to Steuer on the phone, and the suit collapsed.

She could not forget, pouring out her anger at the take-off in a thrust she called "Myself As I Think Others See Me." "The legend has it that we artists are wild, careless, tousled and immoral," she wrote. ". . . We live *en famille*—and such a famille! An organization of idiots—chaotic, arty, self-conscious, thinking theater, breathing theater, smelling theater. To these half-baked intelligences a theatrical family is *only* a theatrical family—it is not an association of normal, healthy human beings."

Ethel the aristocrat had always prided herself on being at home in circles having nothing to do with the stage. "When I'm not in the theater," she insisted now, "I don't think of the theater. . . . the theater is the theater, and life is life, and never do the twain meet except between the hours of eight and eleven. . . ." And yet, contrarily, Ethel had been furious when the critic Percy Hammond that year dubbed Helen Hayes "the First Actress of the Theatre" for her work in *Coquette*, bestowing upon Ethel the, to her, lesser title "First Lady."

At least if Kaufman and Ferber were going to parody the Royal Family they could have got it right. "All that eating and eating done by the Cavendishes in the play," snorted Ethel. "As everyone knows, eating was never the Barrymores' besetting sin!" It was some comfort that the playwrights had found Julie Cavendish almost impossible to cast. Ina Claire refused to be a walking Barrymore advertisement. Laurette Taylor declined as a friend of Ethel's as, for various reasons, did every other noted actress between the ages of thirty and fifty, until the comparatively unknown Ann Andrews played the part. On the other hand, infuriatingly, the play was a hit. Ethel was no longer on speaking terms with Kaufman and Ferber, but Lionel's was the biggest grievance. *The Royal Family* left him out completely. "What the hell."

Ethel stayed with Jack two weeks during which she was photographed looking slim, elegant, and extraordinarily youthful for someone almost forty-nine. Jack considered the visit a great success, writing Ned happily, "Ethel has just left, and we had a grand family reunion. . . . I think she is ever so much happier than she was, thank Heaven! . . . It was like old times with the added Cromwellian accent that we were all on the wagon, which made it all much more fun and in no way impaired the hours we kept. Ethel and I went over on the boat to Catalina before Lionel got back, which she adored. She ate enormously and slept thirteen hours, which she apparently had not done in years. . . ."

He had stopped drinking; now only a divorce stood between him and happiness. In late June he went East again to see Blanche.

Blanche had given no public sign that their break bothered her. She was constantly splashed across the society pages; celebrities like Cole Porter, Thornton Wilder, Eugene O'Neill, and Alec Woollcott frequented her apartment on Beekman Place. It was little Diana's duty to usher these guests into the drawing room saying, "Miss Strange is expecting you." She wore an accordion-pleated party dress for these occasions; her enunciation was perfect because Blanche had taken pains to have her cured of "Jack's nasality." At seven Diana had everything but love.

Blanche had been busy pursuing an acting career, debuting in a small role with the American Theatre Company in a Salem, Massachusetts, repertory production of Clyde Fitch's *Barbara Frietchie* "on the advice of Bernard Shaw who told her she was suited to his Saint Joan, but must learn the mechanics of stage craft." She funked her next appearance as

Gwendolen in *The Importance of Being Earnest*, then appeared in Strindberg only to be judged inexperienced, stilted, and wooden. Nothing daunted, she then managed to persuade John D. Williams himself that she could perform *L'Aiglon* on Broadway. Though Edmond Rostand had written the role of Napoleon's son for no less an actress than Sarah Bernhardt, Williams obligingly presented Michael Strange in *L'Aiglon* in December 1927. Jack telephoned congratulations that the press did not echo. Not even Blanche had enough friends to fill the huge Cosmopolitan Theatre, and *L'Aiglon* folded its wings after eight performances. Still undaunted, Blanche decided on a series of lectures titled "The Stage as an Actress Sees It."

Now Jack's hand shook as he rang her bell. He was not at all sure how one went about persuading a wife to divorce him so he could marry another woman. Blanche was out; when she came in she scanned him: "My God, you've gotten gray!" When he finally broached the subject, Blanche took it with shocking calm. A man might treat divorce casually, thought Jack, but "it seemed rather immoral for *her* to be so indifferent." She agreed to get the divorce quietly out of town; Jack need pay no more than the $18,000 he already paid for their support. Jack was fond of the view that "a man must pay the fiddler," though in his case "a whole symphony orchestra had to be subsidized." But though Blanche demanded regular payments, the orchestra in this case was chiefly Tower Road and the *Mariner*. Anyway she was planning to marry an American attorney she had met in London named Harrison Tweed.

A friend of both, Mercedes de Acosta remembered Blanche's vow. "It was she who did do Jack in, yet she did herself in at the same time. I never knew two people who loved each other more and hated each other so much. I never knew two people more incapable of living together who could not live apart. I am convinced neither one ever loved anyone else and that, spiritually speaking, neither one survived their divorce."

Hurrying back to Dolores, Jack would not have agreed.

BACK IN HOLLYWOOD Jack wrote Ned that he was concentrating entirely on The Dane, which he would produce early in September at the Bowl and at the Greek Theatre in Berkeley. Yet on July 13 the papers announced that John Barrymore was returning to Warner Brothers which, ironically, he had left just when that studio was pioneering sound. Jack knew he had a voice and was disillusioned with the solidly silent United Artists; Warner Brothers needed good voices and would welcome back the prodigal. Moreover, he had filmed only two pictures for United Artists in two years which, because they were not box-office hits, failed to kick back the expected 25 percent. Worse, they had failed to satisfy him artistically. Finally, United Artists was studded with stars whereas, with the exception of Rin-Tin-Tin, he had been top dog at Warners. And he wanted to get back to film comedy, he announced; he had made several very funny pictures recently, none of them intentionally. Yet first he had to do a third and last movie for United Artists directed by Ernst Lubitsch. "A lot of it will be done in the snow," Jack wrote Ned, "which will be fun."

On August 18 Blanche obtained a divorce in Kingston, New York, on the obligatory grounds of adultery. Free and still on the wagon, Jack could marry his madonna.

The first announcement said that John Barrymore's September production of *Hamlet* in the Bowl was postponed; the second that it was canceled. And why not, said everybody: Jack had beautiful Dolores, Tower Road, a yacht, and a Warner contract for five films in two years—$150,000 a picture and 10 percent of the gross. But that wasn't the reason for the canceled *Hamlet*. John Barrymore was afraid.

TWENTY

1928–1929

JACK'S CHIEF ADDITION to 6 Tower Road had been "The Marriage House," a six-room hacienda connected to the main quarters by an arbor. The blue and gold second floor was for Dolores, who could walk out her bedroom door onto a balcony overlooking miles of hills and sea. Jack had an even more spectacular view from a tower study accessible only by ladder and trap door, another attempt at "a divine room at the top of the house where the sun always comes in and where one went to play as a little boy when one wanted to be alone." Though it gave him the illusion of escape, it is certain that he spent very little time there.

To this house he would bring Dolores after the simple ceremony on November 24, 1928. Since this was Hollywood, however, they could not escape sensationalism. The day before, a heavily veiled woman turned up at the county clerk's office to announce that John Barrymore was commiting bigamy since Blanche refused to get a divorce. Reporters rushed to the Costello home at 1388 Schuyler Road. "Mr. Barrymore asked me to marry him," said Dolores simply. "For that reason I believed, and still believe, that he is legally free to marry." "Even in this superb climate," said Jack, "there are crazy people."

At the Costello home the next day Dolores wore cream lace over bisque, the spray of lilies at her shoulder secured by a diamond bar, Jack's gift. Although Dolores was Catholic and Jack nominally so, a Unitarian minister performed the ceremony impossible in the Catholic church. They were photographed, Dolores looking wistfully happy, Jack (though he claimed forty-one) all his forty-six years. But then friends noted how he could look half his age one day, twice his age the next. Certainly his "silk," fluttering bravely for the occasion, was tattered.

He had wanted to spirit Dolores away immediately on the *Mariner*, but Dolores was filming and Jack himself had to endure the making of *Eternal Love* at Banff and Lake Louise in Canada. He should have been in the mood but, ironically, this tale of lovers separated in life until they are united in death by a friendly avalanche was a disaster. The famous "Lubitsch touch" this time was a blow that left the picture "staggering about the arena, punch drunk, and out on its feet."

Passing now from the unpleasant duty of panning Mr. Lubitsch to the equally distressing but rather more familiar one of roasting Mr. Barrymore [ran a typical review]—let us proclaim it as our belief that in "Eternal Love" he gives the worst performance he has ever messed up a screen with. He looks terrible and acts worse. We can think of only one thing Jack Barrymore can do for the movies that will adequately make up for this shabby trick on his admirers. He can make a talkie of "Hamlet."

In this projected entertainment he shall appear in his natural (and not uncelebrated) face. No effort shall be made by himself or his dresser to lift, smooth, rejuvenate or otherwise distort the aforesaid face, and Mr. Barrymore shall not jump around in gleeful abandon or register dismay by opening his mouth a foot.

He shall on the contrary play "Hamlet" exactly as he played it on the New York stage, and if and when he does so we shall publish a retraction of this notice.

Apart from money, the movies had not served John Barrymore well— and vice versa. *Don Juan, When a Man Loves, The Beloved Rogue*, and *Eternal Love* sat on the public stomach like too much rich food. Only *Dr. Jekyll and Mr. Hyde, Beau Brummel*, and *The Sea Beast*—films made, significantly, when he was either on the stage or had just left it—could be claimed the work of a great artist. Hollywood, somehow, had tempted him to excesses that he had curbed in his earlier films. Another problem was attitude. He had been inspired by *Justice, Peter Ibbetson, Redemption, Richard the Third*, and *Hamlet*; clearly, much of what Hollywood offered him left him cold. Even when he was enthusiastic about a film—*The Sea Beast, The Beloved Rogue*—the finished product disappointed him. He was essentially a creative artist. In the theatre his creativity had emerged whole. In movies the director, the camera, and the film cutter did the creating, and Jack had to live with the results.

Which, unlike Arthur Hopkins's ventures, were always aimed at making money. Much to the dismay of Warner Brothers and United Artists, however, John Barrymore's movies were not box-office smashes. They drew well in New York, but were generally considered too highbrow in the provinces. He was not a popular film star like Gloria Swanson, Chaplin, Pickford, Fairbanks, or Gish.

ON DECEMBER 30, Jack and Dolores finally escaped aboard the S.S. *Virginia* on their way to meet the *Mariner* at Balboa. "I am thrilled to death," wrote Dolores in her journal the first day. "—It is such fun spending a vacation of almost three months away from everybody with some one you worship."

Dolores had fallen under Jack's potent spell. She was a good person, not excessively bright, with none of Katherine's chic or Blanche's egocentric vitality. She was the least threatening woman Jack had married and therefore offered him the illusion of security. She looked up to him, wanted to believe in him. She imitated him, calling herself "she" and "her" in her journal as he used the third person in his, calling him "Winkie," "Cat," and "my Egg" as he did her.

On January 9, 1929, the *Mariner* with Otto Matthies at the wheel dropped southward along the Panamanian coast, anchoring frequently in bays so that Jack and Dolores could explore the islands. Jack taught Dolores how to shoot and fish, and when she got a curlew with her first shot she made "her Winkie" very proud. January 13: "What a divine day!!—Otto rowed us ashore in the Skiff for a bath. I don't believe any two people ever spent such a Honeymoon—As soon as Otto left us— we took off our bathing suits & had our bath in the most heavenly small deep pool in a mountain stream—ending in a waterfall—having never giggled so much or been so happy—The natives were washing the laundry from the boat at the end of the stream—They gave us a dried coconut shell to pour water to rinse ourselves. We later visited them in their huts—Had dinner on deck while the sun was setting."

The *Mariner* trailed a shark hook and stocked every weapon from harpoons to rifles. Jack killed eagles, kingfishers, sharks, swordfish, rays, alligators, wahoos—and every day Dolores loved him more: "My darling looks like the brownest Hindu and I worship my dear husband . . . my own Winkie looks like Huckleberry Finn with Funny knives very elaborately attached to his belt . . . My darling and I are married three months today and I only hope it will be for all our lives."

Dolores was not the only one in love. She and Jack kept a log for Mae, whom she missed "terribly":

> The small egg is sleeping on deck in the moonlight [wrote Jack]—curled up with its head on its hand and looks about seven. She had a grand day. We went ashore on this Enchanted Island

with long water falls all over it falling like white-silk ribbons into the sea about three hundred feet high. It is really glorious—We all have to come here some day—She caught lots of fish but the sharks got the big ones so we are going to get Mama a fish big enough to put in the dining room! She insists upon catching it herself!! . . . The small egg is very happy I think—I love her more and more every day. . . .

At Guayaquil their solitude was shattered by crowds and photographers, and they found it difficult to leave the hotel because of the throngs. Girls chattering in Spanish came to their room with presents, one walking straight into Jack's bedroom despite Dolores's protests. The owners of the local theatre gave them a dinner and there was a carnival. Dolores had early relented and they were both drinking, though moderately. From Guayaquil they traveled inland to Quito, where they waved to crowds from their hotel balcony like visiting royalty. Yet it was so cold at 9,300 feet that Dolores could hardly walk; on February 14 she went to bed at six, feeling guilty she could not make love on Jack's birthday. Back in Guayaquil Jack made a speech in Spanish at a showing of *Beau Brummel*, then they sailed away, Dolores delighted to be alone again with her "Jiggie Wink." They finally ended their voyage on March 17. It had been an idyll. Jack was sober, Dolores gave him no cause for jealousy (though he noted in the log one man "who climbed up Winkie as if she was a cliff with daisies on top"), Dolores was still new, their life together still to be created.

NINETEEN TWENTY-EIGHT, the last year that pictures were completely silent, produced at least two masterpieces: *The Last Command*, starring the German actor Emil Jannings, and *Sadie Thompson* with Gloria Swanson and Lionel Barrymore. Jeanne Eagels's steamy performance had made *Rain* a smash on Broadway in 1922 in just the kind of sordid play that so distressed Irene Fenwick. Now at Swanson's insistence, Irene's husband was playing the fanatical minister who tries to reform Sadie in the retitled Somerset Maugham play. Swanson, the producer, and her director, Raoul Walsh, knew they couldn't get *Rain* past Will Hays and the Motion Picture Producers and Distributors of America without laundering, so they bought the rights to Maugham's book and passed their scenario off as a "classic."

Filmed on Catalina Island and studio sets, with art direction by William Cameron Menzies, *Sadie Thompson* has the concentrated atmosphere of a play. Rain pelts remorselessly on the tin roof of the small Pago Pago hotel where Sadie and Reverend Hamilton are holed up waiting for the ship. Repelled and fascinated, Hamilton cannot take his eyes off the strutting, gum-snapping prostitute. Gradually he wakens her to a sense of sin until she promises to return to San Francisco and face the charges waiting her there. But Hamilton has fluttered too near the flame. That night he forces his way into her room and rapes her. The next morning his body is washed up into the nets of a fisherman, his throat slashed.

Gloria Swanson found that with two pros like Lionel and Raoul Walsh (also playing the part of Marine Sergeant Tim "Handsome" O'Hara) she was turning in the best performance of her career. At first she'd had doubts about Lionel: he was obviously a slave to some kind of painkiller for some kind of infirmity and was distant, unkempt, unresponsive. But when Walsh started shooting, "he could shake off his customary lethargy and disorder in an instant and be a half-mad zealot with eyes ablaze, roaring at Sadie Thompson in a voice big enough for the biggest theater that she would be punished for her wickedness." He never, decided Swanson, showed any nerves whatsoever; with no visible effort he simply turned into Hamilton. A slight problem, however, developed.

It rained frequently on Catalina, and Swanson's sensitive nose detected the fact that Lionel was letting his week-old clothes dry right on him. Dilemma. On the one hand, she admired him too much to tell him to his face that he stank. On the other, she couldn't stand it much longer. Finally she instructed two crew members to invade his dressing room at lunchtime when he was napping and strip him. Maybe when Lionel woke up starkers he would put on something else or even bathe. During the last week's shooting Lionel smelled like a rose. Swanson thought him merely careless, but Lionel was carrying on a tradition handed down by Maurice to him and Jack, whose Hamlet tights perfumed the stage.

Swanson's performance as Sadie won an Academy Award nomination, though not an Oscar. Maugham thought Lionel's Hamilton "a show-stopper"—and indeed, Lionel's performance was a work of art. "In Mr. Barrymore's slightly bent body, carried upright on the legs slightly bent themselves by their eternal toil up the stony hill," wrote an appreciative critic; "in his facial mask behind which dance libidinous images, flickering up from the darkness of his being against the will that would drive them down into that darkness; in the stern mouth with its looseness of lower lip; the sharp, sniffing nose with its profile of emaciation; in the eyes that are ready to burn with the fire of the zealot and the horror which they reflect from the inner depths of his soul, you have the perfect picture of a tortured spirit struggling with itself and torturing others."

That same year Lionel teamed with D. W. Griffith, widely reputed to be "through" in films, to make *Drums of Love*, badly titled but "marvellously acted by Lionel Barrymore in the role of the deformed brother. It is his picture any way you look at it." On the eve of talking pictures, therefore, Lionel seemed to be getting better and Jack worse.

ETHEL HAD BEEN impressed enough with Hollywood to submit to a voice test. ("Speech has been a success for thousands and thousands of years," said Lionel. "And now they are testing it.") A limousine chauffeured her to Paramount's Astoria, Long Island, studio: Paramount, which had begun as Famous Players–Lasky, had kept its Broadway tie. She was ushered into the presence of a microphone surrounded by heavy black curtains inside a noise-proof glass cage. She addressed it. Hearing the result she forgot that she had been an early endorser of Edison's invention. "I consider that an excellent imitation of Elsie Janis giving an imitation of Barrymore," said the great lady coldly. "Talking pictures? The public won't put up with them. People don't want their ears hurt or their intelligence insulted."

So Ethel returned to the theatre—and not just any theatre, *her* theatre, the Ethel Barrymore. The Shuberts had bestowed her name on their new playhouse on West Forty-seventh Street, at the same time securing her under their management for Gregorio Martínez Sierra's play *The Kingdom of God*. At its opening Ethel dedicated the 1,100-seat theatre and was presented with a key to the star dressing room. Mummum would have been proud, yet this was not Ethel Barrymore's theatre as in Philadelphia the Arch had been Mrs. John Drew's. Ethel, however, felt the new distinction enough to insist on directing *The Kingdom of God*—though anonymously under the name E. M. Blyth to protect herself.

Ethel played Sister Gracia, a member of the voluntary Order of Saint Vincent de Paul. Phyllis Powell, a young actress in the cast, long remembered the impact of that opening night. Sister Gracia and Sister Julianna enter lugging a big basket of potatoes between them. As Ethel is recognized there is a tremendous wave of applause. When the sisters upset the basket, spilling potatoes all over the stage, the audience goes wild. The play is a tour de force for Ethel: those who think her only the high priestess of gay drawing-room gallantries eat their words.

Heywood Broun called Ethel's performance "the most moving piece of acting I have seen in a theatre"—words that critics would repeat to monotony over the years as Ethel triumphed in plays that were judged unworthy of her great acting. Critics who dismissed *The Kingdom of God* as just a series of scenes, however, missed the plot: the evolution of a gently bred Spanish girl's marriage to Christ. At nineteen, Sister Gracia is passionately in love with her new Bridegroom and the task of serving Him. At twenty-nine, disillusioned and suffering, she is on the brink of leaving Him for a real man who loves her. Denying him with supreme effort, she can say serenely at seventy, "Ah . . . sweet Savior, it's little time we get to talk to each other, you and I. But we're an old couple now. . . ." This was Ethel's first role as a nun; she played it superbly.

Ethel followed *The Kingdom of God* with the gay gallantries of *The Love Duel* with the fine actor Louis Calhern, a worldly comedy that critics took lightly. Ethel did not agree. She thought *Kingdom* and *Duel* dramatic contrasts, took them and Calhern on tour and played them successfully for eighty weeks.

Like all the young actors in her company, Susan Harley was awed by Miss Ethel Barrymore. No one could miss the difference between the coach that carried cast, crew, and dressers and the drawing-room car that housed the star and her adored Siamese cats, Sheila and Shawn. Though calling her "Miss B" among themselves, the cast would have drunk poison rather than address her as anything but Miss Barrymore to her face. The great star was formal, standoffish—such a contrast to Katharine Cornell, for example, who gave her casts big holiday dinners on the road and could be called "Kit."

Ethel had always been reserved, taking to heart Mummum's example of never displaying one's feelings in public. As she grew older the reserve deepened, became almost fanatical. The actress whose real tears moved audiences to tears could not in private give emotionally. Her tremendous self-sufficiency isolated her, as did her dedication to her art. She had faced and was facing the bitter, inevitable loneliness "of all those who are trying to create"; to this creation she had sacrificed married happiness, even her children. "Oh, you have no idea what a great woman she was," said Ruth Gordon who, with her husband Jacques, had known Ethel for years. "She was a great woman in the true meaning of greatness, that isolation of the great who live on peaks. And the great have no friends; they merely know a lot of people." Ethel was very much Sister Gracia, only her divine bridegroom was her art.

She was perhaps secure only with those who served her. She clung to servants: Britt, her faithful chauffeur; her maid Berthe, finally replaced by Anne Patterson, who had now been with her twenty years. Anita Rothe, a trusted confidante, acted with her constantly. She would retain her stage manager Edward McHugh for more than twenty-five years. And Georgie Drew Mendum for more than fifty.

Not a servant, yet not an equal, "the Mutt of the Drews" worshipped Ethel, who was happy to put her cousin in her pocket. If there was an unfilled part in a play, Georgie filled it. When Ethel wanted someone to talk to after a performance, Georgie talked. If Ethel didn't want to answer the telephone or write a letter, Georgie answered, wrote. Eventually Georgie even rehearsed casts for Ethel, who would come in at the last moment to perform. Georgie was just the "wife" Ethel needed: uncompetitive, serviceable, there. Year by year this little wisp of a woman became quainter, wearing Ethel's too-large hand-me-downs inches longer than the fashion, sporting old-fashioned black stockings. She had long ago given up any notion of starring on her own.

"You ought to be supremely happy," an admirer told Ethel. "You have everything that anybody could want—physical, mental, material. Yet you don't give the impression of radiant happiness. You're not like some of these other actresses who look as if God had climbed into his heaven solely for their benefit in order to prove to them—and to their press agents—that all [is] right with the world."

No, thought Ethel: one could listen to all the most beautiful music, saturate oneself in all the loveliest things of the earth—and the play would still be a tragedy or, at the very best, a problem play whose meaning eluded one. And one would still be sitting in an empty theatre, the occupant of a solitary stall, bitterly conscious of the emptiness of the gallery and the boxes and the seats around one. . . . It was at dark moments like these that she thought again that the three children were the only excuse for her life.

THE DARLING CHILDREN . . . Ethel was putting all three through some of the most expensive Catholic private schools in the country: Portsmouth Priory, the Fay School, St. Bernard's, Canterbury, Notre Dame de Namur. Sammy had gone to Andover and now to Brown. He was going on twenty and unsure what he wanted to do. Ethel called him "S-s-ambo" in those "inimitable sibilants," adored him, spoiled him. He was docile, but then it would have taken a bold son to compete with a mother like Ethel Barrymore.

Sister was different: smart, capable, extroverted; she had her feet on the ground. Like her brothers, however, she was painfully conscious of the Barrymore name. Since childhood she had been badgered with the inevitable questions. How did it feel to be the sixth generation of an acting family? Did she want to act? Did her mother want her to act? Did she want to play Juliet? She was so sick of it she could throw up.

Yet at her graduation after eight years at the Academy of Notre Dame de Namur that June 1929, young Ethel (or Chee-Chee, as Jack had nicknamed her) announced that she had decided to go on the stage. She had resisted—she was very stubborn—yet clearly her family and friends expected her to act. Ethel attended the ceremony with Sammy, who hovered shyly behind his smartly dressed mother, so much more elegant than her plump-faced daughter. Chee-Chee was thrilled: "to think that for the first time in her life she called off a performance to come over from New York—well, it's simply wonderful." Ethel professed herself delighted that her daughter had chosen the stage. She had never tried to influence her. Chee-Chee, however, would first go abroad for a year to be polished at a fashionable Catholic school in Verona, then come home and make her debut at the Colony Club. Clearly Ethel considered her daughter a Colt first, a Barrymore second.

Ethel was able to keep up with her rich acquaintances, but while they lived off their incomes she spent her principal and more. She had rented an apartment from the humorist Don Marquis in his house at 125 East Sixty-second Street so that she would not have to drive to Mamaroneck after the theatre, yet several months went by and he received no rent. Undoubtedly the matter had just slipped Miss Barrymore's mind: one knew theatre people, after all; a friendly reminder slipped under the door would do the trick. Marquis wrote a pleasant, apologetic little note and sent it under. Passing her door sometime later, he was astonished to find the note shredded on her mat.

Prose having failed, Marquis took to verse:

> Were I a wealthy codger
> You'd be a rent-free lodger.
> But since I'm not, Miss Barrymore,
> In case you'd like to tarry more,
> Please heed the message of my lyre
> And be a paying occupier.

Silence.

Ethel was on the second floor, Marquis had an office on the first. To leave the house she had to descend a stairway close to his room. Marquis left his door open; one day he heard footsteps. He sprang into the hallway. Ethel saw him and instantly retreated. They played this game for some time. One day, however, when Marquis was deep in his work, Ethel tiptoed down the stairs and was out the door before Marquis could confront her. He had to concede her that round. The humor of the situation began to appeal to him.

One day he was sure he had her. He knew from a message the exact hour she would be leaving the house. This time he let her get almost to the front door before he leapt out of his office and faced her. They stared at each other. Marquis began to laugh. Ethel herself smiled, then broke into a delightful chuckle. When the door closed behind her, Marquis realized he had forgotten to ask for the rent.

Ethel moved out a few months later. Like all good Barrymores, she was careless about bills, far too philistine a concern. Rules were made for other people; besides, Marquis had been an old drinking pal of Jack's at the Players. Surely old ties counted for something.

JACK HAD INSTALLED Dolores on top of Tower Road along with numerous victims of the hunt which he hung in a specially built trophy room. He continued to lavish money on the estate and on possessions: if he owned enough objects he might discover who he was. He built an aviary to house hundreds of rare tropical birds, and designed for it a stained-glass window depicting himself and Dolores as modern saints gazing out over the sea. He designed a Barrymore crest, which he affixed to the front gate and anything else a crest could embellish. He was hurt that Dolores was amused, but then the Costello family had a real crest. He and Dolores were photographed in their baronial quarters looking small and lost.

Now that they were back in Hollywood his terrible jealousy erupted. He was reminded that she had been a model for James Montgomery Flagg; he knew what that meant. (Flagg once confided to a friend that Dolores's underwear was sometimes less than freshly laundered.) They attended a party at which Dolores accepted David O. Selznick's invitation to dance. In an ecstasy of fear, Jack hurried her home where he kept up an inquisition till past three in the morning. "What did he say? *What did he say to you?*" Dolores wept: "I want to be your friend. Didn't you ever have a woman who was a *friend?*" He and Blanche had once been comrades, but the thought only angered him more. He ordered bars installed across windows and doors so that Dolores could not secretly tryst with a lover. He began to refuse social invitations for them. Like Katherine and Blanche, Dolores discovered she had married Dr. Jekyll and Mr. Hyde. Sober, Jack could be almost proper. Drink released demons of jealousy, insecurity, paranoia. Dolores loved him, tried to help him, endured.

In August *The Kingdom of God* tour took Ethel again to Los Angeles and another reunion with Jack and Lionel. This one was not as cozy as the last. For one thing, Jack was now married, never a situation Ethel appreciated. For another, they were all off the wagon and not as well behaved. "Why is Jack drinking so heavily?" Ethel, worried, asked Hotchener. "I don't know," said Hotchener. "Is there always a reason?" And then Jack had not done his Hamlet in the Bowl, something she had encouraged. Something of Sister Gracia's asceticism must also have seeped into Ethel's soul. Sitting on Jack's patio overlooking the pool which overlooked palms and hills, waited on by Athelito Estalialla, Jack's butler, Ethel suddenly exploded. Working in films was shoveling trash compared to working in the theatre, she informed Lionel and Jack. In the theatre there was terrific responsibility. One had always to be on top. One couldn't let down for a moment or everyone else automatically let down too. She had gone on with raging temperatures, with excruciating pain—but by God, she had gone on! And what were they doing but perpetrating a lot of trashy movies and lolling about their pools—

Here Ethel looked at her watch and at cousin Georgie, odd and mouselike among the fountains and the palms. She rose. "We'll be late for the theatre, Georgie! Hurry."

Jack tried to pour Benedictine, but Ethel refused. Lionel and Jack escorted the two women to Ethel's hired car.

"Mike," said Jack mournfully, "what a tragedy it is that you and I have become bums and have deserted the glorious old theatre for the utterly low movies. Here are these two women who are going to go downtown and work, carrying on the tradition of the family. They'll recite lines they have been reciting for weeks and have a magnificent evening, while you and I, having become shovelers of trash, will be forced to sit in a patio under the stars and sip genuine Benedictine."

"Ay," said Lionel. "Let us return to our Benedictine and try not to be envious."

Said Ethel, "Go to hell, both of you!" and jumped into her car.

During Ethel's visit that month Mae Costello died of a heart attack, robbing Dolores of her main support. Mae was only forty-five, two years younger than Jack. Her death hit Jack hard too. He had called her Mamma, had felt she was the kind of warm family that Lionel and Ethel, for all their clan pride, were not. Mae's quiet funeral at St. Andrew's drew few of Hollywood's perennially curious, though she was the mother and mother-in-law of stars. Ethel attended, and the actor Lowell Sherman, in love with Helene Costello. Dolores must have suspected, if not known, that she was pregnant.

Mae's death did not reconcile Maurice Costello to his daughter's marriage. From his modest home down the hill, he would often look up at the lights of 6 Tower Road and curse John Barrymore for having taken his daughter and divided his family. "I used to drive into the hills and cry myself to sleep," said Costello. "Sometimes I would take a newspaper and read myself to sleep. Sometimes I cried myself out of the idea of murder. I would wake up there in the hills and look at the sunshine and decide this was better than San Quentin, that after all John was not worth murdering."

MGM HAD BEEN a happy family in the silent picture days. Lionel had a dressing room in an old frame building, and when not shooting tilted back his chair on the porch and jawed the hours away with Lionel Belmore, Lew Cody, and Lewis Stone while the bottle changed hands. A picture in the can, the studio used to pack producers, directors, cutters, stars, and cast into a streetcar and rattle out to San Bernardino to see a preview. On the way back everyone got a chance to pick the movie apart and put it back together a dozen times. It was all real homey.

The advent of sound sent shock waves through the industry. Actresses who had emoted chiefly with their eyes now faced the subtleties of locution. Actors wondered whether their voices were as virile as their physiques. Hollywood's large colony of émigrés from Europe and Brooklyn panicked: Pola Negri, Vilma Banky, and Camilla Horn were among those who knew their American careers were over. Screenwriters had the jitters: would titles like "Unhand me, you dastardly villain!" go over as dialogue? Top brass groaned: few directors had stage experience. Lionel the theatre veteran was calm.

Not that talkies arrived overnight. United Artists, MGM, and the smaller studios, for example, lagged behind Warner Brothers and Fox—uncertain whether talkies would catch on. Studios with completed films hastily did "goat-gland jobs" (extract of goat gland was a health fad of the twenties), injecting these silents with sound scenes as pressure mounted from Warners' sound on disc—Vitaphone—and Fox's sound on film—Movietone. Part-talkies came next from studios unequipped to meet the sudden demand for all-talkies. A good year after Warners' first all-talkie, *The Lights of New York*, Lionel spoke in a few scenes of MGM's *The Mysterious Island*, pantomimed the rest.

Predictably, however, Lionel first spoke from the screen for the pioneering Warner Brothers. In *The Lion and the Mouse*, he was excellent as Ready Money Ryder, a rapacious villain who enjoys contemplating a large bust of himself inscribed POWER. Like Jack's, Lionel's face is extremely flexible: his jaw thrusts, his creases crease, his eyebrows could row a boat. Most importantly, his voice has texture, range, and power. Obviously here is an actor who has nothing to dread from talking pictures.

With the release of *The Lion and the Mouse*, Lionel's stock soared. Listening to that resonant voice, studios, public, and critics were at last convinced that talking pictures were "not only possible, but virtually on the wing." MGM woke up. They had made a silent called *Alias Jimmy Valentine* starring William Haines as a reformed crook, Lionel supporting as a tough detective. Now they yanked Lionel back to MGM for a goat-gland job on the last two reels. Lionel, said Haines, was sweet to work with as he guided the nervous young actor through the mysteries of projecting into microphones hidden in potted plants, behind screens, and under tables. Undoubtedly Lionel was sweet, knowing he would walk away with the picture—as he did, demonstrating again, said one critic, "the superiority of a trained stage actor over ordinary players."

Then why in the next years did MGM use Lionel only in the silent *West of Zanzibar* and the part-talkie *Mysterious Island*? Perhaps talkie directors were even more needed than stars. "Why relax from your bad dreams," Lionel told the studio brass. "As an old and experienced hand to whom nobody has paid any attention these many years, let me explain. Sound won't make quite as much difference as you fearfully expect. Action will remain the chief ingredient of these cultural dramas of ours. The main difference will be that the titles will from now on be uttered—hopefully in something approximating English." His confidence impressed Louis B. Mayer and his brilliant young associate, Irving Thalberg. Lionel found himself behind a megaphone.

After Lionel's directorial debut with a short called *Confession*, Mayer trusted him with the major star Ruth Chatterton in a remake of the French tear-jerker *Madame X*. Lionel found himself increasingly dissatisfied with the way his actors had to scurry like chickens from one hidden microphone to the next before they could speak. He thought of the property man, who always had his favorite sporting equipment at hand. "Get me one of those damned fish poles and tie the microphone on one end. Then prop it out of camera range over Miss Chatterton's head. When she walks, move the pole along with her, keeping the mike right over her." The sound engineers protested, but Lionel succeeded in having Chatterton rise, walk across the room talking, and continue her conversation while a guitar made music over the dialogue. Though eventually Cecil B. DeMille, among others, claimed he invented the sound boom, Lionel believed his fishing pole was first. At any rate, Louis B. Mayer shed copious tears over *Madame X* in the projection room, as did the public with whom it was a hit.

With two successes, Lionel now was given a star against whom, some claim, Mayer had a personal grudge: the matinee idol John Gilbert, famous after *Flesh and the Devil* as the screen lover of Greta Garbo.

Off screen Garbo and Gilbert were in love, and Garbo had agreed to marry him. Since King Vidor and Eleanor Boardman were also marrying, Garbo and Gilbert decided to make it a double wedding. Louis B. Mayer was among the guests who waited for Garbo to appear. As the minutes passed, Gilbert became increasingly distraught, until finally Eleanor Boardman told him gently that they could wait no longer. At that point Mayer stepped out of the guest bathroom, clapped Gilbert on the back, and said, "What's the matter with you, Gilbert? What do you have to marry her for? Why don't you just fuck her and forget about it?" Enraged, Gilbert attacked Mayer, who fell backward into the bathroom. When he got to his feet he was bleeding. Mayer, the son of a junk dealer, was already the most powerful boss in Hollywood. Now he told Gilbert, "I'll destroy you."

One way to destroy his biggest male star was to assign him an inadequate director for his first full-length talkie. Fred Niblo directed *Redemption*, but Lionel was brought in for retakes. Gilbert was comparatively relaxed in Niblo's scenes, embarrassingly bad in the reshot Barrymore's. Lionel's fiscal irresponsibility enslaved him to Louis B. Mayer, from whom he constantly borrowed against his salary. Perhaps Mayer did not actually take him aside and say, "I want you to wreck that bastard Gilbert." But the head of MGM had other ways of enforcing his will, and Lionel was in no position to refuse him.

Redemption, however, wasn't bad enough; so MGM assigned Lionel to direct a second Gilbert talkie, to be released before the first. *His Glorious Night* did destroy the film idol. Audiences who had thrilled to his silent lovemaking now screamed with laughter as Gilbert told Catherine Dale Owen, "I love you, I love you, I love you." Legend has it that what destroyed Gilbert was an effeminate voice. Actually his voice was quite low, though lacking warmth. What seems to have sunk him is how he was made to use it.

The actor's tension is evident on the screen; he is rigid in the love scenes, his eyes staring. Worse, someone counseled him to deliver every word in pear-shaped tones; the effect was hilarious. If Lionel's intentions were honorable, where was he during the dailies, where he certainly would have recognized that Gilbert's diction was absurd: *he* didn't talk that way in movies, why should Gilbert? Moreover, dialogue like "Oh, beauteous maiden, my arms are waiting to enfold you" was stilted and inane. Why not hire someone to rewrite, like Dorothy Parker, who had been brought in to revamp *Madame X*?

"I watched John Gilbert being destroyed on the sound stage by one man, Lionel Barrymore," said Hedda Hopper, who was also in the film. Louise Brooks blamed Lionel's addiction. "Barrymore was taking heavy doses of morphine in those days, and was hardly responsible for what went on. Anyone could have manipulated him and someone did. It was common talk at the studio before the picture came out. Everyone knew it but Jack." Douglas Fairbanks Jr. believed Lionel's extraordinarily choppy cutting ruined the film. "If there was any intention to punish Jack in *His Glorious Night* and to bring his romantic image crashing down, one sure way to do it was in the cutting room. An awkward break or an extended pause, a jerky transition, or love words run together too quickly would have an audience howling. . . . And no one could prove sabotage. I'm not saying that's what happened, but it could have been done."

Though Lionel was not squarely blamed, many agreed with Gilbert's former wife Leatrice Joy that "he couldn't have done much worse if he tried." Mayer's role in Gilbert's destruction is clearer. His daughter, Irene Selznick, remembers Mayer tossing the bad reviews of *His Glorious Night* onto the dining-room table with a smile. "That," said Mayer, "should take care of Mr. Gilbert."

Garbo gallantly tried to rescue her former lover in *Queen Christina*, but Gilbert hurried his career downhill with suicidal drinking. Says the film historian Kevin Brownlow, "Producers like Mayer behaved like scrapyard proprietors, wrecking cars with the drivers still at the wheel." If Lionel was part of the wrecking crew, he could also reflect that Mayer could at any time junk him. He had better not draw the boss's blood.

BESIDES THE ILL-FATED *Eternal Love,* Jack appeared in only one film in 1929, but it was, in a sense, momentous. Warner Brothers decided to showcase Vitaphone with a huge variety bill called *The Show of Shows.* The actors' trauma at speaking for the first time is evident throughout; with a few exceptions, everyone seems ill at ease. The host, Frank Fay, is infrequently funny, Myrna Loy is a Florodora girl, someone sings a song about bad breath, and the inimitable comic Beatrice Lillie fails to amuse. Dressed as Dutch girls, Dolores and Helene dance and sing in an act featuring all the sister teams in Hollywood. Finally, in the midst of this tasteless welter, a sinister figure in black armor appears in swirling mist: John Barrymore as the villainous Duke of Gloucester, who eliminated his enemies "with the graceful impartiality of Al Capone." Nursing the head of one of those enemies, John turns a pale, leering face to the camera and for the first time on film sends his beautifully resonant voice into the movie houses of America. The textural difference between Barrymore and what has gone before is the difference between velvet and polyester. And yet John's Richard is too rich for the screen; it is a stage performance transmitted by a medium hostile to stage acting. But one thing was established: the talkies were made for John Barrymore.

Jack knew it. "Will you do something for me? (N.B. It seems to me I have asked this question before)," he wrote Ned. "Will you try to think of some more movies for me, ones where the talking device might possibly be used. It seems to be coming in, and apparently now is the time for me to make a killing in it." Jack himself wanted to do a Gustave Flaubert story about Saint Julian containing his favorite trope, a transformation scene from leper to a regenerated Christ figure made "as beautiful as God, gauze and the camera can make him." Certainly Jack had reason to want a good sound vehicle: in 1929 Warner Brothers uncorked *Disraeli*, its first prestige talkie—not with John but with George Arliss re-creating his stage triumph as the British author-statesman.

Warners sent Jack to New York for the premiere of *The Show of Shows* at the Winter Garden. Not the kind of stage appearance John Barrymore was used to making: a modest, unannounced introduction of his Shakespeare turn sandwiched between Ted Lewis and Rin-Tin-Tin. But the audience was surprised and delighted.

"Come and see me, Daddy," Diana had written Jack two years before. "I would like so much to see you." According to Diana, this New York visit was the first encounter with her father that she clearly remembered. Blanche had married Harrison Tweed and taken a luxurious apartment at 10 Gracie Square. One day Diana came home from the Brearley School, where her mother had gone before her, to find Blanche waiting impatiently.

"Catkin, your father is in town. He'll be over in a few minutes. Get out of that uniform and into your blue dress. Be quick about it."

Diana was quick. What would this unknown father think of her? As a small child she had thought herself supremely ugly, a "Japanese doll with jaundice." Every night she prayed, "Please, God, make me beautiful like Mummy," but her stepbrother Robin was the beautiful one, so beautiful that Blanche had kept him in long golden curls until he was nearly eight, loving him best. Robin liked to put on Diana's dresses, boasting that he looked prettier in them than she did, which was true. (When Blanche complained of Robin's androgynous looks to a psychiatrist, he said, "Madam, have you ever looked at yourself in the mirror?")

What would Diana think of this unknown father? She had a photograph of him in *The Sea Beast* hung in the place of honor over her bed. He had become an icon: "half-God, half-man." Blanche would not talk about him, yet once in a while Diana overheard snatches of conversation.

"Poor Jack," Blanche would be saying. "He's starting another motion picture, I understand. When I think of what they're doing to him in that monstrous factory—what's happening to that genius in Hollywood. . . ."

He seemed tall to Diana when he came into the room, an elegant man in an overcoat, his head tilted to one side "as if he were questioning someone." He shook hands formally with Blanche. "Hello, Treepee," he said. He held her briefly and she smelled after-shave, "tangy, like peppermint."

He studied her face. "Who does she take after, Fig?"

Blanche was strangely quiet. "I don't know, Jack. I think she has my eyes, but there's something of you in the expression about the mouth—"

He made himself comfortable on the floor. Diana perched uneasily on a chair. "I understand you like to paint." He indicated a Daumier on the wall, a Monet above the fireplace. "Do you like that?"

"Oh, yes, Daddy." She was listening instead to his voice. Blanche had forced her to do endless vocal exercises to get rid of "your father's nasal voice." *But his voice wasn't nasal.*

"Michael says you draw very well. She showed me one you made of the castle of Ludwig of Bavaria. I thought it ver-ry good. That's what I used to do."

She nodded: Blanche had told her that.

"Would you like to be an artist? I wanted to be once."

"I think so, Daddy."

He went on talking technically about the way Monet got the effect of moonlight reflected on windows, then Blanche reappeared and said, "Catkin, your father and I want to talk. He's got to make a train very soon. Say good-by to him."

Blanche's word was final. Diana kissed her father goodbye and left the room. There was so much she'd wanted to say.

TWENTY-ONE

1930–1932

NOT EVERYONE WELCOMED the coming of sound. Silent films, after all, spoke a universal language that many felt a tragedy to lose. For John Barrymore, who compared silent acting to a man pantomiming a message behind the window of a moving train, sound was a decided blessing. His first feature for Warners was *General Crack*, the romantic story of a soldier of fortune whose adventures at the court of Leopold II elevate him to archdukedom. Unlike most stars, Jack actually read the novel, penciling ideas as well as self-sketches in the margins. Though there was still too much profile, Jack's Crack had dash, brilliance, and more subtlety than he had previously displayed because he had, at last, a larynx. Warners heralded the talking Barrymore:

> JOHN BARRYMORE—YESTERDAY A SPEECHLESS SHADOW—
> TODAY A VIVID, LIVING PERSON—THANKS TO VITAPHONE. . . .
> NOT FIGURATIVELY, BUT LITERALLY, JOHN BARRYMORE "COMES
> TO LIFE" IN GENERAL CRACK. FOR HERE FOR THE FIRST TIME,
> VITAPHONE RESTORES THE PENT-UP POWER OF THE THRILLING
> VOICE THAT MADE HIM THE STAR OF STARS OF THE SPEAKING
> STAGE. . . .

Critics agreed about "the wonderful voice clear and perfectly attuned to dialogue," agreed that John Barrymore had "at last found the medium which suits him best." Not a critic, little Diana went to the movie with her grandfather Charles Oelrichs who, unlike Blanche, did not seem appalled at Jack's screen career. All through the film Diana never took her eyes off the screen; from time to time she murmured, "My Daddy . . . my Daddy," as though Jack were speaking to her too for the first time.

Just as sound first realized him fully on the screen, Jack received the first real warning that the body he tortured so cavalierly with alcohol, cigarettes, irregular eating, and too little sleep was rebelling. Severe stomach pains forced him to stop filming; he was rushed to a hospital where x-rays disclosed a duodenal ulcer. Doctors prescribed rest, bland foods and liquids, but in two weeks Jack was back to hard liquor and chain-smoking. Nothing—not a new career in talkies nor Dolores nor the approaching birth of their child—could stem the tide of despair and self-hatred washing Jack Barrymore ever further out to sea.

Yet he was full of plans. A sound remake of *The Sea Beast* followed by *Peter Ibbetson* with Dolores as the Duchess of Towers, and *Kismet*, if taking it away from Otis Skinner, now with Warner Brothers, would not be a discourtesy. And, of course, *Hamlet*—for now surely the time had come to immortalize John Barrymore's great Hamlet on film.

Hamlet was not filmed. The real reasons may never be exhumed, but clearly Jack angered Warner Brothers when he announced through Henry Hotchener that he had received an offer of more money for *Hamlet* from another studio and expected Warners to match it. Jack Warner replied curtly, adding dark words about managers "benefitting their own positions":

> There was never any question of my *breaking* my present contract with you [replied Jack], but only of *modifying* it, and it seems to me that considering the especial knowledge and experience I have with this play, and the attitude of the public towards my association with it all over the world (and particularly the success in England, which was so widely advertised in this country because it was the only time an American actor had ever accomplished it), and considering also the extra labor and concentration it would require from me, an additional $50,000 and 5% more of the gross are not unreasonable in view of the tremendous possibilities of this picture and the fact that we both realize that it is undoubtedly my "ace in the hole."
>
> I do not quite understand the phrase in your letter about managers "benefitting their own positions," but if it means what I think it does, let me assure you that you are doing Hotchener a very great injustice. . . .

The reasons for Jack not filming *Hamlet* seem purely contractual, yet had he really wanted to make the film, Warners' refusal of an additional $50,000 and 5 percent would not have stopped him. There was also "the extra labor and concentration" *Hamlet* would require—labor and concentration that Jack had not exercised for five years. Quite possibly Jack felt unequal to meeting the challenge of filming his great stage success, as well as fearful of the results.

He followed *Crack* instead with *The Man from Blankley's*, by all accounts a gem of a film which has since been lost. As Lord Strathpeffer, a mild-mannered beetle collector who has drunk too much wine, Jack sets out to dine with a fellow coleopterist whom he has never met, but staggers instead into a house where the hostess has hired an extra guest from Blankley's rental agency to avoid seating thirteen at dinner. While the company readily accepts Lord Strathpeffer as another guest, the hostess is bewildered that a man from Blankley's should discourse at such length on the domestic life of the Egyptian scarab. *The Man from Blankley's* was so subtle, original, and delightfully insane, in fact, that it never won a wide audience, but Myrna Loy's testimony that the film was "one of the most brilliant movies" John Barrymore ever made rings true since many people found him an even more brilliant comedian than tragedian.

Charming on the screen, often less than charming at home. Dolores found herself increasingly isolated, her contacts having to be approved by her jealously insecure husband. Jack had personally chosen her obstetrician, Dr. John Vruwink; had personally ordered him to clock Dolores's progress day by day, as though a true royal heir were expected. Yet when Vruwink followed instructions, Jack exploded. "Good night and *goodbye*, you son of a bitch! Don't come back. If I ever find you in this house again I'll break your goddam jaw." When Dolores numbly begged an explanation, "I don't want him around here because he's stuck on you," said Jack, "and I don't want anybody stuck on you touching you, especially the way this guy has to touch you." He had been drinking; sober, he allowed Vruwink back in the house.

Another of Jack's responses to Dolores's pregnancy was to replace the *Mariner*, dead of dry rot at a $110,000 loss, with a 120-foot, $225,000 diesel luxury yacht. In January Jack and Dolores, accompanied by Fox Movietone News, christened the boat at Long Beach before Jack left for salmon fishing off Seattle. Jack is impeccable in fedora, overcoat, and gloves; Dolores, beautiful in a head-hugging cloche, clutches a bouquet decorated with fluttering ribbons. Jack tries to be at ease. "Speech making is a little like childbirth," he tells the camera; "it's of semi-occasional importance, but the sooner it's over the better." He admits they are about to produce on their own account. Dolores has nothing to say; she smiles and looks at her husband. She can hardly lift the magnum of champagne provided for the christening. "Go ahead," says Jack. "Just think of me." They are the right words: Dolores smashes the bottle into a million pieces—"Damn near wrecked the boat." Jack wanted a son with Blanche, he wanted one now. For a superstitious man how dire, then, to christen the new boat the *Infanta*.

Jack reserved a room next to Dolores's at the Cedars of Lebanon Hospital. Filming the sound remake of *The Sea Beast*, he roamed the halls in dank seaman's garb and unshaven face like the vision of a drowned whale hunter. On April 8 he filmed overtime; despite all intentions of keeping the vigil at Dolores's bedside, he kissed her and staggered off to his room where he immediately went to sleep. A nurse roused him to announce the birth of a daughter. "Splendid," said Jack and rolled over. Or so the legend goes.

He denied his disappointment for the press.

"And who does the new baby look like?"

"I think a little like Lon Chaney."

"Are you sorry to see a girl?"

"A Barrymore sorry to see a girl? You know the tradition in our family—the girls are the only ones we don't have to worry about. And don't forget—*I* understand women so much better. . . . No, I haven't yet entered her at Miss Spence's school for girls or hired a duenna for her first trip to France. I haven't anything written on her birth certificate about the possibilities of her becoming an actress, either. If she wants to go on the stage when she's old enough, fine. If she wants to take up tatting or blow smoke through her ears at church socials, that'll be her affair."

Sitting on the patio weeks later with Dolores, an acquaintance asked, "Do you think you'll make any more pictures?"

Dolores looked down the garden where Jack was happily shooting clay pigeons. She smiled her wistful smile.

"Would you?"

The birth of Dolores Ethel Mae Barrymore, her name honoring three women in one, reunited Maurice Costello with his family. He could now stop gazing up the hill at Dolores's lights; Jack welcomed him with open arms, their feud a thing of the past. At the same time Jack quarreled with a newcomer to the family, Lowell Sherman, who had married Helene. "We were the best of friends until he became an in-law," said Jack, "then something happened. God knows what." The feud seems to have started, however, when they filmed *General Crack* together, Sherman as Leopold II. Sherman was a supreme movie villain, his suave cruelty making Jack's outbursts seem often rather, well, young. Their rivalry grew. One night at a vastly liquid bash at Tower Road, Jack launched into *Hamlet*. He did this often: the more the stage receded from him the more he tried to grasp it. But Sherman had had a bellyful of Jack and Shakespeare. "To hell with you and Hamlet!" he bellowed. Jack lunged at him. "To hell with you and Hamlet!" He took off running, Jack in hot pursuit. When the host failed to return, the guests who went to look for him found him passed out under a hedge. But Jack and Sherman feuded even when they weren't drunk, and Sherman forbade Helene to visit her sister, further isolating Dolores.

Pregnancy had prevented Dolores from making *Moby Dick* with Jack; a young actress named Joan Bennett, looking rather like her in a blond wig, took her place. To little avail. "*Moby Dick* is a *bad* film," said the great Russian director Sergei Eisenstein, and so it is: a seesaw between the cosmic and the comic, a travesty of Melville as well as a silly film all on its own. Compared to his appearance in *The Sea Beast* only four years before, Jack is shockingly older, something which his opening acrobatics up in the crow's nest only emphasize. This Ahab is more than a caricature of John Barrymore as a drunk and a make-out artist: Jack seems drunk from beginning to end. Joan Bennett said that he did not drink a drop throughout the entire filming—no evidence at all since Jack, like all alcoholics, was diabolically clever at tippling in secret. If, however, making Ahab a drunk was the director Lloyd Bacon's idea, then it was a bad one.

Also inexplicably, Jack decided to make Ahab one of Lionel's old men with lots of cackling and heh-hehing that have little to do with the character. Early sound was notoriously poor, but that does not explain why Ahab talks like an old cowhand: "Beg pardon, ma'am. . . . Ain't'cha friends anuf ta intraduce me?" Looking as though he is about to break out laughing, Jack seems aware of the perversity of his performance. If it is true that only a very good actor can be a very bad actor, then *Moby Dick* is negative proof that John Barrymore was great. Perversely, it was one of his most successful movies at the box office.

After filming, Jack took Dolores and baby Dede on a week's cruise to Santa Barbara accompanied by Lionel. Irene was spending a good deal of time in New York. Lionel was not working much: only two films in 1930 released to his credit: *The Rogue Song*, in which he directed the great baritone Lawrence Tibbett, and *Free and Easy*, making only a brief guest-star appearance. Hardly enough to keep Irene and 802 North Roxbury Drive in the style to which they were accustomed.

A solitary man, Lionel still had a few male companions with whom he liked to drink and jaw. Louis Wolheim was one favorite. Lionel had discovered him teaching mathematics at Cornell University back in the early twenties when he was touring and had got him a small role in *The Jest*. Wolheim had a philosopher's mind and a face that looked as though a tank had run over it, unevenly. He made a decided success in Eugene O'Neill's *The Hairy Ape* and appeared with Jack in *Dr. Jekyll and Mr. Hyde, Sherlock Holmes*, and *Tempest*, as Jack's sidekick, Sergeant Bulba. He was Lionel's sidekick off screen, flying the Barrymore colors "pale beer and yellow cheese." Occasionally both men would descend upon the director Lewis Milestone, who had a Czechoslovakian cook, devour Slovakian boiled beef, wipe their chins, and promise, "We'll let you know when we'll come again."

Another friend of Lionel's, Raoul Walsh, preferred livelier entertainment, such as a San Pedro–to–San Francisco boat known as the "seagoing brothel." Inevitably on one of these cruises two prostitutes asked whether they could join the gentlemen.

Lionel waved them into seats. "Bear in mind, ladies, we are not gentlemen. I am an author—my books have been published in many languages. My friend here is a motion picture director. He has directed most of my novels and has become internationally famous." In proof he ordered French wine. His latest novel, he assured them as he filled their glasses, had good parts for them both.

"What's the book called?" one wanted to know.

"*Free Love*," said Lionel solemnly.

"It must have been written about this boat!" said the tart indignantly. "This boat is so loaded with free ass that an honest hooker hasn't got a chance to earn a buck."

Lionel did not intend she should earn one off him. Four bottles later he rose magnificently if unsteadily to his feet. "Beesark, they're all yours," he said, bestowing the women on Walsh with a sweep of his arm as he disappeared in the direction of his stateroom muttering, "To be or not to be. . . ."

Walsh was often amused at his friend's seeming naïveté. Once he introduced Lionel to a prosperous-looking, flossy woman of great charm to whom Lionel took an instant liking.

"Why," said the woman, "you must come to my house sometime in San Francisco. Your brother Jack is a frequent guest."

Lionel promised to look her up, then asked Walsh after she left what the obviously wealthy woman did for a living. When Walsh told him she ran one of the classiest brothels in the country, Lionel was devastated. She had seemed such a nice lady.

Professionally, Lionel was struggling. An actor may be on drugs and still manage, as Lionel had in *Sadie Thompson*, a good performance. But a director has to be the first on the lot and the last off: the film is in his hands. And now Lionel was at Columbia at the request of studio chief

Harry Cohn to direct Cohn's new find, Barbara Stanwyck, in *Ten Cents a Dance*. Stanwyck was a businesslike performer who came to a set to work, period. Her director, she discovered, was a zombie. "Do you know how morphine was discovered?" Lionel once asked a friend. "Ah, it's a most interesting story. Serturner named it morphine for Morpheus, the Greek god of sleep. Beautiful, isn't it?" Stanwyck and her leading man Ricardo Cortez did not think it beautiful to have their scenes constantly interrupted by deep, regular breathing. Despite Lionel, the frustrated Stanwyck gave a good performance. "He tried his best," she said. "As a performer, you just had to try harder." To make things worse, the reels were transposed at the premiere, making Lionel look like a total incompetent. He turned grim, "sulked in his tent and hummed funeral marches." He was rescued again by Maury Small, who begged Irving Thalberg to take him back into the MGM fold as an actor before he lost all self-confidence. When *Ten Cents a Dance* was finally shown in sequence it was a hit for Stanwyck, but Lionel was dead as a director, especially since by now there were plenty of directors who had mastered talkies. Lionel's film career was in jeopardy.

AFTER THE PREMIERE of *Moby Dick* and the christening of Dolores Ethel Mae, Jack and Dolores finally escaped for a long voyage on the *Infanta*. Yet the romantic honeymoon atmosphere of the *Mariner* was completely absent. There were several scientists aboard: Jack was intent on bringing back museum specimens, particularly a rare white seal or two. Then there was the baby. She commanded a stateroom with a crib designed with round edges to prevent injury in high seas; the aft deck, which Jack had fenced and netted for a play area; and cold-storage compartments specially designed to preserve supplies of orange juice, milk, baby food, and cod liver oil. She was also attended by a baby specialist and the capable Nurse Smith. Headlines announced JOHN, DOLORES, AND INFANT DAUGHTER SAIL AFTER HERD OF WHITE SEALS ON GUADALUPE ISLAND as though at five months a harpoon was already in the infant Barrymore hand.

The trip was not the escape Jack and Dolores had hoped. In November off the coast of Guatemala his ulcer flared, causing severe gastric hemorrhaging. The baby specialist with the help of a doctor from the mainland pulled him through the attack, but Dolores was terrified. Then in December he had a relapse, reported in the press as a recurring attack of "jungle fever." At that point, the *Infanta* turned her prow northward, her owner confined to his stateroom, Dolores spending the long days in the company of Nurse Smith.

Paradoxically, the illness prepared Jack physically and mentally for his next film, *Svengali*. The alcoholic bloat so evident in *Moby Dick* disappeared with weeks of abstinence and a bland diet. When Jack stepped before the cameras as the Polish Jew who mesmerizes a young girl into becoming a great singer, he was lean and controlled. His performance, blurred in *Moby Dick*, is now in sharp focus. As the dirty, sly, magnetic Svengali Jack transformed himself into the personification of seductive guile—Lucifer as serpent. He allows enough male sexuality to burn through a repellent exterior to attract. The nose is the key. His own long, quivering nose was phallic; Svengali's nose is an exaggeration of that symbol, rapacious and sensual. This time the make-up department succeeded brilliantly. Jack has a sexual power he lacked in glamour roles like Don Juan and the Chevalier des Grieux. He is like a tomcat watching a mousehole; one believes that he can wipe a young girl's mind free of everything but "Svengali, Svengali, Svengali." His final vulnerability—he cannot make Trilby love him—only adds to his fascination.

Still, Hollywood marred the film. Vaudeville lines:

Svengali: "What did we do last?"

Pupil: "Don't you remember?"

Svengali: "I am speaking about music."

A hodgepodge of nationalities: posters in French, Svengali calling girls "Liebchen," Svengali playing a "tallyho" hunt song—where *are* we? And much criticism fell upon the head of Marian Marsh as Trilby, a role immortalized onstage by the radiant Dorothea Baird playing opposite Beerbohm Tree. Yet what could one expect when a seventeen-year-old novice was given the difficult role and then made up to look like a Hollywood starlet rather than a real young woman. Marsh gave Trilby all she had; she just didn't have enough. But none of this, including Bramwell Fletcher's uninspired Little Billie, could detract from Jack's virtuoso performance. In *Svengali* John Barrymore won back all the acting laurels he had lost. Incredibly he was not even nominated for an Academy Award.

It was Lionel who won an Oscar in 1931, Lionel who had seemed washed up, hopelessly overdrugged, incapable of sustained effort. He had mere third billing in *A Free Soul*, but there was a big courtroom scene in which he had to make a long emotional appeal to the jury and then fall dead that provided him with an opportunity for bravura acting. "It was a wonderful, clever, theatrical, extended scene," said Lionel, "almost an entire reel long, and it frightened me as much as the first night of *Macbeth*."

The day the scene was to be shot Lionel arrived on the set in a stupor. He spoke to no one, seemed oblivious, wanted only "to drop into some corner and be forgotten and go to sleep"—but Clarence Brown, the director, was ready. Lionel knew his words, but no one believed he could get through the ordeal. Lionel approached the jury of extras, began to argue quietly, steadily built a crescendo of emotion, at last pulled out all stops. When he finally collapsed, feeling that he actually *was* dying, cheers and bravos burst from the cast and crew. He hadn't heard them for a long time; they sounded very sweet. Yet picking himself up from the floor, he groaned to think of the retakes. "I am sorry to tell you," he told Brown, "I don't think I could possibly do it again." "You don't have to," said Brown who, well aware of Lionel's condition, had shot the scene from eight different angles.

Adela Rogers St. Johns, on whose novel the film was based, had wanted Joan Crawford for the lead, but the role had predictably gone to Norma Shearer, Irving Thalberg's wife and Crawford's chief rival. Shearer was an intelligent actress, yet when studio heads saw the preview they realized that Lionel's performance had upstaged the star. The picture was rushed back to the drawing board: Shearer's part was padded, Lionel's trimmed. In vain. "Norma Shearer may be the star of this film," said the *New York Times*, "but Mr. Barrymore steals whatever honors there may be."

There were other acting honors. Lionel had liked young Clark Gable in the Los Angeles production of *The Copperhead* and had persuaded Gable to let him direct his screen test. Thalberg had deplored Gable's batlike ears, but watching his performance as a hard-mouthed, woman-bashing gangster in *A Free Soul*, he realized that Gable had created a new kind of screen lover. His impact was confirmed by audiences. The brutality of the Great Depression, now in full swing, demanded tough new heroes. The lovers of the twenties—Valentino, John Gilbert, Ramon Novarro, Antonio Moreno—who had made women faint and men gag were passé. They were the kind of actor Jack despised, the kind of actor he had tried not to be: he preferred men's admiration to women's adoration. Now Gable had achieved with relative ease what Jack admired—he pushed women around, and both male and female audiences loved it. Gable reportedly had spent lean Hollywood years hustling in gay bars; now MGM polished his image as a rugged guy. He took up horseback riding, hunting, fishing, high-powered auto driving, and did skeet-shooting with Jack on his range. Ruggedness, as well as dominating women on screen, came more naturally to Gable than to Jack, a far more diffident, sensitive personality.

George Arliss and Shearer, Oscar winners in 1930, presented the 1931 statues to Lionel and Marie Dressler. In a rented dress suit and white tie, sporting a mustache, Lionel was his usual truculent self, acting more as if he were about to be hanged than paid the industry's highest honor. Lionel's performance in *A Free Soul* was very good, yet it was typical of the Academy to reward big and fundamentally sentimental pieces of acting. In *Svengali*, John Barrymore was always subtly ironic. Who was he mocking—himself, the role, the cast, Hollywood? Oscars didn't go to mockers.

WHILE LIONEL AND JACK were collecting critical honors, Ethel made one of those bad decisions people can make when they have done it all and want to try something new. That summer of 1930 she had a play called *Scarlet Sister Mary* with her in England where she was vacationing with Sammy, Jackie, and the properly finished Sister. Between social engagements with Churchill, the du Mauriers, Anthony Hope, and Tallulah Bankhead, who was making a big hit in London, Ethel would go through the script, sometimes with Sister. Still she claimed she was totally unprepared when Sister announced on the boat coming home, "Mother, I don't want to come out. I want to go on the stage. I want to play Seraphine in *Scarlet Sister Mary*."

A thousand emotions assaulted Ethel; she managed to say only, "Are you sure?"

"Oh, yes, I'm sure. I've thought about it a lot."

But *Scarlet Sister Mary* was an unfortunate play for anyone's debut. Ethel had been visited with the awful desire to collect a company of white actors, blacken their faces with cork, Gullahize their speech, and star herself as the young Si May-e. Of course *Show Boat* had been a tremendous Broadway hit, yet some small still voice should have warned Ethel not to attempt blackface or a dialect like "W'en oona duh de-day, duh dee' duh no de-dey."

A glittering and curious first-night audience packed the Ethel Barrymore Theatre on November 25, crowds jostling on the sidewalk, photographers going up and down the aisles flashing bulbs at celebrities. Everyone wanted to see how Queen Ethel would pull off blackface. By the end of the evening the verdict was in: Ethel Waters might have just as successfully played Lady Helen Haddon. Ethel was "amazingly unsuited" to the role, but of her three bad judgments—playing the lead, introducing her daughter in such a vehicle, and recruiting a distinguished white Broadway and London cast—the last was the worst. *Scarlet Sister Mary* lasted thirty-four performances into 1931; on tour the reaction was the same: "Why did Miss Barrymore do it?"

By Chicago Ethel was wondering the same thing. She was infuriated that her entrances were never applauded because audiences didn't recognize her. As the weeks went by she modified her make-up to a high brown, meanwhile refusing to let photographers near her ("God," said Sister, "we weren't able to get ourselves clean for six months!"); she modified also the muddy Gullah dialect. But nothing could make *Scarlet Sister Mary* less than a disaster.

Circumstances now seemed to be gathering like rain clouds about Ethel's regal head. The Great Depression had hit the theatre hard: a play ticket was now a luxury that many of her devoted fans could not afford. Talkies had further thinned theatre audiences. Her age was fatal to many actresses not of her caliber; if not fatal to her, it certainly limited the number of suitable plays available. And it was not pleasant to hear debates about who were to be John's and Ethel Barrymore's successors on Broadway, even when the answer was encouraging.

John's eminence was not yet really threatened, one critic decided: other actors were either too old or too young, too foreign or too domestic, too fat or too dramatically thin. Walter Hampden was a contender, but Hampden lacked John's divine versatility. That left Alfred Lunt, immensely versatile thanks to experimental Theatre Guild productions, yet an actor who still had to attempt Shakespeare, who still had to "fit his bulging personality into so spiritually tight a part as Peter Ibbetson."

As for Ethel, three actresses were knocking at her door. Helen Hayes had charm, Katharine Cornell warmth, Lynn Fontanne style. Yet none of them could draw across America like Ethel Barrymore because "Ethel Barrymore captured her public while that public was still there to be captured. Now it's at the movies. . . . For years she toured the country appearing 'in person' in cities and towns to which flesh-and-blood theatrical troops are now unknown. She made herself remembered and loved in the homes of the nation. . . . There undoubtedly will be other grand ladies, and they may be on the stage, but none of them will replace 'our Ethel' in the sense that she has replaced the great names of the theatrical past." Ethel was not comforted. "Mother's rivals were never discussed in her presence," said Sister.

Ethel now decided to draw on that public, to take *The Love Duel* to the Broadway-forgotten towns of the Midwest, the South, and the Southwest. Sister was not transferred to the cast. It had become clear to her that her mother was not going to help her become an actress because "she could not bear the thought." Sister considered a singing career: at least no one could say she did not sing as well as her mother. But at least one family friend believes that Ethel pushed Sister toward a singing career because she couldn't bear competition. Naturally if it was announced that a Barrymore was going to be a singer, she was as good as one already.

George White engaged Sister to appear that fall in his *Scandals*. She was a disaster, and Ethel Merman was rushed in to replace her.

On the *Love Duel* tour Ethel began to drink again, perhaps because the charming Louis Calhern, very much her "escort" and a heavy drinker himself, gave her the excuse, perhaps because she was lonely and still upset over the failure of *Scarlet Sister Mary*. Fortunately they were seldom both drunk for the same performance. When Ethel was sober and Calhern tight, Ethel would say her lines, then proceed glibly, "And I know what I would say in your position," upon which she would deliver Calhern's reply. He did the same for her. On one unfortunate occasion when they were both drunk nothing much was happening onstage as the two stars stood looking at each other blankly and the voice of the prompter rang through the house. Finally Ethel turned grandly to the wings. "We *know* the line, young man," she said in a loud, clear voice. "We want to know who says it!"

Meanwhile Ethel read and turned down script after script as she desperately searched for a new vehicle. Fewer and fewer plays appealed to her; the new "realism" disgusted her: one of the "dirty words scripts" she returned with the note "Opened by mistake." So she revived *The School for Scandal*, directing herself, using the faithful Georgie to feed her cues. Anne Seymour, related to the Barrymores through the Rankins and Davenports, had the part of Maria. She did not get close to Ethel. "I was terrified of her," said Anne.

Ethel was terrified at the Denver opening. "On her entrance," said Anne, "Miss Barrymore went down on one knee and found she couldn't get up. When she did, she staggered as she walked across the stage. The cues she received made little impression on her. Backstage, between the acts, she was in an absolute panic. 'I've lost my mind,' she told us. 'I can't remember anything!' "

Denver was horrified. "Miss Barrymore first amazed and then utterly shocked her hosts of Denver friends by a bizarre and unorthodox portrayal," said the *Post*. "She took the unusual liberty of making the historic Lady Teazle a more-than-slightly-tipsy character." The news flashed around the country via wire service: Ethel Barrymore had disgraced herself. Everyone knew, of course, about the unfortunate family weakness.

Furious, Ethel wrote the *Post*. A strained ligament in her left leg had capsized her as she attempted a deep curtsy. When she got up she was dazed but thought she could get through the play. There had been other hazards: the long trip from New York, the terrific Denver heat wave, the strain of rehearsals, the high altitude. She was politely disbelieved; a packed house the next night waited for another debacle—in vain. But on the last night of the engagement, Ethel "fainted" onstage. She could not be revived in time, and the last act was played without her.

When Lionel met Ethel in Santa Barbara he took a long look and recommended that she cancel the tour for a week. Like John Drew, Ethel did not let her companies down; instead she sent them with pay on to San Francisco where she would join them after a cruise on Jack's yacht. When she had fallen asleep in her cabin on the *Infanta* the first day out, Jack scoured her luggage. "Winkie," he said, "I'm an old, practiced hand at secreting the stuff, but if Ethel is doing it she's better at it than I am. The only thing I've been able to find is this." He held up several bottles of Bromidia, an over-the-counter remedy for nerves. Members of her company too always claimed never to have seen her take a sip of anything alcoholic, but their loyalty did not mean that Ethel did not drink and that alcohol was not a constant temptation.

She went back east with *School*, playing it at her theatre with McKay Morris as Joseph Surface, Arthur Treacher as Sir Benjamin Backbite, and John Drew Colt as Sir Harry Bumper, then toured. In New Haven a teenager named Spencer Berger, long enamored of all three Barrymores, bought a ticket for the Shubert to see Ethel Barrymore. Having also conspired with the local florist to have flowers delivered to her dressing room, he vowed to capitalize on the expenditure. Backstage he was confronted by Eddie McHugh, who said that Miss Barrymore could not be seen. "But," said Spencer, "I sent her flowers." "So you're the one?" said McHugh doubtfully, looking over his shoulder for a father to appear. Yet he was finally ushered into the presence. Ethel was alone and decided to be charming. Spencer heard himself accepting an invitation to tea in her hotel suite the following day.

She was real, after all; his flowers graced a table. She ordered tea with lots of toast, explaining that she would eat nothing more till after the evening performance. She chatted easily about her own sons and their schools, drawing him out until, after a magical half-hour, she confessed that she must have her nap. She gave him her crescent smile. "Thank you for the flowers," she said in that sobbing voice. "I don't get many flowers anymore."

Or good plays. After *Scandal* there was nothing to do but pull *The Twelve Pound Look* out of mothballs again for vaudeville. She was desperate for money. She had leased an apartment in a brownstone at 128 East Thirty-sixth Street for three years; she treated the landlord as cavalierly as she had Don Marquis, but this landlord was demanding his rent in plain and unamusing terms. So that when Irving Thalberg unexpectedly telephoned to offer her $35,000 to star in a movie with John and Lionel,

Our Lady of Disdain had no choice but to swallow her contempt for Hollywood and accept.

JACK COULD HAVE HAD nothing but contempt for the *Svengali* spin-off Warners next handed him. *The Mad Genius* is a wretched film. Again Jack plays an impresario with an unidentifiable Eastern European accent, but whatever the flaws in his performance it is gold compared to the tin acting of the rest. And then the wonderful Hollywood authenticity: European "ballerinas" looking like chorus girls in possibly the tackiest costumes ever to mar the screen. And the dialogue! Fedor is a Nijinsky of ballet, Nana his cosmopolitan wife; here is what they say:

"That's right, dear. Now come eat your breakfast. . . . Drink your milk and hurry: you'll be a bigger star than you ever were in Berlin."

"Aw, thanks, darling."

"All right, dear."

"Bye, darling."

It just may be the worst scene ever filmed. Jack smokes constantly and nervously throughout the movie, as well he might. At least he has a spectacular death, a long hurtle down a flight of stairs in front of an audience's horrified eyes. Obviously he is delighted to be released from the torture.

As was Warner Brothers. Jack Warner remembered how seven years before he and his brother Sam had gone backstage after *Hamlet*, determined to be the first to bring the Barrymore magic to the screen. John's dressing-room door had opened a couple of inches and a Barrymore eye had appeared.

"You saw the play?"

"Yes," said Sam. "You were marvelous."

"In that case, you two bastards, you've seen enough of me for the day!" and Jack literally shoved them out the stage door.

Unlike Sam, Jack Warner had never been convinced that John Barrymore had played that scene for laughs. But then he had made *Beau Brummel*, so profitable that unpleasant impressions had been dispelled. Still, when they'd signed him for fabulous terms, Jack Warner hadn't realized that Barrymore drank his meals—not until the visit to his Ambassador Hotel bungalow. Then he knew more or less what to expect, that is until John fell in love with Dolores and became a prima donna for both of them. Admitting that Barrymore had given some great performances, Warner Brothers also had to pay attention to arithmetic: Barrymore box-office receipts did not justify his salary. Now Warner

Brothers declined to renew his contract on their old terms, and in 1931 its long association with John Barrymore ended.

Predictably the break inspired waves of rumor: JOHN BARRYMORE QUITTING FILMS FOR GOOD . . . JOHN BARRYMORE SERIOUSLY CONSIDERING RETURN TO STAGE. That perked the ears of theatrical producers still eager for his return. Paul Bonner wanted him for Robert Sherwood's *Acropolis*. Jed Harris was dreaming of a one-night *King Lear* at the Metropolitan Opera house, tickets from $200 to $500. Alexander Pantages offered 50 percent of the gross to tour his circuit in a play of his choice. The Palace offered him $12,500 a week on the vaudeville circuit, $6,500 more than Eddie Cantor was getting. Theresa Helburn naïvely hoped to sign him with the Theatre Guild. Jack's reply to Helburn was his reply to all: MANY THANKS FOR YOUR CHARMING WIRE AM AFRAID THAT THE IMPRESSION THAT I AM ABOUT TO RETURN TO THE THEATRE IS SO FAR MERELY A RUMOR BUT I DEEPLY APPRECIATE YOUR INTEREST.

He could not return. Mortgage payments were due on Tower Road and the *Infanta*. Dolores was pregnant again. He was drinking too heavily. His memory was not what it had been. He was terrified of a live audience. He kept up the pretense, however, that he could go back to the stage whenever he chose. Hollywood was "that dermoid cyst," "Hollywoodus in Latrina," "the flatulent cave of the winds," "this goddam sinkhole of culture." All talk. He was hooked. Death was the only escape. Well, he was trying.

TWENTY-TWO

1932–1934

T AKING A $25,000 CUT per picture, Jack moved to MGM where Irving Thalberg had the happy idea of teaming him with Lionel as gentleman-thief and detective in *Arsène Lupin*. Jack discovered that glamorous, artificial MGM tolerated no greasy beards or nasal accents. "Got a dress suit?" Thalberg asked him. "Well, you'd better trade in your whiskers for one right away, for that's what you're going to wear from now on." Jack Warner would not have dared to talk that way to John Barrymore.

As the light-fingered Duke of Charmerace, Jack looks properly elegant in top hat and gloves. Neither he nor Lionel has to do anything they haven't done before, yet they do it superbly, complementing each other as Jack's eyebrow arches, Lionel's lowers, as Jack scintillates and Lionel growls. Yet there was friction.

On his best behavior for his new employer, Jack had his lines pat; Lionel battled the drugged numbness that had almost washed up his career. "Well, I've learned *my* lines, Lionel," Jack would say, "now you can learn yours." That would make Lionel growl and fume and forget more lines until Jack Conway, the director, would throw down his script crying, "Is there any law against two Barrymores knowing their lines at the same time?" There seemed to be: Lionel would wander from the script, forcing Jack to invent quickly to keep the scene going. "He's changing his lines!" Lionel would roar. "He's giving me the wrong cues!" Jack took the blame.

Then, though Lionel's role was almost as important, there was the glaring discrepancy between their salaries. Lionel earned $2,500 a week with a forty-week guarantee: $100,000 a year compared to Jack's 1931 wages of $460,500. For the six weeks' shooting of *Arsène Lupin*, Lionel earned $15,000, Jack $83,000. Compared to Jack and Dolores, he and Irene lived simply, he complained: no yachts, no mountain estates, just a few valuable paintings and 802 North Roxbury Drive. And indeed Lionel's financial straits would be a mystery if one did not know about Irene's morphia, to which her husband had become partial, and Lionel's cocaine—expensive addictions. Lionel had had to borrow from Jack, repaying him with $150 weekly deductions from his paycheck. He brooded on the inequalities. One day a fellow actor met him shuffling down an MGM byway, scowling blackly. What was wrong, the actor wanted to know.

"I want to know," said Lionel, "how to make some money—some *real* money."

Lionel was an MGM star; the actor laughed. "You do pretty well, don't you?"

"No, I don't. Guess I'll have to change my name to John."

After their successful duet in *Arsène Lupin*, MGM brought Jack and Lionel together again in *Grand Hotel*, a film which also highlighted inequities. Lionel had acted with Garbo in *The Temptress* and *Mata Hari*, in the latter giving a fine performance as a Russian military attaché fatally attracted to the beautiful spy. But as Fredric March remarked, "Co-starring with Garbo hardly constituted an introduction." Now Garbo was cast opposite John in *Grand Hotel*, and suddenly it was the meeting of the gods. On the first day of shooting Jack actually appeared on the set fifteen minutes early so he wouldn't keep the top-billed Garbo waiting. Nine o'clock came and went; Jack fumed: he might have known she would pull rank. Then a prop boy approached. "Miss Garbo has been waiting outside the door since nine o'clock to escort you onto the set. It was an honor she wanted to pay you."

"This is a great day for me," said Garbo in a thick Swedish accent, coming to meet him. "How I have looked forward to working with John Barrymore!"

Jack kissed her hand. "My wife and I think you are the loveliest woman in the world."

They behaved with royal magnanimity. Garbo submitted to publicity stills. She fed him her specially concocted Irak punch for hangovers. She had the crew rearrange furniture so that in their love scene his left profile would be lensward. Garbo's favorite cameraman, William Daniels, was also accommodating.

"How do they light you?" he asked. "How do you want to look?"

"I have no more idea how they light me than I have how they light a firefly's tail," said Jack. "But I know how I want to look. I'm fifty years old and I want to look like Jackie Cooper's grandson." To Daniels's credit he almost allowed Jack to look his age.

Jack repaid Garbo with the greatest gift an actor can bestow: he supported rather than competed with her, speaking with controlled emotion when he tells her he loves her, for example, and turning his face from the camera. For such courtesies as well as whispered assurances like "You are the most entrancing woman in the world," Garbo repaid him by impulsively embracing and kissing him. "You have no idea what it means to me to play opposite so perfect an artist!"

With third-billed Joan Crawford Jack did not stand on ceremony. "John was like Peck's Bad Boy," said Crawford. "He was usually 'hungover' and would appear on the set with a shy appealing quality. He would use four-letter words, then giggle like a little boy. But the play ended the instant the camera started rolling. Then he became beauteous and fiery."

Lionel was very different. "He'd sit hunched in a corner peering over those funny little glasses. He was forever losing his false mustache. We were constantly poking about in corners, peering under the feet of extras, under tables and chairs, hunting the thing. When we'd find it, he'd slap it on his lip without even looking in the mirror, crying impatiently, 'All right, all right, all right, let's go!' As if *we'd* kept *him* waiting." Yet his total simplicity and kindness won her. "Every single day Mr. Lionel Barrymore would say something nice to me. He'd say, 'How are you, baby? I never saw you look so beautiful,' or he'd tell me that I had acted better than any other day that week. I know he didn't mean it, but it was nice to hear. . . ."

The gallant Lionel had his little revenges, however. As in the court scene in *A Free Soul*, he often pulled off a triumph of acting on the first take, making his fellow actors look like amateurs. When the scene inevitably had to be reshot, Lionel somehow lacked fire and conviction. Watching the rushes, the director Edmund Goulding had little choice but to opt for the version in which Lionel had distinguished himself. In some critics' opinion, he stole *Grand Hotel* right out from under Garbo, John, Crawford, and Wallace Beery. Vicki Baum, the book's author, thought Lionel's performance as a work of art the greatest. Those who didn't think it Garbo's picture agreed, though John was also congratulated on lending distinction to what was, after all, a conventional leading man's role.

MGM approached Jack for Garbo's film *Queen Christina* after Garbo vetoed Laurence Olivier's screen test. Jack was eager to do another film with the actress he admired, but Garbo was determined to save her former lover and insisted on John Gilbert. Really it didn't much matter who played Garbo's leading man; she would be at her best in *Camille* with the handsome but weak Robert Taylor. Yet her scenes with John Barrymore in *Grand Hotel* have an inimitable subtlety, grace, and distinction, something she recognized when she eventually described him as "one of the very few who had that divine madness without which a great artist cannot work or live."

ON JUNE 4, 1932, Jack was pacing the corridor of the Cedars of Lebanon Hospital where Dolores was in labor. Under the pathetic delusion that an external event rather than an inner resolve could cure him, he had promised that if a boy were born to him he would give up drinking. Finally a nurse appeared with the glad news. "Thank god!" said Jack, kissing her. "A son!" Instructing Hotchener to arm himself with a pistol against kidnappers, Jack left the hospital "for a few minutes." Hours later he returned drunk. His self-contempt must have been profound.

He now had the son he desired, yet to what was John Barrymore Jr. an heir? Not financial security, certainly. Finding that no life insurance company would touch him, Jack had turned over to Dolores $70,672 in certificates of deposit for his children, yet it was a sum he himself could run through in days. The Barrymore name meant a great deal, yet he had cursed as often as blessed it. An acting career, yet Jack professed only contempt for acting and actors: difficult to wish such a destiny on his son. Perhaps it was the bleak answer to these questions that made Jack drink after the boy's birth harder than ever.

In his next film, *A Bill of Divorcement*, he played father to a young actress fresh from Broadway. Jack immediately invited Katharine Hepburn to his dressing room for "coaching"; the novice could not refuse. Jack met her in his bathrobe with the familiar gleam in his eye, but Hepburn greeted him coolly in her clipped Bryn Mawr accent. "I see," said Jack, "I've made a mistake."

He made a mistake during their very first take together, the recognition scene between the fugitive mental patient and his daughter. Jack came into the family home in hat and raincoat, walked uncertainly to the fireplace, fumbled with some well-remembered pipes while Hepburn gazed at him compassionately with tears in her eyes. When Jack finally turned and registered surprise at seeing her, Hepburn thought with a shock, "That's not very good, he's overdoing it." Jack saw the disappointment in her eyes. When the camera stopped grinding he came over to her, cupped her chin in his hand. "I'd like to do that one again," he told George Cukor, the director, quietly. On the retake his acting shattered her.

David O. Selznick ranked John Barrymore's Hilary Fairfield "the greatest all-time performance on any motion-picture screen." Certainly in Hilary Jack played out many of his own fears: the taint of hereditary madness that he might have passed on to his own child, the disruptiveness of his presence in his own home, the bouts of madness that were like the bouts of drinking, his extreme vulnerability. "You know we mustn't talk about these things," says Hilary as Jack might himself have said. "It isn't safe, I tell you. When I talk I see a black hand reaching up through the floor. You see that widening crack in the floor to catch me by the ankle and drag, drag"—and the actor loses control as he envisions the forces of darkness pulling him down to destruction. A great performance not really appreciated by American audiences, though *A Bill of Divorcement* made Katharine Hepburn a star.

ETHEL HAD BEEN the first Barrymore signed for *Rasputin and the Empress* and insisted on top billing. This raised problems since Jack, after sharing star billing in *Arsène Lupin* and *Grand Hotel*, wanted his name as sole star. Sister and brother held out stubbornly, finally deciding that Thalberg should decide. The final billing was John, Ethel, and Lionel Barrymore—third place had never been in doubt. Still imperative, Ethel insisted that MGM command her services only from June 15 to September 1 with no more than eight weeks' shooting. She had a theatre commitment with Arthur Hopkins that fall; she made it clear that this Hollywood business was only slumming. Terrified of the camera at almost fifty-three, of her first talkie, and of her first film in fourteen years, Ethel collected her three children for the trip to Los Angeles.

Jack had told Ethel to detrain at Pasadena to avoid the press, but since most stars used that ruse the press was waiting. Jack kissed her as shutters clicked, keeping his left profile resolutely toward the cameras, Ethel no less resolutely facing them with a smile, hand on hip. "Get Bill Daniels!" Jack hissed in her ear, Jack's favorite cameraman since he had magically eliminated "the sweetbreads" under his eyes in *Grand Hotel*. Certainly he had need of a good cameraman, thought Ethel, but if his gray hair and weary dissipation shocked her she did not say so.

"What poor son of a bitch is going to direct this picture?" asked Lionel; and indeed MGM milked the phenomenon of three temperamental Barrymores together to the last drop. Well, they *were* difficult: Jack on drink, Lionel on drugs, Ethel on her high horse. She arrived by limousine every day, swept onto the set like Empress Alexandra. Extras went on tiptoe, the crew resigned card playing and profanity for the duration. They had named a new sound camera on the set "Grandma," but Ethel did not know this the day an assistant director called, "Is Grandma ready?" Ethel stopped dead in her tracks, smote the director with a glare that demanded retribution. Explanations were vain; cast and crew tiptoed in wider circles. She subdued Jack. Photographers approached them between scenes where they sat slumped in their chairs. "Show some animation, Mr. Barrymore," ventured a publicist. "Tell Miss Barrymore something."

"*Tell* her something?" said Jack, wagging his eyebrows in horror. "Certainly not. I'll *ask* her something."

From the beginning there was trouble with the script or rather with six scripts, for though this was to be the Film of Films it had yet to be written to anyone's satisfaction. Thalberg wanted Charles MacArthur, vacationing in Hollywood with his wife, Helen Hayes, to write it but, said Thalberg gloomily, "He won't do it."

"I'll make him do it," said Ethel. She descended upon the Hayes-MacArthur bungalow and seized Charlie by the shoulders. "You are going to write *Rasputin*!"

Ducking behind his small wife, MacArthur declined.

"Do you think you're too good to write for the Barrymores?" demanded the Great Lady. "You lazy good-for-nothing Broadway hack, you're going to write *Rasputin* for us or else I'm going to tear this bungalow apart with my bare hands!" And she kicked Charlie smartly in the shins.

Helen Hayes came only to Ethel's pearls, but was feisty. "Charlie, no woman ever talked to you like that. What are you going to do about it?"

Ethel swept a pile of books off a table and grabbed a lamp. "I'll throw this lamp right through the wall!"

"Look out, Charlie! She's going to do it."

"All right, I'll do your damned show," said MacArthur. "What's it about?"

And since Ethel was not only a great reader but had met Czar Nicholas and Alexandra through the Duchess of Sutherland, she told him.

As Rasputin Lionel suffered the application and removal twice a day of a formidable thatch of beard and whiskers that the make-up department copied from 1916 newspaper photographs of the Russian along with the deep-shadowed eyes and lank hair. As usual Lionel disappeared into the character of Rasputin, though he never lost track of what his brother was up to. In one scene when Jack kept laying his hand on Lionel's arm with the obvious intent of upstaging him, Lionel suddenly doubled up, groaning, "I can't do it! I can't go on!" Alarmed, the director, Charles Brabin, told Lionel to go lie down until he recovered. Two hundred souls waited an hour and a half before Brabin telephoned Lionel's dressing room. Lionel was playing the piano and felt fine.

"But why in the world did you leave the set?"

"But didn't you *see?* That brother of mine was stealing my scene!"

Ethel was not impressed with Brabin's forbearance; she wanted to make the bloody picture and go home. "See here, Mayer," she announced one day into a set phone in a voice that could have filled Madison Square Garden, "let's get rid of this Brahbin or Braybin or what's-his-name." Brabin was immediately replaced, at her suggestion, by Richard Boleslavsky, congenial to Ethel as a former member of the Moscow Art Theatre. She was pacified until an émigré Russian imperial court official had the gall to correct her impression of the Czarina. Witheringly, Ethel reminded him that she had known Her Majesty personally.

"*Relax*, Ee-thyl, and enjoy the climate," said Jack, but Ethel did not relax. Terror inspired the hauteur. As a stage actress she overpowered the camera and microphone with her large voice and grand gestures.

"What the hell are you doing?" asked Jack, watching her moan and flail.

"I haven't the faintest idea."

When Lionel told her bluntly that all she had to do was whisper, she took him so literally that at times her heavy breathing was more eloquent than her lines. She never did reconcile herself to the haphazard method of shooting and the commotion on the set, so unnerving that she demanded black flats be erected to shield her more intimate scenes from onlookers. Worst of all was the script, or lack of it. She was handed lines on scraps of paper with no clue as to how they fit into the whole scheme; the next day the lines would be changed. Still she made it clear that at memorizing she was a pro. Handed three pages and told to learn her lines in an hour, she drawled, "I'm expected to take an *hour* to learn three pages? What am I supposed to do, recite it *backwards?*"

Though Ethel had come to Hollywood because she needed money, she was bound to spend it renting P. G. Wodehouse's lavish layout on Benedict Canyon Road. When she came home from a day's shooting she could hear the children's laughter coming from the tennis courts or garden, though she was too tired to join them. To get more Barrymores into *Rasputin*, MGM had offered her trio three silly parts that they had contemptuously refused. At least Sammy, now twenty-two, had begun to draw $2,500 annually from his trust fund; he also had been got a little work at a studio, though he didn't seem to know exactly what. Handsome Jackie was an instant hit with all the young women, Sammy with the older. All three Colts were amply amused.

Occasionally Ethel amused herself: a lavish party at the Contessa Dorothy di Frasso's, an intimate dinner at George Cukor's, a party at Tallulah's. Garbo came to one of Tallulah's soirees, startling Ethel with her beauty, though it was Ethel who offered her hand, Garbo who diffidently took it. Effortlessly, Ethel was always *the* presence in any room, drawing people out as though they had walked onto a stage without a script and she was feeding them their lines. Now Garbo literally sat at her feet with the other guests and let herself be magnetized. When both Ethel and Jack were guests one evening at Pickfair, however, "the experience was comparable," said Douglas Fairbanks, "to trying out airplane motors in a drawing room."

Russell Colt came out for the Olympic Games. Ethel had taken Russell back as an occasional dinner companion, a testimony to her loneliness but also to the mutual interests they had rediscovered after the divorce. Yet he could still hurt her. His second wife, Gwendolyn Moran, had a son of eleven.

"Have *you* ever known an eleven-year-old boy?" asked Russell.

"Yes. Two."

"Who?"

"Sammy and Jackie Colt," said Ethel evenly. He had forgotten all about them.

They went to the opening Olympic March of Nations where she was curiously impressed by the black-clad Italians who threw up their arms in the Fascist salute as they passed the presidential box. Somehow she was reminded of the crowd at a recent motion picture premiere. She'd been told how the big stars' cars were always applauded as they drove up, but there had been no applause this time as the crowd stared at the furs and jewels and limousines, only a sullen silence that frightened her, as though in spite of the sunshine and the glamour, dark forces were stirring in the land.

Rasputin dragged on into September, Ethel spending every cent she was earning and more: at one point MGM advanced her $3,000 against her next paycheck; she would make $57,500 from the movie but incur expenses of $65,482. The longer she played Alexandra the more imperial she became, ordering that all set calls be given to her maid, Anne Patterson, because she refused to be disturbed. Attempts to deliver dialogue to her home evenings were repulsed: she could *not* learn dialogue after dinner, she would *not* get up at the crack of dawn. Occasionally some MGM unfortunate got Miss Barrymore on the phone in person.

"Now listen," said Her Highness. "I'm at home listening to the World Series and it's far more interesting than anything MGM ever did. And I'm not coming down until I'm good and ready!"

In October her scenes were finally in the can. Despite the ballyhooed reunion of America's Royal Family of Actors, filming *Rasputin* had not been a pleasure. Lionel was always holed up in his dressing room, etching or composing at the piano. Jack was busy trying to seduce the young actress Jean Parker or getting drunk and keeping the huge cast and crew waiting. The change in him since *Svengali* was shocking: he was bloated, so corseted into his prince's uniform that he could not sit down between takes. "If I find that drinking is doing something harsh to my features," Jack had boasted to Monty Flagg, "I can stop—just like that!" He couldn't. All the kohl, lipstick, and camera wizardry in the world could not disguise the dissipation of the once ascetic face, a dissipation only underlined by the studio's attempt to reconstruct with lights, filters, and make-up a spiritual beauty that had been corrupted. Unlike Dorian Gray, Jack had no secret portrait after all.

Off the set the Barrymores had seen each other seldom. There was a famous photography session in Ethel's garden, Ethel center stage in a huge rattan chair, Lionel and Irene occupied with baby John to her right, Dolores and Sister with Dede to her left, her three bad boys—Jackie, Jack, and Sammy—lurking behind her chair. There was an afternoon party at Tower Road which a reporter from *Modern Screen* was allowed to attend. Lionel held the baby and gurgled and cooed at it. "Got to be careful about baby's eyes!" he insisted, shielding the tiny face with his straw hat. But little John's nurse was there to see to all that. As the sun dropped behind the cypresses they all trooped inside. "Got anything new?" said Lionel, studying Jack's shelves. Jack pointed to a couple of volumes and Lionel promptly immersed himself in literature. *Modern Screen* noted that Dede called both Lionel and Irene "Uncle Lionel" and that the Colt boys were interested in Jack's trophy room. There didn't seem to be much more to say.

"Of course there was no truth in the nonsensical publicity stories about quarrels between us," said Ethel. No: they did not know each other well enough to quarrel; they had, with a few lapses, been frighteningly polite. Back east, she gave out scornful interviews about Hollywood, "her first vacation in fifteen years." "You work about two minutes, then go to your dressing room and read a detective novel," she laughed. As for the community: "The people are unreal. The flowers are unreal: they don't smell. The fruit is unreal, it doesn't taste of anything. The place hasn't been thought in. There is no sediment of thought there. The whole place is a glaring, gaudy, nightmarish set, built up in the desert. It looks, it feels, as though it had been invented by a Sixth Avenue peep-show man. Come to think of it, it probably was." Well, LAH-de-dah, thought Jack and Lionel.

Like so many big, ballyhooed, overbudget blockbusters, *Rasputin and the Empress* was not a runaway success. Critics were divided: "Barnum, Bailey, and Barrymore," said some, yet *Film Daily*'s 1933 poll put it in the top ten. In 1975 *The New Yorker* decided that in *Rasputin* all three Barrymores were at their absolute worst; others thought that the writing of the picture prevented the Barrymores—had they been supported by Mummum, John Drew, and John Jr. as the Tsarevitch—from making anything of the muddle. In the event, *Rasputin and the Empress* was a financial disaster for MGM. True to Ethel's prediction, the Yousoupovs took umbrage at the film's handling of Rasputin's murder, and MGM had to pay almost a million-dollar libel award.

No one analyzed how the trio acted together, yet their technique was simple. Resolved: if I—John or Ethel—do not look at my sibling then the audience won't either. Ethel keeps her eyes so resolutely downcast throughout the film that she might be a blushing maiden rather than Empress of All the Russias. Not all Lionel's cajoling or John's assurances can lift those huge orbs to their faces; when she does deign to glance at them briefly, she does something distracting like rotating a large picture hat in her hands. John is even more adept at the game. In the long "I know my destiny" scene, Lionel as Rasputin is forced to orate the whole time to John's back as John poses on a table, cocks his leg, plays with his sword, and keeps his face so militantly toward the camera that finally the scene must be construed not as a confrontation between Rasputin and Prince Chegodieff but as Mike pleading with Jake to for Christ's sake give him a break and look at him. But then Lionel gets his revenge by playing with his long wavy beard so determinedly throughout the film that it becomes a fourth Barrymore.

Ethel looks beautiful. Her vowels are as long as words and her cadences have a fainting fall. Thanks to Lionel's instructions to whisper, she is very subdued, yet one graceful movement of her hand as she leaves her sick son's chamber may be worth the whole movie. And yet Lionel plays a wonderful Mad Monk, even though one wonders after *Svengali* what Jack could have made of the part. Lionel's Rasputin is filthy in mind, body, and habit, making Alexandra's acceptance of his charlatanism all the more tragic. And his prolonged death at Prince Chegodieff's hands is masterly—even though the camera is Jack's friend in the struggle, not his.

Ethel never saw the film until it appeared on television in the fifties; then she telephoned George Cukor to say that she rather liked it. "My, my," she added, "and wasn't Lionel naughty?" She meant that Lionel had stolen the show; and, in fact, *Rasputin and the Empress* is Lionel's film from beginning to end. Ethel and Jack were too busy ignoring each other.

MGM thought Ethel had been naughty. Eight days before the New York premiere of *Rasputin and the Empress* on December 23, 1932, the option on her contract for two more pictures at $40,000 and $45,000 came due. Louis B. Mayer handed down the word: do not exercise.

HAD ETHEL KNOWN what grim years lay ahead she may have regretted alienating Hollywood, though it had taught her how emphatically her place was in the theatre. Or was it. Introduced at a luncheon for the Boston Professional Women's Club as "a member of the Royal Family of Broadway," Ethel had bridled. She was not "of Broadway," she informed her audience. Broadway produced "only bilge water by the scum of the earth."

Poor frightened Ethel. In these years Broadway sizzled with talent. Alla Nazimova in *A Month in the Country* and *Mourning Becomes Electra*. Lunt and Fontanne in *Elizabeth the Queen*. Noel Coward and Gertrude Lawrence in *Private Lives*. Katharine Cornell in *The Barretts of Wimpole Street*. Lunt and Fontanne in *Reunion in Vienna*. Paul Muni in *Counsellor-at-Law*. Conway Tearle and Constance Collier in *Dinner at Eight*. Ina Claire in *Biography*. Humphrey Bogart and Maureen Sullivan in *Chrysalis*. Katharine Cornell and Brian Aherne in *Lucrece*. Raymond Massey in *Hamlet*. Edith Evans in *The Lady with the Lamp*. Just ahead were *The Children's Hour*, *Dodsworth*, *Romeo and Juliet* with Cornell and Basil Rathbone, *Winterset*, Judith Anderson in Zoë Akins's *The Old Maid*, Lunt and Fontanne in *The Taming of the Shrew*, Nazimova in *Ghosts*, Leslie Howard in *The Petrified Forest*, and Helen Hayes in *Victoria Regina*. Where did Ethel Barrymore, a star since 1901, belong in this exciting surge of theatrical vitality?

Just nowhere. Her vaunted engagement with Arthur Hopkins proved to be a weak play called *Encore*. Ethel thought it funny: an opera singer gets younger and younger as she marries and remarries, finally marching down the aisle in a child's white organdy and blue sash. *Encore* opened in New Haven with a rough performance and Ethel obviously suffering from a cold. Subsequent performances were canceled, as was the Providence engagement; the Broadway opening was postponed indefinitely. But then, Ethel didn't trust Broadway any longer.

Instead she set out with it cross-country, at every point reminded of the sullen crowds that had frightened her at the Hollywood premiere. Times were bad and getting worse: people using scrip for money, lines at soup kitchens stretching around the block. The day after Christmas she wired a shoestring producer named Chamberlain Brown (she who had been Frohman's star) that she would do his play *Mrs. Moonlight* for

$500 a week and traveling expenses for her maid; he wouldn't pay it. In March the newly inaugurated Franklin Delano Roosevelt declared a "Bank Holiday," closing institutions nationwide, at which point Hopkins washed his hands of the tour. Ethel's response was to change the name *Encore* to *An Amazing Career* and manage it herself. She announced an opening March 15 in Springfield, Massachusetts, preparatory to coming into New York. She did not get east. In May Chicago greeted *An Amazing Career* tepidly, though Miss Barrymore looked ravishing and Josephine Hull shone in a minor role. The tour folded shortly after, and five cast members filed claim with Actors Equity for unpaid salary. On March 4 Roosevelt had gone on national radio to tell the American people, "The only thing we have to fear is fear itself." Ethel was afraid.

Back in New York she had her own Delano, William Adams Delano, to whom she owed rent for the apartment she had leased since 1930 at $4,500 a year. She could not pay him; she packed her belongings, had the company collect the rented piano, and fled to Mamaroneck where taxes, upkeep, and a staff of servants continued to bleed her. When Delano sued for $4,437 she could pay only $1,000. No wonder that she herself was brought to suing Chamberlain Brown for a paltry $276.90 that summer when the only theatre work she could find was stock in *The Constant Wife*. (Brown's check bounced at the bank.) Nineteen thirty-three was the first year since 1894 that she did not appear either in New York or London or tour with a Broadway play. Her title "First Lady of the American Theatre" seemed a mockery.

Desperate, she dusted off *The Twelve Pound Look* for the Capitol in New York. In the past she had performed twice a day with other live acts; now she had a four-times-daily stint sandwiched between the movie *Storm at Daybreak* and short subjects featuring a jazz band and a kangaroo. The faithful Georgie and Eddie McHugh supported her in this weird limbo in which theirs was the only live act among the talking shadows. Because she was, after all, Ethel Barrymore, the *World* sent a reporter to cover the event. "You admire her for it," he wrote. "You admire her in spite of this, of that, and of the other thing."

This was as close as the press got to saying the unsayable: Miss Barrymore had taken to the bottle again. Jack could publicly boast that he had to leave the stage in *Hamlet* to vomit into the wings; for a lady to drink was—déclassée. Ethel refused to act déclassée, though she was reduced during her Capitol appearance to living in a third-rate hotel on upper Broadway. She did not apologize, though she gave the Algonquin as her address and met people there. A brandy bottle began to go everywhere with her.

"We took a house in Connecticut in 1933 . . . ," said Ruth Gordon, "and Ethel once came to visit us there. She seemed strange to me in her manner, and [Jacques] noticed it too and said to me privately, 'She's drinking.' 'You're crazy,' I told him, for I had never seen her do more than sip at something placed in her hand at a party. But we noticed how frequently she went upstairs to her room. I decided to search the room and finally I found the brandy bottle she had hidden."

But it was not necessarily the bottle speaking when at the end of this frustrating year Ethel suddenly lashed out at the citizens of her own Philadelphia. Eva Le Gallienne had failed to appear for a lecture there; when she rescheduled, she brought Ethel with her. Le Gallienne discovered that the crowd who had waited a few days ago to hear her felt decidedly cheated. With Ethel listening in the front row, Le Gallienne defended herself as someone who had never broken a professional engagement in twenty years in the theatre, then went on to speak feelingly of having worked with Ethel Barrymore in the past and to outline her plans for a National Repertory Theatre. Then suddenly she said, "I have a big surprise for you. I have asked Ethel Barrymore to come here with me, and she will say a few words."

Surprise indeed. Ethel rose, trembling with fury even during the burst of applause. "I don't see why we bother to speak to you at all," she said, her voice rough with emotion as she glared at the audience of society women. "Miss Le Gallienne and I do you an honor to be here. You don't know anything. You don't understand anything. You don't appreciate anything. You never have known anything and you never will.

"I found this child," she continued, looking at Eva. "She has done more for the American stage than anyone else in the world. And yet you dare criticize her, a woman of her intelligence, because she doesn't appear at some meeting or other that she doesn't know anything about.

"I have given thirty-five years of my life to the theatre. Pffft! What difference does it make? I don't know why we do it, we get no thanks. My grandmother had a theatre here in Philadelphia—in the days when people still had manners. Yes, it's been written about in books. But then you wouldn't know anything about that. It doesn't matter. What's the difference?

"You should be happy to come here two or three times in order to hear Miss Le Gallienne once. I think Miss Le Gallienne does you an honor. I don't know why. I don't know why anyone should honor you. You do not come to see my plays. . . ."

Uproar. But the translation of Ethel's outburst is simple: "I am unemployed, I am unemployed, I am unemployed. How could you forsake me?"

During these years her old friend Ashton Stevens had innocently regaled her with a story about Mrs. Patrick Campbell, the once proud beauty of the English stage. Mrs. Pat had had a suitor who pursued her in vain for years. One day the man, now a wealthy widower living in Florence, had read her name in the English papers. The old passion stirred. Impulsively he traveled to London, hired an open Rolls-Royce, loaded the back seat with orchids, and drove unannounced to the theatre. But when Mrs. Pat appeared onstage his heart sank. She was old, she was fat—and he was cured. He left the flowers and the theatre before the first curtain. He wished he had not seen her that way, and he never wanted to see her again.

Stevens stopped. Ethel's eyes were brimming with tears. "Never tell that story again," she said, her voice husky with pain, "to an actress over forty."

Adding insult to her real professional injuries, the IRS now dunned her for 1921–1929 income taxes. Examining her affairs, they found only a minimal bank balance, no safe-deposit box, no securities, no real estate, no household articles or anything that could be converted into cash except a pencil portrait by Sargent valued at $5,000. She was living with her three children, one of whom was supporting her on an inheritance from his grandfather. Ethel now turned to the brother she had helped "a thousand times out of a thousand":

> Dearest Jake—
> Will you be an angel and lend me quite a big sum. . . . I will ask for $25,000—I know it sounds fantastic but my state is fantastic. I have a chance of going to London and sort of starting all over again—but I have to set my house in order here. . . . Oh Jake—I don't want to be maudlin . . . don't think I don't realize about your family and everything—I am going to have my life insured tomorrow which will cover this loan—in case I die—before I can pay it back, but please help me get away from this dreadful palace [sic]—You know how humble I feel when I am afraid you don't like me any more & still I am doing it . . . and I can't ask anybody else and I will promise to pay you back soon—will you send me a wire and relieve my mind—

No record survives of Jack's response, only rumor that he did not send money. Ethel's arrogance about Hollywood had driven a wedge between them. Jack knew in any case how much his leaving the theatre had hurt her; convinced now that he could never "live up," he had withdrawn. In years to come, from a sense of guilt and resentment, he would avoid her.

In the event, Ethel's starting over again in London meant only doing what she had done since 1912—playing *The Twelve Pound Look* in vaudeville. She tried to take courage: she had Nigel Playfair and Beatrice Terry, two good English actors, to support her, she was bringing them their own Barrie. And London had once loved her.

She was featured at the Palladium with Roy Fox's Kit Cat Band, Max Miller the "Cheekie Chappie," sixteen Palladium girls, and Billy Russell "on behalf of the working classes." She came on to a wonderfully warm burst of applause; then, as soon as she began to speak, the audience realized that she was stone drunk. She mumbled and muffed as she wove unsteadily across the stage, inaudible beyond the first few rows. Vaudeville audiences react quickly to what they interpret as a performer's lack of respect for them. There were boos and shouts from the gallery, and when the curtain finally came down to whistles and catcalls it did not rise again. Though the press as a rule gallantly ignored the disgrace, one paper noted, "Her Palladium turn was removed to make way for a dog act."

Ethel defiantly saw a few friends, motored down to Chartwell to visit Churchill. He was currently out of power, and her bruised heart swelled with sympathy for this brilliant leader, "a voice crying in the wilderness" against the feeble temporizings of a Ramsay MacDonald who thought that Hitler could be appeased by soft answers. Meanwhile at a small but exclusive hotel she was running up a bill she could not possibly pay. Douglas Fairbanks Jr., a friend and admirer of the Barrymores, had been in the Palladium audience that night; he now discovered her plight. Marshaling Ethel's London friends, he suggested they all chip in to deposit money anonymously in her bank account. Suddenly Ethel discovered she had "stupidly misunderstood" her bank balance. Liberated (and apparently unquestioning), she sailed home on the *Berengaria*.

And now there was nothing to do but wait out the summer at Mamaroneck hoping for a play; she was too discouraged to take *The Twelve Pound Look* into summer vaudeville again. She paced the rooms like a caged tigress; she drank. Her children learned that much as work had robbed them of a mother, mother out of work was a scourge.

FOR JACK THE YEAR 1933 was artistically profitable as he actually made five superior films in a row: *Topaze, Reunion in Vienna, Dinner at Eight, Night Flight*, and *Counsellor-at-Law*. His diffident charm too seldom emerged on screen, but it did in *Topaze* in his portrayal of an ingenuous middle-aged professor with a pince-nez who is duped into lending his name to a spurious health drink called "Sparkling Topaze." Refreshingly, Jack neither makes a pass at nor kisses a woman in the whole film; refreshingly, he is neither stuffed into a tight uniform nor profiled on the screen. His performance is subtle, nuanced, and beautifully controlled. Myrna Loy is smashing as the exploitative tycoon's mistress Coco. *Topaze* is a jewel.

He returned from RKO to MGM for *Reunion in Vienna*, the Robert Sherwood play in which Lunt and Fontanne had dazzled Broadway in 1931. As the deposed Archduke Rudolf von Hapsburg, Jack expertly runs a gamut of emotions from narcissism to humiliation, but the sparkling, sophisticated comedy bombed in Dubuque and with Depression audiences everywhere. Jack's contract with MGM was now up. The studio felt disinclined to renew.

Selznick saved him, Selznick who, as Louis B. Mayer's son-in-law, was successfully challenging Irving Thalberg, the boy wonder of MGM. There had been personal and artistic enmity between Mayer and Thalberg; now Mayer offered Selznick a contract that gave him first choice of the studio's vaunted stable of stars. Selznick considered John Barrymore still one of these and particularly suited to the role of Larry Reynault, a washed-up alcoholic actor in *Dinner at Eight*. In this play Kaufman and Ferber had pushed their Tony Cavendish of *The Royal Family* to the end of his rope. It was not a kind assignment.

Fortunately the theatre-and-Barrymore-experienced George Cukor was assigned to direct, yet even Cukor did not prevent the character of Larry Reynault from merging with the public John Barrymore. There are references to Reynault's "divine profile," Jack is profiled in his first shot, we are treated to his famous *Hamlet* photograph in profile. Like Jack, Reynault has had three wives. Like Jack, Reynault drinks himself stiff. Finally his manager tells him, "You know, you never were an actor. You did have looks. But they're gone now. You don't have to take my word for it. Just look in any mirror. They don't lie. Take a good look. Look at those pouches under your eyes. Look at those creases. You sag like an old woman. Get a load of yourself! Wait till you start tramping around to the offices looking for a job because you know no agent is gonna handle you. Sitting in those anterooms, hour after hour, giving your name to office boys that never even heard of you. You're through, Reynault. You're through in pictures and plays and vaudeville and radio and everything. You're a corpse and ya don't know it. Go get yourself buried."

Though blessed with a mordant sense of humor, Jack still had to find a way to deal with this double. He decided to play Reynault as a combination Maurice Costello, Lowell Sherman, and himself. He made Reynault, unlike John Barrymore, second-rate, misquoting Oswald's "Mother . . . give me the sun" in *Ghosts* as "Mother dear, give me the moon." And he stage-managed Reynault's death. Cukor wanted him to die in "an ugly, middle-aged awkward sprawl"; Jack did not agree. As it was finally played, Reynault dons a white tie and dinner jacket. He preens in the mirror. He turns on the gas. He composes himself in a chair and trains a reading lamp on his face. He smooths his hair, then leans back, presenting his profile to the spotlight. In death he recaptures his youthful beauty— another transformation.

With a Depression-licking cast that included Marie Dressler, Jean Harlow, Wallace Beery, Billie Burke, and Lionel Barrymore, *Dinner at Eight* was a hit. But the film did not do Jack much good, professionally or psychically. There was a real chance that mocking himself might become his only role.

Cukor had found Jack open, flexible and, curiously, very gentle; Clarence Brown, the director of *Night Flight*, did not, and Selznick was forced to intervene. Jack had refused to give MGM additional shots for the British version of *Dinner at Eight*. Now, said Selznick, MGM should demand those free shots "as compensation for Barrymore's drunkenness today, resulting in our inability to shoot on *Night Flight*. Mr. Hotchener and Barrymore have been so ungenerous about conceding any points that there is no occasion for us to be generous about the matter." Clarence Brown was so fed up, in fact, that he was ready to use an unknown actor in Jack's role rather than put up with his behavior; Selznick was ready to go along with any action Louis B. Mayer decreed, to the extent of discharging Barrymore and suing him for damages.

Fortunately for Jack, Mayer was disposed to be generous since this was the actor's "first serious offense." This *was* generous, for Jack despised Mayer as he did all Hollywood brass with talent for making nothing but money. "Don't you shake that finger at me," he'd sneered at one Jewish mogul; "I remember when it had a thimble on it." Lionel mollified Mayer; Jack, though he knew he was cutting his own throat, brushed him aside. This did not endear him to the chief any more than his sailing away on the *Infanta* that August when he was supposed to be doing retakes endeared him to the harassed Clarence Brown.

Lionel appeased Mayer, but then Mayer controlled Lionel, and both knew it. During the panic set off by Roosevelt's Bank Holiday, MGM had called a meeting to ask its employees to take a 50 percent cut in salary. Lionel was among the stars, directors, writers, and department chiefs who waited for Mayer to address them. Mayer fancied himself an actor; once, portraying a weeping mother, he had fallen on his knees before Lionel and covered his hands with kisses. ("Good God!" said Lionel.) Now Mayer entered, red-eyed and unshaven. "My friends," he began, then broke down, raising his hands in supplication.

It was Lionel who broke the silence. "We all know why we are here," he said huskily. "Don't worry, L.B. We're with you." Emotionally, he declared himself ready to take the cut, urging other MGM employees to follow suit "for the good of MGM, of Hollywood, and of the country."

The screenwriter Ernst Vajda was not buying the company line. "I read the company statements, Mr. Mayer," he said. "I know our films are doing well. [They were: MGM was the only studio not to lose money during the Depression.] Maybe these other companies must do this, but this company should not. Let's wait; there's no reason to cut our pay at this time."

Then Lionel rose and pointed dramatically at Vajda. "Sir," he rumbled in his sonorous, stage-trained voice that sent shivers of apprehension down spines, "you are acting like a man on his way to the guillotine who wants to stop for a manicure."

The group broke into laughter and applause. Mayer beamed, having—thanks to Lionel—won the day. A broke actor is a cowardly actor, and now Lionel's perennial embarrassments were compounded by the fact that after years of drastic anorexic dieting and medicating, Irene was seriously ill.

So Lionel was safe at MGM, but when Jack returned from his cruise with Dolores and the children he found that the studio had no work for him. The market, Selznick had decided, was so flooded with Barrymore pictures that "we should not permit an additional one." First Warners, now MGM. Thalberg at least had had regrets.

With head unbowed, Jack went to Universal to make *Counsellor-at-Law*. Elmer Rice, author and screenwriter, didn't think Jack with his overbred collie face right for the part of the Jewish lawyer George Simon; Universal had wanted Paul Muni to repeat his stage success, but Muni refused to be typecast as a Jewish actor. Only the young director William Wyler was enthusiastic about Jack, a feeling Jack returned as he put his arm around Wyler. "You and I are going to get along fine, you know," he said. "Don't worry about all the temperamental stuff you've heard about the Barrymores. It all comes from my sister, and she's full of shit."

Universal had offered Jack a handsome $25,000 a week, with the catch that he was allowed only two weeks to film a part not only "longer than the Old Testament" but delivered at lightning speed. "It was mad," said Wyler. "In every scene, I shot only Barrymore, skipping close-ups of anybody talking to him for later. It's a terrible way to make a picture." Contrasted with the careful nurturing Arthur Hopkins had given a Barrymore production, *Counsellor-at-Law* illustrated the price that mass entertainment extracts from its actors. Jack's fast, abrasive, angry, and very moving performance reflects the harassment he suffered while filming it even as it testifies to the histrionic powers of an almost-finished actor.

For although he would live nine years more, Jack had imperceptibly drifted across the line. Margaret Carrington and Robert Edmond Jones, now her husband, came to Hollywood to supervise Jack in a film test for a Technicolor *Hamlet* financed by the multimillionaire board chairman of Selznick International Pictures, John Hay Whitney. All these Hollywood years Jack had recited *Hamlet* at the drop of a hat, clinging to his former triumph as to a rock in fast current. Now he pulled tights over thin legs. His face sagged, his thin mustache and the lipstick with which make-up men continued to afflict him made him look like an aging dilettante. He was twenty years too old (onstage not fatal), yet his resonant voice still imbued the lines with the clarity that had enchanted the public eleven years before. When he could remember them. Time and again the cameras had to stop while he groped for the once familiar words. "God knows I've said them onstage hundreds of times with no trouble," he cried to Margaret Carrington. Obviously there could be no *Hamlet* film nor stage *Hamlet* either, though in October of that year came the now pathetic announcement that John Barrymore would play *Hamlet* in the Hollywood Bowl early in 1934.

Margaret had really come to Hollywood to ask Jack to come back to the theatre, to return to build a real Barrymore theatre where he, Lionel, and Ethel would act singly or together. But when she "climbed the hill to his house and saw how he lived in the sunshine," saw the beautiful Dolores and the two beautiful children, her heart sank and she knew she had come on a lost cause.

But it wasn't Tower Road and Dolores and the children and the California sunshine that made Jack a lost cause. After all the energy and money he had poured into his estate, he remembered Mrs. Nicholls's top floor as the last home he had ever known. His marriage to his madonna was the disaster the others had been: Dolores was only human. His children gave him neither joy nor peace nor the will to stop drinking; he was almost the stranger to them that he was to Diana. Owning the largest dinosaur egg in the world outside a museum didn't make him happy, nor did his fabulous gun collection nor even his rare first editions. In the rathskeller he had intended for happy evenings he sat alone night after night drinking himself into insensibility. Had he ever feared that Hopkins, Carrington, and Jones might lure him back to the theatre, he had taken precautions to make that return impossible. During the filming of *Night Flight*, Helen Hayes had told him he had an obligation to return to the stage. Jack had turned deathly white. "I've completely lost my nerve," he told her. "I could never appear before an audience again." It was tragically true.

Were even films possible? Jack was called back to Universal for more shooting on *Counsellor-at-Law*. He'd had two glasses of beer that day (that Hotchener knew of), but he was tired. The scene called for a long speech, a response from the actor John Qualen, a short reply from Jack. He tripped over the short reply, made a face, and got laughs. The cameras ground again, Jack came to the reply and stumbled again. No laughs. He tried it again and blanked. He became furious, throwing Qualen off his lines. He flubbed again. He began to sweat. After twenty-five takes, Wyler called it quits. But John Barrymore was a marked man from that day. "If they say you drink," said the actress Laurette Taylor, "or take dope, you can get over it. But when they say you're forgetting your lines, you're *finished*." No wonder that Jack began more and more to feign drunkenness to cover his mental confusion. Better to be thought a drunk than senile.

Years later Lionel confided to John Huston that he dated Jack's decline from the day he brought back a totem pole from Alaska and installed it atop his mountain retreat. Up until then, said Lionel, Jack could do no wrong; then his luck turned bad. Obviously some Eskimo god had hexed him. Jack had brought back the totem pole the summer of 1931, the year Warners did not renew his contract. Yet Jack had gone on to do brilliant work at MGM and RKO.

Impossible to pinpoint precisely when Jack turned the corner because it was a big bend, not to say bender. It had to do not only with the personal matter of his drinking and memory loss, but with the gradual impingement on the public mind that John Barrymore was a drunk. At first there were arbitrary scenes such as that in *Tempest*, for example, when Jack gets tight on champagne for no good reason. In *The Man from Blankley's* Jack was drunk as part of the plot. Yet why make Ahab a drunk in *Moby Dick*? Then came *State's Attorney* in 1932. Although Jack plays a candidate for governor, he is drunk in the first scene and tosses down drinks so steadily from then on that he is obviously acting not Tom Cardigan but John Barrymore in his usual condition. In the twenties and thirties alcoholism was not considered an illness. The alcoholic might be admired as a witty drunk, or dismissed as pathetic or disgusting—often fatal to the image of a star. And as alcohol steadily ravaged the celebrated face and body, Jack looked like a heavy drinker even in clean roles like Prince Chegodieff. Finally in *Dinner at Eight* role and actor merged. Though Cukor's skillful directing and Jack's ironic approach to Larry Reynault prevented simple parody, *Dinner at Eight* could well have fixed it in the public's and MGM's mind that John Barrymore was a drunken has-been.

Thus in 1934, a year after a magazine biography extolling "Those Incredible Barrymores" had regaled readers with the glamour of their lives, the Barrymore future looked bleak. Lionel broke and desperate over Irene's illness and his own addiction. Ethel out of work. Jack's marriage over in all but fact, his reputation as a reliable actor in shreds. The Barrymores may have denied they were close, but they were suffering together, symbiotically, the worst crisis of their lives.

TWENTY-THREE

1933–1935

ABOUT THIS TIME Laurette Taylor was trying to negotiate with George Cukor to film *The Harp of Life*, one of her husband's plays. She wanted John Barrymore, refusing Lionel because "Lionel isn't as good an actor as John—now." Laurette's and John's careers parallel each other eerily. The formula "Artists to give their best to their creations should be born without a sense of self-preservation" describes them both. Each appeared comparatively seldom on the stage, both had a magical appeal when they did, each was extraordinarily vulnerable and self-destructive. Woollcott thought their positions identical for the identical reason: Laurette was denied the title of foremost actress of the day only because, like John Barrymore, the torment of her personal life almost wrecked her professional. Actresses like Helen Hayes, Ruth Gordon, and Tallulah Bankhead, however, believed Laurette Taylor *was* the greatest actress of her day. Ethel, a close friend of Laurette and her husband J. Hartley Manners, agreed: "I have simply never seen anyone like her on the stage. What she did was indescribable."

Like Laurette, Jack did terrible things to those who loved him. Laurette's daughter Marguerite has described "the featureless terrain of alcohol that asks no effort, harbors no loves, spurns those who come with love to help. . . . When it comes into a home everything goes, love, affection, loyalty, all decent human feeling—it leaves nothing. That is its terrible curse." For five years now Dolores had borne the torrents of suspicion and abuse, the arguments ended only by Jack's passing out, the nights alone and awake in bed, the abject morning-after apologies as she sobbed that she was leaving him.

Amazing that he could continue to make films, and yet his 1,000-volt vitality had always helped him stage impossible comebacks. His next two films scored a low and a high. In *Long Lost Father*, his first B, Jack worked with a second-rate cast and fourth-rate story (but a good director, Ernest

Schoedsack, unhappy with the assignment) and airily pretended not to know he was slumming.

He wanted better things. He had recently been a guest at a luncheon for Bernard Shaw during the playwright's brief touchdown in Hollywood. Despite the *Hamlet* letter they had been civil, and now Jack wrote him that he would love to do a movie of *The Devil's Disciple*—it was one play, thought Jack, in which Shaw did not build up a male character, then, like an Indian-giver, snatch the drama away from the man and throw it to the woman. Years before, Shaw had wanted all three Barrymores for *The Devil's Disciple*; he wanted Jack now, but as usual was more concerned about protecting his play than casting it. The RKO script confirmed his worst suspicions about Hollywood. "It can't find the spiritual *track* of a story and keep to it," he wrote Jack. ". . . And it doesn't know the difference between a call boy and a playwright." Negotiations collapsed.

And then Jack bounced back with something pure Hollywood: Howard Hawks directing, Ben Hecht and Charlie MacArthur turning their play *Twentieth Century* into a movie script about a wildly theatrical producer named Oscar Jaffe—"the next biggest ham in the world," said Hawks, "after John Barrymore." Carole Lombard was scared stiff when told she would co-star with Barrymore; perhaps this is why this cousin of Howard Hawks could not seem to act. Jack held his nose behind her back as she emoted; hard to believe, as Hawks knew, that with a few under her belt Lombard was an uninhibited soul with a wacky sense of humor and a lot of charm. Finally Hawks flagged her down.

"Now forget about the scene," he told her; "what would you do if a man said ——— to you?"

"I'd kick him in the balls," said Lombard, suddenly awake.

"Well, Barrymore said that to you. Why don't you kick him?"

Carole stormed back onto the set, aimed a spike heel at Jack's crotch. Jack sprang back, shielding himself with his hands; the scene was shot in one take.

"She's a star," Hawks told Jack. "But I need a lot of help from you." Jack gave it. Carole was trying to be Katharine Hepburn. "Why don't you be yourself?" he challenged. "Just remember you're a distinct personality. You don't need anyone else. You've got everything." And he walloped her behind.

In Jaffe, Jack delivered a broad caricature of himself: dyed hair, thin mustache, rolling eyes and *r*'s. Oscar makes bravura suicide threats, flaunts an imperious public manner, always has one eye on his own performance. The frantic pace of Hawks's direction whirls Jaffe and Lily through crisis after crisis, yet nothing is real: their tantrums, quarrels, and reconciliations are all a glorious act. Jack plays with relish: the camaraderie of Hawks, Hecht, and MacArthur—three hard-drinking pals and all ardent "masculinists" like himself—sparked his zanily brilliant performance. Though many considered it one of his greatest, he was not even nominated for the 1934 Oscar that Clark Gable won for *It Happened One Night*. *Twentieth Century* was a pioneer "screwball" comedy—too frenetic, too sexually cynical, too off-the-wall to be popular.

After such a display of artistry it was tough to be demoted to another B picture, but John Barrymore just wasn't reliable anymore. In May he reported to RKO for *Hat, Coat and Glove*. He seemed listless, detached. His first scene required him to walk into a department store, purchase the title items, and say seven lines. He could not even remember the name of the character he was playing. Dazed, he stumbled away from the camera. Worthington Miner, the director, gave him ten minutes to pull himself together, then rolled again. Again Jack remembered nothing. At the end of three working days the first scene had not been shot. Production was halted while RKO fumed over mounting costs. Dolores consulted Dr. Samuel Hirschfeld, who had treated her in the past; he asked the producer Kenneth Macgowan, the former Broadway critic gone Hollywood, to suspend shooting. RKO reluctantly agreed. Jack underwent some kind of treatment, came back, got out a word or two, folded.

"Come to my dressing room," he told Miner and Macgowan. "I'll show you I know the whole thing." He struggled for a bad hour. Finally he turned on them. "I know what's going on here. With a few successes under your belt, you're delighted to be in on the fall of John Barrymore! It would never have happened but for the antagonism you made me feel."

Miner had worshipped John Barrymore since the day he had been taken backstage at the age of eight to meet the star of *A Stubborn Cinderella*, had looked forward to working with his idol. The reality shocked him. "The appalling recognition of his own deterioration—it was awesome, terrible, harrowing to observe. For a long time I could not remember it without a shudder." Macgowan informed Hotchener regretfully that RKO was canceling Jack's contract: "I know he isn't drunk. His trouble is more serious than that. Please make him take a long rest."

Because he recognized that something terrible was happening to him, Jack agreed to enter the Good Samaritan Hospital on May 17. The *New York Times* reported that the actor was hospitalized with a throat infection incurred while cruising Mexican waters, but by now everyone could decode "throat infection." Dolores took an adjoining room, as he had for her first baby. Because Maurice had invented "injuries to the head in boxing" as the cause of his memory failure, Jack tried to believe the same.

Actually he feared either his father's paresis or a brain tumor. Tests disclosed neither. Hirschfeld naturally concluded that alcohol had caused the memory loss; he also diagnosed enlargement of the liver and Korsakoff's syndrome, loss of memory of recent events due to toxemia. It is also possible that lack of alcohol triggered Jack's memory loss; people close to him report his either not drinking or drinking minimally before his blackouts during *Counsellor-at-Law*, the *Hamlet* test, and *Hat, Coat, and Glove*. Jack may have suffered hypoglycemia, low blood sugar: when he was drinking, alcohol supplied that sugar; when he abstained, his blood-sugar level dropped dramatically, triggering memory loss. If so, then Jack's addiction had reached the point at which not drinking injured him as much as drinking. What is certain is that he was a very sick man.

During his two weeks at Good Samaritan, Jack suffered violent withdrawal pangs, verbally and physically assaulting his "enemies," the nurses. Unmoved by the Barrymore mystique, Hirschfeld bluntly advised Dolores to have him committed, like Hilary Fairfield, to a sanitarium for the mentally ill. Knowing Jack's horror of ending like Maurice, Dolores could not bring herself to do it. "I sometimes think it was my fault," she said, "that all that happened afterward happened."

Instead, she thought of their happy days when the sea and adventure and her company had stilled Jack's demons. Jack quickly agreed: on his own yacht at least he felt master. Dolores's chief goal was to get him away from drinking cronies like the writers Hecht, MacArthur, and Gene Fowler; she was distressed, therefore, when Jack told Hotchener to keep in touch by telegraph or wireless. By now she fully realized that the Hotcheners had more power over Jack than she had; she viewed them as "evil outside influences" over the husband she still strove to save.

The cruise did not work any more than "geographical cures" ever do in such cases. Though she armed herself with a young nurse named Margaret Hastings, and though she and Otto Matthies scoured the ship for liquor, Jack's ingenuity got him drunk on Dolores's perfume, mouthwash, and spirits of camphor ammonia. The cruise became in microcosm all Jack feared and hated about marriage: prolonged contact with one woman, children who ultimately were not entertaining, no male companionship, and above all no booze.

Jack had not forgotten that he had to make money. When a letter arrived from an associate of the filmmaker Alexander Korda, Hotchener wired Jack to wire him as soon as possible. Jack replied that he would meet him at Vancouver on July 25.

When the *Infanta* anchored that day, Hotchener was waiting at the dock. Jack fell upon him with relief; Dolores recoiled.

"Why did you come?" she demanded.

"Why should he not come?" said Jack quickly. "He's my business manager."

Despite Dolores's pleas that Jack was in no condition to discuss business, Hotchener stuck. Later, at the Georgia Hotel, when Jack defiantly asked for a beer, Dolores protested vehemently. If she ever caught him drinking again, she would take the children and leave him. Jack winced and ordered a ginger ale. Finally Dolores left to do some shopping. Jack seized Hotchener.

"I am being kept a prisoner on the boat. Until today I have not been permitted to go ashore. I am being given sedatives, especially when in port. Why?"

Fully aware of Jack's condition, Hotchener might have sided with Dolores, but he did not. A Barrymore not working was a Barrymore not paying. Beyond that was male bonding. The women in Jack's life tried to sober him up and settle him down; the men championed his god-given male right to heroic dissipation. Hotchener therefore persuaded Dolores that a trip abroad would be good for the family. Jack immediately brightened, telling Hotchener to make steamship reservations and start negotiating with Korda. The family then reboarded the *Infanta* to cruise Alaskan waters until August 17, when they again docked at Vancouver. That night Jack slipped out and stayed all night ashore. The following morning the chugging of a motor launch woke Dolores; she heard Jack calling to her to remain below. Hurrying into her robe, she alerted Margaret Hastings; they reached the deck to see Jack in full evening dress climbing unsteadily aboard. "Oh, Mr. Barrymore—" the nurse began. Jack struck her, breaking her nose, then turned on Dolores.

Dolores left the yacht with the children and the nurse the same day. "The Pacific is too rough," she told reporters. Meanwhile Jack wired Hotchener:

FAMILY LEFT VANCOUVER SATURDAY BY MOTOR TO SEATTLE, THENCE BY TRAIN LOS ANGELES. . . . IF THEY INTERVIEW YOU LISTEN, BUT BE AS NONCOMMITTAL AS POSSIBLE. WILL YOU MEET ME LONG BEACH ABOUT EIGHT FRIDAY MORNING? USE YOUR OWN JUDGMENT ABOUT SEEING THEM AT HOUSE, AS IF CASUALLY, NOT MENTIONING THIS WIRE. REASON FOR THEIR LEAVING, IN CASE OF ANY INQUIRY, WISHING AVOID BAD WEATHER ON ACCOUNT OF CHILDREN.

LOVE TO BOTH.

Jack's version of what had happened on the *Infanta* was understandably different: he had accidentally put his elbow in the face of the nurse, who staggered, knocking down Dolores. At the same time he told Hotchener, "This incident gives my wife sufficient grounds for leaving me for good." It gave Dolores grounds, certainly, for insisting that Jack see a doctor. He was not normal, and he was getting worse. The irresolution of Dolores as well as the absence of Lionel and Ethel in this crisis are almost as pathetic as Jack's own behavior.

Back at Tower Road Jack overheard Dolores telling Dr. Hirschfeld that something must be done to protect her and the children. To Jack that meant only one thing: committal. One morning Dede and her little brother were eating breakfast in the nursery when angry voices erupted from her parents' bedroom down the hall. She knew that they were breaking up, that this was final. She looked at her father's empty place at the table where his fried eggs, smothered in pepper the way he liked them, were getting cold. Greedily she attacked his plate and devoured them.

For Jack flight was the only answer. He was certain, as he told Hotchener, that Dolores no longer was in love with him. He had truly loved her; he agonized over leaving his children and Tower Road; but all he could think of now was evading the long arm of the California courts— pronto. Serious as he believed the situation, it also appealed to the actor in Jack. All would be deepest conspiracy. They must get away without Dolores suspecting, consulting Helios's charts for an auspicious day. The plan included a telegram to Dr. Hirschfeld saying that Jack had to leave immediately to fulfill radio engagements in the East. Every precaution must be taken to make it clear he was neither deserting Dolores nor acting irrationally. Finally, on the way to the Glendale airport, he telephoned Dolores from a drugstore booth. He repeated the fabrication about pressing radio engagements, emphasized that he was depositing $3,500 in the bank for her with instructions that the bank notify him when her balance dropped below $1,000. Then as a final diversion, he told her he was leaving Los Angeles by train.

The plane flight brought no relief: a court order might be waiting at the Newark airport. Hotchener had wired his attorney brother Maurice to meet them; together they got the nervous escapee to the Hotel New Yorker where Helios eventually joined them. On August 30 Hotchener opened a wire from Dolores: I HOLD YOU PERSONALLY RESPONSIBLE FOR ANYTHING UNTOWARD THAT MAY TRANSPIRE. Jack took the wire to mean she thought him incapable of managing his own affairs.

On Maurice Hotchener's advice, Jack was examined by Dr. Lewis

Stevenson, neurologist and neuropathologist; incredibly he was given a clean bill. Still threatened, he announced he would sail at once. "I want to put a lot of ocean between myself and my worries. I need a moat for my castle. The Atlantic is just about the right size."

His caretaker-secretary, Emmet D. Camomile, sent on his trunks. One was the "honeymoon trunk" that had ridden the seas with him and Dolores in the *Mariner*, the other an old battered box patched with labels bearing the initials "J D," borrowed long ago from Uncle Jack. "This is the better trunk," said Jack, fingering the initials; "it is part of me."

Camomile had packed the black *Hamlet* tunic, the dagger, and the little red Temple edition that Jack and Margaret Carrington had labored over twelve years before. "Why do we need to worry," Ellen Terry had told Henry Irving when financial disaster threatened the Lyceum. "We can tour the world forever with Shakespeare's magic golden book." But Irving and Terry had treated the magic book with reverence; for them its powers were intact. Jack had stained his till half the lines were obliterated. It could not serve him again.

ONE OF LIONEL'S ESCAPES was to load his sketching materials into the car and drive north or south along the coast until he found some picturesque cove or seawall, set up his easel, plant an old, battered, broad-brimmed hat on his head, and sketch until the sun dropped low over the Pacific. In his studio dressing room, where he kept a supply of copper plates, acids, and burnishers, he would transfer the sketches to metal, then meticulously scratch in the lines, perhaps with a gramophone needle stuck in a pen. In 1933 one of his etchings had been chosen one of the 100 best prints of the year by the Society of American Etchers, a source of some satisfaction, though he worked mainly to please himself. If any criticism can be made of these extremely professional drypoint etchings it is that they lack flow: objects are static, isolated, rather as the etcher himself was static, isolated. When pressed, Lionel would drag himself reluctantly from his etching or composing and step before the camera.

Actually he made eight movies in 1933, giving sterling performances in all and impressing the veteran actress Marie Dressler, who starred with him in *Dinner at Eight* and *Christopher Bean*. "When Lionel is on the set, you have to stretch yourself, do better than you thought you could do," said Dressler. "I've never played with him that I didn't envy his consummate art."

The trouble was, the characters that Lionel played had become predictable. The actor whose signature on the stage had been an immense versatility was settling into a character actor in the less favorable sense of the term. Now he was inevitably a crusty middle-aged man older than his years, sometimes a husband or a father, more often a loner. Even his splendid performance in *Sweepings*, the story of a man who built a retail empire from a dry-goods shop, did not stretch him: aging credibly twenty or thirty years in a performance was nothing new for Lionel. His characters all called for similar mannerisms: vigorous rubbing of chin, grasping of lapels, throwing out of chest; much running of hand over hair, thrusting of chin, and plunging of eyebrows. Whereas it had taken the young Lionel weeks to get the feel of vastly different parts like Giuseppe, Kid McCoy, and Neri, his characters were now very familiar. They were all a great deal like Lionel Barrymore.

This would seem no crime. Clark Gable, Jimmy Stewart, Cary Grant, Gary Cooper, and Henry Fonda constantly played themselves. Perhaps the difference is that their repertoire of gesture is limited: they are screen actors. Lionel was still essentially a stage actor: he *did* more on screen than most actors. After 120 pictures, Lionel's gestures grooved themselves on the public's consciousness like etching on copper. Add to this Hollywood's ruthless typecasting, MGM's failure as a studio to challenge its stars, and the fact that Lionel for financial reasons made far too many films, and it is no wonder that some moviegoers felt "plagued with Barrymores." Most things Lionel did he did superbly, but he did and said the same things too often. Complained Jack, "As my brother Lionel says in every single picture to some ingenue: 'You have spirit—I like that!' " And Jack himself did not stem the "Barrymore plague" by investing his characters with Lionelisms.

In 1933 Lionel and Irene suddenly began to appear together at Hollywood social functions. Obviously Lionel was indulging her, for Irene was sick. She poses at Lionel's side, her face gaunt, her arms mere sticks, grotesque in a short gingham frock that exposes rather than camouflages her emaciation. When she contracted pneumonia that fall, his devotion deepened. He hurried home after shooting, always bringing flowers, sometimes costly jewelry. In Mamaroneck Ethel watched the outpouring of Lionel's films grimly and misunderstood. "Perhaps someday Lionel will be able to ease up," her colleague Anita Rothe, who had been with her since *Jinks*, remarked. "Not he," said Ethel. "Not until that bitch has collected every pearl in the world."

Since not a kind word survives about Irene except her husband's testimony that she was "a wonderful woman," Lionel's adoration seems inexplicable. George Cukor and Mrs. Samuel Goldwyn, who knew them both, believed that Lionel and Irene were linked in a masochistic-sadistic bond. Mrs. Goldwyn even speculated that Irene's anorexia stemmed from a deep desire to punish Lionel for loving her. Lionel brushed off accusations of idolatry. "Nothing unusual or worth comment in a husband's devotion to his wife," he said when Jack disgustedly called him "Hollywood's Greatest Lover." But now his devotion seemed fanatic. If Irene was at an afternoon tea or fashion show, Lionel might suddenly appear like a bull in a china shop, go up to Irene, lay his hand on her shoulder, and murmur, "I just wanted to see if you were enjoying yourself."

He continued to be broke. In 1934 he was contracted at $3,265 a week to plug *This Side of Heaven* with personal appearances at Loew's theatre chain in his great *Copperhead* scene. MGM had to warn Loew's against advancing Lionel any money beyond what he actually earned: ". . . his personal financial difficulties have complicated our accounting with him. He just manages to keep his head above water and some day I expect a small wave to hit him and knock him completely under." Lionel considered the memo's sender, M. E. Greenwood, one of his best friends; indeed, he had put himself childishly into the hands of the patriarchal Mayer and his minions. Mayer himself valued Lionel; as Frances Marion said, "Lionel Barrymore, the old darling, never complained about anything." Such devotion in these perilous times when actors were threatening to unionize was rewardable, and Mayer could be generous with Lionel. At the same time by loaning out Lionel to, say, Fox for *Carolina*, MGM might ask ten times Lionel's weekly salary and pocket the difference. MGM, in fact, knew Lionel very well: since the actor always spent more than he made, he had to keep chasing the carrot. Yet Lionel, strapped, was better off than Jack, whose net income in 1934 was $75,000, expenses $260,000.

Lionel's success stumping *The Copperhead* gave MGM the idea of filming it, but Lionel refused, firm enough because of Irene's illness to hold Mayer to his promise that 1934 would not repeat the exhausting grind of 1933. Instead, he took Irene to Hawaii, a holiday spoiled when Irene was stricken with a stomach ailment, again the result of years of fanatic dieting. She seemed to recover, then early in 1935 suffered another attack. The doctors advised an operation. Lionel paced the corridors of Good Samaritan trying to stifle the thought that his Renie might never recover. "I feel as if I've dived under a raft," he told Gene Fowler, "and can't come up."

ON HER FIFTY-FIFTH birthday Ethel permitted an interview on the porch of her rambling Mamaroneck house in Taylor's Lane. Her hair gleamed with russet highlights; her eyes that day were dark blue; she smiled her "curious, close-lipped, crescent" smile. But her words were bitter.

"Who cares what happens on Broadway in surroundings like this?" said the actress, still smarting from the debacle of *Scarlet Sister Mary* and *Encore*. Her professional plans were . . . vague. The summer theatre people had liked her in a play based on the life of Isadora Duncan. "But Broadway? I don't know what's come over Broadway. It makes me ill to see it. The other day I saw 'Dodsworth' with Walter Huston. . . . The audience frightened me. They looked alarming. Where do these people come from? No, I don't mean the glossy, painted theatre-party people who rush in from the speakeasies and rush right back again. I mean the rank and file. . . . They don't laugh. They don't cry. They don't seem to understand anything. Why are they there? Who are they anyway?"

What, the reporter asked hastily, was she doing for her birthday?

There would be a quiet dinner with her cousin Georgie, Sammy, and her former husband, Russell Colt. No, Mr. Colt had no idea it was her birthday; he generally dined with her on Wednesdays. If he gave her a diamond bracelet? She'd pawn it to get rid of the sheriff. . . .

Eva Le Gallienne, pioneering founder of the Civic Repertory Theatre and one of the severest critics of John Barrymore's defection to Hollywood, had long wanted to play *L'Aiglon* with Ethel as the mother of Napoleon II, since how many women were there who could realize one's ideal of an empress? Though *L'Aiglon*'s translator, Clemence Dane, laughed at the idea of securing La Barrymore for such a small role, Le Gallienne deferentially approached Ethel at Mamaroneck that summer of 1934. Ethel accepted the part as Eva, who knew about the lean times, hoped she would.

Le Gallienne did everything possible to make her empress happy. She engaged the devoted, heroically tactful Eddie McHugh to work with her own stage manager. She gave Georgie a small part. Though it meant ballet lessons, she let Sister play Fanny Elssler, the dancer. She gave Sammy the parts of A Young Countryman and Fifth Conspirator; she was fond of Sammy because Sammy adored his mother and was good to her. Though she was the star, she insisted that the star dressing room at the Forrest in Philadelphia, where they would open in October, was Ethel's. Clemence Dane came for rehearsals and "billowed up and down incessantly," but Ethel was exempt from her ministrations.

Ethel rewarded Eva with encouragement, acute criticism, and the magic of her presence. Though her performance was judged restrained compared to Le Gallienne's magnificent L'Aiglon, Eva attributed much of the power of her playing to Ethel: "To see Miss Barrymore's noble, beautiful face, which gets more beautiful with every year that passes over it, bending over me, to feel her tears falling gently on my hair! No wonder people thought I played it well; a stick or stone could not have failed to play well under such conditions. . . . To die in the arms of Miss Ethel Barrymore—what a privilege!"

Yet after *L'Aiglon* there was again nothing. Ethel had intermittently suffered insomnia; now white nights became the rule. She drank for unconsciousness; sometimes it worked. Her guilt was profound. She was the custodian of her family's theatrical tradition, yet she was failing that trust. She knew very well that her drinking had made her untrustworthy on Broadway; she lived with the shame of that knowledge. There were other failures. As a woman—at fifty-five, alone. As a mother—Sambo at twenty-five little more than her glove carrier. Sister bright, vivacious, earnest—none of the magic, none. Jackie handsome, irresponsible. No one to whom to pass the torch.

Alec Woollcott rescued her temporarily with a series of guest appearances on his popular radio show, "The Town Crier." "There are certain sounds that seem to me characteristically American," he told millions of listeners. "One of them is the soughing wind in the pine forest. Another is the voice of Ethel Barrymore." Ethel enjoyed doing scenes from *The Kingdom of God* with the script securely in her hands. But radio work did little to fill her coffers. New York State demanded back taxes. The government's claim against her amounted to almost $100,000. A reporter turned up at Mamaroneck to ask whether the state had issued a warrant.

"Tut, tut, there's not a word of truth in it," said Ethel.

"But we've checked the transcript in the county clerk's office and it's there."

"*Isn't that sweet of you*," said Ethel. "You'd better see my lawyer. I have several. I won't talk to any more rotten newspapers."

A London establishment served a summons and complaint for $442.36 owing on clothes purchased in 1930; the process server came eight times to Taylor's Lane but could rouse no one, though he'd seen a hand pulling back a curtain. Milliners, liquor and grocery stores followed suit. Ethel retaliated by suing a Los Angeles theatre manager for improperly using $11,423 of her wages in 1932–1933. The manager counterfiled for $10,918 representing loans and wages paid. She had muddled everything since the days that Frohman and Hayman doled out her salary weekly because "otherwise, Ethel, you'd just spend it." But all the Barrymores were childishly irresponsible about money. She decided to take *The Constant Wife* on tour.

The production was decidedly sleazy, William Eppes, a theatre enthusiast, noted from front row center at the Temple Theatre, Birmingham, Alabama, though even in leftover costumes Ethel had style. To even a charitable observer, however, Miss Barrymore was clearly smashed. "It became," said Eppes, "a tense, personal involvement for each of her admirers. With the total support of cast and audience, she managed to manoeuver herself from chair to chair with a firm hand, never missing a line. At the final curtain she was literally supported by the cast during the tremendous ovation." Eppes waited for the notices. Not a word, not even in the gossip columns; evidently the local critic, "dragon lady" Lily May Caldwell, had corked the bottle. Ethel told everyone that her hotel suite had been sprayed with lethal bedbug killer. Her excuses became increasingly bizarre.

Occasionally the press pulled off its velvet gloves. In New Orleans Ethel arrived late one night, refused to see reporters or photographers. The next morning, emerging late from her Pullman, she found one young woman still waiting. "Get out of my way, you little rat," Ethel was reported as shrieking. Sue Bryan came from a prominent New Orleans family, however, and wasn't going to be pushed around. "You can't talk to me like that," she said. "The hell I can't, you little bitch!" said Ethel, grabbing her by the chin. "If you call me that again I'm going to slap your face," said Bryan. At this, according to the press, Ethel "wheeled and fled." Sadly enough, the episode in some form or another probably occurred.

Ethel always said that all Barrymores had a low alcohol threshold (patently untrue of Lionel), but there are conflicting accounts of her tolerance. Ruth Gordon watched Ethel balance one glass of champagne in her hand an entire evening; when she finally took a sip an ugly red flushed her neck and bosom. "You are witness," said Ethel, "to how much I drink." But Ruth also found a brandy bottle in her room. In Washington, when Ethel stayed with her friend Cissy Patterson, Cissy watched Ethel drink potent martinis all afternoon, then give a smashing performance the same evening.

Then there was the Christmas Eve dinner with the Harrison Tweeds, mass at St. Patrick's to follow. "Catkin, when Aunt Ethel comes, let's all be charming," said Blanche. "We don't like each other particularly, but, after all, it's Christmas."

Regal in gray silk, Ethel offered her hand, palm down, for Diana to take. Over martinis in the drawing room Ethel gazed more and more rapturously at the tracery of bridges over the East River. "Isn't that the most divine view," she kept exclaiming, unable to look away. During dinner, with which there was considerable wine, Ethel swiveled repeatedly to the window, each time crying, "Isn't that the most divine view!"

"My God, I wish she'd take it with her!" said Blanche under her breath, shocking Diana, who thought her aunt awesomely beautiful.

After dessert, brandy. When it was time to leave for mass, Ethel rose, then sat down abruptly. "Oh, dear!" she said. Harrison Tweed gave her his arm, she rose, took a step, slipped and fell. As Blanche apologized for newly waxed floors, Robin helped Ethel to Blanche's bedroom.

"Mummy," said Diana on the way to St. Patrick's, "is Aunt Ethel very sick?"

"Oh, I shouldn't worry, Catkin," said Blanche gaily. "It's just a Barrymore headache."

Obviously Ethel's reaction to alcohol depended a great deal on her emotional state. What is certain is that she fought drinking—alone, willing herself for weeks, even months, not to succumb. She did not turn to her religion for help. Unlike the opera singer Grace Moore, converted by Bishop Fulton J. Sheen, or the newly Catholic Clare Boothe Luce, who always bragged about "My Monsignor this and my Archbishop that," Ethel had no intermediary between her and her religion. Her faith was simple: "I suppose the greatest thing in the world is loving people, wanting to destroy the sin and not the sinner. And not to forget that when life knocks you to your knees, which it always does and always will—well, that's the best position in which to pray, isn't it? On your knees."

IN LONDON JACK SIGNED a film contract with Alexander Korda for $60,000 for six weeks' work. Korda wanted *Hamlet*. Jack unpacked his black tunic, studied himself in the mirror. He tried the soliloquies, Henry and Helios cueing. And then he knew, finally, that his silk was in shreds; he could not play *Hamlet*. Terrified, he let Helios persuade him that a Dr. Srinivasa Murti in Madras might heal him through the ancient art of Ayurveda. The chance of visiting the scenes of Maurice's childhood was an added incentive. Before leaving he made his will: his entire estate was to be converted to government bonds, the interest divided among his three children.

But there was nothing spiritual after all about Jack's visit to India, where he was royally welcomed and entertained as a celebrity. When he reached Madras in November, he discovered that Dr. Murti's treatment consisted of scattering flower petals on an altar, burning sacred oils and incense, chanting incantations, massaging, and frequent aromatic bathing

designed to cure a nasty skin disease that was another symptom of his
deteriorating condition. Jack endured the treatment for some weeks, then
did a bunk. What really happened will never be known, but Jack wove
a tale that eventually assumed the mythic proportions of a tale from *The
Arabian Nights*:

> I always dreamed of meeting a saint and learning from him the
> true secrets of Heaven. . . . I never met him. On the morning I
> arrived in Calcutta, eager for spiritual communion with the young
> saint, I was picked up by a pimp and led to an amazing whore
> house. The most delightful I have ever seen to this day. . . . I
> would like to describe this pelvic palace so that you will not think
> me totally an idiot for giving up my saint in its favor. It had a great
> central room with a floor of pink and white marble which was
> covered with fleets of pillows. You have never seen such pillows.
> They cooed at your buttocks. There were tall silver columns, and
> clouds of colored silks ballooned from the ceiling, giving it the
> look of a heaven of udders. Incense pots gave forth smells capable
> of reviving the most dormant of Occidental phalluses. And music
> came from somewhere. . . . Gentle music that went directly to the
> scrotum and cuddled there. . . . A gong sounded. Bong! Ahzee-
> zee-zee. Beautiful women appeared in twos and threes. They
> moved slowly and their bellies were like serpents. I recall that
> they were hung with little bells and when they moved they made
> a noise like a swarm of bees. These delightful creatures sang and
> danced for me and then draped themselves around me in artistic
> clusters until I felt like a pubic chandelier. . . .
>
> I remained on the pillows for four busy weeks, never leaving
> them except to make use of a small plumbing contrivance within
> staggering distance. I lived and slept on those wonderful pillows
> and was fed like Elijah, but by ravens bearing a superior type of
> food. I would be happy to describe the dainties that were supplied
> me—but there are ladies present. . . .
>
> And so I never met my saint. I met only dancing girls and
> singing girls, all of them devout students of the Kamasutra, which
> teaches that there are thirty-nine different postures for the worship
> of Dingledangle—the God of Love.

The truth seems to be that Jack hired a brothel for one perhaps not
so busy week, but delivered with many flourishes, the Calcutta whorehouse became one of his greatest performances.

ABOVE: Ethel with Dexter Fellowes, Jerome Kern, Jack Dempsey, and George Gershwin at a 1933 radio broadcast. BELOW: Lionel and Irene at Kay Francis's Hollywood barnyard party, 1933

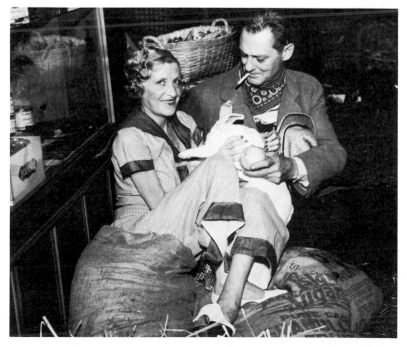

ABOVE: Myrna Loy and John in *Topaze*, 1933. BELOW: A *Topaze* set

ABOVE: John as Oscar Jaffe in *Twentieth Century*, 1934, with Herman Bing, at right, and Lee Kohlmar. BELOW: John and his daughter Diana at the forbidden dinner in Baltimore, February 1935

ABOVE: Lionel and Garbo in *Camille*, 1936. BELOW: John as Mercutio beguiles nurse Edna May Oliver in *Romeo and Juliet*, 1936

ABOVE: Ethel with Dudley
Digges in *The Ghost of Yankee
Doodle*, 1937. RIGHT: Lionel
creating his famous Scrooge
for radio

ABOVE: John and his wife Elaine nightclubbing with her parents, Louis and Edna Jacobs. BELOW: Left to right, Joseph Schildkraut, Robert Morley, John as Louis XV (and INSET), and supporting players in *Marie Antoinette*, 1938

ABOVE: Lionel and Vivien Leigh on the set of *A Yank at Oxford*, 1938. BELOW:
Ethel as Miss Moffat and Richard Waring as Morgan Evans in the 1940
production of *The Corn Is Green*

ABOVE: Ethel applying the notorious *Scarlet Sister Mary* make-up on her daughter, Ethel Colt. RIGHT: John welcoming Diana to Chicago, where he was appearing in *My Dear Children* and she would play in *Outward Bound*, 1940

LEFT: John, 1941. BELOW:
Diana supporting Lionel at
John's funeral, 1942

ABOVE: Ethel and Cary Grant in *None But the Lonely Heart*, 1944. The photograph on the wall is of Ethel at twenty-four as Cousin Kate. BELOW: Lionel cuts a cake at MGM as Mickey Rooney, Robert Montgomery, Clark Gable, Louis B. Mayer, Robert Taylor, Norma Shearer, and Rosalind Russell look on

Humphrey Bogart, Lauren Bacall, Lionel, and Edward G. Robinson in *Key Largo*, 1948

ABOVE: Ethel Colt meets her mother's train in New York, 1946.
BELOW: Merle Oberon, Dana Andrews, Ethel, and Hoagy
Carmichael on the set of *Night Song*, 1947

King Vidor, Lionel, D. W. Griffith, and Lillian Gish on the sound stage of *Duel in the Sun*, 1947

ABOVE: Ethel and her son Sammy Colt on a Hollywood set
BELOW: Lionel the composer

John Barrymore Jr.,
playing Romeo at the
Pasadena Playhouse, 1957,
poses before a photograph
of his father as Mercutio

Drew Barrymore,
grandchild of John
Barrymore, daughter of
John Jr. and Ildiko
Barrymore, in *Irreconcilable
Differences*, 1984

Ethel Barrymore, circa 1928

Lionel Barrymore, 1926

John Barrymore, 1925

He did not get to Agra, Maurice's birthplace, but in January 1935 found himself in Genoa on his way back to London, no better for his quest. There he suddenly changed plans, canceling his film contract with Korda and sailing for New York. (Korda was so disappointed that he would never discuss filming *Hamlet* again, thus losing the chance to produce Laurence Olivier ten years later.) On January 31 Jack arrived in New York, very drunk and spouting bluff: he was going to film *Hamlet*, no truth to marital rift, he had gone to India to see the birthplace of his father. At the Hotel New Yorker with the Hotcheners, he wrote a farewell letter to Dolores against Henry's advice, insisting at the same time that his manager go immediately to Hollywood to protect his property from his wife. In fact, Dolores had already moved from Tower Road to a smaller house in Los Angeles, taking some furniture but leaving the bulk of Jack's possessions intact. He also wrote a stumbling note to Lionel: he couldn't *say* anything in a goddamned letter—but not to worry— "Everything will be *Jake.*"

Apart from assorted hangers-on, Jack was very alone now in New York and drinking heavily. When it occurred to him to visit Diana at Garrison Forest School outside Baltimore, Blanche gave permission on the condition that he not leave the grounds with their daughter. Jack hired a limousine and descended upon the school at teatime. Unlike Maurice at Seton Hall, he did see his child.

Diana saw a man in a tan polo coat over a gray suit, a gray hat tilted rakishly over one eye, just like in his films. She had still not got over the pain of watching Katharine Hepburn play her own daddy's daughter, but now he was here at last.

"Treepee!"

She had planned to be very sophisticated, the other boarders looking on; instead she ran into his arms. He hugged and kissed her. "Well," he said, "you've grown into rather a young lady! . . . I've brought you the most di-vine records from India, and a machine to play them on."

The magic hours sped by, Diana making the most of being the daughter of a celebrity. When dinner was announced she was thrilled when he ignored both headmistresses and led her on his arm into the dining room. She hadn't been popular at Garrison Forest, but that was going to change now.

Later, in her room, she opened the presents from India. She had been in a play, she told him, acting a man's part with pillows stuffed in her front.

"Ah." Jack frowned. "They've saddled you with the Barrymore curse. Pillows and false faces, like your father." He pulled out one of the eternal cigarettes. She noted how he rolled his *r*'s and exploded his consonants like firecrackers. "Do you like that, Treepee? Do you enjoy standing before strangers and saying lines you've memorized?"

She didn't know; her best marks were in art.

"Perhaps you take after me," he said with a smile. ". . . Well, when I was a young man, I wanted to do for Edgar Allan Poe what Doré did for Dante. . . . But somehow"—he ground out his cigarette—"I never did much with it."

An irreproachable visit. The next day, however, the headmistress told Diana she would be allowed to go to dinner with her father in Baltimore accompanied by a friend. Diana was ecstatic. Miss Marshall was a brick and Mummy didn't matter.

Fourteen the next month, Diana practiced on borrowed high heels for the event; Pamela Gardiner, seventeen, was almost as thrilled at the thought of dinner with John Barrymore. But this time Jack was accompanied by a nightclub entertainer and a musician. They were going, he told Diana, to a rather di-vine restaurant, not the schoolgirl kind. Diana pulled out a lipstick. "Are you supposed to be wearing that?" Jack asked doubtfully.

Jack ordered cocktails for four and, after some debate, a Brandy Alexander for Diana, then another. Photographers were outside wanting to scoop John Barrymore and his teenage daughter. Diana objected: Mummy didn't like her photographed for the papers. Jack overruled and flash bulbs popped. They celebrated Diana's ordeal under fire with another drink. He had a large brandy, then another. "Well, young ladies, this is your party. What would you like to do now?" They wanted to see Fredric March in *Les Misérables*.

In the movie house Jack maneuvered Pamela alone into a row, leaving Diana to sit between his friends in the row behind. After a few minutes the musician put his arm around her shoulder. Terrified, she stared at the film without moving. She saw her father put his arm around Pamela, then she saw him kiss her.

When the movie was over Jack wanted another drink and some music. Diana protested that they had to be back in forty minutes. "We have time, Treepee," said Jack. "Never hurry your father."

At the nightclub Jack ordered a double brandy and pressed one on Pamela. He greeted Diana's request for sarsaparilla with feigned horror. "Sarsa-parr-illa? Good God, do they permit it? Did that not go out with Prohibition? Why, Treepee, don't you know that sarsa-parrr-illa erodes your kidneys, gives you pyloric spasms, and turns your liver the color of ochre?" She laughed, uneasily.

They were almost an hour late when the taxi pulled up in front of the school. In the back seat Jack and Pamela were entwined, Jack's face smeared with lipstick. When Diana couldn't wake him she begged the driver to take him home, but the driver didn't know where home was, so Miss Marshall had to be faced. She eventually sobered Jack up with coffee and sent him back to Baltimore, but Blanche was furious and transferred Diana the next year to another school. Pamela had plenty to "tell around" the next day, but Diana was deeply upset by her father's conduct, which had taught her, primarily, that liquor and sex interested him far more than she did.

But the alcoholic exploits everyone. By virtue of his admiration for the Barrymores and the New Haven flowers, Spencer Berger had actually been introduced to Jack on the *Rasputin* set. Now he again encountered the actor, who professed to remember the meeting and immediately commandeered the flattered eighteen-year-old into purveying the liquor that some of his friends were trying to keep from him. Jack had many such acolytes; when Hotchener returned to New York at the end of February he found Jack so near total collapse that one evening he showed no discernible pulse. On the twenty-sixth, Jack was rushed to Doctors Hospital and booked indefinitely for a cure.

But the hospital brought little peace of mind, for as soon as he revived Hotchener entertained him with horror stories about Dolores gutting Tower Road in his absence. As a result Jack wrote fearfully to Colonel William Neblett, the attorney he had hired to represent him in the forthcoming divorce. "I feel uncomfortable that my home and many valuable and salable possessions of mine should be at the mercy of unfriendly people. . . ." He was afraid that when Dolores realized he was not sending her any more money she might retaliate by selling his treasures. Immediate steps must be taken to safeguard his property.

Actually the prudent Dolores had her movie career savings intact: the financial binge of their marriage had been all Jack's. Yet Jack had cause for worry. He hadn't worked since making *Twentieth Century* the year before; he had lost money in shaky investments; he was in debt. Money in the abstract meant little to him except to spend, but the treasures he had collected for years he still needed to own; they defined him. Whether or not Dolores was plotting against him, his own guilt made anything seem probable. And he was pathetically vulnerable to exploitation on all sides.

ON MARCH 11 the *Daily News* columnist Ed Sullivan informed his readers that John Barrymore had collapsed and lay ill at Doctors Hospital.

His column was read by a Hunter College sophomore named Elaine Jacobs. At fourteen she had seen *Svengali* and developed a mad crush on Barrymore. Since then she'd daydreamed about the actor, researched his family history, cut his photographs from movie magazines. In the back of her mind was the thought that if Svengali could turn Trilby into a great singer, perhaps John Barrymore could turn a stage-struck girl into a Sarah Bernhardt. Neither had John's role as a star-making impresario in the recent *Twentieth Century* been lost on her.

Now with her idol only blocks away from Hunter, Elaine decided to meet him at all costs. According to her, she wrote Jack a letter saying she was required to interview a celebrity for a college newspaper assignment. In better days Jack probably would have tossed the letter away with "There's nothing in it." But these were bad days, and he consented to see her.

Appropriate that a romance which turned out to be chiefly a media event should have been sparked through the media.

TWENTY-FOUR

1935–1936

G RUDGINGLY ALLOWED three minutes by the nurse, Elaine stayed three hours. Only her account of these magical hours exists: Jack, relaxed and charming, smoking in an armchair; the famous voice drawling, "Miss Jacobs, I presume?"; his astonishment at finding her bright and articulate; his parting wish to meet her mother and his vow to telephone her at home that very evening. The incredible thing is that with one blow she had attained her goal of attracting John Barrymore's attention.

Jack must have felt he'd been thrown a lifeline. A nubile girl, not beautiful but exotic; a sexual transfusion. Intelligent (she seemed to know as much about the Barrymores as he did). Spirited, yet, through her ambition, pliable. Unlike Katherine, Blanche, and Dolores, an unconnected nobody who could look up to him. Above all, a fan whose vision of John Barrymore as Great Artist might renew his own.

On her second visit he kissed her on the mouth, she said. On the third she brought her mother. And Edna Jacobs too seemed blind to the fact that this was a sick alcoholic thirty-four years older than Elaine. Jack told her he loved her daughter. John Barrymore should love her daughter! She was impressed. In the dozens of photographs of the trio that would grace the papers, Edna Jacobs's dark eyes sparkle with voracious pleasure. She always looks as though she's having much more fun than Elaine.

When Elaine read the Lady Anne scene from *Richard the Third*, Jack declared she was meant for the stage and even promised they would act together. And as the flowers and phone calls tumbled over one another to reach her, she began to realize that her dream was coming true. Barrymore had chosen her, a little Hunter College student, as his consort in greatness.

And why not, said this intensely pragmatic young woman. After all, what good were human relationships if not for mutual benefit? Give-and-take was the rule of life. She had, she believed, as much to give John Barrymore as John Barrymore had to give her. She told Edna she was not in love with John but adored him. If John wasn't already in love with her, she was going to make him fall. She shed the Jewish-sounding Jacobs for Barrie. Elaine Barrie—almost Barrymore.

Jack left Doctors Hospital on the first day of spring and traveled with a doctor, nurse, and Diana to Miami to begin a cruise that Blanche only permitted Diana to join because Harrison Tweed would be along as watchdog. The cruise, according to Diana, turned out to be no cruise at all. With the *Infanta* anchored off Bimini, every morning Jack, Tweed, and the doctor went off in the launch to fish, every evening returned for late dinner. Apart from a daily warning not to swim in the ocean, Jack exchanged hardly a word with his daughter except when, after siphoning a pint of alcohol from the engine cooling system, he appeared on deck roaring drunk and happily cursed everyone. After two weeks he wired Elaine that he was hurrying back to her.

On April 15 Jack breezed into the Jacobs apartment looking tanned and well. Though Edna was sick and wind and sleet roared outside, Jack insisted, "We are going out on the town, my proud beauties." At the Stork Club, at the Cotton Club, the solicitude of waiters and the curiosity of the clientele convinced Elaine and Edna that with John Barrymore they had arrived at last. In the taxi going home Jack swore to the mother: "I will never hurt her. I can only do good things for her. I beg you to give me the chance to prove it." Elaine had always got her way; now Edna agreed to let Jack court her. At the same time she vowed she would be his shadow, ever on the alert to protect her precious daughter. In the event, Edna practiced a great deal of "judicious astigmatism." She was bored with her cipher-husband Louis, who traveled on business most of the time. She was also, humiliatingly, younger than the man who wanted her daughter and determined to get in on the fun. Jack would find Edna Jacobs a sticky shadow indeed.

In the teeth of press accounts that Barrymore planned to return to Dolores and the children and be "just the way we were," Jack swept the Jacobs women into a flurry of evenings on the town. He was sane enough, however, to avoid Ethel who, alarmed at the conflicting publicity, called at the Hotel New Yorker. And then Jack suddenly disappeared.

Elaine claims she hadn't the slightest suspicion that John Barrymore had a drinking problem, an impossibility. Still she was shocked when he stumbled into her apartment one night delirious with flu and drink. During long days of recovery on the sofa at 280 Riverside Drive, her disgust was tempered with pity and, finally, the realization of her power as he told her again and again, "You are my last chance." The words went to her head. Nothing stood in her way, then: she would not only be Mrs. John Barrymore, she would be Elaine Barrymore—a star. When she consummated her seduction, she was grateful that he was gentle, but physically unmoved; on the other hand, the enormous publicity generated by divorce rumors and John's encampment at Riverside Drive ravished her. Reporters surrounded the building: overnight she had become a household word. But, as she would discover, "so was poison."

The press covered, would cover, the John-Elaine—or Caliban and Ariel, as they quickly became known—romance as though it were World War II. Dolores was cast as the beautiful Mother of Sorrows, Jack as the aging Clown Prince of Denmark, Elaine and Edna as the dark villainesses. Why was the press so hostile to this self-possessed but naïve young woman?

She was too aggressively ambitious, true, yet ambition is no crime. She was blamed for breaking up the Costello-Barrymores, that beautiful couple who had enchanted the public on screen and in movie magazines, yet Jack had not seen Dolores for ten months prior to his meeting Elaine. She photographed unfortunately, always smirking with half-closed eyes like a cat with cream; between the sloe-and-sparkling-eyed Jacobs women Jack somehow managed always to look innocent and amused. (He would later look weary as hell.) There was probably anti-Semitism in the double-edged descriptions of "the sultry, dark-eyed beauty." Though the Barrymores had been managed for most of their careers by Jews, the Royal Family did not consort with them romantically. Elaine claimed that throughout their courtship she felt confident and in control, yet the press would do everything in its considerable power to make her absurd and detestable. Inexperienced, she cooperated beautifully.

Toward the end of May, Elaine and Edna "Barrie" sailed with Jack on the *Infanta* for Havana as a Los Angeles paper announced that Jack would no longer be responsible for Dolores's debts. Dolores responded on May 25 by suing for divorce, accusing Jack of extreme cruelty, physical abuse, habitual intemperance, and desertion. "The magnificent silence of Mrs. Barrymore which aroused the admiration of all Hollywood was broken today," announced Louella Parsons with relish. "She has grown so thin and is so beautiful that if Barrymore could see her one feels he would take a fast plane to Hollywood." Louella (whom Jack called "a quaint old udder") recalled a dinner given by Lionel a mere year ago when Jack had told her, "I can smoke in my room and drop ashes. I can sit up all night and read a book. I can ask Dolores to be ready to sail for the West on a moment's notice and she will go with me." Barrymore was mad to leave such a beautiful and devoted wife, Louella told her readers. Lionel had told Jack the same thing: "Dolores is your only chance." Interviewed about her brother in Washington, Ethel, appalled, said firmly, "Whatever Jack does is right."

In Havana the Barrymore party's host was Arturo del Barrio, Helene Costello's third husband, now separated. When they arrived at his hacienda, the pool was surrounded by guests in various stages of undress sipping drinks as they telephoned their brokers in Brussels and Hong Kong. Arturo's younger brother Mario welcomed Elaine with no more than the traditional *"Mi casa es su casa,"* but it was too much for Jack, who turned on Elaine and slapped her face. It was her first taste of his insane jealousy.

And now all the warning flags had flown: the disappearance, the drinking, the jealousy, the battering, and still Elaine pressed on, blinded by ambition, the Barrymore glamour, and the lavish generosity, gaiety, and charm of Jack Jekyll. At no time did she seem to realize that Jack's career was on the rocks and that he had little influence or power. By the time they left Havana, Elaine had acquired a nine-carat yellow diamond, purchased from a pawnshop, and Jack's pledge to marry her. "I needed John," she decided, "but he needed me more."

WHAT JACK NEEDED was medical care and someone who did not want to exploit him. Dolores could have helped had Jack trusted her; had he been hospitalized for any length of time she could have returned to films and supported the family. But Jack saw her only as another enemy who wanted to use him. All his life he had been pulled between competing forces, each camp wanting something. The Barrymore Board of Regents wanting him to be the world's greatest actor, his drinking pals the world's most amusing drunk. Hopkins wanting him for his theatre, Warners for their studio. The Hotcheners wanting him to feather their nest; Dolores wanting him as husband and father. And now Elaine wanting him for her own reasons. She would discover the competition still fierce over this floundering man.

Dolores. Dolores's dignified silence about Elaine had further solidified public sympathy for the rejected wife. True, Dolores no longer wanted Jack. "It is impossible," she said in September when Jack reportedly wanted her to take him back. But to Elaine Dolores was the ex-wife after Jack's money. Afraid that she might add adultery to her divorce grounds and win an even larger settlement, Elaine perjured herself by signing an affidavit swearing to the strictly platonic relationship between herself and John Barrymore.

The Hotcheners. Elaine loathed them at first sight. Henry with his cold eye and preacher's cant, Helios radiating a spirituality that she found transparently phony. "Business managers" indeed! She would more accurately describe the Hotcheners as prime beneficiaries of the John Barrymore charitable trust.

Jack was sleeping in the traveling Louis's bedroom. At night Elaine watched him muddle over his checkbooks and ledgers—bewildered, bored, helpless. She tried to suggest economies; she had money sense and a thoroughly practical mind. One day, seeing him casually sign away $1,000, she urged him to call Henry and ask him what the check was for. Jack had never questioned. Dragging nervously on a cigarette, he telephoned Hotchener. "What was that one grand check for, Hank?" he asked shyly. "I'm just curious."

Hotchener, Jack's manager for ten years, retaliated. In the next weeks, Henry, Helios, and Maurice Hotchener closed ranks against the Jacobs women, adding to their troops Frank Aranow, a colleague of Maurice's, as consultant. In concert, they sat down to prove to Jack that a chippie he'd known barely six months was out to fleece him.

Item: $5,000 for a ring, originally $1,800, additional duty and penalties for failure to declare at customs $3,200

Item: $5,363.15 to Saks, etc. for gowns

Item: $14,000 in checks made to cash, endorsed by Elaine or Edna Jacobs

Item: a $3,000 check, supposed to have gone to Captain Matthies, which the Jacobs women cashed, giving only a few hundred to Matthies

Item: a La Salle car purchased by John Barrymore in the name of Edna Jacobs

Item: $1,000 for a large Capehart radio and phonograph console, delivered to 280 Riverside Drive

Item: weeks of support at John Barrymore's expense on his yacht and in Havana, etc.

Item: $9,600 for lease of a nine-room Jacobs-Barrymore apartment, payments $400 a month for two years, signed in the name of John Blyth—

And, Jack later claimed, $300,000 he had entrusted to the Jacobs women during these months and which he could not account for.

And Elaine had questioned a $1,000 check made out to Hotchener. One evening Jack burst into the Jacobses' apartment and began throwing clothes into a suitcase. "I wish to Christ I'd been born a pansy," he snarled when Elaine and Edna confronted him. "You're all poison, you dames. . . . I've given you gifts and money and now you're out to bleed me. You don't love me. You don't give a damn about me. You're just playing me for a chump."

Edna was enraged. What about hundred-dollar phone calls he had made from their apartment. What about food and rent—

Jack had paid the phone bills. "The mother!" he hissed. "There's always the mother, Christ! I'm going to comb the orphanages for my next piece." At the last minute he remembered to demand the ring. The door slammed.

Elaine claims she was not really shaken. She had invested time, thought, and emotion in the relationship, besides surrendering her virginity to Jack. If he would not marry her, then she was disgraced, a nobody again. He may have lost sight of the glorious life they would lead together, he may have forgotten his promises—but she had not. Her response now was to sue Jack for $3,500 for the ring on the advice of her lawyer, Aaron Sapiro.

Jack had been spirited away by Frank Aranow to Connecticut, out of Elaine's reach. At the same time, Aranow had worked out an agreement, acceptable to Sapiro, that Jack place $5,000 in escrow to be paid to Elaine after one year—if, during that time, she did not follow, annoy, or in any way communicate with him and if neither she nor Edna talked to reporters. Jack also agreed to return the ring if Elaine acknowledged it merely as a gift, not a pledge of marriage. Still feeling that Elaine was too close for comfort, the Hotcheners persuaded Jack that he was safest in Hollywood. And he might have skipped clean had not Julia McCarthy of the *Daily News* been thrown off the train at Grand Central Station by Hotchener and decided to get her revenge and a story at the same time. She telephoned Elaine that John was being shanghaied that day, September 19, on the Twentieth Century for Chicago.

Wiring Jack that nothing could keep them apart, Elaine flew to Chicago on a plane chartered by the *Daily News*, while Sapiro wired Nat Gross, a reporter for the *Herald Examiner*, to help Elaine track her quarry in Chicago. Trailing reporters and directed by Gross, Elaine located Jack's train and stateroom at Englewood Station. "John," she cried, pounding on the door while flash bulbs popped, "this is your Ariel! John, John, I love you!" A bulky black porter grinned out at her. "Honey, I love you too, but I'm not the John you want."

Confident, however, that she was within striking distance, Elaine booked a compartment next to John's on the Santa Fe Chief. By Kansas

City she discovered that she had been riding next to none other than her archenemy, Henry Hotchener. Jack had slipped the Twentieth Century before Englewood with Camomile, his Tower Road caretaker, and boarded another train west. Now, however, informants persuaded her that John would rejoin Hotchener in Kansas City. With her press entourage at her heels, Elaine paced the Union Station platform. "He doesn't realize, he doesn't know what he's doing," she wailed when he failed to appear. And then, egged on by the press, Elaine did an extraordinary thing.

"I address this appeal in an effort to reach John Barrymore, whom I love dearly," she recited into a microphone at the Kansas City radio station. "I also address this to the people of Kansas City and the Middle West who have been so sympathetic and understanding. John, dear, I know you need me now—more than ever before. I realize that certain people are keeping you from me. When you were with me I was able to nurse you back to health. I want now to help and save you from those who would destroy you. My messages to you have not been delivered. Please, please, dear John, don't think I have deserted you. I am here in Kansas City waiting for your call. Please come to me. I am waiting. We have each other. That is all that matters."

Jack phoned her from New Mexico, perhaps amused to find her almost as big a ham as himself. Loiterers around the phone booth at Zuñi Pueblo testified that he began abusively, gradually yielded, and ended by murmuring sweet nothings. Elaine "gloatingly" informed the press of the reconciliation. Appeased for the moment, she returned to New York where she found herself something of a celebrity. Offers came in, and Elaine went to Boston to play in repertory. But she had by no means given up.

Lionel was waiting at Pasadena on the twenty-fifth when a derelict in wrinkled suit, dark glasses, and hat pulled over his face emerged unsteadily from the train. Believing that Jack was returning to Dolores, Lionel greeted his shockingly haggard little brother warmly. Jack leaned wearily on Lionel as reporters crowded round them. How did it feel to make the pit as the winner? Was he going to marry Elaine?

"None of your goddamned business," snarled Jack.

"Here, here," said Lionel, shocked, leading Jack to his waiting car, "that's not the thing to say."

Jack holed up at Roxbury Drive, but that night—much to the disgust of Lionel, who thought Elaine a hormonal infatuation—he telephoned Elaine. "I never think about such things anymore," grumbled Lionel. "Seems to me that Jack would get to that age, too." As a result of that phone call, Jack sued Hotchener for an accounting and return of business records, advised by his new lawyer, Aaron Sapiro, who still had a lawsuit against him on Elaine's behalf. Hotchener immediately countersued, asking $6,400 in salary, $13,500 in commissions, and $10,000 for "special services." Trapped between Hotchener and Elaine/Sapiro, Jack turned on Dolores and had all new locks installed at Tower Road, convinced that the "shanty madonna" was out to ruin him.

Actually Dolores's terms were not in themselves crippling. She had sacrificed nine prime years of filmmaking at the height of her beauty. Now she asked, and got, custody of the children, $850-a-month child support, and the premiums from $235,000 in life insurance policies that Jack would maintain for the children. "She was too beautiful for words," Jack said dryly, "but not for arguments," and she won this one. Jack retained some $100,000 in bonds (a fraction of what he had once held), the title to No. 6 Tower Road, a vacant Beverly Hills lot, and the *Infanta*. But he was deeply in debt, delinquent in taxes, and strapped by the upkeep of Tower Road and the yacht. Sapiro was already deep into his pocket. And he was still making child support payments to Blanche. He had no film contract, the major Hollywood studios considering him washed up, and only miscellaneous radio work.

On October 9, 1935, Dolores obtained an interlocutory decree, final in one year. Their marriage, like Jack's two others, had lasted legally seven years. Actually each had begun to disintegrate after three, the last four years being nightmares of quarrels and reconciliations. But Elaine was undeterred by Jack's track record. When the divorce was announced, she dropped her lawsuit against him, which had included breach of promise, and in late December set out for Hollywood. With, of course, Edna. "I understand that *Elaine* is on her way," snorted Louella. "If she thinks we're going to welcome her with open arms. . . ."

When Jack was not there to meet her, she knew that somebody had got to him since their last phone call. Daughter and mother finally tracked him to the Countess di Frasso's where a party was in full swing, and sent their names in with the butler. Ben Hecht and Charlie MacArthur immediately shoved Jack into a closet and locked the door, while the butler returned and shut the door in the Jacobs women's faces.

But they caught up with Jack: the punch-drunk man could not defend himself from anyone very long. He rented them a house in the Benedict Canyon area. "Why shouldn't we see each other frequently in Hollywood?" he told the press. Sensing hostility on every side, Elaine quickly despised Hollywood, yet at the same time she longed for its recognition.

As Mrs. Barrymore, she tried to believe, she might improve the social tone of movieland as stars like Norma Shearer and Ronald Colman had done. And when her career was launched at last, she would show Hollywood!

THE 1935–1936 Broadway season was the most brilliant since the talkies and the Depression had dimmed its lights: Helen Hayes, Lunt and Fontanne, Judith Anderson, Jane Cowl, Katharine Cornell, Maurice Evans, Leslie Howard, Tallulah Bankhead, and Alla Nazimova all made striking successes in a rich assortment of drama. Ethel herself was scouring the cities of America in *The Constant Wife*, a grueling tour that earned her comparatively little money. She was still drinking; there were more incidents. "Newspaper reporters have been very very good to Ethel Barrymore in times past and time present," said one of the tribe. "Not in what they said but in what they didn't—if you know what I mean. . . ." During the summer she played *Déclassée* at the Berkshire Playhouse, where Chamberlain Brown wrote that he had nothing for her in the autumn. That July too she heard that the Arch Street Theatre, once the proud stronghold of Mrs. John Drew, was being demolished. Profoundly discouraged, the titular First Lady of the American Theatre decided she could no longer go on. She chose to make her announcement as a guest on Ben ("Yowsah, yowsah, yowsah") Bernie's popular radio program, if an inappropriate medium for La Barrymore, still an apt comment on the dissolution of American culture. "This is my last public appearance," said Ethel. "I will devote the rest of my life to teaching others the art of acting." Then she turned to Bernie.

"Knock, knock."

"Who's there?"

"Saul."

"Saul who?"

"Saul there is, there isn't any more."

The phone jangled immediately; reporters wanted to know more. "I hope," said Ethel largely, "that any and all young people who want help or encouragement in the line of speech, dramatics, radio or public presentation will call on me. I'll be so happy to help them." Sipping iced tea a few days later on her Mamaroneck porch, she confirmed that she was really through with the stage: no annual farewell tours, she wished "to leave them smiling." About the actual teaching she was vague. "There will have to be a number of courses. Fencing for one—if actors are going to play Shakespeare they must be at home in Shakespeare—and dancing and languages. There are four little theaters in Mamaroneck, and we will put on plays with an audience, because not even a rehearsal is any good unless it's on a stage."

Mail deluged Mamaroneck. Some petitioners wanted advice, others assurance that her course would guarantee them a Broadway hit. Hundreds appeared at her front door ready to sit at her feet. One young man walked from Boston to Mamaroneck; Ethel gave him a private audience only to discover that he wanted to write popular songs. She took down names and addresses, yet suddenly the whole project seemed frightfully ambitious. She had always said that one learned acting by doing, by starting young. She was also, perhaps, not the ideal teacher. "You would never use her as a model for acting," said Barbara Robins Davis. "Ethel Barrymore always assumed she had the right to do whatever she wanted onstage. By the power of her personality, she made audiences love it." Now she felt she had uncorked a monster.

She was saved when the Studio of Acting offered her an honorary position on its faculty; she accepted with relief and no little guilt. After all, she apologized, the Studio had a working plant. "It's all so organized. And I was so overwhelmed in Mamaroneck."

The IRS had also heard "Saul there is." Ethel owed the government $98,660 as a result (said the IRS) of deducting too much for traveling and entertainment expenses between the years 1921 and 1929 when she was earning from $17,652 to $64,258 a year. Ethel had paid $7,500 on her debt, which the IRS now, amazingly, even considered refunding to her since she was unemployed. But, they decided, she would only squander it as she had vastly greater amounts in the past. They kept the $7,500, concluding that she was not guilty of "willful evasion" but was a victim of her inability to manage her financial affairs. They would forgive the balance, since clearly Miss Barrymore "had no future on the stage."

IN APRIL 1936 Irene contracted tuberculosis. Praying that a dry climate might help her, Lionel took a house for his wife in Phoenix while he himself continued to slave in front of the cameras: *Ah, Wilderness!*, *The Voice of Bugle Ann*, *The Road to Glory*, *The Devil-Doll*, *The Gorgeous Hussy*, *Camille*.

Mayer almost managed to ruin *Ah, Wilderness!* by insisting the part of drunken Uncle Sid be padded for his favorite Wallace Beery at the expense of Lionel's role as the father; Mayer and Beery were "a splendidly matched duo." With the aid of the producer Hunt Stromberg's distortion of O'Neill's play, Mayer succeeded in justifying Beery's top billing, but Clarence Brown, the director, had the artistic sense to attempt to balance the parts in the cutting room, permitting Lionel's expert portrait of Nat Miller to hold the screen against Beery's bleary soak. Still, Lionel's part suffered. He was fully aware of Mayer's machinations, expressing regret but no surprise over the fact that the boss had destroyed what could have been one of his finest acting opportunities. The film was such a critical and popular success that MGM next moved the combination of Lionel, Spring Byington, and Eric Linden to Missouri with Lionel as a fox hunter in *The Voice of Bugle Ann.*

The Devil-Doll was completely different, an offbeat special-effects film with a revengeful Lionel inventing murderous foot-high dolls which he sics on the man who wronged him. To sell the dolls to his quarry he disguises himself as an old woman—worth the price of admission, for there *are* old women who look like Lionel Barrymore: ax-jawed and smiling with deceptive sweetness. The devil-dolls themselves, climbing up bedposts, crawling up a victim's chest, are triumphs of special effects. A B movie, but a quirkily memorable B.

While he was cackling in a white wig, Lionel was agonizing over Irene. Fearing she would be lonely and bored in Phoenix, he borrowed a movie projector and reels of Walt Disney (all the Barrymores adored Mickey Mouse) and drove all night to provide her with a few hours' distraction. She seldom went out now, though she would make trips to the beauty parlor attended by a nurse. Pursing her mouth at the gaunt face in the mirror, Irene saw pretty little Irene Frizzelle, the "Pocket Venus" of Broadway. Waiting in the car for Venus's reappearance, Lionel spared her disillusionment.

Making *The Gorgeous Hussy*, Joan Crawford found Lionel changed. He had grown older, seemingly arthritic, gloomy. She was not the only one to notice that Lionel was testy and in pain. Robert Montgomery had the dressing room next to Lionel's. He would hear him painfully climb the stairs one at a time and shuffle past his door. Soon the notes of a Brahms intermezzo or one of Lionel's own compositions would filter through the wall. Back in the Biograph days, Lionel had suggested to Griffith a story about "How the mind of an unfortunate was brought to reason by music." Music helped him now. One day Mike Cantwell, a boxing trainer and friend, took the stairs two at a time and knocked at Lionel's door. He found him lying on a couch, obviously in pain. Lionel waved him to a seat.

"Just sit a while with me, Mike," he said. "I'm resting between scenes."

Mike was lost for conversation.

"Mike," said Lionel at last, "I'd be all right if only my wife had good health. I'd be all right then."

Lionel went on to play Monsieur Duval, as he had with Ethel for an Actors Equity benefit, in Thalberg's production of *Camille*, directed by George Cukor. He had only a cameo, but a powerful cameo. As the voice of bourgeois realism, Duval is yet the only one who realizes that he can appeal to Marguerite in the name of a code of honor reserved for gentlemen; in Duval Marguerite finally meets her match. It is all Garbo's film, as usual: the drooping eyelids and shoulders, the forehead puckered in incredulity or pain, the untutored laugh with flung-back head—all nourished and expanded by Cukor until the film becomes above all a flowering of her beauty. Lionel's part in her triumph is small, but in its way perfect. And Garbo actually spoke to Lionel on the set where he sat hunched over a drawing board, obviously in pain. She asked:

"Are these for sale?"

"No, I paint them for my wife. They give her pleasure."

BEFORE THE FILMING of *Camille*, Thalberg and Cukor had decided to gamble on Jack for Mercutio in their big-budget prestige film *Romeo and Juliet*. They realized that he might blank out completely, that at best he would be hell to handle, but he had been America's greatest Shakespearean actor and Cukor had successfully directed him in the past.

Elaine later took credit for Jack's performance, whereas in reality she was an irritant during the weeks of filming. Impatient to launch her own career, she constantly urged him to act on her behalf, arousing his suspicion that she had only come to Hollywood to further her own interests. With Sapiro, she also egged him on to legal battle with Hotchener, hardly a soothing effect. And he was drinking. Though he had once again put himself in Margaret Carrington's hands, she now impressed him as "Christ's elder sister." For Carrington too the old magic had vanished. "If only drink would kill all the Barrymores," she said only half-humorously, "what a better world this would be!"

Pressured by Thalberg, Jack agreed to move into a dry-out lock called Kelley's Rest Home. A male nurse and studio police guarded him from drink and Elaine, who was also barred from the *Romeo and Juliet* set. For a time Jack had to be a good boy. But Hecht, MacArthur, and Fowler grew indignant over the violation of their pal's right to drink himself to death as well as ruin Thalberg's picture. While Hecht and MacArthur decoyed the police with witty Broadway dialogue, Fowler tied a bottle to the bedsheet Jack lowered through the bars. The next morning he was to film Mercutio's great Queen Mab speech.

Jack had never wanted to play Romeo, not only because he disliked acting the lover but because Juliet and Mercutio were far more powerful parts. Mercutio was a man's man; to him Jack gave what he had left of Shakespearean acting. He was drunk when he reported for shooting, yet went through the Mab speech, cut to thirty-one lines, in one take, exciting a burst of applause at the end. "Fuck the applause," said Jack. "Who's got a drink?"

Thalberg was not enchanted. Then one Sunday, again with a morning's shooting ahead, Jack was reported missing from Kelley's. Studio aides fanned out for the search until someone found a cabbie who had driven Jack up Tower Road. They found him pacing the yawning rooms of his deserted fortress, his footsteps echoing; they escorted him back to the sanitarium. He was, as he told Fowler, having a hard time finding "a bridge to Terra Firma" in his present state of "slightly swirling levitation."

Mayer now wanted Barrymore replaced at any cost. Thalberg appealed to William Powell, who had made his film debut in 1922 in John's *Sherlock Holmes*. Powell was flattered, but declined to replace the star who had given him his start in pictures. Thalberg and Cukor had to resign themselves to nursing Barrymore through a performance.

"Jack was absolutely on the wagon but gaga when he reported for *Romeo and Juliet*," said Cukor. "He was very vain at the time, still witty and intelligent, but rather helpless. He was defensive, worried about his condition, and would say, 'Where do I go?' in a snappish way."

He was also uncontrollable. Mercutio has the lines "He heareth not, he stirreth not, he moveth not." "He heareth not, he stirreth not, he *pisseth* not," declared Jack roundly.

"All right, Jack," said Cukor patiently, "let's try it again, shall we?"

"Strange how me heritage encumbereth me speech," said Jack. "Dear Mr. Shakespeare, I beg you hear me yet awhile. I am but an impover-r-r-ished actor and yet I would beg you to consider an undeniable fact. I have improved upon your text. 'He moveth not' is not so pertinent to the occasion as 'he pisseth not.' "

After two hours Thalberg was called. He begged Jack to say the line just once as written. On that once they finally got their take.

Thalberg was making *Romeo and Juliet* for Norma Shearer who, he had decided, should bow out of films at the height of her beauty. He also intended *Romeo and Juliet* as a monument to his own career which, he knew, heart disease could end prematurely. Opposed bitterly by Mayer, who knew that Shakespeare wouldn't pay, Thalberg exhausted himself trying to achieve a production he hoped would be his masterpiece. But though critical reaction to the film was positive (audiences, as Mayer predicted, stayed away), he did not really succeed. Although Jack, Leslie Howard (Romeo), Basil Rathbone, and Cedric Hardwicke had Shakespearean experience, Thalberg, Cukor, and Shearer had not. Thalberg took the precaution of hiring Cornell University's Professor William Strunk Jr. "to protect Shakespeare from us." But Strunk could not finally protect Shakespeare from that glossy MGM mentality that prettified and mediocritized so much of what it touched. *Romeo and Juliet* opens like an MGM musical. All the sets are brand-new: "Verona made in a day." Thalberg could have used Jack's skill at antiquing. Friar Laurence's cell looks like a Beverly Hills estate. The costumes have all just been taken out of their boxes, including Jack's white cape and bespangled doublet that asks us to believe that a man-about-Verona in the sixteenth century when the streets ran filth always looked fresh from the cleaners. Norma Shearer was eager to play Juliet and, with the coaching of Constance Collier, achieved within her limits surprising lyrical freshness if not passion. But she looks Hollywood 1936: lipstick, perm, and false eyelashes.

Sets and costumes reflected Thalberg and Cukor's fear of this powerful drama of passion and death. Their effort had, within limits, sincerity; they played it straight and cautiously, but as a result Cukor did not bring out the potential of actors like Rathbone, Hardwicke, and Howard, who knew, however, that at forty-two he was not the ideal teen-aged lover. Or of John Barrymore.

It is debatable whether any director at this point could. Critics have called Mercutio John Barrymore's last great role. And it is true that his guzzling, belching, snorting, and cavorting add texture and depth to a too glossy production; that his delivery and breath control surpass anything Shearer and Howard can muster. But he seems, beneath the bravado, profoundly weary. Why is this old man, we ask (Shakespeare's Mercutio is in his twenties), rioting about Verona like an aged delinquent? Moreover, John is either drunk or acting drunk; perhaps by now the two had merged. Thus John's Mercutio is himself: a blasphemous, witty, dissipated, Rabelaisian fellow who masks his vulnerability beneath a scoffing pose. No matter what the merits of his performance, however, MGM did not rush him into another film.

MEANWHILE ELAINE WAS champing at the bit. She had not come 3,000 miles to shop at Bullock's Wilshire. She was frustrated by Jack's jealous insistence that only he launch her career, maddened by his refusal to do so. She posed for a publicity still and Jack swept aside the hand of the photographer trying to adjust her furs. Before she could take dancing lessons she had to convince Jack that the instructor was homosexual. When a headwaiter bent over her décolletage, Jack snatched the menu and waved the waiter away. If she watched a nightclub entertainer too closely, he demanded *"Why are you looking at him?"* Flattering in a way, yet a decided obstacle to the career she burned for.

For her twentieth birthday she decided to give a party, inviting her maternal grandparents from New York. Jack turned up drunk hours before the celebration was to begin. When she asked him to leave, he demanded, in that cold, menacing tone she had come to dread, what man she was hiding. He left, but in the hours before returning brooded on her infidelities which, he was certain, included an affair with an actor in Boston. He came in smiling, seething underneath. He had invited the Thalbergs; sitting down to dinner Elaine felt her future was made at last. Dinner was going well, though Jack ignored his food for the wine. Then during a lull, he turned to Norma Shearer.

"Tell me, Norma, I'm curious. I can't stand whores—can you? . . . These whores who are never seen in public without their lady mothers."

Elaine and Edna returned to New York. According to Elaine, Thalberg telephoned asking her to come back. Jack was a wreck; they wanted him for *Camille*. According to Elaine, she was not thrilled.

Then, said Thalberg, how would she like an MGM contract?

Elaine and Edna hopped the next train, and the terrible, destructive tug of war began again.

Jack was contrite, sweet, grateful. For days he groomed her for the scene Madge Evans had played opposite him in *Dinner at Eight*; for the actual test, Elaine claimed, he hammed, upstaged her, and cut into her lines. But the sabotaged test was only one tilt of the crazy seesaw. Jack continued to battle with Hotchener, meanwhile urging Sapiro to sue Warner Brothers for $30,000 he claimed due him from *Moby Dick* and *Svengali*. Sapiro was happy to do so, sometimes paying himself more than $4,000 in two weeks. Jack fumbled more and more for that bridge to terra firma. Finally, Thalberg coaxed him again to Kelley's.

He begged Elaine to visit him, and she drove to Culver City with visions of a *Camille* part dancing in her head. Instead she found an abject, terrified man in a little iron-barred cell reeking of paraldehyde. He sobbed as he told her that Thalberg had refused him the Baron de Varville. He went down on his knees, begging her to love him. The thought of sex in a place like that nauseated her. She fled all the way back to New York.

That Labor Day weekend, Irving Thalberg caught a chill that became a cold that turned into pneumonia; he died on September 14, only thirty-seven. Jack and Lionel went together to the funeral, appropriately, for it had been Thalberg who first united them on the screen in *Arsène Lupin*, Thalberg who had appreciated the quality a Barrymore brought to film. For years he had struggled against the merchant mind of Louis B. Mayer to produce sophisticated, adult, quality films. Both Lionel and Jack had lost an ally.

Jack still had one in David O. Selznick. Despite all that Thalberg and Cukor had suffered on the *Romeo and Juliet* set, Jack had turned in a performance, and Selznick now wanted him for the role of the drunken has-been actor in *A Star Is Born*, a character in part inspired by John Gilbert, who had died alone surrounded by bottles the previous January. William Wellman, the director, was skeptical about Jack. "If we use him, we'll have to blackboard him." Selznick overrode the objection: "We can do it that way. Let's try it." Norman Maine was not a part, however, that could be reduced to blackboards, nor could a fallen actor portray an actor's fall. "I can't tell him," Selznick told his business manager. "You tell him." Daniel O'Shea called Jack into his office and broke the news. Jack sat in bewildered silence, then got up and walked out without a word.

Fredric March, who had acted John Barrymore as Tony Cavendish, got the role. But Cukor continued to see only John Barrymore as Norman Maine. When he directed a remake of *A Star Is Born* in 1954 with James Mason playing Maine, he constantly urged Mason to emulate Barrymore. Mason balked: he didn't like Barrymore in films, he couldn't do it. But Cukor was still under the spell. "The only actor he ever talked about," said Mason, "was John Barrymore."

In October Dolores's divorce was final, and Jack telephoned Elaine. He was single again, and lonely. He was on the wagon, he swore, and would stay on if only she would forgive him and return. He insisted he was a wiser and a better man. . . .

Now he would marry her. Elaine and Edna this time took a plane. Jack met her carrying orchids, wearing a camel's-hair topcoat and tennis shoes, and looking tired. He was sure that Lionel intended to block the wedding.

With the indefatigable Aaron Sapiro, they flew to Yuma, Arizona, on November 8, where Jack borrowed two dollars from Elaine for the license. He gave his age as forty-eight (he was fifty-four), Elaine's as a legal twenty-one. Trailed by the press, they breakfasted on scrambled eggs and beer at a greasy spoon. Not the celebration Elaine had imagined, but Edna's eyes sparkled and Elaine could congratulate herself that she was Mrs. Barrymore at last.

Shortly afterward, Jack was lunching at the Brown Derby with Errol Flynn, who idolized him, and David Niven, who did not. Jack's plangent voice, accompanied by extravagant gestures, attracted all eyes to their corner. Flynn deliberately threw him an opening.

"But tell us, Jack, what do you *see* in Elaine?"

Jack banged the table. Conversation stopped.

"You want to know what I see in my wife?" he roared. "Well, I'll tell you! You put it *in*, and it goes right through the main saloon and into the *galley*; then the cabin boy comes down a ladder and rings a bell. . . . In other words, you stupid bastard, *it fits!*"

She would find herself hated and ridiculed. Hated by Jack's male friends, hated by the Hotcheners, hated by the Hollywood press, hated by the Barrymores and even the ex-Barrymores. And she hated heartily in return.

VERY ILL, Irene came home to Roxbury Drive. Fortunately, she had relatives living in the Pacific Palisades: Mary Ellen Wheeler and her daughters Murdie, Benson, and Florence. The Wheelers had sometimes hosted the Barrymores for two-month visits; though Mrs. Wheeler was younger than Lionel, she called him "Son" and he called her "Mother." Now they all pitched in to keep Roxbury Drive running smoothly for the invalid and her semi-invalid husband.

The usual round of Hollywood Christmas parties began. Lionel stayed at home with Irene. He bought a tree and had it trimmed; there were plenty of gaily wrapped presents beneath the boughs. He skipped the annual MGM bacchanalia, which, after L. B. Mayer had officially blessed the turkey dinner, rioted into the small hours. On the morning of Christmas Eve Irene was much weaker. Dr. Speik was sent for and went upstairs to her room. Lionel was sitting in the garden in the sunshine with the Wheelers when at one-thirty Irene slipped away.

Lionel's annual Christmas Day Scrooge had become a holiday radio institution, but not even a trouper like Lionel could face a microphone the day after his wife's death. Jack not only took over for Lionel but managed to sound exactly like him. Then he went to Roxbury Drive to share Mike's grief. He came home shortly after, according to Elaine, pale and shaken.

"He threw me out of the house."

Two days later Mike telegraphed to say he was sorry.

ON NEW YEAR'S EVE Jack and Elaine were at the Trocadero when she broke the news that she had accepted a play offer in San Francisco, a few lines and a voluptuous dance. Jack unleashed a verbal assault that stopped the nightclub in its tracks. Furious, Elaine demanded an apology. It was not forthcoming. Elaine immediately served him with a divorce summons and complaint demanding $2,525 a month temporary alimony. They had been married less than two months.

But for Jack a lawsuit was not the crisis of 1936. In England an important new actor had emerged, an actor who played not only Hamlet, but Romeo, Orlando, Richard II, Oberon, Hotspur, Macbeth, Prospero, and Lear. His theatrical lineage was impeccable: he was a Terry. As long as John Gielgud kept his Hamlet on the other side of the Atlantic, John's went unchallenged. But in the autumn of 1936, Gielgud, supported by Lillian Gish as Ophelia and Judith Anderson as the Queen, opened on Broadway. The actor's rich voice, his poetic delivery of Shakespeare's verse, and the intellectual strength of his whole conception brought cries that here was the greatest Hamlet of them all. The run was extended again and again, until finally Gielgud with 132 performances achieved a new record for Shakespeare, for *Hamlet*, and for Broadway.

Not everyone succumbed. "My standard of excellence," wrote Richard Watts Jr., ". . . is frankly Mr. Barrymore. His was to my mind, not only the finest portrayal of the role I have ever seen but was also the most magnificent piece of acting within my memory. If I think that Mr. Gielgud's performance is somewhat less impressive, it is because he fails to capture the demoniacal humor and thrilling theatrical eloquence that Mr. Barrymore brought to the role. . . ." And yet, when often a whole generation lapses between one great Hamlet and the next, John's Hamlet had stood a mere fourteen years. The notion that he did not care that his Hamlet was challenged is absurd: he lived on his reputation as a great Hamlet. He too could have played *Hamlet* 132 times—200 times—but he had closed shop and run to Paris after Blanche.

Now he responded to Gielgud's triumph with his usual generosity. On "Pipe Night," a distinguished company gathered at the Players Club to honor the young actor. John sent a warm but sadly garbled message:

MY DEAR MR. GIELGUD
MAY I MOST GLADLY BE ONE OF THE MANY TO CONGRATU-LATE YOU ON YOUR MOST BRILLIANT SUCCESS. AS THE GREAT GENTLEMAN WHO IS PRESIDING TONIGHT [Walter Hampden] CAN TELL YOU AND WHICH I AM SURE YOU AND I BOTH KNOW BUT ALTHOUGH TO A GREAT EXTENT WE WHO HAVE THE TEMERITY TO ESSAY HIM THINK WE ARE PLAYING HAMLET BUT STRANGELY DIRECT THINKING ON CHARMING PERSON IS IN MANY RESPECTS PLAYING US STOP OCCASIONALLY THIS COMES UNDER THE HEAD OF A TOUGH BREAK AND IT IS NOT ONLY

STIMULATING BUT THRILLING THAT YOU HAVE SO SUPREMELY
MADE HIM YOUR OWN.

MAY I ASK YOU ON THIS ONE OF THE MEMORABLE NIGHTS
OF YOUR LIFE TO GIVE MY LOVE TO THE PLAYERS STOP I CANNOT
TELL YOU HOW MUCH I WISH I WERE WITH YOU ALL.

Ethel was not as generous. When introduced to John Gielgud at the
Websters' flat in Bedford Street a few years later, she cut him dead.

TWENTY-FIVE

1937-1939

W ITH ELAINE GONE, the Western Board of Regents closed ranks about their wounded hero, presenting him on his fifty-fifth birthday with a naked girl wrapped in cellophane as well as providing a toothsome creature for him to be photographed with in public. Furious, Elaine blamed them for widening the breach, evidently not viewing her divorce suit a serious irritant. She thought them all—Fowler, Hecht, MacArthur, the artist John Decker, the savant manqué Sadakichi Hartmann, W. C. Fields—a pack of sodden juveniles and John, when egged on, the worst of all. And she was right about Decker, "a bastard"; Fields, "a mean bastard"; and Hartmann, "a degenerate fraud."

Lionel had no bawdy boys to rally round after his loss, nor did he wish them. At the Wheelers' invitation, he sent his personal belongings to their home. The rest of 802 North Roxbury Drive he left intact— Irene's toiletries on her dressing table, her clothes in her closets. He retained a caretaker to mow the lawn and trim the shrubbery, a housekeeper to dust the rooms and polish the brass door knocker. Just as Irene lay embalmed in the Calvary Mausoleum, her house stood outwardly the same, but lifeless. He could not bear to live there again. He suffered torment day and night. He wanted to die.

Two days after his birthday, Jack was declared legally bankrupt. Though he had made nearly $3 million as an actor, he could not now meet some $160,000 in debts. He determined to try to pay back his creditors, who included Dolores with a $55,000 trust deed on Tower Road—an uphill task with his earning power fractioned, his reputation fractured.

MGM had agreed to advance Jack $4,000 on his salary for *Maytime*; hearing he was bankrupt, however, the studio withheld payment, fearing they would have to make a duplicate payment to his creditors. With a new lawyer, Henry Huntington, Jack signed an indemnity agreement protecting MGM. He was not as good at protecting himself. *Maytime* was a Jeanette MacDonald–Nelson Eddy epic, John again playing an impresario in love with his pupil. He admired Eddy but not MacDonald, who constantly posed and preened and flourished a chiffon scarf so flagrantly during his speeches that in cold fury he threatened to gag her with it. Had MacDonald had the diva temperament, Jack might have been evicted from MGM sooner than he was. Actually his performance in *Maytime* is subdued, respectable. He is too tired to ham; his voice is tired, gravelly from severe emphysema, yet his "How do you *do!*" when he recognizes his wife's lover flashes with the old spirit.

Except for a sadly brief but very fine appearance as Louis XV the following year in *Marie Antoinette*, Jack was washed up at MGM. Mayer, who nourished Lionel because Lionel was docile, had little affection for blasphemous Jack. Not all the fifteen films he had still to grind out at Paramount, Universal, RKO, and Fox were trash, but twelve were, or nearly. The contrast to his stature a mere nine years before as reflected in his 1928 Warners contract was shocking:

> Producer agrees that Artist shall be the sole star and principal actor in each photoplay and that no director, author, artist or artists or person other than the Artist shall be starred or co-starred or featured therein without the written consent of Barrymore. . . . Producer agrees that the manner of production, release, distribution and exhibition and exploitation of each photoplay and the advertisement, publicity, and printed matter in connection therewith shall be strictly in keeping with the Artist's standing, reputation and prestige and shall be of high order, first-class, and dignified in every way.

Lionel stoutly defended his brother for the cinematic atrocities he would commit. "Against all the errors that can be properly charged against Jack Barrymore, this can be entered in his record: he was consumed with a passion to remit what he owed." Perhaps—but Jack was also consumed with a passion to act. He couldn't stop doing it, off screen and on. Both his public and boudoir battles with Elaine were performances; a pity no camera captured them. Furthermore, much of the insistence on paying bills came from the pragmatic Elaine, even as she ran them up.

Elaine's San Francisco play, *The Return of Hannibal*, ran a week. *Variety* was succinct about her performance: "She looks like Salome; acts like salami." She attributed her failure to Jack's professional and sexual jealousy. Sexual, yes, but Jack had nothing to fear from Elaine as acting competition, though he did have a lively fear, as did Ethel and Lionel, of the damage she could do to the Barrymore name. Back in Hollywood, Elaine appeared on April 24, 1937, in Superior Court to testify to Jack's cruelty, unreasonable jealousy, and impairment to her physical and mental health. "Better luck next time," said the judge.

According to Elaine, the minute she decided to divorce him, Jack wanted her again, invoking his long-slumbering Catholic faith to argue that their marriage in the eyes of the church was forever. On June 22, they were officially reconciled, but there was nothing mystical about their reunion. Jack had invited her to join him for an NBC Shakespeare series. "When John no longer objected to my career," said Elaine, "I came back." As a second condition to her dismissing her divorce suit, Jack had to promise to shape up sartorially: to shave, wear clean suits and neckties, and dye his hair which went white between pictures, though Elaine let him keep a white streak "to make it look real."

Cleaned up and temporarily out of a sanitarium, Jack now faced selling Tower Road and the *Infanta*. The yacht sold quickly for $77,500, settling a $40,000 mortgage and $35,000 tax lien against the boat. Tower Road was a different matter. Though Jack had poured some $500,000 into his creation, he had lost interest when it was complete and his "Chinese tenement," with neither upkeep nor repairs for years, attracted not a single bidder. He was stuck with it.

Jack found himself at Paramount appearing in the first of a series of Bulldog Drummond B movies as Inspector Colonel Neilson. There are the by now wearisome references to John Barrymore that have nothing to do with the role: Colonel Neilson to thug: "You surely wouldn't impair a profile that has endured this long, would you?" Like Jack too, Neilson has a penchant for elaborate transformations. These disguises perhaps gave Jack a little fun, but his whole demeanor shouts his fatigue. Because he could not remember his lines, or feared he could not remember them, he acted completely from blackboards held aloft behind the cameras. Jack claimed he used them because he did not choose to clutter his mind with "the etymological ordure" of the scripts he was given, but was franker with friends: "At that, I am one of the few actors out here who can read and act at the same time."

Paramount also tapped Jack to appear in *Romance in the Dark*, the final picture of the beautiful diva Gladys Swarthout who, unfortunately, the studio had discovered, could not act. He came in the first day, said the young director Henry Potter, with an "Oh, God, here beginneth another crashing bore of a job" look on his face.

"Mr. Barrymore, this is a great moment for me."

Jack looked tired.

"I thought your Hamlet was the greatest acting I've ever seen."

The left eyebrow shot up. "God, you must have been *wheeled* in!" From that moment they were friends.

Most vivid to Potter was a half-hour on the set with the actor at Christmas time, a day when Jack's *lapsus memoriae* was rampant, even with the blackboards. They were talking about the commercialization of the holiday when, without prelude, Jack began to tell of one particular Christmas Eve with Dolores and the children. "Suddenly," said Potter, "all his miasmas were gone. Suddenly he was lucid, beautifully articulate, mellow. The acid, rasping sarcasm faded away and his voice was tender and warm. The lines on his face softened as he described his family gathered around the fireplace as he read them Dickens' 'Christmas Carol' and the love, the kindness of the man and the uncomplicated peace of that evening was almost tangible. I had the feeling that that year—perhaps just that day—had been the only time in his life when he had been truly and completely happy."

Carole Lombard remembered Jack's goodwill and insisted on him for *True Confession*—a sparkler—with Jack adding a deft portrait as a washed-up criminologist with a penchant for cadging drinks and obscenely deflating balloons. In a dirty white suit, his dyed hair curling beneath a cocked fedora, Jack's shuffle out of the bar—cane twirling, rump wiggling—is a wonderful Chaplin take-off. Despite Lombard's fireworks, Jack steals the show.

He had enthusiastically admired Chaplin from early silent days and had got to know him at United Artists. Occasionally, egged on by Chaplin's current wife Paulette Goddard, they spent evenings trying to outstunt each other. Privately, however, Chaplin had his own take-off of John Barrymore which he performed at small gatherings. It was a devastating hit because it captured both John's beauty and obscenity. He did John in his dressing room rehearsing the "To be or not to be" soliloquy and, as the great periods rolled forth, picking his nose and eating it.

IN A SMART BLACK COAT with silver fox collar and ostrich-plumed hat, Ethel had made a grand entrance at a cocktail party given in her honor by the Studio of Acting. Chain-smoking and sipping tea, she launched into her acting credo for the benefit of the assembled trustees and reporters. "In teaching here," she said, "I am going to do the same as I've done in my own productions. I always get the whole company on the stage and say: 'Now, ladies and gentlemen, no one in this play is to act. You're going to simplify yourselves to try to be like the characters are supposed to be. No one is going to have any accent unless the part calls for one." When a reporter asked her what she would be paid, Ethel laughed. "I really don't know. You see, I haven't gone into it with them." Incorrigible.

But she never taught drama classes, nor did she retire. "I believed I would," she said, "for about a week."

Instead she began a twenty-six-week broadcast series of her old stage roles, beginning with *Captain Jinks*. "I'm thrilled to death and crazy about it!" she was quoted. "On the air I can be—oh, my dear—a youngster again!" Expecting temperament or nerves, the radio crew found her outwardly calm about acting for the mike, though her script was typed on heavy cardboard in case her hands shook. She sat engrossed in *Gone with the Wind* until she heard her cue; then she shut her book, rose, and started speaking as she walked toward the microphone. There was only one problem: the plays were reduced to thirty minutes less "Genuine Bayer Aspirin" commercials, hardly time for her to do them justice. She made some money, however, the pressing concern of the moment.

More important, that fall she would have a Broadway opening. The Theatre Guild had decided to risk Ethel Barrymore in *The Ghost of Yankee Doodle*, playing a part written for her by Sidney Howard—Sara Garrison, a charming woman who presides over a family of wealthy liberals concerned about the rising tide of fascism in the world. John Drew Devereaux, Ethel's young cousin, had a part and was awed by The Presence.

"It was the first time I had ever seen the workings of Aunt Ethel at close range," said John. "It was very exciting and also terrifying . . . she seemed to have, as I suppose all great stage stars do, at least five different points of concentration. She could be playing a scene with you and seemingly looking right into the innermost depths of your eyes, but if somebody moved over on the other side of the stage she would notice it immediately. They say that eyes can flash, but I've only known two people who had that sort of eyes—my mother (Louisa Drew) and Aunt Ethel. They could both, as we used to say, quell you with a look. They'd just look at you and all of a sudden fifteen hundred watts would blaze out at you. Most people, when this happened, just stopped what they were doing. . . ."

Also in the cast, Barbara Robins discovered on opening night the terrifying Ethel. John had a line "What would you do in Paris with all us boys!" that got a laugh, but then at the last minute Theresa Helburn had told Barbara to really hurl herself into her reply. Barbara hurled and squelched John's laugh, and suddenly everything on stage came to a halt. Ethel took two or three steps toward the apron, turned. *"Don't you ever do that again!*" she said. In seconds the scene was moving again, but Robins had not recovered by the end of the play. After the curtain Ethel went to Eddie McHugh. A laugh once killed seldom can be revived, but for a Drew-Barrymore it had better. "Tell the director *to get it back*," Ethel ordered. "Don't mind," John comforted Barbara. "She gets like that." She did rather often, Barbara discovered, but Ethel Barrymore fascinated her, particularly the time when she forgot her lines and just went on making beautiful, plausible vowels and consonants until the words came back to her. The audience never noticed.

Critics did not like *The Ghost of Yankee Doodle*, but they loved Ethel's "famous magic and authority," the "luminous glow of her most radiant comedy," the "glint and the quiet grace of the celebrated Barrymore style." Ethel had kicked into a corner the notion that she was through on Broadway. And yet, as Richard Watts Jr. observed, Ethel clearly shared the critics' opinion of the play, which she didn't really seem to be *in* but hovering over sardonically, mocking it. If she couldn't get a good play, perhaps she had to take that step so many middle-aged stars balk at; she had to accept unglamorous roles. She had not been against these. "I want to be a scrubwoman again," she'd said, affectionately remembering *The Silver Box* after too much *Constant Wife*. But her audiences had wanted the glamorous Ethel Barrymore.

Appropriately it was the militantly old Lionel who now cabled from London that she must play the role of the matriarchal "Gran" in Mazo de la Roche's adaptation of her novel *Whiteoaks of Jalna*. When Ethel heard he was in New York on his way back to Hollywood, she telephoned him, asking politely whether she could come to see him.

"No, no," said Lionel with equal formality, "I will come to see you."

He arrived, leaning heavily on a cane. They had not met since the filming of *Rasputin* almost six years before; he was older and infirm. He was also a widower. Perhaps that is why Ethel seemed to like Lionel so much better these years—or perhaps Jack's reputed coldness as well as the distressing Elaine had disillusioned her about her younger brother. She defended Lionel in print when informed that he had been dropped from Actors Equity for failing to join its sister organization, the Screen Actors Guild; she had called him recently for publication "the best actor, the best everything." He returned the favor now, urging her to persuade the British producer Victor Payne-Jennings to let her do the role that he had so admired in London.

When Payne-Jennings called, he asked whether she would mind playing a woman of 101.

"I'd be perfectly delighted," said Ethel. "That's just what I feel."

Directing would be the young British actor-producer Stephen Haggard. "The mere prospect of it terrified me out of my wits," he said, "even though Ethel Barrymore was still four thousand miles away." He knew the position the Barrymores held "at the apex of the American theatrical pyramid"; he knew that Ethel Barrymore had been a star of the first magnitude before he was born. Now she was also a legend.

Haggard had been deeply influenced by the starless repertory system of such groups as the Moscow Art Theatre. Now he confronted a company of adequate players, including Ethel Colt in the small role of Pheasant, over which Ethel Barrymore towered. She had a technique of her own, a technique, he knew, that belonged to the generation of the giants: Irving, Terry, Duse, Bernhardt, Richard Mansfield, Mrs. Patrick Campbell, Otis Skinner. Personal magnetism was its core. Oh, yes: Ethel Barrymore always claimed that she excelled at the democratic art of "listening" onstage, but how she listened! Standing quite still frowning down at the boards, pretending to be thinking about what another actor was saying, then tossing her head (still "listening" of course), narrowing her eyes, flying them wide open—until there wasn't an eye in the house not glued on her instead of the hapless speaker. And Stephen Haggard passionately found this all wrong.

Apart from one huge tantrum, Ethel conducted her relations with the modernist with complete dignity, yet *Whiteoaks* turned out exactly as Haggard had feared. Her hair hidden under a white cap, her teeth whitened to make them look false, Ethel gave a magnificent solo.

"The golden age returned again!" sang one critic—but why go on. For the next four years critics would repeat the same formula with rhapsodic monotony. Ethel Barrymore was magnificent, wonderful, the best she had ever been—in a play sadly unworthy of her genius. "When Miss Barrymore dies at the end of the second act," said one, said all, "the play suddenly becomes as empty as a room built around a portrait that has been removed."

She kept *Whiteoaks* on Broadway for the rest of the season, then set out on a forty-four-week tour. Though she wired her agent that May, AM SORRY BUT NO SUMMER STOCK IN ANYTHING NOT FOR GOLD OR PRECIOUS STONES THANK ALL THE GENTLEMEN BUT HONESTLY I'D RATHER DIE, she ate her words as she brought her own *Whiteoaks* company into stock, an innovation in summer theatre. She needed the money after all, she growled, because "that bloody Equity blackmailing Communistic stuff keeps me broke no matter what I make."

The complaint indicated the reactionary drift of Ethel since the days Equity members had kissed the hem of their leader's skirt. Floundering in dramatic backwaters for years, Ethel had come deeply to resent the theatrical trend that "communistically" claimed that the play and a strong company were more important than a star. Seeing herself as a Broadway outsider, she had even come to resent paying Equity dues; certainly she resented that Actors Equity forced actors to be members to get work: "that bloody Equity blackmailing Communistic stuff." What Ethel needed was a strong play and a strong company, but Frohman's star system which had bred her now played her false with the notion that she could carry any play alone. She always had, she always would. The notion was, well—reactionary.

IT WAS A TESTIMONY to John Barrymore's greatness that even now people imagined him in roles. Cukor wanted him for Cascart in *Zaza*. Ben Hecht wrote a part for him in *Nothing Sacred*, but Jack failed the screen test. Hecht was a friend, yet Gabriel Pascal also wanted him for Shaw's *Caesar and Cleopatra* and (still) *The Devil's Disciple*. In 1939 the great novelist Theodore Dreiser would write:

> Hearken, shining individual that you are!!
> Do me the honor and the favor to characterize *Hurstwood* in *Sister Carrie*. . . . Universal . . . is going to film it. Get well. Decide to. Don't die. Live to present Hurstwood for me. I have, for so long, thought of *you* treading—in art—his sorrowful way—his via dolorosa. *They* so much need and so truly desire you. *I do.* If you *will* to live and do this, you will. My sincere affection as well as admiration underlies this. And they bespeak for you many more years and many more distinguished labors.

Jack himself had bouts of wild, forlorn hope, telling his friend John Decker that he wanted to play *Macbeth* in the Hollywood Bowl.
"How would you get blackboards big enough?"
"I'd have airplanes skywriting."
He was very serious about wanting to play "the ophidian and fearless son of a bitch" brother in Robert Louis Stevenson's *The Master of Ballantrae* with Lionel. He had for years broached the subject to Lionel who, however, dexterously avoided it. He had written Gene Fowler from Kelley's Rest Home, begging him to persuade Lionel, "even intimating it might be a bridge to Terra Firma for his little brother" in that state of "slightly swirling levitation." More realistic was Selznick, who thought of Jack for *Intermezzo*: "a great deal of acting to do and not very many lines of dialogue." This too did not come to pass, but in 1949, when *Sister*

Carrie was at last being cast, Selznick warned William Wyler that "saying 'no' to Olivier is in my opinion exactly the equivalent to having said 'no' to Jack Barrymore for any role he could have played. In years to come it's likely to seem incredible to you that you turned down the suggestion."

Instead of *Sister Carrie, The Master of Ballantrae*, or *Caesar and Cleopatra*, Jack cavorted as Governor Gabby Harrigan in a second-string football farce called *Hold That Co-ed*. Compared to his *Bulldog Drummond* series, Jack is *awake*, but to little purpose, a Gulliver surrounded by Lilliputians. At least he is spared doing "The Limpy Dimp," an embarrassingly uninspired marching dance led by the unpleasant George Murphy and the trying Joan Davis. In future he would be spared nothing.

His next film, however, was another effort to star him in a serious vehicle. Garson Kanin, a new director at RKO, saw Barrymore and only Barrymore as Gregory Vance, an alcoholic ex–Harvard professor turned night watchman in *The Great Man Votes*.

"Nothing doing," said RKO producer Pandro S. Berman.

"Why not?"

"We don't want him here."

"You don't want him here. The greatest actor in America?"

"Was."

"Could be again. In this part."

"He's not going to work on this lot. He's unreliable and irresponsible and impossible."

But Berman owed Kanin a favor, and Kanin went to Jack's house in Bel Air. When Jack finally answered the door, he was stark naked. "They keep leaving," he said, excusing the lack of servants. "More of them leave than we ever hire." Then suddenly he looked down. "Would you excuse me while I slip into something more comfortable?" he fluted, and minced off up the stairs. But when Kanin outlined the script and came to the surprise conclusion, Jack roared, "When do we start?"

Before shooting they met again at Chasen's for dinner. Jack was as usual early so he could get a head start on "the giggle water." Kanin tried to order dinner, but Jack kept tapping the rim of his glass until the bartender had poured eight or nine martinis. When Kanin protested he was starving, "I'm sorry," said Jack with dignity, "but I simply cannot eat on an *empty stomach*!" He was indifferent to dinner when it finally came, but as he got into his chauffeured car he thanked Kanin for the splendid repast.

"Thank *you*, Mr. Barrymore."

Jack gave his short, barking laugh. "*Mr.* Barrymore!" he said derisively, and was driven away.

It was as though he were embarrassed at being reminded of his lost dignity by a stranger, thought Kanin, but it gave him an idea of how to handle John Barrymore for *The Great Man Votes*.

When Jack arrived on the set the first day he was "Mr. Barrymored" from the gatekeeper to the make-up man. Finally a cameraman who had worked with him before offered his hand.

"Good morning, Mr. Barrymore."

Jack snorted. "What the hell is all this Barrymore shit? Who's Mr. Barrymore, for Christ's sweet sake? You must think I'm *Lionel*."

Kanin found him prompt, cooperative, and prepared, though he insisted on the notorious blackboards. Often reading them required unusual gymnastics, like turning his head sharply to scratch the back of his neck. Kanin suggested the boards were more trouble than they were worth since Mr. Barrymore seemed to know his lines perfectly.

"Of course I know my lines," said Jack with a cold stare. "I always do." But this unbalanced verbal highwire artist needed a safety net.

He amazed Kanin the way he could produce tears, floods of tears, discrete tears. "What did you think?" he asked Kanin. "Did you like that little one first and then the big one or would it be better with the big one first and then the little one?" In the next scene he produced the big tear first and then, just when the camera was about to stop grinding, the little one sprang out of his eye.

"Oh, Christ!" he told the fascinated director. "The crying thing is nothing. All women can do it. *Can* do it? Hell, they *do* do it! And kids. . . . When I was about seven, I watched Ethel do it, and Lionel, and that gave me the idea. I went off into the bathroom for an hour or so every day and practiced. But it isn't acting. It's crying." Some people, he assured Kanin, could fart at will, a trick he'd regrettably been unable to master. He boomed with laughter. "Did you ever hear of Le Pétomane? The great French cabaret performer? That was his act. Farting. He was a tremendous hit. I saw him once when I was a kid. He'd come out and give a sort of dissertation on the subject and illustrate the different kinds. I remember that for a finish, he farted La Marseillaise. How could I forget it? But I mean to say, I wouldn't call that acting, would you?"

The only problem on the set was Virginia Weidler, a child actress so adroit that Jack immediately dubbed her "Mrs. Thomas Whiffen" after the old pro who had acted with John Drew on his last tour. In one scene, Jack has Virginia on his lap as he tells her and her brother about their dead mother. Jack was playing beautifully, but Kanin found himself watching the cunning way little Virginia was twisting Barrymore's necktie around her finger. Suddenly Jack screamed.

"God damn it! What the hell do you think you're doing, you hammy little bitch!" He hurled the terrified child across the set. "Who the hell do you think you're acting with, you silly little brute. Silly, hell!—crafty, God damn you, *crafty!* I ought to kick you right in the—"

"Mr. Barrymore, *please!*" said Kanin.

"Don't tell *me!*" Jack shouted. "Virginia. I've messed it up with bitches like her before. They don't fool me."

Perhaps because satire never appeals to the masses, perhaps because John Barrymore had long ceased being a box-office draw, *The Great Man Votes* went nowhere, a fact that depressed Jack, who had given his best. Gregory Vance was also simply too verbal. Alec Woollcott had called the pre-talkies period "the last time in America that the written word was paramount." By 1939 even the spoken word in movies was no longer paramount, a trend that would hit rock bottom in "method actors" like Marlon Brando and James Dean. When Joseph Mankiewicz was asked why he no longer wrote and directed films like his brilliant *All About Eve* (1950), he said, "People no longer come to films to listen—they come to stare." John Barrymore was above all a verbal actor, flinging phrases like roses in *The Great Man Votes*: "my bacchanalian buddy . . . rancor in the breast . . . the plethora of my fragrance . . . chameleon whimsies . . . I seem to detect in you a perspicacity only too rare these days." Certainly the public's tolerance of these verbal gymnastics was only too rare. It gave *The Great Man Votes* a cold shoulder.

SINCE THEIR RECONCILIATION Elaine had made a movie debut of sorts. In the one-reel *How to Undress in Front of Your Husband*, she demonstrated the "art" of taking off clothes. "Miss Barrie is unquestionably an authority on undressing," says a slimy male voice that goes on to tell how "this little lady," unlike most women who do everything to trap a man and nothing after, tantalizes her husband night after night with her striptease. "She must have 'It,' " says the narrator, "because didn't she capture the world's greatest lover?" Unfortunately, Elaine did not have "it," only a flat chest and thick waist. These were not her fault, but appearing in such trash was. She claimed she thought *How to Undress* would advance her career, at the same time insisting she wanted to be a serious actress. Furious at this tasteless exploitation of the Barrymore name, Lionel, Ethel, and Jack tried to suppress the film or have "Barrymore" removed from the credits—without success. New York State, however, banned *How to Undress* as "indecent and tending to corrupt morals," whereas it was really silly and sexist.

Lionel's reaction to Jack's reconciliation with Elaine had been to boycott her and, unfortunately, his brother. He simply stayed away. Ethel recognized Elaine's existence. "It's Ethel Barrymore, my dear," she purred into the phone when a manager failed to catch her name; "you know, Elaine Barrie's sister-in-law!"

Elaine returned Ethel's hatred. They had met when she and Jack went east in 1938. They had seen *Whiteoaks* (Ethel was wonderful, admitted Elaine), then Jack had insisted on a meeting. Ethel was already seated at a table at the Plaza when they arrived, behaving as though the hotel were one of her lesser castles. She had decided to be charming—was her tea spiked, wondered Elaine—and ended by inviting them both to Mamaroneck. Elaine was about to accept when Jack kicked her ankle.

"Baby, my sister is very dangerous," Elaine claims he told her after they had left The Presence. "You mustn't see her again. I wouldn't take you to that awful house for anything. That was one of her performances. Don't trust her."

Elaine hardly needed persuading. She had quickly discovered that both Ethel and Lionel were enemies, but of the two the more formidable was Jack's sister. La Barrymore had been spoiled by years of public adoration and acclaim: that accounted for the hauteur. Equally accountable, however, was Ethel's love of the bottle; surely her queenly airs were magnified by a perpetual alcoholic high. She was, thought Elaine, "far more unquenchable than her brothers"—yet at the same time tougher mentally and physically. As for Ethel's famous loyalty to Jack, Elaine decided it did not exist. During the filming of *Spawn of the North*, when Jack had collapsed with bleeding ulcers, Elaine had wired Ethel JOHN ON MEND. DON'T WORRY HAVE WONDERFUL OPENING. When Ethel did not reply, Elaine concluded she cared nothing for Jack, whereas Ethel was only furious to be told anything by a wife she had never acknowledged. Jack didn't always get high marks for loyalty either, however. According to Edna Jacobs, he told her he considered Ethel "the biggest ham on the stage. All she can do is walk across the stage in a dignified manner." In fact, all three Barrymores were jealous of each other, each wanting to be *the* Barrymore.

Jack and Elaine lived in a fourteen-room Tudor in Bellagio Road in Bel Air with the ubiquitous Edna. As he had Mae Costello's, Jack often enjoyed the mother's company: they were, after all, the same generation, and life can be lonely with a young wife who hasn't lived thirty-four years of your world. Edna claimed that her relationship with her daughter's husband was more than platonic, however. Showing off the house one day to Spencer Berger when Jack was gone, she led him to the Empire-style master bedroom and, eyes sparkling, pointed at the big bed. Jack, she confided, preferred *her* to her daughter on occasion. Edna had divorced the peripheral Louis, quite content to share Jack's home. When they went out together Edna was sometimes escorted by Russell Colt, on holiday from his second marriage. The thought of Ethel's fury had she known gave Elaine distinct pleasure.

Outwardly there were signs of stability. Jack was working, $5,000 of each $6,000 he earned going to his creditors. He had periods of not drinking. The Bundy Drive Boys, that pseudobohemian band of tipplers who drank together at John Decker's Bundy Drive studio, stayed pretty much away. But they were living on the slope of a volcano.

Jack continued his bouts of maniacal spending. He would suddenly *have* to have something, cost no object. He continued to loan money to anyone who touched him, and there were many: "Don't ever, Binky, allow yourself to become the kind of person who can't be a sucker for people." He got frantic cravings—for loganberry juice or suckling pig— that *had* to be gratified. And then just when an evening would be going pleasantly, Jack would decide that one little beer couldn't possibly do any harm. The one little beer ended in fury and perhaps a bruised arm or blackened eye for Elaine, which, when he saw it the next morning, he would either ignore or try to excuse with fawning amends. She found herself less wife than bodyguard: buying a capping machine so she could uncork the beer and water it, conspiring with bartenders to pour him weak drinks, following him when he got up at night in case he was headed for the liquor. He continued to collapse regularly, often being rushed to emergency rooms. Then just when she was about to call a priest, he would sit up in bed shouting for "the goddamn butchers" to let him alone. His jealousy and his sexual hankerings tormented her. Elaine was paying dearly for the prestige of being Mrs. John Barrymore.

A career was the only compensation for life in the snake pit: she was determined to restore John Barrymore to the stage and star with him there. But her movie career refused to get off the ground. Her first and last feature film was *Midnight*, in 1939; she spoke her few lines as a milliner with cool assurance. Jack loved *Midnight*, thought it the most fascinating screenplay he'd ever read, though as Mary Astor's jealous old husband he played third to Claudette Colbert and Don Ameche. Mary and Jack had both been battered by life, and one day as they sat side by side on the set she reached over and laid her hand on his arm for old times' sake. "Don't do that," said Jack, his eyes filling weakly with tears. "My wife is terribly jealous."

In the summer of 1937 Jack had teamed with Elaine in a series of "streamlined Shakespeare" radio broadcasts over NBC. They had to build a fence around the mike to keep John's sonorous voice at broadcasting distance; all his coaching had not rid Elaine of her Riverside Drive accent, yet the series was quite successful and *Variety* called Elaine "not a hopeless trouper." Compared to the 1928 recordings, however—to say nothing of his original performances—Jack was burned out, a fact he tried to disguise with floridity and flourish. In the fifties Audio Rarities records released excerpts from the 1937 NBC programs, unfortunately many people's only exposure to the acting of John Barrymore. In 1982 Eva Le Gallienne came to his defense.

"The greatest actor we ever had was Jack Barrymore. I saw him four times in 'Hamlet.' Don't listen to those terrible recordings because he did them when he had a terrible hangover and was making fun of himself. His 'Hamlet' wasn't a bit like that. He was extraordinarily simple, and he played the whole range of the character." Jack too dismissed the records as the stuff of hangover—sheer bravado. Actually he was cold sober and worked like the devil at the series. He had to; he needed the money. Just because he was desperate he pressed too hard and ended by caricaturing, not capturing, his great Shakespearean acting.

Elaine's ambitions were more exalted than radio, however, as the inscription in the biography of Madame Curie she gave Jack in 1938 indicated: "To Mac—with greetings from his dearest partner in greatness Lady M." Jack had long wanted to play *Macbeth*, not least because it would be pleasant to succeed where Lionel had failed. It was too late now, something that Elaine in her obsession with playing Christ to Lazarus could not comprehend. At her urging, Jack now appealed to Ned Sheldon.

Ned sympathized with Jack's futile search for security in marriage and forbore comment on his fourth; his mission was to support, not criticize. He was horrified, however, at the thought of Jack attempting *Macbeth* in his state with a twenty-three-year-old Shakespearean novice. There were three strikes against *Macbeth*, he wrote with consummate tact: the play had never been popular in America, no actor had ever made a great personal success as Macbeth, and there was danger in Elaine making her first Broadway appearance in so exacting a role as Lady Macbeth.

But then another script came into Elaine's hands. *My Dear Children*, by the novice playwright Catherine Turney and Jerry Horwin, a Hollywood press agent and screenwriter, had been shunted from producer to producer without success. Its central character, Allan Manville, is an aging Shakespearean ham with three children and five wives, all conveniently forgotten. Currently he hangs out in a chateau in the Swiss Alps with a mistress and a portrait of himself as Hamlet at the height of his career. Complications arise when his three daughters arrive independently at the castle. They are followed by three suitors. Further complications. Finis.

The producer Richard Aldrich thought it one of the worst scripts he had ever read, but if John Barrymore could be got to play Manville, he would consider backing it. Hearing of Aldrich's interest, a Hollywood agent sent *My Dear Children* to the Barrymores. Elaine read it first and knew she had struck gold. Allan Manville was a one-dimensional portrait of John Barrymore. What's more, Jack's drinking, memory loss and, by now, incorrigible hamminess would not break and might even make the flimsy play. And Cordelia, the leading daughter role, offered her the chance she'd been longing for.

The William Morris Agency, Jack's representative, was strongly against such a vehicle, but Elaine pushed blindly on. In New York Jack read the play to Ned, who tried to disguise his certain knowledge that *My Dear Children* would be only one more headline in the lurid Caliban-Ariel affair, and failed. When Jack objected, Ned urged him to get the advice of people like Charlie MacArthur, Ben Hecht, Arthur Hopkins, and Robert Sherwood.

Jack consulted MacArthur and the others; all were aghast at the thought of Hamlet returning to mock his ghost in a tacky stunt like *My Dear Children*. But Elaine had more power. Aldrich chose the young Austrian refugee Otto Preminger as director. Elaine's contract gave her $500 a week and 25 percent of the net profits; Jack got 12½ percent of the gross and half the net, with the possibility in a good week of making more than $4,500. Haggard, senile, drinking heavily, Jack set forth on degradation.

"I have always felt that considerably insufficient censure has been voiced against Aldrich and [Richard] Myers' [Aldrich's partner] cold-blooded exploitation of Jack," said H. C. Potter, who had directed Jack in *Romance in the Dark*, "—to say nothing of Elaine Barrie's. Apparently Mr. A.'s tender guidance of 'Mrs. A.' [his wife, Gertrude Lawrence] did not extend as far as Mr. B. in their heartless contrivance of a travelling Macy's-Window-At-High-Noon, in which Jack might exhibit his already well-advanced compulsion for self-degradation. And the sadists flocked to enjoy. Both [Aldrich and Myers] profess[ed] themselves aghast at the circus that ensued. All they intended, they [said], was a production designed to give Jack an opportunity to make a financially profitable comeback. Neither of the gentlemen could have been that naive."

PART FOUR

LAST BOWS

1939–1959

TWENTY-SIX

1939–1940

THERE ARE SEVERAL WAYS to view the tour of *My Dear Children* which opened at the McCarter Theatre in Princeton, New Jersey, on March 24, 1939, and closed in New York at the end of May 1940.

As the gallant attempt of a sick and bankrupt actor to pay his debts even at the expense of his reputation.

As the cold-blooded exploitation of an actor no longer able to protect himself.

As a sorry display of self-exhibitionism.

As Elaine's fault.

As the only work John Barrymore was capable of doing.

As a triumph of acting.

As a journey through Hell without a Virgil, illustrated by Doré—or John Barrymore.

On opening night the McCarter Theatre was jammed to the aisles. John Barrymore had not been seen on the stage for fifteen years, during which time his name had become a scandal. Among the audience curiosity, nostalgia, and hostility were probably evenly mixed. Nevertheless, at the actor's entrance the house exploded with applause that was obviously sincere.

He began by playing it straight, ad-libbing the few lines that eluded him. The break came when, suddenly bored with Allan Manville and the silly play, he turned and called to the prompter, "Give those cues a little louder, sweetheart. We can't hear you." The house roared with laughter, no one more so than Albert Einstein (who once, after a long talk with Jack, declared that no one else had discussed his theories more intelligently). From that moment he ceased being an actor playing a role; he became John Barrymore cracking the whip over a circus that jumped to his tune. At the end the house stood and cheered his brilliant self-mockery. Visibly moved, he appeared before the curtain. "I can scarcely tell you, not having heard that beautiful sound for more than fifteen years, how deeply it affects me," he said with a catch in his voice. "It is pure music to my ears." He then thanked Otto Preminger, his manager Captain Pierce Power-Waters, and each cast member, stagehand, and electrician by name: he could remember when he chose. He had reached the wings when he came back to the footlights. "I almost forgot," he said, faking distraction. "I almost forgot to thank my producers, my, ah, producers . . . let me see, ah, what *are* their names? Has someone got a program? Yes, yes, here it is: Richard Aldrich and Richard, ah, Myers." The audience ate it up. "I don't mind being held down by a script written by a gentleman named Mr. William Shakespeare," John would explain, "but I see no reason to be held down by any other script, particularly a farce comedy."

Because no one felt ready for New York, *My Dear Children* set off on a pre-Broadway tour. With Elaine aboard, publicity was guaranteed: publicity which would strip any rags of dignity from the enterprise. Once a hard man to interview, Jack now participated freely in the spectacle. Not all their battles reached the press, but many did, until readers were driven to protest the squalor.

Jack's jealousy flared almost immediately. As he had confined Dolores to her dressing room while filming *The Sea Beast* for fear she would look at a man, now he wanted to confine Elaine while he was onstage so that she would not look at the handsome actor Philip Reed. Drunk before the Washington opening, he turned on them. When Elaine protested her devotion, he exploded. "Bah! You've come along for the ride like a carhop!"

With each performance he hated the play and the woman who had trapped him in it more, and the more he hated, the more he drank. Power-Waters replaced his nurse with a six-foot-six-inch bruiser named Karl Steuver to serve as Jack's driver, drink-rationer, and bodyguard. By the time the tour headed into Ohio, Jack and Elaine occupied separate Pullman cars and separate hotels. At each train stop, Power-Waters managed to get them to smile together for photographers before they darted for separate cars.

His edema-swollen legs itched tormentingly; his sheets and legs were streaked with blood from his violent scratching; eczema was an added torture. Drinking, of course, aggravated the misery. Onstage his ad-libs, aimed at Elaine, became sadistic. By Memphis on April 20, he insisted, "I can't act with her." One night in New York Jack's old drinking friend and colleague Jack Prescott answered the phone. "I'm going to kill Elaine,"

Jack told him. Hotchener also received a phone call in Hollywood. "Can't we get together on the same basis as before?" asked Jack.

Aldrich and Myers sent Preminger on a plane, accompanied by Charlie MacArthur, whom Jack had asked for. Jack and Steuver were at the airport to meet them, each with a bottle protruding from his pocket. That night a horrified Preminger watched a production that had nothing to do with the original. For most of the play Jack sat slumped on a bench whether or not he was supposed to be onstage. Sometimes he appeared to be sleeping. The audience didn't seem to mind.

On the train to St. Louis that night, Preminger, MacArthur, and Steuver debated Elaine's demerits in Jack's compartment. Surprisingly, MacArthur came to her rescue: "Even if you don't love her anymore, you shouldn't mistreat a lady." Steuver announced that if MacArthur said that again he would stuff him into the five-inch space under the lower bunk.

Meanwhile Elaine had sent for Edna. Later that night Preminger was almost asleep in his own compartment when the curtains parted and two women crawled in and sat on his chest. Edna began to curse Jack in coarse, abusive language. She told Preminger that if he took Elaine out of the play she would tell the press that Jack had raped her not once but several times, and as recently as yesterday. "But who would believe you, Mrs. Jacobs?" said Preminger nastily. Edna made a fist. "If my daughter doesn't stay in the cast I will destroy Barrymore!" Preminger requested them to get off his chest and leave.

Elaine tells a different story: that she told Jack *she'd* had enough, that Jack ripped the dress off her back and struck her, screaming that he would inform her when she could leave the tour. That when the company reached St. Louis, Preminger begged her to stay for the sake of the play and the large presale. That she made the sacrifice.

Finally Elaine agreed to remain another week, during which time Preminger would find and rehearse a replacement. (Actors Equity would rule that Elaine be paid full salary plus the 25 percent for the run.) That day at a luncheon given him by three hundred of St. Louis's first citizens, Jack followed his kiss on Elaine's cheek with a kick in the shins, then launched into a speech pillorying Elaine as the "little wife" who looked so delightful that day, but with whom he couldn't live. That evening at the point near the end of the second act when Manville takes Cordelia over his knees and spanks her, Jack grabbed Elaine and spanked her hard enough to raise welts. She retaliated by biting his wrist until it bled. They thus entertained each other, but between Jack's fooling and memory lapses, the play dragged on till one in the morning.

The next day Preminger told Jack his performances were abominable. "Well, come tomorrow," said Jack into the hush that had fallen among the cast. The next evening he played the part as written, lines and business impeccable. Preminger groaned. "Jack, why can't you do this every night?" Jack grinned. "B-o-r-e-d, my dear boy. Bored."

A vivacious blond actress named Doris Dudley flew in from Hollywood to take Elaine's part, and Elaine and Edna left the tour. Elaine had imagined *My Dear Children* would introduce her to New York audiences and prepare the way for her Lady Macbeth with John but, as she discovered, the applause was all for John, hers the contumely.

On April 29 from St. Louis Jack sent a desperate letter to Maurice Hotchener:

> At my expense, follow up all clews regarding adultery and start a divorce suit if you procure evidence. Start an action against Elaine and her mother to make them accountable for a quarter-million dollars filched from me since 1935.
>
> If you can work out some peaceful financial and matrimonial settlement with Elaine do so. But get rid of her. Select some tax lawyer to work on my messes with the United States and California authorities. Once I carried a half million insurance; what became of it? Look into the mess on my Beverly Hills place costing $250,000, and my Bel Air place into which I sank $25,000 cash. [The Bel Air home on Bellagio Road was in Elaine's name.] Also my $250,000 yacht Infanta, which is gone. Protect my priceless Sargent, my art works, my first editions and other valuable personal belongings which cost me a fortune. . . .

With Elaine gone, Jack turned his self-contempt against the public. The next stop was Omaha, where he told listeners of radio station KOIL, "I want to tell you something about your town. It is one of the most enchanting places I have ever been in." He held his nose for the studio audience. "I never saw so many quiet homes, well-kept lawns, trees with no dust. I can't see why you want to go to the theater at all." That afternoon when the cast was rehearsing at the high school, he took pains to insult a teacher who asked whether he did not find Channing Pollock's play *The Fool* wonderful. "Madam," bellowed Jack, "I think it is a goddam abortion. If you say one more word about Channing Pollock, you will be puked on by one of the greatest, if not the greatest actor in the world."

What was it Woollcott had said so long ago? Something about truly great actors respecting their audiences. . . .

The performance that evening was sponsored by the Omaha Drama League, the kind of women's group that brought out the icon-smasher in Jack. In the scene in which Manville answers the telephone, his butler standing attentively close behind, Jack suddenly wheeled, shrieked in falsetto, "Albert, how many times must I tell you not to goose me!" Dorothy McGuire, a young Omaha actress, was playing his daughter Portia. Jack stroked her bottom appreciatively: "You know, you have a very nice fanny." Finding himself headed by mistake up a flight of stairs instead of into the greenhouse for an amatory session with his mistress, he said quickly, "Ah, we must go upstairs. There are no towels in the greenhouse." Laughter, but a number of Drama League women stalked up the aisle. "I am glad I amused you," he told the audience when the curtain finally came down, "but you have no idea how you amused me." He then went on to deplore marriage as "mankind's greatest calamity" and accuse women of lacking mental and artistic ability: "Of course there are fewer women artists than men because it is difficult to ride Pegasus sidesaddle."

In Sioux Falls, South Dakota, on May 2 Jack filed for separation and an accounting of $300,000 against "Elaine and Co." "In every marital proceeding brought against me by my previous wives," he told the press, "I have always, out of a sense of chivalry, not contested them. But this time I am taking the initiative." He wanted Elaine and Edna to explain what they had done with $300,000 he had entrusted to their management in the spring of 1935, eighteen months before Elaine became his wife. As far as he could tell, they had bought themselves a bit of a mansion in Bel Air and a pair of Packards. Besides that, he charged that Elaine and Co. had commandeered valuable possessions, including "works of art, books, manuscripts, jewelry, paintings, rugs, furniture, guns, pianos, fishing tackle, furs, and wearing apparel."

As Elaine and Edna in evening dress entered the Hotel Navarre the next evening, a process server posing as an autograph hound served them papers. Both women bowed with dignity and kept walking. Nine days later, Elaine retaliated by filing for divorce.

Meanwhile Power-Waters was finding America's Heartland weary of Barrymore's flying circus. Box-office receipts had fallen off; some theatre managers were threatening to cancel bookings. At the same time, hearing that Barrymore was a success on the road, RKO's Pandro Berman made him a sizable film offer with another to Aldrich and Myers to release him. The producers saw it as an excuse to close the show and cut $7,000 in losses, but now it was Jack who persuaded them to wait until Chicago, "a Barrymore stronghold": "I think it important to prove that I can make a success of this play, particularly since Elaine has left the cast." Since Aldrich and Myers declined to sink more money into the enterprise, Power-Waters ended by paying costs and salaries out of his own pocket.

On May 5, touring the Midwest with *Whiteoaks*, Ethel telephoned Jack to say that she had read attacks on his behavior in the press and that she wanted to give him her love and encouragement. Deeply touched, Jack wired her as soon as he hung up: DEAREST EETHEL: I HAVE ALWAYS LOVED YOU MORE THAN ANYONE SINCE MUM MUM WENT. MY ADMIRATION STARTED WHEN WE WERE KIDS, AND YOU SUDDENLY WONDERED WHAT YOU WOULD LOOK LIKE IN A PARTY DRESS. YOU TOOK SOME WHITE LACE CURTAINS DOWN FROM A WINDOW AND DRAPED THEM ABOUT YOURSELF IN SO AMAZINGLY DEXTEROUS A FASHION THAT I THEN AND THERE FELL IN LOVE WITH YOUR BEAUTY. YOU LOOKED AS DIVINE AS SOMETHING OUT OF HEAVEN, AS INDEED YOU WERE AND ARE, AND I NEVER FORGOT IT. DEAREST LOVE TO YOU AS ALWAYS. JAKE.

On May 8 Jack steamed into Chicago ready to deliver the show it was looking for. And he was right about America's number two city, which welcomed stars more warmly than New York. But it wasn't all love by any means. People who would not have come near his *Hamlet* crowded greedily to enjoy this "spiritual striptease of Gypsy Rose John." Word quickly flew about that *My Dear Children* was a laugh-riot. What stunts would Mad Jack pull tonight? "Is Mr. Barrymore drunk today?" patrons began asking. "Oh, what a pity, we shan't have any ad-libs." Drunk or sober, Jack knew perfectly well what they wanted. He gave it to them.

To fashionable latecomers: "Where the hell have you been, darling?"

To a man who laughs as Jack is making love to his mistress: "Ah! I see you've done this sort of thing yourself."

When a fire truck screamed past the Selwyn: "My God, my wife!" A following truck backfired. "And she's got her mother with her!" Or he might stop the play in its tracks and suddenly talk about Mummum. He said that he liked to imagine that old Mrs. John Drew was calling to him from the wings, "Go on, Jack, give them everything you've got!" He did. Snorting, strutting, bellowing, leering, hiccuping, prancing, swearing, wildly ad-libbing, he turned *My Dear Children* into a smash hit. He gave the audience everything it came for, said Ashton Stevens, except actually collapsing and dying onstage.

At that he suffered a coronary on May 30 and was whipped into an oxygen tent installed in his suite at the Ambassador. "The first time I've ever been in a tent show," said Jack. Garson Kanin wired; Jack replied,

"For a man who has been dead for fifteen years I am in remarkable health." Fifteen years: the fifteen years since he had left the stage.

Elaine phoned messages of sympathy that were not relayed; when she flew to Chicago Jack refused to see her. As his condition seemed to worsen, Power-Waters sent for Lionel and Ethel, who hurried to what they thought was their brother's deathbed. When they got to the Ambassador, however, Jack was missing. Orson Welles, who loved and admired Jack, also turned up on the same mission and found only Lionel and Ethel. The three had dinner and then went looking for him. They finally found him in a cathouse on the South Side and got him back to the Ambassador. "He wasn't dying at all," said Welles, "—of course he *was* dying, but he wasn't dying any *more* than he was any other day." Ethel came to a performance of *My Dear Children*, "rocked with laughter at his antics and told him definitely that it was one of the greatest performances of his career." Loyalty could go no further.

Booked for two weeks, *My Dear Children* ran thirty-three. Chicago went Barrymore-mad: Washington Park celebrated Barrymore Day with each horse race named for a member of the cast, Comiskey Park observed Barrymore Baseball Day, Ringling Brothers declared a Barrymore Circus Day. Bored, weary, often so ill that he had to perform the whole play sitting down, Jack endured the nightmare. Offstage he had his revenge. It is unnecessary to dwell on his sad, degraded behavior: how he distracted the actors from the wings with loud, drunken dirty stories, belchings, and hawkings. How no actress was safe from his pawing, though Power-Waters had provided him with three women. How he talked loudly and endlessly about fucking. How he urinated out windows, in sinks, in automobiles, in private elevators, in the sandbox in the lobby of the Ambassador so that he had to be removed by Power-Waters to a house in suburban Glencoe, where he offended his neighbors by urinating on the lawn until Power-Waters removed him to Winnetka where, apparently, the neighbors pulled their blinds. How he made the rounds of the sleazier bars after each performance, staggering home with Steuver at dawn. How his conduct in those bars was often revolting.

One night at the Club Alabam on Rush Street, he realized that the hard-faced woman singing in the spotlight through which cigarette smoke drifted like fog was the passion of his youth, Evelyn Nesbit. And she saw that the damaged man nursing a drink in his shaking hand was her beautiful lover. They both wept at what time and life had done to them, and Jack stood up and declared to the whole nightclub that she was the first girl he had ever loved.

On other occasions, too, the charm shone through. Spencer Berger and his wife-to-be Jane found him chain-smoking in his dressing room after a relatively subdued performance, hunched in a threadbare robe, his feet swollen in old slippers. His dressing table was strewn with pills, make-up, eye drops, and throat sprays, all liberally dusted with ash. "Funny thing about actors and booze," he said, as though trying to explain the sorry tableau to someone who still idolized him. "John McCullough once showed signs of being tiddly at the Arch Street Theatre. He was summoned before my grandmother, who berated him at length. After the lecture, damned if she didn't tell him she'd searched his dressing room, found an inferior rye, and replaced it with a choicer brand. Said he might as well get drunk in style! Can you blame me for being confused on this whole question?"

He dragged deep on his cigarette, coughed, tried to brush off the future. "I'm enjoying this Chicago run mainly because it affords me a chance to visit with another old pal, Ashton Stevens. But I know this play is a bit of cheese and I don't relish taking it into New York." As for *Macbeth*, "It's a possibility, I suppose, because I like the part. But it seems that Lady Macbeth has stepped out for a moment. If it's put on right—Lionel was crucified by a bad production: Bobby Jones lifted the whole concept from a production he'd seen in Germany; something soured in mid-Atlantic because Bobby—and Arthur Hopkins—let him down very badly—it could scare the hell out of audiences, which is what they love.

"Some other genius has suggested *King Lear* for me, but it has only one good scene—between Lear and the Fool on the heath. Besides, Lear is a tiresome, bellyaching old bastard.

"So we shall do what we can with this dish of tripe and then see what tomorrow brings." He pulled slowly on his cigarette and stared through the floor.

He had not seen Diana for six years, though in the last ten he had paid something like $180,000 for her support and only bankruptcy had prevented his financing her New York debut to the tune of $25,000. Though Diana had been named "Personality Debutante of 1937," the lost young woman had decided that acting would "build bridges" to her father's world, and Blanche had permitted her two years at the American Academy of Dramatic Art while continuing to fulfill her debutante duties. With the Manhattan Repertory at Ogunquit, Maine, the past summer, she had earned praise that had Jack (as he telegraphed) RUFFLING MY TAIL FEATHERS LIKE AN OLD HEN. Now he read that she was coming to the Harris Theatre with Laurette Taylor in Sutton Vane's *Outward Bound*.

He wired her enthusiastically: CAN'T WAIT TO SEE YOU LET'S SHARE THE SAME DRESSING ROOM LET ME KNOW ARRIVAL YOUR TRAIN LOVE DADDY.

He met her at the station, "dignified as a judge" in a dark overcoat and homburg—very gray, very weary but not, she saw with relief, drunk. He turned her toward the crowd and the cameras. "You had your face hidden. My dear, you ought to know better than that." He had filled a room in his Winnetka house with flowers for her, but Diana preferred the Ambassador where Blanche had reserved a suite for her and her maid. If Laurette Taylor hated her, as Diana claimed, it may have been because she was not a trouper but Diana Debutante.

Jack was determined to shock Diana Debutante out of her Newport ways. They dined at his favorite restaurant, Ricardo's, where he drank until Diana wanted to beg him to stop but could not because, after all, he was a stranger. On further encounters he continued to disillusion her. Dining at Henrici's, for example, with Laurette, her stage manager Eloise Sheldon, and Ashton Stevens and his wife Kay, he behaved normally until a table of matinee ladies arrived. Then, "You know that fish bowl in the window?" he asked the waiter loudly. "Bring me a Bacardi that size." Guzzling it, he launched into a reverberating account of the Calcutta whorehouse, watching Diana's face for her reaction. Another evening he took her to Harry's New York Bar where he had been making time with a blond dancer named Winnie Hoveler. Winnie danced over to him, perched on his knee, and began to caress him. Diana rose, pulled her furs around her shoulders. Without upsetting Winnie, Jack pushed Diana back into her chair. "Miss, sit down! You-will-leave-when-your-father-tells-you-to-leave. And not before! Don't you get grand with me, Miss Newport!"

At the special matinee he gave in her honor, she did not know what to think. Blanche always spoke of him as though he were dead: "Just remember that he was the greatest Hamlet and one of the most extraordinary men who ever lived." Now, hearing him parody the great soliloquy that once had turned audiences hot and cold, she knew that what he was doing was disgraceful. And yet he was debasing himself so brilliantly! Listening to the audience laughing at her father, feeling their furtive glances asking her how she was taking this exhibition, she decided that she hated them all.

Her opening was canceled: Laurette, drunk, had gashed her forehead and could not go on. Diana perhaps did not connect the fact that she was the daughter of and acting with the two greatest and most tragically wasted actors in America. They themselves, however, felt their bond. Walking down the street together, Jack's arm flung over Laurette's shoulder, they were jostled off the sidewalk in the crowd.

"Oh, Jack, no!" said Laurette. "Not both of us in the same gutter!"

Eloise Sheldon adored Jack: "He broke my heart he could be so wonderful, but by the time I knew him he was already destroyed. We shared the alley where the Selwyn and Harris Theatres joined, and I could have cried daily to see the curious that came around just to see what shocking things he'd say or do. Because he could be so simple and dear, it was one of the saddest things I've ever seen." Among the curious were Jack's colleagues: Charles Laughton and Elsa Lanchester, Fredric March and Florence Eldridge, Douglas Fairbanks Jr., Orson Welles, Mary Pickford. Welles liked to have dinner with Jack after the show. "He was so generous to a young theatre man like myself, and so kindly and so gentlemanly and so warm. He was such a *good* man." This made *My Dear Children* the more painful. "He was so sick he could hardly get through it, and pretended to be drunk. He knew he was prostituting himself, and that everybody he cared about was ashamed of him, but he managed to play it as though it were a great lark, and to bring the audience into it as though they were at a party. A great performance, really." Not to Mary Pickford. She became so hysterical raging at Jack backstage for debasing his art that she had to be sedated.

Lying rigid, blind now, Ned Sheldon heard about the Chicago carnival and tried to dissuade Jack from bringing *My Dear Children* into New York where he once had reigned. "I wish you would cut through and out of this Chicago engagement, head straight for California, let Lionel find you a quiet and economical place to live, then concentrate on the best pictures, best part, and best salary available. . . . Good luck, dear Jack. . . . I wish I could go to Chicago and talk with you for about five hours. Please consider that I am right beside you when you read this letter."

Why didn't Jack take Ned's advice? Despite good business in Chicago, he was left with so few dollars in his pocket after paying his debts that at the circus he'd had to borrow a dime to buy peanuts. He could make more in films. He was not only bored with the play but knew it was a "dish of tripe." Elaine had obtained her second interlocutory decree that November; that was finished. The answer would seem to be that John Barrymore wanted to play before a Broadway audience again even in a piece of rubbish. "Those whom the gods would destroy. . . ."

Dorothy McGuire resigned in Chicago. She thought *My Dear Children* not such a bad play and Preminger a good director, but Jack terrified her because "he was not afraid of anything." At the same time, she marveled how audiences came to feel for him a special closeness, as though by exposing himself he allowed them to possess him, and they were surprised and grateful, like a man to whom a woman unexpectedly gives herself. Still, she could not bear the production any longer. "I had a great admiration for John Barrymore when we started," she told Preminger, "but I cannot watch this man make a fool of himself." And then at the curtain of her last performance Jack touched her deeply with his poetic salute to the actress as "a young pear tree in the silver rain."

His last performance brought tears to the eyes of many in the audience. He was so drunk that he could not remember his curtain speech. Instead, he fastened on Winnie and her sister in the front row and launched into an incoherent, lewd, sentimental monologue. Ashton Stevens was among the people who left before the stage manager finally persuaded Jack to let the curtain fall. In the street Stevens wept for the "complete obliteration of Dr. Jekyll by Mr. Hyde."

Around the corner at the Opera House Maurice Evans was playing *Hamlet*.

HOUSES IN DETROIT, Cleveland, and Pittsburgh broke records, but it was New York that waited the most hungrily for the once great John Barrymore to enter the arena in chains. One of the biggest advance ticket sales in Broadway history generated queues stretching all the way around the Belasco block on West Forty-fourth Street. Special bronzed tickets were made up for the first night—though, because of the actor's supposed unreliability, they bore no date. As Jack's train neared New York, more and more reporters jumped aboard to scoop the return of the Has-Been Hamlet, the Clown Prince of Denmark. With Yonkers behind, Jack went wearily to shave himself for his arrival at Grand Central Station. Wearing big carpet slippers to ease his swollen feet and looking like death, he stumbled off the train into a barrage of flash bulbs. For them he kissed a policeman, the Power-Waterses' daughter Patricia, and Patricia's dog. A gang of children with autograph books screamed and clamored. Reporters shouted questions. Then Ethel emerged and bore him off to a house in Bayside, Queens, where Power-Waters hoped he could be kept sober and well enough for the January 31, 1940, opening. Ethel stayed with Jack three days, then Jack Prescott took over.

Broadway offered a good deal of light fare that season, but New York's taste was for tragedy at the Belasco. On opening night scalpers fought through the throngs, shouting tickets for $100 apiece. Making for the entrance, Brooks Atkinson thought the crowd "looked as if they hoped to be present at the final degradation of Icarus. Standing behind police barriers, they looked sinister. The crowds that watched the tumbrils pass in the French Revolution could not have been more pitiless or morbid."

Ethel was acting that night, but even so would have died rather than grace this performance with one of her late appearances. Her children were there, however, as was Diana, sitting between her half brothers Leonard and the beautiful, homosexual Robin, whose passion for Jack had inspired his calling himself "Robin Barrymore." Like Ethel, Blanche could not bear to see Jack debase himself. But old friends were there: James Montgomery Flagg, Herbert Bayard Swope, and Constance Collier. Movie colleagues: Jack Warner, Gladys Swarthout, Ernst Lubitsch. Theatre people: Dudley Digges, Stella Adler, Harold Clurman. And the critics, of course, including Atkinson and Stark Young who had seen John Barrymore's *Hamlet*, as had many of the audience. And there were enemies: people who deplored John Barrymore and wanted to be in on the kill. Jack was terrified of the New York critics, terrified of the audience, and yet had pursued these terrors relentlessly.

He entered unsteadily, blinking rapidly. The audience saw a man chronically ill—girdled, dyed, eyes bloodshot, feet and ankles swollen, hands shaking with a permanent tremor. Nevertheless, the applause lasted a full five minutes. But as Jack realized, the applause that greets an actor means only that the audience once loved him. He cannot rely upon past affection. He must win his public anew.

The applause had scarcely died when Elaine, with perfect timing, swept down the aisle to a third-row seat, confident of attention in plunging gold lamé, red fox, scarlet nails and lips. The press had declared emphatically that Caliban was through with Ariel, but Ariel knew that the helpless, hapless man would never be through with her until she was through with him. She had, moreover, a letter the press knew nothing about: a letter from Chicago that began "Dear enchanting and slightly nebulous bastard" and ended "For Christ's sake and your own, try to be good and know that I really adore you. You know we really can have fun, dear one."

Had the curtain come down after the prolonged and affectionate greeting it would have been merciful. But the tragedy had to be played out. To the relief of some but the disappointment of most, Jack played cautiously, intimidated by Broadway after so many years. Without his antics the play died. The audience snickered uneasily for a time, then gave up the pretense. The only affecting moment came, as it always did, at the rise of the third-act curtain revealing the portrait of John as Hamlet by James Montgomery Flagg. Jack gazes at it, very depressed, then sits down heavily and begins to recite the "To be or not to be" soliloquy. At this, the final travesty, some wept at the memory of what he had been.

Jack's own eyes were wet as he acknowledged an ovation compounded of sentiment and relief; he began a tremulous curtain speech. Then, as though he were to be spared no indignity, a motley figure with white painted face and orange shoes and stockings leapt from nowhere onto the stage crying, "Stop! Stop! This is Hamlet's ghost talking. I have always wanted to stand on the same stage with the greatest Hamlet." The audience held its breath; Jack himself was confused yet, suspecting a Bundy Drive boys' joke, went along. "You took a long time getting here," he said, putting his arm around the apparition's shoulders; "you look as if you'd had a tough winter. I say, old man, can't you come back tomorrow night." When the curtain finally came down, stagehands converged on the intruder who turned out to be merely an unemployed actor seeking publicity. But the mockery symbolized how far John Barrymore had fallen.

When Elaine hurried backstage, she found a crush of celebrities and Diana blocking her way. "Go away, Miss Jacobs," Diana said fiercely. "Just go away. Nobody wants you here."

"Please allow your father to dismiss me, my dear," smirked Elaine, "—if he does."

Father couldn't dismiss a flea, but was already engaged by family and friends for a party at the Monte Carlo. Elaine followed him there, and patrons of the nightclub stood on chairs to get a view of John Barrymore's fourth wife and daughter pulling him like taffy.

"Look, Miss Jacobs! This is my father. We are Barrymores and you have nothing in common with us. Please go."

"Maybe so," said Elaine, "but I know him a lot better than any Barrymore. I'm staying."

Weeping, Diana pleaded for someone to rescue her father. Frank Chapman, Gladys Swarthout's husband, took him to the men's room, but when they emerged Elaine was waiting. Jack stopped to buy cigarettes, but found his pockets empty. "I'll pay for them," said Elaine promptly. "I might as well pay for your cigarettes—I paid for our marriage license."

Still crying, Diana asked her father to take her home.

"No, I prefer to stay," said Jack. The few times Jack was ever with his daughter he always made it clear that any sexually available woman was more important, one of his more callous crimes. Diana made a frantic call to the Players Club where Prescott and Steuver were waiting. "For God's sake," she sobbed, "come and get my father."

They came. "We have a car," said Steuver to Elaine, "so we'll take you home."

"*I* have a car," corrected Elaine, securing Jack's arm, "so we'll take *you* home."

Photographers asked Jack to kiss Elaine. As he did a passer-by muttered, "Nutty!"

"Sure I'm nutty!" shouted Jack. "Of course I'm nutty. I've been nutty for years. . . . And, so, good night all; may angels lull you gently to sleep. . . ."

When Jack made it clear he was overnighting at Elaine's suite at the Hotel Navarro, Prescott glared. "Well, after all, I am not committing a statutory offense," said Jack, shooting an eyebrow. "She is still my wife." According to Elaine, she begged Jack to be discreet because she didn't want her divorce invalidated and that Jack's remark to a reporter the next morning—"And since when, Miss Ferguson, is it illegal for a man to sleep with his wife in the State of New York?"—forced her to take him back.

She forced Jack to get her back into the cast of *My Dear Children*. Doris Dudley joined Diana in consoling herself over Elaine's victory. "I am in the peculiar position of trying to fight sex with talent," said Dudley.

> I hope [she continued] that Miss Barrie is not doing all this for publicity, because it will hurt John. He needs somebody so badly. He's a very lonely old—no I won't say he's old—he's a very lonely man and he has a spent mind.
>
> I like John. I've hated him and I've loved him. He's not a person you can be on an even keel about. I can understand how this all happened. John is the kind of person who can be easily influenced by people if he likes them. All you have to do is cater to him and flatter him. And did that woman flatter him the other night! It was amazing to see a man of his intelligence fall for it.

Not everyone was so tolerant. "Who in the world gives a damn about the affairs of John and Elaine Barrymore?" complained a jaded reader, echoed in verse by another's "It nauseates me, with my breakfast bun / To read of old John, and what he has done / His wives and his debts and his kittenish capers / I think that I'll stick to the good funny papers." Columnist Natalie Jenkins Bond took up the refrain:

> John Barrymore and his spouse . . . are at it again. The same dreary nonsense of an aging actor making himself ridiculous over a not even attractive young woman less than half his age but old enough to know better all the same. . . . With the array of wives that he's had this last one is one of those things that only he

can explain. . . . a silly little non-entity whose main forte is vulgarity. . . .

One newspaper went so far as to promise its readers on the front page that they would not be insulted by another Caliban-Ariel story inside.

This third reunion with Elaine did nothing to stabilize Jack, who collapsed and had to be taken to Mount Sinai Hospital. When Jack Prescott found himself prohibited, he knew who had issued the orders. Telephoning, he presented himself as "Ned Sheldon trying to get Mr. Barrymore." Jack came on the line. "Come back in five minutes, you sweet-scented bastard!" If Prescott told the staff John Barrymore was expecting him, he would be shown up to the room.

And so the battle over the remains raged. "I didn't feel quite the animosity for Miss Barrie other people did because I thought she did at least try to take some care of John and keep him cleaned up," said Eloise Sheldon. Attending a strictly nonalcoholic musicale and supper at the Barrymore apartment on Easter Sunday, Hume Cronyn agreed. Elaine had insisted that they mix with people, and though John called the guests "those poops," he was looking better and thinking better. As for Elaine, she had no taste, thought Cronyn, but "beauty, a sense of humor, and oomph."

For better or worse, Elaine also kept at him about a real comeback. "Jack," said Laurette, "when are you going to put on your spangled tights and give us King Lear?" "Well, Puke here in the pink bonnet and I were talking about that today," said Jack who, despite calling him a "bellyaching old bastard," was haunted by Lear and sketched himself as the tormented old man stripped of kingdom and crown. ("All that's necessary for a great *Lear,*" said Richard Watts Jr., "is to find three John Barrymores and get them to play Lear, the Fool, and Edgar.") Jack was also talking about putting together a company to present *Hedda Gabler,* among other plays, for Elaine. In reality nothing was possible any longer but four more dreary weeks of clowning to less than full houses. The novelty had worn off. And the first night Elaine made her return appearance as Cordelia she was hissed and booed.

The New York critics in a body had thrown up their hands and wept.

Burns Mantle: ". . . you who have tears to shed over the loss of the American theatre's one-time leader may prepare to shed them."

Stark Young: "He practically slides down the banister of his own reputation."

Sidney B. Whipple: *My Dear Children* is "an open invitation . . . to witness the humiliation of a fallen idol and the abasement of a once magnificent talent."

Richard Watts Jr.: "The recent offstage spectacle of Mr. John Barrymore and his shrinking, sensitive wife has been of such a repulsive sort that I am afraid it has destroyed most of the pleasure that came from Mr. Barrymore's long-awaited return to the theater. Even at best there was something saddening and embarrassing in the sight of the man who is undoubtedly the greatest of our actors appearing as an extravagant buffoon . . . when he should have been trying out his incomparable talents after all these years in a work worthy of him."

But for Brooks Atkinson *My Dear Children* proved that John Barrymore was "still the most gifted actor in this country." For seventeen years he had held his talents cheap; the record was not a pretty one: he was now a ravaged figure. "But the fact remains he can still act like a man . . . who knows the art. . . . The Barrymore breeding keeps him master of silly material, and the tricks he plays on it are the improvisations of a man of sharp and worldly intelligence. . . . Although he has recklessly played the fool for a number of years, he is nobody's fool in *My Dear Children* but a superbly gifted actor on a tired holiday."

Atkinson's remarks inspired Jack to write a stumbling but heartfelt note of thanks:

> To begin with I beg you to believe that I am not in the habit of writing to the Critical Cognoscenti in this—or any other—vein!
>
> It is difficult—I imagine—in such communications not to detect—in spite of the most ingenuous intentions—a certain coy note of speciousness! I somehow or other—do not believe—you will for a moment invest—this screed with that quality—!
>
> I wish merely to most sincerely thank you for your very charming—sane & understanding attitude—and to tell you how deeply grateful I am to you for it—It is more stimulating than you can possibly imagine!

Now he was offered a contract guaranteed to debase him further: Darryl Zanuck wanted to exploit him openly in an autobiographical film called *The Great Profile*. Since he was again $100,000 in debt, thanks in part to the "lovely, big terraced apartment at 325 East Seventy-ninth Street" Elaine had insisted they move into, Jack accepted Zanuck's offer. But it was a season of contrasts. In a *Billboard* poll of the five greatest performers, John won handily over Chaplin, Hayes, Muni, and Caruso, though some respondents ruled out his current vehicle. And he proved he still was a great classical actor, holding fellow actors spellbound at the Associated Actors and Artists of America ball with a Hamlet soliloquy for which he spurned a microphone as "an inverted spittoon."

Jack spent his last night in New York with Prescott, insisting they go to the Hotel Knickerbocker where he remembered discussing the art of caricature with Caruso beneath the Maxfield Parrish painting of Old King Cole. When Prescott reminded him that Caruso had died in 1921, that the Knickerbocker had been razed long ago, and that *Old King Cole* was now hanging in the St. Regis, Jack immediately insisted that they track the portrait to its new home.

The St. Regis bar was nearly deserted, but for Jack that night the place was crowded with familiar faces, and Prescott fell willingly into his friend's mood. Through the door came Jim Hackett, the Shakespearean actor, followed by Uncle John Drew and Nat Goodwin, hearty drinkers all. Caruso was there and "Gentleman Jim" Corbett and Kid McCoy, whom Lionel had impersonated so brilliantly, and old Frank Butler and Rip Anthony, who'd always been good for a meal or a bunk. Willie Collier, the master comedian, materialized along with George M. Cohan, Sam Harris, Monty Flagg, and Frank Case, who had literally given Jack the shirt off his back.

It was late when they kissed each other goodbye. Jack walked away with a jaunty wave of his hand into the night. They would not see each other again.

Thoroughly sick of the dung heap on which he'd been crowing, Jack left with Elaine for Hollywood where Edna was waiting. But why prolong the dreary tale. This reconciliation was no more permanent than the others. Sober for a few weeks, Jack plunged into drinking. He became sure that Martha, their cook, was trying to poison him and made Elaine taste his food before he would touch it. There were violent quarrels, threats of mayhem, disappearances. Finally Jack fled from Bellagio Road to his abandoned castle on the hill. On November 27 Elaine was granted her last interlocutory decree. "Ah, it's wonderful!" said the frightened man, pouring himself whiskey in the office of still another lawyer (Huntington had refused further involvement in the domestic felicities of John and Elaine). "Even if, after all, it's no new experience for me. I'm glad for her, too. It's no particular distinction being called 'Mrs. Barrymore.' There have been too many of them. Now I'm free to resume my search for the perfect mate."

Elaine retained title to Bellagio Road; Jack would pay $15,000 in tax liens and a cash settlement of $8,500. She asked for no alimony, but Jack was not impressed. "Dear, dear Elaine. The sentimental little girl. Why, just to show you how sentimental she is, she once asked me for my false tooth. I wondered why. So I took it out and looked at it and I found it contained five ounces of gold."

In five years Elaine had managed to generate more publicity for John Barrymore than he had attracted in his entire life. Ugly publicity. Jack, of course, participated, being offstage an incorrigible ham, but the energy behind the headlines was Elaine's. She had a zeal for litigation: "Soon I shall be unable to count them on my fingers," said Jack of her many suits. Suffering from inflated ambition, she could be pushy, blatant, and cheap.

She was also practical and tried to introduce some kind of middle-class order into the shambles of Jack's life. And she said two true things (at least). She said, "You couldn't hate him because he was such an abomination to himself." And she said, "You can't live with a man like that." The amazing thing is that she tried, but as she freely admits in her memoir, her ambition knew no bounds. And Jack could be warm, enchanting. During one of their separations he stalked the house on Bellagio Road, dashing from one bit of shrubbery to another until he was surprised by the unexpected emergence of Elaine and Edna. All three of them stood immobile, staring at each other. Coming to her senses, Elaine demanded that he leave the premises immediately or face arrest. In answer, Jack "impishly balanced on one foot and started playing an imaginary pipe." Moments like these made the agony seem worthwhile. But Hyde always reemerged. For her trophy in the five-year battle she took away the name "Elaine Barrymore": Jack specifically forbade her to call herself either privately or professionally "Mrs. John." Ironically she had played a vital part in the name's tarnishing.

JACK STILL HAD in his possession the frontispiece he had painted for Michael Strange's *Resurrecting Life*. Above a landscape of tortured men caught in the toils of monsters erupting from black waters, a naked female—the Eternal Feminine as Poetic Spirit—rises toward a Grail ringed with light and flowers. A tribute to Blanche as poet, the Freudian allegory also embodied the destructive war in Jack's own nature between higher and lower, feminine and masculine. Now, however, he saw the woman only as Elaine-female-destructor. In a rage he obliterated both the female figure and the Grail, substituting the male symbol of a large bird with crest rampant and wings outstretched. A few white flowers of the original shone faintly through.

WHILE JACK WAS LABORING in *My Dear Children*, Ethel chalked up two flops. Not personal failures, but as plays washouts.

She had spent her sixtieth birthday on Alec Woollcott's small, wooded island in Lake Bomoseen, Vermont. Actually it belonged to the Neshobe Island Club, a handful of old Algonquin Round Tablers; since Woollcott was the only permanent summer resident, however, he ruled the island and decreed its guests—and he decreed Ethel often. When she arrived this August, the author Vincent Sheean and his wife, Diana Forbes-Robertson, were among the visitors. Diana was awestruck at Ethel's beauty as she stepped out of the launch in flame-colored lounging pajamas, the sun striking copper glints from the waves of her strong hair. "If Winston could see her now!" thought Diana, for Ethel Barrymore seemed impervious to the years. Vincent Sheean fell in love with her before she told him caressingly how much she admired his writing. A few months later he handed her the first act of a war play called *An International Incident*. Ethel was intrigued. That October she had heard Neville Chamberlain's unhappy voice announcing that once again Britain was at war with Germany. She wanted to do something timely.

First, however, she opened at the Cort in November in *Farm of Three Echoes*—and yes, the critics said the play had only Miss Barrymore to give it life and excitement, and what a job she did! They did not mention the real triumph. Ethel had stopped drinking. No more mysterious collapses onstage, no more ugly scenes with reporters, no more lawsuits over unpaid bills. Somehow Ethel had summoned the discipline that eluded Jack: the nightmare years were over. Vincent Sheean liked to say that it was his *International Incident* that reestablished Ethel Barrymore's reliability in the theatre, but she had already proven herself with *Whiteoaks* and now *Farm of Three Echoes*. A true alcoholic, Ethel had at last told herself she *could* not drink. "We Barrymores were all great drinkers in our day," Georgie Drew Mendum confided wistfully to a colleague. "But now we get together for Christmas dinner, take one look at the plum pudding, and fall flat!" Ethel stopped even looking at the plum pudding. Instead she became a devotee of strong black coffee and iced tea.

On April 2 *An International Incident* came into the Ethel Barrymore Theatre, where she had not played in nine years. Hundreds of her adorers cheered her entrance wildly; indeed, the whole play again turned out to be Ethel Barrymore: Ethel commanding a scene without lifting her voice or even a hand, Ethel tossing in a line that glittered like a diamond amidst dross. But "If Sheean's name had not been on the program," rebuked one critic, "we should have guessed the play was written by an ambitious college boy." Not even Ethel could help this lame dog over the stile; *An International Incident* closed twelve days after its opening. But it had put Ethel back on Broadway as her enchanting self, not the white-haired matriarchs of *Whiteoaks* and *Farm of Three Echoes*—"service enough," said Brooks Atkinson, "for any drama to perform."

Meanwhile the producer-director Herman Shumlin had bought the American rights to a play by the Welsh actor Emlyn Williams. *The Corn Is Green* would probably not go down well with Welsh nationalists today, but in 1940 the story of the English schoolteacher whose human faith lifts a Welsh lad from the coal mines into Oxford had both truth and charm. Helen Hayes and Katharine Cornell both refused the play before Shumlin offered it to Ethel. When he came to the Colony Club to discuss it with her, she said firmly, "You can't be Stanislavskyish about this. It's a simple play about a simple Englishwoman with the gift of teaching, who gets a wonderful chance." Shumlin looked rather surprised, but they quickly came to an agreement.

Shumlin assembled an excellent cast, including Mildred Dunnock, Rhys Williams, Rosalind Ivan, and Edmond Breon. He found the perfect Bessie Watty, the slut who seduces Morgan Evans, in Thelma Schnee and the ideal Morgan Evans in the handsome young actor Richard Waring, of whom Margaret Carrington said, "I haven't been so enthusiastic about anyone since Jack Barrymore did *Hamlet*." Ethel would play Miss Moffat, "about forty, a healthy Englishwoman with an honest face, clear, beautiful eyes, a humorous mouth, a direct friendly manner, unbounded vitality, and complete unsentimentality." Shumlin had had marked successes with *The Children's Hour*, *The Little Foxes*, *The Merchant of Yonkers*, and *The Male Animal*. Everything seemed auspicious, therefore, for the November 26, 1940, opening at the National Theatre.

Except that Ethel took a dislike to Herman Shumlin. She found it unforgivable that he allowed "that terrifying woman" Lillian Hellman in the theatre for the first read-through. (Most people found Ethel far more terrifying than Hellman.) Rather often the words "How *dare* you!" were on her lips. More insultingly, she sent Eddie McHugh to read her part at rehearsals. True, Shumlin's metallic voice barked out directions in a sometimes less than tactful manner. But Ethel's antipathy was emotional-political, inspired both by Shumlin's pro-Soviet stance and her friend Tallulah Bankhead's quarrel with both Shumlin and Hellman over their refusal to let her perform *The Little Foxes* for the Finnish relief fund. Shumlin endured.

Broadway had been longing to welcome Ethel Barrymore looking her age in a strong play. When she made her entrance in her simple school-marm's straw hat, pushing a bicycle, the theatre rang with welcome. Not long into the first act, the audience realized that after the thin theatrical fare they had been starving on, here at last was something solid. The people were real, the Welsh setting real, the problems real. When the second-act curtain, which so often falls on boy-loving-girl or girl-losing-boy, came down on the scene of Morgan Evans sitting down to take his entrance exam for Oxford, Miss Moffat looking tensely on, the audience was gripped by the strong drama of Williams's play. At the end they gave thanks with fourteen curtain calls, eight for Ethel alone. Perhaps the happiest were those who had been unhappy with *My Dear Children*, for *The Corn Is Green* was a Barrymore triumph.

"With the first real snow of late Autumn comes the first real play of the season," wrote Brooks Atkinson happily. "It is 'The Corn Is Green,' and it was superlatively well played at the National last evening with Ethel Barrymore at the peak of her talents. . . . After a long round of mediocre parts, she knows that something of rare quality has come her way and she has risen nobly to the occasion. She plays it forcefully, but she also plays it with deep compassion, and from now on she can wear Miss Moffat as a jewel in her crown. . . . Everything about 'The Corn Is Green' reawakens enthusiasm for the theatre."

Ethel's impact on audiences was enormous. Eloise Sheldon called one matinee "one of the most electric times I ever remember in the theatre. Ethel Barrymore was truly magnificent—even her hands seemed to have the chalky look of a true school teacher. It made me shiver." Michael Redgrave looked back on a performance as his real induction into the theatre. On leave from the Royal Navy, he went on a theatrical tour of New York. The last night in town he paid a dollar for standing room at *The Corn Is Green*. For the first few minutes he was disappointed, "Then something happened that does suddenly happen with great performers—

you get up on their plane. I thought she was marvellous, and I was stage-struck." Redgrave had bought an autograph book at Macy's; he took it backstage humbly for Ethel to sign.

Besides its dramatic appeal, *The Corn Is Green* also reawakened hope for sanity and civilization. Though Williams's play is set in the late nineteenth century, it caught the essence of what Britain and its allies were fighting for far more successfully than the new crop of war plays. As bombs fell on London, obliterating history, Miss Moffat's faith in Greek and Latin, in Shakespeare and Voltaire seemed to embody faith in Western culture. Fascism was enslaving, like the black coal mines or the lust of Bessie Watty; Miss Moffat's belief in the individual mind seemed a reassertion of freedom and democracy. Not that audiences analyzed the play for its contemporary significance. Yet no one could leave the National Theatre without feeling heartened by a Welsh boy's vision that was also the vision of a nation at war: "So the mine is dark. . . . But when I walk through the shaft, in the dark, I can touch with my hands the leaves on the trees, and underneath . . . where the corn is green."

For this reason, a transatlantic broadcast on December 17 between Emlyn Williams in London and Ethel, Waring, Shumlin, and Williams's wife Molly in New York proved one of the most affecting pieces of broadcasting of that or any other year. Originally conceived as a publicity stunt for the play, the program instead captured both the agony of war and the symbolism of Williams's play. Communication by phone or radio was minimal between London and New York since Britain had gone to war so that the impromptu exchange between Williams and his wife was that much more moving—he assuring her that their home was still standing, she assuring him that she and their two sons were as happy as possible. This unexpectedly dramatic broadcast, framed by the singing of the Welsh chorus from the play, won a Peabody Award for the best special events program of the year.

As *The Corn Is Green* settled into a long run, Richard Waring learned a great deal about the Great Lady who, though aloof with most of the cast, liked him because he could act and because he knew Sammy. He was astonished by her sang-froid onstage. "Don't move," she ad-libbed on one occasion. She rose, walked to the door at the back of the stage, opened it. Eddie McHugh was there with the script. "I thought someone was at the door," she said, returning to resume the scene without the audience knowing she had dried up. Or the way she could manage any scene. Shumlin complained one night that he didn't like the hand that Waring got on an exit because it came too near the end of the first act. The next night Waring hadn't closed the door before Ethel turned, radiant, and lifted her arms, crying "Miss Ronberry! Mr. Jones! . . . we are going to start the school!" Waring's exit was never applauded again.

Her sports mania amused him: "Dicky, Dicky, find out about the fights!" In the next scene he would report under his breath that Joe Louis had scored a knockout in the second. Once she was removing her make-up in front of the mirror when he knocked and entered. "I hear the Bums blew two today," said the Great Lady, swabbing cold cream.

She was ritualistic. She never missed a performance, she never varied the excellence of a performance. She always stayed in her dressing room, immaculate with its crisp chintz and handsome light-framed mirror, be-tween a matinee and an evening performance, reading or listening to the radio. During the play she had one brief interval offstage when she did not have time to go to her dressing room; for this McHugh set up a card table covered with a cloth in the wings. Every night the articles on that table were identical: a glass of iced tea, one Vocalzone pastille, one Par-liament cigarette, one box of matches in a Scotty-dog holder, a brush, a comb, a mirror. Her obsession for routine could create difficulties. For realism, Shumlin had obtained actual student essays from a Lafayette High School English class. When Ethel read Morgan Evans's essay every night, she was actually holding pages written by a student named Vincent Infuso. The papers gradually became limp, and one night McHugh made a sub-stitution, throwing her off stride. Ethel was furious. From then on McHugh painstakingly ironed the Infuso papers before each performance. (When they were finally rain-damaged on tour, Ethel bowed to the inevitable.)

Waring was very aware of Ethel's dislike of Shumlin, including his insistence that Waring kick the door open in the scene when he comes in from the tavern. Ethel thought it a terrible bit of business, and Waring usually omitted it. But when Shumlin was in the house, "Dicky, Dicky, kick the door!" Ethel would hiss. "The Gestapo's out there tonight." On another occasion Shumlin told Ethel that her reaction to Morgan Evans's homecoming in the third act wasn't coming through. Ethel froze. "I think," she said, "it is clear that the audience got it—*and* the critics."

"*I* didn't get it," said Shumlin.

Ethel stalked off the stage.

"You can't talk to Miss Barrymore like that!" said the appalled Eddie McHugh.

Every night Ethel was escorted from the theatre either by McHugh or Sammy. Waring got used to the rap, the blond head looking in. "Dicky! What mood is Mother in? Look, can you lend me ten? I didn't get home last night." He would spend the ten at a bar next door waiting for the play to end; he did not hold his liquor well. Playing Romeo, Waring had met Sammy in Eva Le Gallienne's company where she had given Sammy the small part of Paris as a favor to Ethel. But at the read-through Sammy clearly was hopeless. How to tell Ethel? "Oh, give him a costume and a walk-on," said Ethel grandly when informed. "Lazy, untalented, but very lovable," thought Waring. Certainly Ethel loved him.

When not squiring his own mother, Sammy squired older women, mother figures. The often paid. Chronically short of money nevertheless, he and Jackie used Sister to coax money out of their mother. Sammy hated his father, who was so tightfisted that he once sent him a bill for a ten-cent phone call he made from the Yale Club. Still, he managed very well. The Barrymore name had its advantages. With wit, Sammy Colt dubbed himself "The World's Guest."

Jackie might have done something on the stage, but did not. After a few minor parts in his mother's productions, he sat back waiting for the offers to come pouring in. They did not. He was a crack tennis player. Waring thought him charming and warm. Women tumbled for him. He drank too much. Some say Ethel loved him best; if so, Jackie never seemed to know it.

Ethel's and Sister's relationship was the most complex because mother did not overwhelm daughter as thoroughly as she did her sons. "I want her to work," Ethel told the press. "I certainly wouldn't want her around with nothing to do but play bridge and tennis, or whatever it is that idle people do"—apparently a message her sons never received. Sister had ambition, talent, charm. Yet an agent could reduce her to tears: "You think you're a Barrymore, but you don't have the looks, you don't have the talent, you don't have the *stuff*, baby!" She decided that nightclub singing might pave the way to better things, got a job in Philadelphia. The first night she asked them to remove the microphone.

"Hey, you can't sing here without a mike!"

"I don't need one."

She didn't, holding the audience with a warm, strong voice. She packed them in at the Tic Toc in Montreal, they loved her at the Beachcomber in Miami—and it wasn't just the Barrymore name. "She had guts," said Babette Craven, a close friend who met Sister during the Philadelphia engagement, "and no illusions. She knew she was a Colt not a Barrymore, yet she refused to let her mother extinguish her." It had been Sister who had gone with Ethel to the Long Island treatment center where she conquered her drinking problem. They talked religiously on the telephone once a week. Yet Ethel was often acidulous about her daughter's short-comings and, curiously, Sister's ultrapious Catholicism alienated rather than pleased her. In short, Ethel found herself in the position of the dominating mother who cannot bear her children's competition but must live with their failures.

If Sister could only make a brilliant marriage. . . . During one of her tours, Ethel had been wined and dined in Detroit by a rising, unmarried Catholic judge named Frank Murphy. Sister also met him; by the time Murphy was elected governor of Michigan, Sister was dating him seriously. Ethel was impressed. True, Sister would have to go into exile in Lansing if she married him, but then, Ethel decided rather heartlessly, that was her league. And then Franklin Delano Roosevelt made Frank Murphy attorney general of the United States, ticketed for the Supreme Court.

Frank Murphy was now America's premier Catholic catch; moreover, the scene was set in Washington, one of Ethel's favorite stamping grounds. Ethel had always been "more Republican than Democrat"; now, however, she became an ardent supporter of FDR's. She framed the invitation to his third-term inaugural ball, which Sister attended with Murphy; with Charlie Chaplin, Raymond Massey, and Nelson Eddy, she graced the president's Inaugural Concert ("Please, however," warned the chairman, "don't go and steal the Inauguration away from our President"). Suddenly Ethel was very much in touch again with "Princess Alice" Longworth, Teddy's Republican daughter who, though officially out of power, knew everything in Washington worth knowing. Alice was able to report that Frank Murphy was an awkward host; both Ethels seized upon this as a sign that a wife was needed. And whenever a function demanded a couple, Murphy squired Sister.

In all, 1941 was a brilliant year for Ethel. On February 5 *The Corn Is Green* was selected by the Drama Critics Circle as the best foreign play of the season, and on that same day a special radio broadcast honored Ethel Barrymore's forty years in the theatre as a star. Arthur Hopkins, Alec Woollcott, and Helen Hayes were on hand for the tribute, as were Lionel and Jack, broadcasting from Hollywood. Lionel wanted to say, "We bought a big red apple for you, but John drank it"; that was censored. Instead, he managed to make his "Both of us have a great deal to be thankful to her for" sound homely and sincere. Jack, however, who had arrived at the studio an hour early and cold sober, pranced from beginning to end—Jack who once played clean and simply because he hated the mouthings of old-time hams. Ethel wept at the beginning and end of her speech, which had been written for her by Woollcott: "Thank you, thank you all for this treasure you have stored up for me in my particular heaven. Thank you, thank you again." An event "choked with kindliness, good feeling, and admiration" for green, enduring Ethel Barrymore—the only star of four decades still a star in the theatre.

In May a luncheon for five hundred at the Hotel Astor and Ethel accepting the Barter Theatre Award for "the outstanding performance given by an American actress during the current New York season." Significantly, the award was presented by Eleanor Roosevelt, who now saw Ethel almost as one of the liberal Washington family. Ethel heard herself praised as a symbol of America's heritage, a figure of grace, nobility, love, and toughness in "the perfectly horrible, unspeakable, stinking world in which we live"—so said Dorothy Thompson—"unbearable for any one with any sensitivity or imagination." Privately, Ethel was not carried away by all the adulation. "Now that I'm a hit, people I haven't seen or heard from in years are banging at my door. They're crawling out from under the rocks, and worming their way out of the woodwork. What scum!"

The Corn Is Green was still running on Broadway when the Japanese bombed Pearl Harbor on December 7. With something to do at last, Sammy enlisted; Jackie followed. After 475 performances—Ethel's longest run, any Barrymore's longest run—the company set out on a tour that crisscrossed the country for more than two years, Ethel supremely thankful for "the blessing of hard work."

They stayed for eight weeks in Chicago where Ashton Stevens—and all the critics—said "Ethel Barrymore has reached her zenith." (Still, Jack had lasted thirty-two weeks in that abominable *My Dear Children*.) As the tour progressed, Thelma Schnee's acclaimed performance as Bessie Watty grew more and more exaggerated, throwing her into grotesque relief among the naturalness of the others. Ethel began to smolder, but the more Schnee sensed her disapproval, the more she caricatured the part. "I saw Alfred and Lynn in Milwaukee," Ethel wrote Woollcott. "They were so overwhelmed with horror at our Miss Thelma Schnee that I don't think they saw the rest of us."

"Can't you do something?" Ethel asked Fontanne. "She's lost all reality."

Fontanne tried to work with the young actress, whose penciled brows and tip-tilted nose made her such a plausible tart, but Schnee was bafflingly resistant. "I can't do anything about it," she would say with a shrug. As the tour went on, Schnee became anathema to Ethel, who confided to Richard Waring that she couldn't stand her.

Dicky Waring remained a favorite with the critics and with Ethel. "You're not going to leave!" she said when he told her he might have to enlist. "If you leave, *I'll* quit!" He stayed. Sometimes she would talk to him as their train rattled through the night, though more often she was lost in a detective novel or a biography. When they talked, Waring would say again how much he'd love to meet her brother John. "Oh, you should meet Lionel," Ethel would say. "Lionel's the real one. Of course, you'd probably have a wonderful time with Jack because he's always very nice and all that. But Lionel, Lionel's the real one."

"I'LL NEVER QUIT motion pictures as long as they'll have me," Lionel was heard to say these years. Terror of being useless, like a lamed horse, now dominated his life. "God in his infinite mercy knows what I am going to do. I do what I am told."

Lionel was now in a wheelchair. How he got there is not entirely clear since Barrymores are possibly even less truthful than studio publicity departments. In 1951 Lionel told his autobiographical collaborator, Cameron Shipp, that one day in his studio dressing room he had leaned heavily against a metal drafting board, tripped, fallen, and found himself in the hospital "hoisted and trussed like a chicken." Being a Barrymore, he does not specify the hip injury or date the accident, but perhaps his hip was broken or dislocated sometime in 1936. Lionel then says that his hip had healed from the studio fall when, filming *Saratoga* in the summer of 1937, he tripped over a sound cable, fell, and again ended up in Good Samaritan in ropes and pulleys. He left the hospital in a wheelchair where, he says, he stayed.

Not quite. After *Saratoga* he used two canes in *Navy Blue and Gold*, then left for England in September 1937 to film *A Yank from Oxford* using those canes. When he returned, stopping in New York to consult with Ethel about *Whiteoaks*, he was leaning heavily on one. Meanwhile, Selznick had definitely set him for the part of Dr. Meade in *Gone With the Wind*, impossible had Lionel been confined to a wheelchair at the time. Something was now seriously wrong, however, for he did not make *Gone With the Wind*, played all his scenes seated in *Test Pilot* (1938), and was again in the hospital when Frank Capra approached him about playing Grandpa Vanderhof in *You Can't Take It With You*. "His body was a mess," said Capra. "But not his verve."

"I can play the part on crutches," pleaded Lionel. "Just put a cast on my foot to alibi them. That'll do it."

Lionel did play Vanderhof on crutches and seated, his benign rendition of the wacky old gent contributing heavily to the picture's winning the 1938 Academy Award—even though Capra built up Jimmy Stewart's and Edward Arnold's parts to the detriment of Lionel's.

Since Lionel did walk after his purported fall in *Saratoga*, it would seem that he became wheelchair-bound from complications: the hip not healing properly or perhaps inflammatory rheumatism aggravating the fracture. The studios certainly did not know how to handle his condition. Columbia leaked the news that he had slid too fast down a banister, Grandpa Vanderhof's excuse in *You Can't Take It With You*. MGM, denying he had dislocated his hip, sent out word he had arthritis, then decided to pass off his affliction as "an old knee ailment." Most people came to believe that Lionel had arthritis, yet he himself said, "*I do not have arthritis* or rheumatism or any other goddamned ailment!" Instead he talked about complications from an old New York gymnasium injury and once told reporters he had fallen in the bathtub. "I haven't had a drink in twenty years," he added. "If I'd have been drunk when I fell I probably wouldn't have been hurt." At least drunk in the bathtub would have had a more authentic ring than sliding down banisters or the euphemistic tripping over cables.

Lionel's manager, James Doane, however, told certain people that Lionel was confined to a wheelchair because of syphilis. This reminds one of Gene Fowler's statement that Lionel had suffered from syphilis since 1925 though, according to Fowler, it responded to treatment. Mercury and arsenic were used to treat syphilis, sometimes effectively, until 1940 when penicillin became the first reliable treatment for the disease in all its stages; Lionel's infirmity became evident in 1936. Late syphilis can affect any part of the body, including joints—Lionel's knees were noticeably huge and inflamed. Although the truth will probably never be known, it is as difficult to disregard the statements of two of Lionel's closest associates as it is to make sense out of the reasons offered publicly for Lionel Barrymore's being in a wheelchair. Especially when Lionel himself refused to cooperate.

At any rate, as Selznick noted in one of his ubiquitous memos, Lionel Barrymore was now severely limited as far as films went and far more available than he used to be "when MGM was keeping him busy fifty-two weeks a year." No one knew it better than Lionel. Though his salary of $138,000 had put him on the 1938 *New York Times* list of top-paid Americans, he continued to be broke. He owed the government back taxes; since Irene's death he had to get his morphia from illegal sources that were not cheap. He had to work: MGM refused to put him on its pension plan because, he said, he was "too goddamned old when it started." Instead Louis B. Mayer presided over seemingly endless birthday parties with Lionel cutting prop cakes and accepting gold watches and ship's clocks. On these occasions more than two hundred stars, directors, and producers might show up to watch the old boy blow out his accumulating candles and shake each gift to see if it gurgled. Lionel would have preferred a pension. He struggled with black moods and fear.

Every Thursday Lionel would drive through the gates of the Culver City Studio in his specially fitted Oldsmobile, nestle up to the window of the accounting office, and honk his horn. At this signal, a small basket attached to a fishing pole would emerge. The basket contained Lionel's $1,500 paycheck. Lionel would fish out the check, endorse it, and return it to the basket which would disappear and reappear, this time containing the small sum of cash MGM decreed he needed for the week. Daddy doling out Sonny's allowance. What MGM did with the difference between check and cash is not entirely clear, since certainly the studio did not use it to pay the star's state and federal taxes. The cash Lionel would take home and give to Mrs. Wheeler who in turn would dole out beer and gas money for the week. As Frohman had told his sister long ago, "You'd only spend it, Ethel."

Eventually Louis B. Mayer took pity on Lionel and paid a visit to his dressing room. The U.S. government, he told him, supplied morphine to confessed addicts far more cheaply than what he now paid for it from drug dealers. He strongly urged his impoverished star to appeal to Uncle Sam. But Lionel was so horrified at the idea of going public and so ashamed to discover that the studio knew of his addiction that he checked himself into Good Samaritan instead to try and kick the habit. Spencer Tracy, hospitalized at the same time, encouraged his battle. It is unclear whether Lionel succeeded. He kept using cocaine—according to one source encouraged by Mayer, who wanted to keep him pain-free and working—and the liens on his salary lasted till the day he died—and after.

As for the wheelchair, Mayer came through—not nobly but practically, and for MGM very profitably. At Mayer's encouraging, the team who had written the immensely popular Judge Hardy films came up with the idea of a hospital series, with Dr. Kildare, a young intern, pitted against the crustily philosophical Dr. Gillespie, confined with cancer to a wheelchair. MGM thus literally gave Lionel a vehicle for fourteen films which he dominated with grumbling sarcasms, gnarled truths, and violent propulsions of the chair, which became the most formidable prop on the MGM lot. Inevitably, however, the immensely popular, cheaply made series made Lionel even more of a drug on the market. Critics accused him of playing Dr. Gillespie in his sleep, while Ethel observed more tactfully that acting for Lionel was now so easy that it was "almost a sideline to his etching and composing." Certainly by the second Kildare film Lionel was on holiday.

Now that he could not manage stairs, MGM had installed him in an old cottage, a relic of the days when Culver City was a low-income residential area instead of a 117-acre plant. Lionel's new quarters soon looked like the old: upright piano, record player, and a jungle of painting, etching, and composing equipment liberally strewn with cigarette butts from overflowing ashtrays. The cottage next door housed the school for contract kids like Judy Garland and Mickey Rooney, who dashed in and out at odd hours, creating a terrific racket and causing Lionel "to gripe with monumental indignation," said the writer Anita Loos, sharing the cottage with old Gruff-and-Grum. But Loos admired Lionel. He was the only actor she ever knew who extemporized better lines than he was given. It amused her to hear some second-rate scrivener fume about Lionel changing his script, because Lionel generally improved it.

In a rare respite from *Kildare*, Lionel propelled his wheelchair onto the set of *On Borrowed Time* to face off Sir Cedric Hardwicke as an old man who battles "Mr. Brink"—Death—only to find that a world without death to end human suffering is unendurable. Originally from Chaucer's story about the old man who "gets Death up a tree," the fable according to Hollywood had to end with Gramps and his loved ones reunited in eternity, thus reducing Death to an escort service. Apart from the ending, the film has originality and charm.

Bobs Watson played Lionel's grandson, faring about as well as any child actor confronted by the Master. Compared with Lionel's snarling in *Treasure Island*, for example, Jackie Cooper's "Bless my soul, sir!" sounds as though he's reading from cue cards. Similarly, Lionel's impeccably acted Colonel exposes Little Colonel Shirley Temple's phony routine: line, pout; line, dimple; line, frown; line, finger to lips. In *Captains Courageous* with Spencer Tracy miscast as a Portuguese fisherman who calls Freddie Bartholomew "Leetle Feesh" ad nauseam, Lionel's Captain Disko is the only real character. And in *On Borrowed Time* if one had never seen Lionel Barrymore before, one would call his performance a masterpiece. He chuckles, snorts, and talks with his jaw. His eyebrows have a life of their own. He turns lines like "You squid-faced old bird stuffer!" into vicious invective. He is tender and fierce and contemptuous and irreverent. But one has seen this Lionel Barrymore many, many times.

In the spring of 1939 Lionel moved with the Wheelers from the Palisades to a twenty-two-acre "ranch" on Independence Avenue in Sycamore Woods, Chatsworth. "I'm no gentleman farmer," Lionel told the press. "I'm an actor and I bought that place for a hideout. It's way up in the hills, five miles from nowhere. Nobody can ever possibly find it— and that has plenty of advantages in Hollywood. If I didn't have a driver, I couldn't find it myself." Indeed, few people knew the route: straight along Sepulveda almost to San Fernando, then left onto Devonshire Boulevard until Pope's Market where you turned right on Canoga and then onto a dirt road past orchards till you came to a gate with brick posts, turned in and drove on till the fork in the road where you split right and down the hill to his door. Lionel did try a little farming: chickens and a cow, then settled down to roses, corn, razor-backed hogs, and the company of his black Scotties, Sally and Johnnie, and four cats, including a favorite mixed gray named Becky Barrymore. Though Lionel bought the property, he put it in the Wheelers' name so that it could not be confiscated for debt. Dolores Costello called the Wheelers "Lionel's Hotcheners."

He continued to visit Irene's shrine at 802 North Roxbury, where he would spend an hour or two alone with his memories. Although it was costly to maintain, he was reluctant to let it go or even rent it. Yet with tales of Nazi persecution abroad and the Hollywood housing shortage, he began to feel guilty. On inspiration he wrote the great Richard Strauss that if he should decide to come to America, he would turn over his house and staff to him and his family. To his astonishment the composer he worshipped replied that he had made reservations on the *Queen Mary*. As a formality he asked Lionel to swear an affidavit with the American consul in Switzerland so that he could obtain an immigration visa.

Lionel's lawyer refused to touch it. "My God, Barrymore, don't you know that it would not only ruin you but would be an injury to him to bring him to this country where people remember seeing him photographed with Goering and Goebbels?" On reflection Lionel decided it might be difficult to explain to Louis B. Mayer that he was sheltering a Nazi. Yet he deplored the tragedy of mixing art and politics. Surely a genius like Strauss was above petty nationalism.

Yet he himself had become increasingly political and, after years of toeing Mayer's line, conservative. "He was so voluble," said Lew Ayres who, as Dr. Kildare, spent the time between scenes jawing with the old man about art, music, acting, and FDR's proposed third term. "I would make liberal suggestions just to watch the effect, to hear him take off. . . ." In 1940, when Roosevelt was indeed up for an unprecedented third term, Lionel joined the Hollywood anti-Roosevelt "We the People" committee and even appeared on a Los Angeles platform to excoriate the Democrats in what he later admitted was undoubtedly purple prose. On the eve of the election, the committee took out half-page ads in the *New York Times* to refute the notion that all "the Mighty Motion Picture Industry" supported a third-term candidate. The accompanying list of 164 Hollywoodites for Wendell Willkie included Wallace Beery, Gary

Cooper, Bing Crosby, Walt Disney, Hedda Hopper, Mary Pickford, Lew Ayres, Adolphe Menjou, George Murphy, and Lionel.

Lionel's conservative politics drove a wedge between him and Ethel and Jack, who said publicly that he "adored" FDR. At the same time, Jack's increasingly debased antics outraged Lionel: Jack seemed to have no regard for the great family name. And yet, as he cranked out more and more *Kildare*s, Lionel himself was doing nothing to gild it.

TWENTY-EIGHT

1941–1942

JACK HAD NOTHING to sell now but his own degradation. *The Great Profile* was based so blatantly on Jack's exploits with Elaine and *My Dear Children* that Twentieth Century–Fox signed Adolphe Menjou to play Barrymore, thinking that the actor would refuse to libel himself. But Jack signed without even reading the script, forcing Fox to pay Menjou *not* to play the role.

Lionel would say later—at the time he deplored the spectacle—that Jack was heroically trying to pay his debts. It would have been more heroic had he tried to pay them in vehicles that did not debase him; the sad fact is, however, that Hollywood offered him large sums only on the condition that he make a fool of himself. But there was more to it than money. Jack was a willing victim, displaying in these last years an intensification of his self-destructive urge. He took perverse delight in vomiting upon himself in public.

Drinking had brought him to this point, drinking helped him bear it. "God, he was loaded all the time," said Mary Beth Hughes, playing Elaine's role in *The Great Profile*. "He got there at 8:30 every morning and began drinking and when we were ready to shoot he was flying." Flying helped Jack forget that he "hated and despised" Gregory Ratoff, cast as his manic agent, and "hated and despised—but despised" Anne Baxter, cast as a young playwright. When he wasn't flying he was in a daze. Anne Baxter wondered at the "distance in his eyes, as if he were sleepwalking." But it was better to be asleep making *The Great Profile* than awake.

The opening credits roll to "Oh, Johnny, oh Johnny, how you can love!" John's film name is Garrick, a slap in the acting profession's face. Garrick is a vain old queen, wearing a chin strap to bed to lift his sagging jowls while a photograph of the young Barrymore mocks him. Garrick mocks Shakespeare: Life "is a tale told by an idiot, full of sound and fury, signifying"—belch—"nothing." The whole dreary business of Barrymore drunk and ad-libbing through a trashy play while headlines blare his domestic tilts is gone through again. Garrick hams and hams, rolling his *r*'s like thunder, "meselfing" himself to death. The only happy note about *The Great Profile* is that it lost Fox a lot of money. Older people stayed away because they did not want to watch a great actor degrade himself. Young people stayed away because they didn't care. The review that claimed "this is going to be one of the comedy hits of the year" was as accurate as Jack's telling *Photoplay* "I love doing this film."

For years Hollywood's elite had sealed their stardom by pressing their hands and feet into wet cement in the forecourt of Sid Grauman's famous Chinese Theatre. John Barrymore had neither won an Oscar nor been invited to immortalize himself in concrete. Now, however, as a publicity gag for the second worst film he ever made, Fox arranged to have Jack leave his Great Profile to posterity. The invitation was insulting, yet Jack showed up sober in a dark blue suit, accompanied by Mary Beth Hughes and the press. He knelt obligingly, pretending to press his face into the sludge; heckled, he dipped his nose and cheek gingerly into the muck. Not good enough. Sid Grauman leapt forward and pushed his face into the cement, holding Jack down while flash bulbs popped. When Jack was pulled out, he was shaky, scrabbling at hardening cement in his hair and eye. Mary Beth Hughes darted across the street into a bar and came back with a drink that she slipped him. Jack gulped it and stopped shaking.

Late in 1940 he became a permanent guest on the Rudy Vallee "Seal-test Hour" radio show, where he continued to make fun of his vaunted reputation as an alcoholic Shakespearean actor, lover, four-time loser in the divorce courts, and bankrupt. On these shows Vallee was always the hero, Jack his sidekick. And did he get kicked:

"With you, John, a penny earned is a penny attached."

"Is that your original face or a retread?"

"John's vision is double or nothing."

And then Lionel—"Li-o-*nel*" as Jack now roundly called him—who deplored his brother's antics, would put in guest appearances. Calling them "boys," Vallee egged Lionel on to insult his brother:

"Why don't you scatter some subpoenas around so John will feel at home?" Or:

"I'll wager you could tell me a lot about John's childhood."

"First or second?"

Etcetera. As the *New York Times* observed, John's was "fast becoming a twice-told tale."

Some people applauded Vallee for hiring Jack at all, but Vallee was not inspired by charity. The Barrymore name still made people tune in;

many listeners thought his wheezes, snorts, and snores rib-tickling fun. *Movie-Radio Guide* was among those who believed that "today we need laughter much more than we need art. We believe that John Barrymore, who permits himself to act and sound like a fool, knows exactly what he is doing. We believe that his current clowning on the kilocycles is doing more for people than his classic profile ever did."

"I am doing the work of a whore," Jack told Gene Fowler. "By necessity—or so it would seem—I am occupied with what is loosely called 'Radio,' and an occasional frothy picture. I have been told that no one will lock me up if I earn big money—money that nobody but my creditors get. So I do it. And I find it the work of a whore. There is nothing as sad in all the world as an *old* prostitute. I think that every artist somewhere along the line should know what it is to be one, a *young* one, but reform."

One night after a broadcast, Jack and Lionel began to speak of the days when, as young actors, they cringed to hear themselves compared to greats like Edwin Booth, Edwin Forrest, and Joseph Jefferson. Hell! they'd been reared among the giants of the theatre; the mighty dead would haunt them for even listening to such audacity. But now Lionel said, "Jack, you don't have to feel self-conscious now. No matter what has happened of recent years, you really did climb up among the stars. You were one of them."

Jack looked at Lionel, then grinned. "This is a hell of a time," he said, "to tell me!"

Another night Mary Astor was on a program that followed Vallee's. "I was on the second floor of the building where the dressing rooms were. A long bleak fluorescent lighted hall. There was no one else around and I saw [Jack] walking alone down the hall ahead of me. I wanted to catch up and say hello, but I didn't. He had stopped, like someone who just couldn't walk another step; he leaned against the wall in sheer fatigue, his body sagged. It was no time to intrude, so I retraced my steps. I couldn't help thinking: Where was everybody? Where were the valets, the little train of admiring hangers-on, the designers with drawings to be approved, secretaries with a sheaf of letters to be signed? . . . This was a giant of a man, one of the few greats of our time. He was a man with enormous dignity, and he never lost it. He occasionally threw it away— for his own reasons. But that was *his* business. And now, in that long bleak hall, I saw a man who was catching his breath before doing battle, and quite a battle it was, with death."

IN THE EARLY THIRTIES, at Professor Gustav Eckstein's laboratory in Cincinnati where people came to listen to Eckstein discourse on everything from Plato to canaries, an aspiring young actor named Philip Rhodes had met John Barrymore. On that day Eckstein's canaries were flying about the room, liberally splattering Jack, who refused to put on one of the smocks Eckstein kept for guests. The actor's insouciance delighted Rhodes, as did the way he chuckled "like a mad insect" and laughed until he had tears in his eyes. Eventually Rhodes came to Hollywood, where he found John Barrymore "as approachable as a park bench." While Rhodes never became one of the Bundy Drive boys, Jack accepted him as an acolyte and fellow drinker. Rhodes himself had classical good looks and wanted to break into pictures, but Jack was cynical.

"Get out of acting. It will ruin your life. And for Christ's sake, don't imitate me. I was a bridge between two periods and my period has passed."

He looked then, thought Rhodes, like something made by a jeweler's art: the small slender body perfectly symmetrical; the facial planes expertly turned; the large greenish-hazel eyes ornamented by black lashes. On the *Infanta* he would quickly burn a deep brown, so deep that Rhodes wondered whether long ago some Blyth had mated with a Hindu.

He was the most intelligent actor Rhodes had ever met, the best equipped to practice his art, which was, at its greatest, thought Rhodes, comedy. Onstage he seemed to sense how an audience wanted to feel, then improvised—lost himself, left himself under the mat like a key, giving himself to the audience's illusion.

In person he was much larger than onstage, yet protean: everyone and no one. Like a mind reader, he could catch the pattern of what someone was thinking and say the very thing that person was about to say. He had great empathy. Rhodes liked a story Lionel told about Jack unexpectedly joining him and a friend at the theatre. Onstage an actress was emoting, her heart breaking. Lionel stole a look at Jack and saw that he was weeping with the woman, his face noble and exalted as he drank in her suffering. He was tragically vulnerable, thought Rhodes; you wanted to protect him from others and from himself. He was a tremendous giver. His hands were open and people took and took.

And then the long fall and Elaine. Much as he loved Jack Barrymore, Rhodes privately could not understand how Elaine had stood him; perhaps she was too young to know any better. And now Jack was alone. He was bloated, as though the booze could no longer drain out of the saturated tissue. His voice had become deep, resonant, and loose—the vocal cords corroding, the lungs filling with water. Chain-smoking had etched his face into thousands of fine wrinkles. His foul mouth was fouler. He slipped ether into his drinks and hard stuff into his wine, though one drink now was enough to stagger him. He lived alone at the top of Tower Road with Mark Nishimura, his Japanese gardener, and Karl Steuver, who steered him around Hollywood accompanied by a small suitcase full of watered vermouth or fruit juice lightly laced with rum. Jack made Steuver open it often and was under the impression he could still hold his drink. Sometimes he went out alone for an evening, humbly asking Steuver for twenty-five dollars. Steuver gave him ten in ones so it felt like more. Sometimes he was accompanied on these sprees by anonymous women. More often he was alone.

Rhodes pitied him, but recalls, "I sometimes went down an alley to avoid him. With Jack it was going to be a hard night. You had to drown with him. He could pull you down faster than you could pull him up one inch. When he got hold of you, he was so terribly lonely that he didn't want to go home. He would do anything to keep you with him all night— talk about what you were interested in, *give* himself. He was an expert at that. After all, it was his trade."

He still practiced that trade constantly—not in studios reading banalities from blackboards, but in bars with Luis Alberni, a friend of five films, where he would recite reams of Shakespeare to the boozy wonder or indifference of customers. Or on his own patio. "There are some fine actors who, like magicians, need lighting and distance to make their illusions successful," said Ben Hecht. "Barrymore was not of these. . . . Before me in the sunny garden Richard appeared, and it required an effort of the imagination *not* to see him." One night after hard drinking at John Decker's studio, Gene Fowler and his younger son Will took Jack home with them. Fowler went to bed, but Jack and Will sat up and read *Hamlet* aloud together from beginning to end. Another night Jack dragged some friends to the Hollywood Bowl to test the acoustics for the *Macbeth* he was going to do with Judith Anderson.

Reality was quite different as Jack was shunted around to three different studios for three films in 1941: *The Invisible Woman* (Universal), *World Premiere* (Paramount), and *Playmates* (RKO). *The Invisible Woman* was inane but inoffensive, Jack in a mustache and old tweeds spoofing Lionel's Kringelein from *Grand Hotel* so obviously that the *New York Times* said the elder brother "would be perfectly within his rights to sue John as an imposter and a plagiarist." "Good old John," mused Lionel, "indestructible but still obscene." With Elaine out of the picture, they had got very clubby. In *World Premiere* "The Great Profile kids the panzers off the Nazis" as head of Miracle Pictures ("If It's a Good Picture It's a Miracle"). This was no miracle, but a meaningless jumble of spies, vamps, bombs, and lions on the loose through which Jack plodded wearily.

Then came rock bottom: *Playmates* starring Kay Kyser "with John

Barrymore." Kyser and Jack play themselves, a band leader and a washed-up actor in need of publicity. Jack is put through every degrading bit of self-mockery of the sort that had already become a drug on the market. As he says, "I have been in the public eye so long it is permanently bloodshot." The inevitable *Hamlet* photograph reminds us how far John Barrymore has deteriorated. He is made to recite "To be or not to be" to the idiotic Ish Kabibble and band singer Ginny Simms. (It is said that he broke down and wept.) He displays "Ethelbert," male padding that he used to fill out his *Hamlet* tights. He duels and falls backward over a bench. Finally, when he is scheduled to play Shakespeare, he accidentally swallows vocal paralyzing medicine. "I've devoted my life to the theatre. It is my first love, my only love," he begins, then clutches his throat. The audience hoots and jeers. Ish Kabibble and Ginny Simms fill in with a corny musical Shakespeare spoof, Barrymore gets a contract because he *didn't* go on and, as the film ends, Barrymore and Kyser embrace.

Looking like death, Jack tries to give this inexcusable film some verve. He fails. *Playmates* was the last film he was able to make. At one point he looks up at a picture of his ancestors above the mantelpiece and says, "Ah, noble forebears, look what they're doing to me!" It is too painful to watch.

One more attempt to star him came at the insistence of Bette Davis, who was convinced he would make a brilliant Sheridan Whiteside in a film of the Broadway hit *The Man Who Came to Dinner*. "I'd love to do that play with Mr. Barrymore—*any* play with Mr. Barrymore," Davis wrote Spencer Berger, "—but I think this one would be excellent for the screen with him. So let's hope my bosses agree. . . ." Bette Davis had enough clout to persuade Warners to make a screen test in May 1941. It was a disaster.

His face is like "a devil's sick of sin," the eyes poached eggs, the pupils dilated with alcohol. His mascaraed eyebrows writhe grotesquely. His hair is too long. In one episode he obviously forgets his lines, waits tensely until the blackboard is brought, blows out his lips in relief when he manages to get through. He is frightfully dissipated, but beyond that he makes Whiteside just one more caricature of an actor. Had he got the part it would have been his first major leading role since *Twentieth Century*, but he could not get the part.

IN 1941 Jack made his will. He expressly made no provisions for ex-wives, ordering that his estate be divided equally among his three children. In a curious clause he stipulated that his executors employ doctors to ascertain "that he was in fact dead and not in any other state having the semblance of death, in order as far as possible, *to avoid all risk of being buried alive.*" Perhaps this was motivated by his miraculous recoveries from seemingly fatal collapses. These had occurred frequently of late: he would lose consciousness, heart action weak—then wake up restored the next morning with no memory of illness. Quite as hard to kill as Rasputin, though he was doing everything in his power to help. Preparing to leave the hospital once, having recovered from a bleeding gastric ulcer, he spotted a bottle of spirits of ammonia in his bathroom and promptly downed it, bringing on severe hemorrhage and shock. "I trust that the good public will forgive me for recuperating," he said ironically when that too failed to kill him. As a point of honor, he insisted on acting a well man: tragically, one of the greatest roles he ever played. But when his doctor told him that he was critically ill, he said, "I'm ready."

During this time Gene Fowler wrote for Jack "The Testament of a Dying Ham." Jack recited it at the drop of a hat, as did all the Bundy Drive boys:

On the eve of his self-immolation—
By means of a rafter and strand—
A Hollywood mime of a happier time
Wrote his will with a resolute hand.

"To the fair-weather leeches who bled me,
Who helped me to scatter and spend,
Who flattered and licked me, but soon enough kicked me,
Who fleeced me while calling me friend . . .

"To the wenches who trumped up a passion
And held a first lien on my cot,
To the simpering starlets and gleet-ridden harlots
Whose sables were masking their rot . . .

"To the preeners who haunt the drab parties,
To the crackpots in snobbish undress,
To those bogus upstarters who flip off their garters
To pay for a puff in the Press . . .

"To those impotent, credit-mad authors,
Whose skulls with manure are be-crammed,
To those clap-trap extollers and stinking log-rollers,
Who mince in the waltz of the damned . . .

"To the charwomen comers to glory,
The fungi adventists to screens,
Who rise from the gutter to clog up and clutter
The boudoirs, the sidewalks, the greens . . .

"To the venomous merchants of slander—
A conclave of pandering gnomes—
Whose seedy portmanteaus are bulging with cantos
To poison the air of your homes . . .

"To the parasite rabble of agents,
Who nibble like rats at the yield,
To those scavenging cravens, the ten-percent 'ravens,
Who croak o'er a gilt battlefield . . .

"To the poseurs who simulate talent—
The nances, the Lesbian corps,
The cultists, the fadists, the blustering sadists,
The slime of the celluloid shore . . .

"To the censors who squat on their dunghills
And loose their petards as the horse—
Political supers, parochial poopers,
Who strangle all art at the source . . .

"To the mountebank clan of producers,
Who hang their dull stars in the skies,
Who rifle the pockets and gouge the eye-sockets,
But never look higher than thighs . . .

WITNESS:

"I leave them the curse of the dying;
I leave them their own foetid crowd;
I leave them the voices of midnight;
I leave them the hope of a shroud;
I leave them the groans of the fallen;
I leave them the culture of swine . . .
All these, but another—bear witness, good brother—
I leave them the *fate that was mine*."

As Jack's public behavior grew more obscene, most people avoided him. George Cukor was an exception, as was the woman he had tried vainly to seduce, Tallulah Bankhead. Jack showed up at Cukor's party for her in cutaway and striped trousers—elegant, mocking. After a few drinks, however, he slipped into the old obscenities. The room went silent. Tallulah made her way through a throng that included Gary Cooper, Marlene Dietrich, Joan Crawford, and Cary Grant. She took his arm affectionately. "Oh, John, darling, we've *all* heard those words. Kit Cornell used them last week on the radio!"

Hedda Hopper, whose friendship with Jack went back to the filming of *Sherlock Holmes*, also remained loyal. "You'll never know how touched and overwhelmed I was and still am over what you did for me yesterday," she wrote in response to a kind gesture from Jack. "That carries friendship to the peaks of Mount Olympus. There never has been, at least to me, and there never will be but one Barrymore and his name is John. Bless you always."

Visiting Hollywood, Somerset Maugham was only mildly disillusioned with Ethel's brother when they lunched. "What a ham! He now wears his hair dark red with a white *mèche* sweeping up from the forehead, but he still has a perfect nose." Also lunching with Jack, Dorothy Gish was horrified at his mockery; then, at the mention of Margaret Carrington, Jack changed completely. He spoke of her tenderly, reverently. "Everything I ever was," he said, "I owed to her."

David Niven's distaste for the actor who went out of his way to shock, was conspicuously unclean, and often "smelled highly" was far more typical. Niven could not understand his friend Errol Flynn's adoration of Barrymore. Fresh in his memory was the time that he, Ronald Colman, and William Powell had put their yacht into a bay on Santa Cruz Island, expecting to be housed and fed at Eaton's Fishing Camp, the only concession on the island. Instead they were confronted by a belligerent Mrs. Eaton.

"You guys movie folk?"

They admitted it.

Mrs. Eaton grabbed the plates she had just set down. "No film people set foot in my camp. Fuck off, the lot of you!"

Colman tried to ascertain the reason for her hostility.

"Barrymore!" she yelled. "Ever heard of a creep called John Barrymore? . . . Well, ten years ago the bastard dropped anchor down there in a big white schooner. . . ." Tears pouring down her cheeks, she told how Barrymore had made such persistent passes at her beautiful seventeen-year-old daughter that "that goddamned Barrymore sailed away that night with my little girl, and I never seed her no more. Lousy actors!" She bombarded the fleeing trio with grapefruit rinds and empty beer bottles. "Who needs you!"

Harpo Marx spent an evening with Jack to his sorrow, inviting him to his house for dinner and afterward the fights. He hired a bartender: John Decker had warned him that you had to drink freely in front of Jack or he'd resent being treated like a child. Jack arrived with his new bodyguard, an ex-boxer named George; a current girlfriend and the girlfriend's husband; Decker; Gene Fowler; and assorted cronies. Harpo noticed immediately that wherever Jack stood, there was the spotlight: he was to the last fiber a masterful actor.

After the fights they all wound up in a crummy jukebox joint off Hollywood Boulevard. The evening wore on. Fowler and Decker said good night; the cronies disappeared. "It was two in the morning," said Harpo. "Barrymore was trying to make time with the waitress, a blondine dame of about fifty with eyes too close together and teeth too far apart.

"Finally I had enough, host or no host. When Barrymore pulled out his handkerchief, the piece of napkin the waitress had written her telephone number on fell out of his pocket. The last time I saw John Barrymore alive he was down on his hands and knees, groveling on the floor, weeping and snuffling, looking through the sawdust for a juke-joint waitress's phone number."

Fowler and Decker tried to chaperone The Monster, as they called him, but could not guarantee his good behavior. One night at a hamburger palace Jack suddenly decided to assault a blowsy waitress with a wart on her nose. "My last Duchess!" he bellowed, lunging over the counter. "Hoist your dresses, Madam, and let me see Epping Forest again!" Both Jack and Decker had to run for it.

On his own he was impossible, for example, the night he decided to attend the gala opening of Earl Carroll's nightclub. He successfully eluded George and picked up a black woman on the street. When the doorman refused them entrance, Jack swaggered. His companion, he informed the man, was no less than a Hawaiian princess descended from the dusky race of demigods who had first inhabited that blessed isle. The doorman hastily consulted. Jack and his lady swept in.

The heat of the crowded nightclub affected Jack's corroded kidneys. He excused himself, pushed aside an assistant manager with a lordly "Pardon me," addressed himself to a pair of new orange velvet draperies, and opened his fly. He was liberally dousing the velvet when half a dozen attendants jumped him.

"How dare you interrupt a man at such a moment," roared Jack. "Even the lowest of savages respects the human bladder!"

They dragged him from the club still roaring and tossed him into the street.

"I'm going to have to keep a closer eye on him," said Decker, who had been summoned by a witness. "A man who will piss at an opening is a great problem."

"Or a great critic," said Gene Fowler.

In New York, Ned Sheldon heard what was happening to his friend and asked Charlie MacArthur to fly to Los Angeles immediately with a letter. MacArthur found Jack with a prostitute, "in woeful state of mind and body." He handed Jack the letter, borne 3,000 miles by personal messenger. Again, at an intensely emotional moment, Jack could not resist a scene. He studied the envelope, frowned, wavered, then walked to the fireplace. With a roll of eye, he tossed the unopened letter into the flames, muttering as it flared, "Oh, Virgil, Virgil!"

He was attached to life by the bonds of male comradeship and the occasional tug of sex. In November 1941 Jack was again in the hospital when he received a bouquet and a note from Elaine. Elaine says that Jack immediately phoned her, urging a reconciliation. At any rate, he left the hospital primed for a romantic reunion. He restored Elaine's photograph to its silver frame. He ordered Mark Nishimura to lay covers for two. He donned evening dress and stayed sober, supervising the arranging of the flowers and the chilling of the wine. The hours dragged on and no car lights wound their way up to his drive. At midnight he flew into a rage, ripped the photograph from its frame, hurled the flowers into the fireplace, and guzzled the wine, hurling invective at "cunts," his favorite word for women.

Yet it is instructive that Jack had informed both Fowler and Decker of his tryst; that they were stationed at Jane Jones's nightclub brothel on Sunset Strip where Nishimura phoned in frequent bulletins, the last at 2:00 a.m. to report the carnage. The reunion was largely a stunt; even when Elaine did not show, Jack's friends were treated to a performance that would quickly become part of the legend. How much duller Fowler's and Decker's lives would have been without Jack Barrymore, who entertained brilliantly even as he was dying.

He heard from Elaine once more. Fowler, Decker, MacArthur, and Thomas Mitchell had convened at Tower Road one evening when the phone rang. Jack jumped from his chair.

"He has a newspaperman's nose for disaster," said Fowler. "That will be Elaine."

It was Elaine, calling about some postdivorce financial problem. Barrymore's voice, "rich and purring," came from the hallway. "Anything you want. There's nothing I have I wouldn't give you. All I ask is one favor in return—don't hang up. Tell me how much you hate me, but keep on talking so I can hear your voice. No, I'm not drunk, my dear. I am a man at the bottom of Hell—please keep on talking—tell me anything—about the man you're with, how much you love him—anything, just as long as I can hear your voice it doesn't matter what it says. Darling—" Elaine had hung up, but another great performance. He could not help acting even at the bottom of Hell.

Jack was now impossible to women, but still could command the admiration of men. As he always had. John Gilbert had imitated Jack on the diving board: tautly poised with head thrown back, plunging with a snarl into the water. Douglas Fairbanks Jr. had copied the cigarette holder and rakishly tilted fedora. Playing Tony Cavendish in the film version of *The Royal Family*, Fredric March found himself possessed by the Barrymore persona on and off camera. Phil Rhodes admired the "essence movements": the way Jack flung his head like a horse, his "bear walk" when he entered a room. Errol Flynn carried a monkey on his shoulder, as Jack had Clementine. Warren William, Edmund Lowe, John Griggs, John Emery, and Ian Keith all tried to be John Barrymore. John Carradine flourished a walking stick like Jack's and exploded his consonants with Barrymore éclat. As Douglas Fairbanks Jr. said, women often hated Jack Barrymore (when they did not love him), but men adored him. And now there was young Anthony Quinn who felt as though Jack were a second father, who caught his idol's passion for books and collecting, who listened carefully to what Jack had to say about acting.

When Quinn came to lunch at Tower Road, Jack took him to a little den off the living room—cracked walls, dozens of photographs, a greasy armchair. Jack went to a corner sink and peed. "This is my favorite room," he said. "It reminds me of all the dressing rooms I lived in when I was traveling around the country." Quinn heard the sound of hammering. "I'll never stop building," Jack explained. "If I stop building I'll die."

He talked about working with Margaret Carrington. "She taught me to make love to words. Don't get carried away with emotion, kid. Caress the word.

"Kid, I'm going to give you the greatest lesson in acting. The best way to learn to be an actor is to read Walt Whitman's 'Two Strangers from Alabama' . . . It's a very painful poem of lost love. . . . Well, kid, if you can read that poem in front of a mirror while you're sitting on the toilet, you'll be an actor."

His advice to Quinn about women was Maurice's to him. "Don't trust any of them as far as you can throw Fort Knox. They're all twittering vaginas."

Then why had he married so often?

"Because I loved the cunts."

And yet Quinn sensed that he had really loved Dolores.

But in the last year of his life, as Jack felt the shame of disintegrating mental and physical faculties—he had become incontinent—he began to avoid those people who had not already turned their backs on him. Only a handful remained faithful, for love of Jack, of course, but also because they were aware that they were participating in the last rites of a life already legend.

Ben Hecht found Jack asleep on a lumpy couch in Decker's studio. Suddenly a roar ripped the room. "God-dam your arse hole of a house, Decker! This shambles of a couch is not fit for a pair of midgets to fuck on! Out of what swill barrel do you furnish your disgusting habitat?"

When he had lapsed into unconsciousness again, Hecht told Decker that he wanted to give a birthday party for Jack.

"In some sewer, I hope?" said Decker.

On the night of February 15 (though Jack was born a day earlier) a butler announced glittering arrivals at the Hechts' posh rented home. Many of the guests were movie moguls who had turned Hecht down cold a month earlier when he'd solicited them for contributions to meet John Barrymore's soaring medical expenses. As the rooms filled with people, the reason for the gathering began to fly from group to group. Hecht could hear the angry muttering of people who discovered they had been duped into honoring a washed-up actor whose behavior was insulting and intolerable.

Sam Hirschfeld, the doctor long acquainted with Jack's condition, was horrified too—for Jack. "It's a sadistic thing to do, to expose him to a thing of this kind. He's completely irresponsible. They'll crucify him."

The butler ushered in two late arrivals. Decker was red and squinting with tension. Beside him in an impeccable tuxedo stood Jack, smiling, relaxed, his ravaged face transformed into almost youthful beauty.

His entrance struck the crowd dumb. Some tried to feign indifference, but their eyes were drawn irresistibly to the graceful figure waiting with a shy, childlike calm. A few of the older guests had the civility to greet him.

At dinner, however, Jack was ignored as he sat over his untouched soup, until Hecht feared that after all his friend was not going to rise to the occasion. Then his old enemy Louis B. Mayer challenged him. Did he remember the time he had run out of his MGM contract—the mighty Barrymore who considered himself above all laws?

"Yes, I recall the incident," said Jack. "It was the time I went to India. . . . I went to meet a saint. I was seized with a great desire to meet a man named Krishnamurti. I had been told he was a saint who could command the ear of Heaven. Have you never in your life yearned to meet a saint?"

It was not the time he'd gone to India, and Jack had known Krishnamurti well long ago in Hollywood, but that didn't matter. He was center stage once more and, embroidered like an Indian temple, the Calcutta whorehouse tale began to roll off his tongue.

"And so," concluded Jack as the entree was removed, "I never met my saint. I met only dancing girls and singing girls, all of them devout students of the Kamasutra, which teaches that there are thirty-nine different postures for the worship of Dingledangle—the God of Love. . . ." By now the story had become a parable of his own life: his search for the saint or, as Ned had called it, the little green door; his failure to wrest more out of life than the material.

The rich flow went on. He talked of Hamlet—"There, if ever, was a scurvy, mother-loving drip of a man! A ranting, pious pervert! But clever, mark you! Like all homicidal maniacs! And how I loved to play him. The dear boy and I were made for each other." Tales of the London opening followed: how he had arrived half an hour before the opening-night curtain dead drunk, having spent the afternoon with a duchess who lowered the drawbridge as he marched in, "gonfalon high." How he had staggered offstage between soliloquies to vomit into the wings. All fantasy: no one—not even John Barrymore—opened drunk in *Hamlet* in London. But the reviews next day had not been fantasy; he'd kept them as a reminder of "the foolishness of fame and the lunacy of life—'A song sung by an idiot running down the wind.' "

He stopped suddenly and shut his eyes. As the guests remained silent and waiting, he whispered to Decker, "You better take me off, Johnny. I've gone up in my lines."

Hecht and Decker helped him to his feet. Smiling shyly, he walked between them out of the room.

"A few minutes later," said Hecht, "the birthday cake with which I had refused to interrupt Barrymore's story-telling was brought in. Its many candles blazed like a triumphant row of footlights."

DEAREST DADDY, Diana had wired her father after her Broadway debut in *The Romantic Mr. Dickens*. THANK YOU FOR THE APPLE FLOWERS AND WIRES. . . . SO DADDY DARLING I AM DOING MY BEST TO CARRY ON THIS STINKING TRADITION. Now Diana was coming to Hollywood, having won good enough notices for Walter Wanger to have offered her a $1,000 a week contract. DEAREST TREEPEE, Jack wired, THE GUEST WING HAS BEEN SCOURED AND FLOWERED AND IS YOURS FOR AS LONG AS

YOU LIKE. Blanche had stipulated that Diana, accompanied by a chaperone, was never to be alone with her father or spend a single night under his roof. Hateful, but then in six weeks Diana would be twenty-one and meanwhile would do just as she pleased. As Blanche knew, though she did not know that Diana was engaged to one of the despised race, the actor Bramwell Fletcher, eighteen years older, British, elegant—a father figure.

"Are you going to be good?" Diana whispered in her father's ear as she stepped off the train to popping flash bulbs.

"Of course not."

"Good. Neither am I."

Diana did not go immediately to the Beverly Wilshire, as ordered, but to lunch at Tower Road where they were greeted enthusiastically on the lawn by the Afghan hound Viola. Inside she was horrified to find her father and George living in three small rooms. Everything else was derelict except a small, cheerful room decked in chintz and flowers. Jack was showing her his efforts proudly when suddenly he blanched and sank into a chair. She found the pantry, brought him vermouth, helped him raise the glass to his lips. Gradually he regained his natural color. "Don't you ever water it either," he said. "Everyone does."

That night they dined at Romanoff's where they were joined by John Carradine. Then at her request they drove to Chatsworth: she was dying to see the uncle she did imitations of but had never met. The door was opened by a Wheeler. Mr. Barrymore was in bed.

Upstairs she saw a man propped in bed. Was this the impressive Lionel Barrymore she knew on the screen? He seemed shrunken, older. "Stand there for a moment, Diana," he said curtly. "Let me see what branch of the Barrymore family you resemble!"

She did not resemble any branch particularly. She looked at the etchings on the walls of his large bedroom. "I saw one of your etchings in the Metropolitan in New York, Uncle Lionel. May I look at these?"

Jack and Carradine had taken chairs next to Lionel's bed. A Wheeler brought champagne. Jack nudged Carradine. "John, tell Mike. Recite that poem—you know the one I mean." Convulsed with laughter, Carradine hesitated, decided that Diana could take it, and threw himself into "The Testament of a Dying Ham" with gusto. All three men found it uproarious. Then Jack said, "Mike, I guess you're tired," and the visit was over.

"Come and see me again, Diana," said Lionel. "I hope you'll be successful here. I wish you were with Metro. That's where we've all been." She kissed him goodbye. He had been kind, yet it wasn't the solid nourishment she craved.

One night Jack grew maudlin over watered vermouth and insisted on telephoning Blanche, though Diana reminded him it was 3:00 a.m. in New York. "Fig? The thing is here. It is divine. It is so beautiful—it looks like you, Fig. She's everything I expected. I'm so glad she's here." But despite Jack's pleading, Blanche would not come out to Hollywood so the three could be together. "Yes, yes," said Jack, disappointed. "I'll take the best care of her I can."

Diana and her newfound father got along, for a time. *Life* photographed them mugging, Diana's contortions commonplace compared to Jack's. He rehearsed her for a balcony scene excerpt from *Romeo and Juliet* for the Rudy Vallee show. "Don't use that made-actress voice," he barked. "Let me tell you something about Shakespeare. The only reason I thought I was successful at it was because I played it as if Shakespeare had written the play for me. . . . Now you think the same way. . . . There's no precedent to follow. The first time these lines will have been read before an audience will be when you read them on the show."

Variety condemned the reading (Vallee as Mercutio) as "mawkish and embarrassing" but, unembarrassed, Vallee aired three Barrymores next as Brutus, Caesar, and Calpurnia. After the program Lionel was helped into his Olds by his driver, Henry Hinkley, and the wheelchair stowed in the trunk. George was waiting for his charge. "Good night, my dear," said Lionel. "We all did very well." The brief conjoining was over.

Diana wanted more than anything to rescue her father with a play for them both. She had Emlyn Williams's *The Light of Heart* about a broken-down matinee idol forced to support his crippled daughter as a department-store Santa. Richard Aldrich had promised not only that she could write her own ticket if she could get her father to do it but that he would forgive Jack $10,000 for having backed out of another *My Dear Children* tour.

"If I could go back, in the right thing . . . this is so right, it is so much me. . . . I'd probably not take a drink till after the theatre." Jack knew he was deluding himself. "But why couldn't it be a film?" said Diana. He brightened.

"You really think so, Treepee? I'll telephone Darryl right now." She listened across the room. "Hello, Darryl? This is Jack . . . Jack Barrymore. . . . I have my daughter here and we've both read a magnificent play which I think would make an extraordinary picture." There was a long silence. "Oh, I see," he said finally. His voice was edged. "Well, thank you, Darryl." He put down the phone. "Treepee, they don't seem to want me."

She went to him, knelt at his side. "Treepee," he said, "*you* are going on to great things. I am already dead."

He caught a cold which he refused to nurse and could not shake. But he was well enough one night to hand Diana a notebook and ask her to telephone a prostitute. All the Miss Newport in her recoiled; the old bitter knowledge that she was never enough overwhelmed her. She dialed the number, packed her bags. When the prostitute clearly knew the way to Jack's room, she slammed the door, leapt into her car, and took the tortuous curves on two wheels. How *could* he ask such a thing of her, his own daughter!

Two weeks later Decker phoned to say that Jack was asking for her. At Decker's studio she found her father slumped between two "common as cat meat blondes."

"You're supposed to be his friend," she shouted at Decker, just as degenerate as her father, more degenerate. "You know he's not to have sex or liquor. Why do you get girls for him?"

"Well, as-I-live-and-breathe!" said Jack, rousing himself. "If it isn't Miss Newport."

She drove him home. The pool that he had filled for her was empty now, symbolically, she thought. Jack stood for a moment looking at her—defiantly, desperately, helplessly.

"Aren't you coming in to check up? Maybe your old Daddy's hidden himself a young lady to diddle with."

"Oh, go to bed, Daddy. You're disgusting, really you are. You're a drunken old fool. You bore me."

Jack swayed, clutched at dignity. "You bore me as much as I bore you," he said haughtily. "Good night."

This is Diana's version of their final quarrel. According to Gene Fowler, the incestuous tendencies which Jack had displayed all his life in his attachment to older women, as well as in his interpretation of *Hamlet*, surfaced in a new form with Diana. The final break came when he tried to take her to bed.

ONE NIGHT Myrna Loy was working late at the studio with Lionel promoting War Bonds when Lionel suddenly said, "Jack's out in the car; I'm sure he'd like to see you. Why don't you go out and say hello?" Loy went out and saw a gray, crumpled man in the back seat of a limousine. He did not know her. "*God!*" thought Loy, and this is the man I saw striding onto the Warners set only sixteen years before?

This was in March. On the afternoon of May 19, Jack phoned Gene

Fowler to say that he couldn't find his gardener Nishi anywhere. Fowler winced. Nishi had been sent weeks before to a camp for enemy Japanese aliens; Jack had forgotten their leave-taking.

More disturbing was Jack's hoarseness, his shortness of breath. Fowler broke his rule and asked him how he felt.

"I feel like hell," said Jack. He sounded cold sober. "That's precisely how I feel."

He had cirrhosis of the liver. His edematose tissues were swollen with fluid due to his malfunctioning kidneys. Water swelling his lung tissue exerted a powerful pressure against his heart. He had chronic gastritis, an ulcerated esophagus, hardening of the arteries, and chronic eczema. Now he had severe bronchitis as well.

Since Jack always kept up the gay deception that he was in top form, Fowler was concerned enough to call Lionel. Lionel too thought Jack's behavior ominous and promised to check up on him.

Ehrling Moss, still another retainer, reminded Jack it was time to go to the broadcasting studio and drove him down the twisting road to Sunset Boulevard. Today he did not stop at Ella Campbell's St. Donat's Restaurant where, over a Pimm's No. 1 Cup in the English atmosphere, he might dream that he was still the world's greatest classical actor. At the studio he was met by his doctor, Hugo Kersten; he had collapsed several times during previous broadcasts but, thanks to Kersten, had managed to complete the program. Today the usual buffoon's script was put into his hands containing, as usual, some Shakespeare to ham, this time lines from *Romeo and Juliet*: "But, soft! what light through yonder window breaks? / It is the east, and Juliet is the sun. / Arise, fair sun, and kill the envious moon—"

Ironically, for one who disliked playing the lover, they were the last words John Barrymore uttered as an actor. As he spoke them he turned white and swayed. As Vallee caught him in his arms, Jack said, "I guess this is one time I miss my cue."

Tears streamed down his face from pain and shock. Kersten drove him to Hollywood Presbyterian Hospital where his condition was diagnosed as bronchial pneumonia, congestion of the lungs, and cirrhosis of the liver. Kersten thought it would be a miracle if he lasted more than a few hours, but the next morning Jack woke from a coma, looked up into the face of an exceptionally plain nurse, and cracked, "Well, get into bed anyway." Kersten urged that he submit to a fluid-draining procedure under local anesthetic. "All right," said Jack. "Stick a stiletto in my belly!" With a trocar Kersten removed four quarts of water from his abdomen.

When Lionel heaved himself out of his car he found the press holding a deathwatch outside the hospital. Unwilling to be photographed as a cripple, he flung his crutches aside and managed to stand erect long enough to be photographed at the entrance. On the fourth floor he found his brother slipping in and out of consciousness, his breathing labored, his eyeballs rolled up in their sockets. Fowler and Decker had mounted a watch across the hall. Lionel chose to conduct his vigil alone in a nearby room. Occasionally Fowler heard a growl: "Why in God's name can't *I* do something for him?" He did, taking Jack's place on Vallee's program on May 21. He should have told Sealtest and Vallee to go to hell.

At Lionel's request Fowler issued regular bulletins to the press. Blanche wired AWFULLY SORRY TO HEAR YOU ARE ILL HURRY UP AND GET WELL FIG. From W. C. Fields: YOU CAN'T DO THIS TO ME. Thomas Mitchell, Alan Dinehart, and Alan Mowbray, loyal acting pals, waited with Fowler and Decker. Elaine sent flowers and telephoned daily, but Lionel barred her absolutely from his brother. Dolores called and spoke with her former husband. Anthony Quinn came with a Chinese carved ivory boat that he knew Jack had once longed to own. "You little shit, how did you know?" said Jack and burst into tears. Diana had rushed off the set of her second movie *Between Us Girls* when she got word; on subsequent visits Jack lay insensible except once when he opened his eyes and said clearly, "Treepee." Again in a moment of consciousness he told Lionel, "Tell Ethel to go on, not to come." Over and over in his dying sleep he murmured, "Mummum, Mummum."

By Friday twelve quarts of fluid had been drained from his body and his condition had worsened. The Reverend John O'Donnell came as a friend; then, perhaps at Lionel's urging, returned to Jack's room as a priest and gave Jack extreme unction. Jack had told John Carradine once that he was not a good enough Catholic to go to church but too good to kill himself; superstitious, he would not have objected to the last rites. When the priest came again, however, Jack had recovered enough to totter once more onstage.

"Father," said Jack, "I have carnal thoughts."

O'Donnell looked at the dying man incredulously. "About whom?"

Jack nodded at the new nurse, older and plainer than the first. "Her," he said, a comedian to the end.

He hung on, incredibly. One afternoon Fowler discovered a nurse trying to brush his teeth, which remained stubbornly clenched. She assured Fowler it would make the dying man more comfortable. Fowler bent over Jack.

"Listen, you obstinate bastard! A beautiful woman is trying to brush your teeth, which, by some miracle, still remain in your possession. Open your eyes and see for yourself what you are missing, you—"

The Monster opened his eyes; the nurse had no further trouble.

Late in the afternoon on May 28 Jack raised himself on an elbow and asked for Fowler, who was sitting in the hall. "Will you hold my hand while I sleep?" he asked. He rambled on about his children and about Ned, then lapsed into incoherence except for the words "Mummum, Mummum." Then suddenly he said quite clearly, "Lean over me. I want to ask you something." Fowler bent over, steeling himself for a heart-wrenching last request.

"Tell me," said Jack, "is it true that you are the illegitimate son of Buffalo Bill?" They were the last words he spoke to his most faithful Hollywood friend.

He became delirious. They put white mittens on his hands to keep him from clawing at his inflamed skin. He fought so hard that he had to be restrained. Lapsing in and out of consciousness he called for Lionel. His brother dragged himself on crutches to his room and bent over him but could not understand his words.

"What did you say, Jake?" asked Lionel.

"You heard me, Mike," said Jack clearly and fell asleep.

On Friday, May 29, Lionel called Dolores to tell her that Jack could not last much longer. "What do you want me to do?" asked Dolores. "Bring his children?"

"No," said Lionel. "I want them to remember him as he was."

At the same time Fowler was telephoning Diana. "Get out to the hospital right away. I believe your father is dying."

"I can't possibly do it," said Diana, who was scheduled that evening to attend the premiere of her first film, *Eagle Squadron*. "I have a very important appointment."

"So has your father," said Fowler.

According to Diana, she looked in at the hospital on her way to the Pantages Theatre, but was assured by the doctors that her father could hang on for many more days. Either she lied or the doctors did.

Jack's breathing now changed in timbre, becoming, said Fowler, "like the sound made by a knife-blade being ground on a stone wheel." At nine o'clock that evening John Decker went into his room and made a sketch on wrapping paper of the dying man.

At twenty minutes past ten the long suicide of Jack Barrymore was at last accomplished.

THE NEXT DAY Lionel telephoned the box office of the Colonial Theatre in Boston. Ethel was resting in her dressing room between performances of *The Corn Is Green*. As she ran up the aisle of the empty theatre she fell and broke her ankle, though she didn't know it at the time. When she picked up the phone, Lionel told her that Jack was dead.

She went on that evening, in pain, her ankle strapped, giving another inspired performance in a role not unlike that she had played with her younger brother in life. During the prolonged applause she knew that the audience was acknowledging not only her triumph but her loss.

"I am feeling—as I am sure you know—laid low," she wrote Alec Woollcott. "So many memories of my little brother, so long ago, when we were all so young and knew and expected so little, and it didn't matter." And then they had grown up, and expected so much, and it had.

The Corn Is Green closed the following day due to the heat and the uncertainty of Ethel's appearing that evening. But she went on, as she always had. Stella Adler remembered getting off the train one midnight in Pennsylvania Station and seeing ahead of her a tall, straight figure in a dark coat. It was Ethel Barrymore returning from an out-of-town performance, lugging her suitcases, all alone.

TWENTY-NINE

1942—1945

WANTING TO GET BACK to Mummum, Jack had requested cremation and burial in the family plot in Philadelphia. Abetted by the Catholic Ethel, his executors—Lionel, Gene Fowler, and the lawyer Gordon Levoy—did not honor that request. Instead his body was taken to the Pierce Brothers Chapel on West Washington Boulevard. Fowler and his son Will sat with the body all night, interrupted only by Jane Jones, the three-hundred-pound former prostitute who ran an after-hours drinking club on Sunset Strip. She asked to spend ten minutes before the bier, where she knelt with difficulty and prayed. Jack was a great patron of prostitutes. He would have appreciated one praying over him.

At ten o'clock on June 2 a limousine in which Lionel sat slumped picked up Diana. They rode in silence to Calvary Cemetery where an enormous crowd had collected. As Lionel got out of the car he looked at the cloudless sky and spoke for the first time: "Well, it's a nice day for Jack." Maurice Costello and Helene were there; Dolores, now Mrs. John Vruwink as Jack had divined she would be, and the children stayed away. Not so Elaine, who arrived in clinging, low-cut black and a sleek fur cape. During the brief ceremony she and Edna wept befittingly. It was their last moment in the spotlight. All Elaine's attempts at stardom had failed, including a vaudeville turn at the Palace Theatre in Akron, Ohio, where the last two minutes of her act had been lost in a chorus of unpolite hisses.

The thousand-odd spectators were in holiday mood. Long ago Jack had realized the anonymity of the stage actor compared to the movie star when crowds had surged past him to surround a celluloid idol like Valentino. But few of the spectators today were here to honor the movie star John Barrymore; they had come instead to gawk at Clark Gable, Errol Flynn, and Spencer Tracy. For them it was just another show. Jack would have understood.

Fowler, Decker, the MGM executive Eddie Mannix, W. C. Fields, C. J. Briden, and Stanley Campbell carried the coffin to the hearse. Fittingly, Briden and Campbell were make-up men; Jack had been forced to rely on them excessively in his film career. Fields was serving under protest—"The time to carry a pal is when he's still alive"—and refused to ride in the undertaker's limousine which did not have a portable martini bar like his own chauffeured touring car. It was part of the Bundy Drive boys' mystique to treat death as a bad joke, but today young Tony Quinn found their wisecracks jarring. Jack would have understood.

Jack understood a great deal about Hollywood, which is why during his seventeen years in Babylon-by-the-Sea he kept trying to return to the stage. Hollywood was not good for John Barrymore. It plucked him from the center of a New York group who wanted to foster, not exploit, his genius. Hollywood exploited Barrymore, paying him too much money for doing the wrong things, reducing him to a profile. His fabulous salary gave him a sense of false power, for his career was not in his own but in the hands of the camera, the director, the make-up man, and the studios which, with a few exceptions, saddled him with mediocre directors and leading ladies. Hollywood encouraged the most superficial overindulgence while it starved him for the kind of work he wanted to do. It rewarded the great work he did do by denying him not only an Academy Award but even a nomination. It fed his self-contempt, already potent enough. It nourished his cynicism, bitterness, and contempt for others. "Jack wasn't really like that," said Ethel of the Hollywood John Barrymore. "You should have known him before he went out there. He was so lovely, so wonderful, everybody adored him." And at the end, Hollywood joyously trampled on the remains.

Posterity is grateful for a handful of films that managed to capture his versatility: *Dr. Jekyll and Mr. Hyde, Svengali, A Bill of Divorcement, Topaze, Reunion in Vienna, Counsellor-at-Law, Twentieth Century*. No one would claim he should not have made films: Laurence Olivier, John Gielgud, Charles Laughton, and Ralph Richardson made films. But motion pictures should have supplemented the stage if only because John Barrymore was the best American stage actor of the twentieth century. When he left Broadway there was no one to take his place.

Unlike Gielgud, Olivier, and Richardson, John Barrymore was not sustained by a venerable tradition of acting and a national theatre. He needed such a tradition badly: the Drew-Barrymore heritage was not enough for so unstable a personality. He needed strong guidance and reassurance of the kind Ned Sheldon gave him. Even though Arthur Hopkins got great things from John Barrymore, he was not, ultimately, the sort of producer Jack could look up to; Jack needed the kind of discipline dealt out by Mrs. John Drew at the Arch Street Theatre. He needed to be taught responsibility to his audiences and profession; had he learned that lesson he would not have left the theatre permanently nor travestied his art in later years. Yet he probably could not have been taught: some corrosive spirit of mockery and self-hatred blighted him early. And that is why Hollywood was so dangerous to him.

Certainly it had not made him rich, the reason most actors go Hollywood. "I never knew a man who played Hamlet," said Humphrey Bogart (who hated what John Barrymore did to his genius), "who didn't die broke." Jack had sixty cents in his pocket when he was taken to the hospital, personal debts totaling $200,000. After his death claimants crowded the court, fighting among themselves for priority of suit. A month after his death, his wardrobe and the remaining furniture at Tower Road were auctioned, netting a nominal sum: his girdle $4.50, his Hamlet shirt $7.00, his gray sack suit $35.50, his pearl-gray fedora $6.50. His bequests to his children could not be honored. On August 24 by order of the U.S. District Court, his entire estate was auctioned to pay back taxes.

A 1425 manuscript of the Froissart *Chronicles* for which Jack had paid $5,000 went for $750. Lionel secured the Paul Manship bust for $160, Viola for pennies. Dolores bought some of Viola's pups. The San Diego Museum of Art paid a mere $250 for the Sargent. A local collector bought Lincoln's letter to Mummum for $325. Tony Quinn paid $250 for the Richard III suit of armor, John Carradine $226 for a silver service. Edgar Bergen bought the shrunken heads. Columbia Pictures bought furniture. Spencer Berger paid $100 for John's painting *Resurrecting Life*. Hogarth prints went on the block, ancient weapons, sporting equipment, stuffed wild animals, old theatre programs. Yet this was only the dregs of a fabulous collection that had melted away like snow. As Phil Rhodes said, "His hands were open and people took and took." Even when they were not open, people took. There are stories of Dolores backing up her station wagon to Jack's door when he was in New York, her abductions including a Gutenberg Bible which she ignorantly sold for peanuts. The Hotcheners dipped lavishly into the honey pot for years. And Jack himself wondered what had happened to $300,000 entrusted to Elaine and Co.

Loss, waste. Perhaps John Barrymore should have died in the Hotel New Yorker in 1935, the night Hotchener came and found no pulse. He would have spared himself and the public the Caliban-Ariel spectacle, *My Dear Children, The Great Profile, Playmates*, pissing publicly, and all the other pitiable degradations of the last seven years. Yet Jack himself never asked for pity and laughed at life even as he drank to end it.

He was, as he said himself, an actor whose time had passed. Sir Cedric Hardwicke called John Barrymore the last of the great spellbinders. "They couldn't fit into the theatre today. Life was *thundering* away for them not going off in little pops. If Henry Irving and Edmund Kean were alive today, they would probably be in business as executives or tycoons. The theatre wouldn't be big enough to hold them. Laurence Olivier and John Gielgud are the last of the great romantic actors. But even they are mild compared to the great actors of the past. . . ." Olivier agreed: "I'm not a genius. There's no room for genius in the theatre, it's too much trouble." John Barrymore was a genius—and infinite trouble.

Ironically, his New York appearance in *My Dear Children* reminded the theatre world of that genius. Brooks Atkinson had lost interest in the actor who had become for him just a scandalous tabloid name until he witnessed John's expert clowning in that wretched play. For Richard Watts Jr., who had seen *Hamlet* five times, *My Dear Children* reminded him that everything John Barrymore did was epic, whether giving the most stirring performance that critic ever witnessed in the theatre or making a fool of himself wholesale. Paradoxically, too, the gargantuan buffoonery and dissipation of the later years convinced a public who had never seen *Justice, Peter Ibbetson, The Jest, Richard III*, and *Hamlet* that this indeed must have been a prince among actors, for even his self-destruction had been a consummate performance. "At his best," wrote Watts in memoriam, "he made acting seem something so memorable and important that it belonged in the cultural heritage of all of us lucky enough to have encountered it. Although he took his film acting scornfully, he could be splendid on the screen, too. His scene from 'Henry VI' in a foolish revue called 'The Show of Shows' and his great comic performance in a neglected photoplay known as 'The Man From Blankley's' were of true Barrymore stature." After John Barrymore's death, said Watts, "The feeling seemed universal that a man of stature and quality had perished."

THE DEATH OF JACK did not much alter Lionel's external life. Jack on his hilltop and Mike in his valley had lived physically apart. Hard to gauge the emotional impact of Jack's death: for the most part Lionel refused to talk of the past or of his feelings. He seemed to have forgotten Doris Rankin; he had not forgotten but did not speak of Irene. The brothers' competition went back to childhood; later Irene and then Elaine had soured their relationship. Perhaps Lionel's deepest regret was that they had not been closer. In the limousine coming back from the funeral, he had looked at Diana and said, as though completing some thought, "Yes, Miss Barrie knew him better." Diana thought he meant, "Better than you, his daughter," but Lionel meant, "Better than I, his own brother."

Ethel Colt called her uncle "the least like the man-next-door of anyone you ever met." Certainly Lionel was an eccentric. He was capable of sudden ferocities, of haughty contempt for human stupidity. He was far more interested in art and music than in people; art and music were his passion and escape. Now that lack of mobility prevented his ranging up and down the coast in search of sketching scenes, he threw himself into composing, a kind of creation that finally allowed him to disappear completely into his art. Ethel once said, "Stokowski conducting and Rachmaninoff playing his own music was as close to Heaven as I'll ever get." Lionel felt music just as passionately: "It seems to be the only truth, after all is said and done. The only thing left us for comfort." He reverenced Beethoven, Brahms, Bruckner; called Sibelius "the dullest genius" (but sent him cigars during the war). He hated Schoenberg's "well-organized noise," got misty over "Smoke Gets in Your Eyes"—Jerome Kern, but "It could have been written by Schubert." He owned thousands of records, could recognize a composer in the first two bars, made passable music on the oboe and the violin. Now more than anything he wanted to compose a good piece of music. When his suite "Tableau Russe" had been played in the Hollywood Bowl in 1940, Lionel had dismissed the small triumph: "Some people play solitaire, I write music." He began now to compose "In Memoriam" for Jack.

He was assisted by an exiled Hungarian named Eugene Zador with whom he would spend several hours a day, five days a week for the next ten years. A honk of the horn would announce Lionel's arrival in the battered Olds. Some days he would sit in the car talking and chain-smoking cigarettes that he kept loose in an old two-pound coffee can next to him in the front seat, spilling ash down his vest. He emptied almost as many cans of beer. On these days he might shove a score at Zador before he left, grumbling that he knew it wasn't worth the goddamn paper it was written on. Other days he'd whip out his crutches and swing up Zador's front steps "wheezing with eagerness." Zador would play what he had written. "You see," Lionel would crow, "in spite of the fact that I did it, it's good." Sometimes he would call Zador in the middle of the night and play over the phone something he'd just written.

"Does that sound familiar?"

"Yes, it's Brahms's Fourth Symphony."

Bitter swearing, ripping of paper. Zador got to know more than the

musical Lionel. Under the cranky cynicism, he thought, the man was a
sentimental idealist. He worshipped physical Woman, for example: the
lovely limbs, the lovely bodies. If only he could write a ballet for those
limbs, those bodies. . . . He loved children, could be foolish about young
girls. "Dear Daddy," wrote a young thing he had befriended, "A flood
has swept away my home, my car has been destroyed in a collision. . . ."
Not deceived, Lionel bought her a new car, feeling like "a vicarious
lecher."

Yet he was not a happy man. He despised Hollywood—"Like Monte
Carlo, a city of gambling . . . a nervous place full of telephonites who
call just to call." Zador saw him as "a falling star, crippled, aging, hating
impoverishment and the flight of time." His almost fanatic efforts to
compose—he would write more than four hundred pieces of music—
spoke of desperation. Music was all he had.

He tried everything: symphonies, preludes, fugues, fantasias, operas,
romances, elegies, and airs for orchestra, piano, strings, horn, clarinet,
bassoon, cello, and voice. Obviously Zador helped him considerably with
orchestration. Obviously, too, Lionel borrowed shamelessly from his musical gods. Only a great musician breaks new ground; Lionel was a crow
who followed many plows. Besides, he "hated anything new," an ingrained
conservatism that discouraged innovation. He was also deeply sentimental. One imagines tears staining his cheeks as he set to music "So Waits
My Heart":

> Like stars that wait for night to shine
> Like love that waits for love like thine
> Like eyes that wait to see your lovely charms,
> So waits my heart, dear, to hold you in my arms.

For Irene, probably: a melody reminiscent of romantic turn-of-the-
century parlor music.

Yet Lionel commanded respect among Hollywood's musical colony.
Mario Castelnuovo-Tedesco, a colleague of Zador's, had been amused to
find that most Hollywood actors had musical ambitions and dreamed of
writing a piano concerto, though they only knew Grieg's and Tchaikovsky's. Even Mickey Rooney wanted to write a symphony. "The only one
who possessed a certain musical culture, and studied music seriously . . .
was old Lionel Barrymore," said Castelnuovo-Tedesco. ". . . His was a
refined and cultured spirit; he was a courtly person and a true artist. I
enjoyed conversing with him and I used to go to visit him often in his

dressing room. He had a curious fascination for Russian music and had memorized Tchaikovsky's entire thematic catalogue."

WITH THE DEPARTURE of Lew Ayres to serve in the Army Medical Corps, the *Dr. Kildare* became the *Dr. Gillespie* series, except for billing no change for Lionel, who had always lent the series its only distinction. Van Johnson took Ayres's place to no discernible advantage. The female love interest was even more expendable: Laraine Day, Ann Ayars, Donna Reed, Susan Peters, Marilyn Maxwell, and Gloria DeHaven came and went, though not on to stardom. Lionel's favorite was none of these, however, but a wisp of a child with freckles, dark braids, and a winning lisp. "Next to Miss Garbo," vowed the smitten man, "the most awesome actress I have encountered in Hollywood is Margaret O'Brien. She's the only actress besides Ethel who's made me take out my handkerchief in thirty years." Like Jack, who called little scene-stealing Virginia Weidler one of the thirteen most fascinating women he had known, Lionel attributed great powers to little Maggie O'B: "If she'd been born 200 years ago, she would have been burned as a witch!" And there *was* something uncanny about this child who could steal any picture out from under the old pros. Awed by her cunning charm, Lionel presented her with a sapphire and pearl brooch, his only keepsake of Mummum. He meant it as a tribute from one actress who had begun as a child to another. Unlike stage children, however, Hollywood child actors seldom stay the course. Margaret O'Brien eventually would play Juliet to John Barrymore Jr.'s Romeo at the Pasadena Playhouse, then disappear from the scene, taking Lionel's token with her.

During these war years, Lionel as Dr. Gillespie on film and Scrooge on radio functioned as a symbol of courage and survival; it is not too much to say that to the American public he was a powerful symbol of traditional values. But it was his weekly CBS program "Mayor of the Town" that Washington deliberately used as propaganda for home-front morale. Supported by the tart Agnes Moorehead, Lionel as the Mayor of Springdale dispensed not only wisdom, patriotism, and fortitude to Americans at war but also practical exhortations to collect scrap iron, save fats, and abolish hoarding. Even the great Barrymore voice lauding the virtues of the sponsor's Rinso seemed "right" and "American"— though Mummum would have died at Lionel's puckering up to whistle the "Rin-so white!" ditty. Jack hadn't really known there was a war on; Lionel did his part to keep the home fires burning, under his gruff exterior the most passionate of patriots.

And then when many believed that Lionel had found a permanent niche in B pictures and radio serials, he turned in one of the best acting performances of his film career as the fanatical, unscrupulous, silver-tongued Thaddeus Stevens, the congressional leader who locked horns with President Andrew Johnson over post–Civil War reconstruction. *Tennessee Johnson* was "one of Hollywood's grown-up moments," the credit going to actors Barrymore and Van Heflin. The old man could still rise to an occasion, though less and less easily.

And, though Diana believed he cared nothing for her, he had risen to the occasion of her wedding to Bramwell Fletcher two months after John's death, showing up in the Olds two hours before the fashionable ceremony planned by Robin and attended by Blanche, looking more radiant than anyone there, though Harrison Tweed had just told her he was divorcing her. Lionel couldn't stay—hundreds of extras were waiting on the *Tennessee Johnson* set—but he wanted to greet the bride and deliver his gift of two silver compotes. "My dear," he said to Diana, lovely in a wedding dress designed by Universal's Vera West, "I only wish Jack were here to see you now. It would have been a very happy moment in his life." That made Blanche cry, as she had cried when Diana had called to tell her Jack was dead; and then they had champagne and Lionel kissed the bride. It was the first time, thought Diana, that he had acted like an uncle.

Aunt Ethel, on the other hand, didn't seem to know she was alive. In January 1943 Ethel arrived in Los Angeles with *The Corn Is Green*. The tour was making a handsome profit for Shumlin, with concomitantly low salaries for the rest of the cast: he had never before so completely relied on a star to carry a production. On opening night at the Biltmore Ethel did what John Barrymore never could have done: she gave an inspired performance in a role she had now played 800 times. Several nights later, after the enormously applauded curtain, she told Dicky Waring she had a surprise for him out front. It turned out to be Lionel. "My god, it was something, you know," said Waring: "two Barrymores there in the eighth row!" Between them they stood for ninety-nine years of acting; that April Lionel would be sixty-five, fifty years an actor. But brother and sister did not necessarily draw closer after Jack's death, even though Ethel had told Waring, "Lionel's the one."

The Corn Is Green stayed in Los Angeles two and a half weeks, but there is no evidence Ethel saw either Diana or her second movie. Designed to exhibit Diana's virtuosity by casting her as an actress who plays everything from a girl in pigtails to Queen Victoria, *Between Us Girls* proved instead that at twenty-one Diana Barrymore lacked control. Obstreperous as a child, awful as Sadie Thompson, utterly improbable as

Joan of Arc, Diana frays the nerves. She is also too virile to fit Hollywood's feminine ideal. Though she has Jack's dimples and pretty dark hair and eyes, her face is too mobile, her features irregular, her knees fat. She has potential, but everything from her whinnying giggles to adenoidal head cold is overdone. Yet *Between Us Girls* wasn't Diana's fault. "They shouldn't have given me the part, no matter how much I wanted it, no matter how promising my tests," she said correctly. "Even a greatly experienced actress would have thought twice." It was the old story—expecting miracles because the name was Barrymore. But something more: Diana had too much power for films; the stage was her métier.

After *Between Us Girls* Hollywood cooled toward Diana Barrymore. No one told her she was washed up, but the signs were unmistakable. One day she discovered that Universal's star bungalow was no longer hers. Three sleazy pictures followed: *Nightmare, Frontier Badmen, Fired Wife*. She was billed third after Loretta Young and Geraldine Fitzgerald in *Ladies Courageous* in 1944 and not billed at all the same year for a brief appearance in *Hollywood Canteen*. (In 1949 she would be on screen in *D.O.A.* for only seconds as a woman checking into a hotel.) Commendably, she refused work in B-rated Sherlock Holmes and Abbott and Costello films. But it wasn't only Diana's acting that turned Hollywood off. Trying pathetically hard to be a Barrymore, she was running wild—too many men, too much partying, too much arrogance, far too much drinking. Still shuddering from her father's excesses, Hollywood washed its hands. Diana and Bram Fletcher went east.

AS ETHEL CAME WEST again, wheeling out her bicycle for the one thousand and fiftieth time, booming business in February 1944 at the Biltmore to record takes—the only one left of the original cast. But Ethel was in Los Angeles for another reason. For the first time since *Rasputin and the Empress* in 1932 she was going to make a picture.

Cary Grant had wanted Laurette Taylor for Ma Mott in *None But the Lonely Heart*, the movie that was going to prove him a serious actor, but Laurette was bloated from heavy drinking. Ethel did not think Ma Mott the right part for her, but changed her mind when RKO's casting director came to Portland, Oregon, with Clifford Odets's script and an offer of full pay for her road company while she was filming, reimbursement to Shumlin and theatres for lost box-office revenues, all her scenes shot together, and $75,000 for four weeks' work.

Rasputin had been an unhappy experience, and Ethel approached *None But the Lonely Heart* with dread. Instead, she found herself enjoying the work. For one thing, the director Clifford Odets was not Hollywood but theatre; this was his first film. For another, his excellent script was finished, not handed to her on scraps of paper moments before shooting. And Cary Grant was not trying to steal the film like Lionel and Jack; he even tried to get her top billing. She was still very nervous about the camera, but Odets shot her final takes without telling her until her tension evaporated. Still the NO VISITORS sign was quickly hoisted on the set. Apart from a privileged few like Lillian Gish, D. W. Griffith, and Katharine Hepburn, Her Highness did not tolerate intruders.

Filming *None But the Lonely Heart* had been Grant's idea, the novel having stirred memories of his own cockney origins as Archie Leach and his relationship with his own mother after his father died of drink. The big question was whether Grant could drop slick comedy to play a rebellious drifter and whether La Barrymore could disguise her elegance as his junk-dealing mother. In the end it was Grant who didn't measure down. Though Odets complained that Ethel's seventy-five-cent Salvation Army hat made her look "like a dowager countess" until he threw it down and stamped on it, Ethel made the role of the tired, sad, but courageous old mother her own.

In 1975 the film critic Pauline Kael reapplauded Ethel's performance. Kael had found Ethel Barrymore in films "a hollow technician," substituting "presence and charm and hokum for performance."

> Not this time, though. In a few scenes, she and Grant touched off emotions in each other which neither of them ever showed on screen again. . . . there are viewers who still—after three decades— recall the timbre of Ethel Barrymore's voice in the prison hospital when she cries, "Disgraced you, Son." . . . Grant is not as vivid in the memory as Ethel Barrymore.

Cary Grant was nominated for an Academy Award but lost to Bing Crosby for *Going My Way*. And Odets's sensitive, brooding movie failed dismally at the box office. As a result, Grant renounced heavy roles forever, and the gifted Odets was not given another chance to direct for fifteen years. Ethel won an Oscar for Best Supporting Actress, she who hadn't "supported" anyone for forty-three years, much less in Hollywood. Yet it gave her wicked pleasure to have invaded Hollywood and walked off with the prize when so many resident actresses had come to Hollywood and failed. Was it fair? "Perhaps," said Ethel with her crescent smile, ". . . perhaps they shouldn't have gone."

During her brief Hollywood stay she declined large parties in her honor, hobnobbing instead with elect friends like Garbo, Cukor, Zoë

Akins, Spencer Tracy and Hepburn. And Lionel. One topic was Gene Fowler's recently published biography of Jack, *Good Night, Sweet Prince*—Horatio's farewell to Hamlet and also the words Lionel had inscribed on Jack's tomb. Fowler had approached Lionel for the biography and got anecdotes. "Too bad we are not all dead," Lionel had said; "then you would be free to write a *real* story." Indeed, Fowler left out much he wanted to say, not only because he wanted to spare the living such bons mots as Jack calling Irene Fenwick "a lousy lay" but because his avowed mission in writing the biography was "to raise the shattered idol of Barrymore from the dirty cobblestones and place it once again on a pedestal." To that purpose he avoided all critical debate about Jack's achievement as an actor, as well as a hard look at the Hyde side of the Barrymore character, concentrating instead on Barrymore the bon vivant, the charmer, the man's man, the vulnerable genius. A frank "masculinist," Fowler did not go to women about his subject: Ethel had not met him when she received one of twenty-three special first edition copies, inscribed "To Ethel, the sweet genius, with affection from your little brother's friend." Fowler indeed was rather hard on Jack's wives (as Jack had been), especially one, and Elaine promptly threatened to sue. Ethel did not mind the wife-bashing; she told Louella Parsons, "I admire Gene Fowler, and I like his story of John very, very much."

About two things—at least—Ethel and Lionel did not agree. He had plotted a play, *Old Buddha*, with a star part for Ethel as the Empress of China, and was hurt when she said firmly, "I don't think it's right for me." More contentious was politics. Ethel ardently supported FDR for a fourth term. Lionel, on the other hand, greeted Thomas E. Dewey in his wheelchair when the New York governor made a campaign stop in Los Angeles. How furious he would have been had he known the impact of Ethel's remark at a dinner party one night: "How can anyone vote for a little man who looks like the bridegroom on a wedding cake!" Her widely circulated, though unattributed, remark inspired a malicious cartoon in *The New Yorker* and played some small part in the reelection of Franklin Delano Roosevelt.

Lionel's politics did not escape the Roosevelts. After FDR's death he tested for the part of the president in a film about the making of the atomic bomb, winning it with an expert characterization down to the jutting cigarette holder and flashing smile. Eleanor Roosevelt immediately telephoned her son James in Beverly Hills, asking him to inform MGM she objected to Mr. Barrymore having the honor of playing her late husband because of "private statements reportedly made by Barrymore during the last presidential campaign." Startled, MGM asked Lionel to write Mrs. Roosevelt a denial. The president of Loew's, Inc., himself, Nicholas Schenck, delivered the letter to Mrs. Roosevelt in New York, but she refused to withdraw her objection. Meanwhile her son Elliott and his wife, the actress Faye Emerson, had started talking "ethics," splitting Hollywood into pro and con factions. The alarmed studio pulled Lionel out of the picture.

Lionel would spend a good deal of time in his memoir trying to dispose of "the embarrassing gossip which made me out a bitter and vindictive personal enemy of Franklin Roosevelt's," claiming he always had and still had nothing but the highest personal admiration for FDR. But everyone in Hollywood knew Lionel's politics. In *Key Largo* (1948) he had a scene—later cut—in which he hauled himself from his wheelchair and delivered an impassioned speech lauding the late president. "Now that," said Lauren Bacall, "was acting!"

ETHEL FINISHED FILMING *None But the Lonely Heart* on April 5, 1944, and at one o'clock the next day was on the Santa Fe Chief bound east, more emphatic than ever about the joys of the touring actress. "I never know what some theatre people mean when they complain about the rigors of the road. Lord, they must be very faded lilies indeed if they mind touring. I look forward to it, the drafty dressing rooms, the rats, everything. . . ." She throve on trains; as she wrote Zoë Akins, "It is divine traveling in a private car. The most restful thing I've ever done— no telephone no nothing but 3 grinning happy coons who only live to please." Yet from her train window she saw the service stars in the windows of countless homes, some mere shacks, and at every station long lines of too young men in uniform kissing mothers and sweethearts goodbye. Typically, her boys were out of danger: Jackie in Utah teaching squash to servicemen, Sambo in Virginia driving a jeep. Often oppressed by loneliness in these *Corn Is Green* years, she who never wrote wrote often to Woollcott—"Alec mon brave," "Darling and Dearest Al," "Darling Aleeko," signing herself "Rachel," "Gaby Delys," "Vesta Tilley," or simply "Ethel the Lonely."

On June 23, 1944, she ended the phenomenally successful tour of *The Corn Is Green* in Boston, its third visit there. One thousand dollars a week against 7½ percent of the gross had put her back into very comfortable circumstances, though as usual she spent every penny she made. More than that, it had established her again as a draw. She had a radio engagement with Alcoa that would pay $2,500 a week; she had a contract with the Theatre Guild that fall. That August she was sixty-five: fifty years in the theatre. She was a legend, the most distinguished and loved actress in the land. A Personage who satisfied whatever American craving remained for tradition, endurance, class. As a friend observed, "If Queen Mary and Ethel Barrymore were to enter a room at the same time, it's even odds which would drop the first curtsy."

OCCASIONALLY LIFE OFFERS coincidences both graceful and symbolic. *Embezzled Heaven* opened that October in Philadelphia at the old Walnut Street Theatre where Louisa Drew had made her debut 117 years before when she was seven. It had been from the Walnut Street Theatre balcony that a voice had called on the first night of *Captain Jinks*, "Speak up, Ethel. We loved your grandmother, Ethel, and we love you too!" She had not played there since. And now, though she did not know it, *Embezzled Heaven* was the last play she would take to Broadway.

Ethel had succumbed to another Catholic play chosen less for its dramatic merit than for its appeal to her taste for religious heroism. In this dramatization of Franz Werfel's novel, she is Teta, a simple Czechoslovakian cook who believes she can buy her way into heaven by putting her worthless nephew through the seminary with her hard-earned wages. Unfortunately, the contrivedly simple play lived up to neither its actress nor the Theatre Guild's production—though Ethel Barrymore had never been "more magnificent" and though it was "a privilege to see such acting in our time."

She had, in fact, swept the capacity audience away, this "by long-odds, First Lady of the Theatre." Ethel hated the term, that "terrible tag pinned on me by Percy Hammond." Though John Drew had been called "The First Gentleman of the Stage," Ethel believed the title "First Actress" suited her better. Was she right?

After John Barrymore left the stage in 1925, the most exciting work in the theatre was done by actresses: Laurette Taylor, Helen Hayes, Lynn Fontanne, Tallulah Bankhead, Katharine Cornell, Ethel Barrymore. All had claims to First Actress. But before any of them stepped on a stage, there had been Ethel Barrymore. Ethel Barrymore did not excel at Shakespeare, true: there had been too many *Jinks*es and *Cousin Kate*s before her belated outings as Juliet, Ophelia, and Portia. But for the quantity and sustained quality of her work in the theatre, for the genius of her technical craft which after a thousand performances could look spontaneous, for the magic she exercised over audiences, for the adoration she commanded, and for her service to the American public as a touring actress for fifty years, the title First Actress was well merited.

But that theatre career was virtually at an end. Despite sudden collapses and arthritic attacks, Ethel had an amazingly strong constitution.

Now, a week after the New York opening, she was felled by chills and fatigue followed by a high fever. On November 10, the National was dark. Three days later she was rushed to the hospital with pneumonia. A ten-day battle ensued, her victory announced by the electric signs winking across the face of the Times Building: GENERAL MACARTHUR LANDS AT LEYTE ETHEL BARRYMORE'S TEMPERATURE LOWER. On November 22 she was sent to Hot Springs, Virginia, to recuperate. She did, but she had had a close call. She began to wonder how long she could go on trouping.

BECAUSE SISTER HAD DARED marry on December 1 while her mother was still recovering, she spent her honeymoon in Hot Springs with Ethel. Her husband was not Frank Murphy but Romeo Miglietta, an oil and mining engineer who, though spending much of his life in England and America, retained his Italian citizenship. Meeting him at a dinner party, Sister had been immediately drawn by his sophisticated charm. She was thirty-two, Romeo sixty-one, a substitute for the father she had resented. Perhaps his chief appeal was that he was unafraid of Ethel Barrymore.

Sister married because she fell in love, yet marriage was also an antidote for failure. "That Barrymore Colt girl falls flat at every moment she ventures New York," Stark Young had written in 1939; "no talent, plenty of nerve." It took nerve to compete with Ethel, John, and Lionel Barrymore. "The Barrymore name *killed* Sister," said Barbara Robins Davis. And her mother's attitude toward her career was dauntingly ambiguous. At one moment, "Oh, my child doing *that!*" when Sister ran the Jitney Players, a traveling repertory group headquartered in Madison, Connecticut. Yet Mother would have been equally withering had she not made the effort. In fact, Sister had to live with a mother who was embarrassed that her daughter had not made the big time, but who would have resented it if she had.

Sister had turned to music because no one could say she didn't sing as well as her mother, but even in music "living up" took its toll. Believing that Sister had real talent, Barbara Robins staged *London Assurance* as a musical to showcase her talents with the idea of taking it to New York. Sister gave some beautiful performances, then, as they neared New York, began to tighten: she never recaptured the magic. Similarly, Barbara remembered one New York Town Hall concert with a relaxed Ethel Colt giving a stunning performance; then tension would overwhelm her and she inevitably "fell flat."

Though she did not give up singing or her many supportive activities in the arts, Sister would view her marriage as her triumph. "I long ago made peace with myself," she said nine years after her mother's death, "[and decided] I didn't have the drive for stardom. I don't know anybody who can have a really top career and a happy marriage. At some moment your husband is going to ask that crucial question, 'Which is more important, me or your career?'" But Ethel Colt Miglietta *did* have the drive for stardom. She tried again and again, but that elusive commodity, star quality, was missing. Romeo Miglietta absolved her from what, among the Drew-Barrymores, was a crime. She would look back and say that she had succeeded where her mother failed.

ETHEL'S RETURN to the National was marked by *two* red apples and a two-minute ovation. But by January 1945, the Guild's losses on *Embezzled Heaven* exceeded $50,000 and directors Helburn and Langner were looking for another play for their star. Ethel was renting a duplex on East Fifty-second Street, having closed Mamaroneck for the gas-rationing duration; she missed it terribly, along with little things like Atkinson's White Rose perfume, "delicate—like faded roses," that she had not been able to get from England since the war. Since her Oscar she had received any number of long-term contract offers from Hollywood—though no offer to film *The Corn Is Green*, even though Bette Davis wanted her to have the part and though Ethel's fans saw in Davis's Miss Moffat "just a big hole where Miss Barrymore had been." Ethel hedged: "I wouldn't sign a seven-year contract with God. No—you'd better make that 'only with God.'" But since her illness her thoughts turned more and more to the Hollywood she had detested. She could ask $100,000 a picture. Her radio program "Miss Hattie" paid well but offered mediocre material. She owed the Guild another play but they hadn't come up with one. A one-picture contract might be just the thing.

"Really tough to find a place to live," George Cukor wrote her on April 7. However there was a penthouse apartment in the shabby-genteel Chateau Marmont off Sunset Boulevard, "very nace, refaned." The $325 rent included daily maid service, gas, electricity, laundry, and switchboard services, and two hundred palpitating people were waiting to grab it.

"George darling," Ethel replied. "Bless you. I am leaving here May 13." That day too she had heard the news. "I am over-powered today with grief," she said of Franklin Roosevelt's death. There had been a time she had seemed likely to belong to his inner political circle. "My beloved man!"

She went west, bringing her own silver and monogrammed silk sheets and Sammy, who might find something to do in Hollywood. Cukor had also found her a Hungarian-Austrian cook with magnificent recommendations and had induced his artistic friends to redo the Chateau Marmont apartment with antiques borrowed from homes like Lady Mendl's. RKO had suggested the possibility of filming a delightful fantasy, *Miss Hargreaves*, but Ethel was committed to nothing: this was a reconnoitering mission undertaken at her own expense. "Mother liked to be independent," said Sammy.

Instead, she chose *The Spiral Staircase* for her second RKO film, a wonderful Victorian thriller which, however, gave her far less to do than *None But the Lonely Heart*. The cast was decidedly to her taste: Rhys Williams and Kent Smith, who had both acted with her onstage; Sara Allgood, from the Abbey Theatre; Elsa Lanchester; George Brent, whom she'd admired in stock in Denver; Dorothy McGuire, who had had the good taste to leave *My Dear Children*. Ethel was cast as the bedridden stepmother of a psychotic killer who can't tolerate young women with deformities. Ethel's Mrs. Warren is meant to be ambiguous, a sibyl who even with her eyes closed seems to be watching. Usually the huge eyes are open; the voice is hypnotic as it delivers such standard horror-film lines as "Leave this house tonight if you know what's good for you." Amazingly, there is still the sidelong glance and smile that bewitched audiences thirty years before. Many women of sixty-five are unrecognizable as the beauties they were, but the young Ethel Barrymore does not take much imagining. Though Ethel would win an Oscar nomination for the little she had to do, *The Spiral Staircase* is Dorothy McGuire's film, with the thunderstorm that snarls throughout a runner-up.

After all Cukor's labor, Ethel found the Chateau Marmont more shabby than genteel and rented a tiny, secluded house off Laurel Canyon Drive, leaving Sammy to run about town returning all the borrowed antiques. Sammy had got a job, through Lionel, working for Lionel's agent, Maury Small. Ethel was still uncommitted to another film when an old siren song was heard. Arthur Hopkins staging and producing, Robert Edmond Jones designing—names that evoked the magic days of great theatre with John Barrymore, though not one play Ethel had done with them had been a popular success. The play now was a revival of Philip Barry's "ancient flop" *The Joyous Season* with another religious role for Ethel, a Mother Superior, indeed, who returns to her bickering family at Christmas time and with tender humor straightens out their lives.

The Joyous Season opened in Bridgeport, Connecticut, on November 9, Ethel having locked herself in her hotel room the night before, refusing to see anyone when she heard that advance ticket sales amounted to only eight hundred, including two hundred passes. Had Ethel ever read them, the reviews next day would have been too, too familiar. Play: unexceptional. Ethel Barrymore: superb. Hopkins's earlier production of *The Joyous Season* had inspired little critical enthusiasm. "But then he had Lillian Gish," said one critic; "now he has Ethel Barrymore. And what a difference that makes."

She took it to Chicago in January 1946, where business boomed because Catholic parish priests urged their congregations to see it. Both she and Hopkins knew it would not survive New York. "I loved it," said Ethel, "and did not want it to be buffeted, so I closed it at the end of the run in Chicago."

"I don't want to sound like Tallulah," she wrote Sammy, "but they only come to the theatre to see me & it's awfully hard carrying the play. . . . It's cold in Chicago. I think I'll come to California. Find a house for us—not like David Selznick's—something a little simpler."

She still had an obligation to the Theatre Guild, and as she traveled west she told herself she would never stay in Hollywood. At the same time, "fifty years in the theatre" had a final ring. Jack had played *Hamlet* 101 times to best Edwin Booth's record, but "fifty-one years in the theatre" would shatter no mark. And Jack was gone, and she didn't have to prove anything anymore. And so Ethel Barrymore—the chief reason why the Barrymores today are still called a theatrical family—stayed in Hollywood. Except for a benefit performance in New York in 1950 she had taken her last bow.

"I don't think it's true to say that, because of Hollywood, people of real talent have been lost to the theater," she said. "Nobody is lost to the theater unless they want to be. And if they want to be lost, let them." She excepted Jack and Lionel. "What I minded about my brothers coming to Hollywood was that I felt it was such a loss for the public. Jack and Lionel had both been superb in the theater. To think that Jack could be the great Hamlet and then to see him in endless *Something Loves* was distressing. . . . I don't think he was ever satisfied. I don't think yachts and swimming pools make up for other things. Perhaps he always had a feeling that Mummum was looking down, disapprovingly. There was a great bond there." At sixty-five, Ethel refused guilt. And yet, looking back at her last Broadway appearance in *Embezzled Heaven*, she would say, "Perhaps I ought to have died, when everybody was saying such nice things about me."

THIRTY

1945-1949

WHILE ETHEL WAS DECIDING to give up the stage after fifty years, Lionel was having the satisfaction of hearing his music performed from West Coast to East. Elected to ASCAP, his face on the cover of *Pacific Coast Musician*, royalties coming in, he had achieved something he had dreamed of since Henry Hadley had told him as a young man in New York, "It's plain you're never going to be a pianist. You'd better take up composing."

On April 22, 1944, Eugene Ormandy and the Philadelphia Orchestra had broadcast nationwide Lionel's "In Memoriam" to Jack, a warm, nostalgic tone poem weaving together melodies that brought Jack to mind: Gypsy strains, a little song, "Blue Forget-Me-Nots," that the brothers used to listen to at the Café Boulevard in New York when they were young and life lay ahead. "If the great masters were listening," said Lionel, "I'm sure they'd be gentlemen enough to consider the intent of my music rather than the execution." But the high point of musical attention came when Artur Rodzinski and the New York Philharmonic played his "Partita" on national radio. Even Ethel was impressed.

"Lionel, have you *seen* that program?"

"No, I just listened to the radio." He had wanted to be alone so that no one would see his tears.

"I think you should look hard at this."

A symphony by Beethoven. An overture by Brahms. A partita by Barrymore.

Lionel knew he was not the fourth B. "I've borrowed from everybody except the studio gateman, and I'll get around to him later." Yet he defended borrowing: "If your modern composer wants something, what does he do? He goes back to Scarlatti and Corelli and Couperin and borrows their style and dresses it up. When it comes out, it's the last word." The trouble was, Lionel didn't dress up his music enough. Olin

Downes called his "Preludium and Fugue" not of particular originality, then sweetened the censure by adding, "Here, one of the most distinguished figures of the American stage, at the age of 66, writes music with the zest and gusto of the gifted amateur, and this with a surprising degree of technique and an inherent sense of form." Lionel's mentor, Eugene Zador, dodged the question by calling his friend "an amateur professional not a professional amateur."

Inevitably there were a lot of silly headlines these years, such as LIONEL BARRYMORE, FAMED AS ACTOR, MAY BE KNOWN BEST AS COMPOSER. And of course there was generous encouragement for the wheelchair-ridden old actor who had become a national symbol of crusty good heart. Very seldom did the press snarl, an exception being the performance of his Piano Concerto No. 1 by the thirteen-year-old June Kovich in Chicago's Rochester Hall. "Mr. Barrymore's battered themes would have been happier growing up into tunes such as might grace a Hollywood musical comedy," said the *News*. Claudia Cassidy was kinder: "Mr. Barrymore has nothing to say here that has not been better said before, but the man has a flair. Barrymores always do."

There is no question that had Lionel Barrymore not been Lionel Barrymore his music would not have won national recognition. It was pleasant that he had a little success, but for Lionel that was secondary. What thrilled him was mastering the technical forms of music, no mean accomplishment. The content he poured into those forms was derivative, but the triumph of actually composing a symphony or a fugue immense. It is not too much to say that he lived for composing. Lost in chords and counterpoint, Lionel could work six drug-free hours at a stretch.

Toward his sixty-seven-year-old body Lionel displayed typical Barrymore contempt. He refused to discuss his health, became savage when anyone inquired after it. Except when he was in front of the camera, eating, or asleep, he had a cigarette between his lips. He ate enormously: potato salad, malts, hamburgers, cookies. He consumed barrels of beer. Although he told numerous people he had kicked his cocaine habit, Gene Fowler was present one fire-burning winter evening in Lionel's den at Chatsworth when Lionel suddenly began rummaging through his desk drawers and pulled out a bag of cocaine. Propelling himself to the fireplace, he hurled the bag on the fire. "If I need this goddamned stuff to live," he growled, "then I don't give a goddamn about living!" Fowler, who knew a good scene when he saw one, suspected it was not the finale— and there are other stories about Lionel "discovering" bags of cocaine and dramatically renouncing the habit forever.

At the same time, he could drive himself to physical limits. Selznick signed him to play Senator McCanles, the hard-nosed cattle baron of Spanish Bit in an 1880s epic western meant to eclipse *Gone With the Wind. Duel in the Sun* featured "three really hot and really new personalities"—Jennifer Jones, Gregory Peck, and Joseph Cotten—as well as premier actors playing second string—Lionel, Lillian Gish, Herbert Marshall, Walter Huston, and Charles Bickford: the worn-out illusion that an all-star cast and a huge budget (an unprecedented $7.5 million) will make a great movie.

Lionel played most of his scenes in a wheelchair and for long shots had a double, but McCanles's face-off with the railroad officials demanded the real man on horseback. With the assistance of a ladder and extras, Lionel managed to hoist himself onto a white horse, then endure hours of shooting in 110-degree Arizona heat under a director, King Vidor, who was driving Selznick crazy with his ambling pace. Lionel declined to be removed at lunchtime: "No, I'll stay on, because when I get off I'm going home." At the end of the afternoon's filming Vidor asked Lionel whether the next day he would be willing to let himself be dragged by the horse. "All right," said Lionel, "but do it today. You won't see me around here tomorrow." They laid him down, roped his legs like a steer's, then bounced him along the ground behind a car while the cameras ground. His grit drew cheers from the crew but, good to his word, Lionel disappeared for the next few days of shooting.

His eyes gleaming slits, his mouth drawn down in discontent, Lionel is meaner in *Duel in the Sun* than MGM usually allowed, though naturally he turns out to have a heart in the end. Compared to his old Biograph co-player Lillian Gish, acting opposite him as his wife, Laura Belle, the years have dealt harshly with Lionel: he is crippled, bloated. When Vidor suggested that McCanles would not be the type to wear a wedding ring, Lionel's gold band, buried in flesh, had to be surgically removed. With typical stoicism, he submitted silently to the violation of the sentimental symbol.

Gish, Cotten, Huston, and Lionel turned in excellent performances, but in Selznick's own words *Duel in the Sun* cost him "great loss of prestige with the trade and press and public." Raw-sex westerns weren't really Selznick's métier. As the half-breed Pearl, Jennifer Jones tried embarrassingly hard to smolder; the lurid publicity surrounding the film's release broke all Selznick's rules of dignity. But violently negative reviews only meant that the film was a hit with the public.

As was Lionel's next, a film that has since become a Christmas classic, Frank Capra's *It's a Wonderful Life*. On loan from MGM, Lionel was delighted to get his teeth into a real villain, "the skinflint who owned half the town and coveted the other half," but Lionel's Senator McCanles had been a more natural and therefore more sinister portrait of a hard man. Then it was back to MGM for a last wheel down hospital corridors as Dr. Gillespie in *Dark Delusion*. Lionel's paid vacations were over. Suddenly MGM seemed to have nothing more for him to do.

WHEN SAMMY made no headway in finding Ethel a house, Zoë Akins said one day, "Have you ever been to Palos Verdes?" Ethel found it magical, green and high with the Pacific blue to the horizon. At first she fell in love with a Tuscany-style estate in Rolling Hills, but inspecting the house she was repelled to find a snake sunning itself on the balcony off the master bedroom. Fleeing from that bad omen down Chelsea Road as it skirts the coast, she had her driver stop to look at a house with a brick wall blazing with geraniums. A man was standing at the gate. "Have you come to look at the house?" he asked. It was for rent. She walked in and took it.

She moved in with Sammy; her Siamese cats Wingo and Monkey-face; her maid Anna Albert; her butler Fred, who was also her chauffeur; and Fred's wife Edna. Everyone said she was too far away, but she didn't care: she *wanted* to be far away, and the people who mattered would come. And they did. Cukor, Billy Haines and Tommy Douglas, who had decorated the Chateau Marmont apartment, Orry-Kelly the dress designer, Clifton Webb, Cole Porter, Whitney Warren the millionaire—gay men, for whom she had a decided affinity. Zoë Akins, Gladys Cooper. The Artur Rubinsteins. Hepburn. Constance Collier. Garbo carrying her yogurt and soybean patties in a brown bag. Ethel's Sunday luncheons became famous; she staged them like a scene from *Déclassée*: drinks around the goldfish pond, the butler appearing: "Luncheon is served, madam." There was good talk—not "cocktails or parlor movies or that awful thing called canasta." According to the writer-producer Charles Brackett, "Her parties were the best anyone gave."

One of the few Palos Verdes couples Ethel got to know were Elin and Kelvin Vanderlip, the developer of Rolling Hills. Ethel was particularly enchanted with a Norwegian Christmas Eve party that included a huge candlelit tree and presents for the servants Elin had brought with her from Norway. As usual, Ethel was the center of attention, more regal than Queen Mary in fawn-colored lace and pearls. Sammy trailed after her. The little boy who had wept in *Peter Pan* when Maude Adams flew away with the children because "How will their mother know where they are?" did not give his own mother cause to worry on that point. "Sammy did whatever Ethel wanted him to do," said Mrs. Vanderlip. "Every time he'd get a job or a girlfriend, Ethel would sabotage that. She killed all Sammy's projects. . . . He adored her." In turn, Ethel tolerated Sammy's drinking, which he tried to disguise by downing colorless martinis in tall water glasses; his extravagance; his long golfing weekends with conservative Republican cronies from Pasadena and Santa Barbara; his indolence, which she had done much to create.

She would venture into Hollywood for select occasions. A Beverly Hills dinner party, for example, "elegant down to the last rose petal," hosted by Somerset Maugham on whose right she sat as the woman with whom he'd been smitten and who had built his Cap Ferrat house. On another occasion a screening of *The Best Years of Our Lives* at the Samuel Goldwyns' inspired the guests—Cukor, Whitney Warren, Hedda Hopper, Ethel—to wire congratulations to its author, Robert Sherwood: THIS IS THE AMERICAN MOTION PICTURE AT ITS BEST. But she was very choosy and made it perfectly clear that on the whole Hollywood was not top-drawer.

She supported her decidedly comfortable style of living with three pictures: *The Farmer's Daughter* (a critical and box-office success), *Moss Rose* (a pleasant Gothic thriller), and *Night Song* (a high-brow soap). Ethel drove up to the set of RKO's *The Farmer's Daughter* in "a black Cadillac three blocks long—and a liveried chauffeur yet!" and was greeted deferentially by cast and crew. Loretta Young, the star, would get her coffee or bring her her chair between scenes. "My dear," Ethel rebuked her, "there are plenty of people to do that."

Joseph Cotten, the only actor allowed to call her "Miss B," discovered the never-sleeping humor under the dignity. They had a scene in which he takes leave of his mother to go to the capital to see the governor. In the twenties there was a famous vaudeville skit in which a high-toned governor's wife tours a state asylum guided by an old inmate. As they inspect the place the inmate pours out his woes, shocking the governor's wife, who promises to bring his plight to the governor's attention. As she turns to go, the old man boots her smartly in the behind, crying, "Don't forget to tell the Governor!" Now as Cotten took leave of Ethel he got a smart goose in the rear. "Don't forget to tell the Governor!" leered Ethel, flourishing her prop cane. "Our director Hank Potter and I literally fell on the floor laughing," said Cotten. It was some time before cast and crew could pull themselves together.

Ethel plays the political matriarch in *The Farmer's Daughter* expertly without really giving herself to the role. *Moss Rose* gave her far more to do as the murdering Lady Margaret Drego of Charnleigh, and she did it. Yet in the scene where she discovers an intruding Peggy Cummins in her beloved dead son's room, she quickly subsides after her hair-raising *"What are you doing here!"* when a crescendo of anger is wanted. Perhaps she was remembering Lionel's warning that for the camera one need only whisper. In *Night Song* she plays Miss Willy with obvious enjoyment. She has some good lines: "My heart's an old wastepaper basket, filled with unpaid bills and paperback novels," and "Tonight I'm going to take a hot bath and read a detective story. You can't imagine what profound pleasure there is in the prospect." She is imperturbable. Her smile slides up her face into her cheeks and eyes. She smokes a lot. Her strong hands are beautiful. She is androgynous. One loves her and mourns the fact that Hollywood has no leading part worthy of her. One wishes the tedious Merle Oberon and Dana Andrews would take a powder and leave the story to Ethel and Hoagy Carmichael, so much more lively and entertaining.

In September 1946 she went east to be present for the birth of Sister's child, who was named with dynastic pride John Drew Miglietta. Though a devout Catholic, Sister did not feel obliged to produce a trio of offspring like Mummum, Georgie, and her mother. Johnny would be her only child.

Ethel put off the Theatre Guild this visit, promising to do a revival of *The Corn Is Green* as soon as she finished her next picture. At the same time, "Oh, yes!" she told a reporter who asked whether she intended to stay in Hollywood. "I have given a large slice of my life, practically the whole of it, to the theatre—compared to my brothers, I have certainly done my duty by it! . . . I shall miss going all over the country; I loved traveling and I love the theater. . . . Of course—if a great play comes along. . . ." "If someone only had a tempting part for her," sighed Brooks Atkinson. But when she was offered *The Madwoman of Chaillot*, she turned it down.

And yet she was never comfortable in films as she was in the theatre, just as she was never the star in films that she was on the stage. "Why are you nervous?" asked Alfred Hitchcock, directing the much-postponed *Paradine Case* that Selznick had once wanted for all three Barrymores. "It's only a motion picture."

"Suppose," said Ethel promptly, "I said that to *you*."

Nervousness could only help her play the browbeaten Lady Horfield to Charles Laughton's hanging judge. Bored with the miscast Valli and Louis Jourdan, Hitchcock devoted most of his time to the Laughton and Barrymore scenes. Memorable are the two at dinner just before the Paradine verdict comes in. Still displeased with Lady Horfield's coughing that day in court, Lord Horfield scathingly discourses on the resemblance between the convolutions of a walnut and the human brain while Ethel hangs her head. He dismisses her sympathy for the murderess: "You silly woman . . . the Paradine woman will be hanged after three clear Sundays." Surely the first time Ethel Barrymore had ever been called silly, though once a woman reporter preparing to interview her announced that she wanted "all those silly little characteristics which make up the person." "My God, girl," said the horrified agent, "don't you know Miss Barrymore *hasn't* any silly little characteristics?"

Selznick scrapped most of Ethel's footage in the cutting room, added constant rewriting and overspending to that folly, and finally turned out a talky $4 million box-office failure. Ethel was nominated a third time for Best Supporting Actress, losing to Celeste Holm for *Gentleman's Agreement*—predictably, since most of her performance was on the cutting-room floor.

In Selznick's *Portrait of Jennie* she was more herself as Miss Spinny, a shrewd and kindly art dealer who lends most of the solidity to a metaphysical love story Selznick described well when he desperately telegraphed Ben Hecht to write a prologue to the film in "the type of cinematic foreword journalese of which you are the only master I know, combining a certain artistic tone with old Hearst Sunday-Supplement type of hokeypokey, Pseudoscientific approach. . . ." Yet Joseph Cotten was sure from the look in Ethel's eyes in a final scene with him that she believed in a love that transcended space and time.

Having canceled a seven-year contract with Selznick by mutual consent, Ethel after eight pictures still had no long-term contract because, she said, "The first thing I know, they would be lending me out for a lot of money and a couple of outfielders"—as MGM had done with Lionel, trading him to Warner Brothers for his only 1948 film, *Key Largo*.

"We rehearsed three weeks, the whole cast, Lionel in his wheelchair, in pain, never complaining," said Lauren Bacall. "I adored him. He was wonderful—*wonderful*. He was one of those people who pretends he doesn't need anyone and doesn't care, but is so thoughtful, so kind. I used to serve tea in my dressing room every afternoon, and the whole cast would come in—Eddie Robinson, Bogey, Claire Trevor. Lionel had to sit outside the door in his wheelchair, but he looked forward to those tea parties, always came, really enjoyed himself. And when Bogey's and my first son was born, he sent him a silver engraved porringer and cup which—I mean—from Lionel Barrymore was something!

"But he was terribly lonely, I think. And I never saw him with Ethel's friends—Cukor, Maugham, Cole Porter, Constance Collier. You know, Ethel gave these wonderful Sunday luncheons, an enormous mélange of people. And I remember one Sunday Lionel was there in his wheelchair, and he was left alone. Lunch was announced and nobody took him in. So when we were all in the dining room I said, 'Ethel, should I get Lionel?' And she said indifferently, 'Yes—oh yes, get him.' There was something wrong between them. I never asked what, of course."

Hank Potter, a friend of Jack's who directed Ethel in *The Farmer's Daughter*, also felt Ethel's discontent with her older brother.

"I had lunch with Lionel," she told him one day. "You know, he's getting to be such an *old maid*. We were talking about Jack and Lionel said, 'Why, do you know that toward the end they had to put every line of his on *blackboards!*'" The huge eyes flashed. "I just *looked* at him, and I said, 'You mean the way they had to do for *you*, when we did *Rasputin!*'"

Elaine accused Lionel of excesses that made Jack's drinking look like minor truancy; Ethel felt the same. Both her and Jack's careers had been damaged by their drinking—Jack's finally—but not only had Lionel's public image never suffered, despite his addictions, but to that public he was the Grand Old Man: honest, benevolent, straight-shooting. Well the last at least, thought Ethel grimly, was true.

Certainly it was clear to the Bogarts which brother she preferred. A friend had sent Bogey a record he had made of Jack reading Shakespeare. Ethel was coming to dinner, and Bogey knew how Ethel adored Jack. "Don't say anything. We'll just put the record on. She'll be thrilled." "Are you sure?" asked Bacall doubtfully. "Oh, yeah," said Bogey. "She maybe doesn't even know it exists." Ethel made her entrance, more beautiful with her radiant face and erect carriage, thought Bacall, than a girl of twenty. Bogey went to put the record on. Ethel heard half a word. "*No!*" she cried, clapping her hands over her ears. "She *could not bear it,*" said Bacall.

Ethel's settling in Hollywood, therefore, was little comfort to Lionel. His solitary ways, his battered Olds, his rumpled ash-strewn clothes, his politics, his Wheelers—all alienated Ethel, who was just as much of a social success with elect Hollywoodians as she had always been everywhere. Asked about her brother, she dismissed him: "He lives in the valley and I live on the coast, so we don't get together very often." Jack trying to escape on his hilltop, Lionel hiding in his valley, Ethel facing the sea: the Barrymores' choices of homes in Hollywood says something about their natures.

Ethel was better with Jack's children, however, than Lionel, who might not have known that Dede and John Jr. existed. When John saw his uncle for the first time in many years, Lionel grabbed his lapels, just as he did in the movies, and said, "Ee, how are you, boy?" Yet he did not seem much interested in the answer. Dede claimed that when she telephoned Chatsworth the Wheelers would not let her talk to her uncle. In Lionel's words, the Wheelers presided over him "in a state of not unpleasant feminine tyranny." His collaborator, Cameron Shipp, said tactfully that Lionel was always conducting vendettas with the Wheelers that sounded like quarrels to outsiders but were not. What emerges is the picture of three women very solicitous of Lionel, but even more solicitous for their share in his affection and property. Obviously they discouraged Lionel's contacts with his family.

Ethel, on the other hand, sent her car every Friday to collect Dede from Palos Verdes College. "She did everything to make me cozy and comfortable," said Dede, but relaxing with an Empress wasn't easy. "I'd think, 'My God, this is Ethel Barrymore. . . . This is my aunt! I used to sit there and just look at her—her nose, her neck. She was glamorous. Even her bath was glamorous—like Cleopatra's—with a lucite tray that fit over the bathtub holding oils, cosmetics, and a huge natural sea sponge, and Edna always hovering over her like a Nubian."

Yet Ethel liked things her way, as her children and niece and nephew knew. She insisted on family reunions; they held the family together. But what reunions! The children all terrified of the Barrymore name, all sensing they were failures. Sister dreaded these "cozy and comfortable" times, never knowing whether Ethel would greet her lovingly or coldly. Dede felt that powerful authority when she told her aunt she wanted to take modern dance lessons. Ethel would not hear of modern dance. Dede took ballet.

Ethel's son Jackie seemed more independent. He had come to see what Hollywood offered, leaving behind his socialite divorcee wife, Marjorie Dow, older than he by significant years. (Ethel never spoke publicly of this marriage.) In Tinsel Town the wildest and handsomest of Ethel's children immediately became part of a young fast set. Women adored him; he had affairs all over town. To please Ethel, Cukor gave him the part of the stage manager in Ronald Colman's Oscar-winning *A Double Life*, but clearly Jackie was not serious about acting unless in the tough gangster movies he admired. He looked like a movie gangster with his five o'clock shadow and slick dark hair, his pinstriped suits and pointed shoes. He was very much at home at parties at Jack's old hangout, the Ambassador, where there was too much drinking. There were drunken driving charges. "I don't drink beer," he haughtily informed an arresting officer. "I have been drinking bourbon." Like Sammy he drank a lot of "water" at social functions. "Straight gin," he'd tell a friend with a conspiratorial wink. "Don't tell Mother." Of the three children who haunted the mother's dream, Jackie, so much like his Uncle Jack without the gift, tormented her most.

IN 1949 MGM celebrated its twenty-fifth birthday. On the world's largest sound stage Louis B. Mayer presided over a bash for a thousand movie press and salesmen regaled with stuffed squab, molded MGM lion ice creams, and long perorations about the glory of Hollywood's starriest studio. But might does not make right, and there was a good deal wrong with MGM. Behind the scenes, a bitter power struggle was being waged between Mayer, the vice president in charge of production, and his challenger, Dore Schary. In Hollywood independent producers were rapidly undermining the power of the major studios. And nationally television now terrorized the movies the way the movies had terrorized legitimate theatre and vaudeville forty years before. "There was an air of impending disaster," said Adolph Green. "We sat through the long speeches, looking at all those lions melting."

Ethel contributed to MGM's image that January 1949 by signing a one-year contract, forty weeks' guarantee at $2,000 a week. Lionel did his bit by narrating *Some of the Best*, a short feature commemorating the studio's anniversary. And then the Academy of Motion Picture Arts and Sciences, on the urging of George Cukor, decided to honor Ethel on her seventieth birthday with local celebrations and a national radio broadcast. Louis B. Mayer kicked off the festivities with a luncheon for Ethel with MGM stars studding the flower-banked tables. Sammy was present, and John Jr. and Lionel. When it came Lionel's turn to congratulate his sister, he said, "Well, Ethel, I'm awfully happy you are with us and I wish you many happy returns."

"Gosh, that's a heck of a speech," Mayer rebuked him. "You can say more than that."

"I'm sorry," said Lionel, paying Ethel back for not wheeling him in to lunch, "but my writer has gone to San Francisco."

Billie Burke, who had become a star of the stage acting with John Drew, did better. "We are making a kind of history here today, paying homage to the most beautiful woman and the finest actress of our day. You don't just love and adore Ethel. You worship her."

Mayer then rose and grew maudlin over the great honor of having Ethel Barrymore with MGM and the honor MGM did by having her. "America has known and loved you. Now the whole world will know and love you as we do. That you have come to MGM is only fitting. As long as I have been here your brother Lionel has been here. We hope to have you with us always. God bless you and keep you for many years. You are an inspiration to us all."

Ethel, noted the director Vincent Minnelli, tolerated the gush with her usual dignity. She thought Mayer "clever" but hardly an equal—and didn't mind showing it. As Katharine Hepburn observed, "Ethel in Hollywood made appallingly accurate observations and simply didn't know the meaning of caution."

Cukor invited a select group to a prebroadcast party: Lionel, uncomfortable in black tie, Constance Collier, Billie Burke, Lucille Watson, Katharine Hepburn and Spencer Tracy—all people once connected with the theatre. Judy Garland was there, just back from undergoing psychiatric treatment in Boston. When the blazing cake was brought on, Judy stood up, stunning in a white Grecian gown, fixed her enormous brown eyes on Ethel, and in apricot tones sang "Happy Birthday" to her alone. "It was to die," said Katharine Hepburn.

The broadcast which mustered celebrities from all walks of life to pay homage to the First Lady of the American Theatre (*why* can't they say Actress, fumed Ethel) had taken a good deal of coordinating. DEAR WINSTON [Ethel herself had cabled on July 28] IT WOULD BE WONDERFUL IF YOU WOULD WISH ME A HAPPY BIRTHDAY ON AUGUST 15 WHEN I SHALL BE ALL OF 70 YEARS MORE THAN 50 OF THEM MADE PROUD BY HAVING KNOWN YOU. Churchill might have had second thoughts had he been privy to a certain exchange between Ethel and Louis Calhern. Calhern had met Churchill in London where the prime minister, on mention of Ethel's name, had grown misty. Back in New York, Calhern confided that he had spoken with Winston. "How *is* the old sonofabitch?" said Ethel cheerfully. To the end of the shocked Calhern's life, Ethel's words exemplified female treachery.

President Harry Truman made a personal bow to Culture. "I am here to pay tribute for myself and for countless of my fellow countrymen to a great lady and a great artist. I have seen her in most of her roles, and I am eternally indebted to her for the pleasure she has given me. To Ethel Barrymore—first lady of the American stage—many happy returns of the day."

"It's far more than I deserve," replied Ethel graciously, "but believe me, it's not more than I can take to my heart."

From England Emlyn Williams, Dame Sybil Thorndike, Lewis Casson, Clemence Dane, Fay Compton, and Maugham sang their praise. From New York Tallulah, Kit Cornell, the disillusioned Calhern, Gladys Cooper, Ruth Gordon, Arthur Hopkins, and Lunt and Fontanne sent their greetings.

"When I met Alfred," said Lynn Fontanne, "one of the more endearing acts of his courtship was when he rushed me to see the woman he loved, in a matinee. You were playing *Déclassée.* . . ."

"The year 1924. The play, *A Royal Fandango.* You, Miss Barrymore, were the star. I had one line. On the opening night I stood waiting for my entrance, shakily wondering whom they'd get to replace me the second night. Suddenly you stopped beside me and said quietly, 'Relax. That's all you have to do—just relax.' This is Spencer Tracy. I've been capitalizing on that advice ever since."

"In *The Constant Wife* there was one line which I shall never forget," said Somerset Maugham. "It wasn't even a line. It was a single word, the word 'when.' I had written it because it was the natural, obvious word for the heroine of my play to say, and it had never occurred to me that there was anything more in it than the inquiry it made. But Ethel Barrymore put such a wealth of meaning, humor, innuendo and malice—none of which I had seen—into that little word that the audience rocked with laughter until I thought they'd never stop. . . . If I hadn't fallen madly in love with Ethel during the rehearsals, I should have fallen in love with her then. . . ."

Herbert Bayard Swope: "There is in her today the same fire, the same charm, the same alertness and the same ability to make those she meets glow and thrill at seeing her that she had when I first became her willing subject, and that was one day when I, as a young reporter, saw her for the first time. She was with Richard Harding Davis, in front of the old Weber and Fields Music Hall. She then had that utterly irresistible attraction. She has it today: She will always have it. . . ."

Elsie Janis did a last imitation of Ethel's voice. Mysterious to the end, Maude Adams refused to speak on the air but sent surprise greetings. Churchill cabled simply "Winston," word enough.

Finally, Lionel's familiar growl. "It's time for the family now, Ethel." Humbly, knowing their place in the shadow of this Olympus, Sammy, Sister, and Jackie greeted her as "Mother," "Mother darling," "Mamma." Then little Johnny Miglietta piped, "Happy Birthday, Mummum!"

Ethel sat very quietly listening with the others at Cukor's. "She looked so beautiful," said Zoë Akins, "so young and strong and beautiful—that it seemed for the moment intolerable that she was not in her own theater in a play which made full demands on her beauty and her art."

It was intolerable, but this tribute was meant to comfort a once great stage actress who had succumbed to Hollywood. It was an acknowledgment that what Ethel Barrymore stood for was gone. It was encouragement to brave the future.

THIRTY-ONE

1949–1954

LIONEL WOULD MAKE seven more films in his long movie career: 205 pictures not counting those he authored and directed. Of the seven only *Down to the Sea in Ships* had any claim to distinction, though Lionel's performances in all were of the expected excellence. "Gilt-edged," scenarist Frances Marion called Lionel Barrymore's acting stock. *Down to the Sea in Ships* was a film he almost didn't make. Twentieth Century–Fox was in a quandary over the casting: "What we need for the part of the captain is somebody like Lionel Barrymore. He has to look like a captain and bellow like a bull." None of the actors tested measured up. Finally, light broke on the casting department. "We want somebody that looks like Barrymore and can holler like Barrymore and act like Barrymore. . . . Why don't we just get Barrymore?" But this was risky: both the wheelchair and the *Kildare* series had convinced many that Lionel could not rise to a major dramatic role again.

The first days of shooting seemed to confirm director Henry Hathaway's worst fears. For three days he tried to capture the short opening scene of Lionel's uttering a prayer for the successful voyage of the whaler. Lionel blew lines, blanked out. After dozens of takes the scene still was not in the can. Hathaway kept his temper until, in the middle of discussing another scene with Lionel, he discovered the 220-pound actor in the arms of Morpheus.

Hathaway shook him awake. "Lionel, I saw you at lunch. You had two beef stews and at least a loaf of bread. How can you expect to keep awake when you eat like that? You know how things are around here: the rushes are a mess. When Zanuck comes back and sees them he'll probably give us all the heave-ho!"

Lionel thought for a moment. "Henry," he said finally, "you aren't telling me anything I don't know. I've been terrible. I'll tell you what let's do. I'll eat cottage cheese for lunch and I'll go home for two weeks and think things over. You can shoot around me and then I'll come back and we can start over." When Hathaway agreed, Lionel vowed, "By Christ, I'm going to master this if it's the last thing I ever do in life!"

Lionel returned to Fox a different man: awake, powerful, and motivated enough to abandon many of the acting tricks he had leaned on so long like crutches. He did more. One day Frank Stevens, his friend and double for twenty-five years, was stunned to hear Lionel roar, "Frank, you low-down, scoundrelly, idiotic imposter. Get out of the way and let the old man walk!" Heaving himself up, he threw aside his crutches and limped across the set. From then on he refused to use the platform constructed to hoist him to the ship's deck, dragging himself up the gangplank instead.

"No-o-o-o-o!" he cried in disgust when people congratulated him on his gameness. "It has nothing to do with the show must go on. That's nonsense. In the movies they can always yank you and get somebody better. It's this darned leg showing a little sense. If I can just get this damned pot down. . . ." In *Down to the Sea in Ships* Lionel gave a standout performance, his last piece of sustained acting. "The part was so long and tough I doubt that Saint John the Baptist could have done it, but Henry Hathaway and Buddy Lighton, the producer, rammed it down my throat," grumbled Lionel, proud to have met the challenge.

He gave another great performance for California's 1950 centennial celebration, a five-day pageant in the Hollywood Bowl with a cast of a thousand. Seated in a sound booth in his battered felt hat, Lionel narrated "The California Story" against an 85-piece orchestra and a 150-voice chorus and, as his well-known voice rose above the music in great sonorous Churchillian periods, 25,000 people spontaneously rose to their feet and cheered. "Lionel Barrymore has reached the apex of his career," rhapsodized the Los Angeles *Times*, "as a great citizen of a great land, as an American of Americans."

There were penalties attached to being "an American of Americans," however. MGM at that time was the flagship of the anti-Communist phobia that had run through Hollywood like a plague. In reality the number of genuine Communists in Hollywood was small, but fanatics saw them everywhere. Lionel's utter dependency on MGM as well as his own conservatism forced him into defensive postures. His letters these days bore the logo FIGHT COMMUNISM FEARLESSLY on the envelopes. But it was Lionel who was afraid.

To those who wondered why he continued to act at seventy after fifty-five years at the trade, Lionel growled, "I work for one reason only, to keep that man Synder in Washington happy." MGM records show constant loans to Lionel for "urgent debts"; indeed, his last years were made miserable by financial worries. When a mild heart attack complicated by pneumonia canceled a movie called *The Bradley Mason Story*, Lionel refused to go to a hospital because of the expense. He attributed his recovery to his creditors, "who prayed so hard, I got well." That year he was dunned $156,076 in federal and $21,500 in California back taxes; the IRS refused his Offer in Compromise of $30,000. It is preposterous that MGM or Lionel could not submit his finances to a capable tax accountant; it is baffling that Lionel even *had* back taxes since the studio had been controlling his paycheck for years. When Lionel received $750 for a radio broadcast, for example, MGM deducted $141.25 for AFRA dues, $150 for federal withholding, $119.05 for current taxes, $75 to his manager, James Doane, $25 to Boyle and Wood (lawyers?), and $150 to the Franchise Tax Board—leaving Lionel $89.70. Given the deductions and the fact that Lionel was still deeply in debt, it's no wonder he told MGM that if his present weekly salary was increased there would be no use his working at all.

The claim that in 1951, his twenty-fifth year with MGM, the studio gave him a lifetime contract seems to be contradicted by a memo in MGM's files: "His contract will expire 31 July 1951. No options." Why would Metro dump its veteran star at this point? One answer is MGM's pension fund: after twenty-five years an actor was entitled to retirement benefits—a safe bet given the brevity of stars' careers; in fact, William Powell would be one of the few ever to collect. Lionel was due to collect—unless. He did make three more films for MGM, if the memo is correct on a single-picture basis. But he could not retire. Louis B. Mayer, long Lionel's champion—though not averse to sabotaging a Barrymore role—himself was forced out in 1951 and may not have acceded to the betrayal. Lionel's relations with MGM, however, were unalterably embittered.

He decided to write his autobiography in hopes a best-seller would fatten his coffers, or at least the government's: he had been so terrified that the Feds were going to toss him in jail for unpaid taxes that he had actually gone to Washington to plead with them. Cameron Shipp, a well-known journalist, would do the writing, Lionel the reminiscing. Eccentric as ever, Lionel wouldn't let Shipp come to Chatsworth. Instead he drove to Shipp's house and parked the Olds under a grapefruit tree. Shipp sat next to him in the front seat while Lionel chain-smoked his memories and in the back seat a University of Southern California student named Maynard Smith took shorthand notes and made frequent forays into the

Shipp house for beer and cheese. Lionel came daily, though on Saturdays he liked to listen to the Metropolitan Opera broadcasts. On one of those Saturdays Shipp tried to press him about other members of the Barrymore family. "Oh, to hell with the Barrymores!" said Lionel, glaring over his glasses and turning up the volume. During the heights of Verdi he wept abundantly, at one point crossing himself, murmuring, "Jesus Christ, isn't that gorgeous?"

But the Metropolitan Opera wasn't Shipp's only diversion. Lionel was garrulous, rambling, profane. He loved long stories about days with John L. Sullivan or Billy Muldoon, the good old days when there was free lunch at Gilsey's famous bar at Thirtieth and Broadway, where you could rub elbows with theatre stars like Henry Dixey and Nat Goodwin all afternoon before winding up at Brown's Chop House or Martin's and from there going on to make the nightly rounds.

"We'd come out of a bar and start working our way up Broadway, another saloon every few steps. Hell, in Hollywood if you leave one bar you may have to go six miles before you hit the next."

This was not exactly the image Shipp wanted to present to a public who thought of Lionel Barrymore as Dr. Gillespie, the Mayor of the Town, and the benefactor of Tiny Tim. Another problem was Lionel's apparent secrecy: Shipp could not get him to account for eighteen whole years of his life. Finally Shipp discovered that these were the Doris Rankin years, but when he introduced her name Lionel did not seem to remember her. When Shipp offered some facts that he himself had dug up about the first marriage, "Well, you don't say," said Lionel, dropping the matter.

Mrs. John Drew and her son John Drew had both produced memoirs, John Drew's a particularly innocuous list of plays and casts. In 1949 when Lionel began talking to Shipp, autobiographies were by no means the spill-gut confessions they are today, yet *We Barrymores* was called dull, insipid, and vastly disappointing upon publication in 1951 (though it went through several hardcover printings). Critics mourned Shipp's failure to tell the real Barrymore story, but there had been formidable obstacles to anything like a serious book. One was MGM, which demanded that Lionel submit the autobiography for approval before publication. Another was the compulsively reticent Lionel Barrymore himself. Yet a text may be read just as closely for what it does *not* say as for what it does. An autobiography that omits his parents' quarrels, Maurice's death, his daughters Mary and Ethel, says virtually nothing about Doris Rankin, skirts Irene's illness and, except for ritualized compliments, avoids Ethel—to name only a few key omissions—says a great deal about the failures in

Lionel's life. Yet there are genial excuses for Jack, trenchant reasons for leaving the stage, encomiums to Louis B. Mayer, and rationales for Lionel's politics.

One revelation *We Barrymores* makes quite unintentionally. "I cannot recall it," said Lionel of the audience that welcomed so enthusiastically his return to the stage in *Peter Ibbetson*, "without emotion." Lionel spent his Hollywood years bah-humbugging the old days, running down acting as a profession, and vowing he never regretted leaving the theatre. Yet of *We Barrymores'* 296 pages, 231 are devoted to the theatre. The ten-page appendix chronologizes Lionel's plays; no movies are listed. And the book ends with the "Tomorrow, and tomorrow, and tomorrow" soliloquy from *Macbeth*, the humiliating failure that ended his stage career.

PERHAPS THAT FAILURE made Lionel hold his tongue when John Jr. made headlines that summer of 1951 for funking his stage debut at the Salt Creek Summer Theatre in Hinsdale, Illinois. The previous year Jack's son had made his movie debut in a western, *The Sundowners*, though Dolores had fought bitterly against his becoming an actor. Retired herself, married to her former obstetrician John Vruwink, she hated the thought of young John adopting the career that ruined his father. John fought her, going into hiding for two weeks until Dolores panicked and agreed. "Acting is not easy," he told his Aunt Ethel, who had encouraged him. "I know, my dear," said Ethel, "but I thought I'd better let you find that out for yourself." Great things were expected of him instantly, of course, and he found himself constantly compared to "The Great Profile." John was very handsome in an immature way, but at seventeen naturally lacked the charismatic presence of the actor who had been called the handsomest man of his day.

Wanting to live up to the Barrymore name, John had accepted the lead in Salt Creek's production of *The Hasty Heart*. Ethel was pleased, but thought he really should call himself John Smith and start in small parts. His cousin Ethel Miglietta solicitously signed on for the play herself to give him moral support. Tickets were sold, posters stuck up. But how could a young man be a leading actor with no stage experience? John stuck it for two weeks, then told the producer, Marshall Migatz, that he couldn't go through with it. Who could blame him? Ethel did. "It's so awful, we can't stand it," she told the press. "He let the Barrymore family down. I don't know what Equity's going to do. I've never thought about it. Nobody in our family has ever had to think about it. This business of being a star without any apprenticeship is just ridiculous."

John forgave his aunt for denouncing him in public, taking refuge with her for six months when Dolores's marriage to Vruwink began to fall apart (Vruwink was, Dolores said, alternately quarrelsome or giving her the monastic treatment). Though Ethel gave John the run of the house, he was tongue-tied with his formidable aunt until she began to call him into her room before she went to sleep to talk. Ethel urged him to read, insisted that she had faith in him. Their friendship ended abruptly one day when John lost his temper, seized Ethel by the shoulders, and began to shake her. Anna, her maid, ran for Sammy, who threw young John out of the house. Again he had failed the family. "He's so nervous, so jumpy—and he doesn't read—I'm always suspicious of people who don't read," Ethel said sorrowfully. "None of us is like that. We were never nervous, not even old John Drew over there [indicating his photograph], or my mother . . . or Lionel—he is the most relaxed man I know." She did not seem to understand that following the Royal Family's act would make anyone jumpy, and she seemed at pains to stress the fact that John Jr. did not belong.

John would call Lionel "the sweetest man who ever lived." He was more temperate about Ethel, "A wonderful woman, but a mass of contradictions. You know . . . the whole family was competing with each other. I'll never forget the first time I saw Ethel and Lionel together. True love or friendship implies a form of giving that has no desire of getting something back. But everybody wants something back."

AS ETHEL SAID, radio was a godsend to old actors whose voices hadn't aged, and in 1952 MGM permitted Lionel to host CBS's *Hallmark Playhouse*. Whitfield Connor, a regular on the *Playhouse*, got to know Lionel better than the rest of the cast. "Not everyone liked him," said Connor; "he could be pretty testy and uncaring of human feelings." Perhaps Connor had in mind such irascibilities as Lionel's advice to a young actor: "Work hard, save your money. When you have enough money saved, buy an axe. Use it to chop your head off and stop bothering me!" If the crustiness came from pain, Connor didn't know it. "I've got no complaints," Lionel would say; "it's just that I can't see at night."

Lionel had always been publicly modest about his acting. "No, I don't think so," he told a reporter who asked about his great talent. "Jack had; Ethel has. I just happened to keep on coming back to acting because that was what I did better than anything else. Does that mean talent? Certainly not." With Connor he dropped the gallantry. "Ethel's success," said the brother who had always attributed his success to her, "is because of my talent and Jack's brilliance." That was the only time he mentioned Ethel to Connor, though he talked fondly of Jack.

A different side of Lionel emerged one day when he announced that he had sixty-four cats at last count at his Chatsworth ranch. Connor admitted he was looking for a kitten for his daughter Erin.

"Kitten? Kitten?" rumbled Lionel. He turned away, thought fiercely, spun round. "Would you be good to it?"

"Yes, sir," said Connor, but no more was said about kittens that Sunday broadcast or the next or next.

Finally one Sunday in the studio Lionel beckoned. "I think I've found a kitten for you."

"Fine," said Connor. "I can come out to Chatsworth and get it any time you say."

"No," growled Lionel. "Kitten's got to have its shots."

Connor knew a vet.

"No-o-o-o-o. Shots got to be from *my* vet."

Several more weeks elapsed before the Connor phone rang. "I'm comin' over," barked Lionel.

When the Olds pulled up in front of the house five-year-old Erin ran eagerly out, Connor following. But Lionel had no kitten. Instead he glared suspiciously up and down the street until it became obvious that he was casing the neighborhood to see whether it measured up to his standards of kittendom. Without indicating his verdict, he drove away, leaving a very disappointed child.

Ten days later the phone rang again. This time Lionel had the kitten. He also had brought six weeks' supply of kitty food and kitty litter and a two-page letter dictated to his secretary Sadye Coon detailing care and feeding. This he went through painstakingly with Connor. Finally he put the kitten in Erin's arms.

"What are you going to name it, honey?"

"Its name is Lionel," said Erin promptly.

"Honey," chuckled Lionel, "it's a girl cat."

"I don't care, its name is Lionel."

Lionel laughed and laughed. Finally he said, "What's its last name, honey?"

"Brown. Lionel Brown."

Suddenly Lionel was red-faced and furious. "But my name is Bar-r-r-a-more!"

"I know," said Erin imperturbably, "but that's too long."

Lionel glowered, then relented. "And I watched him," said Connor, "become completely captivated by my little daughter." Oddly enough,

Lionel Brown turned out to be very much like Lionel Barrymore: very prickly, struggling when you tried to pick her up, but hungry for love even while spurning it.

FOR HIS SEVENTY-FIFTH birthday Lionel put on a polka-dot tie and permitted an interview. Naturally he was asked what actors he thought the greatest. "Garbo was one of the best I have seen anywhere," said the veteran. "Charles Chaplin, David Warfield, Margaret Wycherly, Alice Brady. James Herne (who had fired him from *Sag Harbor*), Jay Florence, Nat Goodwin, Joseph Jefferson." Of the younger generation he thought Laurence Olivier and Julie Harris the best. And the ten best plays? "Tut! There haven't *been* ten good plays." He was peppery about his own achievement: "I'm half-dead anyway!"

A month after his seventy-fifth birthday, Little, Brown published Lionel's novel, *Mr. Cantonwine: A Moral Tale*. Apparently Lionel wrote it himself, though Maynard Smith typed it and may have cleaned up mechanics like punctuation. Reviewers evaded the novel's merits, or lack of them, by labeling it "hardly to be measured by the standard criteria." And indeed *Mr. Cantonwine* is as unusual as its creator.

Martin J. Cantonwine, a journeying lay preacher and medicine man traveling with two Indians, a bear, and a raven, arrives in the small Kentucky community of Taylorville in 1835. There he meets the beautiful, unfeeling Mary, twenty-nine years his junior. He saves her from the clutches of Admiral, the bear, only to be almost killed himself. While he convalesces, Mary tempts him by bathing naked in his view and he falls passionately in love. Her rascally father gladly gives her in marriage and Mary gladly accepts, intending only to use Cantonwine as a passport to Chicago. She does not permit her husband to sexually consummate their marriage and in Chicago deserts him for a handsome scoundrel after killing his beloved raven, Anthony Wayne.

Cantonwine travels on with the two Indians. In a dark cemetery somewhere in Illinois he wrestles with a young man about to plunge a knife into his heart, dissuading him from suicide. Years pass. Cantonwine comes to a mining town where he is asked to perform a burial service for a local prostitute. This Magdalene turns out to be his Mary, whom he still loves. He carves her headstone himself: "MARY Age 21 1819–1841 Beloved Wife of Martin J. Cantonwine Rest In Peace."

Years pass until, at the age of seventy-five, Cantonwine finds himself in Washington. *Our American Cousin* is playing at Ford's Theatre. As President Lincoln passes through the lobby he recognizes Cantonwine as the man who saved him from suicide in the cemetery many years before and warmly invites him to the White House the following day. Later that evening Cantonwine hears that the president has been shot by an actor named Booth. Suddenly he feels very old and feeble. He is making his way back to his van when a perfumed woman named Mary Magdalene accosts him and chides him for not remembering her. In his van Cantonwine dies and the novel ends with Immanuel Kant's "Time passeth not, but in it passeth the existence of the mutable."

Mr. Cantonwine can be read as allegory, the itinerant preacher standing for the spirit of America which is killed with Lincoln's assassination. Yet from this strange novel more familiar themes emerge. An itinerant lay preacher traveling with Indians, a dancing bear, and a talking raven is a kind of touring vaudeville act; Lionel did a great deal of touring. Cantonwine at one point in the novel is mistaken for an actor from Philadelphia and, again significantly, is Lionel's age when he dies. The Barrymore children, furthermore, were impressed with the fact that Lincoln had honored Mummum's performance with his attendance; his letter was her most precious possession. More significant, Lionel's greatest stage role had been the Copperhead, in which he does indeed help save the Union (Lincoln's life) and is invited to the White House. *Mr. Cantonwine*, therefore, seems a reincarnation of Lionel's years as a touring actor, culminating in a replay of his great *Copperhead* scene with Lincoln. After that scene Cantonwine dies. Is there the suggestion that after his great *Copperhead* success Lionel too spiritually died?

But the greater part of the novel is devoted to the cruel Mary Donovan. She is young, ignorant, ambitious. She can sympathize with the mating passion of Admiral the bear, yet deny herself to her husband. In Chicago she leaves a note, "I have gone for good. To hell with you." When Cantonwine finds her again she is dead in a brothel. In his last hours a prostitute or actress calling herself Mary accosts him, saying "You remember me, surely, Reverend?" As he dies she turns mysteriously into a Miss Dunton (Donovan?) who puts her hands over her face and weeps, merging into the figure of the repentant prostitute Mary Magdalene.

Nothing about Mary Donovan can be read literally, but she resonates. Her name is the name of Lionel's first-born daughter. Irene married Lionel opportunistically. Jack called her a whore. Lionel was not deserted in Chicago but deserted Doris there, having become sexually involved with the cruel Irene. Georgie told Maurice, "I am going to church. You can go to hell." Lionel lost Irene in death and buried her, in a sense carving her inscription. If Mary Donovan represents woman to Lionel, his view of her is bleak: she is callous, sadistic, treacherous. In fact, *Mr. Cantonwine* is a novel of violence and sex, an unusual production for a man of seventy-five. Its theme is stark: animals, including the human, are born, driven by a powerful sex urge to reproduce, die—the premise, not incidentally, of the Hopkins-Barrymore *Macbeth*. Cantonwine has God in his mouth when he dies but Kant's mutability rules the world.

IN 1953 Lionel and Ethel appeared together for the second and last time in a movie, appropriately a tribute to the theatre featuring stage personalities like Tallulah Bankhead, Shirley Booth, Louis Calhern, Rex Harrison, Mary Martin, and Helen Hayes. *Main Street to Broadway* did little for the cause of the theatre, however, or for Lionel and Ethel's relationship: when they were photographed together, Ethel—sure enough—refused to look at her brother. Perhaps this last film turned Lionel's thoughts to the theatre again, for that December when Hedda Hopper telephoned him to chat, he was unusually reminiscent about Mummum and his fiasco at fifteen in *The Rivals*.

"She was a wonderful woman, see? Oh, she was the salt of the earth. She had a hell of a time. And she used to have one glass of whiskey—a little coloring of whiskey and a little rat-trap cheese every night, see. . . . Christ! I didn't want to be an actor anyhow—I never was—so when I got downstairs, see, I found a letter in her handwriting—purple ink. Jesus Christ, what on earth is this! . . . Oh, I did everything—anything but act. . . . My grandmother was the sweetest woman in the world. . . . That was the one and only time I ever played with my grandmother, but then I'm glad I didn't, because honestly, Hedda, I wasn't worthy of it. I really mean it. Oh, she was one of the greatest actresses—she and Mr. Jefferson, you know. You know Jefferson said the greatest line that was ever said—'There is nothing deader than a dead actor.' So I said, 'All he's gotta do is come to Hollywood. . . .'"

Inevitably the subject turned to Hollywood and MGM.

"You're older than the lion."

"Oh, Christ, yes. . . . I'd land in San Quentin if I ever tried [retirement]. I've gotta make at least the pittance I made last year to pay the goddamned income tax."

"What's your favorite picture, or don't you have one?"

"My favorite picture? Well, I guess, I think the one—that one I got the Academy Award on—you know—that, what the hell's the name—"

"*A Free Soul*."

"*Free Soul*, yeh."

"It was a good picture. Metro used to make good pictures; they don't anymore. Aren't these horrible pictures they're turning out?"

"Well, Jesus, I don't know. I—"

"You never go to see them; how the hell could you know!"

"That's true."

"Are you going to fight Metro since they won't allow you to do television?"

"No, no, no. I'm superstitious. Christ, if I ever—if Metro ever fired me, I think that would be the end of me."

"No, it wouldn't—you'd be snapped up next for TV and you'd be wonderful. . . . Lionel, you're on the Metro retirement plan, aren't you?"

"No."

"Why not?"

"Because Lew Stone and I were too goddamned old when it started."

"Well, I promise you that in 1954 you're going to put your footprints in the forecourt of Grauman's Chinese Theatre."

"Well, bless you."

But Lionel was not invited to put his footprints in the forecourt of Grauman's Chinese. Never mind: there wasn't the life-sized statue of D. W. Griffith on Vine that should have been there either—Griffith the master, whose very presence on the *Duel in the Sun* set had reduced both Lionel and Lillian Gish to nervous silence and whose funeral Lionel had reverently attended in 1948. Nor was his seventy-sixth birthday marked by any festivity: MGM was too embarrassed to note it and Lionel reported to the studio to rehearse "Hallmark Playhouse" as usual. He pretended not to care. "Barrymores don't celebrate birthdays. I bet I don't even get a phone call from Ethel." *Some* Barrymores celebrated birthdays: Ethel's seventy-fifth, hosted by George Cukor, was a poshly exclusive event with Ethel at the chief table between Cole Porter and David Selznick, and Elsie Mendl, Somerset Maugham, Lucille Watson, Orry-Kelly, Garbo, Hepburn, Elsa Lanchester, Zoë Akins, the Irving Berlins, and Constance Collier in attendance. Sammy was there too, and Lionel, seated between Hepburn and Ellin Berlin, an oddity in his high-button shoes.

He wanted to get into television, but MGM had a hands-off policy concerning its actors and TV. So he watched it instead in his Chatsworth house which, according to Maynard Smith, who was one of the few to get inside, was exquisitely and elegantly furnished down to the last detail. The fights, *Dragnet*, and old movies. He had begun writing again, this time a loosely woven narrative called *The Shakespeare Club*.

Once again the actor who proclaimed vehemently all his Hollywood years that he never regretted the theatre betrays his real sentiments. *The Shakespeare Club* describes the meetings of a group of old stage actors in a little apartment reeking of plumbing on Formosa Street near United Artists. This battered but courageous old lot discuss philosophy and life and Shakespeare, including John Barrymore's great performances. At seventy-six Lionel can neither sustain plot nor develop character (both shaky in *Mr. Cantonwine*). He begins bravely enough: "Life itself is not an overly pretty thing," then throws away consistency for a jab: "But as capricious, frequently ironic, and occasionally downright hopeless as it can sometimes be, it is not as bad as it can be on television."

Along *The Shakespeare Club*'s rambling way, however, Lionel emerges: his deep pessimism thinly coated with a bromidic frosting of faith in the "Bon Dieu," his hatred of change even as he forces himself philosophically to accept it, his distrust of nature even while he feels intense pleasure in driving the nineteen miles to Chatsworth alone through the night under the stars. The manuscript is studded with quotations from Wilde, Coleridge, and Shakespeare, but it is the tone of "The Rubáiyát of Omar Khayyám" that prevails:

> One thing is certain and the rest is lies;
> The flower that once has blown forever dies.

In May 1954 the IRS finally accepted Lionel's Offer in Compromise of $30,000, an ominous sign. At seventy-six Lionel was not only crippled but suffering chronic myocarditis and inflammation of the kidneys. In July his manager, James Doane, recommended that he start seeing a doctor regularly, and Lionel began to come to the office of Dr. Philip Kalavros at noon, at first daily, then every other day. Kalavros would come out to the car and give him his injections. Lionel was always in a sport shirt and a pair of old brown pants covered with cigarette ash. He would take off his shirt for the injections, exposing still powerful shoulder muscles. When Kalavros asked whether the needle hurt, Lionel shook his head emphatically no. He was feeling pretty well, but "these damned bowels! You know, Doctor, it's like the sensation of ants walking on you."

Gradually they began to talk: of the French doctor Fournier, of Balzac, Churchill, Wagner, Coleridge, and Byron. "He was a strange, unhappy fellow," said Lionel of the flamboyant poet. "He reminds me of my brother Jack."

One day Kalavros presented Lionel with a 2,600-year-old cup, filled it with imported Greek wine, offered it to him. Lionel accepted the cup eagerly in his powerful, deformed fingers. "Now, isn't this wonderful, to drink wine from a 2,600-year-old cup! This is something I never did." He drank deeply, but as he handed back the cup to Kalavros it shattered to pieces.

"Oh, my God! What did I do now? It's terrible, terrible! This is a bad omen. We actors are a superstitious lot." Suddenly he asked, "Do you believe in God?" Before Kalavros could answer, Lionel said, "I am agnostic. I don't know. Who knows?"

He talked until fog began to creep into the valley, banishing the sun. Suddenly he launched into lines from *Hamlet*—"But that the dread of something after death, / The undiscover'd country from whose bourn / No traveller returns. . . ." His strong, freckled hands clasped the wheel tightly; he pounded it with his fist.

"Foolishness! What is all this, what's the meaning of all this?"

"You have accomplished so much; you have done so much. People admire and love you."

"I know, I know, but don't you see? I am not better than when I started." As he groped for a cigarette a tear rolled down his cheek.

The next morning James Doane telephoned Kalavros to say that Lionel had smashed his car against a brick wall, though he had been pulled out with only bruises. Kalavros told Lionel to quit driving. Lionel laughed. He told him to quit smoking. "I have," said Lionel, flinging his cigarette out the window. Ten minutes later Kalavros caught him lighting another.

In early November Lionel finished *The Shakespeare Club*. He could not end it fatalistically after all. "The only way [we] will find out what it is all about, is when we lay our heads on the Savior's breast. . . ."

"These are the important things," Lionel now told Cameron Shipp: "youth and health, and someone to love you." He had none of these. It might have been different—he wept at the thought—had his daughters lived. On November 13, sensing perhaps that he hadn't much longer, he visited Ethel at her home in the Pacific Palisades; unable to afford Palos Verdes, she had moved north into a rambling house built by Gladys Cooper that overlooked the sixth hole of the Riviera Country Club golf course—so convenient for Sammy. She too had produced an autobiography which was about to be serialized in the *Ladies' Home Journal* before publication by Harper & Brothers. That day Lionel scoffed at her concern at the bruise over his left eye but could not prevent her seeing that he looked old and ill. It would be pleasant to think that warm words passed between them, but their reticence was deeply ingrained.

Lewis Stone had died, leaving Lionel the oldest MGM employee. He was tired, ill. Like Gramps in *On Borrowed Time*, he had discovered that death is a primary human need, that he no longer wanted to keep Mr. Brink up the tree. "I don't care to go on any longer," said Lionel.

The next day, Sunday, he seemed in good spirits at the dinner table, though he quoted Macbeth's soliloquy "Out, out, brief candle." Later, watching television, he began laboring to breathe. Florence Wheeler and a nurse who happened to be visiting helped him outside for air, but air did not help. Florence called the doctor, who took him by ambulance to Valley Hospital and put him in an oxygen tent. There was talk of his pulling through even when he sank into a coma, but acute edema of the lungs and uremic poisoning brought on a heart attack. On Monday, November 15, at 7:15 p.m. he died without recovering consciousness.

IN 1953 Dore Schary had presented Lionel with a gold key to his dressing room. Though Lionel made no films for MGM in 1954, he prepared his "Hallmark Playhouse" broadcasts there and still had his half-bungalow crammed with piano, etching and painting materials, ship models, and books. This dressing room had come to the attention of MGM personnel. There was a shortage: James Cagney needed quarters for his current film. Consent to dismantle Lionel's suite, store his belongings, and reassign the bungalow was granted in a memo of November 15. MGM couldn't even wait for its most durable star to stop breathing.

HEARING OF Lionel's death, Ethel's *Ladies' Home Journal* editor, Hugh Kahler, telephoned to ask whether she would like to add something to her autobiography about her brother. She agreed, thought about it, then called him back. "Please say, 'Since I have finished this book, Lionel has died. I would like to think that he and Jack are together—and that they will be glad to see me.' "

There was deep silence on the other end of the phone.

"What's wrong?" asked Ethel.

"I'm crying," said Kahler.

Said Ethel, *"So am I."*

THIRTY-TWO

1953-1959

L IONEL HAD ONCE BEEN ASKED whether he was afraid of the public.

"Nope," he'd answered. "Just curious. The public has a trick of setting somebody on a pedestal, just to tear him down again. It's natural—old as the ages. The trick is to keep off the pedestal if it looks too high."

Lionel had strenuously avoided pedestals, just as he had always modestly insisted, "All my successes were due to the suggestions of others. I have never been too successful with any project of my own creation." Yet the outpouring of grief at his death testified to the place he had carved for himself in the hearts and lives of the American people. There was a grit and texture to Lionel Barrymore that his younger brother always lacked, just as Lionel lacked Jack's "divine spark" and Ethel's unfailing theatre sense. Always contemptuous of acting, he had nevertheless been a thorough actor. To the New York theatre critics of the 1910s and 1920s the *Times*'s judgment at his death that Lionel was a great character—not a great actor—would have been incomprehensible, but that is what twenty-five years of Hollywood typecasting had accomplished.

Ethel sent a blanket of gardenias for the casket that was laid next to Irene's at Calvary Cemetery. Reportedly prostrated with grief and in bed under doctor's orders, she did not attend the funeral. Surely guilt and remorse played a part in her prostration, if such it was. And then, queens mourn alone.

But Ethel was not the queen in movies that she had been in the theatre. Of the twenty-one films she had made since 1944, she starred in only one: *Kind Lady* (1951). MGM had done her the favor of lending her to Fox for *Pinky* (1949) and a fourth Best Supporting Actress nomination; her career with MGM itself was rocky. After *Kind Lady*, which had to suspend production because she fell ill and then proceed slowly because she could only work two or three hours a day, with retakes when her voice developed an inexplicable whistle, MGM decided against another year's contract though it used her again in *It's a Big Country*, *The Story of Three Loves*, and *Main Street to Broadway*. Except for *Kind Lady*, a wonderful film in which she finally acted with someone of her own stature, Maurice Evans, MGM did not use her well. Had *Kind Lady* succeeded at the box office . . . but it did not because, according to its producer, Armand Deutsch, the intimate suspense film premiered in New York's biggest barn of a movie house.

Ethel's own attitude toward films did nothing to promote her Hollywood career. As Katharine Hepburn said, "You met Ethel on her terms"—and they were not terms that Hollywood was used to accepting. She discouraged familiarity; she could be contemptuous and harsh. She condescended, making it clear that she was slumming. Directing her in *Pinky*, Elia Kazan fortunately admired the "grand old battlewagon" who replied to his request for another take, "Why? I can't do it better, boy," and to his further urging, "What do you want it for, your collection?" Underneath the arrogance was fear and the realization that at seventy-five she was lucky to be employed at all. Hollywood could snap its fingers at Ethel Barrymore; in Hollywood you were only as good as your last picture. As Lionel said, "In the movies they can always yank you and get somebody better." The Barrymore name was nothing if it didn't glitter at the box office. MGM had tried to package her for mass consumption as a kind of hip grande dame, constantly photographing her with young stars like Janet Leigh and Kathryn Grayson to prove that she was young at heart. But as a box-office draw, Miss Ethel Barrymore wasn't worth a nickel.

As her move to the Pacific Palisades indicated, she was always short of money. At one point Maury Small, who had also been Lionel's agent, recommended that MGM prorate her salary so she could not spend it all at once. For a person of fairly simple tastes, Ethel went through large sums effortlessly, but then in Hollywood one had to look affluent. She was furious when the IRS now announced that in 1937 it had allowed her to settle a $98,666.38 tax claim for $7,500 because she had "no future" as an actress. "I think it's foul of the papers to print such stories" she said. "The press must be hard up for news if it must go back to 1937. Why don't they go after Senator Nixon?" Certainly it was bad luck in Tinsel Town to have your name coupled with the words "no future."

With less to do in films, Ethel had decided at last to write her life, since everyone else seemed to be doing it. Hermitage House had sued her for $250,000 in 1948 for reneging on a contract to write her *Major and Minor Memories*, but now she believed herself ready. She had written nine or ten pages about her childhood in Philadelphia and read them to the co-editor of the *Ladies' Home Journal*, Bruce Gould, who asked for the whole story. He had no idea what a struggle it would be to get it. Ethel Barrymore always said that unlike her brothers she wrote her memoirs herself. Untrue. And she threw up formidable obstacles to those who did write them.

Since after the first nine pages, Ethel had sent Gould no further material, Hugh Kahler came out to Los Angeles in the summer of 1953 to try to draw her story from her. She had had a heart attack and was sleeping in the library so that she didn't have to climb the stairs. Kahler spent days in that library, but getting her to say more than superficialities was like "pulling an earthworm out of hardpan." Kahler pulled as much as he dared to keep the story coming but was afraid to really tug for fear of snapping the thread altogether. He finally returned with about 25,000 words. Gould and Cass Canfield at Harper's were deeply disappointed. Gould tried flattery:

> This LIFE is a performance by you on which the curtain will never ring down [he wrote in December 1953]. Therefore, it should be the best performance Ethel Barrymore ever gave. To that end I'm sure you are willing to give every help in your power.
>
> In a play, even a play enhanced by your magnetic presence, even with its emotion conveyed by the magic of your eyes, your hands, the stand of your body, few playwrights—none worth your attention—would dare write a scene like this:
> "The child is dead."
> "Dead?"
> "Yes—I suppose, Horace, you will be going to Cincinnati next Wednesday. . . ."
> Too often, Miss Barrymore, your book, as now written, is simply a recounting of the itinerary of your life. It does not fill in what, on the stage, you have understandably relied on your presence to suggest. . . .
> All this can be done without, I believe, violating, or even threatening, the standards of good taste which have governed your life. . . . It is simply that the reader must be permitted to see you rise from the printed page, at least as clearly as the parting curtains reveal you on the stage.

Gould then turned the project over to Laura Lou Brookman, the *Journal*'s managing editor. She would go over the whole manuscript, jotting down questions that logically arose while Harper's compiled its own list. The next step was getting Ethel to see Laura Lou. Gould did not want to send Kahler back to Los Angeles, fearing that Ethel would simply say, "I've already told you I don't want to answer those questions." Besides, Brookman was good at working with difficult authors.

In Los Angeles Ethel wrestled with her aversion for frankness and her desire to see her autobiography published. In the middle of one night Kahler answered his phone to hear Ethel sounding rather desperate and "more or less" yielding to a Brookman interview. Laura Lou and an assistant went west.

They met Ethel Barrymore at her most difficult. Imperious, stubborn, insulting, and in the end almost completely uncooperative, Ethel refused to reveal, delve, expand, analyze, or even respect chronology. Desperate, Brookman interviewed Zoë Akins about the *Déclassée* years, but got little further with Ethel's private life. The result was a gossamer narrative liberally sprinkled with names and places but offering little for a reader to grab hold of. *Memories* had charm: nothing Ethel touched could lack it. But as Gould said, she avoided the truth: about her father's madness and death, about her marriage (passages about which, however, had to be submitted to Russell Colt's lawyer), about her drinking, about Jack's decline, about her children—about virtually everything private as opposed to the public Ethel Barrymore.

Shortly before publication by Harper's, Ethel phoned Cass Canfield with a complaint and an addition. Someone had deleted a little passage about the *Jinks* tour in spring with "little lambs, colts, and dogwood blossoms." She had written that herself and wanted it in. She also wanted to add something about her daughter:

> I never realized then that Sister was to become something new in our family—a wonderful singer. She was the only private pupil Maggie Teyte ever took in America, and she has gone on to a long and successful career of most beautiful singing in concert and opera. Her voice has extraordinary range and she uses it with magnificent artistry. And she has been equally successful in her private career of marriage and motherhood.

Of Sister, Ethel had once said to Barbara Robins Davis, "She's worth the whole lot, you know." Barbara doubted that Ethel ever told her daughter how much she valued her, and even the fond words in *Memories* were an afterthought.

In February 1955 Ethel's health was not good enough for her to make a promotional tour with the book. *Memories*, which should have been the American actress-autobiography of the century, was received cordially and sold well, though disappointment at too many little lambs, colts, and dogwood blossoms was obvious. Gene Fowler refused to praise it in print, a slight that Ethel did not forgive. Zoë Akins called it "a masterpiece of understatement." Eleanor Roosevelt dismissed it as "delightfully easy reading." *Memories* was chiefly dedicated to those glorious years when the doors of the London aristocracy flew open to lovely Daphne, when heads turned on Fifth Avenue to see our Ethel, "swanlike and eager," descending from a hansom. When she reigned as the newest princess of the footlit realm.

There were reasons for the superficiality. One was the powerful legacy of Mummum, who decreed that one's deepest feelings were never to be disclosed. Another was her own disinclination to analyze; she lived, she did not care to know how or why. "I remember only what I want to remember," she said. "Why clutter up the house with a lot of dead history?" Which is another way of saying, "I deny everything that I wish to deny." She kept no scrapbooks, few letters. She lived avidly in the present—hovering over the radio to hear Joe DiMaggio homer in the ninth, smiling over Hollywood gossip columns, devouring Book-of-the-Month Club selections.

In a sense her life had been vicarious. Onstage her huge tears had moved audiences to floods of weeping. Her stage life was full: she loved, wept, lost, renounced, died. Her private life was tragically devoid of emotion. No love for her stranger-parents, no real closeness to either Jack or Lionel. A marriage whose emotional growth ended almost before it began. Children who loved yet feared her. Thousands of friends, but no one to telephone in the middle of the night in distress. Devoted servants, but no equal.

Although *Memories* was criticized for telling little about the real Ethel Barrymore, one extraordinary passage seemed to go unnoticed—extraordinary because it did tell a great deal:

> Sister had the part of Fanny Elssler, the dancer [in *L'Aiglon*], and although she was over nineteen, she went through the painful process of taking ballet lessons in order to make her entrance on the points of her toes. It was beautifully done, but nobody ever noticed. They just took it for granted that she could walk on her toes. That always gave me a pain around my heart. There were so many times in my life when there have been pains around my heart! In fact when I began to write this book, every now and

then I thought of calling it *So Many Tears*, but I decided that this would be rather a melancholy title and also I had managed through the years to dam up the tears. . . .

Laura Lou Brookman was eternally ashamed of the manuscript she produced but, as Bruce Gould said, "Ethel was the one to be ashamed." But Ethel was not. "I didn't keep any notes at all, nor did I have many photographs," she boasted. "But I have a phenomenal memory, and I wrote it as I remembered, and after I started it all came easily." News to Gould, Kahler, Canfield, and Brookman. Why did Ethel lie about writing her life herself? Perhaps because Jack and Lionel had their celluloid immortality assured and she who did not really believe in movies wanted to pretend that she had created a literary immortality for herself. But finally she summed up her attitude toward her memoirs when she said, "The nice thing about an autobiography is that you can leave out certain things."

IN THE MONTHS FOLLOWING the publication of *Memories* came reminders that even actors who don't play *Hamlet* die broke. In May 1955, Gordon Levoy, Lionel's lawyer (and Jack's), arranged for a transfer company to pick up the belongings from Lionel's bungalow that MGM had stored. Rumored to be in six figures, Lionel's assets proved a mere $25,000, all of which he had left to Florence Wheeler in addition to the Chatsworth house and furniture already in the Wheelers' names. But his debts far exceeded $25,000, so that like Jack's his belongings were auctioned to satisfy six figures in debts. His creditors were hardly satisfied. Whereas Jack's estate amounted to more than seven hundred items, Lionel's possessions were minimal: treasured things like books, paintings, and records of little value to anyone else. Cameron Shipp and others were disgusted with the numbers of curiosity seekers pawing over Lionel's effects and spurning them. "This is an obscenity," said Shipp, "an invasion of a great gentleman's privacy after his death." A few things brought cash: the Whistler and Rembrandt etchings Lionel had bought on his 1937 visit to London; some of his own etchings: "Point Mugu," "Point Pleasant," "Purdy's Basin." John Jr. bought the Manship bust of his father for $180. John's *Hamlet* skull sold, as did Lionel's bulging scrapbooks of old theatre programs and photographs. But the auction was a sad affair. In the end James Doane had to be content with twenty-two of Lionel's etchings and plates instead of the money the actor had died owing him.

FOR ETHEL THESE were years of tribute, bittersweet because tributes tell of ends rather than beginnings. In January 1950 she had returned to

New York for an emotional reunion with Eddie McHugh, her stage manager for twenty-five years and now managing her one last time in a benefit performance of *The Twelve Pound Look* for the ANTA "Album." Charles Frohman had first produced Barrie's play for her at his beautiful Empire Theatre; it had served her many years. Bert Lahr, also performing at the Ziegfeld that night, was asked by another actor, "Bert, when does Ethel Barrymore go on?" At that moment came the spontaneous roar of an audience rising to its feet, followed by a thunder of applause that reached their sixth-floor dressing room. "She's on," said Lahr. Ethel stood there holding Kate's typewriter for five minutes, listening to New York love her.

Back in Hollywood she presented the award for Best Actor at the Academy Awards ceremony in March. Regally she accepted the envelope, opened it, and read out, "Laurence Olivier for *Hamlet*." If the Academy thought it was doing her a favor by giving her Olivier to announce, however, it could not have been more mistaken: *Hamlet* for Ethel still belonged to Jack. "I didn't sound too Sonny Tufts, did I?" she asked Charles Brackett when she came off, referring to a famous radio gaffe when a host, handed his evening's guest list, said incredulously, *"Sonny Tufts?"* Privately, she referred to Olivier in his blond Hamlet curls as "Gorgeous George." When John Gielgud met her at a party at Cukor's, however, she was completely gracious, apparently having forgiven him his 1936 New York *Hamlet*.

In June 1952 she had been awarded an honorary doctor of fine arts degree from New York University. She went east for the ceremony and saw a sea of graduates in hoods and tassels rise in her honor. "From the bassinet in her mother's dressing room in the theatre, to the throne of long reigning queen of the Drew-Barrymore dynasty," a reverent voice declaimed, "her tour of the hearts of the theatre-loving public has been an uninterrupted processional of glory in crescendo. The magnetism, the witchery, the power of her personality infallibly enchant us. . . . For her personal family devotion no less than her superlative contributions to the precious architecture of make-believe, we adore her, and so welcome her into this academic communion with fervent satisfaction."

Less than a year later she was back in New York touting *Main Street to Broadway*. She held court in the Empire Theatre which, with American contempt for history, was slated for demolition: she no longer gave interviews, she gave audiences. Wrapped in mink, hiding the weakness left from a bout of flu, she greeted well-wishers, children of old friends, and an electrician who had lit her at the Empire fifty years before. Shirley Booth was currently inhabiting the star dressing room in *The Time of the*

Cuckoo. "It's a crime they have to tear down this theatre," said Ethel. "It's the loveliest theatre in New York. All red and gold—in the English tradition, thank god. No Swedish block here. I suppose they'll be putting up another office building." She condemned as faddish the business of young actors spending so much time at school studying Stanislavsky: "My grandmother would have killed me if I'd had such fads. I am convinced that Stanis, if he were alive today, would be horrified at what is being done in his name. I imagine Stanis must have needed money once and written a book, never thinking anyone would take it seriously."

In some ways the theatre had not changed. "There were just as many people late to the theatre in carriages as there are in automobiles. There were just as many rude people then as there are now, and I hate them just as much today as I did then." But then a reporter got around to playwrights. Were the modern ones better than the old?

"Certainly not," snapped Ethel.

Were they worse?

"I have answered your question!"

Back in Los Angeles Edward R. Murrow invited himself into her home for a *Person to Person* television interview. Sammy conducted a tour of her modest Pacific Palisades house, focusing on the library and on the front porch where she liked to sit looking out to sea. Ethel charmed viewers reciting Hilaire Belloc's comic poem about the Yak but was only moved herself when recalling Murrow's heroic broadcasts from London during the Blitz. Emlyn Williams had made one too and now at last was able to thank her in person for what she had done for *The Corn Is Green* at a party he and Molly gave in Hollywood. At that party, Charles Brackett remembered, Ethel sat in queenly dignity while the guests swirled around her, always a little aloof, a little sad.

Ethel called television "hell," but once a trouper always a trouper. She was so disgusted with one show she'd done with Tallulah, however, that she refused to accompany Cukor's guests to a studio viewing, staying behind wrapped in a rug on Cukor's couch, reading. She ended her thirteen-episode 1956 television series, *The Ethel Barrymore Theatre*, because she found the material mediocre, though ratings may have played a part. In 1954 she had been nominated for Best Actress in a single performance as Madame La Grange, the medium, in the Edwardian thriller "The Thirteenth Chair." The setting was supposed to be an English country house, and Ethel in long black with a rope of jewels, her patrician accent—"fakahz" for "fakers," "ha" for "her"—her remote smile, and the dignity which set her off like a Rembrandt among magazine illustrations could indeed have been its chatelaine. But this "Thirteenth Chair" was cheaply modern with characterless actors in business suits and actresses in fake bouffant Diors trying to act "refaned." "Her style, her skill, her bearing and assurance only serve to accentuate the professional flaws in the rest of her associates," said Tallulah. "So many sparrows trying to roost with an eagle." At one point in the drama a look of intense suffering comes over Ethel's face, so real that one knows once and for all that she has suffered, and deeply.

Her beauty in her seventies had become legendary. Her hair was thick, her skin still lovely, her white hands unfreckled by age. Charles Brackett called her "the most beautiful older woman you ever saw in your life." The actress Dorothy Stickney, meeting Ethel for the first time, agreed: "She was not only warm, simple and gay, but the most beautiful woman I have ever seen." "When you compare her with women today in this age of non-stop facelifts," said Lauren Bacall, "and realize that she never even considered such a thing! Her head was always high, she radiated." Eliot Janeway, whom Ethel had charmed as a boy by treating him like an equal, was impressed with the inner beauty: "Of all the people I have known, Ethel was the most urbane, the most civilized, the most interested, the most articulate." It was these qualities that made people like Katharine Hepburn glad to rise when she walked into a room. "She *fascinated* everyone," said Hepburn, "—and I'm not sure that anyone knew why. It's what you imagine as a child it would be like to meet somebody absolutely fascinating. Then when you meet them it usually isn't. But with Ethel Barrymore it was much more fascinating than I can possibly describe."

Katharine Hepburn wanted to pay tribute to Ethel, however, in a tangible way. Realizing her growing frailty and her incessant debts, Kate proposed to George Cukor that they establish a fund. She herself would contribute, and Spencer Tracy, and she believed there would be others. But the important thing was that the money must seem to come only from Cukor: Ethel might accept money from a director and friend of many years that she would spurn from fellow actors. And so in August 1956 the Ethel Barrymore Fund was established, an enterprise known only to the contributors, who over the next three years would donate thousands to keep the wolf from Ethel's door. Kate, Cukor, Irene Mayer Selznick, and Whitney Warren were the group's nucleus, but Ina Claire Wallace, Charles Brackett, Spencer Tracy, Cary Grant, Ruth Gordon, and Garson Kanin also contributed. Thus on August 7, Ethel received from Cukor's lawyers the startling communication that "Mr. George Cukor has instructed us to forward to you the enclosed check payable to your order."

Her feelings may be imagined. That is probably why, late in 1956, she signed with the independent company Clarion to make *Johnny Trouble*, proving that she was not wholly dependent. Though Ethel was presented with a resolution passed by the Los Angeles City Council congratulating her upon her emergence from semiretirement, and though she was at last starred, the cheap production was a sad way to end a long and distinguished acting career. Not that her performance is lacking. Fragile, and playing in a wheelchair, she acts an elderly woman convinced that her long-missing son will return and prove himself after all not a bad boy. How many times she had wished that of her bad boys . . .

Like her last movie, her last public salute—a Texaco *Command Performance* on November 23, 1957—was a travesty, misconceived and muddled from beginning to end. Invited to co-host the program with Joseph Cotten, Tallulah Bankhead quit over confusion about "the extent of her participation." Though she had never appeared in a movie with Ethel and hardly knew her, Claudette Colbert substituted as an embarrassingly and insincerely effusive host. Eventually the chief entertainment was provided by random entertainers under contract to NBC-TV. Even performers who professed to adore Ethel forgot the purpose of the broadcast. Frank Sinatra, for example, making a surprise appearance to sing "Accustomed to Her Face," turned *his* blatantly to the camera instead of looking at the woman he was supposed to be honoring. For that matter, most of the performers, especially the pointlessly energetic dancers, seemed not to have the faintest idea why they were there. And Ethel herself was pretty much limited to listing her stage successes as posters flashed on the screen.

There were a few redeeming moments. Ethel introduced her grandson, Johnny Miglietta, and shook hands with baseball greats Leo Durocher and Casey Stengel, who stole the show. Ethel Colt Miglietta and Hoagy Carmichael contributed to the singing and dancing—which again, however, had little to do with Ethel Barrymore. Some genuine warmth was provided by her family, however, and by sincere admirers like Orson Welles, Joseph Cotten, and Lauren Bacall, who chided walkouts Tallulah and Peter Lawford. But as *Variety* said, anyone not briefed in advance on the program's purpose would have been bewildered: "Strictly on its merits as entertainment, it was shoddy and uninspired. As an attempt to recapture some of the grandeur, the magnetism and the sheer artistry of one of the great performers of the 20th century, this 60-minute hodgepodge was, at best, a cheap exploitation of a name." What was more painful, however—and explained the failure—was that only a handful of people realized any longer what that name meant.

She tried to carry on, contracting early in 1958 to play Jesse James's mother on TV's *Playhouse 90*, but had to give up the role when she fell at home and broke her arm. She had had to give up something far more important: Mamaroneck, to which she knew now she would never return. Fourteen acres, a fireplace in every room because even in bed she loved to watch flames dancing on the walls. Being a Barrymore, she had no idea of its worth. An investor snapped it up and promptly turned the property into a housing development, adding insult to injury by naming it the "Barrymore Estates."

The Ethel Barrymore Fund, desperately needed now, was in danger of drying up. "You asked me to tell you when the pump needed priming," Cukor wrote to Whitney Warren in August 1958. "As you can see, the Fund is getting dangerously low. . . . I know I've written you this before, but I must say it again, that the assurance that her everyday needs will be looked after has given Ethel the greatest comfort and security. It helps make these trying days much easier for her. She's realistic, brave, and philosophical. She certainly knows the score about herself at all times, even though she never speaks about it. I'm not as aware of her growing frailty as Kate is, who spends more time away from California than I do. Another thing I want to say again is that I feel guilty about masquerading as her sole benefactor, but I'm sure it's better this way."

By then Ethel had received $12,500 from the Fund, about $500 a month. That year, 1958, Cukor, Hepburn, and Warren also undertook to establish Orpheus Recordings, with Ethel as one of the recording artists. It would supplement her income as well as provide her with work not too taxing. Ethel happily began going over things to record. She had for years recited the Twenty-third Psalm and Saint Paul's First Epistle to the Corinthians at the drop of a hat; she had read the "Passion, Death, and Resurrection of Our Lord" over the radio at Easter time in a voice that was a haunting moan of pain. Now she could immortalize these on record.

But a heart condition and rheumatism forced her to stay more and more in bed, beside which there was now an oxygen tank. Frequently Sammy would appear at Philip Dunne's door—Philip, the son of Ethel's great friend Finley Peter Dunne, and a screenwriter. "Do me a favor," Sammy would say; he meant, "Come and sit with Mother so I can leave." Like Cukor, who had given Sammy a part in the 1954 *A Star Is Born* for Ethel, Dunne had also got Sammy work in pictures when he had to prove to the IRS that he was an actor. Now he, or more often his wife Amanda, would make the short trip up the hill. Amanda was terrified at first, hardly knowing what to say to the great lady, but found Ethel interested in everything from a local fire to studio gossip. At the end of a visit, said Amanda, "*She* made me feel that she had had a wonderful time."

Finally Ethel had to leave the Palisades, which she could no longer afford. She and Sammy took a duplex at 135½ South Linden Drive in Beverly Hills. Surveying the hundreds of boxes of books needing garaging, Sammy said, "Mother, either give up reading or go on tour"—for though on tour Ethel had abandoned books in trains and hotels, she had accumulated them since 1945 in staggering numbers. Her chauffeur and his wife and her personal secretary had long gone, and now it was Anna Albert, her maid of ten years, who nursed and cooked for her. Ethel gave up going downstairs, but had her radio next to her pink satin bed and a television on which she watched, for the first time, herself in movies. "I wasn't too greatly upset," said Ethel. Of course, she still *reigned* even from her pillows, and for company kept up her witty spirits. "May I see the most beautiful woman in California?" Charles Brackett called at her bedroom door one day. "And *why*," shot back Ethel, "have I been demoted?" Outwardly she refused complaint or sorrow, even though those closest to her were gone: her cousins "Bee" Drew Devereaux and dear old Georgie Drew Mendum had died in 1954 and 1957.

Katharine Hepburn visited her often. "I never knew the number of the street she lived on because it seemed such a silly little neighborhood for Ethel Barrymore. It didn't have any connection with Ethel . . . but then I don't think I'd ever associate anything with Ethel but a castle on the moon.

"The door was always unlocked, and there was a mean old Siamese cat that would scratch at me. . . . I'd go up the stairs, which had a sort of contraption on it that Ethel could ride up and down on (she never used it), and I'd stick my head inside the door.

"The room had windows in three directions and Ethel sat in a violent breeze the entire time she was desperately ill, no covers over her. . . . There was a beautiful bed with a round head that Ethel had had for a long time, and she sat in a sort of circle, very bad for her back but a wonderful background, and there she sat. She always had silk sheets. I said, 'Ethel, they're very uncomfortable,' but she said, 'I *like* silk sheets.' She had a beautiful bedcover always covered with books; tables all around the bed filled with books, and a little table on the right with a pitcher of water and a gold clock with a glass case so that you could see the works inside ticking away, just like the clock in my house that I'd taken apart as a child and ruined. Once in a while the clock would be stopped when

I came in, so I would set and wind it, and it became a custom that every time I came in I'd wind the clock.

"She had always several vases full of beautiful flowers which had been sent her and which she seemed to like more than anything else. I never felt she liked material things. I wouldn't know what to bring her because she didn't care about anything. I might bring her a flower that I'd picked out of a ratty old border in her own garden. . . . I might bring her a book, which she liked before she got very ill. Once I brought her some towels that were initialed E M B the way she wanted them, and I think she really used those . . . but other things, no interest, no interest in material things.

"She was *beautiful* to look at. . . . Wonderful hair—strong hair, lots of it and well fixed. Exquisite skin. Not much make-up and eyes that, well, scared you to death sometimes, and at other times I'd look and think, 'Where have you been and what are the lives you have seen, and what really goes on in your mind—because although she was a great actress and a great personality and had known everyone in the world, she had a very odd look about her. She was religious. She never talked too much about it, but I think she had great faith in—something. . . . I don't know what the dickens it was. A kind of faith in life, I think. She made you feel that there was something about the human race that was thrilling.

"She never gave in to the, to her, unimportant distresses. She had trouble breathing and sometimes she would cough and when she'd cough I'd get the maid and leave the room with no comment. When she was better I would come back and we would go on with our conversation as though nothing had happened. There were no pills, no medicines around of any kind, and yet she was a very, very ill woman.

"I would go away and I'd always come back. And people would say to me, 'You're so nice to go and call on Ethel.' And I would think, 'How *lucky I am* to be able to see Ethel!' She seemed much more important to me in this phase of her life than people I've seen at the peak of their careers because she was able to cope with what she knew were the last years of her life in a way that gave confidence to others. . . . I always had a feeling of elevation at having been with her. Every time I went I would look at her and think, 'I might never see you again.' And yet there she was, sitting up in bed and looking as though something wonderful was in her future.'"

In March 1959 Cukor admitted to Irene Selznick that his plan of having Ethel make records was impossible. "I don't think she's up to it. The poor darling seems weaker every time I see her. It's a struggle just to keep going day by day. Sadder is a gradual diminution in her interest in life. For the first time she doesn't seem to be as alert mentally as she's always been. Occasionally she gets confused about dates or people. I'm convinced she couldn't cope with the exacting and concentrated work of making recordings."

She could not. She needed oxygen frequently now. In early June her heart condition suddenly worsened, and her doctor, Clay Barton, told Anna she could not pull through. She was losing weight rapidly, and her eyes were enormous in her face. But her wickedness could still flash. Ottie Swope, the son of her friend and staunch admirer Herbert Bayard, finding her in a room that Orry-Kelly had banked with pink carnations, was distressed at her frailness. Uncertain that she was even listening, he made conversation. "And you know," he concluded, "Bette Davis and her husband, Gary Merrill, are touring in *The World of Carl Sandburg*, reading his poetry." Ethel's eyes flew open.

"Thanks for the warning," she whispered.

She could rise to less and less, though on June 12 tears ran down her cheeks as she watched John Gielgud on television in Terence Rattigan's *The Browning Version*. She could not sleep, so Anna and Sammy too would not sleep for nights, and sometimes Anna held her in her arms like a child. Yet she did not complain and Lady Helen Haddon's words could have been hers: "No, no one knows . . . but it's part of the adventure to keep one's courage, and not to care too greatly how the wheel of fortune turns; for we must all go from the game, empty-handed at the end, and if we've played fairly I don't believe that we will mind, really, when the moment comes to blow out our candles, and sleep."

On Wednesday, June 17, Ethel listened to a Dodgers–Milwaukee Braves doubleheader. At ten that night she asked for her doctor. After Barton left, Anna sat with her and talked until she fell asleep. Suddenly at three in the morning, she woke and grasped Anna's hands. There was no pain. "Are you happy?" she asked. "I'm happy. . . ."

She died at nine. The priest came in time, but Anna was glad little Ethel was not there to see how her once beautiful mother had suffered.

AFTERWORD

THE CROWD at Lionel's funeral had trampled the floral pieces in its eagerness to gawk at celebrities like James Stewart, Red Skelton, Jimmy Durante, Mickey Rooney, Walter Pidgeon, Robert Taylor, and Spencer Tracy. But to such cultists Ethel Barrymore's funeral was a huge disappointment. A mere 250 to 300 people attended the requiem mass at the Church of the Good Shepherd in Beverly Hills, the pallbearers were all unrecognizable, and Joseph Cotten, George Murphy, and Irene Dunne the only stars worth ogling. Those inside the church too were disappointed: an impersonal high mass, no mention at all of the dead woman, no words of farewell.

The crowd might have been titillated had it known that when Ethel was transported to the Calvary Cemetery Mausoleum to be laid next to her brothers, she found no room. Lionel had made arrangements for two crypts when Irene died so that he could be buried beside her. Oddly enough, Jack's executors had expected to bury him next to Lionel, but Irene had been found in that crypt. Now Ethel discovered—or rather Sammy and Sister did—that the crypt next to Jack was occupied. The best the family could do was announce that they would try to obtain it for Ethel. But the recently appointed cemetery director was puzzled. How could Ethel Barrymore have expected burial next to John Barrymore when she had not bought the space nor even had it held for her?

Ethel would not have minded that her Hollywood funeral did not rank with Valentino's, Harlow's, Lombard's, or Jack's. After all, she was seventy-nine, hardly a glamorous star. Besides, she had never been of Hollywood but of the theatre, and it was the theatre world that mourned her now as the lights dimmed for five minutes at the Ethel Barrymore Theatre before the performance of Lorraine Hansberry's hit play, *A Raisin in the Sun*. "All of us work hard in the theatre," said Helen Hayes, "but none of us can ever give it the luster that she did." "She lifted the standards

521

of American acting and gave all who knew her an impetus to live on her level," said Cornelia Otis Skinner. Said Guthrie McClintic, "This is the passing of an era." Said Tallulah, "I loved her with all my heart. We'll never see her like again."

This was true. Because during Ethel Barrymore's long, long career the world had changed and the theatre had changed. She had reigned over a theatre that was "gilded and gay" with red velvet and crystal chandeliers, a theatre to which matinee girls came to weep into their boxes of chocolates and young men in gleaming white shirt fronts to present their roses at the stage door. A theatre that was *the* entertainment, unrivaled by radio, motion pictures, or television.

And yet Ethel had been flexible. She had bobbed her hair and done risqué plays like *The Constant Wife*, whitened her hair to play matriarchs, come back at sixty-two to make perhaps the greatest success of her career as a simple schoolteacher in *The Corn Is Green*. Eulogies lauding her as "The Great Lady" or "the most glamorous actress ever to appear on the American stage" or "the royal queen of the American theatre" seemed to forget what a versatile trouper she was, what a survivor in four branches of entertainment—theatre, movies, radio, and television.

Yet there was a sense in which Ethel Barrymore was irrevocably linked to a world that had died to the stuttering of World War I guns. A world in which royalty was still plausible. A world of Empire manners and values. A world in which the written word was paramount. A world in which the words "lady" and "gentleman" had meaning. A world of cultural and moral certainties. A smaller, more leisurely world when only the wealthy traveled and none of one's friends could be black. This is why the title "First Lady of the American Theatre" stuck to Ethel, much as she hated it. Mrs. Patrick Campbell once said that the greatest actresses have to have a bit of the gutter in them. Ethel never dipped even a toe.

Her age corseted Ethel against the shocks of change, as did her innate good sense, her sense of duty, her faith. Lionel withdrew into himself and rode out the rough spots; less stable, Jack felt the shocks of change profoundly: they accelerated his self-destructiveness. But no one felt the break between past and present more than the following generation, the pathetic and tragic children who understood from childhood that they were supposed to pick up the flaming Drew-Barrymore torch and run with it—without, however, having anywhere to go.

Analyzing why a tradition that had sustained an acting family for more than two hundred years suddenly collapsed is as complex as trying to analyze society itself. Yet surely a primary reason for the failure of the next generation is that a theatre of superstars no longer existed. They had taken themselves to the movies (and when movies declined would take themselves to rock). Diana Barrymore wanted to be an Ethel Barrymore, but no one could have been Ethel Barrymore in the American theatre of the 1950s and 1960s. The day of the giants was past. The personal power of the actor had dwindled: from the all-powerful actor-managers to the stars created by impresarios like Charles Frohman and David Belasco to the screen images created by Hollywood make-up and publicity departments, the director, and the camera. Mrs. John Drew had more power as an actress-manager than her son John Drew, controlled first by Augustin Daly, then by Charles Frohman. John Drew had more power, however, than Lionel Barrymore in Hollywood, controlled by Louis B. Mayer, a producer, a director, and the camera. Had John Barrymore been able to manage his own theatre and career as had Irving, Tree, and Mansfield, he might not have detested his calling.

The six children of Ethel and Jack also failed because none was given a chance to develop his or her talents by long apprenticeship. Though a Drew-Barrymore, Lionel toured and played minor roles on Broadway for eight years before scoring in the small role of Giuseppe, which by no means made him an overnight star. Ethel and Jack had had the same necessary apprenticeship long before the term "Royal Family of American Actors" was coined. But the Barrymore and Colt children inherited that title and were raised in such a glare of publicity and overblown expectations that their failure was almost inevitable. The very names of the current generation of Barrymore descendants laid on them an impossible burden: Drew Lord Devereaux, Louisa Lane Devereaux, John Blyth Barrymore, John Drew Miglietta, Drew Barrymore.

Then there is the family curse—not madness or syphilis but susceptibility to alcohol and drug addiction. The older generation, living in a more stable society, drank and still managed careers, yet John Drew Sr., Sidney Drew, Maurice Barrymore, Georgie Drew Mendum, Ethel Barrymore, and John Barrymore were all alcoholics. John Drew and Lionel were heavy drinkers, and Lionel was addicted to morphine and cocaine. Sammy and Jackie Colt were heavy drinkers, Diana Barrymore an alcoholic and drug addict. Only Mummum, Georgie Drew Barrymore, and Ethel Colt seemed to have escaped.

While a tendency to alcoholism appears to be genetically transmitted, Lionel scoffed loudly at acting talent being passed from one generation to another. He viewed acting as a trade like any other and was fond of saying that had their father been a plumber, he and Jack would undoubtedly have flushed drains for a living. And acting ability is undoubtedly more nurture than nature. And here Ethel Barrymore, if she wanted to follow in Mummum's footsteps as the matriarch of an acting dynasty, made a mistake. Mrs. John Drew and Georgie had married actors: to their children the family trade was clear. But Ethel married a millionaire's son, confusing her children about their destiny.

Jack too married in Dolores Costello a woman whose heart was not really in acting. She readily gave up her career after marriage; she returned briefly to films after their divorce, then retired as Mrs. John Vruwink, reportedly using a canister containing a print of *The Sea Beast* as a door-stop. She sent her children to private prep schools, hoping they would go to college, discouraging them from being actors. It did not simplify life for John Jr. and Dede either to be told that acting had torn their father's life to pieces or to know about his suicidal flight from acting in drink.

Jack's marriage to Blanche Thomas also created powerful conflicts between stage and society for Diana. She grew up hearing her mother revile actors, was sent to the most expensive finishing schools, made a dazzling New York debut. But because her mother didn't love her, she pledged allegiance to her father and his world, not knowing he could not love her either. Powerful, "virile," she might have had the force to succeed had she not imitated her father's excesses in hopes of being an instant Barrymore. Of the six children, she had by far the most acting talent for the stage. She appeared in twenty-five plays on Broadway, touring, or in stock: she did serious acting in Tennessee Williams's *Cat on a Hot Tin Roof* and *Garden District*. As Brooks Atkinson said, "Any time she wants to stop fooling around and learn the difference between acting and per-forming, she can be an exciting actress. The stuff is there." But the discipline was not.

It is unnecessary to dwell again on the tragedy of Diana Barrymore's life. It was splashed before the public in her 1957 confessional *Too Much, Too Soon*, in a watered-down movie version, with Dorothy Malone and Errol Flynn as John the following year, in countless ugly headlines. If she could not achieve she could destroy, blaming the Barrymores and her own futility:

> Damn them for giving me nothing and taking it away before I had
> it! Damn Mother for her grandness and her indifference and her
> disdain of me, and damn Daddy for the crazy, mixed-up life he
> led and the daughter he never gave a damn for, and damn Uncle
> Lionel for treating me like the boarding-school bitch I am, and
> damn Aunt Ethel who doesn't even know I'm alive, and damn me

for being a silly, arrogant, affected schoolgirl! God damn us all! We deserve everything we get!

Constantly after men to prove to herself that she was desirable, Diana racketed from East Coast to West, leaving trails of empty liquor and sleeping pill bottles in her wake. Booze, drugs, worthless men, and above all, self-hatred. "I don't mind being punched," she bragged. "Noel Coward said women should be struck regularly like a gong and he's right. Women are no damn good." She's heard the same from her father. On the afternoon of January 25, 1960, a maid found her face-down and naked on the bed in her New York flat. Police concluded there was no evidence of suicide or foul play, but whether a random drinking partner of the night before had done her violence or not is almost irrelevant. Diana was determined to kill herself.

Of Ethel's three children, Jackie had the looks to succeed at acting, dreamed instead of being a prize fighter or tennis champ, drank himself into early retirement. After his Hollywood binge he and Marjorie moved into magnificent Linden Place with Sister and Romeo, who took over the Colt property after Ethel sold Mamaroneck. Both husband and wife were alcoholics, and Marjorie let the poodles she raised pee on all the Aubusson carpets. Sister handled the situation with her usual finesse: since Jackie loved swimming pools, she had one installed at a smaller house on the Colt acres. After Russell Colt died in 1960, Jackie shared the multimillion Colt pot, marrying Edith Hope in 1966 after Marjorie's death in 1964 and moving back to an apartment over the Linden Place garage. He died in obscurity of cancer and drink in 1975 at the age of sixty-one.

Sister said that her favorite quotation was Goethe's "That which thy ancestors have bequeathed, earn it again if thou wouldst possess it." She tried, taking her one-woman revue across the country, singing concerts and opera in New York, succeeding notably in Europe, where the Barrymore name did not haunt her. Yet ambiguous reviews such as "She is not Ethel Barrymore's daughter for nothing" continued to plague her; she never achieved Drew-Barrymore fame. But no one compared herself more rigorously to Ethel Barrymore than Sister herself, or better knew the difference. Admirably, she refused to write a life of her mother. "She was the greatest woman I knew," she said of Ethel instead, "nine times bigger than life." As for airing her grievances, she dismissed the notion as "a fine way to treat your mother." As a promoter of the arts, a teacher, and a reliable performer, she was a pro in her own right. She was a superb cook, a gracious hostess, and a warm personality—"A doll!" said one

Bristol neighbor enthusiastically. Two years before her death in 1977 she sang with Beverly Sills in Donizetti's *The Daughter of the Regiment*—a trouper like her mother to the end.

Sammy was the least tormented of Ethel's children because he set his sights low. He did not try to excel or buckle down to anything more strenuous than escorting his mother while enjoying himself as much as possible. Fifty when Ethel died, he continued the life of a bachelor about towns—Palos Verdes, Palm Beach, Pasadena, Santa Barbara, Palm Springs—wherever the rich gathered. In love with his mother, he did not think of marrying until he met Eleanore Phillips, the West Coast editor of *Vogue* and a woman of talent and energy. Elin Vanderlip takes credit for bringing the two together; they married in 1981. In Sammy, Eleanore found what had charmed his mother and friends: a willingness to accede to her wishes, a sense of fun, loyalty. Sammy died after a long illness in 1986, forfeiting the Colt fortune to a daughter of his father's brother.

Dede escaped headlines without escaping the conflicts of being a Barrymore. As a child in photographs she looks wistful, lost. She enrolled in some drama and radio courses in junior college, but quit a school play at the first rehearsal when the director chided her for nerves. She clashed with her mother when she decided to leave college at nineteen to marry Thomas Fairbanks, the son of a Viennese émigré musician named Fuchs. Dolores in this case was right: Fairbanks was not keen to support a family and, pregnant with their second child, Dede divorced him in 1952, complaining that her husband believed "work is only for peasants." Eventually she married Lew Bedell, a comedian turned record company president, bearing two more children. But marriage does not necessarily mean tranquility; passions still swirl around the Barrymore name and heritage to which Dede is not immune.

Jack's son John tried to conquer the acting urge, but when he was sixteen, he recalls, "I couldn't sleep one night. I went for a long walk. I looked up at the stars for a long time and all of a sudden I knew I had to be an actor." Dolores resisted and John promised to finish high school, but signed his first picture contract before he was seventeen. "Why shouldn't he start at seventeen?" his Aunt Ethel had demanded. "*We* all started sooner than that." By eighteen he was giving turgid interviews: "On my father's side I come from a long line of tragedians. . . ." The *Time* critic said encouragingly that in *The Big Night* John Barrymore Jr. "earns his right to his famous name," but when faced with a stage debut, he twice pulled out at the last minute, saying he was not ready. And how could he be ready to play the lead with no stage experience, though eventually in 1957 he did play Romeo to Margaret O'Brien's Juliet at the Pasadena Playhouse.

An impossible hothouse atmosphere, forcing him like a plant to flower unnaturally, generated inner turmoil that soon erupted into headlines: embattled marriages and divorces, drunk and disorderly charges, lawsuits, arrests for reckless driving and hit-and-run. Though he gave creditable performances in movies like *Never Love a Stranger* and *Night of the Quarter Moon*, the less than box-office hits could not satisfy a young man so profoundly anxious and insecure. Hounded by headlines, finally serving a three-day jail sentence, he left for Rome where Hollywood has-beens could crank out pictures that (as he said himself) he hoped no one would ever see. In Rome another marriage, more scandalous headlines. John had discovered it was much easier to make news by being bad than by being good.

He returned to Hollywood in 1964 without his Italian wife and child and, interviewed by the old Barrymore fan Hedda Hopper, appeared chastened: "I lost half my ego somewhere around the block." He'd finished two screenplays, had eleven other stories in his head. "I want to work—create and do things . . . to make a film that is not a lie. They've only made ten in the last twenty years." For fifteen years, he admitted, money had come into his hands and gone so quickly that he hadn't felt it touch his fingertips. Now he wanted to know himself. He had been through psychoanalysis at twenty-five, but still wasn't sure if he knew how to love.

Always thin and nervous, he had put on some much-needed weight, thought Hedda. His hair was still too long (was he trying to copy the Beatles?) and already gray. His eyes were piercing blue; his hands, unlike his father's, long and sensitive. He repeated again that he had never known his father. "I only saw my father in person once. I was about seven then. He came to the house the day before Christmas. Of course I saw him when I was very young, but I don't remember it." He wanted to do *The Jest* with Jack Palance as Neri, himself playing his father's role, Gianetto. He seemed hopeful about the future.

But John could not take hold. He became notorious for breaking contracts, standing up producers. For a career he began to substitute drugs and a kind of mystic fatalism: "We live our lives out the way we live them out, and that is it." His natural eloquence, grace, and style awed the druggies he gathered around him—"Saint John," they called him and took his words as revelation. In 1966 he was arrested for possessing marijuana . . . sixty days in jail; in 1969 an auto accident . . . "narcotics found in car." Eventually came word that John Drew Barrymore, as he now called himself, was panhandling for drinks in L.A., that he had sold his father's gun collection for drugs and traded his parents' love letters for a bed to sleep in, that he would greet anyone trying to write a biography about the Barrymores with a shotgun.

Phil and Marie Rhodes, great admirers of Jack Barrymore, are still fond of John. They say he is a gentle, sensitive man, not promiscuous like his father, a disaffected soul still searching. He still carries about with him, they say, the silver baby cup engraved "1888 from Mummum to Jack"; and it was John who, in 1980, finally had his father cremated and carried the ashes himself back to Philadelphia to be buried in Maurice's grave: "I gave my father his last wish." "Gentle," however, is a word John's third wife and his daughter Drew would hardly recognize. According to their testimony, John is an abusive, violent derelict who only contacts Drew when he needs drug money.

Dolores carried memories as well as many souvenirs from Tower Road: the Rhodes were horrified, visiting her once at her Fallbrook ranch after a flood, to find a good deal of Jack's precious library floating in her basement. Even during her movie career her cheeks had been eaten away by harsh studio make-up, posing a challenge for make-up men in a later film like *The Magnificent Ambersons*. Toward the end of her life, said Phil, she looked like an old Irish washerwoman—except when she got out her scrapbook and began to reminisce. And as she turned the pages and spoke of the old days with Jack "her face underwent a transformation and she became young and beautiful again."

FOR YEARS AFTER Jack's death, friends, idolators, and imitators held yearly wakes in his memory. Today the Barrymore legend continues to thrive, and destroy.

As a child, John Barrymore III, the son of John Jr. and his first wife Cara Williams, fell under his father's spell. Raised in the drug culture of the sixties, he was soon "painting the line down the fast lane"—hanging out with heavy addicts, stealing cars, serving time. When his father decided in 1980 to cremate John Barrymore and take the ashes to Philadelphia, John III readily went along with the "caper" that involved, he says, getting a genuine dispensation from the Catholic Church and some not-so-genuine family signatures. In the mausoleum, the stinking casket had leaked, gluing it to the marble slab, until his father, very drunk, pushed the gravediggers aside, put one foot up on Lionel and one on Ethel and yanked hard. Before turning the casket over to the crematorium, they were compelled to look inside: though the face was recognizable, transportation had not improved the corpse. John Barrymore's ashes were eventually put into a book-shaped urn; to get them to Philadelphia John Jr. pawned a good deal of the Belleek, the silver, the illuminations . . .

But for John III, life with Father eventually palled. To his son he is no longer "Saint John" but a bum with style, occasionally inspired but spouting lunacy 90 percent of the time. John III swears he is off drugs now and wants to act again. He also admits that his personal reputation keeps him unemployed, although—unlike his father—he claims he never burned anyone professionally. Still, there are no offers. "Maybe I'll have to change my name."

At two and a half, Drew Barrymore, the daughter of John Jr. and Ildiko Barrymore, appeared in a television movie. At four, "I told my mother I wanted to be a movie actress. . . . I thought it would be neat to be a Barrymore. I thought it would be a little hard to follow up on them, but I tried and tried." Drew went on to make *E.T. The Extra-Terrestrial*, *Firestarter*, *Irreconcilable Differences*, *Cat's Eye*, and *See You in the Morning*. The pressure—from her mother, agents, producers, her own aspirations—was intense. "Have you ever thought of knocking off for six months?" asked John III, who once was close to Drew. Drew looked at him as though he were mad. Then in 1988, at thirteen, Drew went into therapy at the ASAP Family Treatment Center in Van Nuys, California. She admitted that she had had a glass of champagne at eight, marijuana and cocaine at eleven. It was easy to sneak out to nightclubs and drink with friends, she said. "I really was a party girl." Everyone to whom the names Drew and Barrymore still mean theatre and acting was sorry, and the media made a meal.

Drew Barrymore will perhaps not be permanently damaged. But since the deaths of John, Lionel, and Ethel Barrymore, the little story with which John Drew ended his memoir *My Life on the Stage* seems particularly relevant:

> In Japan there has been for almost two hundred years the family of Ichikawa, the family of the best actors in Japan. In this family, if the son was not a good enough actor to represent the family, the best actor of the time was adopted into the family to bear the name of Ichikawa.

A sane alternative to heartbreak and destruction.

THEATRE AND FILM CHRONOLOGIES

NOTES

SELECTED BIBLIOGRAPHY

INDEX

THEATRE AND FILM CHRONOLOGIES

Film titles appear in *italics*. The (au) indicates author, (d) director, and (v) vaudeville.

LIONEL BARRYMORE

1893: The Rivals (debut Kansas City)

1894: The Road to Ruin (walk-on New York and tour)

1895: The Bachelor's Baby (tour)

1896–97: Mary Pennington, Spinster (New York debut); Squire Kate; Georgia Cayvan tour with Pennington, Goblin Castle, and The Little Individual

1897–98: Cumberland '61

1898: A Wife's Peril; Magda; Oliver Twist; East Lynne; Camille (Rankin-O'Neil summer stock, Minneapolis, St. Paul)

1898–99: Uncle Dick
The Honorable John Grigsby

1900: Arizona
Rain Clouds; The Rivals; An Arabian Night (Bond Stock Company, Albany)
Sag Harbor

1901: The Brixton Burglary
The Second in Command

1902: The Mummy and the Hummingbird

1903: The Best of Friends
The Other Girl

1905: Pantaloon

1909: The Fires of Fate

1910–11: The Jail Bird (v)
The White Slaver (v)
Bob Acres (v)
The Battle

1912: Stalled (v)
The Still Voice (v)
Friends; So Near, Yet So Far; The One She Loved; The Painted Lady; Heredity; Gold and Glitter; My Baby; The Informer; Brutality; The Unwelcome Guest; The New York Hat; The Burglar's Dilemma (also au); A Cry for Help; The God Within; Three Friends; The Telephone Girl and the Lady; An Adventure in the Autumn Woods; The Tender-Hearted Boy (au); Oil and Water; A Chance Deception; Fate; The Wrong Bottle

1913: *Near to Earth; The Sheriff's Baby; The Perfidy of Mary; A Misunderstood Boy; The Little Tease; The Lady and the Mouse; The Wanderer; The House of Darkness; Just Gold; A Timely Interception; Death's Marathon; The Yaqui Cur; The Ranchero's Revenge; Red Hicks Defies the World; Almost a Wild Man; The Well; The Switch-Tower; In Diplomatic Circles; A Gamble with Death; The Enemy's Baby; The Mirror; An Indian's Loyalty; The Vengeance of Galora (au only); Under the Shadow of the Law; I Was Meant for You; The Work Habit; The Crook and the Girl; The Strong Man's Burden; The Stolen Treaty; His Secret (d only); Chocolate Dynamite (d only); Where's the Baby? (d only); Just Boys (d only); No Place for Fa-*

ther (d only); All for Science; Classmates; Strongheart; Men and Women

1914: *The Massacre; Judith of Bethulia; Brute Force; The Woman in Black; The Span of Life; The Seats of the Mighty*

1915: *Wildfire; A Modern Magdalen; The Curious Conduct of Judge Legarde; The Romance of Elaine; The Flaming Sword; Dora Thorne; A Yellow Streak*

1916: *Dorian's Divorce; The Quitter; The Upheaval; The Brand of Cowardice*

1917: *The End of the Tour; His Father's Son; The Millionaire's Double; Life's Whirlpool (d and au only)*
Peter Ibbetson

1918: The Copperhead

1919: The Jest

1920: The Letter of the Law
The Copperhead; The Master Mind; The Devil's Garden

1921: Macbeth
The Claw
The Great Adventure; Jim the Penman

1922: *Boomerang Bill; The Face in the Fog*

1923: *Enemies of Women; Unseeing Eyes; The Eternal City; Decameron Nights*
Laugh, Clown, Laugh!

1924: *America; Meddling Women; I Am the Man*

1925: The Piker
Taps
Man or Devil
The Iron Man; Fifty-Fifty; The Girl Who Wouldn't Work; Children of the Whirlwind; The Splendid Road; The Wrongdoers

1926: *The Barrier; Brooding Eyes; Paris at Midnight; The Lucky Lady; The Temptress; The Bells; Wife Tamers*

1927: The Copperhead (Los Angeles);
The Show; Women Love Diamonds; Body and Soul; The Thirteenth Hour

1928: *Drums of Love; Sadie Thompson; The Lion and the Mouse; Road House; River Woman; Alias Jimmy Valentine; West of Zanzibar*

1929: *Confession (d only); Madame X (d only); The Hollywood Revue of 1929; His Glorious Night (d only); The Unholy Night (d only); The Mysterious Island*

1930: *The Rogue Song (d only); Free and Easy*

1931: *Ten Cents a Dance (d only); A Free Soul; Guilty Hands; The Yellow Ticket; Mata Hari*

1932: *The Man I Killed (Broken Lullaby); Arsène Lupin; Grand Hotel; Washington Masquerade; Rasputin and the Empress*

1933: *Sweepings; Looking Forward; The Stranger's Return; Dinner at Eight; One Man's Journey; Night Flight; Christopher Bean (Her Sweetheart); Should Ladies Behave?*

1934: *This Side of Heaven; Carolina; The Girl from Missouri; Treasure Island*

1935: *David Copperfield; Mark of the Vampire; The Little Colonel; Public Hero No. 1; The Return of Peter Grimm; Ah, Wilderness!*

1936: *The Voice of Bugle Ann; The Road to Glory; The Devil-Doll; The Gorgeous Hussy; Camille*

1937: *Captains Courageous; A Family Affair; Saratoga; Navy Blue and Gold*

1938: *A Yank at Oxford; Test Pilot; You Can't Take It With You; Young Doctor Kildare*

1939: *Let Freedom Ring; Calling Dr. Kildare; On Borrowed Time; The Secret of Dr. Kildare*

1940: *Dr. Kildare's Strange Case; Dr. Kildare Goes Home; Dr. Kildare's Crisis*

1941: *The Penalty; The Bad Man; The People vs. Dr. Kildare; Lady Be Good; Dr. Kildare's Wedding Day; Dr. Kildare's Victory*

1942: *Calling Dr. Gillespie; Dr. Gillespie's New Assistant; Tennessee Johnson*

1943: *Dr. Gillespie's Criminal Case; The Last Will and Testament of Tom Smith (short); A Guy Named Joe*

1944: *Three Men in White; Dragon Seed (narrator); Since You Went Away; Between Two Women*

1945: *The Valley of Decision*

1946: *Three Wise Fools; The Secret Heart; It's a Wonderful Life*

1947: *Duel in the Sun; Dark Delusion*

1948: *Key Largo*

1949: *Some of the Best (narrator, MGM promotional short); Down to the Sea in Ships; Malaya*

1950: *Right Cross*

1951: *The M-G-M Story (narrator, promotional piece); Bannerline*

1952: *Lone Star*

1953: *Main Street to Broadway*

ETHEL BARRYMORE

1893: The Rivals (Montreal)
Oliver Twist

1894: The Rivals (New York debut)
The Bauble Shop

1895: That Imprudent Young Couple

1896: The Squire of Dames
Rosemary

1897: Secret Service (London debut)
The Bells (English tour)

1898: Peter the Great (London)
Catherine (toured in 1899)

1900: His Excellency, the Governor

1901: Captain Jinks of the Horse Marines

1902: The Country Mouse
Carrots

1903: Cousin Kate

1904: Cynthia (London)
Sunday

1905: A Doll's House
Alice-Sit-by-the-Fire

1906: Miss Civilization (Actors Fund Benefit)

1907: Captain Jinks of the Horse Marines (revival)
The Silver Box
His Excellency, the Governor (revival)
Her Sister

1908: Lady Frederick (toured in 1909)

1910: Mid-Channel

1911: Trelawny of the Wells
Alice-Sit-by-the-Fire (revival) and The Twelve Pound Look
Witness for the Defense

1912: Cousin Kate (revival) and A Slice of Life
The Twelve Pound Look (first of many vaudeville appearances, usually in summer, in this play)

1913: Miss Civilization (v) and Tante

1914: *The Nightingale*
A Scrap of Paper
Drifted Apart (v)

1915: The Shadow
Our Mrs. McChesney
The Final Judgment

1916: *The Kiss of Hate; The Awakening of Helena Ritchie*

1917: *The White Raven; The Call of Her People; The Greatest Power; The Lifted Veil; Life's Whirlpool; The Eternal Mother; An American Widow*
An Evening with J. M. Barrie (war benefit)
The Lady of the Camellias

1918: *Our Mrs. McChesney; The Divorcee*
The Off Chance
Belinda

1919: Déclassée (ran and toured through 1922)

1921: Clair de Lune

1922: Rose Bernd
Romeo and Juliet

1923: The Laughing Lady
The School for Scandal (Players Club revival)
A Royal Fandango

1924: The Second Mrs. Tanqueray

1925: Hamlet
The Merchant of Venice

1926: The Constant Wife (toured until 1928)

1928: The Kingdom of God (inaugurating Ethel Barrymore Theatre)

1929: The Love Duel

1930: Scarlet Sister Mary

1931: The School for Scandal (tour)

1932: *Rasputin and the Empress*
Encore (tour)

1933: An Amazing Career (Encore tour)

1934:   The Twelve Pound Look (v:
London)
Laura Garnett (tryout, Dobbs Ferry,
New York)
L'Aiglon
1935:   The Constant Wife (tour)
1937:   The Ghost of Yankee Doodle
1938:   Whiteoaks
1939:   Farm of Three Echoes
1940:   An International Incident
The Corn Is Green (New York and on
tour through June 1944)
1944:   *None But the Lonely Heart*
Embezzled Heaven
1945:   The Joyous Season (tour)
1946:   *The Spiral Staircase*

1947:   *The Farmer's Daughter; Moss Rose;
Night Song*
1948:   *The Paradine Case; Moonrise; Portrait of Jennie*
1949:   *The Great Sinner; That Midnight
Kiss; The Red Danube; Pinky*
1950:   The Twelve Pound Look (ANTA
"Album" benefit, New York)
1951:   *Kind Lady; Daphne, The Virgin of
the Golden Laurels (narrator); The Secret
of Convict Lake; It's a Big Country*
1952:   *Deadline, USA; Just for You*
1953:   *The Story of Three Loves; Main
Street to Broadway*
1954:   *Young at Heart*
1957:   *Johnny Trouble*

JOHN BARRYMORE

1900:   A Man of the World (v;
Cincinnati)
1901:   Captain Jinks of the Horse Marines (Philadelphia)
1903:   Magda (legit debut, Chicago);
Leah the Forsaken; Glad of It (New
York debut)
1904:   The Dictator
Yvette (Actors Fund matinee benefit)
1905:   The Dictator (London)
Sunday (tour)
Pantaloon and Alice-Sit-by-the-
Fire
1906:   Miss Civilization (Actors Fund
benefit)
The Dictator (Australian tour)
On the Quiet (Australian tour)
1907:   The Boys of Company B; His Excellency, the Governor
1908:   Toddles
A Stubborn Cinderella
The Candy Shop
1909:   The Fortune Hunter (toured until
1911)
1911:   Uncle Sam
Princess Zim-Zim (tour)
1912:   A Slice of Life
Half a Husband; On the Quiet; The
Honor of the Family; The Man from
Home (summer rep, Rochester,

Los Angeles)
*Dream of a Motion Picture Director; The
Widow Casey's Return; A Prize Package*
(Lubins?)
The Affairs of Anatol
1913:   *One on Romance* (Lubin?)
A Thief for a Night (Chicago)
Believe Me, Xantippe
1914:   The Yellow Ticket
*An American Citizen; The Man from
Mexico*
Kick In
1915:   *Are You a Mason?; The Dictator;
The Incorrigible Dukane*
1916:   Justice
*Nearly a King; The Lost Bridegroom; The
Red Widow*
1917:   Peter Ibbetson
Raffles
1918:   Redemption
On the Quiet
1919:   The Jest
*Here Comes the Bride; The Test of
Honor*
1920:   Richard the Third
Dr. Jekyll and Mr. Hyde
1921:   Clair de Lune
The Lotus Eater
1922:   Hamlet (toured 1923–1924)
Sherlock Holmes

1924: *Beau Brummel*

1925: Hamlet (London)

1926: *The Sea Beast; Don Juan*

1927: *When a Man Loves; The Beloved Rogue*

1928: *Tempest*

1929: *Eternal Love; The Show of Shows*

1930: *General Crack; The Man from Blankley's; Moby Dick*

1931: *Svengali; The Mad Genius*

1932: *Arsène Lupin; Grand Hotel; State's Attorney; A Bill of Divorcement; Rasputin and the Empress*

1933: *Topaze; Reunion in Vienna; Dinner at Eight; Night Flight; Counsellor-at-Law*

1934: *Long Lost Father; Twentieth Century*

1936: *Romeo and Juliet*

1937: *Maytime; Bulldog Drummond Comes Back; Night Club Scandal; Bulldog Drummond's Revenge; True Confession*

1938: *Romance in the Dark; Bulldog Drummond's Peril; Marie Antoinette; Spawn of the North; Hold That Co-ed*

1939: *The Great Man Votes; Midnight* My Dear Children (tour)

1940: My Dear Children (New York) *The Great Profile*

1941: *The Invisible Woman; World Premiere; Playmates*

NOTES

Frequently cited theatre and film collections are identified by the following abbreviations:

TCMCNY   Theatre Collection, Museum of the City of New York
TCFLP   Theatre Collection, Free Library of Philadelphia
WCFTR   Wisconsin Center for Film and Theatre Research, Madison
AMPAS   Academy of Motion Picture Arts and Sciences
Locke   Robinson Locke Barrymore Scrapbooks, Billy Rose Theatre Collection, Lincoln Center, New York

CHAPTER ONE: 1878–1882, AND BEFORE

Despite the autobiographies of Mrs. John Drew, John Drew Jr., Lionel, Ethel, and John, the early lives of the Drews and Barrymores are characterized by contradiction, confusion, and above all missing pieces. John Barrymore's first biographer, Alma Power-Waters, treats his childhood superficially, relying on anecdotes told her by John, whose mind in 1940 was hardly reliable. Gene Fowler knew John well only in decline, and though he had the advantage of Lionel's memories of his and John's childhood, Lionel too is an unreliable narrator. Maurice Barrymore's biographer, James Kotsilibas-Davis, paints the most thorough picture of the three Barrymores' childhood in his fine *Great Times, Good Times: The Odyssey of Maurice Barrymore* (Garden City, N.Y.: Doubleday, 1977); unfortunately, the book lacks notes. John Kobler has filled in valuable information about John's schooling, again without indicating sources. Hollis Alpert's biography of the three Barrymores lacks not only source notes but even a bibliography. For this biography I have examined birth, death, and marriage certificates as well as the Drew Family Bible, but even with this assistance questions about the family are not necessarily answered.

The most perplexing is the parentage and birth of Sidney White Drew. Louisa Drew in her *Autobiographical Sketch of Mrs. John Drew* (New York: Charles Scribner's Sons, 1899) says that Sidney was an adopted son. John Drew Jr. fails to mention Sidney at all in his memoir, *My Years on the Stage* (New York: E. P. Dutton, 1922). For these reasons, Dorothy E. Stolp in "Mrs. John Drew, American Actress and Manager, 1820–1897" (Ph.D. diss. Louisiana State University, 1953) argues that Sidney was indeed adopted, citing the additional evidence that (1) Sidney was not baptized at St. Stephen's Episcopal Church as were the other Drew children and that (2) the *Catalogue of Matriculates of the College, University of Pennsylvania, 1749–1893* lists Sidney Drew White as the son of Sidney White and Maria Drew, born at sea September 28, 1863. To the argument that Sidney was adopted I can contribute only negative evidence: his birth is recorded neither at St. Stephen's (records before 1860) nor in the Philadelphia City Archives (records after 1860) nor in Borough of Manhattan records for 1863, as the entry in the Drew Family Bible suggests. (Granted there are other boroughs than Manhattan which I did not search.) Also supporting the adoption theory are playbills in the Furness Collection of the University of Pennsylvania and the Theatre Collection of the Free Library of Philadelphia showing Mrs. John Drew before the public almost continually during the time(s) she was presumed to have borne Sidney.

John Barrymore's *Confessions of an Actor* (Indianapolis: Bobbs-Merrill, 1926) does not mention Sidney White Drew's birth; Alma Power-Waters's *John Barrymore: The Legend and the Man* (New York: Julian Messner, 1941) ignores it. It is rather surprising, therefore, to read as fact in Gene Fowler's *Good Night, Sweet Prince* (New York: Viking, 1943) that John and Louisa Drew were married in 1850 and had four children in the following five years: Louisa, John, Georgiana, and Sidney. Lionel was probably the source of Fowler's statement, Lionel who claimed in *We Barrymores* (New York: Appleton-Century-Crofts, 1951) that his grandmother might say what she liked but Uncle Sidney certainly looked like her. Ethel agreed in *Memories: An Autobiography* (New York: Harper & Brothers, 1955). Other Barrymore biographers have taken this line, though placing Sidney's birth a decade later. Kotsilibas-Davis states that Robert Craig, a handsome and talented actor in Louisa's company, fathered Sidney in 1868. As it turns out, however, the only "evidence" for Craig as Louisa's lover is her passing reference to him in her autobiography as "one of the most talented young men I ever met." Also crushing this theory are the facts that (1) Louisa was forty-eight in 1868, somewhat late for childbearing, (2) playbills show her appearing fairly steadily throughout the 1867–1868 season, and (3) far from asking Craig to leave her company, as Kotsilibas-Davis claims she did, Craig remained with her company through the 1870–1871 season. Alpert and Kobler say that Louisa Drew presented John Drew with "a surprise" when he returned from abroad, father of the surprise unknown. To compound the confusion, *Who Was Who on the Screen* gives Sidney Drew's birth date as August 28, 1864, *The Oxford Companion to the Theatre* as 1868, obituaries in *Variety*, the *New York Times*, and the Philadelphia *Inquirer* as 1865.

The Drew Bible, invaluable as a resource, seems, however, to contain some inaccuracies. Eliza Kinlock recorded John Drew Sr.'s death as May 23, 1863; according to his wife's autobiography and newspaper accounts, however, he died on May 21, 1861. While Eliza may have erred about her son-in-law's death, it is improbable that Louisa Drew, who recorded the births of her other two children correctly, should mistake her daughter Georgie's birth date, which she entered as June 11, 1855. Although reference books give Georgiana's birth date as May 21, 1856, and at least one source says that John Drew died on his daughter's birthday on May 21, this is probably an occasion to trust the Family Bible.

Adine Kinlock Stephens Drew ("Aunt Tibby") was born, according to the Bible, in Melbourne, Australia, March 12, 186[0 or 1]; her death on January 14, 1888, is confirmed by a death certificate in the Philadelphia City Archives. She therefore died at either twenty-seven or twenty-eight, not at twenty-two as biographers have stated. Adine's confirmation is also on record at St. Stephen's: March 8, 1874.

Again, in the Family Bible, Louisa Lane married Henry Blaine Hunt in New Orleans, March 30, 1836; George Mossop in St. Louis, May 25, 1848; John Drew in Albany, New York, July 28, 1850. Georgiana Drew and Maurice (Herbert Blyth) Barrymore's wedding date is entered as December 31, 1876.

One necessarily relies on the Barrymores' own accounts of their childhood—sketchy, impressionistic, and undated as they are—with the knowledge that actual events can seldom be fixed and that their accounts must be interpreted rather than merely accepted. It is rare that such concrete evidence survives as the note from Louisa Drew dated September 2, 1891, to F. A. Hoyt & Company: "This suit for Jack requires alteration. His illness prevented my trying it on before last evening. I will call round to the store in the course of the morning. Yrs truly Louisa Drew" (Spencer Berger Collection).

Even the "evidence" of 140 North Twelfth Street may have disappeared. I am grateful to David Spitz who, in 1986, had a frame shop on the premises and showed me the layout of the Barrymores' former home. At that time Spitz said that the property was going to be pulled down to make room for a convention center.

CHAPTER TWO: 1882–1886

Great Times, Good Times is the source of Maurice's antics in the Annex.

In *We Barrymores* Lionel says, "I never saw my mother and father on stage and never went on tour with them as a boy." Helena Modjeska's *Memories and Impressions* (New York: Macmillan, 1910) confirms that the Barrymore children accompanied their parents on the 1882–1883 tour, as do Marion Moore Coleman's *Fair Rosalind: The American Career of Helena Modjeska* (Cheshire, Conn.: Cherry Hill Books, 1969) and Antoni Gronowicz's *Modjeska, Her Life and Loves* (New York: Thomas Yoseloff, 1956). Ethel's memories of Modjeska's acting are either precocious, since she was three when the tour began, or perhaps confused with later Modjeska performances at the Arch Street Theatre. Modjeska herself has a different version of the quarrel with Maurice Barrymore over *Nadjezda*— that Barrymore insisted she play the exhausting drama every day even though its reception was not warm. Kotsilibas-Davis presents Maurice's case.

I am grateful to Jeri Hill, Secretary/Bookkeeper of St. Stephen's in Philadelphia, for providing me with information about Louisa Drew's pew and silver plate and about the family's baptism and confirmation records. Alice Judson's brief memoir (Billy Rose Theatre Collection, Lincoln Center) is the source of Louisa Drew's outrage at hearing that her grandchildren were to be baptized Catholics. About John's baptism in 1884 Kotsilibas-Davis says, "At seven the next morning, the Reverend Doctor Rudder, rector of St. Stephen's, was awakened by Mrs. Drew's coachman. Shortly after eight o'clock, with Aunt Tibby and Uncle Googan as godparents, John Sidney Blyth Barrymore was welcomed into the Episcopal Church." However, Dr. Rudder had died in 1880 and there is no record of John's baptism at St. Stephen's which, had it taken place, would have been performed by Dr. S. D. McConnell.

Ethel is the only one of the three Barrymores who talks about England (Polly, Madame Tussaud's, Oscar Wilde) in her autobiography. Kotsilibas-Davis did a good deal of research about the Barrymores in England to which I am indebted, as well as to Mrs. Susan Shaw and Allen Davies, who directed me to sources for Maurice Barrymore's 1884–1886 sojourn in London. "There was much—too much—good fellowship" and "While he was with you" quoted from Kotsilibas-Davis.

The powerful German actress Emily Rigl played the title role of Maurice Barrymore's *Nadjezda*. While she was unequal to the rigors of the part the first night, the disaster could equally be attributed to a battle between Maurice's noisy claque of partisans and those they annoyed with their cheers and whistles. Actually *Nadjezda* ran for six weeks, Rigl vindicating herself with successively stronger performances, Herbert Beerbohm Tree as Prince Zabouroff launching his great career, and some critics praising the play's power and promise. Still, Maurice's play was considered a failure. Later in life he would become obsessed with the idea that the playwright Victorien Sardou stole the crucial last two acts of *Nadjezda* for his *La Tosca*.

Charles Belmont Davis writes about Georgie and Ethel at Point Pleasant in *Adventures and Letters of Richard Harding Davis* (New York: Charles Scribner's Sons, 1917). Lionel's, John's, and Ethel's statements about not knowing their parents are taken from *We Barrymores*, *Confessions*, and *Memories*.

CHAPTER THREE: 1886–1892

Sources for this chapter include Jerome Beatty's "Those Incredible Barrymores," *American Magazine* (February, March, April, May, 1933), *We Barrymores*, *Confessions*, and *Memories*, nine original pages of which, with Ethel's corrections, are in the Theatre Collection of the Museum of the City of New York (TCMCNY). Ethel also wrote briefly of her grandmother's routine in "Myself as I Think Others See Me," an unpublished manuscript written in 1927 or 1928, kindly lent me by Spencer Berger. Clara Morris described Mrs. John Drew's Arch Street Theatre and her management in "The Dressing Room Reception Where I First Met Ellen Terry and Mrs. John Drew," *McClure's Magazine* (December 1903). Georgie Drew Barrymore was quoted on the red shawl in "The Funeral of Mrs. John Drew," Philadelphia *Public Ledger* (September 2, 1897). Also useful for Drew-Barrymore background are the clipping files on Louisa Drew in the Theatre Collection of the Free Library of Philadelphia (TCFLP); Dorothy E. Stolp, "Mrs. John Drew: American Actress-Manager, 1820–1897"; Rosemarie K. Bank, "Louisa Lane Drew at the Arch Street Theatre: Repertory and Actor Training in Nineteenth-Century Philadelphia," *Theatre Studies* (special double issue, nos. 24/25, 1977–1978, 1978–1979); and C. Lee Jenner, "The Duchess of Arch Street: An Overview of Mrs. John Drew's Managerial Career," *Performing Arts Resources* 13, ed. Barbara Naomi Cohen-Stratyner (1988). Fowler and Kotsilibas-Davis are also useful, of course, for the early years, though Fowler creates conversations that no one could possibly have overheard or remembered. Mr. and Mrs. Clark's memory of the Barrymore children is taken from an unidentified clipping: TCFLP.

I have depended on Fowler for Lionel's brief careers at the Academy and Race, presumably supplied to Fowler by Lionel himself. I am grateful to the Reverend John B. DeMayo, Archivist of the Archdiocese of Philadelphia, and to the Reverend Monsignor Michael E. Kelly and Father William Noe Field of Seton Hall Preparatory School for their assistance in trying to trace the school years of Lionel and John. Kobler says that Lionel attended Seton Hall only two semesters (1889), no source. Lionel says he was at Seton Hall from age ten to fifteen. Seton Hall confirms 1889 (if he entered before April 28 he would have been ten). At fifteen Lionel joined his grandmother on the stage. It is probable (even given Barrymore volatility) that he actually stayed at Seton Hall until the spring semester 1893; both he and John were there after the death of their mother in 1892, according to Kotsilibas-Davis.

John does not clarify his educational picture by saying that he went to the Catholic day school attached to Ethel's convent at the age of nine, thus leaving his education from 1886 to 1891 unaccounted for. He probably attended the convent school in Philadelphia *until* 1891 when, at the age of nine, he was sent to join Lionel at Seton Hall. (Lionel errs in saying that John came to Seton Hall *after* being dismissed from Georgetown Preparatory School.) John perhaps wrote the letter to his grandmother about being attacked in 1891; Mrs. Drew was touring that year. The first source of this letter that I could find is John's *Confessions*, in which he quotes only his last line, "He struck me a blow which felled me to the ground." Fowler, from an unknown source, expanded this to, "I was attacked by this huge fellow and without cause. And, as the great brute advanced toward my desk, I tried to placate him; but he struck me, and as I reeled beneath the cruel blow the world went black before my eyes. . . ." Kotsilibas-Davis has still a different version (no source): "I was attacked by this huge fellow without cause. And, as the great brute advanced toward my desk, I tried to placate him; but he struck me a blow which felled me to the ground." The actual wording of John's letter remains a mystery. Fowler reports that the parallel bars episode took place before the eyes of Father Marshall at Seton Hall, as does Lionel, from whom Fowler probably heard the incident. Kobler has it taking place in front of Father Richard at Georgetown Prep. Father William Noe Field, Curator of Archives at Seton Hall, reports there is a legend at that school that while John was doing "a bird's nest" on the parallel bars before a priest-teacher, dice, naughty pictures, etc. fell from his pockets. According to Kobler, John stayed only two semesters at Seton Hall, leaving therefore in 1892 and attending various New York schools (among them P.S. 43) before he was sent to Georgetown Prep on October 16, 1895. It is possible that Lionel thus left Seton Hall in 1892, John also being withdrawn at his older brother's leaving.

"The difference between what he could do professionally": *Illustrated American* 3, ed. Marwell Hall, 1894. Maurice as "the victim of a culture": the exaggerated creed of manliness in the last decades of the nineteenth century was in part a reaction against the threat of the strong feminist movement of that time. Even a sophisticated writer like Finley Peter Dunne ("Mr. Dooley") complained that profanity was so necessarily a part of a man's conversation that oaths had lost their significance. If one studies the advertisements of the period, one is struck by the amazing number of products that promise to eliminate "male prostration," "male weakness," etc. Obviously many men were terrified of not living up to the aggressive virility of the "man's man."

Lionel on John's resemblance to Maurice in *We Barrymores*. Augustus Thomas analyzed John's and Lionel's resemblance to Maurice in *The Print of My Remembrance* (New York: Charles Scribner's Sons, 1922).

Ethel devotes quite a number of pages to the convent in *Memories*. Mary Hagerty reminisced about Ethel in "The Philadelphia Scene," Philadelphia *Inquirer* (September 7, 1954), and Clare R. Warren also remembered Ethel at dancing school in the *Inquirer* (July 9, 1959).

CHAPTER FOUR: 1892–1897

"This is much worse for me": Philadelphia *Inquirer* (n.d.), clipping files: TCFLP. "Better than any man in the country": A. Frank Stull, a member of Louisa Drew's company, "Where Famous Actors Learned Their Art," *Lippincott's Monthly Magazine* (March 1905). "A lazy, stroll-about school": Louisa Drew to Clara Morris, "The Dressing Room Reception Where I First Met Ellen Terry and Mrs. John Drew."

John Drew defends himself for "betraying" Augustin Daly by going over to Frohman in his memoir, *My Years on the Stage*. Drew's shift to the Frohman management is also discussed in Isaac F. Marcossan and Daniel Frohman, *Charles Frohman: Manager and Man* (New York: Harper & Brothers, 1916). Frohman managed John Drew, Georgie Drew Barrymore, and even Mrs. John Drew; Maurice Barrymore, however, considered Frohman one of the monopolists who were gaining a virtual stranglehold on the theatre, and refused to work for him. Thus although Frohman offered Maurice the lead in *Shenandoah* (which proved one of the biggest draws of all time), Maurice turned him down even though his own career was floundering at the time: his play *Waldemar, or The Robber of the Rhine* failed, and his engagement with Mrs. Bernard Beere ended prematurely when she failed to please

New York audiences. Maurice became a bitter enemy of the all-powerful Theatrical Syndicate and Theatrical Trust, helping to create the Association for the Promotion and Protection of an Independent Stage in the United States.

Since Georgie was called more witty than Maurice, it is a pity that "I'm going to church and you can go to hell!" is one of her few ripostes to have survived. Otis Skinner's opinion of Georgie as the most delicious comedian on any stage is cited by Cornelia Otis Skinner in "The Radiant Ethel Barrymore," *McCall's* (February, March 1950). Kotsilibas-Davis describes the onset of Georgie's illness and Maurice's reaction as well as the leavetaking at the North River pier. Ethel's memories of the trip to and the stay in Santa Barbara can be corrected in some details by notices of Georgie's death in the Santa Barbara *Daily Independent* (July 3, 1893) and *Morning Press* (July 4, 1893) and by her death certificate. Ethel described the train trip home to Cornelia Otis Skinner, "The Radiant Ethel Barrymore." Louisa Drew's "the keenest sorrow of my life" is from her autobiography. John's "She wanted to be alone with me then" is in *Confessions*. Lionel recalling Maurice's stunned behavior at Georgie's funeral is from Fowler.

The episode of Lionel's striking the boy who called his mother disgusting is told in Kotsilibas-Davis. Mummum descending upon Lionel and handing him his fate is in *We Barrymores*. Lionel incorrectly gives the year of his debut in *The Rivals* as 1894 and the place as the Coates House in *We Barrymores*. The Kansas City *Star* (October 20, 1893) announces the engagement of Mr. and Mrs. Sidney Drew, presenting Mrs. John Drew for one week commencing Monday, October 23, at The Auditorium. They offered *The Rivals* on Monday, Tuesday, and the Saturday matinee; *The Road to Ruin* Thursday, Friday, and Saturday night. Lionel's matinee debut, therefore, occurred on October 28. He says in *We Barrymores* that he had to repeat the agony in the evening; the *Star* gives *The Road to Ruin* for Saturday evening. It is possible that the bill was changed; at any rate Lionel seemed very certain that he suffered through two performances. (Mrs. John Drew's performances, incidentally, were highly praised in the *Star*, though Sidney Drew did not fare very well.) Louisa Drew's letter to Lionel is quoted from *We Barrymores*. Fowler gives an entirely different version, source unknown.

Ethel's *Memories* and Cornelia Otis Skinner's "The Radiant Ethel Barrymore" are sources for her debut on June 11, 1894, at the Academy of Music in Montreal, the tour that followed, and her failure to find acting jobs in New York.

"Slim and pale as a church candle" and like a "Siamese office boy" come from Fowler. I am indebted to Kobler's account of John at Georgetown Preparatory School in *Damned in Paradise*. "Do you wish to adopt" is in Kotsilibas-Davis. Dr. Hirschfeld's opinion of John's alcoholism is reported in Fowler, which also tells about John's seduction by his stepmother, John himself the source. John on "the symmetrical lady" is in *Confessions*. "My boy, that kick" cited in Fowler. John's caring for his grandmother and Louisa Drew's "The greatest sorrow" and "Waves and actors" are in Fowler. Louisa Drew's death and funeral were widely reported in Philadelphia papers, clippings: TCFLP.

CHAPTER FIVE: 1895–1901

A chief source for this chapter is *Memories*, again with reservations and corrections. Ethel's chronology is often unreliable: for example, she did not see Irene Vanbrugh in *His Excellency, the Governor* in the summer of 1899, as she states, but in the summer of 1898. William Bartlett Reynolds describes Ethel substituting for Elsie de Wolfe in "A Fellow Player Recalls Ethel Barrymore's First Stage Appearance" (William Seymour Theatre Collection, Princeton University Library). Ethel first appeared as Priscilla in *Rosemary* on August 31, 1896. The actor William Roerick described Ethel's cello-and-caramel-sauce voice in "The Drews and Barrymores: Another Kind of Dynasty," *Equity News* (August 1985). Other sources for Ethel's early work with Frohman are John Drew, *My Years on the Stage*; Marcossan and Frohman, *Charles Frohman: Manager and Man*; Jane S. Smith, *Elsie de Wolfe: A Life in the High Style* (New York: Atheneum, 1982); Phyllis Robbins, *Maude Adams: An Intimate Portrait* (New York: G. P. Putnam's Sons, 1956); and clippings in the Robinson Locke Barrymore Scrapbooks (Locke): Billy Rose Theatre Collection, Lincoln Center, New York.

Ethel makes three trips to London in this chapter: her first long stay of 1897–98, the summer of 1899, and the summer of 1900. Besides *Memories*, other sources include Kotsilibas-Davis; Margaret Webster, *The Same Only Different: Five Generations of a Great Theatre Family* (New York: Knopf, 1969); Charles Belmont Davis, *Adventures and Letters of Richard Harding Davis*; Laurence Irving, *The Successors* (London: Rupert Hart-Davis, 1967); Daphne du Maurier, *Gerald: A Portrait* (New York: Doubleday, Doran, 1935); Ellen Terry, *The Story of My Life* (London: Hutchinson, 1908); Diana Forbes-Robertson, *My Aunt Maxine: The Story of Maxine Elliott* (New York: Viking, 1964); *Ellen Terry and Bernard Shaw: A Correspondence*, ed. Christopher St. John (New York: G. P. Putnam's Sons, 1932); Denis Stuart, *Dear Duchess: Millicent Duchess of Sutherland* (London: Victor Gollancz, 1982); and that invaluable reference work, J. P. Wearing's *The London Stage: A Calendar of Plays and Players*, 3 vols. (Metuchen, N.J.: The Scarecrow Press, 1976, 1981, 1984).

Letters of introduction: on March 23, 1897, Bernard Shaw wrote Sally Fairchild, "If you send any 'nice, pretty, ambitious little girl who is an actress' to me, you will not survive our next meeting." This "little girl" is undoubtedly Ethel, as Bernard Burgunder argues in "Shaw and Ethel Barrymore?" *Cornell Library Journal* (Autumn 1969).

Ethel opened at the Adelphi as Miss Kittridge in *Secret Service* on May 15, 1897, and substituted for Odette Tyler in the female comedy lead on June 9. *The Era* noted that despite the suddenness of Miss Tyler's illness, the news had reached several of Miss Barrymore's friends, who "were on hand, among the 'Standing Room Only' contingent, to welcome her with a little rattle of the palms." The *New York Tribune* congratulated her for going "straight at the difficult fence," but Tyler's role was given to Hope Ross for the remainder of the play's seventy-nine performances.

There are at least three variations on Ethel's account of her last-minute rescue by Henry Irving. Marcossan and Frohman say that the night before she sailed she was dressing to go to dinner at the home of the novelist Anthony Hope when Terry wired DO COME AND SAY GOOD-BY BEFORE YOU GO." John Barrymore in "Those Incredible Barrymores: Blame It on the Queen," *American Magazine* (March 1933) says that Henry Irving sent the wire. Kotsilibas-Davis says that both Irving and Terry were at the last performance of *Secret Service*, after which Terry sent Ethel a note asking her not to leave without saying goodbye. But this last account eliminates the period of anxious unemployment that Ethel describes; then too Irving and Terry seldom visited other theatres, especially the Adelphi and especially together.

Both Ellen Terry and Bernard Shaw comment rather often on Ethel in their collected correspondence, a testimony to the impact that she made in London. They are not always complimentary. Terry observed in *The Story of My Life* that Ada Rehan's voice was "a little like Ethel Barrymore's when Miss Ethel is speaking very nicely," suggesting that Miss E. did not always do so. Shaw did not think very much of Ethel's acting, writing to Terry (January 29, 1898), "Your Tabers and Rockmans and Julia Arthurs and Barrymores are all very well; but you don't catch [George] Alexander and [Herbert Beerbohm] Tree and

Co depending on them." Terry defended Irving's policy on January 31: "Each one of them comes to us for less money than the rest of the Managers would have given them." The Terry-Shaw exchange about Laurence's engagement to Euphrosine took place on January 13, 1898. Though Ethel was too timid to knock on Shaw's door with a letter of introduction she felt brave enough after her great social success to walk up to him one night at the Haymarket and introduce herself: *Memories*. Laurence Irving, Henry Irving's grandson, in *Henry Irving: The Actor and His World* (London: Faber and Faber, 1951) claims that Ethel's engagement at the Lyceum was all Terry's and Laurence Irving's doing: "Aided and abetted by Ellen Terry, Laurence, who had joined the company, persuaded him [Irving] not only to cast Ethel Barrymore for Euphrosine in *Peter the Great*, but to take her on tour to play the burgomaster's daughter in *The Bells*; thus, encouraged by her brother, Jack, who was at Cambridge [*sic*], he was able to conduct his wooing and the rehearsals of his play at the same time." But Irving would not have hired an incompetent actress under any circumstances.

John himself says almost nothing about his years in England, excusing himself in "Those Incredible Barrymores" by saying that he remembered Ethel's and Lionel's triumphs but had forgotten his own. Margaret Webster's *The Same Only Different* provides delightful glimpses of him; both Kotsilibas-Davis and Kobler fill in some of the gaps, though not the source of John's having affairs with a duchess and an actress which, though hardly improbable, must be classified as legend.

Since Lionel's account of his early stage career is sketchy at best, I cannot express too strongly my gratitude to the late George C. Pratt, formerly of the George Eastman House in Rochester, New York, who provided me with several hundred pages of notes of Barrymore plays and itineraries compiled from the New York *Dramatic Mirror* and other contemporary sources.

Lionel joined Georgia Cayvan's company in September 1896, when she played *Mary Pennington, Spinster* and *Squire Kate* in the East, then opened at Palmer's in New York on October 5, 1896, in *Mary Pennington*, followed on October 19 by *Squire Kate*. In 1897 Lionel toured with her company into June, when she disbanded for the summer, pronouncing the tour "highly successful."

The McKee Rankin–Nance O'Neil season of summer repertory in Minneapolis and St. Paul offered an unusual number of plays: *East Lynne, Oliver Twist, Camille, The Counsel for the Defense, The Arabian Nights, The Private Secretary, Leah the Forsaken, A Wife's Peril, The Danites,* and *Magda*. It is uncertain in just how many of these Lionel acted. Nance O'Neil then took *Camille, Leah,* and *Magda* on tour with Lionel in the cast, which, however, he quit for an engagement with Sol Smith Russell for a September 1898–April 1899 tour of *Uncle Dick* and *The Honorable John Grigsby*.

Many companies toured with Thomas's immensely popular *Arizona*; Lionel's company opened in June 1899 at the Grand Opera House, toured extensively, then returned to Chicago in April 1900. The role of Captain Hodgman had been played by the popular actor Arthur Byron, who often acted with John Drew at the Empire; Lionel had decidedly been promoted.

Other sources for Lionel's early career are Spencer Berger's collection of theatre programs, clippings in Locke and TCMCNY, John Perry's *James A. Herne: The American Ibsen* (Chicago: Nelson-Hall, 1978), and Eleanor Robson Belmont's *The Fabric of Memory* (New York: Farrar, Straus, & Cudahy, 1957).

It is interesting to speculate about what Ethel lived on from her return to New York at the end of August 1900 until *Jinks* opened in January 1901: the diamond brooch would fetch only so much. The first edition of *Captain Jinks of the Horse Marines* (New York: Doubleday, Page, 1902) has play photographs from the Garrick production as well as original costume sketches, inspired by *Godey's Lady's Book*, by Percy Anderson. The New York *Dramatic Mirror* reported that the play was only "fairly well received" in Philadelphia; no wonder Ethel tried to persuade Frohman not to bring it to New York. Despite its overwhelming success there, Ethel might read in the February 9 *Dramatic Mirror* that "Ethel Barrymore, to be perfectly candid, played Madame Trentoni not better than probably some score or more of young actresses presently rated as ordinary could have played the role." Obviously the public paid no attention at all to the critics. Other sources for *Jinks* include John's "Those Incredible Barrymores: Blame It on the Queen," Kotsilibas-Davis, Marcossan and Frohman, John Drew's *My Years on the Stage*, and *Memories*. There has been some confusion about a *Jinks* review that Ethel quoted in *Memories* that ends, "Lucky people. Lucky public to have Miss Ethel Barrymore . . . for New York is at your feet! Dear Ethel! Dear Miss Barrymore. Dearest Miss Ethel Barrymore—newest princess of our footlit realm." While accurate in spirit, this paean was written by the actress Ruth Gordon for Ethel's seventieth-birthday radio tribute. The twenty-one-year-old Wallace Stevens's rhapsodies are quoted from Holly Stevens, *Souvenirs and Prophecies: The Young Wallace Stevens* (New York: Knopf, 1977). Some sources say that her brother John was with Ethel when she first saw her name in lights and wept, but Ethel in a 1906 magazine interview said it was her maid, and that source seems more reliable than later ones.

CHAPTER SIX: 1901—1902

Much information about Ethel in this chapter comes from news stories from January 1901 to September 1902 in Locke. Other sources include Ethel Barrymore, "My Stage Life Up to Date," *Metropolitan Magazine* (June 1901), "Ethel Barrymore's Stage Views," *Theatre* (October 1901), Gustave Kobbé, "The Girlishness of Ethel Barrymore," *Ladies' Home Journal* (June 1903), and "Ethel Barrymore: The American Girl and Women's Emancipation," in Albert Auster, *Actresses and Suffragists: Women in the American Theatre, 1890—1920* (New York: Praeger Publishers, 1984). In the nineties the American Protective Association and the Immigrant Restriction League were two organizations concerned with protecting the "lingering type of [Anglo] American" from "the alien element that surrounds us." The great showman Tony Pastor sensed this Anglo-Saxon trend, marketing Lillian Russell, who typified the "fresh, fair ideal of womanhood," as "the English Ballad Singer." Ethel was equally publicized as the ideal Anglo-American type of young woman, an image her frequent trips to England fortified. Ethel's "literary ambitions": It is surprising to find her stating in the Chicago *Chronicle* (January 19, 1902), "I am always writing plays." Not a scrap of this early writing survives, but perhaps her efforts indicate that, like John and Lionel, she also wanted to do something besides acting, even after her great success in *Jinks*. Ethel defended society in W. de Wagstaffe, "Ethel Barrymore—An Impression," *The Theatre* (November 1902).

For Maurice's deterioration and incarceration I have drawn on Kotsilibas-Davis as well as on the Robinson Locke Scrapbooks and current accounts in the New York *Dramatic Mirror*. It is interesting that Maurice had dropped his *Man of the World* vaudeville sketch for poetry recitation in the halls: W. S. Gilbert's "Etiquette," Miss Corey's "The Story of Two Clouds," and George R. Sims's "Told to the Missionary"; this was the program he was booked for at the Lion Palace the day of his breakdown. On May 4, 1901, the *Mirror* reported that "Ethel Barrymore frequently visits her father, Maurice Barrymore, at the Home for the Insane at Amityville, Long Island, and is a great source of comfort to him. Miss Barrymore fainted for the sixth time this season during the performance of *Captain Jinks of the Horse Marines* at the Garrick last Thursday."

Lionel recounts his adventures in "Running Water" and his hiring by Sam Shubert in *We Barrymores*. The Shubert Archives in the Lyceum Theatre, New York City, have scripts and production records of *The Brixton Burglary, The Copperhead*, etc., in which Lionel played. *We Barrymores* is also the source of Ethel's appealing to Frohman to hire Lionel for *The Mummy and the Hummingbird*. Lionel's statement that his ambition was to emulate Maurice comes from Lee Shubert's unpublished memoir, chapter 13 (Shubert Archives).

Ethel says in *Memories* that she met Winston Churchill in 1900, but they actually met at Dunrobin in 1901. Winston's attachment to Ethel was confirmed by Phyllis Moir, Churchill's one-time secretary, in a Washington interview reported in the Philadelphia *Inquirer* (June 24, 1943) and is also noted in Ted Morgan, *Churchill: Young Man in a Hurry, 1874—1915* (New York: Simon and Schuster, 1982), and in Ralph Martin, *Jennie: The Life of Lady Randolph Churchill*, vol. 2 (Englewood Cliffs, N. J.: Prentice-Hall, 1971). Frustratingly, Ethel destroyed all of Churchill's letters. The original run of *Jinks* was 168 performances; Ethel returned to the Garrick on September 16, 1901, for twenty-four additional performances, then toured until May 1902.

John's political drawings appeared in 1901 and 1902 in the New York *American*, the *Evening Journal, Cosmopolitan*, and the Sunday *Herald*. In the *Herald*, Jack satirizes the Food Trust as the Minotaur who threatens the Thesean trust-buster set to slay it. He also satirized *Ignorance* as a hideous giant and *Drink* as a human head riddled with wormy holes. John recalled his early bohemianism in "Barrymore's Adventures When He Was Down and Out," in the *New York Times* (October 5, 1913), incorporating them later in *Confessions*. Ethel M. Kremer in 1940 shared with Spencer Berger her impressions of John in Carl Strunz's art class. John's amusingly disgraceful performance in *Jinks* (*Memories, Confessions*) took place during the October 21–26, 1901, Philadelphia run when he substituted for George Howard as Charles La Martine. John's Press Artists League scholarship was announced in the *Dramatic Mirror* (December 14, 1901).

Evelyn Nesbit herself discusses her involvement with John in *Prodigal Days* (New York: Julian Messner, 1934). "The girls think he's good-looking today," said Evelyn. "They should have seen him then when he was about twenty-two! He possessed an effervescent originality and a Villonesque charm that was like nothing and nobody else." Cecil B. DeMille, whose mother ran the girls' school at Pompton, New Jersey, mentions John's notes to Evelyn in *Autobiography* (Englewood Cliffs, N. J.: Prentice-Hall, 1959).

The murder-suicide that led to John's being fired from the *Evening Journal* occurred when the talented young writer Paul Leicester Ford was shot to death by his jealous brother Malcolm, who then blew his own brains out. John's various employments are described in "Those Incredible Barrymores" and *Confessions*. Ethel's letter to Finley Peter Dunne [n.d.] is in the Manuscript Collection of the Library of Congress, a valuable testimony, since so few of her letters survive, to her constant concern for John.

Lionel's triumph in *The Mummy and the Hummingbird* is described in *We Barrymores, Memories*, and clippings in Locke. Lionel uncharacteristically quoted in *We Barrymores* the very favorable New York *Daily Tribune* review of September 5, 1902. Critics praised him for being able to convey the passion of Giuseppe without exaggerating the role. Ethel, it was reported, applauded Lionel's entrance vigorously (despite Mummum's dictum) and sobbed intermittently throughout his affecting performance. There is another view of Lionel's performance, however, from Frohman himself. Inspired by the uncle-nephew combination, Augustus Thomas wrote *The Pug and the Parson* (later *The Other Girl*) for John Drew and Lionel, but Frohman would not let Drew play the parson because, as in *The Mummy and the Hummingbird*, Lionel would be judged the better actor whereas he only had the showier part, according to Thomas's *The Print of My Remembrance*.

CHAPTER SEVEN: 1902—1905

Maurice's incarceration at Amityville is described in Kotsilibas-Davis as well as reported in the papers of the day and in Augustus Thomas's *The Print of My Remembrance*.

Ethel's apartment on West Fifty-ninth Street is described by W. de Wagstaffe in "Ethel Barrymore—An Impression" and in *Memories*. In December 1904 she moved again, to a house at 94 Park Avenue in the good Murray Hill district, furnishing it with heavy red velvet and oak furniture, black bearskins, and red carpets.

Poil de Carotte, an extremely popular play on which *Carrots* was based, had been presented for the first time in 1900 with Mme. Suzanne Després; by 1934 it had been played 2,706 times and by 1956 filmed three. Frohman avoided the classics: he did present Marlowe and Sothern in Shakespearean repertory in 1904 and 1905 as well as Maude Adams in *Romeo and Juliet* in 1899, but generally he preferred contemporary British plays.

Ashton Stevens recorded "That's you, plus Sargent" in *Actorviews* (Chicago: Covici-McGee, 1923). The Sargent drawing, which appeared on the cover of the *Ladies' Home Journal* (January 1904), was the most valuable item ($700) in Ethel's possession when she died.

Theodore Roosevelt's objection to Alice's pouring tea at a charity event for the Orthopedic Hospital is cited in James Brough's *Princess Alice: A Biography of Alice Roosevelt Longworth* (Boston: Little, Brown, 1972). Wired T.R.: DO NOT LIKE THE ADVERTISEMENTS OF YOUR APPEARING AT PORTRAIT SHOW. THEY DISTINCTLY CONVEY THE IMPRESSION THAT ANY PERSON WHO WISHES TO PAY HIS FIVE DOLLARS MAY BE SERVED WITH TEA BY YOU AND ETHEL BARRYMORE.

Sources for Ethel's 1903 English summer are *Memories* and clippings in Locke and TCMCNY. Ethel does not mention that she was the chief bridesmaid at the wedding of Anthony Hope and Betty Sheldon on July 1—Anthony Hope, who confided to the Duchess of Sutherland, "I should like to marry Ethel myself, if I could make time": Sir Charles Edward Mallet, *Anthony Hope and His Books* (London: Hutchinson, 1935).

John is amusing in *Confessions* about his Chicago fiasco with the Rankin-O'Neil company. "There is no more devastating tragedy than to be awfully bad at a job," he said later, "and still not be able to do anything about it"; but John was still taking acting lightly at the time.

Lionel vented his view of the Great Actor as sublime egoist to Ashton Stevens in the San Francisco *Examiner* (April 16, 1905). His "I'm not as clever as my brother Jack" is from the same interview.

John's "Corse Payton Defying the Drama" has evidently disappeared. Payton was a boozing companion who billed himself as "the world's best worst actor" and was as perennially short of funds as John.

Glad of It, really four skits strung together instead of a play, was something of a family affair, with Georgie Drew Mendum and Phyllis Rankin in the cast.

"The Barrymore Curse" was much publicized. For example, the *American Journal Examiner* (February 12, 1905) featured a sensationalized story about Ethel fainting as the last-act curtain fell on *Sunday*: "alarming cough . . . mother's consumption feared or father's nervous prostration," etc. Actually Ethel did faint a good deal, a result probably of her strenuous professional and social life, or tight corset lacing.

Ethel is frank about *Cynthia*'s London failure in *Memories* and told the story of Churchill's "Oh, my poor darling!" to friends. Churchill also appeared every night after the theatre at the Savoy where Ethel could be found surrounded by admirers. Captain Harry Graham's *Misrepresentative Men* was published in 1904 (New York: Fox, Duffield) with Ethel's photograph as a frontispiece. He also produced *Ruthless Rhymes for Heartless Homes, Etc.* Neither volume convinces the modern reader that he was, as Ethel thought, brilliant. *Memories* is the source for the Irish holiday and the exchange with Henry Irving at the Colonial Theatre.

Sunday was that strange hybrid, an American western written by four English actors under the nom de plume Thomas Raceward. Not surprisingly, critics were astringent about the play's "failure to catch the American atmosphere or to draw plausible American characters." *Life* concluded its review, "It's very remarkable that an American manager could have thought this piece suitable for American audiences, and in this case full credit must be given to Ethel Barrymore for helping both author and manager out of a good opportunity for a failure." At least one source hints that Ethel did not invent "That's all there is, there isn't any more": we choose to believe her statement in *Memories* that she did. Alan Dale in an interview of February 12, 1905, quotes Ethel as saying "I'll make you cry yet." Her February 1905 letter to Clyde Fitch is printed in Montrose J. Moses and Virginia Gerson, *Clyde Fitch and His Letters* (Boston: Little, Brown, 1924).

Kotsilibas-Davis describes Maurice Barrymore's death as do contemporary notices such as that in the *Dramatic Mirror* (April 1, 1905). Cornelia Otis Skinner quoted Joseph Jefferson's judgment of Maurice's Captain Absolute in "The Radiant Ethel Barrymore." John describes his return to 140 North Twelfth Street in *Confessions*.

Lionel talks about his aversion to acting in *We Barrymores*. His exit from *The Other Girl* company was widely reported. By the time Ethel wrote her autobiography, she had evidently forgotten that it was Lionel who persuaded her to do *A Doll's House*: "someone persuaded me . . ." Lionel claims it was he and Doris in *We Barrymores*.

John talked to Ashton Stevens about the audience as Monster in San Francisco in 1905. He reported his sensation of unity with the audience for the first time in *A Doll's House* in "Those Incredible Barrymores," though it is difficult to believe his claim, "From then on, I knew that my flesh was the theatre's flesh."

The Chicago *Record* (April 28, 1905) said that Nora Helmer had revealed Ethel "a thorough artist." In New York the *Evening Post*'s critic was among those who found her out of her depth. The "Open Letter to Miss Ethel Barrymore"—unidentified clipping: Locke.

CHAPTER EIGHT: 1905–1909

The Barrie-Frohman-Adams collaboration is discussed in Phyllis Robbins, *Maude Adams: An Intimate Biography*, Denis Mackail, *Barrie: The Story of J.M.B.* (New York: Charles Scribner's Sons, 1941), Janet Dunbar, *J. M. Barrie: The Man Behind the Image* (Boston: Houghton Mifflin, 1970), Marcossan and Frohman, *Charles Frohman: Manager and Man*, and Andrew Birkin, with Sharon Goode, *J. M. Barrie and the Lost Boys: The Love Story That Gave Birth to Peter Pan* (London: Constable, 1979). The original Peter Pan in London was Nina Boucicault. *Alice-Sit-by-the-Fire* with Ellen Terry and the popular Irene Vanbrugh as Amy was a moderate success in London where it ran 114 performances. Ethel's "the mother thing" in *Memories*; Marcossan and Frohman say, however, that Ethel wanted the mother part from the beginning, just one more of the eternal Barrymore contradictions. Ethel describes Frohman and Barrie at the Savoy in *Memories*. She misdates the cricket weekend in *Memories* as 1904; Mackail and Birkin correct her. *The Dictator* played at the Comedy in London from May 3 to July 15 to great enthusiasm, with John Barrymore listed first among Collier's gifted supporters. "I was so in love with her!": Churchill retrospectively in *Newsweek* (June 29, 1959). Winston Churchill's brother Jack, himself in love with Lady Gwendolyn Townley, wrote to Winston on November 14, 1907: Randolph

S. Churchill, *Winston S. Churchill*, Vol. 2, *Companion: 1907—1911* (London: Heinemann, 1969).

Ethel appeared on the cover of *The Theatre* (August 1905) announcing, typically, both her forthcoming appearance in *Alice-Sit-by-the-Fire* and her engagement to Captain Harry Graham. Ethel's arrival in New York with an engagement ring was reported widely; I quote from the Chicago *Record Herald* (September 8, 1905).

"Nothing but praise for her fellow actors": for example, Ethel was warmly enthusiastic about Maude Adams's Juliet in 1899, and laudatory of Maxine Elliott's beauty. In 1908, however, she allowed herself a hit at an old rival, Mrs. Patrick Campbell: "Olga Nethersole was a 1000 times better Mrs. Tanqueray than Mrs. Pat. How Mrs. Pat will love me": New York *Herald* (January 12, 1905).

There is no doubt that the three Barrymores were a hit at the Criterion despite demurs that Ethel was too young to be convincing as Alice Grey, although the *Tribune* attacked Barrie's play as "often insipid, never strong, has no character, no action, no dramatic effect"—far too severe a judgment considering the quality of current Broadway fare. When Ethel took *Alice* on the road, however, she got panned at least in the Toledo *Blade*: "Ethel can no more play *Alice-Sit-by-the-Fire* than she can play Lady Macbeth. Her personality, magnetism, and youthful beauty blind one to the fact that she loses the essence of the play."

Ethel and John played *Miss Civilization*, an amusing piece about a young girl who surprises a gang of burglars (John is one) in her dining room and outwits them, at the Broadway Theatre January 26, 1906, and again at the Palace Theatre April 23, 1913. The *Dramatic Mirror* interview was published March 10, 1906. The incident of James Kearney finding John drunk is reported in Kobler's *Damned in Paradise*.

Ethel on Lionel's nervous terror is in *Memories*, Lionel's wanting out of the tour is in *We Barrymores*. Neither dates the crisis; however, all three Barrymores were at Powers' Theatre in Chicago with *Alice* and *Pantaloon* beginning March 16, 1906, and on March 31 the *Dramatic Mirror* announced Lionel secluded on Long Island with pneumonia, indicating that he left the tour late in March, perhaps shortly before March 22, when Ethel was reported as breaking down under a nervous attack on account of Lionel's illness. Since Lionel was *not* ill, she broke down (if at all) on account of his leaving the tour. As for John's leaving the tour, he has said that Ethel's appendectomy was the reason; actually, however, he was hired by Collier in March before her attack: *Dramatic Mirror* (March 31, 1906). "Sidney Drew will replace John Barrymore with Miss Barrymore," wrote an unidentified tour manager to Frohman. "I rehearsed him here last week—he promises to be excellent [as] the Clown": Seymour Theatre Collection, Princeton University Library.

I have drawn on John's *Confessions* and Kobler for the earthquake and Jack's Australian tour with Collier. A delightfully illustrated letter from John to the actress Lulu Glaser (n.d. but written during a Powers' Theatre engagement in Chicago with Collier) indicates what Collier had to put up with: Jack draws himself flying for the stage door in pajamas while a furious stage manager shakes his watch at him, and John tells Lulu that he only woke up in time for the matinee by sheerest chance: Seymour Theatre Collection, Princeton University Library. Ashton Stevens described John's physical beauty (teeth "like deep water gems") in an interview of February 4, 1905: Locke.

For Harry Thaw's murder of Stanford White I have drawn on Evelyn Nesbit's *Prodigal Days*, Kobler, and Gerald Langford's *The Murder of Stanford White* (Indianapolis: Bobbs-Merrill, 1962) from which the trial testimony is quoted. Newspaper accounts of February 3 and 9, 1907, have John "at Poland Spring by doctor's advice" (though on February 4 he played a special matinee of *A Doll's House* in Boston with Ethel); of course he was avoiding the trial publicity.

Daniel Frohman (at least) recognized that *The Silver Box* changed Ethel's career by proving she could play serious parts; so also did a few critics like the New York *Telegraph*'s, who said, "She was not just Ethel Barrymore, she was the character the author's lines called for."

"I hate New York critics": interview in the New York *Herald* (January 1908). "Society and I have nothing in common": a February 2, 1908, interview in the *Morning Telegraph*, whose reporter, it should be noted, found her living in still another place: she had given up her Murray Hill house for an apartment over a small shop on West Fortieth Street facing Bryant Park. Burns Mantle criticized Ethel's "extremism" in the Chicago *Tribune* (February 9, 1908).

Amy Leslie criticized John's performance in *The Boys of Company B* in the Chicago *Daily News* (July 20, 1907), retracted her criticism in an interview of August 10. "You see," said John on that occasion, "by some mistake, Lionel has industry; no Barrymore on earth ever had that before." Lionel always denied he had any industry. Of Lionel John also said in a Chicago interview of August 24, 1907, "I wish I were as good a character actor as my brother; I'd like nothing better."

The "Two Bare Feet" review is from the Chicago *Tribune*, which grudgingly admitted, "I suppose [*Toddles*] fixes Jack Barrymore's status as a comedian." "A pronounced personal success" was the verdict of the Cincinnati *Time Star* (March 21, 1908). John himself tells of his rescue by Mort Singer in *Confessions*. Ethel ran up a $180 phone bill having John's reviews transmitted to Grand Rapids on May 27, 1907; she came from Milwaukee to see John in Chicago on May 15, 1908.

Ethel tells about chauffeuring George Baker to Tuxedo Park in *Memories*, as she does the encounter with Russell Colt at Sherry's, her engagement, and marriage. I am indebted to George Howe's account of the Colts, Howes, and DeWolfs in *Mount Hope: A New England Chronicle* (New York: Viking, 1959) as well as to George Howe's niece Evelyn Payson for talking about the Colts and Linden Place. Ethel's outburst against millionaires' sons appeared in the Chicago *Journal* (October 1, 1908); her denial ("I never gave such an interview") in the St. Louis *Republic* the next day. Cornelia Otis Skinner in "The Radiant Ethel Barrymore" has Ethel saying apropos of her "Never, never will I marry a millionaire's son," "What *lady* wrote that?" She had not forgiven the St. Louis reporter. Skinner also says in her excellent article that Ethel had no idea that Russell Colt was even moderately well off, hard to believe since Ethel had been acquainted with the status of the Colt family for almost five years. For her marriage to Colt I have relied on Boston *Chronicle* articles of March 10, 13, 14, and 16, 1909, and the New York *Telegraph* (April 7, 1909). I have also used information from the Columbus *Dispatch Magazine* (November 15, 1914), which profiled Russell Colt for its series "Little Known Husbands of Well-Known Wives."

CHAPTER NINE: 1909–1912

Information about Lionel and Doris in Paris is meager indeed. Lionel discusses Paris in *We Barrymores*, but as usual concentrates on other people. Afterward he would warn interviewers, "Don't ask about Paris!" Apparently he saw a good deal of theatre there, belying his dislike of it. Actually he made one brief return to the States on September 3, 1907. Ethel met the *Bremen* at the Hoboken pier, astonished at her brother's "positively aldermanic girth." Reportedly he brought some of his paintings (if so, contradicting his statement in *We Barrymores* that he wiped out his canvas every Friday), evidently to prove he was really working; at any rate he sailed again on October 4 with Ethel's "blessing and [financial] support."

Information about Lionel and Doris's daughters is almost nonexistent. Answering a questionnaire submitted by the theatre and film historian Daniel Blum in the 1950s (WCFTR), Lionel said he had two daughters, Mary and Ethel, who died at age two and in infancy. I have been able to uncover only a news story about little Ethel's illness (Locke) and the certificate of her death on March 24, 1910, from the Department of Records and Information Services, New York City. Mary's birth and death are not on record in Manhattan, or in Rocky Point, Suffolk County, Long Island, or, apparently, despite my colleague Professor Gabriel Merle's efforts to uncover birth and death certificates, in Paris. Presumably we can trust Lionel's statement on Blum's questionnaire, yet when he and Doris divorced in 1922 at least two newspapers stated that *Doris received the custody of the only child*. Add to this Lionel's nephew John's statement that Lionel's daughter died in the flu epidemic of 1917–1918 and one can hardly consider the mystery solved—though it seems almost impossible that in the twentieth century a child can simply be missing. Doris Rankin Barrymore, who eventually remarried, never spoke publicly about her children to my knowledge.

After the run of the "fresh, wholesome" comedy *The Fortune Hunter* at the Gaiety, the play toured from September 1910 to June 10, 1911—the longest run John ever forced himself to endure. Mary Ryan played Bette Graham, the druggist's daughter whom the fortune-hunting Nat Duncan finally prefers to the wealthy girl. "Oh, Uncle John" reported retrospectively in the Philadelphia *Evening Bulletin* (January 31, 1933).

Ethel tells of her first pregnancy and the birth and baptism of Samuel Colt in *Memories*. Russell Colt has no part in this account except that, significantly, after saying how safe Dr. Danforth made her feel, she follows with an ostensible non sequitur about Russell's irresponsibility at his job. Ethel made frequent public statements about the importance to her of a family. The eleven-pound Master Colt was reported in the *Telegraph* of December 14, 1909. Ethel's "Well, here *I* am" is quoted in the *New York Times* (February 21, 1915). Her best work after the birth of her son: David Gray, "Ethel Barrymore's Little Son," *Ladies' Home Journal* (April 1, 1911.)

The Fires of Fate opened at the Illinois Theatre, Chicago, December 6, 1909. On December 26, Lionel was reported "suffering"; shortly after he left the production. Staying with Ethel, he was reportedly "writing a libretto for a musical comedy dealing with life in the Latin Quarter"—still another attempt at escape.

Mid-Channel with Edward Arnold (known best as a film "heavy") ran at the Empire into April 1910, the road tour beginning April 25. During the New York run in February, Ethel was reported "seriously ill" and taking strychnine to keep going, "risking death to perform." While this is undoubtedly exaggeration, Ethel had an amazing number of attacks and illnesses for a healthy woman who always boasted that nothing kept her off the stage. "As Zoe Blundell she had a triumph": Marcossan and Frohman, *Charles Frohman: Manager and Man*. Ethel's three rules for an actress quoted in the *New York Times* (December 7, 1913).

Russell Colt's scuffle at the Hotel Knickerbocker was reported in the New York *Telegraph* (June 24, 1910). "Felt Russell's fists herself": in her deposition against Colt in 1921, Ethel stated that Colt had begun beating her six months after their marriage. Ethel rhapsodizes about the Mamaroneck house at the end of Taylor's Lane in *Memories*.

John's joining the "Seats for Women" movement is reported in the New York *Telegraph* (October 3, 1909). Discussing the women in John's life is extremely precarious: with the exception of Evelyn Nesbit, many of the women with whom the press connected him were probably "showcase" affairs, John's real sexual-emotional interests being elsewhere. Frederick L. Collins in "The Loves of John Barrymore," *Liberty* (September 19–November 7, 1936), names all the women I mention and more; Collins evidently got his information from Evelyn Nesbit's *Prodigal Days*, early newspaper accounts, Elsie Janis's "Jack of All Maids," *Liberty* (March 2, 1929), and the series in *American Magazine*, "Those Incredible Barrymores." Much of this, it should be stressed, is outside information, even speculation. According to Gene Fowler, John "concealed from me little if any of the tragic thread that was woven into the golden cloak of his genius," including a relationship with a woman that was more a psychological case history than an affair. Writing about this "grim saga" to Dr. Harold Thomas Hyman on January 13, 1944, Fowler still did not reveal the name of the woman; his letter, edited, is included in his son Will Fowler's *The Young Man from Denver* (Garden City, N.Y.: Doubleday, 1962). Will Fowler in a letter to Margot Peters says that the woman was Irene Frizzelle. No one, however, except the late Gene Fowler knows the details of this "sensational" affair, a fact which underlines the fragility of outsiders like Frederick Collins's account of John Barrymore's love life.

Since John was playing in *The Fortune Hunter* when he married Katherine Harris, some thought he was playing the role in real life. Katherine's grandmother was Gabbie Lydig Brady, wife of a New York Supreme Court judge. Katherine's mother Kitty had inherited half a million from a rich uncle, Charles Daly; Kitty's sister May was Mrs. Herbert Harriman, who had previously married into the wealthy Stevens family, occupiers for generations of the feudal Stevens castle on the west bank of the Hudson. Gabbie Lydig Brady's letter to Katherine is quoted from the Frederick L. Collins article. It is said that May Harriman punished Gabbie for her support of John by withdrawing the handsome income she had previously settled upon her. Gene Fowler discusses John's first marriage as though from firsthand information in *Good Night, Sweet Prince*, including John's dismissing Katherine as "the Mental Giantess."

Ethel's marital problems erupted in the story "Tears Hide Tale of Quarrel for Miss Barrymore," New York *Telegram* (November 16, 1910). The press followed the divorce story avidly, but had to admit defeat on August 14, 1911, when both Ethel and Russell denied everything at Mamaroneck. A few days later on August 27, Ethel, Russell, and Sammy "narrowly missed death" in an auto accident returning from a Colt luncheon and tea in honor of Miss Primrose Colt's engagement, another testimony of reconciliation.

It is difficult to assess Georgie Drew Mendum's talent, but from all contemporary accounts she had a great deal. Her career is discussed briefly in "Unto the Fourth Generation of Players," *The Theatre* (August 1915); she made a considerable success in many plays, including *The Girl Question* and *A Modern Eve*. When she died at the age of eighty-two of arteriosclerosis on July 30, 1957, an obituary repeated that "Miss Mendum was said to have excelled any of her illustrious family as a comedienne." Under the circumstances, it is odd that Charles Frohman did not take her into his organization as he had done her comedienne aunt, Georgie Drew Barrymore; evidently he thought she lacked star quality.

After *Peter Pan*, *The Twelve Pound Look* was Frohman's favorite Barrie play because he thought it summed up all human tragedy. Barrie wrote the one-act in Switzerland during his impending divorce, probably portraying himself autobiographically as the unsatisfactory husband, Harry Sims, whose wife (Mary Barrie) leaves him. Ethel's carrying off the year's acting honors (as she had the previous year) is the opinion of the *Green Book* (August 1911). Frohman's letter to Barrie of early February 1912 about *A Slice of Life* is printed in J. A. Hammerton's *Barrie: The Story of a Genius* (London: Sampson Low, Marston, 1929). In London Irene Vanbrugh, Gerald du Maurier, and Cissie Loftus played Ethel's, John's, and Hattie Williams's roles.

I am grateful to Spencer Berger for illuminating John's not very well known dramatic activities during the summer of 1912. Beginning July 1, Oliver Morosco engaged John for five weeks at the Belasco Theatre in Los Angeles, James Neill directing. Katherine replaced Bessie Barriscale as Phoebe Ridgeway in *On the Quiet* during the second week of its run, acting under the name Katherine Blythe. With effort, Katherine might have made quite a success on the stage; the *Dramatic Mirror* (August 27, 1913), for example, called her "very good." During his Los Angeles stay John gave the *Examiner* an interview about the great future of the automobile in that city, direly prophetic.

John's "What the hell has happened?" is reported in Fowler. Will Fowler in *The Young Man from Denver* reports his father as saying that John Barrymore was exactly the opposite of a great man with the ladies. Gene Fowler described John's bedroom scream to Spencer Berger as "a banshee screech." Mercedes de Acosta analyzed John's conflicts in *Here Lies the Heart* (New York: Reynal, 1960). "Jack Barrymore Manages to Lick Someone at Last" is in the New York *Review* (August 2, 1912); the barber sued for $1,550. Sarah Bernhardt called acting "feminine" in her *Memories of My Life* (New York: D. Appleton, 1907). The feminizing of the American stage—or "civilizing of the theatre," as some called it—is revealed in statistics: from 1870 to 1880 the number of actresses rose from 780 to 4,652; from 1890 to 1910 from 4,652 to 15,463. This feminizing is also discussed in Henry Tyrell, "Mary Shaw—A Woman of Thought and Action," *The Theatre* (August 1902), and in Albert Auster, *Actresses and Suffragists: Women in the American Theatre, 1890–1920*. In England, where this feminization had also taken place, a misogynist like the stage designer Gordon Craig looked upon it as a disaster and said the theatre could only recover its greatness by expelling all women from the profession.

Lionel's seasons in vaudeville with Doris and Sidney Drew's family are reported in the *Dramatic Mirror* and *Variety*. His salary is quoted from an article in *Variety* (January 8, 1941) listing some 1910 vaudeville earnings; $500 was the least paid, with a star like Yvette Guilbert earning a top salary of $4,000 a week. "Do Motion Pictures Mean the Death of the Drama?" in *The Theatre* (December 1915) is a typical discussion of the threat from movies. Daniel Frohman on the stage is quoted in Garff B. Wilson, *Three Hundred Years of American Drama and Theatre: From Ye Bear and Ye Cubb to Hair* (Englewood Cliffs, N.J.: Prentice-Hall, 1973). Lionel discusses his capitulation to films in *We Barrymores*, Ethel to vaudeville in *Memories*. Lionel says that he visited D. W. Griffith's studio after *A Still Voice* (1912). Biograph Studio records show, however, that Lionel made *The Battle* in September 1911 while he was playing *Bob Acres* at the Orpheum in New York and that he continued to alternate film work and vaudeville throughout 1912.

CHAPTER TEN: 1912–1916

Lillian Gish and Mary Pickford on making money in the movies are reported in Gish, with Ann Pinchot, *The Movies, Mr. Griffith, and Me* (Englewood Cliffs, N.J.: Prentice-Hall, 1969); Frohman to Marie Doro in Marcossan and Frohman, *Charles Frohman: Manager and Man*. Mary Pickford talked about moviemaking with Lionel in "Personalities I Have Met," Chicago *Daily News* (September 13, 1916), and *Sunshine and Shadow* (Garden City, N.Y.: Doubleday, 1955). The D. W. Griffith papers are on microfilm at the Memorial Library of the University of Wisconsin-Madison, including Billy Bitzer's account of the beer bribe and a tribute to Griffith by Lionel. Bitzer also experimented in *The New York Hat* with cut-back and fade-out, discovering the latter by accident. I am grateful to Spencer Berger for loaning me his print of *The New York Hat*. Lionel's comforting Gish is reported in *The Movies, Mr. Griffith, and Me*.

Lionel discusses filming with Griffith in *We Barrymores*, but his statements must be checked against Cooper C. Graham et al., *D. W. Griffith and the Biograph Company*, Filmmakers No. 10 (Metuchen, N.J.: The Scarecrow Press, 1985), a project instigated and supervised by the late Jay Leyda of New York University. However, even though Graham et al. do not list him among the twenty-eight performers, Lionel can probably be believed when he says he played a number of small parts in *Judith of Bethulia*, Griffith's 1913 ground-breaking four-reeler. Though he did not go with Griffith to California, where much of *Judith* was filmed in desertlike Chatsworth Park north of Los Angeles, Griffith finished the film in New York, where Lionel evidently joined the company. Also informative on early film making is *The American Film Industry*, ed. Tino Balio (Madison: University of Wisconsin Press, 1985), particularly the section "Struggles for Control, 1908–1930." Biograph, a studio which relied on story first, direction second, and competent actors as a class (not individuals) third, capitulated in 1913 when it revealed the identities of leading Biograph players in the New York *Dramatic Mirror* for the first time. Raoul Walsh reported Lionel's sneaking in Biograph's back door in *Each Man in His Time* (New York: Farrar, Straus and Giroux, 1974).

Ethel talks about her vaudeville experiences in *Memories*. "Has your own true wife that Twelve-Pound Look?" Ethel challenged American men in the New York *Mail* (August 21, 1914). "Don't think me gushing": Zoe Beckley, "Has Your Own True Wife That Twelve-Pound Look? Try Dr. Barrie's Remedy," New York *Mail* (August 26, 1914). Alan Dale praised Ethel in "The Most Interesting People of the Theatre, No. 1: Ethel Barrymore," *Green Book* (December 1915).

Ethel's statements about motherhood appeared in the New York *American* (March 7, 1913), the Toledo *News Bee* (March 13, 1913), the *Green Book* (April 1913), *Harper's Bazaar* (November 1913), and the New York *Sun* (November 13, 1913). She herself reports calling Frohman two hours after her third child was born in *Memories*, the source also of the theatre as a "blessed sanctuary."

Written for Ethel by C. Haddon Chambers, *Tante* was based on the novel of the same name by Anne Douglas Sedgwick; the popular Charles Cherry was Ethel's leading man. The play was a success: "Chambers will have many happy returns (box-office) of the season," said Frohman in December, "as Miss Barrymore is doing so well with his 'Tante.'" James Dale's wonderful description of Ethel as Tante comes from his memoir *Pulling Faces for a Living* (London: Victor Gollancz, 1970); I am grateful to Sir John Gielgud, who introduced me to this delightful book by loaning me his copy.

Ethel deposed that Russell struck her "in a New York hotel"; this was perhaps the Netherlands, to which she had moved Sammy and his French nurse because the house on Sixty-first Street that she had rented wasn't big enough for three children and their nurses. The hotel arrangement, she explained (she had always to explain), allowed her "to have all three children with me almost as much as if we all had been under one roof." Ethel on Sammy and Russell's "bronchitis" is in *Memories*. The first "symposium exhibition" of Kinemacolor's celebrities as they appear in private life was given in Kinemacolor's projection room October 20, 1913; photographs from the film later appeared in the press.

The press announced a year before Ethel signed with All Star that she would make a film with Famous Players; untrue, but perhaps an indication that she was thinking of motion pictures. Her first film with All Star was announced as *Captain Jinks*; she did not make it, perhaps because, as she wrote Eleanor Robson Belmont a few years later, "I'm afraid I don't look much like Captain Jinks anymore." Her per picture salary was variously reported as $10,000 and $15,000, which would have been a record sum. *The Nightingale* was filmed in Yonkers, Augustus Thomas directing. Advice to Ethel to "train down a bit" appeared on May 27, 1914. On August 28, 1913, the New York *Mail* reported that Ethel had lost seventy-five [*sic*] pounds in six weeks by swimming an hour a day, horseback riding, and drastically cutting down on food and sleep.

A Scrap of Paper, with Charles Dalton and Mary Boland, was offered for thirty-two performances as a tip of the hat by Frohman to nostalgia. Ethel described the summer of 1914 in *Memories*. Ashton Stevens quotes Ethel's wire about boxing in *Actorviews*. Frohman announced in July 1914 that Ethel's play for the fall would be Edward Sheldon's *The Bridge of Sighs*; instead Ethel played in vaudeville until December 21, when she started rehearsing *The Shadow* (*L'Ombra*) by Dario Niccodemi. Both Ethel's reactions to *The Shadow* and Sammy's were reported in an interview in the *New York Times* (February 21, 1915) titled "An Ancient Confusion Annoys Miss Barrymore"—the confusion being that an actress must live offstage what she acts onstage to play it well. Ethel all her life dismissed the notion as nonsense. Although Ethel made a stunning success in *The Shadow*, it lasted only seventy-two performances at the Empire, Lent (reported *Variety*) knocking the business out from under "the best notices any show had at the Empire this season." Ethel then took *The Shadow* on tour to Philadelphia, Boston, and Chicago, her three strongholds.

Sources for Frohman's last days and death include Marcossan and Frohman's *Charles Frohman, Memories*, John Drew's *My Years on the Stage*, and Andrew Birkin's *J. M. Barrie and the Lost Boys*. Rita Jolivet, the only one of the three with Frohman when the wave hit to survive, quoted him as saying, "To die will be an awfully big adventure." Edna Ferber's secondhand version is "Don't be afraid of death. It's the most wonderful experience in life": *A Peculiar Treasure* (New York: Lancer Books, 1960; orig. pub. 1938). Barrie, however, had more faith in Frohman's memory of his favorite play: "His last words . . . were really, I feel sure," he wrote Pauline Chase who had played Peter, " 'Death will be an awfully big adventure,' " quoted in Birkin. Birkin says that Ethel sent Frohman a last-minute cable begging him not to sail, on what evidence is uncertain. While he may have been fonder of Ethel, there is little question that Frohman's ideal actress was Maude Adams, of whose reclusiveness (which he created) he said, "Some people prefer mediocrity in the limelight to greatness in the dark." "For years he had been": *Memories*.

For the play about the woman who traveled for the T. A. Buck Featherloom Petticoat Company Edna Ferber collaborated with George V. Hobart. The stories originally appeared in the *American Magazine* (1913–14), then in *Cosmopolitan*; they made her reputation, though Ferber tired of writing them. On August 23, 1915, Ferber's friend Sallie Lindsay White wrote about Ferber's creating a play for Ethel: "Why you shd be so excited that you shd by rights be a great trial to yr family. At the thought of consulting, measuring, weighing words, phrases, emotions, situations, etc. with anything as grand as Ethel Barrymore": WCFTR. Ferber's illuminating description of Ethel is from *A Peculiar Treasure*. Ethel herself says that *Our Mrs. McChesney* was a great success everywhere except Chicago: "They preferred me there in serious plays": *Memories*. She talked about the play's inspiring her to go into business in the *Metropolitan* (January 1916) and about "almost acting herself" in the *American Magazine* (March 1916) as she had earlier in "Why I Want to Play Emma McChesney," *American Magazine* (November 1915).

"She believes in pictures": New York *Telegraph* (December 4, 1916). As early as 1913 Ethel had supposedly endorsed "the Talking Pictures," i.e. the new "kinetophone, Mr. Edison's invention for synchronizing the human voice with the motion picture."

It was the late George C. Pratt of the George Eastman House in Rochester, New York, who discovered reviews of three Lubin films with "Jack Barrymore"—*Dream of a Motion Picture Director, The Widow Casey's Return*, and *A Prize Package*—then a review of a fourth, a straggler released after the other three on April 14, 1913, *One on Romance*. Spencer Berger discusses the first three in "The Search for John Barrymore," *American Classic Screen*, Vol. 5 (1980). Linda Kowell and Joseph P. Eckhart, who in 1980 were trying to reconstruct the Lubin story, found two people who observed Barrymore at the Lubin studio, though they were not sure whether John was there to act or to visit friends. Spencer Berger has shared his correspondence with George Pratt with me, including a letter of

June 27, 1983, announcing the fourth Lubin with "Jack Barrymore" billed after Eleanor Caines and Frank DeVernon. Pratt believed that the Lubin Jack Barrymore is "the real thing. It seems to fit in with what we know about Barrymore's adventurous nature, and the lack of publicity is quite in key with the attitude of the stern and anxious stage producers of the time": letter to Berger, July 16, 1969. Kobler and James Kotsilibas-Davis in *The Barrymores: The Royal Family in Hollywood* (New York: Crown Publishers, 1981) discuss John's early picture career (not the Lubins, though Kotsilibas-Davis lists three of them as *a, b,* and *c* before *An American Citizen*). Joseph Garton in *The Film Acting of John Barrymore* (New York: Arno Press, 1980) treats the Lubins at some length. John's description of silent films as "making frantic and futile faces": "Those Incredible Barrymores: Lionel, Ethel and I," *American Magazine* (February 1933). J. Searle Dawley's comment on John as "the best" and John's antics at Famous Players come from Adolph Zukor, with Dale Kramer, *The Public Is Never Wrong* (New York: G. P. Putnam's Sons, 1953).

James Montgomery Flagg talks about his friendship with John and John's marriage to Katherine in *Roses and Buckshot* (New York: G. P. Putnam's Sons, 1946) and on Ethel's being the best company in the world next to John in *Celebrities* (Watkins Glen, N.Y.: Century House, 1960). Flagg was an enormously popular illustrator whose World War I poster of Uncle Sam pointing a finger at the unenlisted was perhaps his most famous work. Flagg did three portraits of John—as a young man about town, as Hamlet, and in Hollywood toward the end of his life—and a not very good painting of Ethel.

I am indebted to Eric Wollencott Barnes's biography of Ned Sheldon, *The Man Who Lived Twice* (New York: Charles Scribner's Sons, 1956). Sheldon's papers in the Special Collections of the Houghton Library, Harvard University, oddly enough do not include any correspondence from John, though Barnes quotes a number of letters. John's outstanding ability "to make *anyone* to whom he spoke or *listened*": Gene Fowler to Dr. Harold Thomas Hyman, quoted in Will Fowler's *The Young Man from Denver*. "And he knew that I was wise to this artful dodge," said Fowler. "Bored with summers of tennis, teas, and foxtrotting": John Ten Eyck wrote an account of John and Katherine at Spring Lake, New Jersey, early summer of 1914, published in the *Green Book* (January 1915). John sailed for Europe to meet Ned on the *Olympic* on June 26, 1914. Barnes gets much of his information about Ned and John in Italy in the summer of 1914 from Gene Fowler, *Good Night*, to which I am also indebted. That fall *Variety* announced John rehearsing for Charles Dillingham in Sheldon's *The Lonely Heart*; then on October 17 Dillingham was reported as having decided "not to present Jack Barrymore in *The Lonely Heart* for the present."

Jane Grey played the romantic lead opposite John in *Kick In*, while Katherine had the lesser part of Daisy. About the play the *Times* (October 20, 1914) said, ". . . a good melodrama, for it has suspense in abundance, it achieves a really stirring climax, and its humor is the robust humor that is compounded of extravagant slang and shrewd observation." *Kick In* moved to the Republic in December, then to the Manhattan Opera House in April 1915. Interestingly enough, John stated while acting in *Kick In* that he was dying to play Androcles in Bernard Shaw's comedy that had failed in London, *Androcles and the Lion: New York Times* (February 21, 1915).

I am indebted to Audrey Kupferberg, former director of the Yale Film Study Center, for loaning me Spencer Berger's print of John's first surviving film, *The Incorrigible Dukane*. *Variety* did not like it, saying on September 17, 1915, "Mr. Barrymore tries for too much comedy in the feature, overdoing it of course in that way. He attempts falls, does a 'funny walk,' and mixes in slapstick until Chaplin is constantly in mind. If there is anything at all much worth while in this film, it will be only Mr. Barrymore's name." Evaluating it in 1970, the distinguished film expert William K. Everson commented on *Dukane*'s harsh film quality and says that but for the film's rarity it is unexceptional, "though it's to

Barrymore's credit that his personality gets through at all." Given John's enormous popularity on the stage at that time and contemporary descriptions of his charm and good looks, I do not feel that his personality *does* get through.

Justice was first performed in London at the Duke of York's on February 21, 1910, with Dennis Eadie as Falder and a strong cast including Edith Olive, Charles Bryant, Edmund Gwenn, Dion Boucicault, Lewis Casson, and O. P. Heggie. Max Beerbohm, critic for the *Saturday Review*, called *Justice* "cinematographic" in a review collected in *Around Theatres* (New York: Simon and Schuster, 1954).

CHAPTER ELEVEN: 1916–1917

John told Gene Fowler that he stopped drinking for two years beginning probably in February or March 1916 with his decision to do *Justice*. Other witnesses to John's drinking the popular temperance beverage Bevo are Whitford Kane and Ashton Stevens. John's techniques for creating Falder are discussed in *Everybody's Magazine* (July 1916). "Acting—all you have to do": quoted in Flagg, *Roses and Buckshot*. Brooks Atkinson remembered John's performance in his introduction to Alma Power-Waters, *John Barrymore: The Legend and the Man*. Cathleen Nesbitt gives her impressions of John's performance in *A Little Love and Good Company* (London: Faber and Faber, 1975). During the New Haven tryout performance, John pounded at his cell door with such passion that the set collapsed, a mischance avoided in New York by sounder construction. The *New York Times* raved over *Justice* in two long reviews, *"Justice* as a Promise" and Alexander Woollcott's *"Justice*: Second Thoughts on First Nights," both calling the play a red-letter night in the theatre. Later Woollcott would describe *Justice* as the watershed between John's career as a young aimless comedian and his maturity as an actor: "The Two Barrymores," *Everybody's Magazine* (June 1920). Financially, *Justice* quickly developed into what *Variety* (April 14, 1916) called "a sensational success": $1,800 average per performance, $12,000 per week. John gave a special matinee on April 24 "primarily in honor of Minnie Maddern Fiske," the actress who more than anyone else pioneered modern realism in the theatre. Nesbitt is the source of John's playing games onstage and of John's mistaking a prisoner for a warder. Though both John and Nesbitt remembered *Justice* doing badly on the road, *Variety* reported it as "doing nicely" at about $10,000 a week in Chicago, where it opened October 16, 1916, and left about a month later. Whitford Kane credits the road cast for persuading John to take theatre more seriously in *Are We All Met?* (London: Elkin Mathews and Marrot, 1931).

Sheldon's *The Lonely Heart*, not a good play, never reached Broadway because the Shuberts did not want Basil Sydney, for whom Sheldon finished the play, to star and Sheldon refused a substitute.

For the staging of *Peter Ibbetson* I have drawn upon Constance Collier's *Harlequinade: The Story of My Life* (London: John Lane, The Bodley Head, 1929), Gene Fowler's *Good Night. We Barrymores*, and *Confessions*, and the very complete account of the business end of the play in the Shubert Archives. Shubert was not endlessly generous: a few nights before the scheduled opening Woods told Constance that there was no money for the two more scheduled dress rehearsals. In fact, they finished lighting the last act just half an hour before the first-night audience came in and had there been adequate dress rehearsals the opera scene would not have collapsed. Constance continually pleaded with Shubert: "I have enough money now to do it in a cheap way but that is no good at all. We must go for the big public in the best way and do the thing splendidly": Shubert Archives. Woollcott reviewed the play in the *New York Times* (April 22, 1917); the *Dramatic Mirror* also called

Lionel's colonel "a flawless characterization." While condemning the play's sentimentality in the *Green Book* (July 1917), Channing Pollock praised John's performance as "wonderfully true and comprehensive" and Lionel's as "ingeniously evil as Svengali, and more plausible," concluding, however, that *Peter Ibbetson* was "a fine and praiseworthy attempt to do something not quite doable." Heywood Broun in the New York *Tribune* agreed: "We lose patience with the adapter of 'Peter Ibbetson' on two grounds—he fails to make sufficiently adequate characterization of Peter and he imparts to the dream scenes an annoying, sirupy quality. . . . John Barrymore does not seem to us naturally suited for Peter": quoted in *The Literary Digest* (June 2, 1917). With tickets as high as four dollars and the house sold out nightly, *Ibbetson* was "the biggest theatrical draw in town": *Variety* (May 11, 1917). Woollcott on the chance of laughter ending John's career is quoted from the *New York Times* (March 21, 1920).

Michael Strange (Blanche Oelrichs Thomas) vividly describes her meeting with and impressions of John in *Who Tells Me True* (New York: Charles Scribner's Sons, 1940); other sources are Nesbitt and Kobler. The friend who observed Blanche and John at Lakewood was Blanche Shoemaker Wagstaff: letter of February 1940 to Spencer Berger.

Ethel refers briefly to "two of the most miserable weeks in my life" in *Memories* and to her war efforts at far greater length in the same source. *Variety* (December 1, 1916) and the *New York Times* (May 26, 1917) also reported her war activities.

The Red Cross Pageant, starring such stage notables as Tyrone Power Sr., Blanche Yurka, Ina Claire, and E. H. Sothern, was filmed in five reels by Christy Cabanne on October 5, 1917, at Rosemary Farm in Huntington, Long Island, as a fund-raiser (*American Film Institute Catalogue, Feature Films, 1911–1920*), with John playing a tyrant in a religious sequence and Ethel an unidentified country. (Lionel's part, typically, is not noted.) I am grateful to James Card, retired director of the film department at the George Eastman House, for bringing this apparently lost film to my attention.

Very few of Ethel's early movies survive. The Library of Congress Film Department has the first reel only of *The Awakening of Helena Ritchie*; the George Eastman House owns *The White Raven* and, purportedly, *The Call of Her People*, though the latter was missing in July 1988, and there is evidence that MGM (Turner Enterprises) has a library positive print of *The Final Judgment*. *Variety* (December 29, 1916) gave *Helena Ritchie* warm praise for unusually skillful narrative technique involving "fade-back," and "uniformly excellent" acting. Ethel considered Somerset Maugham's play *Our Betters* in 1917, the year she spent chiefly filming, but rejected it because, according to *Variety* (November 3), she didn't like it in its present form.

Ethel "would never bare her soul" to Ned Sheldon: she mentions him only once in *Memories*, and there is no other evidence that they were close, as there is, for example, for his friendships with Edith Wharton and Mrs. Patrick Campbell. I have drawn on Barnes for Sheldon's role in the Barrymore *Lady of the Camellias*. The dream version, invoked by prologue and epilogue, was not Sheldon's invention, however, having been devised by the actress Laura Keene in 1856. Ethel's script of *Camellias* was presented to the Billy Rose Memorial Theatre Collection by her grandson, John Drew Miglietta, along with her acting copies of *L'Aiglon*, *The Constant Wife*, *The Twelve Pound Look*, and *Whiteoaks*. "Camille to Be Her Greatest Effort" reported the New York *Telegraph* (August 12, 1917). The play ran for fifty-six performances, with Holbrook Blinn as Georges Duval, Charles Coghlan as Gustav, and Rose Coghlan as Madame Prudence. Ethel makes no mention of the critical reaction to her Marguerite in *Memories*, citing instead the accolades of good friends and her own, "I don't think I have ever played a part that I really loved so much." *Theatre Magazine* (February 1918) called her performance "creditable but not inspired." Sarah Bernhardt's note was quoted in the *New York Times* (January 12, 1918).

Motography (January 20, 1917) announced, "John Barrymore New Brenon Star," engaged to film *The Lone Wolf*, his first picture in nearly two years; John did not make the movie. Spencer Berger lent me his copy of *Raffles*. *Variety* gave the film raves on December 7, 1917. During these years there was considerable conflict between stage and screen: the movie *Raffles*, for example, was delayed release because a Broadway producer liked John so well in the film's preview that he wanted to revive the play with John in Kyrle Bellew's old role before the movie hit the screen. The deal fell through, but it was typical of competition for stories and stars between stage and screen.

Sources for the *Peter Ibbetson* tour include *Variety*; correspondence among Collier, John, Lionel, and Lee Shubert in the Shubert Archives; Collier's *Harlequinade*; Gene Fowler's *Good Night*; and Stevens's *Actorviews*. *Variety* (June 15, 1917) reported that *Ibbetson* would close the next day "for no other reason than the actors won't work any longer. . . . The Barrymore brothers claim their parts are too strenuous. . . ." When the play reopened at the Republic on September 3, it "hung up a record for a return to a New York house," drawing $11,000 a week. This is why Collier called the situation "desperate" (October 12 to Lee Shubert) when Shubert announced that he would send the play down to the 48th Street Theatre on October 27. "Aren't you sorry you haven't more Barrymores?": quoted by Woollcott in the New York *World* (October 26, 1925).

Exactly when John started drinking again is uncertain. Ashton Stevens during the Chicago *Ibbetson* run reports his abstinence, calling John "Bevo, former Barleycorn Barrymore." Constance Collier, however, says he came drunk to the theatre and, of anyone, she would know. That he resumed drinking in February or March 1918 is a good guess.

Lionel's letter to Shubert resigning from the *Ibbetson* tour was written from the Philadelphia Club: "I hope you understand how much I regret having to leave *Peter Ibbetson*. . . . I have been extremely happy . . . under your management and sincerely hope I may have the good fortune to be under it again": Shubert Archives. Shubert remembered his relations with all three Barrymores as pleasant, despite sudden storms that usually, however, could be immediately settled with a personal talk. Lionel's remarks about returning to the theatre were printed in *Vanity Fair* (January 1917).

CHAPTER TWELVE: 1918–1919

Augustus Thomas complained of Lionel's painstakingness in his Preface to *The Copperhead*, his four-act drama based on the novel *The Glory of His Country* by the Honorable Frederick Landis. Opening in New Haven on January 16, 1918, *The Copperhead* ran for 120 performances at the Shubert before it was sent on tour. Lee Shubert's unpublished memoir confirms that Ethel attended Lionel's opening night. Shubert also tells about John's attempting to buy out the *Peter Ibbetson* house, as does "Those Incredible Barrymores," *American Magazine* (March 1933). Rather incredibly, Lionel was not starred on the opening night of *The Copperhead*: at least one source quotes Thomas saying after the play to John D. Williams, "There is nothing to do about the fellow but to star him," to which Williams replied, "The people out front have already starred him, and I am changing the advertisements for tomorrow morning's papers": Locke.

Ethel praised Lionel in the New York *World* (May 20, 1918), P. G. Wodehouse in the April 1918 issue of *Vanity Fair*. The New York *Tribune* complained (March 21, 1918) about Lionel's obsession with privacy: "To interview Lionel Barrymore is one of the twelve tasks fit for a modern Hercules." "I'm glad everybody likes me in it" is quoted from *The New Republic* (March 30, 1918). Doris's comments appeared in *Theatre Magazine* (April 1918) as did Arthur Hornblow's complaints about the actors' poor diction. Both Wodehouse and Heywood Broun (Boston *Globe*, January 17, 1918) praised Doris's acting highly.

Though critics found "the laughs few and the dinginess rather overpowering" in *The Off Chance* that opened February 14, 1918, for ninety-two performances, *Vanity Fair* praised the cast and Ethel, who was "wonderful in a part that gives her no real help. Her playing is an object-lesson in what can be done by a clever woman with very little material" (April 1918). Eva Le Gallienne remembered Ethel's making something out of nothing in the *New York Times* (December 18, 1979) on the occasion of the fiftieth anniversary of the Ethel Barrymore Theatre. *Variety* (May 10, 1918) quoted the *World* on *Belinda*'s being hopelessly beneath Empire standards, but again said that "there is nothing for which to reproach Miss Barrymore." Ethel describes meeting Zoë Akins and reading *Déclassée* in *Memories*. *Variety* of August 23 and 30, 1918, praised *Our Mrs. McChesney*.

John's return to Famous Players–Lasky for *On the Quiet*, based on the 1901 farce-comedy by Augustus Thomas starring William Collier, was ballyhooed in *Motion Picture World* (June 1, 1918): "After a Successful Whirl on the Stage Actor Comes Back to First Screen Love." *Variety* gave John a rave review on August 30, 1918.

"The featuring of Katherine Harris-Barrymore by a picture concern," said *Variety* (August 9, 1918), "is reported to have caused considerable agitation among the Barrymores who object to the professional use of the family name"—an attitude quite consistent with their later protectiveness. Katherine appeared that fall in *The Big Chance* as Harris Barrymore, no hyphen. When she played Mrs. Leslie in *Déclassée* the following year, however, she was billed as Katherine Harris.

Gene Fowler describes John's fantastic apartment in *Good Night*. There are letters from John to Mrs. Nicholls in the Gene Fowler Collection, Special Collections, University of Colorado at Boulder Libraries. John also reminisced to Ruth Rankin about the Top Floor: "Jack the Bachelor," *Photoplay* (May 1934).

The *Times* (April 12, May 7, 1916) reported that John D. Williams had signed John Barrymore to a five-year contract with the stipulation that he not be starred; evidently Williams intended establishing a repertory group. The broken contract was announced in *Variety* (May 31, 1917). Although John did come to Hopkins, his motives were not entirely pure. He had been offered *Dear Brutus*, but was so sure that Barrie's play would run two years at the minimum that he chose Tolstoy instead. William Gillette played *Dear Brutus*, which was indeed popular, but then *Redemption* itself had a long run of 204 performances. John credited the adaptation of *Redemption* to Blanche in *Confessions*. Hopkins discusses *Redemption* at some length in *To a Lonely Boy* (New York: Doubleday, Doran, 1957), including John's misguided Russian-Jewish accent and Tolstoy *fils*'s reaction to the play. Cornelia Otis Skinner said that she could still see John's "incredibly tapering white hands" in the *New York Times* (February 13, 1944). Thomas Mitchell, who had the small part of Artemyev, told Spencer Berger about Lionel's surprise appearance in *Redemption*; Mitchell developed a lifelong admiration of John during the run of the play and became a close friend during John's last years in Hollywood. On February 13, 1919, Eugene O'Neill was still writing that his production of *Beyond the Horizon* was being held up by the unavailability of the Barrymore brothers. Eventually Richard Bennett and Edward Arnold played Robert and Andrew Mayo in a production which won overwhelmingly favorable reviews: Louis Sheaffer, *O'Neill: Son and Playwright* (Boston: Little, Brown, 1968).

Sidney Drew reminisced about his son and the bellhop to William Wellman, also a member of the Lafayette Escadrille, in *Good Night*. Sidney Rankin Drew was shot down over France on May 19, 1918. After the war, Lucille went to look for his grave, intending to honor it with an appropriate marker; finding a flower-covered stone marked SIDNEY RANKIN DREW, HERO, she decided she could not improve upon the tribute. Encouraged by Lionel, S. R. Drew had appeared in twenty-two films in 1913–1914 and in 1915 was Vitagraph's youngest director. Sidney Drew (Uncle Googan) died in New York City on April 9, 1919, the opening night of *The Jest*, from uremic poisoning due to nephritis; he had been appearing with Lucille in Detroit in *Keep Her Smiling* when he was stricken. Most obituaries gave his age as fifty-four (from what source is unknown), which would make his birth year 1865. But see the arguments in chapter one. After her husband's death, Lucille virtually withdrew from films; she died in 1925 at the age of thirty-five after a lingering illness.

Although his *Copperhead* opening in Chicago was a sensation (*Variety*, November 29, 1918), Lionel was soon complaining that the stagehands at the Garrick were making too much noise during his great last act. Although the manager was reported as using every precaution to meet "the star's insistent demand for quietude," *The Copperhead* was transferred to the Studebaker, where it never managed to draw as it had at the Garrick, though $7,500 in mid-January was considered a good week. Lionel talks about the recurrence of his phobia in *We Barrymores*. Lionel's remarks in Toledo, reported in the *Blade* (March 3, 1919), are typical of the mixed signals he always sent publicly about the stage versus motion pictures.

Channing Pollock's criticism of Broadway plays was made to John Galsworthy and reported in "The New Season," *Theatre Arts Magazine* (April 1919).

For accounts of *The Jest* I have drawn on Barnes's *The Man Who Lived Twice, Confessions, We Barrymores*, Hopkins's *To a Lonely Boy*, and Strange's *Who Tells Me True*. *The Jest* received extravagant critical attention, most critics coming sooner or later to the conclusion that the play itself was overwrought but the acting of Lionel and John superb. I have quoted from J. Corbin in the *New York Times* (April 20, 1919), Courtenay Savage in *Forum* (May 1919), Woollcott's "Second Thoughts on First Nights" in the Sunday *New York Times* (September 28, 1919), and Dorothy Parker in *Vanity Fair* (June 1919). Kenneth Macgowan in *Theatre Arts Magazine* (July 1919) typically thought the show all Robert Edmond Jones: "*The Jest* without Jones would be a bare and ugly thing. With Jones, *The Jest* is a sensation." Booth Tarkington's complaint about *The Jest* is printed in *On Plays, Playwrights, and Playgoers: Selections from the Letters of Booth Tarkington to George C. Tyler and John Peter Toohey, 1918–1925*, ed. Alan S. Downer (Princeton, N.J.: Princeton University Press, 1959). Tarkington actually thought very highly of both Lionel and John as actors. Dr. Smith Ely Jelliffe's "Psychotherapy and the Drama" articles appeared in the *New York Medical Journal* in the September 3, 1917, January 18, 1919, and October 4, 1919, issues. John's fourth wife, Elaine Barrymore, told Spencer Berger indirectly in a letter of November 17, 1986, that John was "an intimate friend" of Jelliffe.

As witness to the success of Ethel's tour with *The Off Chance*, her engagement at Boston's Hollis Street Theatre beginning November 18 was extended through December 14; she broke box-office records in Washington in March 1919, and the tour was eventually extended to the West Coast. Chicago was a puzzler, however: some nights below $500 and then "the season's most remarkable reversal" in her second and final week, turning away thousands (*Variety*, January 10, 1919).

Besides an article, "The Actors' Strike," *Outlook* (September 3, 1919), Ethel devotes nine pages in *Memories* to her participation in the Actors Equity strike; obviously it was an important event in her life. *Variety* issued "Strike Bulletins" from August 25 until the end of the strike. I am also indebted to Alan Churchill's discussion of the strike in *The Great White Way* (New York: Dutton, 1962). Ethel was interviewed by Robert J. Cole, "Ethel Barrymore Stands With 'My People,'" *New York Times* (August 24, 1919), the source of her "People understand, I think." On August 29, the New York *Mail* suggested that Ethel and George M. Cohan settle the strike personally since they were the dominating personalities and neither had lost favor with the other side. Cohan remained a holdout, the only actor permitted onstage without an Actors Equity card. Lionel's performance at the benefit drew raves in *Shadowland* (November 19, 1919) and from Heywood Broun in the New York *Tribune* (September 7, 1919).

Ethel on *Déclassée* is in *Memories*. John wrote to Blanche about attending the performance on Monday, October 6, 1919; the letter is quoted in Kobler, no source.

CHAPTER THIRTEEN: 1919–1920

Zoë Akins's fascination with Ethel Barrymore dated from the age of fourteen when she saw a reproduction of John Singer Sargent's drawing of the actress. She was inspired to verse ("To Ethel Barrymore," eventually published in *Vanity Fair*, June 1920):

> The face is like a flower a-bloom in May;
> The head is lifted for a wreath of bay;
> The steady eyes—of what lost world are they? . . .
>
> O, in a world of sadness and despair
> 'Tis good to find a gracious thing and fair—
> A face serene, nor restless with old fears,
> Set calm and star-like toward the coming years!

As for *Déclassée*, many critics objected from the beginning to Lady Helen's melodramatic death. There was a particularly dangerous moment when the servant enters carrying Lady Helen "white and limp," for Ethel Barrymore·was an armful; no one, however, dared laugh. *Variety* reviewed the play on October 10 and November 7, 1919, the latter column even criticizing Ethel for "a bad gown" and for having "touched her hair blonde."

Margaret Case Harriman, the daughter of Frank Case, has written about the Round Table in *The Vicious Circle* (New York: Rinehart, 1951). "Could I maybe": Edna Ferber to Woollcott, quoted in Scott Meredith, *George S. Kaufman and His Friends* (Garden City, N.Y.: Doubleday, 1974). Ferber dubbed Woollcott the "little baby New Jersey Nero." Actually, "*Zowie*, or the Curse of an Akins' Heart" laughed at both *Déclassée* and Akins's current play, *The Varying Shore*. The cast included Kaufman as Mortimer Van Loon (a Decayed Gentleman), Harold Ross as Lemuel Pip (an Old Taxi-driver), John Peter Toohey as Marmaduke La Salle (a Stomach Specialist), and Woollcott as Archibald Van Alstyne (a Precisionist). "*Zowie*" was published in *Vanity Fair* (July 1922).

Tallulah Bankhead talks about her relations with both Barrymores in *Tallulah: My Autobiography* (New York: Harper and Brothers, 1952). In 1922 *Vanity Fair* called her "the world's most subtly amusing imitator of Ethel Barrymore." Her visit to John's dressing room probably took place in September or October of 1919, since *Dr. Jekyll and Mr. Hyde* was filmed in early November. I am indebted to Lee Israel's excellent biography, *Miss Tallulah Bankhead* (New York: G. P. Putnam's Sons, 1972), for detailing Tallulah's eventual marriage to the actor John Emery, who had actually lived with John and Katherine as a boy and who not only remarkably resembled John Barrymore but copied his mannerisms and acting style. Throughout Emery's marriage to Tallulah it was rumored that he was Barrymore's illegitimate son and, as Israel comments, Tallulah had probably been drawn to Emery by the resemblance.

John's letter and cable to Blanche are quoted from Kobler, no source. Diana Barrymore's *Too Much, Too Soon*, with Gerold Frank (New York: Henry Holt, 1957), prints the cable as two separate messages.

The Jest closed for the summer June 14, 1919, reopened just as strong in September and was finally withdrawn February 21, 1920, closing to "the greatest box-office record for drama or nonmusical shows in American theatrical history," having run thirty-one weeks and grossed $549,500—triple the take of most plays. It would have grossed even more had John not dropped out due to illness from January 31 to February 7. During the fall 1919 season, there were strong rumors that John would take *The Jest* to London, which was "waiting with bated breath" to see "the great American actor." It is possible that John wanted to go to London because Blanche was in London and Paris; Hopkins probably dissuaded him, arguing that he should build a repertory, including *Richard the Third*, before storming the British capital.

Sources for the production of *Richard the Third* include *Confessions*, "Those Incredible Barrymores," *American Magazine* (March 1933), Hopkins's *To a Lonely Boy*, Strange's *Who Tells Me True*, Gene Fowler's *Good Night*, and a chapter "The John Barrymore I Knew" by Margaret Carrington, who died before completing a planned book about John (Gene Fowler Collection, Boulder, Colorado). The late John D. Seymour, related by marriage to the Barrymores, described Hopkins's frustration with the stamping horse in a letter of September 13, 1985, to this biographer. Ada Patterson described Blanche at the first night of *Richard the Third* in "John Barrymore's Romance," *Photoplay* (November 1920). Woollcott on the "electric atmosphere" at the Plymouth and the entrance of John Drew, Lionel, and Ethel in the *New York Times* (March 8, 1920). John's face "like a dagger": Ludwig Lewisohn, *The Drama and the Stage* (New York: Harcourt, Brace, 1922). "His voice is now beautifully placed": "F.H." in *The New Republic* (March 24, 1920). Arthur Hornblow's critique appeared in *Theatre Magazine* (April 1920) where he announced 1919–1920 as "the great Barrymore year." Woollcott reviewed *Richard* in the *New York Times* (March 8 and 21, 1920), Kenneth Macgowan in the New York *Globe* (March 8, 1920). As for negative comments, Alan Dale argued that unselfconsciousness was the greatest test of genius and accused John of self-consciousness in the New York *American* (March 14, 1920), while Woollcott's review of March 21 cautioned John that he must take "the last step of his ascent" and respect his audience. "Perhaps a sudden vision would do it," Woollcott concluded. "Or maybe a crack on the head. Anyway, we hope it comes to him before he tries *Hamlet*." *Richard* as a hit: for the first eight days it played to $21,000 a night, unheard of for Shakespeare (*Variety*, March 19, 1920), and continued to pack the house.

I am grateful to Ray Ruehl for making his print of *Dr. Jekyll and Mr. Hyde* available to me. *Jekyll and Hyde* had already been filmed: a Selig version in 1908, a Danish one in 1910, a Universal production in 1912 directed by James Cruze, a 1913 film with King Baggott, and in 1920 an American film with Sheldon Lewis. Both Fredric March and Spencer Tracy later played the dual character in talking versions. On the stage Richard Mansfield's *Jekyll and Hyde* was much admired, though Laurence Irving, the grandson of Sir Henry Irving, said that none of the *Jekyll and Hyde*s, filmed or staged, matched his father Henry Brodribb Irving's stage creation "for credibility, horror and pathos." John's movie introduced a love interest played adequately by Martha Mansfield, Nita Naldi, and a Wildean tempter, Sir James Carew. John expressed disappointment in the film in "John Barrymore Writes on the Movies," *Ladies' Home Journal* (August 1922), while the *New York Times* praised the picture on April 4, 1920. *Variety* reported (March 4, 1921) that the film was not doing so well on the road; in New York, however, it was so popular that the navy used it for recruiting efforts: a poster showed John Barrymore saying, "Don't be a 'Dr. Jekyll and Mr. Hyde'—Stop talking about what you would do—Do It—Join the Navy Now!"

For Lionel's performance in *The Letter of the Law* I have drawn on Arthur Hornblow in *Theatre Magazine* (April 1920), Woollcott in the *New York Times* (February 29, 1920), and *Variety* (February 27, 1920). The play ran until May 8, 1920, having moved from the Criterion to Maxine Elliott's Theatre in April. Of *The Copperhead* film *Variety* (February 13, 1920) said, "As a feature picture, it will never compare to the forcefulness and human interest that the drama held for its audiences as played by Mr. Barrymore several years ago. . . ."

Blanche's poem is quoted from *Resurrecting Life* by Michael Strange, with drawings by John Barrymore (New York: Knopf, 1921); I am indebted to Spencer Berger for lending me his autographed copy. Blanche's exchange with Mercedes de Acosta is reported in Acosta's *Here Lies the Heart*. Blanche on Doris Rankin and Iris Tree's comment on actors' infidelity is in *Who Tells Me True*. In his *Confessions of an Actor* (New York: Simon and Schuster, 1982), Sir Laurence Olivier argues that "sex is a component of an actor's tremendous physical outlay onstage." *Variety* (April 9, 1920) reported on Blanche, then on April 23 chastised actresses for their indecent interest in John Barrymore's inamorata: "Indeed, there is something almost ludicrous in the shameless peeking and preening that has gone on among the distinguished women of the stage in the effort to catch a glimpse of this slender, willowy poetess, so long a queen among the fashionable. Great beauty she has beyond question, and a frank, free, careless stare that searches out hidden meanings and makes whomever she condescends to talk to feel unexpectedly important—these qualities she has, but an artist, if she is to be judged by her occasional lapses into verse, she is not and never will be. But as the complement of an artist, even of a great artist, she would be superb."

Kenneth Macgowan reported in *Theatre Magazine* (October 1920) that Arthur Hopkins's plans were almost complete for a new building to house a repertory company. In this case, John's illness was not a drawback: it would give him an excuse to act only four days a week, disarming the public's prejudice against plays that don't run eight times a week, months at a time. Jacob Ben-Ami was named as an alternating artist, but Hopkins's dream of a repertory theatre with John Barrymore came to nothing.

"He beat her terribly" is from Ethel's deposition as reported in the Toledo *Blade* in 1923, headlined "Resigns as Human Punching Bag." Ethel described her interview with the cardinal in *Memories*, called her three children "justifications" in her unpublished "Myself As I Think Others See Me." Barbara Robins Davis commented on Russell Colt in an interview with this biographer in January 1987; the other friend wished to remain anonymous.

CHAPTER FOURTEEN: 1920–1921

John's self-sketch made at Muldoon's and inscribed to fellow inmate Henry Hunt King is in the National Portrait Gallery, Smithsonian Institution. John's letter to Chapman (Houghton Library, Harvard University) is a good example of what Gene Fowler called his "outstanding faculty" of making the person he was addressing feel as though he were the only one in the actor's confidence.

Blanche described the marriage ceremony in *Who Tells Me True*, where she also talks about their "crazed spirituality." Her poem about the White Plains house appears in *Resurrecting Life*. Gene Fowler describes the damage to Mrs. Nicholls's house in *Good Night*.

Ashton Stevens recorded Ethel's reaction to Sammy's letter in *Actorviews*. Ethel took her children to see *Dr. Jekyll and Mr. Hyde* while visiting Kyalami Cottage in Easthampton the summer of 1920, reported in Kobler. John Drew Miglietta, Ethel's only grandchild, told the biographer that Jackie Colt always felt unwanted; Miglietta says he had the hardest time of the three Colt children. Both Eleanore Phillips Colt (Mrs. Samuel) and Herbert Swope, Jr., a close friend of Ethel and her children, testify that Sammy hated his father. St. John Ervine admitted his falling in love with Ethel in *Vanity Fair* (June 1920). Meeting John on this same New York visit, Ervine said, "He talked better than any actor I have ever listened to."

Lionel's leaving Metro: Marcus Loew bought the financially plagued producer-distributor Metro with which Lionel had made ten movies, while First National had managed to gain control of the biggest theatres in major metropolitan areas, though First National would itself be challenged by Adolph Zukor. Despite *Motion Picture Classic*'s verdict, only *The Great Adventure* of the four films Lionel made with Whitman Bennett was considered something of a failure, Lionel and Bennett having turned Arnold Bennett's comic novel *Buried Alive* into a morality play. Critics also complained that *Jim the Penman* lacked the drama of the stage play, a common complaint of the day since plays did not automatically translate easily into silent movies; *Variety*, however, called Lionel's acting "intelligent, as always." Lionel condemned movies in a 1920 interview with Cedric Belfrage, "He's in Pictures for the Money": Locke.

The unreliable and heavy-drinking John D. Williams seems to have been the contentious party in his scraps with Arthur Hopkins over the services of Lionel. Williams claimed in the New York Supreme Court that Hopkins had agreed to shares losses on *The Copperhead* and profits on *The Jest* because of Lionel's withdrawal to play the latter (*Variety*, March 12, 1920); he lost the suit. In January 1921 Williams announced that he would sue Hopkins if Lionel appeared in *Macbeth* because Lionel owed him another play. The New York Supreme Court refused to grant Williams an injunction, saying that Lionel had fulfilled his obligations to Williams with *The Copperhead* and *The Letter of the Law*. Evidently Williams considered Lionel a hot property.

Hopkins discusses *Macbeth* at some length in *To a Lonely Boy*. Robert Edmond Jones's revolutionary sets are reproduced in his *Drawings for the Theatre* (New York: Theatre Arts, 1925). Percy Hammond quotes Allen to McBride in "Those Very First Nighters" in *But—Is It Art?* (Garden City, N.Y.: Doubleday, 1927). Woollcott on the audience suffering shock is in the *New York Times* (February 18, 1921). "Mr. Barrymore's Macbeth was just a gloomy, uninteresting oaf": *Shadowland* (May 1921). On Lionel making Macbeth insane, *Forum* (April 1921). Kenneth Macgowan excoriated Lionel in *Theatre Arts Magazine* (April 1921), arguing that the proof that *Macbeth* was Lionel's and not Jones's fault lay in the fact that the sets "worked" when Julia Arthur as Lady Macbeth and E. J. Ballantine as Malcolm held the stage. Eugene O'Neill's chief reaction to this *Macbeth* was "a rage at Barrymore. He got between the production and me. That is my main trouble in theatregoing, by the way, and the real reason I avoid the show-shops": Sheaffer. On the other hand, *Variety* (February 25, 1921) gave *Macbeth* a long, positive, analytical review praising it as an allegory of the first law of nature—the perpetuation of the race—as expanded by Dr. Smith Ely Jelliffe in an interview in the New York *Herald* (January 21, 1921). Jelliffe was in the first-night audience, another indication of his and Hopkins's close connection. As for Lionel's own remarks about *Macbeth*, it is clear in *We Barrymores* that he is still hurt by its failure; and, as an old man filling out Daniel Blum's questionnaire, the only "anecdote of interest to readers" he supplies is Allen's "Lay off, McBride!"

Diana Barrymore tells of her naming and of her father being afraid to hold her—presumably Blanche was her source—in her then scandalous autobiography, *Too Much, Too Soon*. The legal papers in which John waived paternal rights over Diana are in the Gene Fowler Collection.

I am grateful to Spencer Berger for lending me his copy of *Clair de Lune* (New York:

G. P. Putnam's Sons, 1921), inscribed "Every good wish to Mr. Barrymore's friend and mine Michael Strange, 1942." Helen Dryden executed the magnificent costumes John designed; the music was Fauré, Debussy, and a piece composed by Blanche. *The Bookman* (June 1921) described the opening-night crowd; *Too Much, Too Soon* and *Who Tells Me True* are also sources. Robert Benchley praised Ethel and damned the play in *Life* (May 5, 1921); Woollcott in the *New York Times* (April 19, 1921). Ethel tells about the phone call to Lionel in *Memories*, a story repeated by Heywood Broun in *The New Republic* (February 2, 1938) with the addition that Ethel also fetched Uncle Jack out of the Racquet Club, improbable since curtain time was imminent. John's unpublished letter to the *Times* and *Tribune* is in the Houghton Library, Harvard University. Ludwig Lewisohn championed the production in *The Nation* (May 4, 1921). John blamed "dwarfs and Barrymores" in *Confessions*.

The *New York Times* complained of the ephemeral plans of the Brothers Barrymore July 31, 1921. Ethel was equally ephemeral these years as far as movies went. Famous Players bought *Déclassée* for her, but nothing came of the projected film. She was supposed to do *Mid-Channel*, but Equity Pictures finally bought it for Clara Kimball Young. Then, in 1920, her four-picture contract with Tri-Star Pictures was abrogated "by mutual agreement." The *Peter Ibbetson* that all three Barrymores were to have made was finally filmed as *Forever* in 1921 with Wallace Reid as Peter, Elsie Ferguson as Mary, Duchess of Towers, and Montagu Love as Colonel Ibbetson.

Colleen Moore gives her impressions of John in *Silent Star* (Garden City, N.Y.: Doubleday, 1968). Kotsilibas-Davis discusses *The Lotus Eaters* in *The Barrymores*.

Ethel's functioning as Colonel Colt's hostess is confirmed in George Howe's *Mount Hope*. Ethel herself talks about his generosity in *Memories*. Colonel Colt's will was made public in the press (Locke) as was his sons' contesting it. Currently more than a dozen Colt descendents are claimants to the trust fund.

Irene Fenwick's "I like clean things" and Alan Dale's and Amy Leslie's comments about her come from clippings in Locke. Irene's rise from chorus girl to Frohman actress, as well as her various divorces, are fairly well documented in Locke though, frustratingly, the sources of the articles about her are seldom identified.

CHAPTER FIFTEEN: 1921–1923

Blanche Barrymore tells far more about their marriage than John who, in his autobiography, mentions her with courteous restraint. The conversations quoted between John and Blanche are largely from *Who Tells Me True* and *Too Much, Too Soon*. Mercedes de Acosta analyzed the Barrymore marriage perceptively in *Here Lies the Heart*.

The Film Study Center at Yale University has a print of John's 1922 *Sherlock Holmes*; I am grateful to Audrey Kupferberg for providing me with a VHS copy as well as her "Sherlock Holmes," a commentary on the resurrection of the Barrymore film after fifty years' loss, notably by the film historian Kevin Brownlow. Everson discusses the film's shortcomings ("no highlights . . . no pictorial style of its own") in "Rediscovery: John Barrymore's Sherlock Holmes," *Films in Review* (February 1976). The *New York Times* (May 8, 1922) said the film as a theatrical composition "falls to pieces"; still, it was a box-office success and was considered—along with *Orphans of the Storm* (which John called "the most wonderful motion picture I have ever seen"), *Nanook of the North*, and *Robin Hood*—one of the better pictures of the year. John himself thought he looked in *Sherlock Holmes* "a little like a predigested onanist" (letter to Sir Gerald du Maurier, September 27, 1926, the Gene Fowler Collection) and complained about motion pictures in general in "John

Barrymore Writes on the Movies," *Ladies' Home Journal* (August 1922), saying that most of them lack imagination. Certainly the attempt to translate William Gillette's stage play virtually whole to the silent screen lacked imagination, since the main charm of the play was its dialogue.

The Claw opened in Boston in September 1921 and moved to the Broadhurst Theatre in October. On November 11, 1921, *Variety* reported that it "counts as one of the dramatic leaders, though no smash, and acting of Lionel Barrymore provides main strength." Critical opinion is cited from *Variety* (October 21, 1921), Woollcott in the *New York Times* (October 18, 1921), and Arthur Hornblow in *Theatre Magazine* (January 1921). Woollcott thought that Irene Fenwick acquitted herself handsomely as the wife, Hornblow that she gave capable support. Spencer Tracy's encomium is quoted from Kotsilibas-Davis, *The Barrymores*. Ludwig Lewisohn compared Lionel and John in *The Drama and the Stage*. There are three telegrams from Lionel to Theodore Dreiser (March 8, 11, and 15, 1922) in the Van Pelt Library, University of Pennsylvania, Philadelphia. Lionel asks Dreiser to meet him in Kansas City for a few days to discuss dramatizing *Sister Carrie* for his next season. The novel was not dramatized at this time, however, because Dreiser was unwilling to sign away all rights and playwrights of the caliber he desired would not do the work for a fixed fee.

John talks about his *Hamlet* in *Confessions*, though it is only his London performance that he discusses at any length. Ethel gave her version of inspiring John in *Memories*. Margaret Carrington's comments are again from "The John Barrymore I Knew." The "little red Temple edition" of John's *Hamlet* is in the library of the Players Club, lightly annotated by John with directions such as "Here look out but not interpret," "in a sort of dream-like voice," "boyishly." John's marginal drawings also sprinkle the text. Writing to Gene Fowler in 1944, Dr. Harold Thomas Hyman claimed that John had consulted with psychiatrists about his Freudian interpretation of Hamlet. Gene Fowler, however, doubts that anyone but Margaret Carrington appreciably influenced his interpretation: letter to Hyman of January 19, 1944, quoted in Will Fowler's *The Young Man from Denver*, which is also the source of John's "That dirty, red-whiskered," his preference for *Richard III*, and his statement that he felt enthusiastic about *Hamlet* for only the first week. "Seriously, I have often wondered": *Confessions*.

Spencer Berger provided me with a copy of John Lark Taylor's unpublished "My Season with John Barrymore in 'Hamlet,'" dated from 142 East 19th Street, New York City, September 1923. Whitford Kane, cast as the First Gravedigger, devotes a chapter to *Hamlet* in *Are We All Met?* He admired John excessively in other plays but thought that Johnston Forbes-Robertson remained the best Hamlet he had seen. Arthur Hopkins discusses *Hamlet* in *To a Lonely Boy*, but with none of the enthusiasm he displayed for John's *Richard III*. Blanche Yurka on *Hamlet* in *Bohemian Girl: Blanche Yurka's Theatrical Life* (Athens: Ohio University Press, 1970). "Only an instrument in an orchestra": John Gielgud's opinion of a classical actor's role in *Stage Directions* (London: Hodder and Stoughton, 1963). Lillian Gish has stated that her interpretation of Ophelia as lewdly mad in the 1936 Gielgud *Hamlet* in New York was the director Guthrie McClintic's original idea and had never been done before, but this was Rosalinde Fuller's interpretation in 1922.

Hamlet evoked a tidal wave of critical response. Quoted are Helen Hayes retrospectively in *Collier's* (September 22, 1951), Stark Young in *The New Republic* (December 6, 1922), Arthur Hornblow in *Theatre Magazine* (January 1923), Heywood Broun in the New York *Tribune*, and Kenneth Macgowan in the New York *Commercial Advertiser* (November 26, 1922). J. Rankin Towse, veteran of the New York *Evening Post*, was the sole critic "outside the high chorus of praise," according to *The Literary Digest* (January 6, 1923); Towse, however, did praise John at the expense of the company, inspiring the letter John posted on the call board, quoted from Taylor's "My Season with John Barrymore in 'Hamlet.' " Showering praise upon Barrymore, John Corbin attacked Jones's set in a long review in the *Times* (January 14, 1923).

There are several versions of John's performance for the Moscow Art Theatre players. John Lark Taylor says John's performance that afternoon was one of the best he ever gave! Ethel, always praiseful of John and eager to demonstrate her influence over him, says in *Memories*:

"He knew he was doing something wrong, and after the first act he sent for me and said, 'What's the matter? What am I doing?'

" 'You're pressing.'

" 'Yes, I guess I am.'

"Then he relaxed and was his usual great self again."

Both Hopkins and Yurka say, however, that John "never got back into the corral." Eventually Stanislavsky wrote to the cofounder of the Moscow Art Theatre, Vladimir Nemirovich-Danchenko, that "John Barrymore's Hamlet was far from ideal, but very charming": quoted in David Magarshack, *Stanislavsky: A Life* (London: MacGibbon and McKee, 1950), also the source of John's skill at finding Stanislavsky's hidden pin.

CHAPTER SIXTEEN: 1922–1925

Ethel in *Memories* and Hopkins in *To a Lonely Boy* discuss their very mixed repertory season, Ethel claiming that she had long been interested in forming a repertory company in New York. Woollcott reviewed *Rose Bernd* in the *New York Times* (September 27, 1922), Hornblow in *Theatre Magazine* (December 1922). McKay Morris played Romeo and Basil Sydney Mercutio to Ethel's Juliet. Glenn Hughes complained that this *Romeo and Juliet* was "a muffled dirge" in "Repressed Acting and Shakespeare," *The Drama* (March 1923), arguing that Hopkins emasculated both *Hamlet* and *Romeo and Juliet* by productions that suppressed their Elizabethan passion though, since *Hamlet* is a meditative drama, it suffered less from the Hopkins-Barrymore treatment. Other criticism of the Barrymore and Cowl Juliets is taken from *The Best Plays of 1922–1923*, ed. Burns Mantle (Boston: Small, Maynard, 1923). John's undated letter to Ethel is in the Zoë Akins Collection at the Henry E. Huntington Library. Akins has jotted on the first page, "A rare item: actually a letter from Jack Barrymore! Not to me but to Ethel B." Jane Cowl's Juliet with the young Rollo Peters as Romeo was acclaimed nationwide and challenged John's record-breaking *Hamlet*, the financial manager of the Philharmonic Auditorium in Los Angeles claiming that Cowl's Juliet drew $32,367 one week compared to John's $30,000 at the Manhattan Opera House: *New York Times* (December 30, 1923).

"She ought to play Lady Teazle. She may take it from me that she would make a success of it": Ellen Terry in *The Story of My Life*. The *New York Times* dubbed Ethel "Our Lady of Vaudeville" (July 5, 1923).

Ethel's divorce, final on July 6, 1923, was widely reported; I have drawn on Locke and articles in the Philadelphia *Inquirer* (June 26, July 6, 1923).

At one point Lionel was reported as contesting Doris's divorce; evidently he changed his mind. Like Ethel's, the divorce was widely reported, though Irene Fenwick's name was never mentioned. The New York *World* (December 22, 1922) said that custody of the only child was awarded to Mrs. Barrymore, presumably an error, though with the Barrymores nothing is certain. Lionel offered his reasons for the failure of the marriage in *We Barrymores*. He and Irene were married by a Captain Ciamarra, an Italian war hero (presumably with the credentials of a J.P.) with many of the cast of Samuel Goldwyn's *The Eternal City* present. Goldwyn interrupted filming long enough for the couple to have a brief honeymoon in Venice; he might have canceled it, *Motion Picture* deciding that *The Eternal City* "is poorly acted by players who never appear in character, with the single exception of Richard Bennett. Its redeeming features are the backgrounds, which show ancient and modern Rome in all its glory and atmosphere. The story and interpretation fail to impress us."

A photograph of Lionel captioned "The star of 'The Fountain,' Eugene O'Neill's latest play" appeared in *Theatre Magazine* (October 1922), indicating that Lionel was at one point committed. Why he backed out (if he did) is uncertain, though the reason is very possibly linked to Irene. Lionel's outburst over *The Piker* is from an article, dateline New York, January 25, 1925: Locke. Woollcott deplored *Man or Devil* in the New York *Sun* (May 22, 1925). Bernard Shaw's casting of *The Devil's Disciple* appeared in the *New York Times* (May 6, 1923). Lionel tells of meeting Maury Small in *We Barrymores*. Hopkins mourned Lionel's leaving the theatre in *To a Lonely Boy* and in a letter to an unidentified correspondent (December 29, 1949) quoted in *We Barrymores*. Gene Fowler told Spencer Berger about Lionel's morphine addiction; Berger believes (as do I) that Fowler was on the inside track with Lionel and would know.

Blanche describes John's jealousy in *Who Tells Me True*. Evidently there was some cause. Duff Cooper wrote his wife Diana on Christmas Eve, 1923: "I don't know of whom else you can be jealous. I hope not of Mrs. Barrymore—I'm not sure she isn't rather K.O. [keen on] me—but she would be safe from me on a desert island, so long as there were a friendly and not unreasonable turtle about": *A Durable Fire: The Letters of Duff and Diana Cooper, 1913–1950*, ed. Artemis Cooper (London: Collins, 1983). Diana did not feel the same about John. Playing "the copulation game," she wrote Duff that John Barrymore was number one on her list of men she would like to go to bed with. Diana Barrymore talks about her half brother Leonard's hostility to John in *Too Much, Too Soon*.

The Museum of Modern Art in New York has a print of *Beau Brummel* in its film collection. I am indebted to an analysis of *Beau Brummel* in Marian Keane's unpublished dissertation "The Great Profile." Spencer Berger has contributed greatly to the documentation of John Barrymore's films in "The Film Career of John Barrymore," *Films in Review* (December 1952), "The Film Career of John Barrymore," *Image* (January 1957), "The Royal Family in Films," *Image* (December 1957), "The Search for John Barrymore," *American Classic Screen*, vol. 5 (1980), and "Tribute to John Barrymore," delivered as an introduction to a Barrymore film series at the George Eastman House, May 1969. Also very insightful is Joseph Garton's *The Film Acting of John Barrymore*.

Mary Astor kept a diary in which she frankly estimated the prowess of her many lovers, but dealt with John tactfully in *My Story: An Autobiography* (Garden City, N.Y.: Doubleday, 1959) and *A Life on Film* (New York: Delacorte Press, 1971).

John Lark Taylor claimed that John took very little part in the rehearsals of the Manhattan Opera House *Hamlet*. He was contradicted by John's valet Paul in an interview by Adele Whitely Fletcher, "After Him There Isn't Any More": Spencer Berger Collection. "We took the train on Monday and arrived in New York the following Saturday morning at nine-thirty. At ten-thirty he was on this stage rehearsing and he rehearsed all day and into Sunday morning. Then all Sunday and well into Monday morning so they could open on Monday night. There ain't nobody else could do that or would do that. In 'Hamlet' too." The *New York Times* did not like the new Polonius, Moffat Johnston, but everyone preferred Reginald Pole as a visible ghost, including Arthur Hopkins, who admitted he had been wrong about the spotlight. In December *Hamlet* was raided on the tip that it was immoral, but Sergeant Stuart De Witt of the West Thirtieth Street Police Station decided instead that the play was both clean and thoroughly enjoyable: *New York Times* (December 14, 1923).

John Lark Taylor's memoir is a major source for the *Hamlet* tour. Blanche Yurka says that John's inscription on the Sargent reads, "From your mildly incestuous son," though the word looks like "wildly." Kobler reports John's exchange with Calvin Coolidge and the threat of "assassination" if he attempted *Hamlet* in London.

CHAPTER SEVENTEEN: 1924–1925

The uncertainty of John's plans during 1924 was underlined by an announcement in the *New York Times* (August 21, 1924) that Arthur Hopkins would present four stars that fall: Ethel Barrymore, William Farnum, William Gillette, and John "in a new starring vehicle." Hopkins did not produce John, who instead was wasting his energies on plans to produce a play by Michael Strange about Edgar Allan Poe, long a hero of John's. This fell through when Blanche was sued by the playwright Sophie Treadwell on the grounds that Blanche had stolen Treadwell's Poe play, which Treadwell had sent to Barrymore. Blanche countersued for $300,000 and the entire case was dropped.

Ned Sheldon is described as "lying like a living corpse on his catafalque" in Barnes's *The Man Who Lived Twice*. Dr. George F. Draper, a pioneer in psychosomatic medicine, argued that Ned's illness was "a sort of self-immolation"; Ned's regular doctor, Carl Binger, agreed: quoted in Kobler. Mercedes de Acosta diagnosed Ned's illness in *Here Lies the Heart*.

Sailing for England, John announced that he would like to act a dramatic version of Wagner's *Parsifal*, adding, "Medieval and churchly plays have a large public appeal at present" (*New York Times*, November 6, 1924); certainly Parsifal was the right kind of role for him. Margaret Webster in *The Same Only Different* describes John at Bedford Street and the rehearsals of *Hamlet*. John devoted the entire last chapter of *Confessions* to the Haymarket *Hamlet*, including Shaw's letter in its entirety, with the restrained comment, "There is always someone who, when you have been regarding a charming this, calls your attention to a not so entrancing that."

James Agate criticized John's *Hamlet* in the London *Sunday Times* (February 22, 1925), reprinted in *The English Dramatic Critics*, ed. Agate (New York: Hill and Wang, n.d.). Agate objected to the "pure reason" of much of John's interpretation, concluding his review, "But all that intellect could do was done." Presumably this was why he found John's "a great though not overwhelming performance," even while he concluded that John *was* Shakespeare's very own Hamlet—confusing, to say the least. The London *Daily Mail* faulted John for "sudden fury" when the text did not justify it, manneristic pauses between words, and "technical faults," concluding, however, that his performance gripped and held: "his Hamlet was personality with rugged edges." The London *Chronicle* praised this Hamlet's dignity, but said it lacked excitement, the very thing audiences responded to in the Barrymore Hamlet. As for the London *Daily News*: "In general the chief characteristic of this new Hamlet is his high strung sensitiveness. He is not an elocutionary Hamlet in the ordinary sense, but it was a pleasure to hear verse spoken with such precision and without any accent, either of America, Oxford, or Kensington. It was just Anglo-Saxon English." Sir John Gielgud's annotated *Hamlet* program, dated March 26, 1925, and quoted with his permission, is in the Mander and Mitchenson Theatre Collection, Beckenham, Kent. Gielgud's Guardian Lecture at the National Film Theatre took place December 14, 1986. Sir Laurence Olivier cited the influence of John's Hamlet in an interview in *Time* (November 15, 1982) and in his autobiography titled, like Barrymore's, *Confessions of an Actor*. Herman Weinberg is quoted from *Close-ups*, ed. Danny Peary (New York: Workman Publishing, 1978). One of John's greatest English admirers was Richard Worth, who wrote in *The Weekly Despatch* (November 7, 1926) that "his genius and love of his art were so manifest that one felt for him a real friendship."

Henry Arthur Jones's tribute to John is printed in *The Life and Letters of Henry Arthur Jones*, ed. Doris Arthur Jones (London: Victor Gollancz, 1930); Jones also praised John for doing "a good turn to a deserving but temporarily discredited dramatist": Richard A. Cordell, *Henry Arthur Jones and the Modern Drama* (New York: Ray Long and Richard R. Smith, 1932). Dame Madge Kendal was quoted in "London Women Pay Tribute to Barrymore," *New York Times* (February 28, 1925). John's "fervor and champagne" recipe was reported in the *New York Times* (May 7, 1925), which also quoted him saying, "I intend to go to Berlin in the Fall and produce 'Hamlet' in German, if they will let me"—another unrealized project. Bernard Shaw's letter, included in *Confessions*, is also printed in *Bernard Shaw: Collected Letters, 1911–1925*, Vol. 3, ed. Dan H. Laurence (New York: Viking, 1985). John's letter to Golding Bright is quoted in Kobler, no source.

As usual, the only source for John and Blanche's quarrels and final split is Blanche herself, both in *Who Tells Me True* and in her daughter Diana's *Too Much, Too Soon*. Her account is, of course, biased, yet she could also call herself "superlatively immature" and, not incidentally, reveal herself as a tough lady. When Gene Fowler came to write his biography of John, he had a hard time with Blanche. In a letter to Lionel of May 1, 1943, he writes, "I have tried very hard to be fair with her, but the more I polish the chapter the more it seems I am trying to be subtly ironical, and sometimes not so subtly. In as much as almost everyone has taken this lady over the knee and applied a barrelstave to her butt, it was my intention not to join this array of flagellators but try to be as objective as possible when discussing the fact that she put our pal, The Monster, through the hamburger machine." Fowler had sent the manuscript to Ned Sheldon. "I hope that the Michael Strange chapter will not offend him in any way as he has a delightful though somewhat naive portrait in his mind of this Sappho, this Little BoPeep. He is such a grand guy that I have tried to remove the brass knuckles when discussing the lethal Mike": Gene Fowler Collection. The separation agreement between John and Blanche is also in the Gene Fowler Collection. Oswald Mosley, who knew them both, once told them, "You both have the same occupation in life, each doing what you want and trying to stop the other doing the same thing; you both win on the first point but both flop on the second": *My Life* (London: Nelson, 1968). Once, when she was talking with Duff Cooper about the need for a great love in people's lives, Blanche admitted she "only adored her husband": *A Durable Fire*.

John's Warner Brothers contracts are in WCFTR. Robert Edmond Jones's letter to John is quoted from Kobler, no source. Lionel said about Shaw's letter, "This depressed Jack. It would have floored me. I might comment *sotto voce* that Mr. Shaw *seemed* to be forgetful in saying that Master Shakespeare did not pretend to play as well as to write, for Shakespeare was known as an actor all his life and was not accredited as a famous playwright until after his death. As an actor, Shakespeare might have looked with more favor than did Mr. Shaw, a writer, upon the necessity to condense a play a little. But Mr. Shaw, in my sincerely humble opinion, was one of the mountain peaks of the world and I think I had better keep quiet": *We Barrymores*. Woollcott described John's "real shyness" in *Everybody's Magazine* (June 1920). John's "Aren't you sorry you don't have more Barrymores?" is quoted in the New York *World* (October 26, 1925). Hopkins on John's quitting the stage is in *To a Lonely Boy*. In a letter of December 29, 1949 (cited in *We Barrymores*), Hopkins quoted Emily (Mrs. Norman) Hapgood's metaphor of the two Barrymores casting gold plates into the river. John told about not being recognized by movie fans in "Hamlet in Hollywood," *Ladies' Home Journal* (July 1927). Arthur Hopkins's belief that Ethel was devastated by John's abandoning the theatre is shared by this biographer.

CHAPTER EIGHTEEN: 1925–1927

Ethel's telegram of August 23, 1923, to Zoë Akins continues PLEASE READ IT TO ARTHUR RIGHT AWAY SO I CAN GET HIS ATTITUDE AND THEN GO AHEAD WITH PLANS YOU HAVE DONE A GRAND AND WONDERFUL PIECE OF WORK BLESS YOU AND MUCH LOVE ETHEL: Zoë Akins Collection, Henry E. Huntington Library. Edward G. Robinson had the small role of Pascual in *A Royal Fandango*; another young actor had only one line as a newspaper photographer, but was very nervous. "Relax," Ethel told Spencer Tracy. "That's all you have to do—just relax. It'll all be the same in a hundred years." This from the actress who suffered severe performance anxiety as described, for example, in Philip Emerson Wood's "Ethel Barrymore Had Stage Fright," *Delineator* (August 1926). But Barbara Robins Davis also heard Ethel dismissing her terror: "Of course I'm not nervous. You see, I know so much more than they do." *A Royal Fandango* lasted a mere twenty-four performances at the Plymouth Theatre. Critical praise for Ethel's Paula Tanqueray is quoted from Robert Downing, "Ethel Barrymore 1879–1957," *Films in Review* (August–September 1959); *The Second Mrs. Tanqueray* had seventy-two performances at the Cort Theatre before Ethel took it on tour.

Pickings are indeed slim for evidence of Ethel's involvement with Tearle and Daniell. Spencer Berger surmises that she and Tearle were lovers: "People invited them together; they were photographed together." Certainly Tearle had a reputation as a lover offstage and on. Alpert in *The Barrymores* calls Ethel's supposedly unrequited passion for Daniell "musty gossip"; others who knew Ethel refer to him as "her escort." Brian M. Chic called Daniell "a gentleman who probably would've been happier in the 19th rather than 20th Century" in "Henry Daniell," *Films in Review* (January 1983). Alpert quotes Ethel Barrymore Colt on her mother's Victorian, nunlike sexual nature, something that Eliot Janeway and Barbara Robins Davis in interviews with this biographer corroborate. Ruth (Mrs. Jacques) Gordon's opinion is quoted from Alpert, who interviewed her.

Ethel sailed for England July 18, 1925, returned August 22; her trip is thinly documented in clippings in the Mander and Mitchenson Theatre Collection, the *New York Times*, and *Memories*. Ethel's abstinence in ·public was noted in the press; she was, for example, reported "refusing a cocktail" at a party in October 1925.

Ethel talks about both her Ophelia and Portia in *Memories*. As one critic said aptly of the latter, "She delivered 'the quality of mercy' as a tête-à-tête not an aria." I have quoted liberally from James Dale's delicious chapter on Ethel in *Pulling Faces for a Living*. It is shocking to find Ethel calling John "That bastard!" however. One can only assume that she was very angry as well as hurt about his leaving the stage. Ethel defends her acting and cites Bourdet and Reinhardt in "Myself As I Think Others See Me," the source also of her grievances against "the classical Mr. Heywood Broun" and "the recondite Mr. Percy Hammond." *The Best Plays of 1925–1926* assessed the Hampden-Barrymore collaboration as "failing to excite."

During a 1949 broadcast celebrating Ethel's seventieth birthday, Somerset Maugham said plainly that he had fallen madly in love with Ethel, reported in Garson Kanin's *Remembering Mr. Maugham* (New York: Atheneum, 1966). Ethel's "Oh, darling, I've ruined your beautiful play" became one of Maugham's set pieces. The Cleveland papers said coldly the day after the opening of *The Constant Wife* that a city of its size and importance deserved an actress who knew her lines; Ethel knew them the second night and had a triumph in New York: "Not since *Déclassée* has any playwright written for her the gay gallantries of which she is the theatre's high priestess," raved Woollcott. Barbara Robins Davis spoke with this biographer about Ethel in *The Constant Wife* and is also the source of Ethel's "Wherever I am is center stage." Maugham on Ethel's paying for his Cap Ferrat house is quoted from a letter from George Cukor to Katharine Hepburn (August 14, 1957): AMPAS. *The Constant Wife* (*The Constant Infidelities*, a critic called it) was considered advanced for its time, particularly lines like a mother's telling her daughter, "You're not in love unless you can use his toothbrush."

Numerous articles about "Hamlet in Hollywood" greeted John's first years in Hollywood, no one letting him forget—or perhaps he not letting Hollywood forget—that he had been a great stage actor: "John Speaks for Himself," *Motion Picture Classic* (August 1925), W. Adolph Roberts, "Confidences Off-Screen," *Motion Picture Magazine* (August 1925), "Hamlet in Hollywood," *Ladies' Home Journal* (June, July 1927) and "Up Against It in Hollywood," *Ladies' Home Journal* (June, July 1928) are examples.

John's nostalgia for the stage is evident in a letter (1925) written to Sir Johnston Forbes-Robertson, given to this biographer by the late Diana Forbes-Robertson Sheean: "I have just read your enchanting book 'A Player Under Three Reigns' and devoured every word of it. It is the most charming thing of its kind I have ever read. If I have Hatchard's send you the first English edition would you be so very very good as to inscribe something in the front of it for me—thereby ineffably heightening the charm of it for myself and later my daughter. If you would then send it back to Hatchard's they will forward it to me in the appalling community of Hollywood where I am making motion-pictures (for my sins) and it will be a real breath of England. . . . I do so hope you don't think this impertinent. I should dearly love it. . . ."

John kept Ned Sheldon's night letter, later showing it to his friend and admirer Philip Rhodes, who memorized the letter and kindly relayed it to me.

"That's a great makeup job" quoted from Jack L. Warner, with Dean Jennings, *My First Hundred Years in Hollywood* (New York: Random House, 1964). "What we are going to do for a love interest": *Confessions.*

Among other sources, I have drawn upon Fowler's *Good Night*, Kobler, Alpert, and Kotsilibas-Davis's *The Barrymores* for versions of John's falling in love with Dolores and the Hollywood years, as well as upon news clippings (usually from the Los Angeles *Times*) in the AMPAS archives. Harry Brundidge described John as the most "cussed and discussed" celebrity in *Twinkle Twinkle Movie Star* (New York: Dutton, 1930). Douglas Fairbanks Jr. defended him in *Vanity Fair* (September 1930).

The WCFTR has prints of both *The Sea Beast* and *Don Juan*, both of which Joseph Garton discusses perceptively in *The Film Acting of John Barrymore*. John's hating "pansy parts": Flagg's *Roses and Buckshot*. John Engstead, the reporter who tried to interview John, is quoted in John Kobal's *People Will Talk* (New York: Alfred A. Knopf, 1985). Philip Rhodes, quoting John himself, told me about the make-up process used in *Don Juan*. Mary Astor tells of her devastation at John's desertion in *My Life: An Autobiography*. Sumner Locke Elliott, who contributed an introduction to her later book, *A Life on Film*, said in a letter to Spencer Berger that even in later life Mary Astor could not discuss the painful filming of *Don Juan*. Elliott is also the source for Mary's "My god-damned angel face." Myrna Loy describes her difficulties with John in "Myrna Loy Attends as History Repeats Itself at *Don Juan* Presentation," *Classic Images* (July 1983), and in her autobiography with James Kotsilibas-Davis, *Myrna Loy: Being and Becoming* (New York: Alfred A. Knopf, 1987). Telegrams from Albert Warner to Jack Warner, quoted in *My First Hundred Years in Hollywood*, report the "tremendous turnout" for *The Sea Beast* in New York. Robert Sherwood reviewed *Don Juan* in *Life* (August 26, 1926). "The Silent Drama: *Don Juan* and the Vitaphone" is quoted in George C. Pratt's *Spellbound in Darkness: A History of the Silent Film* (Greenwich, Conn.: New York Graphic Society, 1973). *Variety* and the *New York Times*, it should be noted, did not join in the general panning of *Don Juan*. Vitaphone was the ace up the Warner sleeve. Though the first demonstration of "talkies" at the 1900

Paris Exhibition had been unimpressive, Jack, Harry, Sam, and Albert Warner had realized that talking pictures were the future. To this end they signed stage actors with good voices, like George Arliss, Otis Skinner, and Barrymore, and popular entertainers like Sophie Tucker and Ted Lewis, meanwhile buying up musical publishing houses to sew up talent like Vincent Youmans and George Gershwin. Though Fox developed its own sound system called Movietone, Vitaphone struck first and made cinematic history. "I made it for money": *Photoplay* (August 1928).

John's log from the December 27, 1925, to January 19, 1926, *Gypsy* cruise, in which he admitted he missed Lionel, the only other person besides Dolores he wanted along, is quoted extensively in Fowler's *Good Night*. The log seems to have disappeared; as Alpert reports: "What ultimately happened to it remains a mystery. Dolores had it for several years before it unaccountably vanished. It turned up again, after John died, in the possession of Henry Hotchener. He sold it for $20,000 to Gene Fowler. . . . Whoever acquired it after Fowler's death in 1960 is unknown." The bulk of Fowler's papers were turned over to the University of Colorado at Boulder by his son Will, but the log is not among them. Indeed, even some materials listed in the catalogue of the Fowler Collection—John's medical records, for example—are missing.

CHAPTER NINETEEN: 1926–1928

Ironically, "clean Irene" played in such dramas as *The Song of Songs*, about which John Drew said, "Such things only happen in Europe and should stay there." "We love the theatre": James Kotsilibas-Davis, *The Barrymores*, no source. Lionel panned films in "The Present State of the Movies," *Ladies' Home Journal* (September 1926). Lionel's movies have been documented by Robert Downing, "Lionel Barrymore's Film Career," *Films in Review* (January 1955), Bert Gray, "The Movies of Lionel Barrymore," *Films in Review* (April 1962), and Kotsilibas-Davis, *The Barrymores*. I am grateful to Spencer Berger for lending me prints of *The Bells* and *Wife Tamers*, the only Roach two-reeler that Lionel made before Maury Small rescued him. Walter Kerr tells of Hal Roach's scheme for hiring down-on-their-luck actors for slapstick in *The Silent Clowns* (New York: Alfred A. Knopf, 1975). Maury Small's reaction is reported in *We Barrymores*. Lionel reacts to being asked to support Lon Chaney in "Those Incredible Barrymores: How I Escaped a Lover's Doom," *American Magazine* (April 1933).

The George Eastman House owns a print of *When a Man Loves*, which did not win much current favor, though Joseph Garton in *The Film Acting of John Barrymore* admires its romantic style. Complaints about John's eternal profile: Heywood Broun, retrospectively, in *The New Republic* (February 2, 1938); *Photoplay* (April 1927); Perceval Reniers, "The Shadow Stage," *The Independent* (April 30, 1927). Stark Young condemns John's films in "A Terrible Thing," *The New Republic* (September 14, 1927), Percy Hammond in "The Barrymore Hamlet" in *But—Is It Art?*

The New York *Post* warned readers not to take John's *Confessions of an Actor* too seriously (April 17, 1926). Other reviews called the book "genial, unconventional, and interesting . . . pleasant hot weather reading": *The Independent* (July 1926). *Literary Digest International Book Review* (June 1926) liked it better: "This is a volume which, escaping by a wide margin the feeble mediocrity of most of its kind, affords the reader a vigorous and sprightly life-story, told with great charm."

John's letter to Blanche about the script of *The Beloved Rogue* is quoted in Fowler's *Good Night*. John eventually persuaded United Artists to pay Blanche $1,250 for the possible use of one of her scenes and the title *They Shall Not Pass*. I am grateful to the staff of the Film Archives of the Museum of Modern Art for screening *The Beloved Rogue, Beau Brummel, Just Gold*, and *General Crack* for me. *The Beloved Rogue* has drawn mixed reactions. Spencer Berger considers it the best of Barrymore's Hollywood silents. Joseph Garton thinks the clown scene contains Barrymore's most memorable acting. Perceval Reniers roundly condemned it as "the weakling" in *The Independent* (April 30, 1927). David Shipman in *The Great Movie Stars: The Golden Years* (New York: Hill and Wang, 1979) says that *The Beloved Rogue* is merely *If I Were King* and *The Vagabond King* all over again, "with the swashbuckling hero—Barrymore—appallingly unattractive in every possible way." John vented his frustration with movies to his niece as reported by Spencer Berger in "Ethel Barrymore Colt," *Hopkins Literary Magazine* (June 1935), in "Hamlet in Hollywood: I," *Ladies' Home Journal* (June 1927), and in "Up Against It in Hollywood," *Ladies' Home Journal* (January 1928).

John comments on the best place to spend Christmas in "Hamlet in Hollywood: II," *Ladies' Home Journal* (July 1927); the description of him as subconsciously embarrassed by Christmas and New Year's is in Fowler's *Good Night*, also the source of John's admission to Henry Hotchener that he would probably drink a lot on the voyage. John's and Blanche's telegrams are in the Gene Fowler Collection. Blanche frequently thanks him for his generosity and kindness as does Diana: "Dear Daddy: Thank you very much for all those nice things you sent me. How have you been? I had a very nice summer and I had swimming lessons. Come and see me, Daddy. I would like so much to see you. Much love and kisses from Diana" (October 15, 1927). John's kid-glove treatment of Blanche is evident in a letter quoted in part in Kobler (p. 233) in which John begs her to sign a paper so that he can take title to the Tower Road property. "I am terribly sorry to have to trouble you about this," he writes, promising to pay any fee attached to her notarizing the paper.

Louisa Drew Devereaux's letter to Georgie Drew Mendum is in the Seymour Theatre Collection, Princeton University; John Drew's *Thespian Dictionary* is in TCFLP. After his uncle's death, John wired David Glasford, a member of the Players Club, which Drew had once headed: DEAR DAVID I WISH YOU TO KNOW THAT I AM IN ACCORD WITH MY UNCLE'S EXPRESSED WISH THAT OTIS SKINNER BE APPOINTED THE NEXT PRESIDENT OF THE CLUB I SINCERELY HOPE THAT THE BOARD WILL BE OF THE OPINION (Gene Fowler Collection); Walter Hampden, however, was elected. Katherine Harris, who, after John, married Alexander Dallas Bache Pratt and then Leon Orlowski, also died in 1927, in May.

His disappointing film career probably inspired Lionel to return to the stage in *The Copperhead* at the Los Angeles Playhouse; he was a great success, the critic Edwin Schallert urging, "Whatever you do, see it." Lionel thought a young man playing a minor role very promising; later he was responsible for getting Clark Gable a screen test at MGM.

John's Tower Road extravaganza has often been described in contemporary newspapers and movie magazines, by other Barrymore biographers, and more recently in *Architectural Digest* (April 1979): "House of Legend: Updating John Barrymore's Former Residence Now Called 'Bella Vista.' "

The documents in the case of Robert Gordon Anderson vs. Joseph M. Schenck et al. are in WCFTR. John claimed that he only submitted to the scenarist H. DeVere Stacpool's 1917 biography of Villon, *The Life and Works of François Villon* by John Payne (1881), and Michael Strange's scenario. He also claimed his idea of Villon to have been influenced by a poem of Frank Butler's which he illustrated in 1905 and Justin Huntly McCarthy's play *If I Were King*. John did admit to reading Anderson's book but thought it "not utilizable." John's answers were obviously prompted by his lawyer; even so, his "I do not remember" and "I have none [records] available" seem typical of his business dealings. The Hotcheners have been described by Fowler in *Good Night*, Mary Astor in *My Story*, and two of John's wives—Dolores Costello quoted in Alpert, and Elaine Jacobs (Barrie) Barrymore, with Sandford Doty, in *All My Sins Remembered* (New York: Appleton-Century, 1964).

Spencer Berger kindly loaned me a print of *Tempest*. Peter Noble discusses Erich von Stroheim's problems with the film in *Hollywood Scapegoat: The Biography of Erich Von Stroheim* (London: The Fortune Press, 1951), pointing out that the film credit "Story from the Austrian" was literally true. Von Stroheim later wrote *The Devil-Doll* with the director Tod Browning, one of Lionel's kinkier successes. Camilla Horn tells of filming with John in Kobal's *People Will Talk*.

John's fight with Myron Selznick on the lawn of the Ambassador Hotel, supposedly started by a slurring remark to Selznick, made the front page of the *New York Times* (March 1, 1928). John had already made news for delinquent taxes, then received a bench warrant for reckless driving on April 10: no wonder Mae Costello was worried.

John was interviewed about his Bowl *Hamlet* in the *New York Times* (May 6, 1928). One of his weirder plans was a projected two-reeler of *Hamlet* starring Charlie Chaplin with Mary Pickford, Douglas Fairbanks, and himself in supporting roles, proceeds to go to the construction of a Shakespeare Theatre at Stratford-on-Avon; the project was scrapped. John made Victor Record No. 6827 on April 13, 1928; it was released in June of that year. John's letter to Ned about his New York visit (n.d.) is quoted in Barnes.

Alpert in *The Barrymores* quotes Dolores on her encounter with Mary Astor. Mary Astor (*My Story*) says nothing about airing her affair with John, writing instead, "And one time when I was alone with her I asked, 'What about you and Jack? Is that all over?' Perhaps it was an understandable bias, but to me her answer seemed rather sly and confident. 'Not—quite!' she said. My sympathy was immediately transferred to Jack, and I thought, 'You're hooked, my friend!' And another thought followed immediately, 'It serves you right!' "

Ethel talks at some length about her 1928 visit to Los Angeles in *Memories*. George Cukor, the director, has commented on Ethel's extreme dislike of Irene Fenwick Barrymore; "married whores" is quoted from Kotsilibas-Davis, *The Barrymores*. Ruth Gordon in *Myself Among Others* (New York: Atheneum, 1971) reports Ethel's reaction to *The Royal Family*. Ethel never forgave Kaufman and Ferber, replying to Kaufman long after when he asked her to do a "Three Ethels" benefit with Ethel Waters and Ethel Merman, "I plan on having laryngitis that day"—Julie Cavendish's line in *The Royal Family*. John's letter to Ned about Ethel's visit is quoted in Barnes.

John describes his confronting Blanche about the divorce in "Those Incredible Barrymores: My Son John," *American Magazine* (May 1933). Blanche says in *Who Tells Me True* that the evening John asked her for a divorce was the most pleasant they ever spent together. Blanche "funking" *The Importance of Being Earnest*: Blanche refused to make her entrance opening night, having it announced to the curious audience that she had missed rehearsals because of illness. Most people left; those who remained were treated, after an hour, to Blanche's doing a "dress rehearsal" with a prompter. As Gene Fowler has remarked, trouncing Blanche is a real temptation. Diana complains about her guest duties in *Too Much, Too Soon*. Correspondence these years between John and his New York lawyer, Henry Root Stern, indicates his concern for Diana. He made provisions for her through an insurance policy on Blanche's life for $30,000 and, since he wanted her to have $3,500 a year for life, also established a trust fund. He assures Stern that she will also receive "by far the largest part of my estate through my Will," one of his more pathetic prophecies: Gene Fowler Collection.

WCFTR has the original papers covering John's return to Warner Brothers: in a contract dated July 7, 1928, John agrees to appear on an exclusive basis in five Warner features "with Vitaphone accompaniment." Not only is he to be "sole star and principal actor" with script approval, but Hotchener as his manager receives $15,000 per picture *direct from the studio,* in addition to what John himself paid him as his manager. Warners approved John's appearance in "spoken drama" (theatre) as long as he was not engaged in or preparing a photoplay. Since the starting date for his first picture was April 1, 1929, his Warner contract had nothing to do with the cancellation of *Hamlet* in September 1928. Fowler in *Good Night* attributes John's canceling *Hamlet* to his sulking because he imagined Dolores had flirted with an old friend of the family, but this does not explain future cancellations or deal with John's powerful conflict about returning to the stage.

CHAPTER TWENTY: 1928–1929

William Cameron Menzies, art director of *The Beloved Rogue* and *Tempest,* designed "The Marriage House" for John. After the charge of the mysterious woman, reported in the Los Angeles *Times,* reporters went looking for Blanche, whom they found vacationing near Cannes. "How interesting," she said, informed John was married. "I wish him happiness." The New York *Daily News* (November 29, 1928) boasted a scoop: "a secret tryst" with "an unknown woman among the roses of the gorgeous gardens of the Ambassador Hotel" had spurred Michael Strange's "sensational testimony" in the divorce court. The testimony was not in the least sensational, Blanche and John having agreed on this course since adultery was the only acceptable grounds for divorce in New York State. John's looking "half his age one day, twice his age the next": Douglas Fairbanks Jr. in "John Barrymore," *Vanity Fair.* Ruth Waterbury in a 1928 *Photoplay* interview described John's face as looking "as thin and worn as a fine gold coin."

Eternal Love was roundly panned; the quoted reviewer is A. M. Sherwood Jr. in *Outlook and Independent* (June 5, 1929). Camilla Horn complained that John had a double for the hazardous scene in which they cross the glacier, while she did not. John told her, "They couldn't care less. As long as they get their shot in the camera, we can go and *drop dead!*" Obviously someone cared about Barrymore, however. "He looks terrible and acts worse": Even given the fact that John could look twice his age on occasion, it seems incredible that the man who was called the handsomest of his generation could come across so badly on screen. One might almost suspect the make-up department of sabotage. John has a three-day beard, fat cheeks, falsely blackened eyebrows, huge eye-whites, lipsticked mouth. He looks dissolute and acts dissolute, *always* drinking, for example. He walks stiffly, poses constantly, and then those limp wrists! Strange that Lubitsch could not get a more attractive performance from him.

Dolores's honeymoon journal, as well as her and John's joint log for Mae Costello, are extensively quoted in Gene Fowler's *Good Night.* Neither document is among John's papers in the Fowler Collection, however.

Gloria Swanson discusses *Sadie Thompson* at length in *Swanson on Swanson* (New York: Random House, 1980). *Sadie Thompson* survives today only because Swanson stored the one remaining print of the film in Mary Pickford's nitrate film vault; many early films produced on chemically unstable nitrate film stock simply disintegrated. Even so, by 1950 the last eight-minute reel—Hamilton forcing his way into Sadie's room to rape her, the discovery of his body, the reunion of Sadie and "Handsome" O'Hara—had decomposed. The refilming of that reel is discussed by Audrey Kupferberg and Rob Edelman in "*Sadie Thompson*: The Restoration and Recreation of a Lost Classic," *Sightlines* (Summer/Fall 1987). The critique of Lionel's Hamilton is quoted from "Exceptional Photoplays: *Sadie*

Thompson," National Board of Review Magazine (February 1928) in George C. Pratt's *Spellbound in Darkness.*

Ethel on talking pictures is quoted in Kotsilibas-Davis, *The Barrymores.* According to *Memories,* Ethel learned from Zoë Akins toward the end of the long run of *The Constant Wife* that the Shuberts wanted to build her a theatre and name it after her, the condition being that they manage her. Since they had a play she loved, *The Kingdom of God,* she accepted. I am grateful to Phyllis Powell for her comments on *The Kingdom of God* as well as to Susan Harley for her observations of Ethel on tour. When I spoke with Mrs. Harley over the phone, I referred to Ethel Barrymore as "Ethel." There was a profound silence, then: *"Miss* Barrymore, *please,* for us older folks. 'Ethel' is shocking!" Nothing brought home to me more clearly Ethel Barrymore's powerful persona. Another example of Ethel's clout, said Mrs. Harley, was the occasion of a dinner in Detroit when Ethel inadvertently was seated next to a woman who, it leaked out, had recently appeared in court for shoplifting. The entire *Kingdom of God* company was in a state of terror throughout the dinner for fear Miss Barrymore would find out and be outraged.

Ruth (Mrs. Jacques) Gordon is quoted from Alpert. The late John Seymour, related by marriage to Ethel through the Rankin-Davenport-Seymour connection, provided me with valuable insights into the Ethel–Georgie Drew Mendum relationship. "You ought to be supremely happy" is quoted from Ethel Barrymore's "Myself As I Think Others See Me," as is her response.

Ethel Colt complained about her publicity-ridden youth in a Washington *Post* interview (September 15, 1968). "Ethel Colt Yields to Lure of Stage," announced the Philadelphia *Evening Bulletin* (June 6, 1929), which also reported on her graduation that took place at Notre Dame de Namur's new location in Rose Valley near Moylan, Pennsylvania.

Don Marquis's contretemps with his tenant are described in Edward Anthony's *O Rare Don Marquis* (Garden City, N.Y.: Doubleday, 1972). Marquis was rumored to have appealed to John Barrymore, who replied, "If she's badgered enough she'll pay, although she won't like it." Anthony does not say whether Marquis badgered Ethel enough.

John's blowup after Dolores danced with David O. Selznick is reported by Alpert, who interviewed Dolores. "Less than freshly laundered": James Montgomery Flagg to Spencer Berger. Fowler's *Good Night* reports Ethel's worrying about John's drinking. "Working in films was shoveling trash": the whole story is told in "Those Incredible Barrymores: Lionel, Ethel, and I," *American Magazine* (February 1933).

Mae Costello died intestate with an estate that did not exceed $1,000; Dolores, however, filed a petition for administration of her mother's estate because Mrs. Costello had in her keeping $61,000 in two banks that belonged to Dolores. Dolores was more prudent with money than John. Maurice Costello's "I used to drive into the hills" is quoted in Kobler, no source.

Lionel devotes considerable space to silent picture days and the coming of sound in *We Barrymores.* I am also indebted to Kevin Brownlow's *Hollywood: The Pioneers* (New York: Alfred A. Knopf, 1980) and *The Parade's Gone By . . .* (New York: Alfred A. Knopf, 1968) and to Spencer Berger, who shared his thorough knowledge about the evolution from silent to sound films with me. Kevin Brownlow discusses "The Rise and Fall of John Gilbert" in *Hollywood: The Pioneers.* Gilbert's daughter, Leatrice Gilbert Fountain, writes at length about *His Glorious Night* in *Dark Star,* with John R. Maxim (New York: St. Martin's Press, 1985); Louis B. Mayer, Hedda Hopper, Louise Brooks, and Douglas Fairbanks Jr. are quoted from that source. Brownlow and Fountain disagree about the direction of *Redemption,* Brownlow saying that Lionel was brought in for retakes, Fountain that Lionel was replaced by Fred Niblo halfway through the picture. As for the sabotage of *His Glorious Night,* Fountain also reports that the director Clarence Brown told her,

"We never turned up the bass when Gilbert spoke; all you heard was treble." Mayer's motive, according to Fountain, was not only revenge but cost-cutting. Mayer was paring his payroll to pay for the studio's conversion to sound; he couldn't break Gilbert's lucrative contract, but Gilbert might himself. "I'll tell you how to get rid of him," Fountain reports the studio boss William Fox telling Mayer. "Give him a couple of bad parts. That'll make him mad."

John received $25,000 for *The Show of Shows*: Warner Brothers Archives, Special Collections of the University of Southern California. His performance was highly praised: "The scene by Barrymore stands out like a fine cameo amid the ambitious and dazzling array of talents and ballets which whirled by with kaleidoscopic speed": *Screenland* (February 1930). John's letter to Ned is quoted from Barnes's *The Man Who Lived Twice*; the Gustave Flaubert story (mistakenly attributed to Anatole France in Barnes) that interested him was "St. Julian the Hospitaler," which, he said, would have to be "monkeyed with if it is not sufficiently Chautauqua."

"Come and see me, Daddy": Diana to John, October 15, 1927. Diana dates her first remembered meeting with her father as 1929 in *Too Much, Too Soon*. However, in a letter to Ned Sheldon that Barnes ascribes to 1928, John wrote, "Diana is adorable, and the three of us will have such fun as she grows up or gets larger, as she is quite grown up enough as she is." John traveled back and forth to New York a number of times in 1928–1929; the exact time of this father-daughter meeting cannot be pinpointed.

CHAPTER TWENTY-ONE: 1930–1932

A silent print of *General Crack* from Czechoslovakian film archives with Czech subtitles is owned by the Museum of Modern Art; sound discs for the film are reportedly in Warner Brothers' Burbank vault. In February 1941 at the end of his career, John gave his copy of George Preedy's novel *General Crack* to Spencer Berger, saying "Who else is interested?" John made notes in the margins such as "All these lines should be acrid and amusing" and "If this is in—it should be a compelling, vital and magnificent speech—(a stunt!)." Charles Oelrichs wrote John on March 25, 1930, about Diana's reaction to *General Crack*, continuing, "Diana is a sweet child, has a brilliant mind, a great imagination, and a happy disposition and with it a promise of great beauty": Spencer Berger Collection.

John's letters of January 25, 1930, to Darryl Zanuck, associate executive in charge of production, about *Ibbetson* and *Kismet*, and March 26, 1930, to Jack Warner about *Hamlet* are in the Warner Brothers Archives, University of Southern California Library.

The trade paper *Harrison's Reports* summed up *The Man From Blankley's* (based on F. Anstey's amusing piece) correctly: "Will satisfy to the core those who enjoy subtle, original comedy . . . [but] it is doubtful that it will draw at the box-office." Joseph Garton quotes Myrna Loy on *Blankley's* in *The Film Acting of John Barrymore*. Though the print of *Blankley's* has disappeared, Spencer Berger owns a cassette of the Vitaphone discs, which gives some idea of the movie's comic tone. The Warner Vitaphone process recorded movie sound on separate sixteen-inch discs, an inferior method to Fox's Movietone sound on film (soundtrack) because film and disc could get out of synchronism; Warners converted to sound on film in 1931.

Garson Kanin reports the John–Dr. Vruwink confrontation in *Hollywood* (New York: Viking Press, 1974). I am grateful to Spencer Berger for loaning me a print of the Fox Movietone News coverage of the *Infanta's* christening at Long Beach on January 15, 1930. John on Dolores's smashing the bottle is quoted in Kotsilibas-Davis, *The Barrymores*. The *Infanta* is now the *Thea Foss*, used by the Foss Launch and Tug Company for entertaining guests; since John owned her she has been used for the defense of Puget Sound during World War II and as a geological survey vessel. As the latter, the murals of tropical fish that John painted on the head of the main deck vanished under a coat of cold gray paint. Catherine Hunter, a sometime secretary for John who claimed to be a friend of Dolores's, reported on the new baby and on Dolores's decision to leave films in "An Heir for the Barrymores," *Screen Play Secrets* (September 9, 1930). John's dislike of Lowell Sherman is reported in Fowler's *Good Night* and Kobler.

Eisenstein on *Moby Dick* in *Immoral Memories: An Autobiography*, trans. Herbert Marshall (Boston: Houghton Mifflin, 1983). Other critics disagreed with Eisenstein (and this biographer): *Theatre Magazine* (October 1930) said, for example, that "unquestionably Mr. Barrymore's new Ahab is one of the best screen performances of his career." Spencer Berger has pointed out that *Moby Dick* was one of the first movies to use the widening and narrowing of the screen to create dramatic contrasts like the limitless sea versus the whale's jaws closing on Ahab, though this innovation was almost wholly confined to first-run movie houses. Joan Bennett's testimony that John was not drinking during the filming of *Moby Dick* is quoted in Kotsilibas-Davis's *The Barrymores*. Joan's father, Richard Bennett, the stage actor, and John were old drinking pals; Joan was afraid of John at first from his reputation but, like Colleen Moore and Marian Marsh, found him kind and helpful.

Raoul Walsh writes about his and Lionel's adventures in *Each Man in His Time*. Lionel complains about the hardships of directing in *We Barrymores*. "Do you know how morphine . . . ?": Philip Kalavros, "I Remember Lionel," *Fortnight* (February 2, 1955). Stanwyck and Ricardo Cortez complain about Lionel's directing in Ella Smith's *Starring Miss Barbara Stanwyck* (New York: Crown Publishers, 1974). Homer Dickens in *The Films of Barbara Stanwyck* (Secaucus, N.J.: Citadel Press, 1984) says, "Poor Lionel Barrymore! He should have stuck to acting. As a director he was pedestrian and flatfooted." Evidently that should read "addicted."

John's "jungle fever" rumors persisted, *Photoplay* (March 1931) reporting euphemistically that "the jungle fever assumes such a form that Barrymore cannot drink while suffering from it."

In Gregory Mank's "Marian Marsh Recalls John Barrymore," *Films in Review* (December 1985), Marsh remembered working with John in *Svengali* as a pleasant experience: "These were happy days for Jack Barrymore. He was on his best behavior, I might add; he was happily married to Dolores Costello, and he wasn't drinking. Dolores would visit the set with their little infant daughter 'Dede,' who was just learning to speak then. The little girl didn't like that beard! When Barrymore would want to kiss her, she didn't like that very much—the beard tickled her!" *Svengali* was almost universally praised, *Motion Picture* (July 1931) claiming, "Barrymore wins back all the laurels he has lost. . . . Here is Barrymore at his best"; the *New York Times* agreeing: "Mr. Barrymore's fine performance surpasses anything he has done for the screen."

Until 1934 Oscars were awarded not on a calendar basis but from the period August 1 to July 31. In 1930–1931 Lionel won Best Actor over Jackie Cooper (*Skippy*), Richard Dix (*Cimarron*), Adolphe Menjou (*The Front Page*), and Fredric March (*The Royal Family of Broadway*), playing the John Barrymore character, Tony Cavendish, in the adaption of the Kaufman-Ferber play.

"Gable reportedly had spent lean Hollywood years": the director George Cukor is the source, though Cukor had reasons for wanting to smear Clark Gable. *Scarlet Sister Mary* was based on the 1928 Pulitzer Prize–winning novel by Julia Peterkin. Ethel's and her daughter's public statements about Sister's career conflict. In *Memories*, for example, Ethel says, "It was lovely having Sister in the [*Scarlet Sister Mary*] company with me. There was a very special kind of happiness in seeing her so charming, so sure in her part. When she first came on the stage, smiling, it always seemed to radiate a glow to every corner of the theater." Yet on September 25, 1968, Ethel Colt gave an interview to the Washington *Post* that made the competition between them clear. Ethel Barrymore's grandson John Miglietta also testifies to his mother's and grandmother's rivalry. At the same time, Sister could say without contradiction, "She was the greatest woman I ever knew, nine times bigger than life."

Frederick L. Collins wrote about John's and Ethel's successors in *Woman's Home Companion* (April 1929). Armand Deutsch, a film producer and a close friend of Louis Calhern's, is the source of Ethel's and Calhern's drinking on the *Love Duel* tour. A gentleman, Calhern would never admit, however, to an affair with Ethel. Anne Seymour on the *School for Scandal* tour is quoted in Alpert. Fowler's *Good Night* reports John's discovery of Ethel's Bromidia. Spencer Berger kindly shared with me his meeting with Ethel in April 1932.

The spin-off *Mad Genius* borrowed Marian Marsh, Carmel Myers, and Luis Alberni from the *Svengali* cast. Anton Grot again did the sets, but they lack the imagination of his *Svengali* designs. John's Tsarakov, the dominating nurturer of genius, would be repeated by James Mason in *The Seventh Veil* and Anton Walbrook in *The Red Shoes*, to name only two variations on this perennial theme. The *New York Times* at least found John "never for a moment off key" so that "it is somewhat distressing when such a brilliant actor is playing in the same scene with Miss Marsh. . . ." Said *Photoplay* (July 1931) mysteriously, "Magnificently photographed and produced, but Barrymore's artistry is so perfect that this picture leaves a bad taste."

Jack Warner writes about his studio's association with John in *My First Hundred Years in Hollywood*. John's theatre offers after his break with Warner Brothers are cited in Kobler. Telegrams between John and Theresa Helburn are in the Beinecke Library Special Collections, Yale University. Helburn replies to John's "merely a rumor": THANKS FOR YOUR PROMPT AND VERY KIND REPLY IF THE IMPRESSION WHICH HAS GOT SO FAR EVER GETS BEYOND THE RUMOR STAGE WON'T YOU CONSIDER THE POSSIBILITY OF RETURNING TO THE THEATRE IN ASSOCIATION WITH THE GUILD I ASK YOU TO KEEP THIS CONFIDENTIAL.

CHAPTER TWENTY-TWO: 1932–1934

There are useful, though incomplete, records of John's and Lionel's MGM salaries in the MGM Archives, Turner Entertainment Company, Culver City. "Got a dress suit?": "Those Incredible Barrymores: Lionel, Ethel, and I." On May 20, 1931, Lionel requested that MGM discontinue deducting $150 a week from his paycheck to repay John. It was by no means the first loan: Lionel wrote John, for example, on February 18, 1927, "Have check. Heaven bless you. Loads of love from Irenie and me": Gene Fowler Collection. "Guess I'll have to change my name to John": Henry F. Pringle, "Late-Blooming Barrymore," *Collier's* (October 1, 1932).

John talks about filming *Grand Hotel* in "Those Incredible Barrymores: Lionel, Ethel, and I." Gene Fowler in *Good Night* reported Garbo's throwing her arms around John; there were half a dozen witnesses to the decidedly uncharacteristic event. Joan Crawford calls John "Peck's Bad Boy" in A *Portrait of Joan: An Autobiography*, with Jane Kesner Ardmore (Garden City, N.Y.: Doubleday, 1962). Joan on Lionel's being a dream to work with is from the same source and from Henry F. Pringle's "Late-Blooming Barrymore," where Pringle also offers the interesting contention that Lionel refused to cooperate on second and third takes. *Grand Hotel*, a box-office success, did not escape criticism: "Why, then, does the presence of a galaxy of stars offer us no guarantee of authentic thrills?" asked Matthew Josephson in *The New Republic* (April 27, 1932). "Why, all working together, do they hit no pitch of sincerity?" His answer is that Hollywood is only interested in entertaining, not presenting truth and beauty. Joan Crawford claimed that the stars' efforts to upstage each other were "historic"—if true, this is certainly one explanation of their hitting "no pitch of sincerity." Sir Cedric Hardwicke, a shrewd critic, faulted the director, Edmund Goulding, for using Baum's story "merely as a series of exercises for the stars," quoted in Robert Payne's *The Great Garbo* (New York: Praeger Publishers, 1976). *Grand Hotel*, however, made a profit of $947,000 for MGM, remarkable for Depression years. John wrote Garbo eagerly about another picture: "I am completely in your hands and gladly so. . . . Whatever your decision is, please believe I will most perfectly understand it, and it can in no way affect my very great admiration for you as an artist and my affectionate regard for you as a personage": Kobler. He does not name the picture, but *Queen Christina* went into production in 1933. Garbo on John's "divine madness" quoted from Fowler's *Good Night*.

Good Night is also the source for John's reaction to the birth of a son, reported to Fowler by Hotchener. Dolores, quoted in Alpert, confirms John's ambivalence about acting: "His very acting career that had made him so successful seemed to turn him inside out."

I am very grateful to Katharine Hepburn for talking to me at length about the Barrymores and about her experience filming *A Bill of Divorcement* with John, which she also discusses in John Kobal's *People Will Talk*. Joseph Garton in *The Film Acting of John Barrymore* calls John's performance "extraordinary . . . human . . . vulnerable," but says that today the film is often laughable chiefly because of Hepburn's performance.

I have drawn on the MGM Archives for contract and billing information for *Rasputin and the Empress*, which Thalberg invited Ethel to make early in 1932. Other sources include *Memories* and *We Barrymores*; "Those Incredible Barrymores" in the February and March 1933 issues of *American Magazine; Time* (March 7, 1932); Kenneth Barrow, *Helen Hayes: First Lady of the American Theatre* (Garden City, N.Y.: Doubleday, 1985); Ben Hecht, *The Improbable Life and Times of Charles MacArthur* (New York: Harper, 1957); Samuel Marx, *Mayer and Thalberg: The Make-Believe Saints* (New York: Random House, 1975); Elsa Schallert, "They're the Royal Family of Hollywood Now," *Motion Picture* (September 1932); Spencer Berger, "Ethel Barrymore Colt," *Hopkins Literary Magazine*; and "The Royal Family Reunion," *Motion Picture* (August 1932). Kotsilibas-Davis, who interviewed cast members like Jean Parker, discusses the filming of *Rasputin and the Empress* at length in *The Barrymores*. Memos about Ethel's refusing to learn dialogue at night and appear on the set before she was ready are in the MGM Archives. "Well, they needn't call *me* for nine," Ethel is reported as saying on another occasion. "I *won't* be called on the set and kept waiting. The others are always late. You won't need me until afternoon and perhaps not then." Obviously La Barrymore gave the studio a lot of trouble. Ethel's earning $57,500 and spending $65,482 was reported in the *New York Times* (September 21, 1952) in a review of her tax record. Sidney Skolsky in the *Times* quoted Ethel's strictures on Hollywood (April 5, 1933).

Prince and Princess Yousoupov sued MGM which, they claimed, had grossly misrepresented the Prince's (Chegodieff in the film) relationship with the Mad Monk. The exact amount of the award was not disclosed, though rumored to be close to a million dollars. "The settlement was for a lot more money than they'll admit at MGM," said the Yousoupovs' lawyer, Fanny Holtzman. Though Ethel thought the lawsuit "painfully cheap," she had tried to warn Thalberg that the Yousoupovs would take umbrage. Ironically, however, Yousoupov sued because he was *not* given credit for the murder in the film; then a real Chegodieff sued MGM for using his name when he had nothing to do with Rasputin's murder. Apart from the lawsuit, the lack of big audiences in America and the fact that *Rasputin* had to be withdrawn in England resulted in huge losses for MGM on its Barrymore venture. The Yousoupovs' lawsuit is discussed in Edward D. Berkman's biography of Fanny Holtzman, *The Lady and the Law* (Boston: Little, Brown, 1976), and Bosley Crowther's *The Lion's Share* (New York: Dutton, 1957).

Ethel's remarks on the bilge water of Broadway were reported in the Philadelphia *Evening Bulletin* (December 21, 1931). The New Haven tryout of *Encore* was a disaster: Ethel had a cold for the November 28, 1932, opening, was barely audible the next night, and canceled the following matinee and evening performances. *Encore* was due at the Plymouth Theatre on December 19, but Hopkins postponed the New York opening indefinitely. In *Memories* Ethel reports the play failing in Chicago because of Roosevelt's "Bank Holiday"; that, however, occurred in March 1933 and she played Chicago in May. Ethel's contretemps with Chamberlain Brown is documented in copies of letters in Locke; Brown offers numerous excuses for not paying Ethel, including his past loyalty. The play *Mrs. Moonlight*, which Ethel wanted, had a very successful 321-performance run in New York. William Adams Delano's suit against Ethel is reported in an unidentified clipping dated October 29, 1934: Locke. In connection with her tax delinquencies, Ethel put the big bed given to her by Colonel Colt up for sale for $3,700; there were no takers.

Ruth (Mrs. Jacques) Gordon's testimony about Ethel's drinking is quoted from Alpert. Ethel's and Eva Le Gallienne's appearance at the Philadelphia Lecture Assembly at the Warwick Hotel raised a storm of controversy. I quote Ethel's angry remarks compositely from the Philadelphia *Evening Bulletin, Record,* and *Inquirer* of December 1, 2, and 3, 1933. "I have suffered a great deal watching plays in which Miss Barrymore has acted," declared one of the insulted Philadelphia society women. "I never considered her a good actress and she proved that she wasn't—much less a lady." Various actors were asked for their response. "I'm sure Miss Barrymore was right," said Fredric March. "She always is, and she is to be congratulated on coming to the aid of a fellow actor." Said Helen Hayes piously, "Oh, my, what a statement. I can't understand why Miss Barrymore should have turned on her audience like that. We actresses have every reason to be grateful to our audience." Told of Ethel's outburst, the musical comedy star Irene Bordoni said, "I think that's cute!"

Ashton Stevens's story about Mrs. Patrick Campbell was told by his wife, Kay Ashton-Stevens, in *Variety* (January 7, 1953), quoting from a 1946 Stevens column. Ethel's "Dearest Jake" letter, written in pencil, inscribed "Private and Personal," and postmarked January 3, 1934, is in the Gene Fowler Collection. Fowler told Spencer Berger that John "ducked Ethel" in the last years because he "couldn't live up to her." Ethel opened at the London Palladium on February 5, 1934. Douglas Fairbanks Jr. writes about her debacle in *The Salad Days* (Garden City, N.Y.: Doubleday, 1988), and I have also drawn on clippings in the Mander and Mitchenson Theatre Collection. In the light of her own inaudibility, an interview Ethel gave in London complaining about slovenly, half-inaudible modern stage voices is rather pathetic.

Quoting his mother, John Miglietta told this biographer that his grandmother Ethel out of work was like "a caged tigress."

Topaze was voted the best American film of 1933 by the National Board of Review of Motion Pictures "with a salute to John Barrymore's memorable characterization." John's performance in *Reunion in Vienna* drew mixed reactions. "John Barrymore steps into Alfred Lunt's shoes and contributes a brilliant portrayal as the wild and amorous Archduke Rudolf von Hapsburg": Mordaunt Hall, *New York Times* (April 29, 1933). "Barrymore . . . takes full license and works feverishly to demonstrate for the customers his prowess as a comedian. He seems a bit self-conscious at times; merely a somewhat elderly actor acting a part instead of losing his identity in the character. He is always Barrymore, never the Archduke. . . . Unlikely money film outside of a few of the larger cities": *Variety* (May 2, 1933). The latter prediction proved too true, but the film probably would have done little better with Thalberg's original choice, the Lunts. *Reunion in Vienna* was the only film Thalberg produced with John as the solo star.

Samuel Marx in *Mayer and Thalberg* discusses the enmity between the studio bosses and Selznick's rescuing John for *Dinner at Eight*. Cukor talks about John at length in Richard Schickel's *The Men Who Made the Movies* (New York: Atheneum, 1975). Selznick sent a memo to M. E. Greenwood on April 12, 1933 (MGM Archives), regarding John's drunkenness. It is incredible that Mayer called this John's "first serious offense": he held up shooting frequently during *Rasputin and the Empress*, according to Marx in *Mayer and Thalberg*. Jack's "thimble" remark quoted by Elaine Barrymore in *All My Sins Remembered*.

Frances Marion, an MGM screenwriter, described Mayer's acting antics in *Off With Their Heads! A Serio-Comic Tale of Hollywood* (New York: Macmillan, 1972). Samuel Marx writes about Lionel's helping Mayer persuade MGM employees to take 50 percent cuts. After the meeting Mayer was heard to remark smugly, "How did I do?" MGM's Depression strategies are also discussed in Leonard Mosley, *Zanuck: The Rise and Fall of Hollywood's Last Tycoon* (Boston: Little, Brown, 1984).

On May 16, 1933, Selznick sent a memo to Nicholas M. Schenck, president of Loew's and MGM, about using all three Barrymores again: "I am trying to make a selection from *The Forsyte Saga* by Galsworthy for the remaining picture we have with John Barrymore. I also plan on using Lionel Barrymore in this picture and at the right time may submit for your consideration something that I fear will offhand have opposition from you—the thought of again using Ethel Barrymore. I think we could get an extremely important picture by having the three Barrymores as members of a single family, and assure you we will not have the grief of *Rasputin*, because it will be a finished script and Ethel, if we decide to use her, and have the right part for her, can take the part or leave it. Also, Cukor, who is very enthusiastic about the idea, has handled the Barrymores on many occasions, without the slightest difficulty—perhaps the only director of which this can be said": *Memo from David O. Selznick*, ed. Rudy Behlmer (New York: Viking, 1972). Less than a year later, a Selznick memo reads, "The market is and will be flooded with John Barrymore pictures and we should not permit an additional one. This was one of the considerations of permitting him to do *Counsellor-at-Law*." Thalberg expressed regrets about MGM's plans to abrogate John's contract to Spencer Berger in mid-August 1933.

John's reassurance to William Wyler is quoted from Kobler, no source. John called his part "longer than the Old Testament" in a letter of September 22, 1933, to a Miss Field: Gene Fowler Collection. Margaret Carrington tells of her hopes of persuading John back to the theatre in "The John Barrymore I Knew." Gene Fowler quotes John saying that Mrs. Nicholls's house was the last home he ever knew. Fowler reports fifty unsuccessful retakes of the *Counsellor-at-Law* scene, Wyler remembers twenty-five. "If they say you drink": Laurette Taylor, quoted in her daughter Marguerite Courtney's biography, *Laurette* (New York: Atheneum, 1968). Lionel to John Huston on John's bad luck in Huston's *An Open Book* (New York: Alfred A. Knopf, 1980). Gene Fowler co-scripted *State's Attorney* with Rowland Brown, tailoring it to fit John.

The 1933 magazine biography was "Those Incredible Barrymores" in *American Magazine*, ghost-written by Jerome Beatty, a friend of John's since the days Beatty was head of publicity and advertising for Famous Players. In 1935 this series, condensed, was published in a cheap edition called *We Three—Ethel—Lionel—John* (Akron, Ohio: Saalfield Publishing).

CHAPTER TWENTY-THREE: 1933–1935

I am indebted to Marguerite Courtney's discussion of her mother's alcoholism in her fine biography, *Laurette*. Ethel knew Laurette's husband J. Hartley Manners in London when he was an actor. According to Courtney, "Many of his early [playwriting] efforts he took to a young friend, Ethel Barrymore, for criticism. A quiet, 'No, Hartley,' from Ethel sent him off again to write another. He had great respect for her judgment." His big success came with *Peg O' My Heart*, written for Laurette. "Alas, poor Hartley," said Ethel of the popular but critically underrated writer, "only the audiences like his plays."

John was scheduled to act a temperamental conductor husband to Katharine Hepburn's composer wife in *Break of Hearts*, but script difficulties shelved the project, which was filmed later with Charles Boyer and Hepburn. *Long Lost Father* was shot in two weeks, John making $25,000 a week.

On March 28, 1933, Bernard Shaw and his wife Charlotte spent approximately two and a half hours in Hollywood. Marion Davies hosted a luncheon for them at her MGM bungalow, Chaplin, Mayer, Clark Gable at the main table, other guests including John, William Randolph Hearst, Una Merkel, and O. P. Heggie, who had acted with John in *Justice*. Shaw then visited the *When Ladies Meet* and *Dinner at Eight* sets. On the way to the latter, John reportedly asked Shaw for his autograph for his son, which, upon learning the child was not a year old, Shaw refused, saying that the child was too young to appreciate it. One source said that Barrymore was "taken aback," another that "he got sore and jumped out of the car, ruining his costume in the rain": Bernard Dukore, "GBS, MGM, RKO: Shaw in Hollywood," *Shaw: The Annual of Bernard Shaw Studies*, 5 (University Park: Pennsylvania State University Press, 1985). Either the sources were wrong or Shaw repented. John added a "Jr" to his embossed "JB" in a letter to Shaw of May 24, 1933: "My dear Mr. Shaw, Thank you so much for your autograph. May I come and see you to thank you for it when I grow up?" I am grateful to Dan H. Laurence, who discovered John's thank-you in the British Library. The *Devil's Disciple* correspondence is quoted in Fowler: Shaw wrote John on November 14, 1933, and January 22, 1934.

The filming of *Twentieth Century* has received a good deal of attention. Garton gives a long analysis, and there are accounts in Gene Fowler and Kotsilibas-Davis, *The Barrymores*. Joseph McBride in *Focus on Howard Hawks* (Englewood Cliffs, N.J.: Prentice-Hall, 1972) and Doug Featherling in *The Five Lives of Ben Hecht* (Toronto: Lester and Orpen, 1977) also discuss the film, Featherling labeling Hecht a "masculinist." Garton argues that the anti-Hollywood tone of the film is all Hecht, not Barrymore, forgetting that Jack called Hollywood, among other choice epithets, "that sinkhole of culture." The Hawks-Lombard dialogue is based on Hawks's account in Richard Schickel's *The Men Who Made the Movies*. Worthington Miner on John's deterioration is quoted in Kobler.

The account of John's breakdown, hospitalization, medical analysis, and treatment are based on Fowler's reporting in *Good Night*. According to Dr. J. Evan Blanchard, the difficulty with the hypoglycemia theory is that hypoglycemia is characteristic of people with end-stage liver disease; more commonly, people with early cirrhosis have high blood sugar due to the inability of the liver to metabolize glucose and to a relative insulin resistance in the cells. However, since John had been, as Hirschfeld concluded, a drunk since the age of fourteen, cirrhosis may have been well advanced. As previously noted, John's medical records, though indexed, are missing from the Gene Fowler Collection. *Good Night* is also the source for the *Infanta* cruise and the final flight from Tower Hill, Fowler using Hotchener, who kept a shorthand diary which he lent for *Good Night*, and perhaps John himself as sources. I have taken into account their obvious bias, which has been to some extent corrected by Alpert, who talked to Dolores, and by Kotsilibas-Davis in *The Barrymores*, which reports Dolores calling the Hotcheners "evil outside influences." Obviously there was a terrific power struggle going on, with John in the middle and Dr. Hirschfeld perhaps the only person of disinterested integrity in the whole sordid business. John's telegram to Hotchener is in the Gene Fowler Collection. Kotsilibas-Davis interviewed Dolores (Dede) Barrymore Bedell; her memory of her parents' breakup is in Kotsilibas-Davis, *The Barrymores*. John finally left the country telling reporters, "I am still very much in love with my wife. We are very happy. . . ."

Marie Dressler praises Lionel in *My Own Story* (Boston: Little, Brown, 1934). "As my brother Lionel says," quoted in Elaine Barrymore, *All My Sins Remembered*. Lionel and Irene were photographed frequently in 1933 at various events, Lionel often looking as strained as Irene. Spencer Berger was present at Mamaroneck on the occasion of Ethel's "that bitch" remark. Cukor on Irene reported by his friends; Mrs. Goldwyn quoted in Kotsilibas-Davis, *The Barrymores*. On Lionel as "Hollywood's Greatest Lover" and his showing up at parties to check on Irene: Sara Hamilton, "Until Death Them Did Part," *Photoplay* (April 1937), an article that has a ring of truth despite a welter of misinformation that includes Lionel's having given up the stage on the death of his two sons! "I feel as if I've dived under a raft": Lionel to Fowler in *Good Night*.

Lionel's perennial financial difficulty is documented in the MGM Archives; he was currently trying to recover $12,619 from a bad investment in a guaranty company, as was John. Naturally Lionel was strongly anti-union during these years that actors, writers, and directors were being wooed by Hollywood branches of the Dramatists Guild and Actors Equity. Studio bosses urged their personnel to repel approaches from "foreigners" and join the company-approved Academy of Motion Picture Arts and Sciences. Many did. In *We Barrymores* Lionel devotes a whole chapter of praise to his boss, "A Bow to Louis B."

Ethel was interviewed on her fifty-fifth birthday by Michel Mok in the New York *Post* (August 15, 1934). Spencer Berger reports Eva Le Gallienne deploring John's abandoning the stage for Hollywood: "She was fanatic on the matter." Le Gallienne writes about her professional relationship with Ethel in *With a Quiet Heart* (New York: Viking, 1953). Eloise Armen, a former stage director of Laurette Taylor's and a friend and neighbor of Miss Le Gallienne's, told me that Le Gallienne's feeling for Ethel approached reverence. Mrs. Arman confirms that there was a definite feeling in theatrical circles that Ethel could not be risked on Broadway because of her drinking.

Woollcott was a thorough Barrymorean. After the second act of the opening in Baltimore of *The Kingdom of God*, Raoul Fleischmann dared to call the play dull and monotonous. "It has," said Woollcott severely, "all the monotony of a great church bell," and turned on his heel: John Baragwanath, *A Good Time Was Had* (New York: Appleton-Century-Crofts, 1962). Ethel's scrimmages over taxes and debts are reported in the New York *Herald Tribune* (April 24, 1934, January 24, 1935) and in the New York *Post* (July 1935). Ethel's "smashed" performance in Birmingham was described in a letter to this biographer; the New Orleans episode was reported locally on November 5, 1935. Ethel gave her own interpretation in Minneapolis (December 10, 1935) under the headline "WOMEN MAKE BUM NEWSPAPER MEN." "I simply told her I never permitted myself to be interviewed by girls." The girl said, "Ah'll crash you daown." Ethel claimed she only "gestured" at the reporter and "quite by mistake" jostled a cameraman. She also claimed that she sent her manager down to the newspaper office and that the managing editor pulled the girl's story out of her typewriter; however, the story was printed. Alpert quotes Ruth Gordon on Ethel's one glass of champagne; Cissy Patterson witnessing the martinis is in Paul F. Healy's *Cissy: The Biography of Eleanor M. "Cissy" Patterson* (Garden City, N.Y.: Doubleday, 1966). Diana reports the Christmas Eve disaster in *Too Much, Too Soon*.

Ethel's "on your knees" is quoted by Adela Rogers St. Johns in "Ethel Barrymore," *Cosmopolitan* (September 1943).

John's will is in the Gene Fowler Collection. John performed the most elaborate version of the Calcutta whorehouse story at a birthday party thrown for him by Ben Hecht, reconstructed by Hecht in *A Child of the Century* (New York: Simon and Schuster, 1954). Michael Korda writes of Alexander Korda's disappointment at losing John in *Charmed Lives: A Family Romance* (New York: Random House, 1979). John's letters to Dolores and Lionel are quoted in Fowler's *Good Night*. Diana reports her father's visits in *Too Much, Too Soon*. Spencer Berger told this biographer about his functioning as an alcohol purveyor to John. John's letter to William Neblett is in the Gene Fowler Collection. "Shaky investments": one of them, John's and Dolores's struggle to retrieve $150,000 from the Guaranty Building and Loan Association, whose officer, Gilbert Beesemyer, ended in San Quentin, made print between 1932 and 1934. The judge overruled their claim for priority, ruling that the 20,000 creditors and certificate holders would share on a pro rata basis the distribution of the Guaranty's remaining assets. The Barrymores tried to overturn this ruling several times, but benefited only their lawyers.

Euphemistic still, the press reported John hospitalized with bronchitis, influenza, and strenuous work before the cameras. Elaine Jacobs ("Barrie") Barrymore describes her meeting in *All My Sins Remembered*. She claims that when she saw *Svengali* it "came over her" that she and John Barrymore were going to be very close.

CHAPTER TWENTY-FOUR: 1935–1936

As with Blanche, John said relatively little publicly about his relationship with Elaine Jacobs. She produced a memoir, *All My Sins Remembered*, with Sandford Doty (who later wrote a devastating account of working with the Jacobs women in *Giving Up the Ghost*). Mrs. Barrymore and Doty certainly capture twenty-four years after the Barrymores divorced the flavor of John's speech and the picture of his tormented behavior. Mrs. Barrymore's account often conflicts with other, more objective, versions of these years, however. There is a Barrie file in the Gene Fowler Collection containing legal documents such as Elaine's affidavit that her relation with John was not carnal, canceled checks, telegrams, letters, etc., that help balance Elaine's version of the relationship. Kobler adds Frank Aranow's previously unpublished "The John Barrymore Case." Kobler and others have emphasized how great a part the press played in the Caliban-Ariel circus, not only overpublicizing it but encouraging it. Clipping files at AMPAS bulge with Caliban-Ariel antics in 1935–1936.

During these years, accompanying the Elaine theme, are John's legal battles. One of his complaints against Hotchener was that the lawyer did not destroy checks, papers, and records so that after the break with Elaine on or about September 14, 1935, "we can start for the West with a clean slate." Why did John want these records—particularly the checks—destroyed? Probably because they testify to his extravagant infatuation with the Jacobses. Hotchener countered by denying that as secretary, agent, business manager, and adviser he had handled any sums above petty cash—patently a falsehood. Hotchener also complained that John had dismissed him in a letter dated April 14, 1935, addressed to Hollywood, though John knew him to be in India at the time. Again we see Elaine's influence: John had just returned from the cruise with Diana and Harrison Tweed and was actually living at the Jacobses' apartment at that time. But then, of course, John rebanded with the Hotcheners against Elaine before fleeing New York on September 19.

Again I am grateful to Spencer Berger for loaning me prints of *Ah, Wilderness!*, *The Devil-Doll*, and *Camille*. Berger wrote about the Mayer-inspired tinkering with *Ah, Wilderness!* in a letter of July 9, 1974, to Jeanine Basinger, a Wesleyan University professor of film studies. Joan Crawford on Lionel filming *The Gorgeous Hussy* is quoted from Crawford, *Portrait of Joan*. Robert Montgomery's and Mike Cantwell's encounters with the infirm Lionel reported in "Until Death Them Did Part," *Photoplay* (April 1937). Garbo's exchange with Lionel is reported by Frances Marion in *Off With Their Heads!*

The Carrington-Barrymore mutual disillusionment is quoted in Alpert, no source. Elaine's account of the *Romeo and Juliet* filming in which she claimed that she persuaded John to stop drinking does not tally with others: Bob Thomas, *Thalberg: Life and Legend* (Garden City, N.Y.: Doubleday, 1969); Samuel Marx, *Mayer and Thalberg*; Cukor, quoted in Carlos Clarens, *Cukor* (London: Secker and Warburg, 1976); Fowler's *Good Night*; and Kotsilibas-Davis, *The Barrymores*. John's hard time finding "a bridge to Terra Firma" is quoted from a letter he wrote to Fowler from Kelley's Rest Home during the summer of 1936: Gene Fowler Collection. "Verona made in a day": Carlos Clarens in *Cukor*. Spencer Berger kindly loaned me a print of *Romeo and Juliet* as well as a specially illustrated "Motion Picture Edition" of the play brought out by Random House (1936) in conjunction with the film, an amusingly naïve publication.

William Wellman wrote *A Star Is Born* which, he claimed, was based on the life of the silent star John Bowers, though Gilbert and perhaps even Maurice Costello were part of the portrait: there was no shortage of silent screen idols whose careers crashed with the coming of sound. James Mason's disinclination to imitate Barrymore in the 1954 version is quoted in Ronald Haver, *A Star Is Born* (New York: Alfred A. Knopf, 1988).

In an undated letter, but undoubtedly written in 1936, John writes the novelist John Erskine from 6 Tower Road (John Erskine Papers, Rare Book and Manuscript Library, Columbia University): ". . . I wish you *were* out here. I have a huge house full of empty yawning rooms in which I live blissfully alone—except for a semi-occasional coryphée—who flits but does not light—and a faithful retainer—an *older* lady—with judicious astigmatism—who runs through the entire play—but NEVER steals a scene!" Elaine is obviously the coryphée, Edna the older lady.

David Niven reports the Brown Derby lunch in *Bring On the Empty Horses* (New York: G. P. Putnam's Sons, 1975).

Photoplay's (April 1937) version of Irene Barrymore's death is dramatic but not the truth:

"Jack's Christmas gift for Renee arrived, Lionel took it up to her.

"She smiled up at him.

" 'It was sweet of Jack,' she said, 'but, darling, I know that there won't be any Christmas for me.'

"He knelt at her side, and even as she clasped his hand and smiled, the end came."

T. A. Speik, who had treated Irene since 1928, gave as contributory causes of death chronic myocarditis and laryngitis. Anorexia was seldom diagnosed in 1936. Irene was interred on December 29, 1936, at the Calvary Mausoleum.

Richard Watts Jr. championed John's *Hamlet* against John Gielgud's in the New York *Herald Tribune*. I am very grateful to Sir John for providing me with a copy of Barrymore's November 23, 1936, telegram, as well as recollections of Ethel Barrymore. Though Raymond Massey and Leslie Howard had both played *Hamlet* since John's 1922 performance, Gielgud was Barrymore's first serious challenger. Interviewed in the *New York Times* (August 18, 1972), Margaret Webster looked back at the Barrymore and Gielgud Hamlets. Although it was almost impossible to answer who was the best, "I would say that the most glittering performance was the one John Barrymore did in London in 1924 [*sic*]. Barrymore's Hamlet had enormous fire and eroticism—it was all fire and ice. But I think the best all-around performance was John Gielgud's first Hamlet, done when he was twenty-five or twenty-six. It was a youthful, poetic Hamlet and John appeared even younger than he was." The debate goes on today.

CHAPTER TWENTY-FIVE: 1937–1939

Elaine's judgment of John's Hollywood friends was not totally inaccurate. Philip Rhodes and Spencer Berger, among others, called John Decker "a bastard," Fowler described W. C. Fields to Spencer Berger as "a mean bastard," and Ben Hecht called Sadakichi Hartmann "a degenerate fraud" in "John Decker's Hollywood," *Esquire* (December 1945).

Lionel's mental state after Irene's death, as well as his preserving 802 North Roxbury Drive, is described in Gene Fowler's notes for *Good Night* in the Gene Fowler Collection. Lionel talks briefly about his closing up the house in *We Barrymores*.

Court records, transcribed by Gene Fowler, and other documents in John's bankruptcy hearings are in the Gene Fowler Collection; the Hampton-Booth Library of the Players Club has notices of the meetings of his creditors, the first on May 5, 1937. Ironically, John had been elected to the board of the Bank of America in 1933: "Decent of them to ask me," he told Spencer Berger, "—and I was decent enough never to attend a meeting." MGM's $4,000 advance, prorated, began February 8, 1937; John executed the indemnity agreement February 27: MGM Archives. Considering his state of health (he collapsed on January 12 on the *Maytime* set) and the brevity of his role, John's $5,000-a-week contract with MGM was decent. John's contract with Warner Brothers, dated July 7, 1928, is in WCFTR. Lionel defended John's making bad pictures in *We Barrymores*.

Headlines in the Los Angeles *Times* and *Examiner* chart the tragic emotional, physical, and economic confusion of John's life during the first half of 1937, from Elaine's claiming him jealous of her career in January to unpaid grocery bills in April to the reconciliation on June 22. Apropos of the divorce-reconciliation-divorce pattern, Edith Hardacre wrote Spencer Berger (February 6, 1940): "One night my husband and I sat right behind John Barrymore and Elaine at the theatre. They had just had their first interlocutory decree of divorce. He was quite disgusting—kissed and pawed her all through the performance."

The *Infanta* was repossessed and sold to the Lowe family, Alaska salmon packers. No. 6 Tower Road was eventually bought by an MGM film cutter, Hugo Grimaldi. Katharine Hepburn, Marlon Brando, and Candice Bergen have since owned or rented the property; Hepburn says that, coincidentally, she has occupied all John's Hollywood houses.

John objected to "the etymological ordure" to journalist J. P. McEvoy, quoted in Kobler, boasted he could act and read at the same time to Gene Fowler, *Good Night*. H. C. Potter recalled filming with John in a letter of February 25, 1970, to Spencer Berger. To Spencer Berger my gratitude, again, for having loaned me the hard-to-find *True Confession*. Philip Dunne, a Hollywood writer and the son of Ethel's great friend Finley Peter Dunne, witnessed Chaplin's imitation of John; I am obliged to him and Amanda Dunne for an illuminating interview.

The Studio of Acting's cocktail party for Ethel was reported in the New York *Herald Tribune* (November 1, 1936). "I'm thrilled to death and crazy about it!" is quoted in "A Barrymore Finds Youth in Middle Age," *Radio Mirror* (Fall 1936). Ethel's radio series was prompted by the success of "Lux Radio Theater" and Helen Hayes's radio shows; Ethel's proved not as popular. The twenty-six-week series began October 7, 1936, over the NBC Blue Network WJZ, 8:30 to 9:00 p.m. Besides *Jinks*, she did *Sunday, Cousin Kate, Déclassée, Camille, The Laughing Lady, The Off Chance, The Shadow*, and *The School for*

Scandal from her repertoire; seventeen more plays were added to flesh out the series.

John Drew Devereaux on acting with Ethel in *The Ghost of Yankee Doodle* is quoted in Alpert; Barbara Robins Davis talked about her experience in the same play in an interview with this biographer. On Ethel's "famous magic and authority," Brooks Atkinson, echoed by John Mason Brown, who thought that Ethel alone made a night at the Theatre Guild rewarding. Ethel on Lionel's part in *Whiteoaks* is in *Memories*. She defended Lionel's anti-union stance in the New York *Herald* (November 1, 1936). Stephen Haggard's experience directing *Whiteoaks* is discussed by Christopher Hassall in *The Timeless Quest* (London: Arthur Barker, 1948). *Whiteoaks* opened in Montreal February 22, 1938, at His Majesty's Theatre where Ethel had made her acting debut in *The Rivals* at fifteen; it had 104 performances at the Hudson in New York before touring. "AM SORRY BUT": telegram to Johnstone Briscoe (May 4, 1939); "the bloody Equity blackmailing" in a note from Boston (n.d.) also to Briscoe, both communications in the Eugene O'Neill Theatre Collection, Waterford, Connecticut.

Today when even the greatest actors descend to advertising endorsements, it is interesting to consider the Barrymore record during these years when all three Barrymores suffered financial embarrassment. Actually, Ethel first advertised petticoats in connection with her role as a petticoat saleswoman in *Our Mrs. McChesney*; later she swore she used only Cutex fingernail polish. In 1938 she did an "Ethel Barrymore Confesses" ad for Libby's. The "confessions" included Worst fault: extravagance; Best virtue: bearing no malice; Favorite actor: Henry Irving; Favorite song: "*Morgen*" by Richard Strauss; Favorite book: The Bible; Pet vanity: my complexion; Favorite food: fresh peaches; Favorite drink: strong black coffee and (surprise) Libby's tomato juice. The entire cast of *Dinner at Eight* appeared in a Coca-Cola ad except John, who would not have lent credence to the testimonial. Lionel also appeared in Rinso newspaper ads in connection with his radio series "Mayor of the Town." John alone resisted going commercial. When a woolen mills company wanted to name a bathing suit after him, for example, he replied that he "never bathed."

"I am going to the Coast at the end of this week and will speak with Joan [*sic*] Barrymore to let you know at once," Gabriel Pascal wrote Bernard Shaw (October 13, 1938); the letter, however, does not make it clear whether he is thinking of John for both *Caesar and Cleopatra* and *The Devil's Disciple*, for which, he tells Shaw, he can get Clark Gable if desired: Library of the British Museum. Theodore Dreiser's June 1, 1939, letter is quoted by permission of the Trustees of the University of Pennsylvania. John on playing *Macbeth* in the Hollywood Bowl is quoted in Fowler's *Good Night*. John's letter about *The Master of Ballantrae* is in the Gene Fowler Collection. Selznick discussed John in memos of October 23, 1938, and November 11, 1949, quoted in Behlmer, *Memo From David O. Selznick*. With his permission, I have quoted liberally from Garson Kanin's account of making *The Great Man Votes* in Hollywood.

Spencer Berger loaned me a print of *How to Undress in Front of Your Husband*. Elaine is invariably harsh with Lionel and Ethel in her memoir; they returned her feelings in spades. Her contention that Ethel cared nothing for John is contradicted by Ethel and John themselves; certainly, however, Ethel was against John's marriage to Elaine, whom she scornfully called "Ariel." Edna Jacobs told Spencer Berger that John called Ethel "the biggest ham." "The Bundy Drive boys . . . stayed pretty much away": Gene Fowler admitted to Spencer Berger that John's friends sometimes kidnapped him because, he said, Elaine was "giving Jack dope." This reminds one of John's complaint to Hotchener in Vancouver that he was being drugged when in port. Perhaps Elaine tried the same ploy to keep him passive and at home, or perhaps the paranoic John only suspected that she was doping him and Fowler believed his story.

Elaine's scenes were cut from *Hold That Co-ed*; she had sixth billing in *Midnight*. Maurice

Zolotow describes John's enthusiastically demanding to read the whole script of *Midnight* in *Billy Wilder in Hollywood* (New York: G. P. Putnam's Sons, 1977). From Zolotow also comes the anecdote of John's rushing into the women's toilet by mistake on the *Midnight* set. "He was pissing away when a lady opened the door. 'This is for women!' she cried in outrage. 'And so is this,' Barrymore replied, shaking his tool at her."

The Barrymore-Barrie "Streamlined Shakespeare" broadcasts were hurriedly put together as an answer to CBS's Shakespeare series. John and Elaine did *Macbeth* (July 5, 1937), *The Tempest*—John as Caliban, Elaine as Ariel (July 11, 1937), and *Twelfth Night*— John as both Sir Toby Belch and Malvolio (July 19, 1937). John Griggs, a Barrymore-admiring actor who worked mainly in radio, told Spencer Berger that John was sober and serious about the broadcasts. CBS outdid NBC with *Hamlet, Much Ado About Nothing, Julius Caesar, The Taming of the Shrew, King Lear, As You Like It,* and *Henry IV,* featuring such actors as Ben Webster, Leslie Howard, Rosalind Russell, Claude Rains, Raymond Massey, Edward G. Robinson, Walter Huston, Humphrey Bogart, Tallulah Bankhead, Orson Welles, Estelle Winwood, and Sir Cedric Hardwicke. John also officiated as master of ceremonies on CBS's "The Texaco Star Theater" from Hollywood in the early winter of 1938. Mrs. James Wallington, whose husband was the announcer, told Spencer Berger that John was inevitably accompanied to the studio by Elaine and Edna. "Barrymore was considered only partially successful, as his tendency to be 'hammy' bothered some. He was popular with all concerned with the program. He was easy to work with—except perhaps his habit of snapping his fingers. He was dependable from all angles, including alcohol. He 'mugged' considerably to studio audiences. He did not appear particularly attractive—for one thing, his tuxedo did not fit."

Ned Sheldon's letters to John about *Macbeth* and *My Dear Children* are quoted from Barnes, *The Man Who Lived Twice.* H. C. Potter gave his opinion about Aldrich and Myers's insidious role in *My Dear Children* in a letter to Spencer Berger of February 25, 1970.

CHAPTER TWENTY-SIX: 1939–1940

Sources are plentiful for the *My Dear Children* tour and New York run. Besides countless press clippings, I have drawn upon Elaine Barrymore's and Diana Barrymore's memoirs; Otto Preminger's *Preminger: An Autobiography* (Garden City, N.Y.: Doubleday, 1977); Gene Fowler's *Good Night,* which uses Charles MacArthur, Jack Prescott, Ashton Stevens, Henry Hotchener, and Spencer Berger as sources; Kobler; and Alma Power-Waters's *John Barrymore: The Legend and the Man.* Power-Waters's naïve biography paints the *My Dear Children* tour as a Sunday picnic; the wife of Captain Power-Waters was there, however, and both Fowler and Kobler have relied on her book for material. As Spencer Berger wrote in a review of her biography, the stories she coaxed out of John himself, however, "indicate that his imagination is now master of his memory."

The Princeton opening was reviewed locally and by New York and Philadelphia papers, the *Evening Bulletin,* for example, reporting, STAGE WELCOMES BARRYMORE BACK, "MY DEAR CHILDREN" WITH ELAINE BARRIE HAS BRILLIANT OPENING, going on to comment on John's remarkable resemblance to the late John Drew: "Those deliciously dry inflections of voice, or a tilt of an eyebrow, a purse of the lips, a significant shrug which the elder actor could introduce with such telling effect, have somehow descended upon his nephew" (March 25, 1939). Elaine's performance was called "well-drilled."

John's letter to Maurice Hotchener was published in the New York press on March 14, 1940, citing papers filed in Brooklyn Federal Court in April 1939 by the law firm of Hotchener and Finn. The same firm in September 1939 was reported seeking to collect

$9,200 from the "harassed Great Profile" for services rendered in getting rid of Elaine, threatening to reveal "certain matters of delicacy" if he did not pay.

I am indebted to Kobler's thorough account of John in Omaha. He was joined there by Henry and Helios Hotchener, who tried to straighten out his marital affairs; their briefly renewed relationship ended, however, coldly. A copy of John's telegram to Ethel is in the Gene Fowler Collection.

Chicago historian Lloyd Lewis, quoted in Kobler, coined the telling phrase "spiritual striptease" to describe John's performance. John's ad-libs at the Selwyn are recorded in current Chicago reviews, in Power-Waters's biography, and in the Random House (1940) publication of *My Dear Children*, dedicated by Turney and Horwin to "John Barrymore: *Never a Dull Moment.*" Orson Welles on John is quoted in Barbara Leaming, *Orson Welles* (New York: Viking, 1985). John called Welles "a really definitely charming oddity" in a letter [n.d.] to Alec Woollcott; "I think he is aces up": Houghton Library, Harvard University. Spencer Berger kindly provided me with records of his two backstage visits with John on July 11 and November 24, 1939, which I have combined. Eloise Sheldon Arman, Laurette Taylor's stage manager for the Chicago production of *Outward Bound*, described her and Laurette's experiences with John in Chicago in a letter to this biographer of May 23, 1986. Winnie Hoveler, the blond dancer to whom Diana objected, made headlines as "Forgotten Girl in Barrymore Case" in the New York *Mirror* (February 5, 1940). John's visits to Harry's New York Bar "are the happiest memories of my life," said Hoveler; unfortunately, John's promise to "put her name in lights in New York" came to nothing. Ned Sheldon's letter to John is quoted in Barnes. Dorothy McGuire talked to this biographer about *My Dear Children* in a telephone interview of January 20, 1987.

John's return to New York was widely photographed and reported, the *New York Times* describing the event in "John, of the House of Barrymore, Comes Home Again" (February 4, 1940). John's "the noise at your entrance" is quoted in *All My Sins Remembered*. In a brief introduction to the Random House edition of *My Dear Children*, John denied that the New York audience and critics intimidated him opening night: ". . . I just didn't think of anything funny. . . . Gosh, I tried hard enough. I kept looking for an opening, but none came." We may be permitted to doubt him in an essay which also declares "I like this play. It is a good play. . . ." Power-Waters, among others, described the eruption of Bert Freeman, the unemployed actor, onto the stage of the Belasco. For the post-theatre battle between Diana and Elaine I have drawn on contemporary newspaper accounts, their memoirs, and Kobler's biography. Doris Dudley's statement appeared in the New York *World Telegram* (February 2, 1940). "It nauseates me": Los Angeles *Times* (February 5, 1940); Natalie Jenkins Bond complained in the Newark *Ledger* (February 5, 1940). Eloise Sheldon Arman's "I didn't feel quite the animosity" and "Jack, when are you going to put on your spangled tights?" are quoted from a letter to this biographer of June 9, 1986. John's reply to Brooks Atkinson's review is in Locke. The *Billboard* polled eighty-five show-business people about their favorite performers; the results (April 13, 1940): John, 86; Chaplin, 77; Hayes, 70; Paul Muni, 64; Caruso, 53. Lionel received 19 votes, Ethel 1, a reflection of how her career had suffered in the thirties. John himself chose (1) Henry Irving, (2) David Warfield, David Belasco's star, (3) Charles Chaplin, (4) Eleonora Duse, (5) Marie Dressler. Besides his recitation at the Associated Actors and Artists ball, reported in the *New York Times* (April 22, 1940), Jack also read soliloquies from *Hamlet* at the fiftieth anniversary of the Shakespeare Club of New York and a National Arts Club event. I am indebted to Jack Prescott's account in Fowler's *Good Night* of John's last night in New York.

All through the tour John was harassed by creditors, including Dolores for unpaid child support and Maurice Hotchener for services rendered. In addition, on January 6,

1940, Deputy Sheriff Ed Kee served a writ of attachment on furniture in the Bel Air house for $3,037 owed. John was not there, but Edna Jacobs welcomed the sheriff: "I'll take good care of him and see that he has a good bed and comfortable quarters. You may not see him again for a couple of months." Deputy Kee reportedly moved into John's home.

On September 23, 1940, Los Angeles papers reported John Barrymore filing suit for divorce from Elaine "in another of the domestic break-ups which have become historic." John charged Elaine with causing him "grievous mental suffering and great bodily injury." Accompanying the suit was a restraining order forbidding Elaine from "harassing, annoying or interfering with the peace, quiet and personal freedom of the plaintiff, Barrymore, or from entering or attempting to enter the premises at No. 6 Tower Road, Beverly Hills, where the plaintiff is now residing." Elaine and Edna were also forbidden to dispose of their properties except for living expenses. "Neither of us is to blame," John was quoted as saying. "I came to the realization we'd both be happier, so I beat it." Actually Elaine obtained the divorce on grounds of cruelty.

Elaine's zeal for litigation: one of her last suits was against a record company selling excerpts from the "Streamlined Shakespeare" recordings she had made with John (for which she read a quite decent Lady Anne to his Richard III). She lost.

Gene Fowler was present when John obliterated the upper half of his drawing for *Resurrecting Life.* I am grateful to Spencer Berger, who loaned me copies of the two versions. Though John was now through with all but casual women, his reputation as a womanizer remained, and *Look* (November 5, 1940) interviewed him for "Confidentially . . . these are the thirteen most Fascinating Women in My Life." "The most glamorous woman I ever knew was my grandmother, Mrs. John Drew," said John. "My sister Ethel always has awed me more and I have dreaded her criticisms more than that of any other person." He then went on to list Carole Lombard, Virginia Weidler, Garbo, Fay Compton (his London Ophelia), his daughter Diana, Katharine Hepburn, Paulette Goddard, and his four wives.

CHAPTER TWENTY-SEVEN: 1939–1941

An undated letter from Ethel to Woollcott says, "I will only go home long enough to hurl some more or less suitable things in bags & proceed to Bomoseen. I should think that would be about Aug 12—so I'll be with you for my ninety-third birthday and we'll say nothing whatever about it": Houghton Library, Harvard University. I am grateful to the late Diana Forbes-Robertson Sheean for her memories of Ethel at Lake Bomoseen. After Ethel's death, Vincent Sheean undertook a biography of the actress for the publisher Bernard Geis but, according to Diana, dropped the project because Geis wanted him to sensationalize the book. Sheean's notes and incomplete manuscript have apparently been lost, most unfortunately, since he interviewed dozens of people now dead.

Farm of Three Echoes was produced by Victor Payne-Jennings, producer of *Whiteoaks*, and by Arthur Hopkins, who also staged it. Critics were unanimously impressed with Ethel's acting, the New York *Sun* writing, ". . . the pungency of Miss Barrymore's brilliant acting gives [Ouma Gerart] depth and breadth and often violently comical life" (November 29, 1939).

The exact moment when Ethel stopped drinking cannot, of course, be known, but she obviously had stopped before undertaking *Whiteoaks*, which ran on Broadway a full season without any personal incidents involving the star. Perhaps it was the Theatre Guild's bringing her back to Broadway with *The Ghost of Yankee Doodle* that provided the impetus. "We Barrymores were all great drinkers in our day": Georgie to Wallace Rooney, who kindly wrote this biographer (September 28, 1985) about his touring with Ethel in *Farm of Three Echoes*. Ethel was gracious except for one night when he altered a line and threw her off stride. As soon as the curtain hit the boards, Ethel seized the unfortunate actor: "How *dare* you! In all my fawty yeahs in the the-a-tah!"

The "international incident" in Sheean's play occurs when the English Mrs. Charles Rochester visits a Detroit strike and gets knocked over the head by a capitalist policeman. Pretty thin stuff but, said Brooks Atkinson (*New York Times*, April 3, 1940), "You can regard the whole incident as a triumph for Miss Barrymore." He was echoed by Sidney B. Whipple (*World Telegram*, April 3, 1940): ". . . she could put on long, white whiskers and play King Lear . . . and the performance would be a fascinating one."

Ethel's "You can't be Stanislavskyish" is quoted from *Memories*. Both Richard Waring and Sol Jacobson, then assistant to Richard Maney, the press agent for *The Corn Is Green* and the best in the business, remember Ethel's prejudice against Herman Shumlin. Waring says that Ethel always called Lillian Hellman "that terrifying woman." Tallulah's quarrel with Shumlin and Hellman is discussed in Lee Israel's *Miss Tallulah Bankhead* and William Wright's *Lillian Hellman: The Image, The Woman* (New York: Simon & Schuster, 1986). Brooks Atkinson's review is from the *New York Times* (November 27, 1940). I am very much indebted to Sol Jacobson for his illuminating comments about *The Corn Is Green* as well as for providing me with a tape of the transatlantic broadcast with Emlyn Williams, recorded live at WOR in New York, December 17, 1940. Emlyn Williams had played the part of Morgan Evans 800 times, had wanted to play it in America, but the war intervened. Williams had met Ethel Barrymore in New York in November 1936 when she came round to his dressing room to congratulate him on the success of his play *Night Must Fall*. "It was like meeting Royalty," Williams wrote this biographer on October 23, 1985. "I half-wondered why I had not been led round to the Royal Box during the first intermission! My awe was considerably intensified by the fact I was playing in the Ethel Barrymore Theatre." Richard Waring gave me a long, intimate account of his years with Ethel in *The Corn Is Green*; I am deeply grateful. Eloise Sheldon Arman described the matinee in a letter to this biographer. Afterward, when she and Laurette Taylor went backstage, Ethel said, "That one was for Hartley" (Manners, Laurette's late husband). Laurette, who always talked too much when she was nervous, told Ethel, "Eloise adores Jack." Ethel got taller. "Don't they all?" she said dismissingly. Michael Redgrave is quoted from Lillian Ross and Helen Ross, *The Player: A Profile of an Art* (New York: Simon and Schuster, 1962). *The Corn Is Green* paid back the cost of production ($14,000) at the end of the third New York week; from then on it made a profit: *New York Times* (June 25, 1944).

I am grateful to Richard Waring, Eliot Janeway, Herbert Swope Jr., John Miglietta, Babette (Mrs. Robin) Craven, and Eleanore Phillips Colt, all of whom talked to me about Ethel's children. Eliot Janeway said that Sammy contracted syphilis, which cut down on his womanizing severely. Both Waring and Miglietta spoke of Jackie Colt's charm and indolence. Ethel's "I want her to work" is quoted in the Boston *Traveler* (March 10, 1941). Ethel Colt's Tic Toc performance drew the following critique: "Introduced as a member of the Royal Family of the Theatre, Ethel Barrymore Colt displays a wealth of personal charm. But her voice is cued too high for the niteries. Girl would do well with specially tailored numbers or pops more suited to her throaty, intriguing voice": unidentified clipping, February 3, 1940, WCFTR. In Miami in December 1940 she was billed as "The Princess of the Royal Family."

Eliot Janeway reported the Barrymores' connection with Frank Murphy in a letter to this biographer of April 11, 1986. Ethel did a decided political turnabout: in September 1924 she had campaigned for Coolidge on the radio, she lunched with Coolidge several times, and in December 1935 urged Roosevelt's defeat in the press. Letters of January 11 and 18, 1941, from an unknown correspondent (Special Collections, Beinecke Library, Yale University) document Ethel's participation in the Inaugural Concert: "The White House called me today, asking me to beg you to appear in the President's Inaugural Concert, which will be given at Constitution Hall in Washington on Sunday evening, January 19th, the night before the Inauguration itself. . . . Mrs. Roosevelt will certainly be there and the President hopes to be there, too. The audience . . . will number about four thousand. . . . The program will also be broadcast throughout the country."

The record "The Great Profile Speaks: John Barrymore Live" contains Lionel's and John's February 5, 1941, tribute to Ethel and her reply: Spencer Berger Collection. Ethel's Barter Award was an acre of land in the mountains of Virginia. Eleanor Roosevelt's and Dorothy Thompson's remarks were reported in the *New York Times* (May 13, 1941) and New York *Herald Tribune* (May 14, 1941). Ethel's "Now that I'm a hit" is reported by Richard Maney in *Fanfare: The Confessions of a Press Agent* (New York: Harper, 1957).

Richard Waring provided valuable information about the tour of *The Corn Is Green*. Ethel wrote to Woollcott about Lunt and Fontanne's horror at Schnee's performance from the Hotel Statler, Buffalo, n.d.: Houghton Library, Harvard University.

Lionel's "I'll never quit motion pictures" appeared in the New York *Sun* (December 14, 1937), which also relayed the bathtub story. A memo from David O. Selznick (October 23, 1938) about the casting of *Intermezzo* dates Lionel's confinement to a wheelchair fairly closely: "Incidentally, the only reason we were able to get Lionel Barrymore is that he is now crippled to such an extent (and I am sorry to say that I understand it is probably permanent) that he is unable to walk, and such appearances as the poor fellow is able to make in the future are going to have to be in a wheel chair. . . ." Besides *Gone With the Wind*, Lionel missed playing Scrooge in *A Christmas Carol*, designed by MGM to capitalize on his radio popularity as Scrooge. Lionel himself recommended Reginald Owen to replace him; Owen also replaced him for the 1938 Christmas Day broadcast, a publicity stunt for which Lionel was paid as usual. Capra quotes Lionel in *The Name Above the Title* (New York: Macmillan, 1971).

One of the people James Doane told about Lionel's being confined to a wheelchair because of syphilis was Oliver Dernberger, a long-time Hollywood resident and collector of Barrymoriana who discussed both Lionel and John with me. I am extremely grateful to Dr. Richard Larson for going over Lionel's case with me in detail. While Dr. Larson stated that old trauma to hips or other joints could certainly cause enough difficulty to confine Lionel to a wheelchair, syphilitic joint disease is not an impossibility. Lionel's death certificate neither proves nor disproves the theory, the causes of death listed being too general.

Katharine Hepburn is the source of Mayer's urging Lionel to go public about his morphine addiction and Lionel's checking into Good Samaritan Hospital instead; Hepburn visited Spencer Tracy there during Lionel's stay. Kotsilibas-Davis in *The Barrymores* says that MGM regularly administered cocaine to Lionel at the studio infirmary to keep him working and pain-free. "When the dosages exceeded legal limits, Mayer saw that an adequate supply was obtained and that the studio absorbed the expense"—no source. If true, Lionel's glowing praise of Mayer in *We Barrymores* takes on added significance.

Anita Loos talks about Lionel in *Cast of Thousands* (New York: Grosset & Dunlap, 1977). Lionel described to Gene Fowler how to get to his Chatsworth place: notes, Gene Fowler Collection. Dolores on Lionel's "Hotcheners" is quoted in Kotsilibas-Davis's *The Barrymores*. Lionel tells of his aborted effort to import Richard Strauss in *We Barrymores*. Lew Ayres describes Lionel's political volubility in *The Barrymores*. Lionel admitted to a little purple invective against Roosevelt in *We Barrymores*. The "We the People" ad appeared in the *New York Times* of November 4, 1940. Lionel expressed his dislike of John's current antics to Laraine Day, playing the love interest in the *Dr. Kildare* series, quoted in Kotsilibas-Davis's *The Barrymores*.

CHAPTER TWENTY-EIGHT: 1941–1942

Alma Power-Waters says in her biography of John that he did not bother to read the *Great Profile* script. Zanuck had originally intended Gregory Ratoff's agent to be the main character because a story "so exact as to the facts in a case" could not be good entertainment, though Zanuck believed that with a fictionalized Barrymore character "it can turn out to be one of the most smashing comedies of the year": February 14, 1940, notes of conferences with Zanuck, WCFTR. Zanuck tried to get Rosalind Russell for the Elaine character opposite Adolphe Menjou. Producers considered Menjou a Barrymore substitute during these years: in 1936 Menjou played John in a Caliban-Ariel spoof called *Sing, Baby, Sing* with Alice Faye as Elaine; in 1938 Menjou was originally scheduled for *Hold That Co-ed*; and late in 1940 Menjou starred in a B remake of *A Bill of Divorcement* with Maureen O'Hara as the daughter Sidney. Actually, John was not supposed to be available for *The Great Profile* at all: Aldrich and Myers had scheduled another season of *My Dear Children* to begin in Chicago September 2, 1940; it is typical of John's mismanaged affairs that he ended up owing the producers $15,000 to get out of his obligation. Mary Beth Hughes recorded her experience making *The Great Profile* and the profile pressing at Grauman's Chinese Theatre in "Notes at Wild Random" (March 25, 1952): Hampden-Booth Theatre Library, Players Club. Anne Baxter on "the distance in his eyes" reported in Kotsilibas-Davis, *The Barrymores*. At one point Baxter was acting with her hands, supplicating John with upturned palms. John stared at her until she had finished, then asked in a bored voice, "Does she have to swim?" *Film Daily* (August 20, 1940) called *The Great Profile* a great picture; few other reviewers agreed. *Photoplay* (September 1940) reported John's "I love doing this film."

My thanks to Spencer Berger for providing me with tapes of some of John's "Sealtest Hour" broadcasts, several made with Lionel. Though the script quality of the programs was usually mediocre, one actually was anthologized in *Best Broadcasts of 1940–1941* (New York: McGraw-Hill, 1939). While *Movie-Radio Guide* (December 29, 1940) applauded John's broadcasting efforts, *Variety* (March 12, 1941) believed that Lionel's radio form topped his brother's. "I am doing the work of a whore": Fowler's *Good Night*, also the source of Lionel's "Jack, you don't have to feel self-conscious now." Mary Astor writes about seeing John at the broadcasting studio in *A Life on Film*.

Philip Rhodes asked me to meet him in the lobby of a Studio City Great Western Savings and Loan office. We talked there for three hours, periodically interrupted by personnel who wondered whether they could be of service. "No, darling," Rhodes would say and promptly go back to his Barrymore imitations. His reverence for the memory of John Barrymore is typical of the idolization John inspired, and I am indebted to Phil Rhodes's insights into Barrymore's character.

Richard Waring, who knew Luis Alberni, on John's reciting "reams of Shakespeare" in bars; Ben Hecht on John's Richard in *A Child of the Century*; Will Fowler describes the reading of *Hamlet* in *The Young Man From Denver*; Harrison Carroll reported John's testing his *Macbeth* in the Hollywood Bowl in the Boston *Daily Record* (May 14, 1941). Judith Anderson had played Gertrude to John Gielgud's Hamlet and was currently playing Lady Macbeth to Maurice Evans's Macbeth on Broadway. For the record, the following are John's announced plans to return to Shakespeare onstage:

December 1928: *Hamlet* in the Hollywood Bowl and Greek Theatre in Berkeley
September 1933: "Willing to play *Hamlet* next summer at Central City, Colorado"
November 1933: *Hamlet* in the Hollywood Bowl with Helen Chandler
July 1937: *Hamlet* in the Hollywood Bowl
May 1941: *Macbeth* in the Hollywood Bowl with Judith Anderson
July 1941: Shakespeare readings with the Philadelphia Orchestra at Robin Hood Dell
n.d.: *King Lear* in the Hollywood Bowl.

To these may be added the aborted *Hamlet* films: May 1930, Warner Brothers; November 1933, David O. Selznick; 1934, Alexander Korda.

John received $5,000 a week for *The Invisible Woman*, most of which went to his creditors; the *New York Times* reviewed it on January 9, 1940. During these last years announcements kept appearing about projected Barrymore films: "John Barrymore Has Last Ambition to Make Film with W. C. Fields" (1940); Cecil B. DeMille negotiating with John Barrymore to play Captain Jason Forbes in *Reap the Wild Wind* (1940); "Mae West, John Barrymore Paired for *Not Tonight, Josephine*" (1941). Bette Davis's "I'd love to do that play" quoted from letter to Spencer Berger postmarked October 16, 1940. I am grateful to Howard Gotlieb, Curator of Special Collections at Boston University's Mugar Memorial Library, for loaning me his personal videotape of John's rare *The Man Who Came to Dinner* test in which he is introduced on the screen as "Mr. John Barrymore," a tribute to his past greatness. Charles Laughton badly wanted the role of Sheridan Whiteside, but was considered too effeminate for the part, which went to Monty Woolley.

John Barrymore's will is in the Gene Fowler Collection and is also discussed in Millie Considine and Ruth Pool's *Wills: A Dead Giveaway* (Garden City, N.J.: Doubleday, 1974). I am grateful to Will Fowler for permission to quote his father's "Testament of a Dying Ham" from *The Young Man from Denver*. Phil Rhodes is one Barrymore admirer who still recites the poem à la John.

Tallulah Bankhead's "Oh, John, darling" from Eugenia Rawls's *Tallulah: A Memory*, ed. James Hatcher (Birmingham: University of Alabama, 1979). Hedda Hopper's letter of June 3, 1941, is in the Hedda Hopper Collection, AMPAS. Somerset Maugham is quoted in Kobler; Dorothy Gish lunching with John is from Lillian Gish's *The Movies, Mr. Griffith, and Me*. David Niven expressed his dislike of John in *Bring On the Empty Horses*. I am very much indebted to Ben Hecht's chapter "A Last Performance" in *A Child of the Century* for the "Epping Forest," the Earl Carroll nightclub, the baffled romantic dinner with Elaine and her phone call, and the birthday party. Harpo Marx recalls his evening with John in *Harpo Speaks!*, with Rowland Barber (New York: Bernard Geis Associates, 1961). Anthony Quinn devotes considerable space to John in *The Original Sin: A Self-Portrait* (Boston: Little, Brown, 1972). They met when Quinn got the John Barrymore part in *Clean Beds*, a play produced by Mae West. "You're a sonofabitch; you're a shit," Quinn quotes John saying when he came backstage after the performance. "You were marvelous there. How old are you? . . . By Christ! You're a kid! Ach! Christ, everybody's doing a takeoff on me, kid, why shouldn't you? At least you do it well." Barrymore had long been Quinn's idol.

Before coming to Hollywood, Diana Barrymore had appeared on Broadway in *Romantic Mr. Dickens* (a flop), Zoë Akins's *The Happy Days* (brief run), and Kaufman and Ferber's *The Land Is Bright*. Brooks Atkinson wrote of the first, "As Caroline Bronson, Miss Barrymore gives a romantic performance that is surprisingly accomplished and lifts the play out of the doldrums. This is the best Barrymore debut in some time." Diana describes her reunion with John and her Hollywood experience in *Too Much, Too Soon*. *Life* (March 9, 1942) had a feature on father and daughter, John looking very ill despite the clowning. Diana and John performed the *Romeo and Juliet* sketch on Vallee's January 29, 1942, show.

Though *Time* thought Diana "a luminously sensitive Juliet," *Variety* (February 4, 1942) said that Diana was "shallow and commonplace" and John "a grotesque octogenarian."

Myrna Loy tells of seeing John again in *Myrna Loy: Being and Becoming*. The basic source for John's last illness is Gene Fowler, who was there. Lionel also kept the watch, as he tells in *We Barrymores*. Elaine Barrymore in her memoir blames Lionel for not letting her speak with John over the phone. Kotsilibas-Davis, *The Barrymores*, reports that Dolores spoke with John, though not what they said. Lionel and Fowler differ on John's finally being received into the Catholic Church. Lionel, nominally a Catholic, says that John asked for a priest, Fowler that the Reverend John O'Donnell came as a friend to visit John, but hearing that he was expected to die soon, returned to John's room, presumably to persuade him to die a Catholic. Kobler reports John's last words to Lionel as "This is wonderful. . . . What a wonderful place," but gives no source. Lionel himself says that John's last words were "You heard me, Mike." Frances Marion in *Off With Their Heads!*, giving no source, says that John asked Diana weakly "Please stay" when he was dying; she did not. John Decker made four copies of his sketch of the dying man, one of which, ironically, Earl Carroll finally owned. Ethel does not dwell on John's death in *Memories*. She wrote Woollcott from Mamaroneck about John; he had invited her to Lake Bomoseen, but she replied, "I don't feel much like moving just yet": Houghton Library, Harvard University. Stella Adler described seeing Ethel at Pennsylvania Station in a telephone conversation with this biographer.

CHAPTER TWENTY-NINE: 1942–1945

As Kobler has already pointed out in *Damned in Paradise*, the story that Raoul Walsh bribed the mortuary attendant to let him borrow John's body for an hour as a prank to frighten Errol Flynn is myth. It fits the nothing-sacred image that both Walsh and Flynn tried to perpetuate, but also suggests "the risen god": Flynn was among the Barrymore idolators who maintained a "cult" for John. There is another story about Flynn raising his glass at a drunken wake for John Decker and saying, "And now Uncle John has gone to join our other dear friend of Bundy Drive, John Barrymore." At that point Decker's portrait of Barrymore tilted on its easel and crashed to the floor. "Well done, Uncle John!" whispered Flynn: Charles Higham, *Errol Flynn: The Untold Story* (New York: Dell, 1981). Sources for John's funeral include Fowler's *Good Night*; *Too Much, Too Soon*; Anthony Quinn's autobiography; and AMPAS clipping files.

Numerous letters as well as Fowler's accounts of court hearings in the dispersal of John's estate (Gene Fowler Collection) document the squabbling that went on among John's lawyers and creditors after his death. Roland Rich Woolley, a lawyer whom Fowler himself brought into John's affairs, was particularly persistent.

Sir Cedric Hardwicke is quoted on John as the last of the great spellbinders in Lillian Ross and Helen Ross, *The Player: A Profile of an Art*. Olivier's "I'm not a genius" is quoted from a review of Simon Callow's *Charles Laughton: A Difficult Actor* in *The New Yorker* (July 25, 1988). In his introduction to Alma Power-Waters's biography of John, Brooks Atkinson said that John had become just a scandalous name; Atkinson, one remembers, was the only New York critic who did not decry *My Dear Children*. Richard Watts Jr.'s memorial tribute to John appeared in the New York *Herald Tribune* (June 7, 1942).

Sources for these years of Lionel's life include *We Barrymores*; *Too Much, Too Soon*; Kotsilibas-Davis, *The Barrymores*; Cameron Shipp, "The Most Unforgettable Character I've Ever Met," *Reader's Digest* (August 1957); Dr. Phil Kalavros, "I Remember Lionel," *Fortnight* (February 2, 1955); Ethel Colt Miglietta interviewed in the Washington *Post* (September 15, 1968); Eugene Zador, "The Musical Barrymore," clipping files WCFTR; a Hollywood interview with Lionel by Kate Holliday reprinted in the New Haven *Register* (March 6, 1943); Mario Castelnuovo-Tedesco's "Hollywood" from an unpublished memoir translated by John Tedeschi; *Variety* (September 9, 1942), and *Time* (January 11, 1943). In 1969 Eugene Zador deposited the bulk of Lionel's compositions (more than 400, including unfinished scores) in the Special Collections of the University of California, Los Angeles. I am grateful to Robin Strausberg, who undertook the copying of some of these scores for me. Ethel rhapsodized on "Stokowski conducting" in conversation with Spencer Berger.

Lionel was paid handsomely for the "Mayor of the Town" series, though he grumbled "$2,000 for the name Lionel, $2,000 for the name Barrymore, and not one cent for my performance." Radio listeners disagreed, voting him Best Actor for 1942–1943 and in *Motion Picture Daily*'s 1945 poll Best Film Player on the Air. He depended on the money: when his manager, James Doane, telephoned him in 1943 to say that he had lost the show, he panicked. "Mayor of the Town," however, returned to the air in March 1944 with new theme music by Lionel. Like many Hollywood stars, Lionel did wartime broadcasting for causes like the United China Relief Fund and put in hours at the Hollywood Canteen. Lionel would have liked to do more broadcasting, but MGM objected, *Variety* (January 31, 1945) reporting that the studio would not let Barrymore take over CBS's "Lux Radio Theatre" as an emcee replacement for Cecil B. DeMille.

On January 29 and February 4, 1943, George Haight, an MGM executive, and Herman Shumlin exchanged letters about the road production of *The Corn Is Green* that opened in Los Angeles January 28, Haight extolling the freshness of the production compared to the shopworn quality of so many long-touring productions: Shumlin Papers, WCFTR. "My god, it was something": Richard Waring in an interview with this biographer.

Eagle Squadron (1942), Diana's first movie, was an average World War II story about an American flier (Robert Stack) fighting for the RAF and his girl (Diana); Diana acted creditably, considering it was her film debut. The mixed reviews *Between Us Girls* received indicated that Diana had definite possibilities as an actress, though not in Hollywood. I owe my discovery of Diana in *Hollywood Canteen* and *D.O.A.* to the acute cataloguing of the WCFTR, which lists them as Diana Barrymore movies even though her name does not appear in the credits.

Cary Grant wanting Laurette Taylor for *None But the Lonely Heart* is in Marguerite Courtney's *Laurette*. Ethel had good things to say about making the film in an interview with Thornton Delehanty in the New York *Herald Tribune* (April 9, 1944). I am indebted to Pauline Kael's discussion of the place of *None But the Lonely Heart* in Grant's career in *The New Yorker* (July 14, 1975), also the source of her assessment of Ethel's performance. Ethel won Best Supporting Actress over Jennifer Jones (*Since You Went Away*), Angela Lansbury (*Gaslight*), Aline MacMahon (*Dragon Seed*), and Agnes Moorehead (*Mrs. Parkington*). "Perhaps . . . they shouldn't have gone": unidentified clipping, New York (March 18, 1945): AMPAS.

"Too bad we are not all dead": Fowler's notes, Gene Fowler Collection. Fowler told Spencer Berger that *Good Night, Sweet Prince* was half the length he had intended, and in a letter to Dr. Harold Thomas Hyman, quoted in *The Young Man From Denver*, defended his exclusion of both sensational episodes in John's life and an assessment of his *Hamlet*. Henry Hotchener, incidentally, continued to collect even after John's death: Fowler paid him $20,000 for the use of John's *Mariner* sea log and also assigned Hotchener 25 percent of the biography's profits since he relied heavily on daily shorthand diaries that Hotchener had kept for ten years after he became John's manager. Fowler stated his mission in writing the biography to Roland Rich Woolley in a letter of September 28, 1942: Gene Fowler

Collection. Ethel's copy of *Good Night, Sweet Prince* is in the Samuel Colt Collection, University of Southern California Cinema-Television Library and Archives of Performing Arts. Elaine accused Fowler of, among other things, anti-Semitism. Ethel told Louella Parsons she liked the book in an interview of March 18, 1944, in the Los Angeles *Examiner*.

The manuscript of Lionel's and Anita Loos's collaborative *Old Buddha* is in TCMCNY; Loos did the writing of Lionel's plot. In a column of October 12, 1944, Westbrook Pegler attacked Roosevelt's Secretary of the Interior, Harold Ickes, for a speech in which Ickes "made merry" over Lionel's greeting Dewey from a wheelchair. Pegler represented Lionel, Gene Fowler, and W. C. Fields, along with other Hollywood Republicans, as defiers of "the insidious terrorism persecution practiced by the native [Hollywood] Communist element, who were among the hosts to Ickes when he guyed an afflicted man." The remark about Thomas E. Dewey looking like the wedding cake bridegroom was attributed to Alice Roosevelt Longworth, but Ethel made it, as Eliot Janeway, among others, confirms. The Lionel-Roosevelt flap was chronicled in both East and West coast newspapers. Lauren Bacall's "Now that was acting!" is from an interview with this biographer.

Ethel's "I never know what some theatre people mean" is quoted from *Parade* (March 25, 1945), but was typical of her attitude toward touring all her life. Ethel voiced her appreciation of private train cars to Zoë Akins in a letter [1944?] in the Akins Collection, Huntington Library. On May 8, 1943, Ethel did a guest appearance on CBS's "Report to the Nation," giving her impressions of "America at War as Seen During Two Seasons of Road Touring."

Telegrams and letters from Theresa Helburn to Ethel (Beinecke Library, Yale University) testify to the ordeal the Theatre Guild had trying to pin down Ethel for *Embezzled Heaven* and even to get the script into her hands. Most believed Franz Werfel's *Song of Bernadette* far more successful as Catholic propaganda, though the *Daily Mirror* critic at least found *Embezzled Heaven* "a sensitive, warming, beautiful play"—Ethel's opinion. Ethel protests the "First Lady" tag in "Myself As I Think Others See Me." She briefly discusses her last two plays and her serious illness in *Memories*. Presumably she did not lay a wreath (as announced) on Edwin Booth's statue on November 13 at the annual Players Club celebration of Booth's birthday, only the second woman after Margaret Webster named to preside over the ceremony.

I am grateful to John Miglietta for discussing his father Romeo (accent on the *e*) with me. "No talent, plenty of nerve" is quoted from *Stark Young, A Life in the Arts: Letters 1900–1962*, ed. John Pikington, vol. 2 (Baton Rouge: Louisiana University Press, 1975). "The Barrymore name *killed* Sister": Barbara Robins Davis in an interview with this biographer. Friends say that Ethel Colt Miglietta was "a straight-shooter"; certainly she was frank about her competition with her mother in her 1968 Washington *Post* interview.

Lawrence Langner discussed the closing of *Embezzled Heaven* and the desirability of finding another play for Ethel so that the backers could recoup their losses in a letter to Ethel of January 10, 1945 (Beinecke). On March 23, 1945, the Guild officer Molly Day Thacher suggested to Helburn and Langner that a program of one-acts for Ethel might be more interesting than trying to find or have written for her another long play. Ethel never did do another play with the Guild. "I wouldn't sign a seven-year contract with God": *Time* (September 23, 1946).

Before the "Miss Hattie" series, Ethel had done (and would continue to do) occasional broadcasts, for example, reading Stephen Vincent Benét's "Listen to the People" on "Cavalcade of America" (July 5, 1943). She debuted in Alcoa's thirty-nine-week "Miss Hattie" series over the NBC Blue Network on September 17, 1944, from three-thirty to four. She said of the role, "It's a sort of female Will Rogers part—a universal American woman, a pretty nice person." This sounds tepid, and *Variety* (September 20, 1944) agreed: " 'Miss

Hattie' is nothing more than a conventional daytime serial treatment of one of radio's well known 'typical American families,' this time the Thompsons. Teeoff show provided little in the way of dramatic highlights, either for Miss Barrymore or other members of the cast. But it did demonstrate that the distaff rep of the 'royal family' can hold her own in radio thesping and without much doubt, could really carve a niche for herself if provided with scripts worthy of her talent." This did not happen.

George Cukor's April 7 and 27, 1945, correspondence with Ethel about the Chateau Marmont is in the Cukor Papers, AMPAS. "Mother liked to be independent": Kotsilibas-Davis, *The Barrymores*. Ethel lost 1946 Best Supporting Actress in *The Spiral Staircase* to Anne Baxter (*The Razor's Edge*), to whom Lionel, obviously chosen in case Ethel won, presented the award.

"But then he had Lillian Gish": Philadelphia *Inquirer* (December 4, 1945). *Variety* reported the Catholic churches of Chicago urging their members to see *The Joyous Season*. "I loved it": *Memories*. "I don't want to sound like Tallulah" quoted from Kotsilibas-Davis, *The Barrymores*. "I don't think it's true" and "Perhaps I ought to have died": *Memories*.

CHAPTER THIRTY: 1945–1949

Some performances of Lionel's music: "Partita," Fabien Sevitzky and the Indianapolis Symphony (March 20, 1944); "In Memoriam," Eugene Ormandy and the Philadelphia Orchestra, CBS (April 22, 1944); "Valse Fantasia," Hollywood Bowl Orchestra (July 23, 1944); "Partita," Fabien Sevitzky and the New York Philharmonic (August 2, 1944); "Fugue Fantasia," George Szell and the Cleveland Orchestra (November 9, 11, 1944); "Valse Fantasia," Vladimir Bakaleinikov and the Pittsburgh Symphony Orchestra (December 1944); "Preludium and Fugue," Fabien Sevitzky and the Indianapolis Symphony (December 5, 1944); "Halloween—A Fairy Tale," Pasadena Civic Orchestra, narrated by Lionel Barrymore (November 11, 1945); "Piano Concerto No. 1," George Dasch and the Chicago Businessmen's Orchestra with June Kovich (November 1945); "Partita," Artur Rodzinski and the New York Philharmonic, CBS (March 31, 1946); "Prelude and Fugue," Fabien Sevitzky and the NBC Orchestra (June 9, 1946).

Pacific Coast Musician featured Lionel for March 16, 1946. Ethel's reaction to his "Partita" is in *We Barrymores*. Lionel defended borrowing from other musicians in a Hollywood interview (July 17, 1944), New Haven *Register*. Olin Downes criticized Lionel's music in the *New York Times* (December 6, 1944). The Chicago critics' reaction to Lionel's Piano Concerto was reported in *Variety* (December 5, 1945); a photograph of June Kovich is among Lionel's papers at UCLA, inscribed "with everlasting gratitude."

"He refused to discuss his health": Cameron Shipp in "The Most Unforgettable Character I Ever Met." Gene Fowler told Spencer Berger about the cocaine-on-the-fire episode at Chatsworth; Kotsilibas-Davis, *The Barrymores*, reports at least one other similar scene. The agony of making *Duel in the Sun* is charted in *Memo from David O. Selznick* from February 28, 1945, to August 13, 1947.

I am grateful to Elin Vanderlip for an interview about Ethel's residence in Palos Verdes and to Enid Coors, who kindly showed me through the house Ethel occupied at 1501 Chelsea Road. Garson Kanin's *Remembering Mr. Maugham* reports Ethel attending Maugham's dinner; the October 29, 1946, telegram to Robert Sherwood is in the Beinecke Library.

I am indebted to *The Barrymores* for the account of Ethel making *The Farmer's Daughter*. *Variety* called her performance in *Moss Rose* "strong"; the picture is a little jewel, with Jack the Ripper overtones. It is not generally known that Ethel still had a contract with the

Theatre Guild to do another play to make up for losses on *Embezzled Heaven*; letters in the Beinecke spell out Ethel's agreement with the Guild, a memo to Langner and Helburn on September 16, 1946, saying that Ethel had agreed to do *The Corn Is Green* after her next film. "I have given a large slice": Los Angeles *Times* (January 18, 1948), which also reported her exchange with Hitchcock. Brooks Atkinson's lament from the *New York Times* (December 1, 1946). The *New York Times* (July 26, 1946) announced her seven-year contract with Selznick, first picture to be *The Paradine Case*. When that was delayed, Ethel was loaned to Fox for *Moss Rose*; subsequently her Selznick contract was mutually canceled because (it was announced) she wanted complete control over her vehicles.

Of course she did not have complete control. After *The Paradine Case*, Selznick began a Technicolor remake of *Little Women* with Ethel as Aunt March, but scrapped the project. She had also been looking forward to working with director John Ford, playing a troublesomely drunk Englishwoman in *The Family*; that movie too did not pan out. Finally, she did not get the coveted Laurette Taylor role in *The Glass Menagerie*, which went, unfortunately, to Gertrude Lawrence. Instead, after *The Paradine Case*, Ethel put on a white wig and aging make-up to play the compassionate grandmother of a young man on the run in a second-rate drama called *Moonrise*.

Selznick's November 24, 1948, telegram to Ben Hecht about the prologue to *Portrait of Jennie* is quoted from *Memo From David O. Selznick*. Ethel's reason for refusing a long-term contract is reported in the Los Angeles *Times* (January 18, 1948).

Lauren Bacall talked about Lionel and Ethel in an interview with this biographer on May 23, 1988. H. C. Potter reported Ethel's remarks about Lionel in a letter to Spencer Berger of October 16, 1969. Lionel's excesses, according to Elaine Barrymore in *All My Sins Remembered*, involved shooting drugs. "He lives in the valley": Los Angeles *Times* (January 18, 1948). John Barrymore Jr. described his rare meeting with Lionel to Sheilah Graham, "Hollywood Today," New Haven *Register* (December 31, 1950). Dede Barrymore Bedell talked to James Kotsilibas-Davis about Ethel, as reported in *The Barrymores*. Lionel's description of the Wheelers is from *We Barrymores*, Cameron Shipp's from "The Most Unforgettable Character I Ever Met." "But what reunions!": Barbara Robins Davis was privy to Ethel Colt Miglietta's terror of those reunions; Eleanore Phillips (Mrs. Samuel) Colt told this biographer that Sammy was terrified of his mother. Jackie Colt had married Marjorie Dow Bancroft in 1940, when he was twenty-eight, after her divorce from the wealthy Bostonian Hugh Bancroft in 1936. Eleanore Colt told this biographer that Jackie's "affairs all over town" were flagrant and well known. "Don't tell Mother": Jackie's instructions at a party to Diana Forbes-Robertson Sheean.

MGM's twenty-fifth birthday celebration is described in Samuel Marx's *Mayer and Thalberg: The Make-Believe Saints*. Ethel's contract with MGM is in the MGM Archives. Interestingly enough, considering Ethel's and Lionel's coolness toward each other, they are the only stars not seated in alphabetical order for the official MGM twenty-fifth Birthday Celebration studio portrait. Lionel and Ethel are both in the front row, but June Allyson is seated next to Lionel, not Ethel.

Ethel's seventieth birthday celebration was widely reported in the press. Katharine Hepburn described George Cukor's party to this biographer. The prerecorded tribute was broadcast over ABC at 10:30 p.m. in each time zone. Much of the groundwork for the broadcast is contained in letters and other documents in the Cukor Papers, AMPAS, including Ethel's cable to Winston Churchill. Churchill was traveling in northern Italy when Ethel sent her plea; presumably this accounts for the terseness of his message. "How *is* the old sonofabitch?": Armand Deutsch quoting Louis Calhoun in a telephone interview with this biographer. Ethel quoted some of the tributes in *Memories*. "She looked so beautiful" is quoted from Alpert.

CHAPTER THIRTY-ONE: 1949–1954

Kyle Crichton tells of Lionel's making *Down to the Sea in Ships* in "Barrymore, the Lion-hearted," *Collier's* (March 26, 1949). California's centennial celebration in which Lionel participated took place September 8–12, 1950.

Lionel's correspondence with the theatre and film historian Daniel Blum (WCFTR), undated but from these years, has FIGHT COMMUNISM FEARLESSLY typed on the envelopes. Lionel's financial difficulties can be discovered from the MGM files: there is a great deal of correspondence about his tax problems, as well as records of his earnings: $13,000 for the first twenty-six "Dr. Kildare" radio series; $27.70 per program for "At Home with Lionel Barrymore," a fifteen-minute offering of cracker-barrel philosophy aired Tuesday, Thursday, and Saturday at 7:15 a.m., which *Variety* (November 2, 1949) thought Lionel lifted above the commonplace. On August 9, 1949, MGM loaned Lionel $3,000 to help settle his tax situation; on February 28, 1950, $715.98 even though he still owed MGM $551.98; on September 5, 1951, there is a $100 loan for urgent debts; on January 28, 1952, a loan for flood damage to his home, and so on. James Kotsilibas-Davis says in *The Barrymores* that Lionel signed a lifetime contract with MGM in his twenty-fifth year, no source. This seems to be contradicted by the studio memo as well as by Lionel's being bumped this year from MGM's pension plan.

I am indebted to Alpert's account in *The Barrymores* of Cameron Shipp's collaboration on *We Barrymores*; Alpert interviewed Maynard Smith, who did the note-taking. Shipp himself discusses the collaboration in "The Most Unforgettable Character I Ever Met."

John Barrymore Jr.'s running out on *The Hasty Heart* and Ethel's reaction are reported in AMPAS clipping files. John's "A wonderful woman" is from an interview of August 10, 1964, with Hedda Hopper: Hedda Hopper Papers, AMPAS.

I am very grateful to the late Whitfield Connor for his Lionel Barrymore recollections as well as his wonderful imitation of the actor. "No, I don't think so": Inga Arvad, "The Youngest Meets Hollywood's Oldest," New Haven *Register* (July 2, 1944).

The seventy-fifth birthday interview appeared in the Philadelphia *Sunday Bulletin* (April 26, 1953). Hedda Hopper's apparently unpublished interview with Lionel took place on December 21, 1953: Hedda Hopper Papers, AMPAS. "Barrymores don't celebrate birthdays": interview with Bob Thomas in the Los Angeles *Times* (April 28, 1954). Bob Thomas also reported (New Haven *Register*, November 17, 1954) a member of the family telling him Lionel wept as he recalled what might have happened had his daughters lived.

The manuscript of *The Shakespeare Club* is in the Samuel Colt Collection, University of Southern California Cinema-Television Library and Archives of Performing Arts. After Lionel's death, the Wheelers had published *I, Becky Barrymore: The Autobiography of a Famous Cat*, as told to Benson Wheeler by Lionel Barrymore (New York: R. Steller, 1959), but neither text nor illustrations did anything to enhance Lionel's reputation.

Dr. Philip Kalavros wrote "I Remember Lionel," *Fortnight* (February 2, 1955). During the last two months of his life, however, Lionel was treated by Dr. John Ewing, who signed the death certificate giving myocarditis chronic as the cause of death due to edema lung—acute, and nephritis—chronic, parenchymatous.

MGM's memo about evicting Lionel's possessions from his bungalow suite is in the studio files. Another memo lists his belongings, which included a conductor's baton, a dog-head cane, a framed self-portrait, and a silver-framed picture of women and a child; one would give something to know who they were.

Ethel's conversation with Hugh Kahler was reported by Louella Parsons in the Los Angeles *Examiner* (April 28, 1955).

CHAPTER THIRTY-TWO: 1953–1959

Lionel on the public is quoted from Ivan St. Johns, "The Barrymore Mystery," *The New Movie Magazine* (July 1932). "All my successes": answer to Daniel Blum's questionnaire (n.d.): WCFTR. The *New York Times* (November 17, 1954) said, "Yet (it can be repeated because he never had any illusions) he was not a great actor . . . but he was a great character." As Lionel requested, the casket remained closed at the service at the Calvary Cemetery Chapel attended by some 700 people; a requiem mass was celebrated by the Reverend John J. Hurley of Our Lady of the Valley Catholic Church. Pallbearers were not celebrities but old friends: George Tremblay, Neville Worger-Slade, Lee Stanfield, Stanley Campbell, William Ball, and James Doane. On November 19, 1954, the day of Lionel's funeral, Gene Fowler hosted a tribute over KNX-Radio in which Dr. Norman Vincent Peale, Helen Hayes, and Edward Arnold (Lionel's frequent rival as a "heavy") participated. The auctioning of Lionel's estate is reported in clippings from the Los Angeles *Times* and *Examiner* and MGM files. Shipp's "This is an obscenity" is quoted from Kotsilibas-Davis, *The Barrymores*.

I am grateful to Armand Deutsch for talking to me about the problems of filming *Kind Lady* and its reception, as well as about Ethel's status in Hollywood (She "wasn't worth a nickel" at the box office), confirmed by a February 15, 1951, MGM memo: "At completion of *Kind Lady* option not exercised, contract terminated, off pay roll." Ethel's contracts are on file in the MGM Archives. In 1949, for example, she had a $2,000-per-week, forty-week guarantee contract for *The Red Danube, That Midnight Kiss*, and *Pinky*, for which she was loaned to Twentieth Century–Fox, receiving $30,000 for the picture. Ethel lost the 1949 Best Supporting Actress Oscar to Mercedes McCambridge (*All the King's Men*). For *The Great Sinner* she was offered $20,000 a week, one-week guarantee. On January 3, 1950, her salary was raised to $2,500 per week "to enable her to meet her financial problems," yet she made no movies released in 1950 at all. Kazan on the "grand old battlewagon" in *Elia Kazan: A Life* (New York: Alfred A. Knopf, 1988).

"Since everyone else seemed to be [writing her life]": Tallulah Bankhead, for example, had produced "My Friend Miss Barrymore" for *Collier's* (April 23, 1949), Alexander Kirkland, "The Matterhorn at Twilight," *Theatre Arts* (November 1949), and Cornelia Otis Skinner, "The Radiant Ethel Barrymore," *McCall's* (February and March 1950). The first nine pages of *Memories* (all or almost all she wrote) are in TCMCNY, donated by Anne Seymour, later curator of the collection. Hermitage House apparently dropped its suit at the return of a $5,000 advance. Correspondence in the same collection among Bruce Gould, Cass Canfield, and Ethel spans the period August 4 to December 17, 1953; "The *Life* is a performance": Gould to Ethel on December 14, 1953. Sol Jacobson informed me of the difficulties Ethel made for his good friend Laura Lou Brookman and also put me in touch with Bruce Gould, who wrote me (February 27, 1987) about his and Harper's difficulties with Ethel and the autobiography. "I remember only what I want to remember": *New York Times* (June 19, 1959). "I didn't keep any notes at all": interview with Bob Thomas, unidentified clipping, August 17, 1954: AMPAS, also the source of "The nice thing about an autobiography." Another reason Ethel might have claimed she wrote her life herself is that she also took credit—and perhaps did dictate much of it—for "My Reminiscences," published in *The Delineator* (September, October, November, and December 1923, January and February 1924), the content of which is similar in part to *Memories*.

Ethel performed *The Twelve Pound Look* at the Ziegfeld on January 29, 1950, with Mildred Dunnock as Lady Sims, Louis Hector as Sir Harry Sims, and Philip Tonge as the Butler. Bert Lahr is quoted by Leonard Lyons, "The Lyons Den," New York *Post* (June

19, 1959). "Too Sonny Tufts" is quoted in Alpert. Ethel's "Gorgeous George" remark was relayed to this biographer by William Dozier. Sir John Gielgud in a letter to this biographer of October 28, 1985, said that Ethel was all graciousness to him in Hollywood; he was also present when Ethel refused to accompany Cukor's guests to a screening of her television program. Ethel's honorary degree is in the Samuel Colt Collection, the Archives of Performing Arts, University of Southern California Library. Ethel was interviewed at the Empire Theatre by the *New York Times* (April 7, 1953). She appeared on Murrow's *Person to Person* May 6, 1955. Ethel hosted *The Ethel Barrymore Theatre* from September to December 1956, appearing in only two of the dramas, "The Daughter of Mars" and "General Delivery." I am grateful to Spencer Berger for loaning me a tape of "The Thirteenth Chair," done for *Climax*, an hour-long series hosted by William Lundigan. Ethel also appeared, in a wheelchair, on CBS-TV's *Eloise* with Evelyn Rudie, Mildred Natwick, and Louis Jourdan.

Charles Brackett on Ethel's beauty is quoted in Alpert. Dorothy Stickney commented in a letter (February 1, 1955) to Cass Canfield (TCMCNY), Lauren Bacall and Eliot Janeway in interviews with this biographer. Katharine Hepburn spoke of Ethel's fascination in a taped reminiscence made at George Cukor's house shortly after Ethel's death.

Letters from Cukor to Hepburn, Irene Selznick, and Whitney Warren about the Ethel Barrymore Fund are in the Cukor Collection, AMPAS, as are numerous letters about founding Orpheus Recordings.

Variety panned the Texaco *Command Performance* on November 27, 1957.

Philip and Amanda Dunne talked about Ethel's invalidism in an interview with this biographer (January 1987). "Mother, either give up reading": Leonard Lyons, New York *Post* (June 19, 1959). "May I see the most beautiful woman in California" quoted in Alpert. I am very grateful to Katharine Hepburn for permission to quote from the tape she made about Ethel, passages from which I have taken the liberty of rearranging and condensing. The tape was made available to me by Spencer Berger, to whom Cukor gave a copy. "Thanks for the warning": Herbert Swope Jr. in a telephone interview with this biographer.

Father William Kenny of the UCLA Newman Club gave Ethel last rites. Anne Seymour wrote on June 18, 1959, to an unknown correspondent about Ethel's death, which she learned about from a telephone call to Anna Albert (TCMCNY). Ethel's death certificate gives the immediate cause as pulmonary infection due to arteriosclerotic heart disease (twenty years) due to generalized arteriosclerosis (twenty-five years). Her name on the certificate is Ethel Barrymore Colt, and she is listed as "widowed" rather than divorced.

SELECTED BIBLIOGRAPHY

For this biography of the Barrymores I have drawn upon published and unpublished materials in the Spencer Berger Collection; the Billy Rose Theatre Collection at the Performing Arts Research Center, Lincoln Center; the Theatre Collection of the Museum of the City of New York; the Shubert Archives; the Hampden-Booth Theatre Library, Players Club; the Rare Book and Manuscript Library, Butler Library, Columbia University; the Manuscript Division of the Library of Congress; the Beinecke Rare Book and Manuscript Library, Yale University Library; Special Collections, Houghton Library, Harvard University; the Harvard Theatre Collection; the Seymour Theatre Collection, Princeton University Library; the Department of Rare Books, Cornell University Library; the Theatre Collection of the Free Library of Philadelphia; the Furness Shakespeare Library, University of Pennsylvania; the Photojournalism Collection, Temple University; the Wisconsin Center for Film and Theatre Research, Madison; the Gene Fowler Collection, Rare Books Room, University of Colorado at Boulder Library; the Department of Manuscripts, The Henry E. Huntington Library; the Academy of Motion Picture Arts and Sciences; the Archives of Performing Arts, University of Southern California Library; the Department of Special Collections, Library of the University of California, Los Angeles; the MGM Archives, Turner Entertainment Company, Culver City; the Theatre Museum, London; the Raymond Mander and Joe Mitchenson Theatre Collection, Beckenham, Kent. For Barrymore films, I have had access to the collections of Spencer Berger, the Wisconsin Center for Film and Theatre Research, the Yale Film Study Center, the George Eastman House, the Film Department of the Library of Congress, and the Film Center of the Museum of Modern Art.

Acosta, Mercedes de. *Here Lies the Heart*. New York: Reynal, 1960.
Agate, James, ed. *The English Dramatic Critics*. New York: Hill and Wang, n.d.
Alpert, Hollis. *The Barrymores*. New York: Dial Press, 1964.
Anthony, Edward. *O Rare Don Marquis*. Garden City, N.Y.: Doubleday, 1972.
Astor, Mary. *A Life on Film*. New York: Delacorte Press, 1971.
———. *My Story: An Autobiography*. Garden City, N.Y.: Doubleday, 1959.
Atkinson, Brooks. *Broadway*. New York: Macmillan, 1970.
Auster, Albert. *Actresses and Suffragists: Women in the American Theatre, 1890–1920*. New York: Praeger Publishers, 1984.
Balio, Tino, ed. *The American Film Industry*. Madison: University of Wisconsin Press, 1985.
Bankhead, Tallulah. *Tallulah: My Autobiography*. New York: Harper & Brothers, 1952.

Baragwanath, John. *A Good Time Was Had*. New York: Appleton-Century-Crofts, 1962.

Barnes, Eric Wollencott. *The Man Who Lived Twice*. New York: Charles Scribner's Sons, 1956.

Barrow, Kenneth. *Helen Hayes: First Lady of the American Theatre*. Garden City, N.Y.: Doubleday, 1985.

Barrymore, Diana, with Gerold Frank. *Too Much, Too Soon*. New York: Henry Holt, 1957.

Barrymore, Elaine Jacobs, with Sandford Doty. *All My Sins Remembered*. New York: Appleton-Century-Crofts, 1964.

Barrymore, Ethel. *Memories: An Autobiography*. New York: Harper & Brothers, 1955.

Barrymore, John. *Confessions of an Actor*. Indianapolis: Bobbs-Merrill, 1926.

Barrymore, Lionel, with Cameron Shipp. *We Barrymores*. New York: Appleton-Century-Crofts, 1951.

Behlmer, Rudy, ed. *Memo from David O. Selznick*. New York: Viking, 1972.

Belmont, Eleanor Robson. *The Fabric of Memory*. New York: Farrar, Straus, and Cudahy, 1957.

Berkman, Edward D. *The Lady and the Law*. Boston: Little, Brown, 1976.

Bernhardt, Sarah. *Memories of My Life*. New York: D. Appleton, 1907.

Birkin, Andrew, with Sharon Goode. *J. M. Barrie and the Lost Boys: The Love Story That Gave Birth to Peter Pan*. London: Constable, 1979.

Brough, James. *Princess Alice: A Biography of Alice Roosevelt Longworth*. Boston: Little, Brown, 1972.

Brownlow, Kevin. *Hollywood: The Pioneers*. New York: Alfred A. Knopf, 1980.

———. *The Parade's Gone By . . .* New York: Alfred A. Knopf, 1968.

Brundidge, Harry. *Twinkle Twinkle Movie Star*. New York: Dutton, 1930.

Capra, Frank. *The Name Above the Title*. New York: Macmillan, 1971.

Churchill, Alan. *The Great White Way*. New York: Dutton, 1962.

Churchill, Randolph S. *Winston S. Churchill*. Vol. 2, *Companion: 1907–1911*. London: Heinemann, 1969.

Clarens, Carlos. *Cukor*. London: Secker and Warburg, 1976.

Coleman, Marion Moore. *Fair Rosalind: The American Career of Helena Modjeska*. Cheshire, Conn.: Cherry Hill Books, 1969.

Collier, Constance. *Harlequinade: The Story of My Life*. London: John Lane, The Bodley Head, 1929.

Considine, Millie, and Ruth Pool. *Wills: A Dead Giveaway*. Garden City, N.Y.: Doubleday, 1974.

Cooper, Artemis, ed. *A Durable Fire: The Letters of Duff and Diana Cooper, 1913–1950*. London: Collins, 1983.

Courtney, Marguerite. *Laurette*. New York: Atheneum, 1968.

Crawford, Joan, with Jane Kesner Ardmore. *Portrait of Joan: An Autobiography*. Garden City, N.Y.: Doubleday, 1962.

Crowther, Bosley. *The Lion's Share*. New York: Dutton, 1957.

Dale, James. *Pulling Faces for a Living*. London: Victor Gollancz, 1970.

Davis, Charles Belmont. *Adventures and Letters of Richard Harding Davis*. New York: Charles Scribner's Sons, 1917.

DeMille, Cecil B. *Autobiography*. Englewood Cliffs, N.J.: Prentice-Hall, 1959.

Dickens, Homer. *The Films of Barbara Stanwyck*. Secaucus, N.J.: Citadel Press, 1984.

Downer, Alan S., ed. *On Plays, Playwrights, and Playgoers: Selections from the Letters of Booth Tarkington to George C. Tyler and John Peter Toohey, 1918–1925*. Princeton, N.J.: Princeton University Press, 1959.

Dressler, Marie. *My Own Story*. Boston: Little, Brown, 1934.

Drew, John, Jr. *My Years on the Stage*. New York: Dutton, 1922.

Drew, Louisa Lane. *Autobiographical Sketch of Mrs. John Drew*. New York: Charles Scribner's Sons, 1899.

du Maurier, Daphne. *Gerald: A Portrait*. New York: Doubleday, Doran, 1935.

Dunbar, Janet. *Barrie: The Man Behind the Image*. Boston: Houghton Mifflin, 1970.

Eisenstein, Sergei. *Immoral Memories: An Autobiography*. Trans. Herbert Marshall. Boston: Houghton Mifflin, 1983.

Fairbanks, Douglas, Jr. *The Salad Days*. Garden City, N.Y.: Doubleday, 1988.

Featherling, Doug. *The Five Lives of Ben Hecht*. Toronto: Lester and Orpen, 1977.

Ferber, Edna. *A Peculiar Treasure*. New York: Lancer Books, 1960; orig. pub. 1938.

Flagg, James Montgomery. *Celebrities*. Watkins Glen, N.Y.: Century House, 1960.

———. *Roses and Buckshot*. New York: G. P. Putnam's Sons, 1946.

Forbes-Robertson, Diana. *My Aunt Maxine: The Story of Maxine Elliott*. New York: Viking, 1964.

Fountain, Leatrice Gilbert, with John R. Maxim. *Dark Star*. New York: St. Martin's Press, 1985.

Fowler, Gene. *Good Night, Sweet Prince*. New York: Viking, 1943.

Fowler, Will. *The Young Man from Denver*. Garden City, N.Y.: Doubleday, 1962.

Garton, Joseph. *The Film Acting of John Barrymore*. New York: Arno Press, 1980.

Gielgud, Sir John. *Stage Directions*. London: Hodder and Stoughton, 1963.

Gish, Lillian, with Ann Pinchot. *The Movies, Mr. Griffith, and Me*. Englewood Cliffs, N.J.: Prentice-Hall, 1969.

Gordon, Ruth. *Myself Among Others*. New York: Atheneum, 1971.

Graham, Cooper C., et al. *D. W. Griffith and the Biograph Company*. Filmmakers No. 10. Metuchen, N.J.: The Scarecrow Press, 1985.

Gronowicz, Antoni. *Modjeska, Her Life and Loves*. New York: Thomas Yoseloff, 1956.

Hammerton, J. A. *Barrie: The Story of a Genius*. London: Sampson Low, Marston, 1929.

Hammond, Percy. *But—Is It Art?* Garden City, N.Y.: Doubleday, 1927.

Harriman, Margaret Case. *The Vicious Circle*. New York: Rinehart, 1951.

Hassall, Christopher. *The Timeless Quest*. London: Arthur Barker, 1948.

Haver, Ronald. *A Star Is Born*. New York: Alfred A. Knopf, 1988.

Healy, Paul F. *Cissy: The Biography of Eleanor M. "Cissy" Patterson*. Garden City, N.Y.: Doubleday, 1966.

Hecht, Ben. *A Child of the Century*. New York: Simon and Schuster, 1954.

———. *The Improbable Life and Times of Charles MacArthur*. New York: Harper, 1957.

Henderson, Mary C. *Theater in America: 200 Years of Plays, Players, and Productions*. New York: Harry N. Abrams, 1986.

Higham, Charles. *Errol Flynn: The Untold Story*. New York: Dell, 1981.

Hopkins, Arthur. *To a Lonely Boy*. Garden City, N.Y.: Doubleday, Doran, 1957.

Howe, George. *Mount Hope: A New England Chronicle*. New York: Viking, 1959.

Huston, John. *An Open Book*. New York: Alfred A. Knopf, 1980.

Irving, M. Laurence. *The Successors*. London: Rupert Hart-Davis, 1967.

———. *Henry Irving: The Actor and His World*. London: Faber and Faber, 1951.

Israel, Lee. *Miss Tallulah Bankhead*. New York: G. P. Putnam's Sons, 1972.

Jones, Doris Arthur, ed. *The Life and Letters of Henry Arthur Jones*. London: Victor Gollancz, 1930.

Jones, Robert Edmond. *Drawings for the Theatre*. New York: Theatre Arts, 1925.

Kane, Whitford. *Are We All Met?* London: Elkin Mathews and Marrot, 1931.

Kanin, Garson. *Hollywood*. New York: Viking, 1974.

———. *Remembering Mr. Maugham*. New York: Atheneum, 1966.

Kazan, Elia. *Elia Kazan: A Life*. New York: Alfred A. Knopf, 1988.

Kerr, Walter. *The Silent Clowns*. New York: Alfred A. Knopf, 1975.

Kobal, John. *People Will Talk*. New York: Alfred A. Knopf, 1985.

Kobler, John. *Damned in Paradise: The Life of John Barrymore*. New York: Atheneum, 1977.

Korda, Michael. *Charmed Lives: A Family Romance*. New York: Random House, 1979.

Kotsilibas-Davis, James. *Great Times, Good Times: The Odyssey of Maurice Barrymore*. Garden City, N.Y.: Doubleday, 1977.

————. *The Barrymores: The Royal Family in Hollywood*. New York: Crown Publishers, 1981.

Langford, Gerald. *The Murder of Stanford White*. Indianapolis: Bobbs-Merrill, 1962.

Laurence, Dan H., ed. *Bernard Shaw: Collected Letters, 1911–1925*, vol. 3. New York: Viking, 1985.

Leaming, Barbara. *Orson Welles*. New York: Viking, 1985.

Le Gallienne, Eva. *With a Quiet Heart*. New York: Viking, 1953.

Lewisohn, Ludwig. *The Drama and the Stage*. New York: Harcourt, Brace, 1922.

Loos, Anita. *Cast of Thousands*. New York: Grosset and Dunlap, 1977.

Loy, Myrna, with James Kotsilibas-Davis. *Myrna Loy: Being and Becoming*. New York: Alfred A. Knopf, 1987.

McBride, Joseph. *Focus on Howard Hawks*. Englewood Cliffs, N.J.: Prentice-Hall, 1972.

Mackail, Denis. *Barrie: The Story of J.M.B.* New York: Charles Scribner's Sons, 1941.

Magarshack, David. *Stanislavsky: A Life*. London: MacGibbon and McKee, 1950.

Mallet, Sir Charles Edward. *Anthony Hope and His Books*. London: Hutchinson, 1935.

Maney, Richard. *The Confessions of a Press Agent*. New York: Harper, 1957.

Marcossan, Isaac F., and Daniel Frohman. *Charles Frohman: Manager and Man*. New York: Harper & Brothers, 1916.

Marion, Frances. *Off With Their Heads! A Serio-Comic Tale of Hollywood*. New York: Macmillan, 1972.

Martin, Ralph. *Jennie: The Life of Lady Randolph Churchill*, vol. 2. Englewood Cliffs, N.J.: Prentice-Hall, 1971.

Marx, Harpo, with Rowland Barber. *Harpo Speaks!* New York: Bernard Geis Associates, 1961.

Marx, Samuel. *Mayer and Thalberg: The Make-Believe Saints*. New York: Random House, 1975.

Meredith, Scott. *George S. Kaufman and His Friends*. Garden City, N.Y.: Doubleday, 1974.

Modjeska, Helena. *Memories and Impressions*. New York: Macmillan, 1910.

Mooney, Michael MacDonald. *Evelyn Nesbit and Stanford White: Love and Death in the Gilded Age*. New York: William Morrow, 1976.

Moore, Colleen. *Silent Star*. Garden City, N.Y.: Doubleday, 1968.

Morgan, Ted. *Churchill: Young Man in a Hurry, 1874–1915*. New York: Simon and Schuster, 1982.

Moses, Montrose J., and Virginia Gerson. *Clyde Fitch and His Letters*. Boston: Little, Brown, 1924.

Mosley, Leonard. *Zanuck: The Rise and Fall of the Last Tycoon*. Boston: Little, Brown, 1984.

Mosley, Oswald. *My Life*. London: Nelson, 1968.

Nesbit, Evelyn. *Prodigal Days*. New York: Julian Messner, 1934.

Nesbitt, Cathleen. *A Little Love and Good Company*. London: Faber and Faber, 1975.

Niven, David. *Bring On the Empty Horses*. New York: G. P. Putnam's Sons, 1975.

Noble, Peter. *Hollywood Scapegoat: The Biography of Erich von Stroheim*. London: Fortune Press, 1951.

Olivier, Sir Laurence. *Confessions of an Actor*. New York: Simon and Schuster, 1982.

Payne, Robert. *The Great Garbo*. New York: Praeger Publishers, 1976.

Peary, Danny. *Close-Ups*. New York: Workman Publishing, 1978.

Perry, John. *James A. Herne: The American Ibsen*. Chicago: Nelson-Hall, 1978.

Pickford, Mary. *Sunshine and Shadow*. Garden City, N.Y.: Doubleday, 1955.

Pikington, John, ed. *Stark Young, A Life in the Arts: Letters, 1900–1962*, vol. 2. Baton Rouge: Louisiana University Press, 1975.

Power-Waters, Alma. *John Barrymore: The Legend and the Man*. New York: Julian Messner, 1941.

Pratt, George C.. *Spellbound in Darkness: A History of the Silent Film*. Greenwich, Conn.: New York Graphic Society, 1973.

Preminger, Otto. *Preminger: An Autobiography*. Garden City, N.Y.: Doubleday, 1977.

Quinn, Anthony. *The Original Sin: A Self-Portrait*. Boston: Little, Brown, 1972.

Rawls, Eugenia. *Tallulah: A Memory*, ed. James Hatcher. Birmingham: University of Alabama, 1979.

Robbins, Phyllis. *Maude Adams: An Intimate Portrait*. New York: G. P. Putnam's Sons, 1956.

Ross, Lillian, and Helen Ross. *The Player: A Profile of an Art*. New York: Simon and Schuster, 1962.

St. John, Christopher, ed. *Ellen Terry and Bernard Shaw: A Correspondence*. New York: G. P. Putnam's Sons, 1932.

Schickel, Richard. *The Men Who Made the Movies*. New York: Atheneum, 1975.

Sheaffer, Louis. *O'Neill: Son and Playwright*. Boston: Little, Brown, 1968.

Shipman, David. *The Great Movie Stars: The Golden Years*. New York: Hill and Wang, 1979.

Smith, Ella. *Starring Miss Barbara Stanwyck*. New York: Crown Publishers, 1974.

Smith, Jane S. *Elsie de Wolfe: A Life in the High Style*. New York: Atheneum, 1982.

Stevens, Ashton. *Actorviews: Intimate Portraits*. Chicago: Covici-McGee, 1923.

Stevens, Holly. *Souvenirs and Prophecies: The Young Wallace Stevens*. New York: Alfred A. Knopf, 1977.

Strange, Michael. *Clair de Lune*. New York: G. P. Putnam's Sons, 1921.

———. *Resurrecting Life*. New York: Alfred A. Knopf, 1921.

———. *Who Tells Me True*. New York: Charles Scribner's Sons, 1940.

Stuart, Denis. *Dear Duchess: Millicent Duchess of Sutherland*. London: Victor Gollancz, 1982.

Swanson, Gloria. *Swanson on Swanson*. New York: Random House, 1980.

Terry, Ellen. *The Story of My Life*. London: Hutchinson, 1908.

Thomas, Augustus. *The Print of My Remembrance*. New York: Charles Scribner's Sons, 1922.

Thomas, Bob. *Thalberg: Life and Legend*. Garden City, N.Y.: Doubleday, 1969.

Walsh, Raoul. *Each Man in His Time*. New York: Farrar, Straus and Giroux, 1974.

Warner, Jack, with Dean Jennings. *My First Hundred Years in Hollywood*. New York: Random House, 1964.

Wearing, J. P. *The London Stage: A Calendar of Plays and Players*, 3 vols. Metuchen, N.J.: The Scarecrow Press, 1976, 1981, 1984.

Webster, Margaret. *The Same Only Different: Five Generations of a Great Theatre Family*. New York: Alfred A. Knopf, 1969.

Wilson, Garff B. *Three Hundred Years of American Drama and Theatre: From Ye Bear and Ye Cubb to Hair*. Englewood Cliffs, N.J.: Prentice-Hall, 1973.

Wright, William. *Lillian Hellman: The Image, the Woman*. New York: Simon and Schuster, 1986.

Yurka, Blanche. *Bohemian Girl: Blanche Yurka's Theatrical Life*. Athens: Ohio University Press, 1970.

Zolotow, Maurice. *Billy Wilder in Hollywood*. New York: G. P. Putnam's Sons, 1977.

Zukor, Adolph, with Dale Kramer. *The Public Is Never Wrong*. New York: G. P. Putnam's Sons, 1953.

INDEX

623

PERMISSIONS ACKNOWLEDGMENTS

Grateful acknowledgment is made to the following for permission to reprint previously published and unpublished material:

Hollis Alpert: Excerpts from *The Barrymores* by Hollis Alpert. Copyright © 1964 by Hollis Alpert. Published by Dial Books in 1964. Reprinted by permission of International Creative Management as agents for Hollis Alpert.

Gwenn Thomas Avillez and Viviane Thomas Trimble: Excerpts of letters and cables of Diana Barrymore and excerpts of published and unpublished works of Michael Strange (Blanche Thomas). Reprinted by permission of Gwenn Thomas Avillez and Viviane Thomas Trimble.

Gwenn Thomas Avillez, Viviane Thomas Trimble, and Gerold Frank: Excerpts from *Too Much, Too Soon* by Diana Barrymore, with Gerold Frank, published by Henry Holt and Company, 1957. Copyright © 1957 by Diana Barrymore and Gerold Frank. Reprinted with the kind permission of Gerold Frank, Gwenn Thomas Avillez, and Viviane Thomas Trimble.

Elaine Barrymore: Telegram from Elaine Barrymore to Ethel Barrymore and inscription from Elaine Barrymore to John Barrymore. Reprinted by permission of Elaine Barrymore.

Eleanore Phillips Colt: Excerpts from letters of Ethel Barrymore. Reprinted by permission of Eleanore Phillips Colt.

Doubleday: Excerpt from *My Story: An Autobiography* by Mary Astor. Copyright © 1959 by Mary Astor. Excerpt from *To a Lonely Boy* by Arthur Hopkins. Copyright 1937 by Arthur Hopkins. Reprinted by permission of Doubleday, a division of Bantam, Doubleday, Dell Publishing Group, Inc.

Antony John Barrymore Fairbanks: Excerpts from diary entries of Dolores Costello; excerpts from letters, telegrams, and cables of John Barrymore and Lionel Barrymore; excerpts from *We Barrymores* by Lionel Barrymore, published by Appleton-Century-Crofts in 1951. Reprinted by permission of Antony John Barrymore Fairbanks.

Donald I. Fine, Inc.: Excerpt from *Child of the Century* by Ben Hecht. Copyright 1954 by Ben Hecht. Copyright renewed 1982 by Charles A. Mantione as Executor of the Estate of Ben Hecht. Reprinted by permission of the publisher, Donald I. Fine, Inc., 19 West 21st Street, New York, NY 10010.

PHOTOGRAPHIC CREDITS

for Film and Theatre Research. *Plate 30:* above, Wisconsin Center for Film and Theatre Research; below, Courtesy of the Spencer Berger Collection. *Plate 31:* above, Courtesy of the Ray Ruehl Collection; below left and right, Courtesy of the Spencer Berger Collection. *Plate 32:* Courtesy of the Spencer Berger Collection.

SECTION III (FOLLOWING PAGE 370)

Plate 33: above, Courtesy of the Spencer Berger Collection; below, Wisconsin Center for Film and Theatre Research. *Plate 34:* above, Courtesy of the Kobal Collection; below, Courtesy of the Spencer Berger Collection. *Plate 35:* above, Courtesy of the Spencer Berger Collection; below, Photojournalism Collection, Temple University Libraries. *Plate 36:* above, Courtesy of the Ray Ruehl Collection; below, Courtesy of the Spencer Berger Collection. *Plate 37:* Courtesy of the Spencer Berger Collection. *Plate 38:* above, Hearst Newspaper Collection, Special Collections, University of Southern California Library; below, Courtesy of the Kobal Collection. *Plate 39:* above, Courtesy of the Kobal Collection; below, Wisconsin Center for Film and Theatre Research. *Plate 40:* above, Wisconsin Center for Film and Theatre Research; below, Hearst Newspaper Collection, Special Collections, University of Southern California Library. *Plate 41:* above, Courtesy of the Spencer Berger Collection; below, Photojournalism Collection, Temple University Libraries. *Plate 42:* above, Courtesy of the Spencer Berger Collection; below, Wisconsin Center for Film and Theatre Research. *Plate 43:* Courtesy of the Kobal Collection. *Plate 44:* above, Hearst Newspaper Collection, Special Collections, University of Southern California Library; below, Courtesy of the Kobal Collection. *Plate 45:* Collection of the author. *Plate 46:* above, Courtesy of Eleanore Phillips Colt; below, Courtesy of the Spencer Berger Collection. *Plate 47:* above, Photojournalism Collection, Temple University Libraries; below, Courtesy of the Spencer Berger Collection. *Plate 48:* above, Courtesy of the Ray Ruehl Collection; below left and right, Wisconsin Center for Film and Theatre Research.

A NOTE ON THE TYPE

The text of this book was set in a digitized version of Garamond No. 3, a modern rendering of the type first cut by Claude Garamond (1510–1561). Garamond was a pupil of Geoffroy Troy and is believed to have based his letters on Venetian models, although he introduced a number of important differences, and it is to him that we owe the letter we know as old style. He gave to his letters a certain elegance and a feeling of movement that won for their creator an immediate reputation and the patronage of Francis I of France.

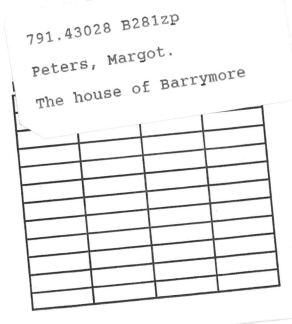